THE Ultimate ACT Tutorial

The Easiest and Most Effective Way to Raise Your Score

By Erik Klass

Klass
tutoring
The Test Prep Experts

Version 3.0, July 2015

About the author:
Erik Klass, owner and founder of KlassTutoring, grew up in Westchester, CA. He studied Mechanical and Manufacturing Engineering at the University of California, Los Angeles, where he holds a Masters in Engineering. He also has a degree in music from Berklee College of Music in Boston, MA. Over the past 15+ years, he has personally tutored hundreds of students for the ACT. This book is the culmination of his work and experience.

Contributor: Jonathan Lotz

KlassTutoring offers full-service, private ACT tutoring. For more information about KlassTutoring, visit our website: www.KlassTutoring.com.

If you have any questions or comments about this tutorial, please email us at: **info@KlassTutoring.com**.

To order additional copies of this book, please visit our e-store at:
www.createspace.com/3646628

Printed by CreateSpace

Printed in the United States of America

A Note from the Author vii
Introduction ix

Part 1: English 1
I English Introduction 3
II Grammar 5
   1. Verb Tense 6
   2. Subject-Verb Agreement 11
   3. Pronouns 17
   4. Parallelism 24
   5. Punctuation 27
   6. Fragments 33
   7. Run-Ons 38
   8. Misplaced Words 43
   9. Redundancies 47
   10. Apostrophes and Confused Words 50
   11. Idiom 54
   12. Adjectives and Adverbs 64
   13. Comparisons 66
   14. Illogical Comparisons 69
   15. Grammar Odds and Ends 71
     Noun Agreement 71
     Paired Conjunctions 72
     More Confused Words 74
     Vocabulary 76
     Nonsense 77
   16. Grammar Quizzes 79
III Usage/Mechanics 87
   1. Avoid Wordy Answer Choices 89
   2. Avoid -*ING* Words 91
   3. No Change 93
   4. Avoid the Passive Voice 94
   5. Avoid New Mistakes 95
   6. Check Your Answers 96
   7. Interrelated Questions 97
   8. Usage/Mechanics Summary 98
   9. Usage/Mechanics Problems 99
IV Rhetorical Skills 103
   1. Main Ideas 107
   2. Transitions 113
   3. Organization 117
   4. Meaning Questions 120
   5. Answer the Question 123
   6. Style 125
   7. Rhetorical Skills Summary 127
   8. Rhetorical Skills Problems 128
V Timing 131
   1. Times 132
   2. Timing Summary 135
VI ACT Practice Tests: Techniques Reference 137
VII English Answers 149

Part 2: Math 157
I Math Introduction and Basic Concepts 159
   1. Introduction 160
   2. Calculators 163
   3. Basic Concepts 166

    4. Basic Concepts Problems 172
II Arithmetic 177
    1. Percent Problems 178
    2. Proportions 186
    3. Ratios 189
    4. Averages, Medians, & Modes 193
    5. Rates, Times, & Distances 197
    6. Patterns 199
    7. Exponents 206
    8. Tables and Graphs 210
    9. Arithmetic Word Problems 214
    10. Arithmetic Problems 215
III Algebra 225
    1. Essential Algebra 226
    2. Algebraic Word Problems 230
    3. The Pick Tricks 233
    4. Simultaneous Equations 248
    5. Factoring 250
    6. Quadratics 255
    7. Algebra Problems 257
IV Geometry 271
    1. Geometry Introduction 272
    2. Area and Perimeter 274
    3. Triangles 283
    4. Angles 291
    5. Coordinates 298
    6. Lines 303
    7. More Circles 315
    8. Solids and Volume 321
    9. Geometry Problems 327
V Functions 347
    1. Function Basics 348
    2. Graphs of Functions 352
    3. Transformations 359
    4. Domain and Range 363
    5. Functions as Models 366
    6. Functions Problems 368
VI Trigonometry 375
    1. Basic Trigonometry 376
    2. Trig and the Unit Circle 382
    3. Graphs of Sine and Cosine 390
    4. The Laws of Sines and Cosines 394
    5. Trigonometry Odds and Ends 398
    6. Trigonometry Problems 403
VII Math Odds and Ends 411
    1. Probability 412
    2. Principle of Counting 415
    3. Complex Numbers 417
    4. Logarithms 421
    5. Matrices 424
    6. Logic 428
    7. Direct and Inverse Variation 429
    8. Sets and Groups 432
    9. Symbol Problems 437
    10. Consecutive Integers 441
    11. Greatest/Least Possible Values 443
    12. Math Odds and Ends Problems 446

VIII ACT Practice Tests: Techniques Reference 453
IX Math Answers 459

Part 3: Reading 513
I   Reading Introduction 515
II Reading Test Strategies 517
   1. The Passage 518
   2. Context 524
   3. Answering the Questions 526
   4. Direct and Extended Reasoning Questions 529
   5. Main Idea Questions 537
   6. Tone Questions 545
   7. Vocabulary Questions 551
   8. Function Questions 555
   9. Odds and Ends 563
      Comparison Questions 563
      Rhetorical Devices 569
      Difficult Passages 577
III Timing 583
   1. Times 584
   2. How to Get Faster 588
   3. Timing Summary 591
IV Practice 593
   1. Reading Questions 594
   2. Questions for ACT Passages 596
V ACT Practice Tests: Context Reference 615
VI Reading Answers 621

Part 4: Science 639
I   Science Introduction 641
II Data Representation 645
   1. Data Representation Intro 646
   2. Graph Basics 650
      Direct Questions 650
      Extrapolation 652
      Passage I 654
   3. New Information 656
      The Second Parts of Answer Choices 659
   4. Trends 660
   5. Make Connections 661
      Passage II 666
   6. Tables 668
      Interpolation 668
      Graphs from Tables 670
   7. Calculations and Math 673
   8. Combining Graphs 677
      Passage III 682
   9. Data Representation Odds and Ends 685
      Descriptions and Headings 685
      Learn 688
      Ratios 689
      Other Figures 690
      Passage IV 694
   10. Data Representation Problems 696
III Research Summaries 705
   1. Research Summaries Intro 706
   2. Data Representation Revisited 708

   3. Research Methods 712
      Terminology 712
      The Experimental Method 713
      Basic Method Questions 713
      Mistakes 714
      Equipment 715
   4. Science Sense & Science Knowledge 717
   5. Research Summaries Problems 720
IV Conflicting Viewpoints 733
   1. Confliction Viewpoints Introduction 734
   2. Direct Questions 739
   3. Indirect Questions 741
   4. Comparisons 742
   5. Strengths and Weaknesses 743
   6. Conflicting Viewpoints Problems 745
V Timing 751
   1. Times 752
   2. Hard Passages 755
   3. Timing Summary 756
VI ACT Practice Tests: Techniques Reference 757
VII Science Answers 769

A NOTE FROM THE AUTHOR

Dear Student,

Congratulations! You now have the most complete and effective ACT tutorial available: *The Ultimate ACT Tutorial*. I know, because I have read just about every other tutorial on the market, and unlike many of the techniques found in other tutorials, the KlassTutoring methods taught here are easy to learn, clearly presented, and proven to work. These lessons and techniques come from my years of experience as a tutor and owner of KlassTutoring. At KlassTutoring, we have tested and perfected every technique in this tutorial. I know they work because I have been watching them work for years.

But this tutorial does not work magic. You must be prepared to work hard, complete your homework assignments, and diligently study the methods and examples. I can't predict how high your score will go. That is up to you. What I can guarantee is that this tutorial will provide you with the tools and information you need to succeed on nearly every problem on the ACT. With practice and effort, you should walk into the testing room prepared and confident.

Study with discipline and diligence as you set your pace toward the college of your dreams.

Best of luck!

Erik Klass and KlassTutoring

INTRODUCTION

THE ULTIMATE ACT TUTORIAL

This tutorial provides you with the techniques you need to excel on the ACT. These techniques will be displayed using clear example problems, and you will have opportunities to practice and master the techniques on literally hundreds of practice problems.

You may have noticed that there are no practice tests in this tutorial. At KlassTutoring, we believe that students will benefit from taking *real* ACTs, not ones made up by a test-prep company. **In order for this tutorial to be most effective, you should purchase *The Real ACT Prep Guide,* 3rd Edition***. This is an official source of *real* ACT tests and problems. While most of our competitors decided to create their own tests, we decided against this for two reasons: (1) it is next to impossible to create a test that truly reflects a real ACT, and (2) we don't have to—there is an excellent book written by the actual testmakers.

So why do you need *The Ultimate ACT Tutorial*? Why not just buy the ACT book? The ACT book is an excellent source of ACT *tests* but not a great source of ACT *techniques*. That's where we come in—we provide the techniques, and you can practice and perfect them on real ACT tests. As you work through this tutorial, you will see assignments for every test question in the ACT book.

There are 5 tests in the ACT book. **We will use 4 of these tests (Tests 2-5) for *timed* practice. We will use the other test (Test 1) as a source of extra practice questions.** The 4 timed tests will give you the practice and experience you will need before tackling the real test on "game day." More test-taking information is found on the following pages. The ACT book also contains a number of additional practice problems that are *not* part of the tests. Many of these will be assigned as you work your way through *The Ultimate ACT Tutorial*. You will usually complete these practice problems untimed and sometimes out of order.

DISCLAIMER

This tutorial is the most accurate and up-to-date ACT guide that we know of, at the time of this writing. But the ACT has been known to make small changes to the test's formatting and content from time to time, often with little or no warning. We recommend that you get the free *Preparing for the ACT* booklet from your school, or download it from the ACT website, to see if there have been any recent changes since the publication of this tutorial.

*ACT is a registered trademark of the ACT, Inc., which was not involved in the production of and does not endorse this book.

THE ULTIMATE ACT TUTORIAL: WRITING

The ACT Writing Test is a separate and optional part of the ACT. KlassTutoring's Writing tutorial (*The Ultimate ACT Tutorial: Writing*) is also separate and optional. If you're planning to take the Writing test, or if you just need to get your essay writing in shape, we recommend you purchase this book. You can find it at Amazon.com and other book sellers.

PROGRAMS

We have prepared three general ACT programs that you may follow as you work your way through the tutorial. The hours below are estimates of *actual tutoring times* (including learning techniques, reviewing homework, taking quizzes, and completing lesson problems). **The hours do *not* include time for completing homework and taking practice tests.** To determine the program that is right for you, consider: (1) how much time you have before you plan to take the ACT and (2) your desired level of mastery.

Throughout the tutorial, you will notice notes **in bold** for each of the programs, such as lessons and questions to complete (or skip), tests to take, and so on. Details for each program are found on the following pages (Tutoring Schedules).

20-HOUR PROGRAM

Our shortest standard program should take about 20 hours of lesson time. Rest assured that the 20-hour program still covers most of the important ACT topics.

30-HOUR PROGRAM

For many students, we recommend the 30-hour program. This program covers most of the questions you will find on the ACT. This is our most popular program at KlassTutoring.

40-HOUR PROGRAM

If you are looking for the highest score possible and if time permits, look at every topic in the tutorial, as covered by the 40-hour program. Students with high starting scores should definitely consider this program (although these students will probably choose to skip easier lessons).

TUTORING SCHEDULES

As you may have noticed in the Table of Contents, *The Ultimate ACT Tutorial* is divided into four main parts: English, Math, Reading, and Science. You should *not* work straight through this tutorial. The tutoring schedules on the following pages will give you an idea of how to plan your work.

TIMES

Take a look at one of the schedules. You can see that each lesson is scheduled for *two hours*. As described before, these hours are estimates of *actual lesson time* (including learning techniques, reviewing homework, taking quizzes, and completing lesson problems). The hours do *not* include time for completing homework and taking practice tests. For most students, completing one to two lessons per week is a realistic pace. Obviously, consider your final test date as you plan your lessons.

Students have different strengths and weaknesses and work at different paces, so treat the schedules as general guides. Don't worry if your actual times don't match the times on the schedules. You may choose to spend extra time on more difficult topics or skip entire sections that you are already comfortable with.

For each lesson, the schedule gives time breakdowns for each part of the curriculum (English, Math, etc.); see the number in parentheses following each list of lessons. These time estimates also include time that you might spend going over the previous lesson's homework.

HOMEWORK

As you work your way through the tutorial, you will notice assignments labeled with a homework symbol:

The following schedules will include *additional* homework assignments: see the homework (HW) row following each lesson. All homework assignments (those labeled with the symbol above and those on the schedules) should be completed *between* lessons—we recommend you "step away" from the material before completing these assignments.

20-HOUR SCHEDULE

Hrs.	English	Math	Reading	Science
1/2	□ Introduction □ Verb Tense □ Subject-Verb Agree. (0.75)	□ Introduction □ Calculators □ Basic Concepts □ Percent Problems (1.25)		
HW	□ Take Test 2*	□ Take Test 2* □ Basic Concepts Worksheet	□ Take Test 2*	□ Take Test 2*
3/4	□ Pronouns □ Parallelism (0.50)	□ Proportions □ Ratios □ Averages… □ Rates… □ Patterns (1.25)	□ Reading Introduction □ The Passage (0.25)	
HW	□ Study for Grammar Quiz 1 (Sections 1-4)	□ Basic Concepts: Correct Test 2**		
5/6	□ Grammar Quiz 1 (Sections 1-4) □ Punctuation □ Fragments (0.50)	□ Exponents □ Tables and Graphs □ Arithmetic Word Probs. (0.50)	□ Context □ Answering the Questions □ Direct & Ext. Reasoning Questions (0.50)	□ Science Introduction □ Data Representation Introduction □ Graph Basics (0.50)
			Optional Writing: Start 3-hour program	
HW		□ Arith. Worksheet 1 □ Arith.: Correct Test 2**		□ Data Rep.: Passage I
7/8	□ Run-ons □ Misplaced Words (0.50)	□ Essential Algebra □ Alg. Word Problems □ Start Pick Tricks (start) (0.75)	□ Main Idea Questions (0.25)	□ New Information □ Trends □ Make Connections (0.50)
HW	□ Study for Grammar Quiz 2 (Sections 5-8)		□ ACT Passage I*	□ Data Rep.: Passage II
9/10	□ Grammar Quiz 2 (Sections 5-8) □ Redundancies □ Apostrophes and Confused Words □ Idiom (0.50)	□ The Pick Tricks (finish) (0.50)	□ Timing (0.50)	□ Tables □ Calculations □ Combining Graphs (0.50)
			Optional Writing: Start 2-hour program	
HW			□ ACT Passage II*	□ Data Rep.: Passage III
11/12	(0.00)	□ Geometry Intro. □ Area… □ Triangles □ Angles □ Coordinates (1.25)	□ Tone Questions (0.50)	□ Timing (0.25)
HW	□ Study for Grammar Quiz 3 (Sections 9-11)	□ Algebra Worksheet 1 □ Algebra: Correct Test 2**	□ ACT Passage III*	□ Data Rep.: ACT Pass. I*

* Tests and passages indicated with asterisks are found in *The Real ACT Prep Guide*. Note: Use KT reading questions for ACT reading passages. Tests are found in the back of the book. Other passages are found in the front sections.

** Problem lists and test correction instructions are found in *The Ultimate ACT Tutorial*: See the "Problems" sections at the end of relevant chapters. All work should be done in *The Real ACT Prep Guide*.

20-HOUR SCHEDULE (continued)

Hrs.	English	Math	Reading	Science
13/14	□ Grammar Quiz 3 (Sections 9-11) (0.25)	□ Lines □ Function Basics □ Graphs of Functions (1.00)	□ Vocabulary Questions (0.50)	□ Odds and Ends (0.25)
HW		□ Algebra Worksheet 2 □ Geom. Worksheet 1 □ Geom.: Correct Test 2** □ Arith. Probs.: Test 1** □ Alg. Probs.: Test 1** □ Functions Worksheet 1 □ Functions: Correct Test 2**	□ Correct Test 2**	□ Data Rep.: Passage IV
15/16	□ Usage/Mechanics (0.50)	□ Basic Trigonometry (0.75)	□ Function Questions (0.50)	(0.25)
HW	□ Usage/Mechanics: ACT Passage I* □ Usage/Mechanics: Correct Test 2**	□ Geom. Worksheet 2 □ Geom. Probs.: Test 1** □ Trig. Worksheet 1 □ Trig.: Correct Test 2**	□ ACT Passage IV*	□ Data Rep.: Correct Test 2** □ Data Rep.: Passage I (KT practice)
17/18	□ Timing (0.50)	□ Review Timing (0.75)	□ Review Timing (0.25)	□ Review Timing (0.50)
HW	□ Take Test 3*	□ Take Test 3*	□ Take Test 3*	□ Take Test 3*
19/20	□ Correct Test 3** (0.50)	□ Correct Test 3** (0.50)	□ Correct Test 3** (0.50)	□ Correct Test 3** (0.50)

*/** See first page of Schedule

30-HOUR SCHEDULE

Hrs.	English	Math	Reading	Science
1/2	□ Introduction □ Verb Tense □ Subject-Verb Agree. (0.75)	□ Introduction □ Calculators □ Basic Concepts □ Percent Problems (1.25)		
HW	□ Take Test 2*	□ Take Test 2* □ Basic Concepts Worksheet	□ Take Test 2*	□ Take Test 2*
3/4	□ Pronouns □ Parallelism (0.50)	□ Proportions □ Ratios □ Averages… □ Rates… □ Patterns (1.25)	□ Reading Introduction □ The Passage (0.25)	
HW	□ Study for Grammar Quiz 1 (Sections 1-4)			

5/6	□ Grammar Quiz 1
	   (Sections 1-4)
	□ Punctuation
	□ Fragments
	(0.50)
		□ Exponents
		□ Tables and Graphs
		□ Arithmetic Word
		   Probs.
		(0.50)
			□ Context
			□ Answering the
			   Questions
			□ Direct & Ext.
			   Reasoning Questions
			(0.50)
				□ Science Introduction
				□ Data Representation
				   Introduction
				□ Graph Basics
				(0.50)

HW		□ Arith. Worksheet 1 □ Arith.: Correct Test 2**		□ Data Rep.: Passage I
7/8	□ Run-ons □ Misplaced Words (0.50)	□ Essential Algebra □ Alg. Word Problems □ The Pick Tricks (start) (0.75)	□ Main Idea Questions (0.25)	□ New Information □ Trends □ Make Connections (0.50)
HW	□ Study for Grammar Quiz 2 (Sections 5-8)		□ ACT Passage I*	□ Data Rep.: Passage II

9/10	□ Grammar Quiz 2
	   (Sections 5-8)
	□ Redundancies
	□ Apostrophes and
	   Confused Words
	□ Idiom
	(0.50)
		□ The Pick Tricks (finish)
		(0.50)
			□ Timing
			(0.50)
				□ Tables
				□ Calculations
				□ Combining Graphs
				(0.50)

HW			□ ACT Passage II*	□ Data Rep.: Passage III
11/12	□ Adjectives and Adverbs □ Comparisons □ Illogical Comparisons □ Grammar Odds and Ends (0.50)	□ Geometry Intro. □ Area… (0.75)	□ Tone Questions (0.50)	□ Timing (0.25)

HW	□ Study for Grammar
	   Quiz 3 (Sections 9-11)
		□ Algebra Worksheet 1
		□ Algebra: Correct
		   Test 2**
			□ ACT Passage III*	□ Data Rep.: ACT Pass.
				   I*

13/14	□ Grammar Quiz 3 (Sections 9-11) (0.25)	□ Triangles □ Angles □ Coordinates (1.00)	□ Vocabulary Questions (0.50)	□ Odds and Ends (0.25)
HW		□ Algebra Worksheet 2	□ Correct Test 2**	□ Data Rep.: Passage IV

* Tests and passages indicated with asterisks are found in *The Real ACT Prep Guide.* Note: Use KT reading questions for ACT reading passages. Tests are found in the back of the book. Other passages are found in the front sections.

** Problem lists and test correction instructions are found in *The Ultimate ACT Tutorial*: See the "Problems" sections at the end of relevant chapters. All work should be done in *The Real ACT Prep Guide.*

30-HOUR SCHEDULE (continued)

Hrs.	English	Math	Reading	Science
15/16	□ Usage/Mechanics (0.50)	□ Lines □ More Circles □ Solids and Volume (0.75)	□ Function Questions (0.50)	(0.25)
	Optional Writing: Start 3-hour program			
HW	□ Usage/Mechanics: ACT Passage I* □ Usage/Mechanics: Correct Test 2**	□ Geom. Worksheet 1 □ Geom.: Correct Test 2** □ Arith. Probs.: Test 1** □ Alg. Probs.: Test 1**	□ ACT Passage IV*	□ Data Rep.: Correct Test 2**
17/18	□ Timing (0.50)	□ Review Timing (1.00)	□ Review Timing (0.25)	□ Review Timing (0.25)
HW	□ Take Test 3*	□ Take Test 3*	□ Take Test 3*	□ Take Test 3*
19/20	□ Rhetorical Skills (0.50)	□ Function Basics □ Graphs of Functions (0.50)		□ Research Summaries Intro. □ Data Rep. Revisited □ Research Methods □ Sci. Sense/Knowledge (1.00)
	Optional Writing: Start 2-hour program			
HW	□ Rhetorical Skills: ACT Passage I* □ Usage/Mechanics: Correct Test 3**	□ Basic Concepts: Correct Test 3** □ Arith.: Correct Test 3** □ Algebra: Correct Test 3** □ Geom.: Correct Test 3**	□ Correct Test 3**	□ Data Rep.: Correct Test 3** □ Research Sum.: ACT Passage II*
21/22	(0.50)	(0.75)	(0.25)	(0.50)
HW	□ Rhetorical Skills: Correct Tests 2 & 3**	□ Functions Worksheet 1 □ Functions: Correct Tests 2 & 3** □ Algebra Worksheet 3	□ ACT Passage V*	□ Research Sum.: Correct Tests 2 & 3**
23/24	(0.25)	□ Basic Trigonometry □ Trig and the Unit Circle (1.00)	(0.25)	(0.50)
HW	□ ACT Passage II*	□ Trig. Worksheet 1 □ Trigonometry: Correct Tests 2 & 3** □ Geom. Worksheet 2	□ ACT Passage VI*	□ Data Rep.: Passage I (KT practice) □ Research Sum.: Passage I (KT practice)
25/26	(0.25)	□ Probability □ Principle of Counting (1.00)	(0.25)	(0.50)
HW	□ ACT Passage III* □ Study for Grammar Quiz 4 (all Grammar sections covered in the 30-hour program)	□ Odds and Ends Worksheet □ Odds and Ends Probs.: Test 1** □ Odds and Ends: Correct Tests 2 & 3**	□ ACT Passage VII*	□ Data Rep.: Passage II (KT practice) □ Research Sum.: Passage II (KT practice)
27/28	□ Review Timing (0.25)	□ Catch up or move ahead (1.00)	□ Review Timing (0.25)	□ Review Timing (0.50)
HW	□ Take Test 4*	□ Take Test 4*	□ Take Test 4*	□ Take Test 4*
29/30	□ Correct Test 4** (0.50)	□ Correct Test 4** (0.50)	□ Correct Test 4** (0.50)	□ Correct Test 4** (0.50)

*/** See first page of Schedule

40-HOUR SCHEDULE

Hrs.	English	Math	Reading	Science
1/2	□ Introduction □ Verb Tense □ Subject-Verb Agree. (0.75)	□ Introduction □ Calculators □ Basic Concepts □ Percent Problems (1.25)		
HW	□ Take Test 2*	□ Take Test 2* □ Basic Concepts Worksheet	□ Take Test 2*	□ Take Test 2*
3/4	□ Pronouns □ Parallelism (0.50)	□ Proportions □ Ratios □ Averages… □ Rates… □ Patterns (1.25)	□ Reading Introduction □ The Passage (0.25)	
HW	□ Study for Grammar Quiz 1 (Sections 1-4)	□ Basic Concepts: Correct Test 2**		
5/6	□ Grammar Quiz 1 (Sections 1-4) □ Punctuation □ Fragments (0.50)	□ Exponents □ Tables and Graphs □ Arithmetic Word Probs. (0.50)	□ Context □ Answering the Questions □ Direct & Ext. Reasoning Questions (0.50)	□ Science Introduction □ Data Representation Introduction □ Graph Basics (0.50)
HW		□ Arith. Worksheet 1 □ Arith.: Correct Test 2**		□ Data Rep.: Passage I
7/8	□ Run-ons □ Misplaced Words (0.50)	□ Essential Algebra □ Alg. Word Problems □ The Pick Tricks (start) (0.75)	□ Main Idea Questions (0.25)	□ New Information □ Trends □ Make Connections (0.50)
HW	□ Study for Grammar Quiz 2 (Sections 5-8)		□ ACT Passage I*	□ Data Rep.: Passage II
9/10	□ Grammar Quiz 2 (Sections 5-8) □ Redundancies □ Apostrophes and Confused Words □ Idiom (0.50)	□ The Pick Tricks (finish) (0.50)	□ Timing (0.50)	□ Tables □ Calculations □ Combining Graphs (0.50)
HW			□ ACT Passage II*	□ Data Rep.: Passage III
11/12	□ Adjectives and Adverbs □ Comparisons □ Illogical Comparisons □ Grammar Odds and Ends (0.50)	□ Geometry Intro. □ Area… (0.75)	□ Tone Questions (0.50)	□ Timing (0.25)
HW	□ Study for Grammar Quiz 3 (Sections 9-11)	□ Algebra Worksheet 1 □ Algebra: Correct Test 2**	□ ACT Passage III*	□ Data Rep.: ACT Pass. I*
13/14	□ Grammar Quiz 3 (Sections 9-11) (0.25)	□ Triangles □ Angles □ Coordinates (1.0)	□ Vocabulary Questions (0.50)	□ Odds and Ends (0.25)
HW		□ Algebra Worksheet 2	□ Correct Test 2**	□ Data Rep.: Passage IV

* Tests and passages indicated with asterisks are found in *The Real ACT Prep Guide*. Note: Use KT reading questions for ACT reading passages. Tests are found in the back of the book. Other passages are found in the front sections.

** Problem lists and test correction instructions are found in *The Ultimate ACT Tutorial*: See the "Problems" sections at the end of relevant chapters. All work should be done in *The Real ACT Prep Guide*.

40-HOUR SCHEDULE (continued)

Hrs.	English	Math	Reading	Science
15/16	□ Usage/Mechanics (0.50)	□ Lines □ More Circles □ Solids and Volume (0.75)	□ Function Questions (0.50)	(0.25)
HW	□ Usage/Mechanics: ACT Passage I* □ Usage/Mechanics: Correct Test 2**	□ Geom. Worksheet 1 □ Geom.: Correct Test 2** □ Arith. Probs.: Test 1** □ Alg. Probs.: Test 1**	□ ACT Passage IV*	□ Data Rep.: Correct Test 2**
17/18	□ Timing (0.50)	□ Review Timing (1.00)	□ Review Timing (0.25)	□ Review Timing (0.25)
HW	□ Take Test 3*	□ Take Test 3*	□ Take Test 3*	□ Take Test 3*
19/20	□ Rhetorical Skills (0.50)	□ Function Basics □ Graphs of Functions □ Transformations (1.00)		□ Research Summaries Intro. □ Data Rep. Revisited (0.50)
HW	□ Rhetorical Skills: ACT Passage I* □ Usage/Mechanics: Correct Test 3**	□ Basic Concepts: Correct Test 3** □ Arith.: Correct Test 3** □ Algebra: Correct Test 3** □ Geom.: Correct Test 3**	□ Correct Test 3**	□ Data Rep.: Correct Test 3**
21/22	(0.50)	□ Domain and Range □ Functions as Models (1.0)	(0.25)	(0.25)
HW	□ Rhetorical Skills: Correct Tests 2 & 3**	□ Functions Worksheet 1 □ Functions: Correct Tests 2 & 3**	□ ACT Passage V*	
23/24	(0.25)	(0.75)	(0.25)	□ Research Methods □ Sci. Sense/Knowledge (0.75)
HW	□ ACT Passage II*		□ ACT Passage VI*	□ Research Sum.: ACT Passage II* □ Research Sum.: Correct Tests 2 & 3**
25/26	(0.25)	□ Basic Trigonometry □ Trig and the Unit Circle (1.00)	(0.25)	(0.50)
	Optional Writing: Start 3-hour program			
HW	□ ACT Passage III*	□ Geom. Worksheet 2	□ ACT Passage VII*	□ Data Rep.: Passage I (KT practice) □ Research Sum.: Passage I (KT practice)
27/28	(0.25)	□ Graphs of Sine and Cosine □ The Laws of Sines and Cosines □ Trig. Odds and Ends (1.25)	(0.25)	(0.25)
HW	□ Test 1: Passage I**	□ Trig. Worksheet 1 □ Trigonometry: Correct Tests 2 & 3**	□ Test 1: Passage I*	□ Data Rep.: Passage II (KT practice) □ Research Sum.: Passage II (KT practice)

*/** See first page of Schedule

Hrs.	English	Math	Reading	Science
29/30	(0.25)	(Back to Algebra chapter) □ Simultaneous Equations □ Factoring □ Quadratics (1.00)	□ Comparison Questions (0.50)	(0.25)
		Optional Writing: Start 2-hour program		
HW	□ Test 1: Passage II**	□ Algebra Worksheet 3 □ Geom. Worksheet 3	□ Test 1: Passage II*	□ Data Rep.: Passage III (KT practice) □ Research Sum.: Passage III (KT practice)
31/32	(0.25)	□ Probability □ Principle of Counting □ Complex Numbers (0.75)	□ Rhetorical Devices (0.50)	□ Conflicting Viewpoints Intro. □ Direct Questions (0.50)
HW	□ Study for Grammar Quiz 4 (Sections 1-15)	□ Geometry Probs.: Test 1** □ Functions Probs.: Test 1** □ Trig. Probs.: Test 1**	□ Test 1: Passage III*	□ Data Rep.: Test 1: Passage II** □ Research Sum.: Test 1: Passage I**
33/34	(0.25)	□ Logarithms □ Matrices □ Logic □ Direct and Inverse Variation (0.75)	□ Difficult Passages (0.50)	□ Indirect Questions □ Comparisons □ Strengths and Weaknesses (0.50)
HW	□ Test 1: Passage III**	□ Arith. Worksheet 2 □ Algebra Worksheet 4 □ Geom. Worksheet 4	□ Test 1: Passage IV*	□ Data Rep.: Test 1: Passage IV** □ Research Sum.: Test 1: Passage III** □ Conf. Viewpoints: ACT Passage III* □ Conf. Viewpoints: Correct Tests 2 & 3**
35/36	(0.25)	□ Sets and Groups □ Symbol Problems □ Consecutive Integers □ Greatest/Least Possible Values (1.00)	(0.25)	(0.50)
HW	□ Test 1: Passage IV**	□ Functions Worksheet 2 □ Trig. Worksheet 2 □ Odds and Ends Worksheet □ Odds and Ends Probs.: Test 1** □ Odds and Ends: Correct Tests 2 & 3**	□ KT Passage	□ Data Rep.: Test 1: Passage V** □ Research Sum.: Test 1: Passage VII** □ Conf. Viewpoints: Passage I (KT practice) □ Conf. Viewpoints: Test 1: Passage VI**
37/38	□ Review Timing (0.25)	(1.00)	□ Review Timing (0.25)	□ Review Timing (0.50)
HW	□ Take Test 4*	□ Take Test 4*	□ Take Test 4*	□ Take Test 4*
39/40	□ Correct Test 4** (0.50)	□ Correct Test 4** (0.50)	□ Correct Test 4** (0.50)	□ Correct Test 4** (0.50)

*/** See first page of Schedule

WHERE'S THE WRITING SCHEDULE?

The optional Writing Test is covered by our companion tutorial: *The Ultimate ACT Tutorial: Writing*. If you are planning to take the Writing Test, please purchase this tutorial. This book contains detailed programs to help you write great essays in no time.

TAKING THE PRACTICE TESTS

Practice tests are found in *The Real ACT Prep Guide*. Each test is really five tests in one: English, Math, Reading, Science, and Writing (optional); the tests will always be in this order. **Make sure to time yourself when you take these tests.** Use the following schedule:

- **English Test: 45 minutes**
- **Math Test: 60 minutes**
  —10-minute break—
- **Reading Test: 35 minutes**
- **Science Test: 35 minutes**
  —10-minute break—
- **Writing Test (optional): 40 minutes (new time)**

You should leave yourself about **4 hours** to take all five tests (or a little over 3 hours for just the first four tests). Because you'll be completing a significant amount of ACT homework as you work your way through the tutorial, you may decide to take some practice tests (English, Math, Reading, Science, and Writing) separately, rather than completing all five tests in one sitting. **You should still *always* time yourself, and never take a break in the middle of a test.**

To closely simulate the actual test-taking experience, take at least the last ACT test of your chosen program in *one sitting* and use the full amount of time available for each individual test. This will help you prepare for the actual test day when you may spend nearly 4 hours completing the test.

Show all work in the ACT book. For practice, cut out and use the answer sheets and lined essay pages provided for each test by the ACT. **Do not look back to the tutorial while taking the practice tests.**

GRADING THE PRACTICE TESTS

To grade a practice test you must find a *raw score*, which is just the sum of all the questions you get correct on a given test, and then convert the raw score to a *scaled score* (between 1 and 36) using conversion charts in *The Real ACT Prep Guide*. Details on how to do this are found at the back of the ACT book, after the last test. Make sure to grade your tests carefully so you can chart your progress as you work your way through this tutorial.

GUESSING ON THE ACT

(!) **You do not lose points for guessing on the ACT.** This means that when you're done with each individual test, you should have filled in a bubble for every question, even if you had to guess. For this reason, you need to create a strategy for answering the questions. You have two options:

1. **Skip questions:** As you work your way through a test, skip a question that gives you trouble (and leave the corresponding answer blank on your answer sheet). Circle the problem number, either in your *test booklet* or on your *answer sheet*, so you can easily find it later (if you circle the number on your answer sheet, you'll have to erase before finishing the test, but of course these circles are easier to spot). But here's the catch: you must diligently watch the clock so that, worst-case scenario, you have about 30 seconds at the end of the test to guess on any questions that you skipped. Of course, you will hopefully have more time than that so you can go back and actually *look* at some of these questions, but *at the very least* you need to scribble in your favorite letters before you run out of time.

2. **Guess as you go:** If you're not sure about a problem when you get to it, take a guess, fill in the answer on your answer sheet, and move on. Again, circle the question number. If you have time at the end of the test, quickly flip through your test booklet and revisit any of the questions you guessed on. The advantage of this technique is that you don't have to worry about guessing at the end of the test if you run out of time (because you've been filling in answers all along). The disadvantage is that, if you do have time to go back to some of these questions, you might spend a little extra time erasing each guessed answer that you decide to change.

We recommend the first option above, but both are fine. Decide which one you prefer, and stick with it. You might experiment on the practice tests in the ACT book to see which strategy you're more comfortable with. Just make sure you have a plan in place before you take the real ACT.

TIMING STRATEGIES

Because the criterion for ordering the questions varies on each type of test, timing strategies will also vary. For example, when you complete the questions on the English Test (questions that are *not* arranged in order of difficulty), a good goal is to get to the end of the test—the last question may be the easiest one on the test. On the other hand, when you complete the questions on the Math Test (questions that generally *are* arranged in order of difficulty), it is important to spend time on the questions that you can answer correctly, even if that means guessing on some of the harder questions at the end of the test. **Specific timing strategies for each test will be discussed later.**

GET A STOPWATCH

Many of the timing strategies discussed in this tutorial require keeping track of *deadlines*, and the easiest way to do this is with a stopwatch. Look online for a stopwatch that does not make beeping noises (the ACT folks do not allow beeping during the test). Also, the watch must be a *wrist*watch, not a watch that is held in your hand. You should be able to find a decent, silent digital watch in the $20-$30 dollar range. It's worth the investment. Silentstopwatch.com offers an excellent watch for less than $30, but there are others out there.

PROCESS OF ELIMINATION

A *process of elimination* is an important, all-around strategy on the ACT. This means physically crossing off the letter in your test booklet when you're "very sure" that an answer choice is wrong. A process of elimination will not only help you focus on the answer choices that may be correct (by eliminating the ones that are *not* correct), but this process will also sometimes lead you to the correct answer simply by removing the three or four (depending on the section) *incorrect* answers. You will undoubtedly identify the correct answer immediately on some questions, without having to scrutinize the other answer choices. This is great. But oftentimes you should aggressively eliminate answer choices to help zero in on correct answers.

FLASHCARDS

There are many opportunities throughout this tutorial to create flashcards. Many of the important and more specific items that should be memorized are indicated with a flashcard symbol:

There are different ways to create flashcards, but, in general, there should be some form of a question on the front of the card and the answer to that question on the back. Create flashcards for any information that you are worried you may forget before taking the test. And, of course, don't forget to study them frequently.

FIVE-STAR REVIEWS? QUESTIONS? COMMENTS?

If you agree that this tutorial really is the *ultimate* ACT tutorial, please give it a five-star review. We sell most of our books on Amazon, and we rely on five-star reviews to help compete with the larger tutoring companies. Of course, work your way through the tutorial and prove to yourself that this really is the best book out there. If you agree that it is, we really appreciate the positive feedback. Thank you!

If, on the other hand, you did not have a "five star" experience with this tutorial, please let us know. The author, Erik Klass, personally responds to every email inquiry (find another book where *that* happens!). If there's anything he can do to improve your experience, or anything that you'd like him to explain better, he'd love to hear from you. He can be reached at: **info@KlassTutoring.com**

Also, if you have any questions or comments, the email above is how to reach KlassTutoring. We appreciate all feedback, and we're always looking for great reviews for our next cover.

UPDATES

We highly recommend that you send us your email address so we can send you occasional updates, including any errors or omissions that we find in this edition of the tutorial. Again, our email is: info@KlassTutoring.com.

THE ULTIMATE GUARANTEE

At KlassTutoring, we believe in our unique approach to ACT tutoring, and we are committed to your success and satisfaction. If, after completing our standard 30-hour program, your ACT score does not increase by at least 12 total points (or 3 composite points), we will refund you 150% of the lesser of the purchase price or list price of the tutorial (not including tax, shipping, and handling). To qualify for a refund, please send us *all* of the following items:

- ☐ The original receipt or proof-of-purchase, clearly showing the purchase date, the purchase price, and the name of the tutorial (*The Ultimate ACT Tutorial*).
- ☐ Your copy of *The Ultimate ACT Tutorial*, with all of the 30-hour program's lesson problems, homework problems, quizzes, and other assignments clearly completed.
- ☐ Photo copies of your official scores of actual ACTs, before and after using the tutorial. The date of the first ACT must be before the date of the tutorial purchase.
- ☐ Your mailing address (where we will send the refund).

Claims for refunds must be received within 120 days of the purchase date of the tutorial, as printed on the original receipt. Incomplete claims will not be processed. Send materials to:

The Ultimate Guarantee
c/o KlassTutoring
3125 Curts Ave., Suite 1000
Los Angeles, CA 90034

Please allow 6-8 weeks to receive your refund in the mail. Limit one refund per customer.

COLLEGE COUNSELING

This tutorial is *not* intended to replace your college counselor. It has only one goal: **to help you achieve the highest score possible on the ACT**. Many students have questions such as:

- How do I sign up for the ACT?
- What do my ACT scores mean?
- To what colleges should I apply?
- Do I even have to take the ACT?
- What about the SAT?

There are a number of places where you can find helpful information:

- The ACT website (www.actstudent.org/) can answer a number of your questions about signing up for the test and what your scores mean.
- Get the free *Preparing for the ACT* booklet, either from your school or from the ACT website. (There's an extra practice ACT here, too!)
- Your school's college guidance counselor should be able to help you make difficult decisions regarding school selections and what tests you need to take.
- Many students seek the advice of private college counselors in their areas.
- You can contact colleges directly to discuss their expectations and requirements, or just review their websites—usually a great source of information.
- Buy or check out a book that specializes in college selection and enrollment.

THE FIRST ASSIGNMENT

OK—it's time to get started. Before completing any of the lessons in this tutorial, we recommend that you take a practice test in the ACT book. This will give you an idea of your starting score and will perhaps allow you to create a sensible program that focuses on your weaknesses. As you make your way through the tutorial and cover relevant topics, you will frequently go back and make corrections to this practice test.

Note the symbol to the left below. We'll use this symbol throughout the tutorial for all practice test assignments.

 All Programs: Take Test 2 in *The Real ACT Prep Guide*. (Remember, we're going to use Test *1* for practice problems.) Review "Taking Practice Tests" in this introduction.

———

PART 1
ENGLISH

I
ENGLISH INTRODUCTION

The English section is divided into six chapters:

    I.   Introduction

   II.   Grammar

  III.   Usage/Mechanics

  IV.   Rhetorical Skills

   V.   Timing

  VI.   English Technique Reference

 VII.   English Answers

TYPES OF QUESTIONS

All questions on the English Test are multiple choice, with four answer choices. The questions fall into one of two general categories:

1. Usage/Mechanics (approximately 50* questions covering punctuation, basic grammar, and sentence structure)
2. Rhetorical Skills (approximately 25* questions covering writing strategy, organization, and style)

Since you will be taking practice ACTs before these questions are discussed in the tutorial, read the test instructions carefully to understand how to answer these questions.

*Based on KlassTutoring's classification

TEST LAYOUT

The English Test includes:

- Five passages
- A total of 75 multiple-choice questions
- A total test time of 45 minutes

A GENERAL APPROACH

You might want to take a moment now to open up the ACT book and see what these questions look like. Read the directions (this should be the only time you have to do this).

ANSWER QUESTIONS *WHILE* YOU READ THE PASSAGES

Unlike the ACT Reading or Science Tests, where all of the questions for a passage *follow* the passage, nearly all of the questions on the English Test show up *next* to the passage. You can, and should, answer them while you're reading the passage.

EXCEPTIONS

Be aware. Sometimes you have to read *beyond* the point where a question shows up before you can answer the question. We'll get more into this later (see Interrelated Questions in the Usage/Mechanics chapter and Main Ideas in the Rhetorical Skills chapter). There aren't many of these, so in general, answer questions aggressively as you read through the passage. This is the best way to maximize your time on the test.

TECHNIQUE IDENTIFICATION

Often, there are clues that will help you figure out what technique is being tested by a specific question. Throughout the tutorial, look for the magnifying glass for information about identifying techniques:

HAPPY FACE TOPICS

Topics that are indicated with the symbol below may be a review for many students. You may choose to move quickly through this material or (for advanced students) skip it altogether and go straight to lesson problems. If you struggle on any lesson problems, go back and review the relevant material.

II
GRAMMAR

This chapter covers the most important part of the English Test: *grammar*. These grammar topics will also help you in your writing, so keep them in mind as you prepare for the ACT's Writing Test (the essay).

1. VERB TENSE

The tense of a verb describes *when* a verb "happens." If events occur at the same time, the verb tenses must be the same. If events occur at different times, the verb tenses should reflect the order of these events.

VERB-TENSE TERMINOLOGY ☺*

Verb – The part of speech that expresses existence, action, or occurrence in a sentence.

TENSE

While there are many different tenses, it is helpful to be familiar with the five most important verb tenses found on the ACT. Since you will not be tested on their official names (such as *past perfect*), we will refer to them by the *times* that they occur, as shown on the time-line below:

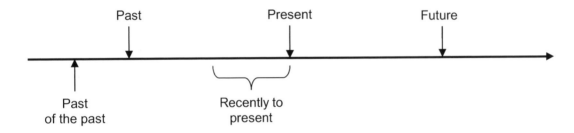

First, let's look at the easy ones. You are probably comfortable with these already. ☺

Present: Today, I *study* with my tutor for the ACT.

Past: Yesterday, I *studied* for several hours for the ACT.

Future: Tomorrow, I *will study* several more hours for the ACT.

Now, for the harder ones—from now on, we'll call these the *"other" verb tenses*:

Past of the past: This tense always uses the word **had**. For example:

> Before Aimee took the ACT last year, she *had studied* for several months. (The studying took place *before* Aimee took the ACT; hence, the *past of the past*).

*See Happy Face Topics in the English Introduction

Recently to present: This tense uses the word *has* for *he*, *she*, *it*, or any *singular* thing performing the action and *have* for *I*, *we*, *they*, *you*, or any *plural* thing performing the action.

> I *have studied* for the ACT for what seems like an eternity. (This has been going on for a while, and it sounds like it still is.)

TO SUMMARIZE

Past-of-the-past tense → use the word **had**

Recently-to-present tense → use the word **has** or **have**

TO BE ☺

The verb *to be* is an irregular verb. Most of its forms don't even resemble the word itself. Luckily, your ear will probably pick up on correct and incorrect uses. You are probably already comfortable with the following:

> Yesterday, I *was* sick.
> Today, I *am* feeling great.
> They *were* the best in the class last year, but now they *are* struggling.
> She has *been* here for hours.

-ING WORDS

(!) Words in the *-ing* form can be used to express continuous action. **However, a word in the *-ing* form—on its own—does not function as a verb.** For example:

> Incorrect: John *running* to the store.

Doesn't sound good, right? To correctly use an *-ing* word as part of a verb phrase, you must use a *to be* verb. The following are some examples:

> Past: Yesterday, we *were emptying* out the cupboard.
> Present: Today, John *is running* to the store while we finish the work.
> Recently-to-present: John *has been working* as a handyman this summer.
> Past-of-the-past: John *had been working* two jobs before he had enough money to buy the bike.

IRREGULAR VERBS

Irregular verbs may behave in unpredictable ways. For example:

present: Today, I *lie* on my bed.

past: Last night, I *lay* on my bed.

past of the past: Before I woke up this morning, I had *lain* on my bed.

recently to present: I have *lain* on my bed all morning.

As you can see, things can get a little tricky. The good news, however, is that the ACT does not put too much emphasis on these irregular verbs. But they *do* occasionally show up, so if your ear tells you that the form of a verb sounds "funny," you may have found one of these irregular verb errors.

VERB TENSE ON THE ACT

Verb tense questions on the ACT almost always ask you to recognize the tense set somewhere else in the passage—usually in the previous sentence or earlier in the sentence in question—and match the underlined verb to the previous verb. In the following problems, make sure you focus on the verbs that are not underlined (and are thus correct).

> To identify verb tense questions, look for questions with answer choices that contain the same verbs in different tenses—for example *look, looked, has looked, will look,* etc.

VERB TENSE LESSON PROBLEMS

Answers to all lesson and homework problems in this chapter start on page 150. You may want to mark this page for future reference.

Built at the turn of the century, the mansion <u>displaying</u> some of the oldest styles of architecture seen in the region today.
₁

1. **A.** NO CHANGE
   B. will have displayed
   C. displayed
   D. displays

The scientists were sure they had uncovered an ancient human skeleton, but they <u>had not been sure</u> of its origin.
₂

2. **F.** NO CHANGE
   G. are not sure
   H. will not have been sure
   J. were not sure

Continued →

Since last night, Paul <u>worked</u> on his history
paper, and he will probably still be working on
it until tonight.

3. **A.** NO CHANGE
    B. works
    C. will work
    D. has been working

Patrick learned to swim before he could walk,
competed in his first swimming contest before
he started kindergarten, and <u>winning</u> his first
race when he was five years old.

4. **F.** NO CHANGE
    G. won
    H. wins
    J. will win

Taking the time up front to properly plan the
project will ensure success. Jumping right in
with no planning, however, <u>leads</u> to failure.

5. **A.** NO CHANGE
    B. will have lead
    C. lead
    D. will lead

Early in the morning, the majestic sun peeks
over the distant hillside. Long shadows
<u>stretched</u> out over the yellow fields.

1. **A.** NO CHANGE
    B. stretch
    C. will stretch
    D. stretching

Before I finish my research paper, I <u>have read</u>
three books on the subject.

2. **F.** NO CHANGE
    G. will have read
    H. read
    J. had read

The teacher looked back fondly on the days
when students <u>come</u> to class free of cell phone
distractions.

3. **A.** NO CHANGE
    B. came
    C. will have come
    D. could have come

Before the rocket was launched, Ken <u>written</u>
dozens of articles about its expected path.

4. **F.** NO CHANGE
    G. had written
    H. had wrote
    J. will write

Continued →

Cobwebs fell from the ceiling of the haunted mansion as Jason carefully <u>crept</u> inside.
₅

5. **A.** NO CHANGE
   B. will creep
   C. creeps
   D. has crept

2. SUBJECT-VERB AGREEMENT

Subjects must always agree with their respective verbs in number. In other words, if the subject is *singular* then the verb must be *singular*, and if the subject is *plural* then the verb must be *plural*.

There are two challenges to this topic. The first one is identifying the subject and its verb in the sentence. The second one is deciding whether the subject is singular or plural.

SUBJECT-VERB-AGREEMENT TERMINOLOGY

Subject – consists of a noun, noun phrase, or noun substitute which often refers to the person, place, or thing performing the action or being in the state expressed by the rest of the sentence.

Preposition – A word that locates things in *time, place,* or *movement.*
Prepositional Phrase – A preposition followed by a noun or pronoun. } See examples below.

Modifying Phrase – We'll get more into modifying phrases later. For now, you should know that a modifying phrase is part of a sentence that can be removed without greatly altering the grammatical correctness of the sentence. A modifying phrase is separated from the rest of the sentence with commas. This makes it easy to spot.

PREPOSITIONS

Since removing *prepositional phrases* will help you find subjects and verbs, first let's look at a lesson on prepositions. If a word sounds correct in *either one* (not necessarily both) of the following sentences, the word is probably a preposition. Memorize these sentences.

The professor walked _____ the desk. (good for *place* or *movement* prepositions: ex. *into*)
The professor talked _____ the class. (good for *time* prepositions: ex. *after*)

Here are some examples of prepositions. Try them out in one or both of the sentences above.

about	beside	in front of	through
across	between	into	throughout
after	by	like	to
against	concerning	next to	toward
around	during	**of***	under
at	except	off	until
before	for	on	upon
behind	in	past	without
beneath			

*The word "of" is probably the most common preposition.

IDENTIFYING THE SUBJECT AND THE VERB

BAREBONES SENTENCES

The ACT loves to trick you by putting prepositional phrases or modifying phrases between the subject and its verb, but the subject is never part of these phrases. So: **Get rid of prepositional and modifying phrases when looking for the subject of a sentence.** After these phrases are removed, you will be left with the "barebones sentence." For example:

> The number of calories recommended for the average person by the Food and Drug Administration, according to a report last year, depend on the age and size of the individual.

First, remove the modifying phrase: "according to a report last year." Notice the commas on either side of the phrase. Next, remove the prepositional phrases (prepositions are in bold below). You should be left with the following sentence. The subject (and verb) become much easier to see.

> The number **of** ~~calories~~ recommended **for** ~~the average person~~ **by** ~~the Food and Drug Administration~~, ~~according~~ **to** ~~a report last year~~, depend **on** ~~the age and size~~ **of** ~~the individual~~.

> The number recommended depend.

The subject is *number* and the verb is *depend*. (Note: "recommended" is an adjective. It is describing the noun "number." The "number" certainly did not recommend anything.) Since *number* is singular and *depend* is plural, the subject and verb do not agree (more on the number of a verb soon). The correct sentence should read:

> The *number* of calories recommended for the average person by the Food and Drug Administration, according to a report last year, *depends* on the age and size of the individual.

VERBS BEFORE SUBJECTS

Sometimes, the verb comes *before* the subject. When you spot a verb, ask yourself what or who is "performing" the verb, and be prepared to look beyond the verb in the sentence. Look for the word "there," especially at the beginning of a sentence:

> There remain questions about the cause of the fire.

Remain is the verb and *questions* is the subject.

Never before has Bill been so successful.

Has is the verb and *Bill* is the subject.

IDENTIFYING THE NUMBER OF THE VERB ☺

Verbs behave in strange ways, as we've already seen in the previous section. In general, the rules that define the number of a verb are the opposite of those for nouns. When a verb is singular, it generally has an *s* at the end:

He eats by himself.

When a verb is plural, it generally does not have an *s* at the end.

They eat together.

If you're ever in doubt, just try out the verb in question with *it* or *they*, and trust your ear.

IDENTIFYING THE NUMBER OF THE SUBJECT

A NOSE SUBJECTS

FLASH CARDS

! **The most commonly missed subjects can be remembered using the acronym: *A NOSE*. These are all *singular* in number:**

- **A** anybody, anyone
- **N** nobody, no one, neither, none
- **O** one
- **S** somebody, someone
- **E** everybody, everyone, either, each, every

Again, these subjects are all *singular*.

COLLECTIVE NOUNS

! **Collective nouns are almost always *singular* on the ACT, even though they may seem plural.** If you can add an *s* to a collective noun to make it plural (for example: *group → groups*), then you know that without the *s*, it is singular:

number	audience	team	city, state, or country
amount	group	company or corporation	staff or department

SUBJECTS WITH "AND" OR "OR"

Make sure you are comfortable with the following rules.

AND

Linking two subjects with *and* creates a *plural* subject. For example:

Elizabeth *and* Jasmine are going to drink coffee. (*plural*)

OR

Linking two subjects with *or* will make the linked subject *singular* if the word closest to the verb (usually the last word) is singular and *plural* if the word closest to the verb is plural. For example:

Elizabeth or **Jasmine** is going to pay for the coffee. (*singular*)

Andy *or* **the girls** are going to the museum. (*plural*)

There is **one can** of soup *or* bagels in the pantry. (*singular*)

———

The following steps outline the method for working with subject-verb agreement errors:

1. Identify the subject and its verb. Find the "barebones sentence," if necessary.
2. Determine the number of the subject (singular or plural).
3. Make sure the number of the verb matches the number of the subject.

Subject-Verb Agreement questions will usually have answer choices that have the same verbs in singular and plural forms (ex: *take* and *takes*, or *has taken* and *have taken*).

SUBJECT-VERB AGREEMENT LESSON PROBLEMS

Each member of the group of scholars <u>has</u> taken a number of courses at the university.

1. **A.** NO CHANGE
   B. have
   C. are going to have
   D. having

Ryan or Mike, no matter what you may have heard, <u>are going to be at</u> the dance.

2. **F.** NO CHANGE
   G. have been going to
   H. is going to be at
   J. have been at

Continued →

The team of representatives, many from as far away as China and India, <u>is assembled</u> in the banquet room.
₃

3. **A.** NO CHANGE
    B. have assembled
    C. are assembled
    D. are in assembly

One of the students <u>is going to the city finals for</u> <u>his or her</u> success in the spelling bee.
₄

4. **F.** NO CHANGE
    G. are going to the city finals for his or her
    H. is going to the city finals for their
    J. have gone to the city finals for their

I counted numerous boats at the docks, but there <u>was not</u> as many boats as the year before.
₅

5. **A.** NO CHANGE
    B. were not
    C. will not have been
    D. is not

HW

Either football or basketball <u>are my favorite</u> <u>sport</u>.
₁

1. **A.** NO CHANGE
    B. are my favorite sports
    C. have been my favorite sport
    D. is my favorite sport

Everyone on the team, even the goalies, <u>have</u> <u>been</u> in great shape.
₂

2. **F.** NO CHANGE
    G. are
    H. is
    J. are going to be

The audience, mostly made up of rich businessmen and politicians, <u>are paying</u> top-dollar for events like this.
₃

3. **A.** NO CHANGE
    B. pay
    C. pays
    D. are payers for

Every nut, bolt, and tool <u>were</u> stolen from the tool shed.
₄

4. **F.** NO CHANGE
    G. was
    H. are
    J. have been

Continued →

The feeling I got after listening to the lecture about the city's traffic jams <u>were that</u> nothing is
going to be done about them anytime soon.

5. **A.** NO CHANGE
    B. is that
    C. was that
    D. are that

3. *PRONOUNS*

PRONOUN TERMINOLOGY ☺

Pronoun – A word that generally stands for or refers to a noun or nouns whose identity is made clear earlier in the text.

PRONOUN CASE

CASES OF PRONOUNS

The two general *cases* of pronouns are *subject* pronouns and *object* pronouns. Subject pronouns perform the actions in the sentence. Object pronouns are the recipients of the actions. If you are ever unsure of the case of a pronoun, plug the pronoun into a simple *performer-recipient* sentence and trust your ear, for example:

<u>He</u> threw the ball to <u>her</u>.

He is performing the action and *her* is receiving the action. Thus, *he* is a subject pronoun and *her* is an object pronoun.

Subject pronouns		Object pronouns
I	→	*me*
he	→	*him*
she	→	*her*
they	→	*them*
we	→	*us*
it	→	*it*
who	→	*whom*
you	→	*you*

The following rules will help you choose the correct case for a pronoun.

PRONOUNS AND PREPOSITIONS

! **Use *object* pronouns when the pronoun shows up in a phrase with a preposition:**

...between *you* and *me*...

...to Sherry and *her*...

...among *us* students...

...from *him* and *her*...

A PRONOUN LINKED WITH A NOUN

When a pronoun is side-by-side with a noun (*we* seniors, *us* students), **eliminate the noun to determine which type of pronoun to use.** For example:

(*We, Us*) seniors decided to take the day off.

We is the correct pronoun since *us* is clearly incorrect when *seniors* is removed.

The award was presented to (*we, us*) students.

Us is the correct pronoun since *we* is clearly incorrect when *students* is removed.

This approach can also help you when a pronoun is part of a linked subject or object. For example:

Toby and me decided to take the day off.

Remove the noun (*Toby*) and you will "hear" the error in the sentence.

Me decided to take the day off.

The pronoun should be in the subject case. The correct sentence reads:

Toby and *I* decided to take the day off.

WHO VERSUS *WHOM*

Recall that *who* is the subject pronoun and *whom* is the object pronoun. For example:

My mom, *who* has the day off, is going to the store.
With *whom* are you speaking?
I am speaking to the telephone repair man, about *whom* I'm sure you've heard a lot.

THAT VERSUS *WHICH*

While *who* or *whom* refers to people, as described above, *that* and *which* are pronouns that refer to groups or things. There is often confusion about whether to use *that* or *which*. There are distinct differences between the two.

That is used as a pronoun to introduce essential information that you absolutely need to understand what particular thing is being referred to. For example:

> Heather likes bananas *that* are still green.

Out of all the types of bananas in the world, Heather likes the particular ones that are still green. Since the information *are still green* is essential to understand what kind of bananas Heather likes, use *that*. In addition, since this information could not be removed without greatly altering the sentence, do not use a comma.

Which is used as a pronoun to introduce nonessential, added information, which may be helpful but is not totally necessary to understand what particular thing is being referred to. For example:

> Heather likes bananas, which are high in potassium.

The fact that bananas are high in potassium is added information that isn't essential to understand what kind of bananas Heather likes (since all bananas are high in potassium). **Which is usually preceded by a comma because it introduces information that could be removed without drastically changing the desired meaning of the sentence.**

––––––

To identify pronoun case errors, look for questions with answer choices that have the same pronouns in different cases. (ex: *he* and *him*)

PRONOUN AGREEMENT

NUMBER AGREEMENT

In a sentence, the pronoun must agree in number with the noun or nouns it is replacing.

> Everyone who plays an instrument knows *they* must practice for hours everyday to master the craft.

This sentence sounds fine, right? But it is incorrect. The pronoun *they* is referring to the noun *everyone*, the subject of the sentence, which is singular. Therefore, *they* should be replaced with a singular pronoun.

Everyone who plays an instrument knows *he or she* must practice for hours everyday to master the craft.

PRONOUN AGREEMENT

If pronouns are referring to the same thing in a sentence, make sure they are the same pronoun type. Watch out for illogical changes to the pronouns as a sentence develops.

When *one* prepares for a concert, *you* should visualize a standing ovation at the end.

Both pronouns should be *one* or *you*, such as:

When *one* prepares for a concert, *one* should visualize a standing ovation at the end.

———

The following steps will help you work with pronoun-agreement errors:
1. Identify the pronoun in the sentence.
2. Identify the noun that the pronoun is referring to. Usually the noun will precede the pronoun in the sentence.
3. Make sure the pronoun and the noun agree in number.

To identify pronoun agreement errors, look for questions with answer choices that contain plural *and* singular pronouns.

AMBIGUOUS PRONOUNS

Pronouns must clearly refer to the noun or nouns they replace. For example:

The early marching music of New Orleans was probably the earliest form of jazz, and *they* used musical elements from both the African and European continents.

In the sentence, *they* is an ambiguous pronoun because there are no groups mentioned in the sentence to which *they* logically refers. The sentence could be corrected by either adding a group of people to the first part of the sentence or replacing *they* appropriately:

The *musicians* of early marching music in New Orleans were probably playing the earliest form of jazz, and *they* used musical elements from both the African and European continents.

Or:

The early marching music of New Orleans was probably the earliest form of jazz, and *the musicians* used musical elements from both the African and European continents.

Another ambiguous pronoun problem occurs when it is unclear what noun is being referred to in the sentence. For example:

Thomas told Jason that *he* was responsible for studying the origins of jazz for their report on American music.

It may sound strange, but for the sentence to be totally clear and unambiguous, it should read:

Thomas told Jason that *Jason* (or *Thomas*) was responsible for studying the origins of jazz for their report on American music.

THEY

The pronoun *they* is commonly used when some form of *experts* is intended; this is also ambiguous:

They say that jazz was originally a combination of African and European musical elements.

The correct sentence should read:

Musical historians say that jazz was originally a combination of African and European musical elements.

IT

The pronoun *it* is also used frequently in ambiguous ways. For example:

The musicians combined African musical traditions with the use of classical European instruments, and *it* started a whole new style of music.

To what exactly is *it* referring? The pronoun *it* is ambiguous. Here's an improved version of the sentence:

The musicians combined African musical traditions with the use of classical European instruments, and a whole new style of music was born.

If the pronoun *it* clearly refers to the singular subject of the sentence or another singular noun in the sentence, its use is probably correct. The following examples are correct:

The *music* of early New Orleans had strong rhythmic characteristics because *it* was played in parades, marches, and other processions.

Many contemporary musicians study *jazz* because *it* is the foundation of American music.

———

To identify ambiguous pronoun errors, look for the pronouns "they" and "it." These pronouns are often ambiguous.

———

PRONOUN LESSON PROBLEMS

I will play the song for Dorothy and <u>he</u>.
₁

1. **A.** NO CHANGE
    B. him
    C. himself
    D. he, who listens

The speaker, about <u>whomever</u> we had been
₂
talking for weeks, spoke with grace and
eloquence.

2. **F.** NO CHANGE
    G. who
    H. whom
    J. OMIT the underlined portion

The after school programs have given the
students something to do with <u>everyone's</u> free
₃
time.

3. **A.** NO CHANGE
    B. their
    C. his or her
    D. one's

Nobody I know who has gone to the water park
thinks <u>they</u> will go again.
₄

4. **F.** NO CHANGE
    G. he or she
    H. he or she, by themselves,
    J. all of them

Continued →

The company was given financial support until <u>they pulled</u> out of debt.
₅

5. **A.** NO CHANGE
   B. they pulled themselves
   C. it pulled itself
   D. the staff pulled themselves

<u>We</u> seniors are proud to be graduates of such a
₁
fine school.

1. **A.** NO CHANGE
   B. We,
   C. We, the
   D. Us

Waiting for over an hour, we wondered what <u>had happened to she</u> and Daniel.
₂

2. **F.** NO CHANGE
   G. had happened to her
   H. happened to she
   J. happens to her

Anyone starting ninth grade knows that <u>they</u>
₃
<u>were</u> thrown from the frying pan into the fire.
₃

3. **A.** NO CHANGE
   B. they have been
   C. they will be
   D. he or she has been

When you stand near the conductor, <u>anyone</u>
₄
must be careful not to get hit by his baton.

4. **F.** NO CHANGE
   G. you
   H. one
   J. the audience members

The Polish accordion tradition known as *polka* has a recognizable rhythmic pattern because of <u>their</u> consistent use of a triplet meter.
₅

5. **A.** NO CHANGE
   B. the pattern's
   C. their pattern's
   D. the tradition's pattern's

4. PARALLELISM

When you are expressing two or more series of ideas or actions, they should be *parallel* in form. In other words, they should be constructed in the same way. For example:

> An excellent employee is open to new ideas, responsive to company needs, and he complies with the company rules of business.

Notice the three phrases that describe the employee:

1. ...open to new ideas... (*adjective-preposition-object*)
2. ...responsive to company needs... (*adjective-preposition-object*)
3. ...he complies with the company rules of business. (*pronoun-verb-preposition-object*)

The first two phrases are similar. In each, an *adjective* ("open" and "responsive") is followed by a *preposition* ("to" in both cases) is followed by an *object* ("new ideas" and "company needs"). In the third phrase, the structure is different. A *pronoun* is followed by a *verb* is followed by a *preposition* is followed by an *object* ("the company rules of business"). The sentence is not parallel in construction.

To correct the sentence, replace "he complies" with the appropriate adjective ("compliant") to match the first two phrases. The words "compliant with" are parallel to "open to" and "responsive to," and the correct sentence reads:

> An excellent employee is *open to* new ideas, *responsive to* company needs, and *compliant with* the company rules of business.

On the ACT, parallelism questions often test the parallelism of *verbs*, so watch out for changing verb forms. Also, look for the following:
1. A series of two or more actions or items
2. Lists, especially when there are distracting phrases thrown in between the items
3. Comparisons (because they always include at least two items)

PARALLELISM LESSON PROBLEMS

Ted would prefer <u>to watch grass grow to</u> finishing his homework.

1. **A.** NO CHANGE
   B. watching grass grow to finishing
   C. to watch grass grow than finishing
   D. watching grass grow than to finish, on time,

While Nick hides in the basement, Louie <u>is looking</u> in the attic.

2. **F.** NO CHANGE
   G. has looked
   H. looks
   J. looked

For most great artists, creative freedom is more important than <u>financially comfortable</u>.

3. **A.** NO CHANGE
   B. being financially comfortable
   C. financial comfort
   D. having a comfortable finance

The coach preaches the idea that all of his players, no matter their current skills, can learn the intricacies of the game and <u>they can become</u> great athletes.

1. **A.** NO CHANGE
   B. become
   C. so they can become
   D. becoming

Jess <u>likes taking</u> the bus more than driving her car because she can read, sleep, or talk to interesting new people.

2. **F.** NO CHANGE
   G. likes to have taken
   H. liked to take
   J. likes to take

For most great artists, <u>being creatively free</u> is more important than being financially comfortable.

3. **A.** NO CHANGE
   B. creative freedom
   C. having the freedom to create
   D. freedom to create

All programs: Now is a good time to review sections 1-4 and take Grammar Quiz 1 (Sections 1-4), which is found in the Grammar Quizzes section at the end of this chapter.

5. PUNCTUATION

The most important aspect of punctuation on the ACT is the correct use of commas and, to a lesser degree, semicolons. The use of apostrophes will be discussed in the Apostrophes and Confused Words section.

Most comma problems on the ACT (over 80%) involve the use of a comma when one is *not* needed. So let's learn about the *correct* uses of commas—once you are familiar with these correct uses, you'll be ready to identify the *unnecessary* uses found on the ACT. First, let's cover some basic terminology. You do not have to memorize any of these terms; they merely aid in teaching the material.

SENTENCE BUILDING BLOCKS

Sentences are generally made up of up to three distinct parts: *independent clauses*, *dependent clauses*, and *phrases*.

> **Clause** – a sequence of words that contains a subject and its verb
>
> **Independent clause** – a clause that can stand on its own and make sense
>
> **Dependent clause** – a clause that cannot stand on its own because it *depends* on the rest of the sentence to make sense

Let's look at an example to illustrate these parts.

> As he looked up at the blimp, William tripped on the curb.

In the example above, *William tripped on the curb* is the *independent clause*, and *As he looked up at the blimp* is the *dependent clause*.

> **Phrase** – a sequence of two or more words that does not contain a subject and a finite (non-*ing*) verb. We can refer to any group of words that is not a clause as a *phrase*.

By changing the first part of the sentence slightly, we can turn the dependent clause into a *phrase*. The *-ing* form of a verb is a common way to do this.

> Looking up at the blimp, William tripped on the curb.

Because there is no subject in the first part of the sentence, *Looking up at the blimp* is a phrase. This phrase is modifying *William* by adding information about what he was doing when he tripped.

Sentences must have at least one independent clause. Good writers will add different combinations of dependent clauses and phrases to these independent clauses to make interesting-sounding sentences.

COMMAS

SEPARATING DEPENDENT CLAUSES FROM INDEPENDENT CLAUSES

Commas must be used to separate a dependent clause from a following independent clause of a sentence. For example:

As he looked down at his untied shoe, Gregg missed the UFO that flew over his head.

       dependent clause   independent clause

When a dependent clause comes *after* an independent clause, the comma is unnecessary. Notice that there is no need to *pause* between the clauses in this situation, which is a good reminder that the comma is not needed. For example:

Gregg missed the UFO flying over his head as he looked down at his untied shoe.

       independent clause   dependent clause

Or:

Gregg missed the UFO because he was looking down at his untied shoe.

    independent clause   dependent clause

SEPARATING MODIFYING PHRASES FROM INDEPENDENT CLAUSES

Commas must be used to separate modifying phrases from the independent clause of a sentence. This topic was introduced in the Subject-Verb lesson.

Looking down at his untied shoe, Gregg missed the UFO that flew over his head.

    modifying phrase   independent clause

If a modifying phrase shows up in the middle of a clause, make sure there are commas on either side of the phrase. This correctly suggests that the phrase could be removed and the sentence would still make sense. Try this in the following example:

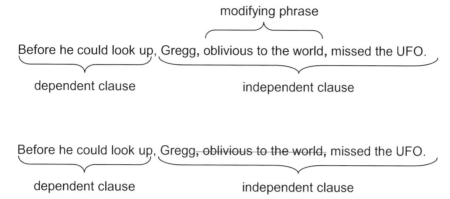

SEPARATING TWO INDEPENDENT CLAUSES

Some sentences will have two independent clauses separated by a conjunction, such as *and*, *or*, or *but* (more on conjunctions later). **A comma must come before the conjunction**, as shown in the following example:

Gregg looked down at his untied shoe, and he missed the UFO flying over his head.

independent clause   independent clause

ONE INDEPENDENT CLAUSE WITH TWO ACTIONS

Make sure there are indeed two distinct independent clauses. The following example does not need a comma because the sentence has only one independent clause containing two actions.

Gregg looked down at his untied shoe and missed the UFO flying over his head.

PAUSING

While you read a punctuation question on the ACT, briefly *pause* when you come to a comma. Listen carefully (in your head, of course) for any awkwardness. This approach will help you identify most of the punctuation errors on the test. As stated earlier, the ACT often places commas in places where pauses are unneeded or sound awkward. As you read the following examples, make sure you pause at the commas:

Gregg, looked down at his untied shoe and missed the UFO flying over his head.

Gregg looked down, at his untied shoe and missed the UFO flying over his head.

Gregg looked down at his untied shoe and missed the UFO flying, over his head.

Are the pauses necessary? Do you hear any awkwardness? Try reading without the pauses and see how the sentences sound. In all three examples, the commas are unnecessary.

OTHER PUNCTUATION

SEMICOLONS

Semicolons (;) are similar to periods; the sentences that they separate, however, must be closely related. **Semicolons are used to separate independent clauses**, which, if you recall, could stand alone as complete sentences. The following example illustrates the correct use of a semicolon:

Gregg looked down at his untied shoe; he missed the UFO flying over his head.

        independent clause   independent clause

COLONS

Colons (:) are used to indicate that what follows is an elaboration, summation, or list of what precedes. For example:

Gregg made a list of what he should have ready for the next time a UFO appears: a camera, a binoculars, a notebook, and a pencil.

When Gregg told his friends that there had been a UFO sighting, you could describe their reaction in a word: incredulous.

DASHES

Dashes (—) are used to note an abrupt break or pause in a sentence or to begin and end a separate phrase or clause. Their uses are similar to those of commas. Unless the break is clearly unneeded—you should use the pause idea discussed earlier—it's hard to get dashes wrong.

Gregg decided he would study UFOs for the rest of his life—that he might need to make a living some day did not concern him.

His parents—both certain that UFOs did not exist—hoped that Gregg's interest was just a passing phase.

————

To identify punctuation errors, look for questions with answer choices that contain changes in punctuation, particularly a variety of comma placements. Watch out for problems that correct one comma error but introduce another.

PUNCTUATION LESSON PROBLEMS

<u>After spending, several years trying to grow a</u>
¹
<u>garden</u> Linda decided she'd rather just buy her
¹
produce from the store.

1. **A.** NO CHANGE
   B. After spending several years trying to grow a garden,
   C. After spending, several years trying to grow a garden,
   D. After spending several years trying to grow a garden

<u>Daniel not a large man by any means</u> somehow
²
seems to dominate our basketball games.

2. **F.** NO CHANGE
   G. Daniel, not a large man by any means
   H. Daniel not a large man by any means,
   J. Daniel, not a large man by any means,

You should watch the <u>road but you should also</u>
³
<u>occasionally,</u> check your mirrors.
³

3. **A.** NO CHANGE
   B. road; but you should also occasionally,
   C. road, but you should also occasionally
   D. road, but you should also occasionally,

She skated with amazing <u>skill, and finesse</u> as
⁴
though she had wings on her back.

4. **F.** NO CHANGE
   G. skill, and finesse,
   H. skill and finesse;
   J. skill and finesse

The weather may seem nice now. In just a few
<u>weeks, however, the ground</u> will be covered
⁵
with snow.

5. **A.** NO CHANGE
   B. weeks, however the ground
   C. weeks however, the ground,
   D. weeks however the ground

Tommy, friendly as always offered to assist the
confused tourist.

1. **A.** NO CHANGE
   B. Tommy, friendly as always,
   C. Tommy friendly as always,
   D. Tommy friendly as always

Skipping through the sprinklers and rolling
through the grass, Katie became a wet and
grassy mess.

2. **F.** NO CHANGE
   G. Skipping through the sprinklers and rolling through the grass
   H. Skipping through the sprinklers, and rolling through the grass
   J. Skipping through the sprinklers, and rolling through the grass,

Even though many voters apparently unaware
of the country's many problems, are happy with
the incumbent, I feel that we are ready for a
new leader.

3. **A.** NO CHANGE
   B. voters, apparently unaware of the country's many problems,
   C. voters, apparently unaware of the country's many problems
   D. voters apparently unaware of the country's many problems

George rocked the boat many people fell out.

4. **F.** NO CHANGE
   G. boat, many
   H. boat; many
   J. boat in that many

Pete's Bistro, the busiest and noisiest restaurant
on the street, caters to a motley crew of tourists
and locals.

5. **A.** NO CHANGE
   B. Bistro, the busiest, and noisiest
   C. Bistro, the busiest, and noisiest,
   D. Bistro, the busiest and noisiest,

6. FRAGMENTS

Several types of fragments show up on the ACT. You can identify them by looking for the specific parts described below.

DEPENDENT CLAUSE

First, let's define the word *conjunction*:

Conjunction – A word that links the parts of a sentence together.

There are several different types of conjunctions (we'll learn about others soon). One kind, called a **subordinate conjunction** (don't worry about memorizing the name), turns an independent clause into a dependent clause when placed in front of the independent clause. Remember that a dependent clause, on its own, is not a complete sentence—it's a fragment.

after	even though	though
although	if	unless
as	if only	until
as if	in order that	when
as long as	now that	whenever
as though	once	where
because	rather than	whereas
before	since	wherever
even if	so that	while

When you spot one of these words at the beginning of a sentence, look out for a fragment. For example:

Fragment: *As* the forest fire burned, bellowing smoke into the air.

The sentence lacks an independent clause. Note that if the word "As" were removed, the sentence would be an independent clause.

-*ING* WORD USED AS A VERB

As taught in the Verb Tense lesson, a word in the -*ing* form—on its own—does not function as a verb. When the subject of a sentence lacks a verb, the sentence is a fragment. For example:

Fragment: The firefighters, many from hundreds of miles away, *preparing* to fight the fire.

The subject "firefighters" lacks a verb. You could fix this sentence by adding "are" or "were" in front of "preparing."

PRONOUN PHRASE

Watch out for phrases that begin with pronouns such as *that*, *which*, *who*, or *whom*. Especially watch out for *that*; the others are easier to identify because they will usually be preceded by a comma. The following are all fragments because the subjects ("fire," "fire," and "residents") lack verbs:

> The fire *that* burned over 1,000 acres last summer.
> The forest fire, *which* was likely started when someone threw a cigarette from his car.
> The residents, *who* lived in the small mountain town all their lives.

"THAT" CLAUSE

Sometimes the word *that* indicates a clause within a clause. This so-called *"that" clause* must have its own subject and verb. For example:

> Fragment: The newspaper reporter said *that* residents returning to their homes.

The subject of the "that" clause ("residents") lacks a verb.

While less common, *question* words such as *why*, *where*, *who*, *what*, *how*, etc. can also create their own clauses, so watch out for them.

MODIFYING PHRASE

The ACT will often use long modifying phrases to disguise fragments. Try removing modifying phrases to find the barebones sentence.

> The fire captain, one of the most experienced firefighters in the county and not surprisingly the first on the scene.

The subject "captain" lacks a verb.

SEMICOLON

Watch out for fragments when two clauses are separated by a semicolon. As taught in the Punctuation section, a semicolon (like a period) separates two *independent clauses*.

Incorrect: Jerry enjoys tree climbing; but quick to warn of its potential dangers.

Incorrect: Jerry enjoys tree climbing; however warning of its potential dangers.

The second clause in each of the previous examples is a fragment.

A fragment usually contains one of the following:

1. Dependent clause (look for a subordinate conjunction)
2. *-ING* word used as a verb
3. Pronoun phrase
4. "That" clause
5. Modifying phrase
6. Semicolon

FRAGMENTS LESSON PROBLEMS

Bertrand Russell's *The Problems of*
[1] *Philosophy, often* one of the first books
[1]
assigned in introductory Philosophy courses
because of its ability to make the abstruse
comprehendible.

1. **A.** NO CHANGE
   B. *The Problems of Philosophy*, is often
   C. *The Problems of Philosophy* is often
   D. *The Problems of Philosophy*, often being

After the committee released its findings on the
[2]
widespread use of cell phones, scientists
warned that there may be a link between cell-
phone use and brain tumors.

2. **F.** NO CHANGE
   G. The committee released
   H. The committee releasing
   J. After the committee releasing

Although better known as a movie star,
Austrian actress Hedy Lamarr, who became a
[3]
pioneer in the field of wireless communications
following her emigration to the United States.

3. **A.** NO CHANGE
   B. Hedy Lamarr
   C. Hedy Lamarr who
   D. Hedy Lamarr; who

Continued →

When choosing a health insurance <u>company;</u>
<u>4</u>
<u>choose</u> carefully.
4

4. **F.** NO CHANGE
   G. company. Choose
   H. company, choose
   J. company, and you should choose

The <u>sculptor, carefully shaping</u> with his hands,
5
transformed clay into art.

5. **A.** NO CHANGE
   B. sculptor carefully shaping
   C. sculptor carefully shaped
   D. sculptor, who carefully shaping

Jerry said that climbing <u>trees, an activity not</u> for
1
everyone because of its inherent risks.

1. **A.** NO CHANGE
   B. trees is not an activity
   C. trees, an activity that is not
   D. trees, not an activity

Most <u>people showing</u> little concern for
2
agriculture and farming, even though these
fields were keys to the rise of human
civilization.

2. **F.** NO CHANGE
   G. people show
   H. people, who show
   J. people, showing

The so-called wind car, possibly the first
automobile, which used a machine similar to a
windmill to drive gears, which in turn drove the
<u>wheels, designed</u> by da Vigevano in 1335.
3

3. **A.** NO CHANGE
   B. wheels, was designed
   C. wheels; it was designed
   D. wheels. The car was designed

When turning <u>right, make</u> sure
4
to look over your right shoulder for
pedestrians and bikers.

4. **F.** NO CHANGE
   G. right; make
   H. right; you should make
   J. right; it is a good idea to make

Continued →

Most of the overnight campers know <u>that the</u> <u>ghost stories being</u> told to scare them from
leaving their bunks in the middle of the night.

5. **A.** NO CHANGE
   B. that the ghost stories are being
   C. that the ghost stories, which are being
   D. that the ghost stories

7. RUN-ONS

FANBOYS CONJUNCTIONS

Most run-on errors on the ACT involve a *compound sentence*, which is just two independent clauses linked with a conjunction called a FANBOYS, or *coordinating*, conjunction (once again, you don't have to memorize the official name). These are the seven FANBOYS conjunctions:

for, and, nor, but, or, yet, so

To help remember these conjunctions, use the acronym **FANBOYS**: **F**or-**A**nd-**N**or-**B**ut-**O**r-**Y**et-**S**o. You might also notice that each conjunction is either two or three letters long. (Many other conjunctions are longer.)

(!) **The FANBOYS conjunctions, listed above, are the only conjunctions that can link two independent clauses. As explained in the Punctuation section, when they link independent clauses, they should be preceded with a comma.** For example:

In his books and essays, Thoreau challenged the traditional ideas of society, **and** he was thus both criticized and praised by his readers.

RUN-ONS ON THE ACT

From the Punctuation section, we know that two independent clauses must be separated by (1) a comma *and* a FANBOYS conjunction or (2) a semicolon—otherwise, the sentence is a run-on. On the ACT, there are three common types of run-on sentences related to this rule:

COMMA BUT NO CONJUNCTION

The first one, called a *comma splice*, involves two independent clauses separated by a comma but lacking a conjunction. For example:

Yoshio thought that his printer was broken, it simply was out of ink.

       independent clause   independent clause

To correct this run-on, simply add an appropriate conjunction:

Yoshio thought that his printer was broken, *but* it simply was out of ink.

CONJUNCTION BUT NO COMMA

The second type of run-on also has two independent clauses. This one correctly includes a conjunction but is lacking a comma before the conjunction. For example:

Yoshio thought that his printer was broken and this was because the page came out white.

independent clause   independent clause

Since the second part of the sentence is an independent clause, a comma must come before the conjunction. The correct sentence should read:

Yoshio thought that his printer was broken, and this was because the page came out white.

A more eloquent and succinct way to correct the error is to turn the second clause into a dependent clause or modifying phrase. The ACT may correct run-ons in this way:

Yoshio thought that his printer was broken because the page came out white.
Or:
Because the page came out white, Yoshio thought that his printer was broken.

NO COMMA, NO CONJUNCTION

Some compound sentences lack the comma *and* the FANBOYS conjunction. For example:

The page came out white Yoshio, thus, thought that his printer was broken.

You can add a comma and an appropriate FANBOYS conjunction—such as "and" or "so"—after the word "white," or just add a semicolon:

The page came out white; Yoshio, thus, thought that his printer was broken.

NON-*FANBOYS* TRANSITION WORDS

Watch out for transition words between independent clauses that are *not* FANBOYS conjunctions. These sentences may sound fine but are often considered run-ons. For example:

I practiced for hours while I taped myself, *then* I listened back to see how I sounded.

This sentence is a run-on. Use a FANBOYS conjunction, such as *and*, to correct the error. A good test is to notice that the word *then* could be moved around within the sentence (a FANBOYS conjunction is generally "stuck" between the clauses):

I practiced for hours while I taped myself, *and then* I listened back to see how I sounded.
I practiced for hours while I taped myself, *and* I *then* listened back to see how I sounded.
I practiced for hours while I taped myself, *and* I listened back *then* to see how I sounded.

Here are some other transition words commonly used (incorrectly) to link independent clauses. This list will hopefully give you an idea of what to look for:

even so	in fact	on the other hand
furthermore	in other words	similarly
however	moreover	therefore
in addition	nevertheless	thus

———

To identify run-on errors, look for questions with answer choices that contain various ways to connect independent clauses, including commas, conjunctions, periods, and semicolons.

RUN-ONS LESSON PROBLEMS

Most people rarely get to see the <u>sunrise they</u>[1] are asleep that early in the morning.

1. **A.** NO CHANGE
    B. sunrise and they
    C. sunrise because they
    D. sunrise, and because they

<u>Kevin had run slowly at first, he</u>[2] then accelerated quickly to avoid the pursuing tacklers, who, to the delight of the crowd, fell harmlessly at Kevin's feet.

2. **F.** NO CHANGE
    G. Kevin had run slowly at first; he
    H. While Kevin had run slowly at first; he
    J. Kevin had run slowly at first he

Many health experts agree that young people are not active <u>enough, this</u> inactivity is likely a result of the temptations of such sedentary activities as watching television or working on the internet.

Many people now watch more shows on their computers than on actual <u>televisions, and I wonder</u> if the end of the television is near.

At the end of the last day of school, the students <u>celebrated; however,</u> the teachers, with stacks of ungraded tests on their desks, had much work ahead.

3. **A.** NO CHANGE
   B. enough this
   C. enough. This
   D. enough and this

4. Which of following alternatives to the underlined portion would NOT be acceptable?

   F. televisions, leading me to wonder
   G. televisions I wonder
   H. televisions. I wonder
   J. televisions, which makes me wonder

5. **A.** NO CHANGE
   B. celebrated, however,
   C. celebrated, however
   D. celebrated however

Playing a sport and learning an instrument offer good analogies for effective <u>studying, because</u> these activities involve considerable practice to master, one can see the obvious benefits of hard work and persistence.

The book was written without regard to punctuation or <u>paragraphs this unconformity</u> made it difficult to understand.

He spoke with his <u>hands, but his voice</u> was silent.

He worked tirelessly to finish the experiment on the health benefits of soy <u>beans because the health conference was</u> only a few weeks away.

The book *Dune*, by Frank Herbert, is the world's best-selling science fiction novel and has won both the Nebula and Hugo <u>Awards, in other words,</u> it's a sci-fi classic.

1. **A.** NO CHANGE
   B. studying because
   C. studying; because
   D. studying, and this is because

2. **F.** NO CHANGE
   G. paragraphs, this unconformity
   H. paragraphs, an unconformity that
   J. paragraphs and this unconformity

3. **A.** NO CHANGE
   B. hands but his voice
   C. hands, his voice
   D. hands his voice

4. **F.** NO CHANGE
   G. beans, the health conference was
   H. beans, the health conference being
   J. beans. The health conference being

5. **A.** NO CHANGE
   B. Awards, in other words
   C. Awards, in other words;
   D. Awards; in other words,

8. MISPLACED WORDS

MOVING WORDS TO AVOID AMBIGUITY

Sometimes the order of the words in a sentence creates an ambiguity. Look at the following example:

> There was a scratch on the new wood table right in the center.

This sentence literally suggests that the wood table is "in the center." Likely, this is not the intended meaning. Move the related words together in the sentence to remove the error, as in the corrected version below:

> There was a scratch *right in the center* of the new wood table.

Here is another example:

> The ice cream competition will be the largest ever with ice-cream samples from over 100 contestants kept in a large freezer.

Our hearts go out to those poor contestants in the freezer. The following sentences remove the ambiguity:

> The ice cream competition will be the largest ever with over 100 contestants. The ice-cream samples will be kept in a large freezer.

MOVING WORDS TO AVOID AWKWARDNESS

Sometimes the order of the words just plain sounds wrong:

> Computer Aided Design offers at the same time opportunities to be artistic and technical.

Perhaps the meaning is clear, but the sentence doesn't sound great, does it? The following corrects the awkwardness:

> Computer Aided Design offers opportunities to be artistic and technical *at the same time.*

IMPROPER MODIFIERS

As we've seen in the previous sections, dependent clauses and phrases can act as modifiers for a noun or nouns in the sentence. On the ACT, *improper modifiers*, which are usually at the beginning of a sentence, appear to modify an illogical noun because of this noun's closeness to the modifying phrase. **You must make sure that the noun meant to be modified is as close as possible to the modifying phrase.** For example:

> With power and skill, the volleyball was spiked over the net by Jill.

The modifying phrase in this sentence is *With power and skill*. It is obviously meant to modify *Jill*, but it seems to modify *the volleyball*. The sentence's intended meaning may be obvious, but the sentence should be corrected to read:

> With power and skill, Jill spiked the volleyball over the net.

There are two ways to identify misplaced words questions:

1. Look for questions with answer choices that give you the option to move the underlined portion to another part of the sentence.
2. Look for questions with answer choices that rewrite a large portion of the sentence, often an entire clause. As you might imagine, words or phrases are repositioned in these answer choices.

APPROACH TO MISPLACED WORDS QUESTIONS

Even though you may use the answer choices to *identify* a misplaced word problem (as described above), try to answer these misplaced words questions without scrutinizing the answer choices right away. Just use the passage. This *aggressive* approach will often help you because the answer choices on Misplaced Words questions can be wordy and confusing.

MISPLACED WORDS LESSON PROBLEMS

You can use this phone card to call your sister and tell her about the fine dinner you had <u>for less than a dollar</u>.
₁

1. The best placement for the underlined portion would be:

   A. where it is now.
   B.) after the word *sister*.
   C. after the word *about*.
   D.) after the word *dinner*.

Corporations are more <u>likely to hire college</u>
₂
<u>graduates with advanced degrees than smaller</u>
₂
<u>companies</u>.
₂

2. F.) NO CHANGE
   G. likely to hire, as opposed to smaller companies, college graduates with advanced degrees
   H. likely to hire than smaller companies college graduates with advanced degrees
   J.) likely than smaller companies to hire college graduates with advanced degrees

After sneaking out the window to play games with his friends, <u>his parents were the last people</u>
₃
<u>Sean expected to run into at the arcade</u>.
₃

3. A. NO CHANGE
   B.) Sean least expected to run into his parents at the arcade
   C.) running into his parents was the last thing Sean expected at the arcade
   D. his parents, at the arcade, were the last people Sean expected to run into

After sleeping through the entire semester, <u>a shock was receiving the A to Chrissie</u>.
₄

4. F. NO CHANGE
   G.) receiving an A was a shock to Chrissie
   H.) Chrissie was shocked that she received an A
   J. Chrissie's A was a shock to her

The writer discussed the negative impact of graffiti <u>in the last chapter of his book</u>.
₁

1. The best placement for the underlined portion would be:

   A. where it is now.
   B. after the word *discussed*.
   C. after the word *negative*.
   D. at the beginning of the sentence (capitalizing *in*, ending the underlined portion with a comma, and making the *T* in *The* lowercase).

After hearing the CD of the live performance, <u>our disappointment in missing the show was</u> <u>unbearable</u>.
₂

2. F. NO CHANGE
   G. our disappointment in having missed the show was unbearable
   H. we were, because of having missed the show, unbearably disappointed
   J. we were unbearably disappointed about missing the show

The new navigation <u>system, when a button is</u> <u>pressed, will speak directions to the driver, on</u> <u>the steering wheel</u>.
₃

3. A. NO CHANGE
   B. system will speak directions, when a button is pressed on the steering wheel to the driver
   C. system will speak directions to the driver when a button is pressed on the steering wheel
   D. system, will speak directions to the driver, when a button is pressed on the steering wheel

---

With strength and endurance not found among any of the other <u>competitors, Greg Lemond's</u> <u>victory was yet again</u>.
₄

4. F. NO CHANGE
   G. competitors, Greg Lemond rode to victory yet again
   H. competitors, to victory yet again Greg Lemond rode
   J. competitors as Greg Lemond rode to victory yet again

All programs: Now is a good time to review sections 5-8 and take Grammar Quiz 2 (Sections 5-8), which is found in the Grammar Quizzes section at the end of this chapter.

9. REDUNDANCIES

The ACT likes to make sure that you're paying attention by testing *redundancies*. A redundancy involves saying the same thing twice, thus using more words than necessary. The ACT typically tests this by using words that mean about the same thing.

> That school's water polo team is favored to repeat and duplicate its championship of last year.

Of course, to *repeat* and to *duplicate* mean about the same thing. Eliminate one of them to correct the sentence

> That school's water polo team is favored to *repeat* its championship of last year.

Here's another example that tests the meaning of a word.

> If you start your report the day before it is due, your teachers will think you are a procrastinator who is always waiting until the last minute to begin working on something.

What is a procrastinator? A procrastinator is one who is always waiting until the last minute to begin working on something. The last part of the sentence is redundant and should be eliminated.

> If you start your report the day before it is due, your teachers will think you are a procrastinator.

To identify redundancy questions, look for questions with some long answer choices and at least one that is considerably shorter than the others.

SHORT ANSWERS

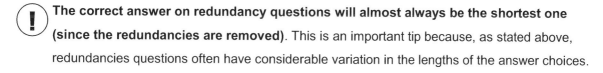

The correct answer on redundancy questions will almost always be the shortest one (since the redundancies are removed). This is an important tip because, as stated above, redundancies questions often have considerable variation in the lengths of the answer choices.

OMIT THE UNDERLINED PORTION

You will often see the words "OMIT the underlined portion" as an answer choice on redundancies questions. This answer choice, which shortens the passage more than the others, is usually the correct one.

REDUNDANCIES LESSON PROBLEMS

The company is able to stay on top of the tech world because of its emphasis on <u>new</u> innovations.

1. **A.** NO CHANGE
   B. the newness of its
   C. new and current
   D. OMIT the underlined portion.

The judge was forced to <u>free the man and let</u> <u>him go</u> after the judge determined that the evidence had been tampered with.

2. **F.** NO CHANGE
   G. free the man
   H. let the now free man go
   J. free and liberate the man

The tree <u>swayed and moved back and forth</u> in the strong wind.

3. **A.** NO CHANGE
   B. swayed
   C. swayed back
   D. swayed back and forth

Because the conference room is flooded, we'll have to have the community meeting <u>later, at a</u> <u>future date</u>.

4. **F.** NO CHANGE
   G. later, in a while
   H. at a future date
   J. at a later, future date

(HW)

You have to score at least 90 points <u>or more</u> on the company's written test to be considered for the job.

1. **A.** NO CHANGE
   B. but no less than that
   C. and no less than that
   D. OMIT the underlined portion.

In the last sentence of the book, the author <u>concluded by hinting</u> that everything had been a dream.

2. **F.** NO CHANGE
   G. concluded and hinted
   H. finished writing by hinting
   J. hinted

Continued →

Diego Maradona is without question one of the <u>fastest and nimblest</u> players soccer has ever known.
₃

Before Sir Edmund Hillary conquered Mount Everest in 1953, many agreed that its steep and treacherous slopes <u>were insurmountable and would never be climbed</u>.
₄

3. **A.** NO CHANGE
   B. fastest, quickest, and nimblest
   C. fastest, nimble and agile
   D. fastest

4. **F.** NO CHANGE
   G. were insurmountably unclimbable
   H. were insurmountable
   J. could not be mounted by climbing

10. APOSTROPHES AND CONFUSED WORDS

Sometimes students confuse words that have similar *appearance* or *sound*. For example, you may come across words such as *principal* and *principle* (a *principal* works at your school—he's your "pal" (get it?); a *principle* is a rule or standard.) There are hundreds of other confused words, but luckily most of the confused words tested on the ACT have to do with the more manageable subject of apostrophes ('). Apostrophes have two general uses:

1. To indicate that letters have been removed from a word—this is called a *contraction*. For example, *they're* is a contraction of *they are* (note the missing *a*).
2. To show possession. For example, this is *Kathleen's* book. (The book belongs to Kathleen.)

APOSTROPHES USED FOR CONTRACTIONS ☺

The most commonly-tested contractions are the ones that sound like other words. For example,

> This is there cooler, so please put it over they're. Their going to be here soon.

If you read the sentence out loud, it sounds fine. But do you see the three errors? The following words may sound alike, but they have different uses: *their* should be used as a possessive for they; *there* should be used to indicate a place; and *they're* should be a contraction for *they are*. The following corrects the sentence:

> This is *their* cooler, so please put it over *there*. *They're* going to be here soon.

Here are a few other commonly-confused words involving contractions:

your/you're
The word *your* is used as a possessive for *you* (This is *your* book). The word *you're* is a contraction of *you* and *are* (*You're* going to have to study hard to raise your score).

its/it's
This one can be tricky. The word *its* is a possessive of *it* (*Its* windows are dirty). The word *it's* is a contraction of *it* and *is* (*It's* a lovely day to clean the windows).

There are dozens of other contractions that might show up, but they typically fall into one of two categories. Either the apostrophe replaces the *o* in *not* (*can't* = *can not*, *wouldn't* = *would not*) or the apostrophe replaces the beginning of a *to-be verb* (*I'm* = *I am*, *he'd* = *he would*, *you'll* = *you will*). Note that the contraction of *will not* is *won't*, an unexpected change in spelling.

APOSTROPHES USED FOR POSSESSIVES

Apostrophes are often used to indicate that something or someone *possesses* something else. For example:

This is Jeff's car. (The car belongs to Jeff.)

There are three general rules to remember when turning a noun into a possessive:

1. If the word is singular, add *'s*. (Most grammarians, including the ACT test writers, require the *'s* even if the word already ends with an *s*; see the second example below.):
    Jeff → Jeff's car
    moss → the moss's growth
2. If the word is plural and ends with an *s*, add an apostrophe to the end of the word:
    girls → the girls' room
    the Smiths → the Smiths' house
3. If the word is plural and does *not* end with an *s*, add *'s* to the end of the word:
    children → the children's hospital
    men → the men's room

PRONOUN POSSESSIVES

As you've already seen (*their*, *your*, *its*), pronouns can be used as possessives. **These words do *not* use apostrophes, even if they end with an s.** The following are some examples:

your = possessive of *you*
their = possessive of *they*
my = possessive of *I*
his = possessive of *he*
its = possessive of *it*
whose = possessive of *who*

The pronoun possessive may change if it comes at the end of a phrase. Trust your ear:

The bike is *yours*, but the skateboard is *mine*.

APPROACH TO APOSTROPHES ON THE ACT

The ACT often mixes contractions and possessives on the same question, so the first step is to decide which is appropriate. Here's a good test: **first check for a contraction.** If, after expanding the word, the sentence sounds correct, then the contraction is correct. For example:

> The day's beautiful at this time—don't you think?

Expand the contraction, and you have:

> The *day is* beautiful at this time—don't you think?

This sounds fine. The word is a contraction and the apostrophe is used correctly. Here's another example:

> My *friend's* are going to be here soon. → My *friend is* are going to be here soon.

Clearly this is incorrect. Either the word *friend's* is a possessive or (as is the case here) the apostrophe should be removed.

————

To identify apostrophe errors, look for questions with answer choices that contain variations in apostrophes for the same word. Also, look for possessive pronouns.

APOSTROPHES AND CONFUSED WORDS LESSON PROBLEMS

The <u>ancient shells shape</u> tells scientists much
₁
about the shape of the organism that inhabited
it.

1. **A.** NO CHANGE
   B. ancient shells' shape
   C. ancient shell's shape
   D. ancient's shell's shape

Nicholson Baker's first book, *The Mezzanine*,
with <u>its</u> copious digressions and footnotes,
₂
influenced many writers to come.

2. **F.** NO CHANGE
   G. it's
   H. its'
   J. their

Continued →

Poison oak is difficult to identify because <u>its</u>
₃
propensity to imitate the appearance of nearby
plants.

3. **A.** NO CHANGE
   B. of its
   C. it's
   D. of it's

Since the members of the science team will
work along the coast, <u>they're going</u> to
₄
focus their report on beach erosion.

4. **F.** NO CHANGE
   G. their going
   H. theirs is one
   J. there will be

<u>It's in your best interest</u> to keep your hands
₁
inside the vehicle during the tour.

1. **A.** NO CHANGE
   B. Its in your best interest
   C. Its' in your best interest
   D. It's your best interest

Only a few of the <u>country's regions</u> are named
₂
using the native language.

2. **F.** NO CHANGE
   G. countries' regions'
   H. country's region's
   J. countries regions

<u>Your going</u> to regret staying up late because
₃
classes start an hour earlier tomorrow.

3. **A.** NO CHANGE
   B. You will
   C. Your
   D. You're going

<u>Giraffes long necks</u> allow them to reach tree
₄
leaves and other foods that most other animals
cannot.

4. **F.** NO CHANGE
   G. Giraffe's long necks
   H. Giraffes' long neck's
   J. Giraffes' long necks

11. IDIOM

Idiom has to do with the manner or style of a language. Idiom rules are less predictable and consistent (and, thus, more difficult to remember) than most of the other grammar rules in this tutorial. The good news is that many of the idiom errors will simply sound wrong to your ear.

PREPOSITIONAL IDIOMS

Most idiom mistakes on the ACT have to do with an incorrect preposition following an adjective or verb. For example:

> We only wanted to look at the paintings; we were *indifferent **of*** the sculpture exhibit.

Idiom dictates that, in general, the preposition *to* (not *of*) should be used after *indifferent.* There is no real way to predict this rule—the choice seems arbitrary. This is why these idiom rules can be difficult. You must either memorize from a long list of rules or (hopefully) rely on your ear. The correct sentence should read:

> We only wanted to look at the paintings; we were *indifferent **to*** the sculpture exhibit.

Here is another common mistake:

> The oil paintings don't look *different **than*** the acrylic ones.

Idiom dictates that the preposition *from* should follow *different*:

> The oil paintings don't look *different **from*** the acrylic ones.

SAME WORD, DIFFERENT PREPOSITIONS

Complicating matters, sometimes the same word can take different prepositions depending on the context. For example:

> We *agreed **to*** go to the museum together, but we could not *agree **on*** how to get there. I hope you *agree **with*** me that walking is out of the question.

Fortunately, most of these rules will sound natural to your ear. For example, you probably would never say: we could not *agree* ***to*** how to get there. It just sounds wrong.

LEARNING IDIOM

The best way to learn idiom rules is by hearing (or reading) correct idiom. Simply put, this is how we all learn to speak correctly. Unfortunately, there is no real shortcut to learning idiom. That's the bad news. The good news is that many students will already "hear" the idiom errors that show up on the test. And for those who struggle with these idiom rules, keep in mind that any one test will probably include only a handful of idiom questions. But we guarantee that they do show up.

The list on the following page displays some of the most common prepositional idiom errors, but before looking at the list in detail, try the homework problems on page 57. If you miss several of them, you may choose to spend some time making flashcards and memorizing the items on the list (especially if you are doing well on most of the other grammar rules in this chapter). If you get most of the questions on the homework correct, your "idiom ear" is probably in good shape and you won't have to put significant time into this lesson.

Remember that some of the verbs and adverbs on the following list may use different prepositions depending on the context of the sentence. When needed for clarification, examples are written in brackets.

———

To identify prepositional idiom errors, look for questions with answer choices that contain a variety of *prepositions* (e.g., *of*, *with*, *over*, *to*, etc.). If necessary, review prepositions in the Subject-Verb lesson.

LIST OF COMMON PREPOSITIONAL IDIOM ERRORS

abide **by** (not **to**)

ability **to** [make] (not **for** [making])

accompanied **by** (not **with**)

according **to** (not **with**—but *in accordance* **with**)

accused **of** (not **over** or **with**)

acquainted **with** (not **to**)

afraid **of** (not **about**)

agree **on**, **to**, or **with** (not **about**)

aim **at** (not **on** or **against**)

alarmed **at** (not **about**)

amazed **at** (not **about**)

amused **by** (better than **at**)

angry **with** or **about** (not **against**)

annoyed **by** (not **about** or **at**)

anxious **about** (not **for**)

argue **about** (not **on**)

arrive **at** (not **to**)

ashamed **of** (not **over** or **with**)

belong **to** (not **with**)

benefit **from** (not **by**)

bored **by** or **with** (not **of**)

careful **of** or **with** (not **for**)

combine **with** (not **to**)

comply **with** (not **to**)

concentrate **on** (not **over** or **in**)

concerned **about** (not **of**)

confident **in** (not **about**)

conform **to** (not **in** or **with**)

confused **by** (not **over**)

congratulated **on** (not **about**)

consistent **with** (not **to**)

curious **about** (not **with**)

delighted **with** (not **about**)

depart **for** (not **to**)

dependent **on** (not **of**)

deprived **of** (not **from**)

detrimental **to** (not **for**)

die **of** (not **from**)

different **from** (not **than**)

dip **into** (not **in**)

dive **into** (not **in**)

divide **into** (not **in**)

disapprove **of** (not **with**)

distinct **from** (not **of**)

embarrassed **by** (not **about**)

essential **to** [succeed] (not **for** [succeeding])

exception **to** (not **of**)

excited **about** (not **at** or **over**)

an expert **in** (not **about** or **of**)

familiar **with** (not **to**)

famous **for** (not **in**)

fired **from** (not **off of**)

frightened **by** or **of** (not **at**)

furious **about** (not **over**)

good **at** (not **in**)

guard **against** (not **from**)

happy **about** (not **of**)

hopeless **at** (not **in**)

ignorant **of** (not **with**)

independent **of** or **from**

indifferent **to** (not **of** or **with**)

insight **into** (not **to**)

intent **on** (not **with**)

interested **in** (not **about**)

intrude **on** (not **in**)

involved **in** (not **with**)

irritated **by** (not **from**)

knowledge **of** (not **about**)

leave **for** (not **to**)

live **in** [a city] (not **at**)

live **at** [a hotel] (not **in**)

live **on** [a street] (not **at**)

look **at** (not **toward**)

married **to** (not **with**)

mourn **for** (not **over**)

necessary **for** (not **in**) [understanding] (not **to** [understand])

oblivious **to** (not **of**)

opposed **to** (not **over**)

part **with** (not **from**)

planning **to** [work] (not **on** [working])

point **at** (not **to** or **toward**)

popular **with** (not **among**)

pray **for** (not **about**)

preoccupied **with** (not **in**)

prohibited **from** (not **to**)

proud **of** (not **about**)

pry **into** (not **in**)

punished **for** (not **over**)

relevant **to** (not **for**)

responsible **for** (not **about**)

satisfied **with** (not **about**)

shocked **at** (not **about**)

shoot **at** (not **toward**)

similar **to** (not **with**)

sorry **for** (not **about**)

succeed **in** (not **with** or **at**)

suffer **from** (not **with**)

suited **to** (not **for**)

surprised **at** or **by** (not **about**)

sure **of** (not **about**)

suspicious **of** (not **with**)

suspected **of** (not **with**)

tendency **to** [work] (not **of** [working])

tremble **with** [cold] (not **from**)

upset **about** (not **at**)

wary **of** (not **about**)

worried **about** (not **over** or **with**)

HW

Do NOT look back to the lesson as you complete this assignment:

If you expect to play in the game, you must <u>abide by</u> the coach's rules.

1. **A.** NO CHANGE
   B. abide to
   C. abide from
   D. be abiding with

The running back <u>crashed through</u> the opposing tacklers and never looked back.

2. Which of the following alternatives to the underlined portion would NOT be acceptable?

   F. fought for
   G. muscled through
   H. ran around
   J. jumped over

The author, Sir Arthur Conan Doyle, is <u>famous for</u> his Sherlock Holmes mystery novels.

3. **A.** NO CHANGE
   B. famous in
   C. famous by
   D. famous of

After years of struggle, the country of Kosovo is finally <u>independent by</u> Serbia.

4. **F.** NO CHANGE
   G. independent with
   H. independent of
   J. having independence from

<u>Over land and sea</u>, the warriors traveled to their destinies.

5. Which of the following alternatives to the underlined portion would NOT be acceptable?

   A. By land and sea
   B. Through land and sea
   C. Across land and sea
   D. On land and sea

COMMON IDIOM MISTAKES

There are hundreds of common idiom mistakes. Again, these rules are generally not as predictable as the other grammar rules in this tutorial. Here is an example:

The reason I can't compete in the track meet today is because I have a sprained ankle.

This sentence may sound OK, but it is actually idiomatically incorrect because *is because* is following *reason*. The sentence would be correct with *that* in place of *is because*:

The *reason* I can't compete in the track meet today is *that* I have a sprained ankle.

There is no universal rule here—just an idiom rule that you may have to memorize.

These errors are hard to predict and are thus potentially difficult to prepare for. But the good news is: they don't show up very often on the ACT. Thus, unless you have a lot of time, you might choose to just read them over—don't worry about making flashcards and memorizing at first. Try the homework at the end of the section. If you struggle, then you should consider spending some time making flash cards and memorizing. If you get most of them correct, your ear is in good shape and you won't have to put significant time into memorizing the rules.

The following lists a number of common idiom mistakes:

a lot → very much

Incorrect: I like track and field events *a lot*.

Correct: I like track and field events *very much*.

around → about

Avoid *around* to designate time, distance, or any other quantity.

Incorrect: The meet starts at *around* noon.

Correct: The meet starts at *about* noon.

at

>Incorrect: Where is the pole *at* for the pole vault?

>Correct: Where is the pole for the pole vault?

at once

The words "at once" are generally used with the conjunction "and" in the following way: something is "at once (this) *and* (that)."

>Incorrect: The book was *at once* unsophisticated because of its everyday writing and themes, but it's certainly enjoyable because of its interesting characters.

>Correct: The book was *at once* simple-minded because of its everyday writing and themes *and* enjoyable because of its interesting characters.

badly → desperately

>Incorrect: She *badly* wants to win the decathlon.

>Correct: She *desperately* wants to win the decathlon.

because (used after *reason*) **→ that**

>Incorrect: The reason she runs so quickly is *because* she trains hard.

>Correct: The reason she runs so quickly is *that* she trains hard.

being as/being that → because

>Incorrect: *Being that* she trains so hard, she is difficult to beat.

>Correct: *Because* she trains so hard, she is difficult to beat.

bunch → group

Do not use *bunch* when referring to people.

>Incorrect: There is a *bunch* of athletes getting ready for the marathon.

>Correct: There is a *group* of athletes getting ready for the marathon

center around → center on

A center is a single, fixed point and as such cannot move or exist *around* something.

>Incorrect: The news conference *centered around* the Iraq war.

>Correct: The news conference *centered on* the Iraq war.

doubt but/help but → doubt/help

Incorrect: I have no *doubt but* that you are the best high jumper on the team.

Correct: I have no *doubt* that you are the best high jumper on the team.

Incorrect: I could not *help but* notice the height of the bar.

Correct: I could not *help* noticing the height of the bar.

flunk → fail

Incorrect: He may be the best at pole vaulting, but he *flunked* his history quiz.

Correct: He may be the best at pole vaulting, but he *failed* his history quiz.

former/latter

Former and *latter* should only be used when choosing between *two* things.

Incorrect: After visiting Paris, Madrid, and London, I prefer the *latter*.

Correct: After visiting Paris, Madrid, and London, I prefer London.

graduate

Graduate should be followed by *from*.

Incorrect: He will probably win 20 tournaments before he *graduates* high school.

Correct: He will probably win 20 tournaments before he *graduates from* high school.

in regards to → in regard to

Incorrect: *In regards to* the javelin throw, I'll stay as far away as possible.

Correct: *In regard to* the javelin throw, I'll stay as far away as possible.

inside of → in less than

Incorrect: He ran the mile *inside of* four minutes.

Correct: He ran the mile *in less than* four minutes.

irregardless → regardless

Incorrect: *Irregardless* of what he says, it looks dangerous.

Correct: *Regardless* of what he says, it looks dangerous.

is when/is where → is/occurs when

Incorrect: The shot put *is when* you throw a heavy metal ball called a shot as far as possible.

Correct: The shot put *is* throwing a heavy metal ball called a shot as far as possible.

Incorrect: A false start is *where* you leave before the gun sounds.

Correct: A false start *occurs when* you leave before the gun sounds.

kind of/sort of → somewhat or rather

Incorrect: She was *kind of* disappointed with her javelin throw.

Correct: She was *somewhat* disappointed with her javelin throw.

like/maybe → approximately, perhaps, or about

Incorrect: There were *maybe* one thousand fans in the stands.

Correct: There were *approximately* one thousand fans in the stands.

lots of → many

Incorrect: There are *lots of* athletes on the field.

Correct: There are *many* athletes on the field.

more … and not → more … than

Incorrect: She is known *more* for her jumping *and not* for her running.

Correct: She is known *more* for her jumping *than* for her running.

most → almost

Incorrect: He runs *most* every day of the week.

Correct: He runs *almost* every day of the week.

nor → or (see the Conjunction section)

Incorrect: If she expects to win, she cannot start late *nor* early.

Correct: If she expects to win, she cannot start late *or* early.

of → have

Incorrect: If you *would of* been here with the stopwatch, I *could of* timed myself.

Correct: If you *would have* been here with the stopwatch, I *could have* timed myself.

plenty → very

Incorrect: You could tell from his long stride that he was *plenty* fast.

Correct: You could tell from his long stride that he was *very* fast.

plus → and

Incorrect: He has huge arms, *plus* his legs are also strong.

Correct: He has huge arms, *and* his legs are also strong.

reason is/was because (see *because*)

so → very

Incorrect: It is *so* difficult to jump over hurdles.

Correct: It is *very* difficult to jump over hurdles.

so as to → to

Incorrect: He uses chalk *so as to* grip the shot more firmly.

Correct: He uses chalk *to* grip the shot more firmly.

try and → try to

Incorrect: *Try and* see if you can run one lap without collapsing.

Correct: *Try to* see if you can run one lap without collapsing.

use to/suppose to → used to/supposed to

Incorrect: He *use* to be the fastest sprinter at our school.

Correct: He *used* to be the fastest sprinter at our school.

Incorrect: She was *suppose* to win the decathlon, but she sprained her ankle.

Correct: She was *supposed* to win the decathlon, but she sprained her ankle.

After reading over the common idiom mistakes on the previous pages, try the problems below. Do NOT look back to the lesson while completing the assignment.

The reason for my late arrival is <u>because</u> the train was running behind schedule due to the demonstration downtown.
[1]

1. **A.** NO CHANGE
   B. due to the fact that
   C. that
   D. for the reason of

I couldn't help <u>but notice</u> the smell of cigarettes on your clothes when you returned from the library.
[2]

2. **F.** NO CHANGE
   G. but to notice
   H. as to notice
   J. noticing

Winning the lottery is a matter of luck, <u>irregardless of what</u> the fortune teller may say.
[3]

3. **A.** NO CHANGE
   B. disregarding what
   C. regardless of what
   D. irregardless what

The grandfather clock was used more for decoration <u>than</u> for time keeping.
[4]

4. **F.** NO CHANGE
   G. and not meant
   H. and not
   J. but not

You should not wear a jacket <u>nor</u> long pants on the raft because both will just get soaked.
[5]

5. **A.** NO CHANGE
   B. or
   C. but
   D. and also not

All programs: Now is a good time to review sections 9-11 and take Grammar Quiz 3 (Sections 9-11), which is found in the Grammar Quizzes section at the end of this chapter.

20-hour program: After completing Grammar Quiz 3, jump to the Usage/Mechanics chapter.

12. ADJECTIVES AND ADVERBS

ADJECTIVES AND ADVERBS TERMINOLOGY

Adjective – a word that describes or modifies a person or thing in a sentence (such as *blue*, *old*, *calm*, or *happy*).

Adverb – a word that modifies a verb, adjective, or other adverb in a sentence (such as *quickly*, *happily*, or *stubbornly*). Adverbs describe *how* something happens.

ADJECTIVE AND ADVERB ERRORS

Adjectives only modify *nouns*. On the ACT, adjective and adverb errors occur when an adjective is used incorrectly in place of an adverb, or vice versa. As you read the example below, first identify the adjective or adverb. If you spot an adjective, remember that it must describe a noun. If you can't identify the noun that the adjective should modify, the adjective is incorrect; replace it with an adverb.

I was surprised how quick she walked to the store.

The adjective is "quick." Ask yourself: what is "quick" modifying? Since it's describing "*how*…she walked," it should be an adverb:

I was surprised how *quickly* she walked to the store.

GOOD VERSUS WELL AND BAD VERSUS BADLY

The words *good* and *bad* are adjectives, and the words *well* and *badly* are adverbs. Following the rules above, if a noun is being modified, use *good* or *bad*, and if a verb is being modified, use *well* or *badly*. For example:

He performed *well* on the test. (*Well* describes how he *performed*.)
He received a *good* score on the test. (*Good* modifies the noun *score*.)

When dealing with any of the five senses, there is an exception to these rules. Use the word *good* or *bad* to modify verbs. For example:

After sketching with a new type of charcoal, the drawing looks *good* (not *well*).
The burnt bread made dinner smell *bad* (not *badly*).

To identify adjective and adverb errors, look for questions with answer choices that contain words in adjective AND adverb forms. You might also see similar words as nouns or comparison words in the answer choices. For example, if you see the words *happy* (adjective), *happily* (adverb), *happiness* (noun), and/or *happier* (comparison) in the answer choices, the question is probably testing adjectives and adverbs.

ADJECTIVES AND ADVERBS LESSON PROBLEMS

No matter <u>how careful</u> tax returns are checked,
₁
there is always a good chance of mistakes.

1. **A.** NO CHANGE
   B. how much care
   C. the more care
   D. how carefully

Trying to find the source of the rumor, Elijah
<u>moved rapid</u> from one group to another.
₂

2. **F.** NO CHANGE
   G. moved rapidly
   H. moved more rapid
   J. moved with rapidness

The speaker once again showed her skills with
one of her <u>typical brilliant</u> dissertations.
₁

1. **A.** NO CHANGE
   B. typically brilliant
   C. typically brilliantly
   D. typical, brilliant

She received accolades for doing a <u>really good</u>
₂
<u>job</u> on the science project.
₂

2. **F.** NO CHANGE
   G. real good job
   H. a job as well as possible
   J. job that is well

13. COMPARISONS

THE *NUMBER* OF A COMPARISON

The *number* of a comparison refers to the number of items being compared. There are grammatical differences between comparing two things and comparing three or more things.

When comparing **two** things, you will use the *-er* form of an adjective (words such as happi*er* or strong*er*) or the word *more* prior to an adjective (such as *more* beautiful). You will also often use the word *than* for these comparisons (not *then*, a common mistake).

Jason is *better than* I am at shooting with his left hand. (two people)

When comparing **three or more** things, you will use the *-est* form of an adjective (happi*est* or strong*est*) or the word *most* prior to an adjective (such as *most* beautiful). For example:

Jason is the *best* player on the team at shooting with his left hand. (three or more people)

DOUBLE COMPARISONS

Make sure to never create a *double comparison* by putting words like *more* or *most* in the same phrase with words in the *-er* or *-est* form. For example, avoid:

more friendlier, most friendliest

TRICKY COMPARISON WORDS ☺

The table below shows some of the tricky comparison words. If you already hear these correctly, don't worry about memorizing them.

adjective	two things	three or more things
good	better	best
well	better	best
bad	worse	worst
little	less	least
much	more	most
many	more	most

The ACT may try to use *more* or *most* when one of the *tricky* comparison words should be used. For example:

Jason's game went from bad to more bad because of his injury.

The words "more bad" are not grammatically correct. They should be replaced with the word *worse*.

Jason's game went from bad to *worse* because of his injury.

These errors are essentially double comparisons, as described above.

———————

To identify comparison errors, look for questions with answer choices that contain the words *more* and *most* or have the same words in the *-er* and *-est* forms.

COMPARISONS LESSON PROBLEMS

An oil candle is both brighter and <u>more longer-burning</u> than a conventional wax candle.
<u>1</u>

1. **A.** NO CHANGE
    B. longer-burning
    C. far more longer-burning
    D. long-burning

On our track team, Evan may have long legs, but he is definitely not the <u>faster of the group</u>.
2

2. **F.** NO CHANGE
    G. fastest of the group
    H. most fastest of the group
    J. group's faster runner

Since he spends all day and night studying, Brian, not surprisingly, is the <u>most intelligent</u>
3
student in the class.

3. **A.** NO CHANGE
    B. more intelligent
    C. more than intelligent
    D. more than anyone else, intelligent

Amanda is definitely the more outspoken of the
                                          1
twins.
  1

1. **A.** NO CHANGE
   B. Amanda is definitely the most outspoken of the twins
   C. Of the twins, Amanda is definitely the most outspoken
   D. More than the other of the twins, Amanda is definitely outspoken

When deciding whether to take the high road or
the low road, the <u>best</u> choice is often elusive.
                     2

2. **F.** NO CHANGE
   G. most best
   H. more better
   J. better

I would be <u>more than happier</u> to take you and
                   3
your friends to the airport.

3. **A.** NO CHANGE
   B. the most happiest
   C. more than happy
   D. a quality greater than happiest

14. ILLOGICAL COMPARISONS

These types of problems don't show up frequently on the ACT, but the rule is good to know. The saying goes that *you can't compare apples to oranges*. For example:

> The science department's projects are much more interesting than the English department this year.

The sentence is incorrect because the science department's *projects* are being compared to the English *department*. The correct sentence should read:

> The science department's projects are much more interesting than the English department's *projects* this year.

You don't always have to restate the noun being compared, as above. Using an *apostrophe-s* (*'s*) or the word *that* (singular) or *those* (plural) is usually acceptable. (Just make sure the comparisons are *parallel*, as in the examples below.)

> The science department's projects are much more interesting than the English department*'s* this year.

> The projects of the science department are much more interesting than *those* of the English department this year.

––––––––

When you spot a comparison, ask yourself: what items are being compared? You might want to underline the two items. **Always compare "apples to apples."**

To identify illogical comparison errors, look for questions with underlined comparisons. The answer choices will contain various comparing options; however, looking for the comparison in the passage is probably the best way to identify these types of questions.

ILLOGICAL COMPARISONS LESSON PROBLEMS

Our school's students are much stronger in math and science <u>than the average school</u>.
₁

1. **A.** NO CHANGE
   B. than the average school is in math and science
   C. than the average school's students
   D. than the students at the average school

The history of Hawaii, <u>like other Pacific islands</u>,
₂
is primarily concerned with the ocean.

2. **F.** NO CHANGE
   G. similar to other Pacific islands
   H. like those of other Pacific islands
   J. in comparison to other Pacific islands

A recent study suggests that eating fish twice a week is healthier <u>than eating other meats</u>.
₁

1. **A.** NO CHANGE
   B. than other meats
   C. than other meats twice a week
   D. than other meats are

Daniel's score on this test, after diligent study and practice, is much better than <u>his last test</u>.
₂

2. **F.** NO CHANGE
   G. his score on his last test
   H. the test he took last
   J. that test that he took last

15. GRAMMAR ODDS AND ENDS

The following grammar rules do not often show up on the ACT, but they are good rules to know. If you have time, look them over.

NOUN AGREEMENT

Nouns must agree in number (plural or singular) with the number of the noun or nouns they are referring to. For example:

Dave and Scott are looking for *a girlfriend*.

Obviously, Dave and Scott are not looking for one girlfriend. *Girlfriend* must be plural so it agrees with the plural subject of the sentence. The correct sentence should read:

Dave and Scott are looking for *girlfriends*.

> To identify noun agreement errors, look for questions with answer choices that contain the same common noun in plural and singular forms.

NOUN AGREEEMENT LESSON PROBLEMS

Once considered a place to meet people and
<u>   </u>
                    1
drink coffee, bookstores are now generally
used just to buy books.

1. **A.** NO CHANGE
   B. Considered then a place
   C. Once it was considered a place
   D. Once considered places

To become <u>a better reader</u>, students are urged
                    2
to read everything they can get their hands on,
including newspapers and magazines.

2. **F.** NO CHANGE
   G. better readers
   H. the best reader
   J. a reader better than before

The cookies all come <u>in an individual box</u>, so
¹
you should have no trouble separating the
chocolate chunk ones from the peanut toffee
ones.

1. **A.** NO CHANGE
    B. in a different box
    C. in different boxes
    D. in different and distinct boxes

<u>The vibraphone, melodic and percussive</u>
²
<u>instruments</u> used mostly in jazz, can be played
²
with two or four mallets.

2. **F.** NO CHANGE
    G. Vibraphones, a melodic and
    percussive instrument
    H. The vibraphone, at once melodic
    and percussive instruments
    J. The vibraphone, a melodic and
    percussive instrument

PAIRED CONJUNCTIONS

These conjunctions or phrases, which always come in pairs, are also called *correlative*
conjunctions. Make flash cards for the ones you don't know.

both...and — *Both* the lions *and* the tigers were putting on a show at the zoo.

not only...but also — The new electric car is *not only* more efficient than a gasoline-powered
   car *but also* much quieter. (Sometimes "but" alone is used on the ACT, but if you have a
   choice, use "but also.")

not...but — The movie is *not* light-hearted or trivial *but* dark and disturbing in the ways it
   portrays drug-use.

either...or — You can be *either* for him *or* against him; there is no in between.

neither...nor — He is *neither* as large *nor* as strong as his father, but he is much faster.

whether...or — *Whether* you go to a good university *or* straight to the work force is up to you.

as...as — Amy was not *as* scholastic *as* her older sister, but she was much more sociable.

not so much...as — It is *not so much* the sound of the breaking waves *as* (not *but*) the smell of
   the sea that characterizes my beach house.

so...that — It is *so* hot today *that* I'm afraid to go outside.

To identify paired-conjunction errors, look for the *first* part of each pair in the passage (the second part will often be incorrect or missing altogether).

PAIRED CONJUNCTIONS LESSON PROBLEMS

The new documentary is not only an important educational film <u>and</u> a pleasurable viewing experience.
₂

1. **F.** NO CHANGE
   G. but it is
   H. but also
   J. but

Both the pencil <u>or</u> the pen are mightier than the sword.
₃

2. **A.** NO CHANGE
   B. and
   C. and also
   D. and, too,

Neither your muddy shoes <u>or</u> your rain soaked jacket will be allowed in this house.
₁

1. **A.** NO CHANGE
   B. Neither your muddy shoes nor
   C. Either your muddy shoes nor
   D. Neither your muddy shoes and also not

Frank, while frightening in his own ways, was not as gruesome or as sinister <u>compared to</u> Drake.
₂

2. **F.** NO CHANGE
   G. as
   H. as compared to
   J. when compared to

I can tell that you are angry not so much by your choice of words <u>but by</u> the tone of your voice.
₃

3. **A.** NO CHANGE
   B. but because of
   C. as by
   D. but from

MORE CONFUSED WORDS

We already saw how words such as *their*, *there*, and *they're* can be confused because of the similar look and sound of the words (see the Apostrophes and Confused Words section). Other words may be confused because of similar *meanings*. For example:

> You can only pay here if you have ten items or less.

Believe it or not, this sentence is incorrect. *Less* should be used when referring to things that cannot be counted, like mashed potatoes or water. *Fewer* should be used in place of *less* when the items can be counted:

> You can only pay here if you have ten items or *fewer*.

The following words are a few of the most commonly confused:

between/among

Between is usually used for two items or people; *among* is used for more than two.

> Just *between* you and me, I don't think the money was distributed properly *among* all the players at the poker table.

each other/one another

Each other refers to two; *one another* refers to more than two.

> While the happy couple kissed *each other* in the darkened room, the people still at the party wished *one another* a happy New Year.

fewer/less

Fewer is for things that can be counted; *less* is for things that cannot be counted.

> I would like *fewer* peas and *less* mashed potatoes.

into/in

Into refers to the motion of going from outside to inside; *in* means within.

After jumping *into* the lake, you will be *in* over your head.

like/as

Like means: of the same form, appearance, or kind; *as* means: to the same degree or in the same manner. *Like* is not an acceptable substitute for *as*, *as if*, or *as though*. A good rule of thumb is to replace *like* with *as* whenever the sentence still sounds correct.

Adam fouls frequently, just *as* (not *like*) Andrew does.
The dog scratched on the door *as if* (not *like*) it wanted to come in.
Nick is *like* his brother in many ways. (*As* sounds incorrect here).

many/much

Like *fewer* and *less*, *many* is for things that can be counted; *much* is for things that cannot be counted.

I don't have *much* patience left—I don't know how *many* more arguments I can handle.

number/amount

Number is for things that can be counted; *amount* is for things that cannot be counted.

Bill had a *number* of hundred-dollar bills in his wallet—the *amount* of money stolen is just a guess.

To identify confused words questions, look for questions with answer choices that contain different word options. Of course, you should also look for the specific words listed above.

Try the following homework problems *after* you have reviewed the lesson material. Do NOT look back to the lesson while completing the problems:

The company's surplus was divided evenly <u>between</u> all twenty hardworking employees.
₁

1. **A.** NO CHANGE
   B. through
   C. around
   D. among

After Matt <u>walked in the theater</u>, his eyes took several minutes to adjust to the dark.
₂

2. **F.** NO CHANGE
   G. walked into the theater
   H. was walking in the theater
   J. walking inside the theater

Spooked by the moonless dark night and the eerily silent alley, we ran <u>like if</u> we were being chased by a mob of zombies.
₃

3. **A.** NO CHANGE
   B. like
   C. as if
   D. as

The members of the internet company had been a bit premature in <u>congratulating one another</u> since just a few months later their company was nothing more than unpaid bills and worthless stock.
₄

4. **F.** NO CHANGE
   G. congratulating each other
   H. their congratulating of each other
   J. congratulations for one another

VOCABULARY

The ACT may test your vocabulary on the English Test. These questions involve words that have similar meanings, not unlike the Confused Words lesson above. For example,

When the blow fish senses danger, it brings in water to make its entire body proliferate.

The word "proliferate" means: to increase in number. It is not the correct word for this context. You could correct the sentence with words such as *expand*, *enlarge*, *grow*, etc.:

When the blow fish senses danger, it brings in water to make its entire body *expand*.

Because there aren't many vocabulary questions on the ACT, we don't think it's worth memorizing long lists of words for this test. However, we encourage you to work on vocabulary outside of our ACT curriculum. A strong vocabulary will certainly benefit you beyond this one test, and it will certainly help your Reading scores on the ACT.

To identify vocabulary questions, look for answer choices that contain different words with similar meanings.

Here's a sample question so you know what to look for:

If I <u>lend</u> the book to you, I expect to get it back
₁
by the end of the month.

1. Which of the following alternatives to the underlined portion would be LEAST acceptable in terms of the context of the sentence?
   A. loan
   B. borrow
   C. entrust
   D. deliver

NONSENSE

Some answer choices create a sentence that simply doesn't make sense. Sometimes you'll hear obvious awkwardness as you read the sentence. Other times you'll have to read carefully and think about the intended *meaning* of the sentence to discover the nonsense. Try the following lesson problem:

Studying history is like going back in time and
learning <u>from the mistakes of those</u> that came
₁
before.

1. Which of the following alternatives to the underlined portion would be LEAST acceptable?
   A. NO CHANGE
   B. about the mistakes of those
   C. from those
   D. DELETE the underlined portion

John Brown made his name in the raid of Harper's Ferry, <u>where he hoped</u> would lead to a rebellion against Southern slave owners.

1. **A.** NO CHANGE
   B. an act that he hoped
   C. a place that he hoped
   D. DELETE the underlined portion

———

30- and 40-hour programs: See the schedules in the introduction to know when you should review all grammar sections, including sections 12-15, and take Grammar Quiz 4 (Sections 1-15), which is found in the next section. For now, skip to the Usage/Mechanics chapter.

16. GRAMMAR QUIZZES

The following quizzes test all of the grammar topics. **Do not look back to the tutorial while taking these quizzes.** Answers to all quizzes start on page 154.

Grammar quizzes:

- GRAMMAR QUIZ 1 (SECTIONS 1-4)
- GRAMMAR QUIZ 2 (SECTIONS 5-8)
- GRAMMAR QUIZ 3 (SECTIONS 9-11)
- GRAMMAR QUIZ 4 (ALL SECTIONS, INCLUDING 12-15)

GRAMMAR QUIZ 1 (SECTIONS 1-4)

Played in a 1989 chess tournament in Belgrade, the longest game in history <u>ends</u> in a 269-move draw.

1. **A.** NO CHANGE
   B. had ended
   C. will have ended
   D. ended

We wanted to give the package to <u>she</u> and Marcus, but they had already left town.

2. **F.** NO CHANGE
   G. her
   H. herself
   J. hers

Everyone on the bus, even the shy and uncomfortable freshmen, <u>were laughing and singing</u> all the way to the museum.

3. **A.** NO CHANGE
   B. laugh and sing
   C. have laughed and sang
   D. was laughing and singing

He reads actively, but when he has to talk in front of a group, he <u>spoke</u> like someone unfamiliar with the standard rules of grammar.

4. **F.** NO CHANGE
   G. speaks
   H. had spoken
   J. has spoken

<u>Enjoying</u> time with family and friends is more important than working all day and night.

5. **A.** NO CHANGE
   B. The enjoyment of
   C. To enjoy
   D. Taking enjoyment from

The country was largely ignored until <u>they decided</u> to build long-range weapons.

6. **F.** NO CHANGE
   G. they had decided
   H. it was decided
   J. it decided

The number of times that I have had to reprimand my employees for wasting time playing on their computers <u>approach</u> the hundreds.

7. **A.** NO CHANGE
   B. have approached
   C. will have been approaching
   D. is approaching

Quiz 1 continued →

He was not only kind to his own children but also <u>showed kindness</u> to the children of others.
₈

8. **F.** NO CHANGE
   G. kind
   H. kindly
   J. had kindness

GRAMMAR QUIZ 2 (SECTIONS 5-8)

One reason to keep your house <u>clean, is that</u> a
₁
tidy environment leads to a relaxed mind.

1. **A.** NO CHANGE
   B. clean is: that
   C. clean is, that,
   D. clean is that

When you <u>eat too much ice cream, as the child</u>
₂
<u>learned the hard way</u>, you might get a
₂
stomachache.

2. **F.** NO CHANGE
   G. eat too much, as the child learned the hard way, ice cream
   H. eat too much ice cream, as learned the hard way by the child
   J. eat, as the child learned the hard way, too much ice cream

<u>Now that you understand</u> the basics of
₃
electricity, particularly the dangers involved
when you are working with bare wires.

3. **A.** NO CHANGE
   B. Now you understand
   C. Now that you have an understanding of
   D. Now you understand that

Considered an expert in her field, the <u>doctor's</u>
₄
<u>research papers</u> were widely read and studied.
₄

4. **F.** NO CHANGE
   G. doctor wrote research papers that
   H. doctor's papers of research
   J. research papers of the doctor

I walked <u>slowly, away from the bear</u> as though
₅
there was nothing out of the ordinary.

5. **A.** NO CHANGE
   B. slowly away, from the bear,
   C. slowly, away from the bear,
   D. slowly away from the bear

One of the best ways to keep your house <u>tidy,</u>
₆
<u>donating</u>, which not only minimizes your "stuff"
₆
but also is good for your community.

6. **F.** NO CHANGE
   G. tidy, which is donating
   H. tidy, by donating
   J. tidy is by donating

Quiz 2 continued →

The storm hit last <u>night, and the</u> electricity was
out for over eight hours.

7. Which of the following alternatives to the underlined portion would NOT be acceptable?

    A. night; the
    B. night and the
    C. night—the
    D. night. The

The lawyer <u>working tirelessly to</u> give her client
a decent chance in court, even though the
evidence strongly suggests guilt.

8.   **F.** NO CHANGE
    G. works tirelessly to
    H. had been working with tirelessness to
    J. tirelessly work and

He thought the math class would be <u>easy, then</u>
his class started working on limits.

9.   **A.** NO CHANGE
    B. easy then
    C. easy but then
    D. easy, but then

The <u>owner or, as he likes to call himself, the
boss,</u> of the business rules with an iron fist.

10. **F.** NO CHANGE
    G. owner, or, as he likes to call himself, the boss,
    H. owner, or as he likes to call himself the boss
    J. owner or as he likes to call himself the boss,

GRAMMAR QUIZ 3 (SECTIONS 9-11)

<u>Its hot enough</u> today to fry an egg on the
sidewalk.

1. **A.** NO CHANGE
    B. Its hotter
    C. Its' hot enough
    D. It's hot enough

Quiz 3 continued →

Karoline Mariechen Meyer broke the world's record by holding her breath for <u>18 minutes and 33 seconds—nearly 20 minutes</u>.
2

2. **F.** NO CHANGE
   G. 18 minutes and 33 seconds, or nearly 20 minutes
   H. 18 minutes and 33 seconds
   J. less than 20 minutes—18 minutes and 33 seconds

As a reader, she <u>has an ability for making</u> even the most mundane prose come alive.
3

3. **A.** NO CHANGE
   B. has an ability to make
   C. has an ability of making
   D. has an ability with making

<u>A puppy's first steps</u> occur three to four weeks after birth, far earlier than a baby's first steps.
4

4. **F.** NO CHANGE
   G. A puppy's first step's
   H. A puppies' first steps
   J. A puppies first steps

Their aggressive and inappropriate actions make it clear <u>that theirs</u> little hope of compromise.
5

5. **A.** NO CHANGE
   B. that theirs is
   C. that there's
   D. that they're is

I was accepted to Harvard, Yale, and Stanford, and because I wanted to stay in California, I chose <u>the latter</u>.
6

6. **F.** NO CHANGE
   G. the last one
   H. the final choice
   J. Stanford

The sight of the movie's star actor on the red carpet <u>excited and invigorated the huge crowd</u>.
7

7. **A.** NO CHANGE
   B. excited the huge crowd
   C. excited the huge and massive crowd
   D. excited the now invigorated, huge crowd

I understood the material when I read the math book but <u>was confused of</u> my teacher's lengthy and boring lectures.
8

8. **F.** NO CHANGE
   G. had confusion for
   H. was confused by
   J. was confused with

GRAMMAR QUIZ 4 (SECTIONS 1-15)*

Elephants, <u>a surprisingly fast creature, have</u>
₁
been known to run forty miles per hour.

1. **A.** NO CHANGE
   B. surprisingly fast creatures, have
   C. a surprisingly fast creature, has
   D. a surprisingly fast creature that has

I almost fell asleep as the raft floated <u>lazy</u> in the
₂
still waters.

2. **F.** NO CHANGE
   G. lazily
   H. lazier
   J. laziness

There are <u>not as much</u> people on the beach
₃
each year because of the erosion caused by the
high surf.

3. **A.** NO CHANGE
   B. lesser
   C. less
   D. fewer

Because she was having such a great time, the
little girl <u>was opposed of</u> leaving the theme park
₄
early.

4. **F.** NO CHANGE
   G. was opposed from
   H. was opposed to
   J. had opposition for

After analyzing the evidence and writing the
research paper about the health risks of living
near a cellular tower, researchers knew
<u>it would</u> cause an uproar.
₅

5. **A.** NO CHANGE
   B. the results would
   C. they would
   D. this would

The <u>MSPCA or Massachusetts</u> Society for the
₆
Prevention of Cruelty to Animals, is a national
and international leader in the protection of
animals.

6. **F.** NO CHANGE
   G. MSPCA Massachusetts
   H. MSPCA—Massachusetts
   J. MSPCA, or Massachusetts

Quiz 4 continued →

* **20-hour program:** You may choose to skip questions 1, 2, 3, 10, 14, & 15.

Each of the three witnesses <u>were wary</u> of
₇
testifying against the frightening gang leader.

7. **A.** NO CHANGE
    B. were warily
    C. was wary
    D. have been wary

The Grapes of Wrath, by John Steinbeck, tells
the story of the <u>Joad family's</u> migration west.
₈

8. **F.** NO CHANGE
    G. Joad's family's
    H. Joad families
    J. Joad's families

It is a <u>usual</u> custom at our family gatherings
₉
to toss the ball around a little after dinner, even
though we are usually too full to run.

9. **A.** NO CHANGE
    B. usual and regular
    C. routine
    D. OMIT the underlined portion.

He is ambivalent about his favorite team going
to the finals, both happy about the chance to
win it all <u>but</u> sad about the fact that he can't
₁₀
afford tickets.

10. **F.** NO CHANGE
    G. and
    H. but also
    J. combined with

Because he <u>hit</u> so many game winning shots,
₁₁
he was considered last season's best closer.

11. **A.** NO CHANGE
    B. hits
    C. has been hitting
    D. will hit

New high-definition <u>televisions that</u> have
₁₂
resolutions far superior to those of the past.

12. **F.** NO CHANGE
    G. televisions
    H. televisions, that
    J. televisions, which

Those <u>citizens which</u> refuse to vote should be
₁₃
the last to complain about the government.

13. **A.** NO CHANGE
    B. citizens, whom
    C. citizens whom
    D. citizens who

Quiz 4 continued →

Last year's company party, which was catered by the best cook in town, was much better than this year.
14

Martin and Sid have similar running styles, but Sid is definitely the fastest of the two.
15

14. **F.** NO CHANGE
    G. this year's party
    H. the one of this year
    J. that of this year

15. **A.** NO CHANGE
    B. the faster
    C. fastest
    D. the most faster

III
USAGE/MECHANICS

We have reviewed the grammar rules, and now it's time to look at the kinds of questions on the ACT that test these rules: the Usage/Mechanics questions. These questions make up a majority of the English questions (about two-thirds, or roughly 50 of the 75 questions on the test). This chapter will discuss some general techniques that will help you tackle Usage/Mechanics questions.

IDENTIFYING USAGE/MECHANICS QUESTIONS

Usage/Mechanics questions are fairly easy to identify. Unlike the Rhetorical Skills questions (to be discussed in Chapter IV), **Usage/Mechanics questions generally lack a written question next to the question number**—the question is *implied*. In other words, you will only see the answer choices. See the examples below.

USAGE/MECHANICS QUESTION:

9. **A.** NO CHANGE
    B. are
    C. is
    D. has been

RHETORICAL SKILLS QUESTION (CHAPTER IV):

10. Given that all of following sentences are true, which one would most effectively conclude the paragraph?

    A. Michael Douglas certainly has been in a lot of movies.
    B. It is no surprise that an actor with this many awards is so highly respected.
    C. Actors come and go, but Michael Douglas is here for the long haul.
    D. Michael Douglas is certainly more than just an actor.

EXCEPTIONS

There are a few Usage/Mechanics questions on each test that have written questions. The two most common ones are:

- "Which of the following alternatives to the underlined portion would NOT be acceptable?" (Look for a grammar error among the answer choices.)
- "The best placement for the underlined portion would be:" (This is likely a Misplaced Words question.)

There are also a few Rhetorical Skills questions on each test that *lack* a written question. The most common of these are *main idea* and *transition* questions, which will be discussed in the Rhetorical Skills chapter.

Again, most of the Usage/Mechanics questions do *not* have written questions, and most of the Rhetorical Skills questions *do* have written questions, but make sure you can identify the few exceptions.

1. AVOID WORDY ANSWER CHOICES

Good writing is usually as concise and clear as possible, with no needless words. Besides being grammatically correct, the correct answers on the English Test are usually the clearest and often the shortest of the answer choices. **In fact, the shortest answer choice available is correct far more than half the time. Certainly, if you find yourself in a guessing situation, guess the answer that is the shortest or has the fewest words.**

DON'T FORGET THE NO CHANGE ANSWER CHOICE

The answer choice labeled NO CHANGE (A for odd problems, F for even problems) refers, of course, to the words in the passage. These words won't be reprinted above the other answer choices—making their length hard to compare to the lengths of the other answer choices—so don't forget to look back to the passage. This NO CHANGE answer choice may very well be the shortest answer choice, but you won't know unless you remember to look.

CLOSE ENOUGH TO CALL A TIE

Sometimes the differences in the lengths of the answer choices are subtle—perhaps a couple letters or one word. Don't worry about wordiness for these answer choices. For example, the verb "is" is shorter than the verb "are," but that's obviously not enough of a reason to select "is" as your correct answer. Look for answer choices that have more significant variations in length.

A NOTE TO SELF STUDY STUDENTS ABOUT "EX" PROBLEMS

Example problems are indicated with an EX symbol:

You will see a boxed solution following each example. For the following sections, try to answer the example question *before* looking at the solution. You may want to cover the solution with a sheet of paper so that you're not tempted to peek.

T.S. Eliot was awarded the Nobel Prize in

Literature in 1948 <u>by the consideration of</u> his
₁

contributions to poetry and playwriting.

1. **A.** NO CHANGE
    B. for
    C. owing to
    D. due to the fact of

Right off the bat, you can see that B is the shortest answer choice (don't forget to look at A, the underlined portion). Also, notice the relative wordiness of A and D compared to B and C. So focus on B and C. Which sounds better? The correct answer is **B**, not surprisingly the shortest answer choice available.

---

2. AVOID -ING WORDS

(!) **Answer choices that use words in the *-ing* form are incorrect about 90% of the time.**

Words in the *-ing* form often create fragments or other awkwardness. As taught in the Verb Tense lesson, it is important to remember that a single word (on its own) in the *-ing* form does not function as an active verb:

> Fragment: John *running* to the store. ✗
> Correct: John *has been running* to the store. ✓

Be especially wary of the words *being* and *having*, which are almost always wrong. Let's look at an example:

The professor argued that although many universities have excelled at training future scientists, <u>the failure is in their not educating</u>₂ humanities majors in the methods of scientific thought.

2. **F.** NO CHANGE
   G. they have failed to educate
   H. the failure they have is in their not educating
   J. having failed to educate

As you go through the answer choices, note that F, H, and J contain *-ing* words. The best answer, indeed, is **G**, the one answer lacking an *-ing* word.

EXCEPTIONS

GRAMMATICALLY CORRECT USES

The *-ing* form of a word is not *necessarily* incorrect, as seen in some of the grammar lessons. Thus, you should be able to recognize *-ing* words that *are* used correctly. As covered in the Grammar chapter, there are two common grammatically-correct uses of *-ing* words:

1. Recall that an *-ing* verb phrase can be used to express continuous action over a period of time, for example:

   Bob *has been working* at the mini-mart since he was in high school.
   Bob *is* certainly *gaining* the respect of his boss.

2. Modifying phrases often contain *-ing* words, as displayed in the Punctuation section. For example:

Using both hands, Bob has become the fastest bagger in the store.

Having the most experience, Bob is certain to become the store manager before long.

PARALLELISM

If you have to maintain parallel construction with *-ing* words that are not underlined (which means they must be correct), then an *-ing* word will be part of the correct answer.

For many a great artist, <u>being free to innovate</u>
<u>is more important</u> than being well paid.
₃

3. **A.** NO CHANGE
   B. having freedom of innovation is more important
   C. there is more importance in the freedom to innovate
   D. to have the freedom to innovate is more important

Notice that the word *being*, usually a clear indicator of an incorrect answer, is found in a part of the sentence that is not underlined. The only answer choice that maintains a parallel construction is **A**: …*being* <u>free to innovate is more important</u> than *being* well paid.

-*ING* IN EVERY ANSWER CHOICE

Obviously, when there is an *-ing* word in every answer choice, one of them must be correct. You should still probably avoid answer choices that have more *-ing* words than the others or ones that contain *being* or *having*.

HARMLESS -*ING* WORDS

-*ING* words that function as simple nouns are usually OK. For example:

When the *going* gets tough, the tough go *fishing*.

There's really no better way to write this sentence. The good news is that when *-ing* words are used as simple nouns, they're usually found in every answer choice.

SUMMARY

Answer choices with *-ing* words are usually incorrect—eliminate them aggressively. Just make sure you understand the few exceptions described above.

3. NO CHANGE

The NO CHANGE answer choice (A for odd problems, F for even problems) is the correct answer about as often as each of the other answer choices (about one-fourth of the time). Students have a tendency to find an error in the sentence at all costs, but often the sentence is correct as written. The ACT folks generally won't try to trick you on these—if the sentence sounds good as written, don't be afraid to select NO CHANGE.

<u>Most experts considered</u> Michael Phelps to be
_4_
the greatest swimmer ever after he won eight
gold medals in the 2008 Beijing Olympics.

4. **F.** NO CHANGE
   G. Almost all experts considered
   H. Absolutely many experts considered
   J. Experts, but not all, considered

Of course, you could probably guess the answer to this one based on the lesson, but look at the answer choices anyway. Notice that none of them are grammatically incorrect, but there's nothing wrong with **F**, right? Go with it. Each of the other answer choices is wordy. Notice that H even changes the meaning of the original sentence slightly ("most" is different from "many"); this is something to watch out for on the ACT.

4. AVOID THE PASSIVE VOICE

The passive voice means that the performer of the action in the sentence is *not* the subject of the sentence. For example,

The books were carefully arranged on the shelf by Dan, a self-proclaimed neat-freak.

The subject of this sentence is *books*, but the books are obviously not performing the action of *arranging*—*Dan* is. This sentence is in the *passive voice*. To rewrite the sentence in the *active voice*, make *Dan* the subject of the sentence:

Dan, a self-proclaimed neat-freak, arranged the books on the shelf.

Look to eliminate answer choices in the passive voice in the following example:

<u>Dan arranged the books on the shelf, he</u>
₅
proceeded to proclaim himself a neat-freak.

 (EX)

5. **A.** NO CHANGE
   B. The books, which were arranged on the shelf by Dan, who
   C. The books were first arranged on the shelf by Dan, who then
   D. After arranging the books on the shelf, Dan

The original sentence (answer choice A) is a run-on because it lacks a FANBOYS conjunction after the comma (review run-ons). Answer choices B and C should be eliminated because they are both in the passive voice. B is also a fragment. The correct answer is **D**. Dan is the subject of the sentence and performs the action in the sentence—he "proceeded to proclaim himself a neat-freak."
Eliminate:
A. Run-on
B. Passive Voice/Fragment
C. Passive Voice

---

5. AVOID NEW MISTAKES

Let's say you're reading a passage on the English Test and you identify a grammar error in an underlined portion of a sentence. When you look at the answer choices, you might pick the first one that corrects the error. But you must make sure that you don't end up selecting an answer choice that introduces a *new* error. How do you avoid these careless mistakes? By being careful! Make sure you read the whole answer choice before picking it, or look at the other answer choices to see if any of them also correct the original error.

His article in the school newspaper <u>challenged,</u>
<u>6</u>
<u>the student body to stop</u> blaming teachers and
<u>6</u>
start becoming accountable for the widespread low test scores.

6. **F.** NO CHANGE
    G. challenged the student body: to stop
    H. challenged the student body in stopping
    J. challenged the student body to stop

Don't forget, if you're working on your own, try answering these example questions *before* looking at the boxed solutions that follow.

> Students who move too quickly might choose G or perhaps H—both answer choices correct the original error (an unnecessary comma after "challenged"), but the best answer is **J**.

6. CHECK YOUR ANSWERS

Immediately after you choose an answer, give the sentence a quick read with the answer plugged into the passage. Sometimes an answer choice sounds fine out of context but doesn't work when you read it in the passage. Listen carefully for any awkwardness as you reread the sentence. Checking answers will especially benefit students who make careless mistakes.

AN EXCEPTION

If you work carefully and find that you rarely make careless mistakes (congratulations, because you're in the minority!) AND if you have trouble finishing the English section in time, you might be more comfortable moving quickly to the next question without checking answer choices. Just keep track of your mistakes as you work on ACT practice problems and practice tests—if you find that you make careless mistakes, you should start checking your answers.

7. INTERRELATED QUESTIONS

Sometimes on the ACT, the answer to one question depends on the answer to another. To make things even more difficult, you may have to answer the second question first. Look at the following example questions:

<u>While eating</u> whole grains—cereal grains that contain bran and germ as well as the

7. **A.** NO CHANGE
   B. Eating
   C. Since the eating of
   D. Because eating

endosperm—is a great idea, <u>but</u> I'm not sure eating whole grain doughnuts and cookies is what health experts had in mind.

8. **F.** NO CHANGE
   G. however
   H. and
   J. but on the other hand

First look at Question 7. For all we know, A, B, and D all could work. We need to know more about the rest of the sentence, so leave 7 blank and look at Question 8.

Look at the answer choices for 8—it's testing conjunctions. The last part of the sentence is an independent clause ("I'm not sure eating…"), so eliminate G ("however" is not a FANBOYS conjunction). The best answer is **F**—"but" is the logical conjunction here (J is wordy).

Now go back to Question 7. Since Question 8 did not give us the option to remove the conjunction, the sentence must be a compound sentence (two independent clauses). Eliminate A, C, and D because these answer choices turn the first part into a dependent clause. The answer is **B**.

The previous lesson discussed checking your answers. After you answer the above questions, quickly read the corrected sentence to make sure your answers make sense:

> <u>Eating</u> whole grains—cereal grains that contain bran and germ as well as the endosperm—is a great idea, <u>but</u> I'm not sure eating whole grain doughnuts and cookies is what health experts had in mind.

Sounds good! ✓

8. USAGE/MECHANICS SUMMARY

As stated before, your knowledge of the grammar rules from chapter II is the most important aspect of the Grammar/Usage questions. If you remember the additional guidelines below, you should be comfortable with these questions:

1. Avoid Wordy Answer Choices.
2. Avoid *-ING* Words.
3. The NO CHANGE answer choice (A or F) is correct about as often as the other answer choices.
4. Avoid the Passive Voice.
5. Avoid New Mistakes.
6. Check Your Answers.
7. Watch out for Interrelated Questions.

9. USAGE/MECHANICS PROBLEMS

PRACTICE PROBLEMS

The Real ACT Prep Guide, 3rd Edition offers three sample passages starting on page 42, and 5 additional passages (that we'll use for practice) from Test 1. Focus only on the Usage/Mechanics problems for the following assignments, as shown below. Skip the Rhetorical Skills questions. We'll cover those in the next chapter.

- ☐ Sample Passage I: 1, 2, 3, 4, 5, 6, 7, 8, 9, 11, 12, 14
- ☐ Sample Passage II: 16^{40}, 17, 19^{40}, 22, 23, 24, 25, 27, 29, 30^{40}
- ☐ Sample Passage III: 34, 35, 36, 38, 39, 41, 43, 44
- ☐ **Test 1**: Passage I: 1, 2, 3, 6, 7, 9, 10^{40}, 11^{40}, 12, 13, 14
- ☐ **Test 1**: Passage II: 16, 17, 18, 19^{40}, 20, 22, 25^{40}, 27, 28, 29, 30
- ☐ **Test 1**: Passage III: 31, 32, 33, 34, 35, 36, 37, 39, 41, 42, 44
- ☐ **Test 1**: Passage IV: 47, 48, 51, 53, 55, 56, 57, 58, 59^{40}
- ☐ **Test 1**: Passage V: 61, 63, 65, 66, 67, 68, 69, 70, 72

[40] Questions marked with a "40" are covered by the 40-hour program.

These practice problems should *not* be completed as a closed-book test. Do *not* time yourself. While you complete these problems, review the lessons from this chapter (summarized on the previous page) and the grammar topics from Chapter II. These practice problems offer you a chance to learn and master the techniques you've learned, in the context of real ACT passages and questions. If you have trouble identifying the best technique to use on a problem, see the Techniques Reference information in Chapter VI, starting on page 138.

You might choose to space the above assignments out over the course of your studies. See the "Schedules" section in the introduction for more details about programs.

PRACTICE TEST

All programs: Now is a good time to take **Test 3** in the ACT book (you should have already taken Test 2, and Test 1 will be used for practice problems), **but before you do, jump ahead and read through the Timing chapter**. The Timing chapter explains that, if you have trouble finishing the test, you may choose to skip some of the Rhetorical Skills questions. It's important to start practicing your timing techniques while you take this practice test. Also consider the following:

- For most students, even though we haven't covered the Rhetorical Skills questions, you should still tackle some, if not most, of them. You'll hopefully get some of the easier ones correct.

- If you're following the **20-hour program**, make sure you aggressively search out and answer the Usage/Mechanics questions. The 20-hour program usually doesn't allow enough time to go over Rhetorical Skills questions, but rest assured that most of the questions on the test are Usage/Mechanics. As we said, tackle some of the Rhetorical Skills questions if you have time; you'll hopefully get some of the easier ones correct.

- After you grade your test, correct any missed Usage/Mechanics questions (see Test Corrections below). Also, make sure you go back and correct any missed Rhetorical Skills questions after you complete the Rhetorical Skills chapter.

TEST CORRECTIONS

As stated above, after each practice test is graded, you should correct Usage/Mechanics problems that you missed or left blank. There are three steps to correcting the practice tests:

1. The Usage/Mechanics questions for each test are listed below (the brackets show individual passages). Go back to your answer sheet for the corresponding test and circle the question numbers below that you missed (or guessed on, if you kept track of your guesses).

   - **Test 2**: [1, 2, 3, 4, 7, 9, 10, 11, 12], [16, 17, 19, 20, 21, 22, 23, 25, 26], [31, 32, 33, 34, 36, 38, 40^{40}, 41, 42, 43, 44^{40}], [46, 47^{40}, 49, 51, 52, 54^{40}, 55, 57, 59, 60], [61, 62, 63, 64, 66, 67^{40}, 68, 71, 72, 73, 74, 75]

   - **Test 3**: [1, 2, 3, 5, 8^{40}, 9, 10, 11, 12, 13], [16, 17, 18^{40}, 19, 21, 22, 24, 26, 27, 28, 29], [31, 34, 35, 36, 37, 40, 41, 42, 44, 45], [46, 49, 50, 51^{40}, 52, 53, 54, 58, 59], [61, 62, 63, 64, 67, 68, 70, 71, 72, 74]

   - **Test 4**: [1, 2^{40}, 3, 4, 6, 7, 8, 10, 11, 12, 14], [16, 19, 20, 21, 22, 23, 25, 26, 27], [31, 32, 33^{40}, 34, 35, 36, 37, 38, 39, 40], [48, 49, 50, 53^{40}, 55^{40}, 57, 59, 60], [61, 62^{40}, 63, 64, 65, 66, 67^{40}, 68, 69, 70, 72^{40}, 73]

   - **Test 5**: [1, 3, 4, 7, 8, 9, 10, 12, 14^{40}], [16, 18, 19, 20, 21, 23, 24, 26, 27, 28, 29], [31, 32^{40}, 33, 34, 38^{40}, 39, 40, 41, 42, 43^{40}], [46, 47, 48, 50, 51, 52, 53, 56, 58, 59], [61, 64, 65, 66, 67, 69^{40}, 71, 72]

   ^{40} Questions marked with a "40" are covered by the **40-hour programs**.

2. Correct the problems in *The Real ACT Study Guide*. As you correct the problems, go back to the tutorial and review the techniques. The idea is to: (1) identify techniques that have given you trouble, (2) go back to the tutorial so you can review and strengthen these techniques, and (3) apply these techniques to the specific problems on which you struggled.

3. If you have trouble identifying the best technique to use on a problem, see the Techniques Reference information in Chapter VI, starting on page 138.

IV

RHETORICAL SKILLS

The Rhetorical Skills questions focus on writing strategy, main ideas, organization, and style. These questions—which make up about one-third, or roughly 25 of the 75 questions on the test—tend to be more difficult than the Usage/Mechanics questions discussed in Chapter III. While the grammar techniques from Chapter II may come in handy, the questions discussed in this chapter, for the most part, do *not* rely on grammar knowledge. This chapter will discuss general techniques that will help you tackle Rhetorical Skills questions.

IDENTIFYING RHETORICAL SKILLS QUESTIONS

Rhetorical Skills questions, unlike Usage/Mechanics questions, generally have a written question next to the question number. In addition, the answer choices tend to be longer than those on Usage/Mechanics questions.

If necessary, go to page 87 to see examples of Usage/Mechanics and Rhetorical Skills questions.

––––––––––

A passage on "Snooker" is found on the following page. Don't read it yet. The questions and related lessons will be discussed on the pages following the passage. For easy reference, you might want to cut the passage out of this tutorial.

[1]

Snooker, a table sport where each opponent uses a cue to hit colored balls into table pockets, has been around for over a hundred years. If you've watched a game of pool or Billiards, then you might be more familiar with Snooker than you think. 1 The game likely originated in India in the late 1800's when British Army officers made variations to traditional Billiards. The word *snooker* was a slang military term for an inexperienced military man. It is claimed that Colonel Sir Neville Chamberlain was playing this new game when his opponent failed to "pot"—or sink—a ball. Chamberlain called his opponent a "snooker." The sport soon took this as its name.

[2]

The history of Snooker is filled with exciting matches and skilled players. The goal of Snooker is to score more points than the opponent. The game includes 15 red balls, one white ball, or cue ball, and six balls of different colors. Points are scored by potting balls. But the hard part is that the balls must be potted in a predetermined order. If you miss a shot on the desired ball, then your turn is done and the next player takes over. Imagine the challenge of having to hit one specific ball with all of the other balls scattered around. 3

(EX)

1. At this point, the writer is considering adding the following sentence:

   > Billiards involves more colored balls than does Snooker.

   Given that it is true, would this be a relevant addition to make here?

   A. Yes, because it gives the reader a better idea of the differences between Billiards and Snooker.
   B. Yes, because it allows the reader to visualize Billiards.
   C. No, because it doesn't help expand the historical background of Snooker.
   D. No, because this paragraph is discussing table sports in general, not *specific* table sports.

(EX)

2. Which choice would most effectively and appropriately lead the reader from the topic of Paragraph 1 to that of Paragraph 2?

   F. NO CHANGE
   G. Billiards and Snooker are not the only games played with cues and balls.
   H. Snooker may have gotten its name from an unskilled player, but the game is not easy.
   J. Every game must have a means to determine winning from losing.

(EX)

3. Given that all of the following sentences are true, which one, if added here, would offer the best transition from Paragraph 2 to Paragraph 3?

   A. No wonder Snooker players are considered to be so skilled.
   B. Tournaments are where Snooker players can show their stuff.
   C. So many balls; so little time.
   D. A major advance for Snooker occurred in 1969 when the balls were used to demonstrate color TV.

[3]

Of the many great Snooker players,
Stephen Hendry stands out. Born in January 13, 1969 in Scotland, Hendry became the youngest player to become a Snooker World Champion— at the age of 21. He went on to win six more World Championships, and he was Snooker's number one player for eight consecutive years, between 1990 and 1998. Hendry's skill as a player lead to amazing riches and fame for him, and helped popularize the sport of Snooker around the world. However, you may not have heard of it. 5
4

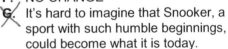

4. Which of the choices would provide an ending most consistent with the essay as a whole?

F. NO CHANGE
G. It's hard to imagine that Snooker, a sport with such humble beginnings, could become what it is today.
H. The possibility of fame is real indeed.
J. Snooker may be difficult, but that shouldn't stop you from giving it a shot.

Question 5 asks about the preceding passage as a whole.

5. Suppose the writer had chosen to write a brief essay that compares Snooker to other table games. Would this essay successfully fulfill that goal?

A. Yes, because the essay discusses pool, Billiards, and Snooker.
B. Yes, because the essay mentions that Snooker is a variation of Billiards.
C. No, because the essay primarily discusses the origins and development of Snooker.
D. No, because the essay fails to mention any other table games.

1. MAIN IDEAS

The most important part of Rhetorical Skills questions is recognizing *main ideas*. As the name implies, a main idea is the central point or message of a passage, paragraph, or even an individual sentence.

MAIN IDEA OF A PARAGRAPH

Think about the main idea of each paragraph while reading a passage. The first or last sentence—often called a *topic* sentence—of a paragraph can often help you identify the paragraph's main idea. But remember that these passages are in need of revision and may lack clear and effective topic sentences. Therefore, you will likely have to look at details within the paragraph as well.

FIND KEYWORDS

You should usually be able to write down the main idea of a paragraph in just a few words. These words, or *keywords*, will help you when you look at the answer choices. **Read Paragraph 1 of the sample passage now.**

The first thing you might notice is that to answer Question 1, you should read the whole paragraph. **You will often have to read the entire paragraph before answering main idea questions, even if the question shows up early in the paragraph.** After you've read Paragraph 1, think about the main idea of the paragraph and come up with some keywords.

What's the first word that comes to mind? (This should be straightforward. Write your first keyword below before moving on.) If you're working on your own, don't forget to cover the boxed solutions so you're not tempted to look ahead.

First keyword for Paragraph 1 = _____

Was your first keyword "Snooker"? This is certainly the focus of the first paragraph.

Now that you have the first keyword ("Snooker"), let's dig a little deeper. What word best captures how the paragraph focuses on Snooker?

Second keyword for Paragraph 1 = _____

> Look at some of the key phrases: "...has been around for over a hundred years...," "...the game likely originated in India in the late 1800's...," "The sport soon took this as its name." The paragraph is talking about the *origin* of Snooker.

So, based on these two keywords ("Snooker" and "originated"), the main idea of Paragraph 1 must have something to do with the **origin** of **Snooker**.

YES OR NO QUESTIONS

Finally, let's look at Question 1. Notice that it is a Yes or No question. These questions have two *yes* answer choices and two *no* answer choices. The first step, *before* you look at the answer choices (in detail), is to decide whether the answer is *yes* or *no*. By doing this, you immediately remove half of the answer choices. Do you think the sentence in question ties into the main idea of the paragraph (circle one below)?

YES or NO

> The sentence focuses on "Billiards," which is not a main idea of the paragraph. The answer is **no**: eliminate A and B.

WATCH OUT FOR OFF-TOPIC ANSWER CHOICES

You will often eliminate an answer choice because it is *off-topic*; in other words, the answer choice does not tie into the main idea of the paragraph. Look at the remaining answer choices (C and D). Which answer choice is better? Consider the main idea of the paragraph.

Choose an answer for Question 1 now. Don't forget, don't peak at the answer below until you've answered the question.

> As stated, the sentence is off-topic because it focuses more on Billiards than Snooker. It has nothing to do with the origin or history of Snooker. The answer is **C**.

TOPIC SENTENCES

A topic sentence, which is usually found at the beginning (but sometimes the end) of a paragraph, can serve two purposes:

1. Summarize or capture the main idea of its paragraph.
2. Transition from one paragraph to another.

Once again, analyzing the main idea of each paragraph in question and looking for keywords will help you solve topic-sentence questions. **Read Paragraph 2 now.** Don't answer any questions yet. When you're done reading, think about main-idea keywords for the paragraph. Can you come up with two or three of them?

Keywords for Paragraph 2 = _____

What keywords did you come up with? Of course, "Snooker" should come to mind again. The passage is still talking about the sport Snooker. Beyond the general topic of Snooker, what is the specific focus of the paragraph? The paragraph talks about how Snooker is played ("The goal," and goes on to say that the sport is challenging (notice the keywords "the hard part" and later "Imagine the challenge").

Hopefully your keywords ("Snooker," "goal," and "challenge") helped you come up with the main idea of Paragraph 2: **how to play** the **challenging** game **Snooker**.

Now, look at Question 2. Which answer choice best transitions from Paragraph 1 and covers the main idea of Paragraph 2?

Answer Question 2 now.

F and H both refer to ideas presented in Paragraph 1 ("history of Snooker" and "its name," respectively), but only **H** also introduces the main idea of Paragraph 2 ("the game is not easy").

To answer Question 3, we'll have to **read Paragraph 3**. Don't worry about Questions 4 or 5 yet. What are the keywords for this paragraph?

Keywords for Paragraph 3 = _____

Your first keyword should probably be "Stephen Hendry." Is there anything else? You might notice that the paragraph transitions, in the last sentence, to the *popularity* of Snooker (thanks in no small way to Stephen Hendry).

The main idea of Paragraph 3 has to do with **Stephen Hendry** and how he helped **popularize** the sport of **Snooker**.

Now, let's tackle Question 3 (go back to Paragraph 2). Once again, note that the question is asking you to consider the main ideas of Paragraph 2 *and* Paragraph 3. What's the best answer?

Answer Questions 3 now.

Only **A** mentions the skill required to play (Paragraph 2) and transitions to an actual Snooker player (Paragraph 3). You might notice that the first sentence of Paragraph 3 gives you enough information to answer the question: "Of the many great **Snooker players**…" You didn't have to read the whole paragraph to answer Question 3.

MAIN IDEA OF THE PASSAGE

Some passages will have a question that relates to the main idea of the entire passage. The best way to tackle these is to think about the main idea of each paragraph. Let's do this with the practice passage:

- Paragraph 1 has to do with the **origin** of **Snooker**.
- Paragraph 2 has to do with **how to play** the **challenging** game of **Snooker**.
- Paragraph 3 has to do with the **Stephen Hendry** and how he helped **popularize** the sport of **Snooker**.

If you were to summarize the passage, you might say that the passage offers a general overview of the sport of Snooker, from its origins to its current popularity.

Now, look at Question 4. What answer choice best captures the main idea of the passage?

Answer Question 4 now.

F seems to disagree with the main idea of Paragraph 3 (that Snooker has become popular). And ask yourself: would this ending help summarize the essay as a whole? Look back to the main ideas of each paragraph; you'll probably agree that F is not correct. H is too narrow—it only focuses on Paragraph 3, not the whole passage (remember, the question asks about "the essay as a whole"). J shifts the focus to "you," the reader, actually playing the sport. This is off-topic—not a focus of the passage. The best answer is **G**, which touches on the origin of Snooker (its "humble beginnings") and its current popularity ("what it is today").

Let's look at Question 5, which is another Yes or No question. First, before you look at the answer choices, does the writer succeed in comparing Snooker to other table games (circle one below)?

YES or NO

Your first thought might be *yes*—you probably remember "pool" and "Billiards" mentioned in the first paragraph. But there are two reasons why the answer is *no*. First, these other table games are merely *mentioned*; there is no strong *comparison* taking place between Snooker and these other games. And second and most importantly, this is a main idea question, a question that asks you to consider the passage as a whole. As we already know, the focus of the passage is *Snooker*, not how Snooker compares to other games. So at this point, eliminate A and B, the *yes* answers.

ELIMINATE FALSE ANSWER CHOICES

Yes or No questions often have *false* answer choices. Check to see if one of the remaining answer choices is false. **Look at Question 5**, answer choice D. Does the essay fail to mention other table games?

Answer Question 5 now.

As stated above, "pool" and "Billiards" are mentioned in the first paragraph. Eliminate D, leaving **C**. Indeed, the essay's focus is "the origins and development of Snooker."

MAIN IDEAS SUMMARY

To summarize, when you tackle main idea questions:

- Look for keywords in the passage that capture main ideas.
- Answer Yes or No questions before looking (in detail) at the answer choices.
- Watch out for answer choices that are off-topic.
- Understand how topic sentences work.
- Eliminate false answer choices.

look for main focus first

2. TRANSITIONS

CONJUNCTIONS AS TRANSITIONS

As we've already learned, conjunctions are words that connect phrases or sentences together. They transition from one thought or idea to another. These conjunctions can be broken into three main types:

CONTRAST TRANSITIONS

although	even so	instead of	rather than
but	however	nevertheless	still
conversely	in contrast	on the contrary	while
despite	in spite of	on the other hand	yet
even though			

SUPPORT TRANSITIONS

additionally	besides	in fact	similarly
also	furthermore	likewise	(colon) :
and	in addition	moreover	

CAUSE AND EFFECT TRANSITIONS

accordingly	for	since	therefore
because	hence	so	thus
consequently	in order to	so... that	when... then

TRANSITIONS AND MAIN IDEAS

To choose a correct transition, you need to recognize the main idea of where you *were* and the main idea of where you're *going*. Whether you're dealing with phrases, sentences, or whole paragraphs, understanding main ideas is the key. Let's look at an example:

Although it may take a long time to understand all of the intricacies of Snooker, you can enjoy watching the sport today if you just understand the basic rules.

6. Which of the following alternatives to the underlined portion would be LEAST acceptable?

   F. While
   G. Since
   H. Even though
   J. Despite the fact that

Do you recognize the need for a contrast? Taking "a long time" to understand how Snooker is played *contrasts* being able to enjoy watching the sport "today." What's the best answer? Read the question carefully.

Answer Question 6 now.

The first part of the sentence talks about taking "a long time" to understand Snooker. The second part says you can enjoy the sport "today." The only answer choice that doesn't reflect this contrast is **G**—"Since" is a cause and effect transition.

Some Transitions questions don't involve conjunctions at all. For example, a question might ask which sentence best transitions from one paragraph to the next. These are usually Main Idea questions, involving the use of topic sentences. We covered these in the previous section (see Questions 2 and 3).

ILLOGICAL CONJUNCTIONS

Conjunctions are often used in *illogical* ways. For example:

CUE

You can easily follow the Snooker action *so that* you understand the basic rules.

Do you see the error? *Following the Snooker action* does not allow you to *understand the basic rules*. Rather, *understanding the basic rules* allows you to *follow the Snooker action*. The direction of causation is wrong. Replace *so that* with a logical word, such as *because*, *since*, *now that*, or *if*:

You can easily follow the Snooker action *because* you understand the basic rules.

Here's another example:

I practiced Snooker for hours every day, *and* I still struggled during the match.

The conjunction *and* is not the best choice here. Can you think of a more logical conjunction? The following sentence reflects the desired contrast:

I practiced Snooker for hours every day, *but* I still struggled during the match.

Let's try an ACT example:

Michael drove as fast as he could, <u>and</u> he
arrived in plenty of time to see the start of the
match.

7. Which of the following alternatives to the
   underlined portion would NOT be
   acceptable?

   A. so not surprisingly
   B. and thus
   C. so
   D. but

Do you see the illogical conjunction? What's the best answer?

Answer Question 7 now.

The use of a contrast conjunction ("but") is illogical here. The best answer is **D**.

SOMETIMES, NO TRANSITION IS BEST

Don't assume that you *must* use a transition. If the flow sounds awkward with a transition, or if
none of the transitions seem to work, look for the answer choice that does *not* have a transition.
For example:

I wanted to learn how to play Snooker.
<u>It seemed</u> the best place to start was learning
how to break.

8. **F.** NO CHANGE
   G. Nevertheless, it seemed
   H. On the other hand, it seemed
   J. In any case, it seemed

Consider the main idea of each sentence and answer Question 8 now.

The flow from the first sentence to the second sentence is clear without a transition. G and H
are clear contrasts and can be eliminated since there is no contrast between the two sentences.
The transition in J, "In any case," is wordy at best and awkward at worst. The best answer is **F**.

SPECIAL SUPPORT TRANSITIONS

Sometimes a transition will be the right type (contrast, support, or cause and effect), but it will not work in the specific context of the passage. There are several support transitions, in particular, that have special uses. Here are a few examples:

First, second...

Stay consistent with numerical transitions. If you don't see a *first*, don't use a *second*. Also, you should usually stay consistent with how the number is expressed: *first*, *second*, *third*..., *number one*, *number two*, *number three*..., and so on.

For example

For example is a support transition, but make sure there is indeed an example following the transition.

In summary

Make sure what follows "in summary" is an actual summary. There should not be any new information presented.

In addition

Make sure additional information is included and not just an elaboration of the previous topic.

Finally

Make sure *finally* precedes the last of several items. It should, not surprisingly, generally show up near the end of a passage when used correctly.

To identify transition questions, look for questions with answer choices that contain various transition conjunctions. Note that transition questions often look like innocent Usage/Mechanics questions, but they *do* require you to go beyond basic grammar and understand main ideas in the passages.

3. ORGANIZATION

Some questions ask you to change the organization of a passage. Usually this involves changing the placement of a sentence or adding a sentence somewhere in a given paragraph. You might also be asked to reposition an entire paragraph, but these questions are less common.

> To identify organization questions, look for questions that ask you to move, reorder, or add a sentence or paragraph to the passage.

LOOK FOR CLUES

The *clues* will be words that suggest something must come before. These clues may either be in the sentence that you're moving (if you're moving a whole paragraph, look at the *first* sentence of that paragraph) or in the sentence that *follows* a potential placement.

For example, if you see a *pronoun* (such as *he* or *they*) or a *possessive pronoun* (such as *his, their, its,* or *these*), the previous sentence probably mentions the noun that the pronoun refers to:

[1] The first World Championship was organized by Englishman **Joe Davis**. [2] **His** efforts moved the game from a pastime to a professional sport.

[1] **New companies are becoming Snooker sponsors** all the time, and the game is showing **huge growth** in the Far East and China. [2] **These** are all signs that the future of Snooker is bright.

In both examples above, clue words "His" and "These" reveal the order of the sentences.

Here's another example. Let's say the first sentence of a paragraph is:

This ranking system for Snooker may be confusing, but most agree that it's fair.

The clue words are "This ranking system." The preceding sentence (perhaps the last sentence of the preceding paragraph) probably has something to do with this ranking system.

Always look for clue words when you're dealing with organization questions.

Let's look at an Organization question. First, read the paragraph below:

[1] The Snooker World Championship, the most important event in Snooker, takes place annually in Sheffield, England. [2] It is televised throughout the United Kingdom, Europe, and the Far East. [3] He or she walks away with status, fame, and riches. [4] The prize money is impressive—over $500,000 goes to the winner.

 9

 9. For the sake of logic and coherence, Sentence 3 should be placed:

    A. where it is now.
    B. before Sentence 1.
    C. after Sentence 1.
    D. after Sentence 4.

Question 9 focuses on Sentence 3. Look for clue words in Sentence 3.

Clue word(s) for Sentence 3: _____He/she_____

> Notice the pronouns "He or she." Whatever sentence precedes Sentence 3 should probably mention a person (someone for "He or she" to refer to).

Considering these clue words ("He or she"), what's the best place for Sentence 3?

Answer Question 9 now.

> Keeping the sentence where it is now is incorrect. While Sentence 2 touches on possible fame for the winner because the Championship is widely televised, at this point no particular person has been mentioned, and there is no mention of money. Sentence 4 mentions "the winner" and discusses money ("$500,000"). Thus, moving Sentence 3 after Sentence 4 is the correct choice. The answer is **D**.

MAIN IDEAS

Besides clue words, you might have to consider main ideas (something you should be thinking about anyway; see Section 1). Make sure ideas flow sensibly from one to another. Look at the following example, which relates to the paragraph on the Snooker World Championship above.

> Question 10 asks about the preceding paragraph.

10. Upon reviewing this paragraph and realizing that some information has been left out, the writer composes the following sentence:

> The event is held at the Crucible Theater, which seats fewer than 1,000 people, but that doesn't mean there aren't a lot of viewers.

The most logical placement for this sentence would be:

   F. before Sentence 1.
   G. after Sentence 1.
   H. after Sentence 2.
   J. after Sentence 3.

First, look for clue words in the new sentence. You might not see anything obvious (no pronouns, for example). At least, from the words "The event," you know that the Championship has already been introduced (eliminate F).

So now you have to think about the main idea of the sentence. It's talking about *where* the event is held, and it's also talking about the fact that there are a lot of *viewers*. Now look back to the passage and try answering the question.

Answer Question 10 now.

Sentence 1 talks about where the event is held. Sentence 2 says that the event is "televised throughout the United Kingdom, Europe, and the Far East." The added sentence would go great between these two sentences. It touches on the main ideas of both Sentence 1 and Sentence 2. The answer is **G**.

CHECK YOUR ANSWERS

As with other English questions, check your answers. Quickly read the part of the passage that you reorganized, making sure that the sentence order sounds sensible and fluid. If you hear obvious awkwardness with your answer, then you should take a look at the other answer choices.

---

4. MEANING QUESTIONS

Meaning questions are sometimes the most difficult questions on the test. They require you to go beyond a general understanding of grammar and structure. You must decide, based on the *meaning* (or main idea) of part of a passage, whether a phrase or sentence should be added to or deleted from the passage.

These questions can take several forms, but they usually ask you to consider one of two questions:
1.   What happens if something is *deleted* from the passage?
2.   What happens if something is *added* to the passage?

Let's go back to Paragraph 1 from the sample passage at the beginning of this chapter to look at an example:

[1]

Snooker, a table sport where each opponent uses a cue to hit colored balls into table pockets, has been around for over a hundred years. If you've watched a game of pool or Billiards, then you have some idea about Snooker. In fact, the game likely originated in India in the late 1800's when British Army officers made variations to traditional Billiards. The word *snooker* was a slang military term for an inexperienced military man. It is claimed that Colonel Sir Neville Chamberlain was playing this new game when his opponent failed to "pot"—or sink—a ball. 11 Chamberlain called his opponent a "snooker." The sport soon took this as its name.

11. The writer is considering deleting the following phrase from the preceding sentence:

—or sink—

If the writer were to make this deletion, the essay would primarily lose:

A.   an anecdote about the naming of a sport.
B.   a brief explanation of a term.
C.   an explanation of why a player is unskilled.
D.   an important distinction of Snooker.

To answer Question 11, consider the function (or meaning) of the words "or sink."

Answer Question 11 now.

The word "sink" probably helps the reader understand the meaning of the word "pot," a word that most readers are probably unfamiliar with in this context. So **B** is the best answer—the essay would lose "a brief explanation of a term," that term being "pot."

Let's go back to Paragraph II from the sample passage to look at one more example. (Recall that Question 2 replaced the topic sentence, as shown below.):

[2]

Snooker may have gotten its name from an unskilled player, but the game is not easy. The goal of Snooker is to score more points than the opponent. The game includes 15 red balls, one white ball, or cue ball, 12 and six balls of different colors. Points are scored by potting balls. But the hard part is that the balls must be potted in a predetermined order. If you miss a shot on the desired ball, then your turn is done and the next player takes over. Imagine the challenge of having to hit one specific ball with all of the other balls scattered around.

 (EX)

12. At this point, the writer is considering adding the following phrase:

> which the player strikes with a stick called the cue,

Given that it is true, would this be a relevant addition to make here?

F. Yes, because it helps the reader understand the term *cue* and better visualize the play of the game.
G. Yes, because it helps explain why the game is so difficult.
H. No, because it is inconsistent with the essay to go into detail about the play of Snooker at this point.
J. No, because this information would be a better addition in Paragraph 3.

 x = right answer

As discussed in the Main Ideas section, try to answer Yes or No questions before looking at the answer choices. Would the added sentence be a relevant addition (circle one below)?

YES or NO

The phrase does add some relevant information—it's certainly as informative as mentioning the kinds of balls found in the sport. You can always go back if you don't like your two options, but at this point, go with **yes**, and eliminate H and J.

So you're left with F and G, right? What's the better answer choice?

Answer Question 12 now.

You can eliminate G because it is false. The phrase really doesn't explain why the game is difficult. It does help the reader understand the term cue and better visualize how Snooker is played. The answer is **F**.

———————

As you see, we used some techniques from the Main Ideas section (Yes or No questions, false answer choices). In fact, having a sense of main ideas—both of the paragraph in question and of the whole essay—will often help you on meaning questions.

5. ANSWER THE QUESTION

This lesson may sound obvious, but make sure you carefully read Rhetorical Skills questions. Sometimes, if you read a question too quickly, more than one answer choice seems to work. The ACT sometimes asks very *specific* questions, so read them carefully and answer exactly what the question is asking.

> These questions often seem to have multiple correct answers. When more than one answer choice appears to work, go back and carefully reread the question.

Let's go back to Paragraph III from the sample passage at the beginning of the chapter to look at an example. (Recall that Question 4 replaced the last sentence, as shown below.):

[3]

Of the many great Snooker players, Stephen Hendry stands out. Born in January 13, 1969 in Scotland, Hendry became the youngest player to become a Snooker World Champion— at the age of 21. He went on to win six more World Championships, and he was Snooker's number one player for eight consecutive years, between 1990 and 1998. Hendry's skill as a player lead to amazing riches and fame for him, and helped popularize the sport of Snooker around the world. It's hard to imagine that Snooker, a sport with such humble beginnings, <u>could become what it is today</u>.
13

13. Given that all of the choices are true, which one would conclude the essay by giving credit to Snooker players for the popularity of Snooker?

   A. NO CHANGE
   B. could become the international phenomenon it is today.
   C. could become, thanks to competitors like Hendry, what it is today.
   D. could provide such wealth to its champions.

First of all, notice that every answer choice is true. According to the passage, Snooker *is* an "international phenomenon" (B) and *does* "provide such wealth" to its players (D). But look carefully at the question. It asks you to find an answer that credits *Snooker players* for Snooker's popularity. Which one does that?

Answer Question 13 now.

Only **C** works. In fact, even if you hadn't read the passage, by reading the question carefully you would have probably been drawn to C.

As you can see, if you didn't read the question carefully, choosing the correct answer would be difficult, if not impossible. By if you "answer the question," the problem becomes straightforward.

6. STYLE

The last Rhetorical Skills topic to consider is style.

FORMAL VS. INFORMAL

Style questions ask you to consider *consistency* of style. For example, if an essay is written as a formal essay, then make sure the answers to questions reflect this formality.

Besides the World <u>Championship,</u> there are a number of other Snooker tournaments held throughout the world. The UK Championship is right behind the World Championship in importance, and The Masters is also <u>a prestigious tournament</u>.

14. Which of the following alternatives to the underlined portion would NOT be acceptable?

    F. a celebrated event
    G. definitely a lot of fun
    H. high on the list of renowned tournaments.
    J. highly-acclaimed

The paragraph above is formally written (as is the entire passage on Snooker). Do any of the answer choices contradict this formality?

Eliminate any answer choices that are too informal.

> You probably spotted **G**. The words "a lot of fun" work grammatically, but the style is too informal for this paragraph.

POINT OF VIEW

The point of view of a passage describes the narrative voice of the writer. Each offers a different style of writing.

I

Some passages are written in the first person, using *I*, the writer, as the narrator. This allows the writer to tell a personal, and perhaps intimate, story.

YOU

Some passages are written in the second person, directly addressing *you* the reader. These passages give a sense of advising the reader, often in an informal way.

ONE

Some passages are written in the third person, where the writer, as an observer, discusses a thing or person (*one*). These passages are the most formal of the three points of view.

All of the above are viable stylistic options for an essay. Just make sure the essay stays consistent. Don't choose an answer choice that deviates from the point of view set by the rest of the passage.

7. RHETORICAL SKILLS SUMMARY

The following summarizes the techniques that will help you tackle Rhetorical Skills questions:

1. Main Ideas

    - Look for keywords in the passage that capture main ideas.

    - Answer Yes or No questions before looking (in detail) at the answer choices.

    - Watch out for answer choices that are off-topic.

    - Understand how topic sentences work.

    - Eliminate false answer choices.

2. Transitions

    - Learn the three types of transitions.

    - Consider main ideas.

    - Watch out for illogical conjunctions.

    - Sometimes, no transition is best.

    - Make sure the conjunction works in context (special support transitions).

3. Organization

    - Look for clue words.

    - Consider main ideas.

4. Dig beneath the surface of the passage for meaning questions.

5. Answer the question.

6. Keep style consistent.

8. RHETORICAL SKILLS PROBLEMS

PRACTICE PROBLEMS

The Real ACT Prep Guide, 3rd Edition offers three sample passages starting on page 42, and 5 additional passages (that we'll use for practice) from Test 1. Focus only on the Rhetorical Skills questions (shown below):

- ☐ Sample Passage I: 10, 13, 15
- ☐ Sample Passage II: 18, 20, 21, 26, 28
- ☐ Sample Passage III: 31, 32, 33, 37, 40, 42, 45
- ☐ **Test 1**: Passage I: 4, 5, 8, 15
- ☐ **Test 1**: Passage II: 21, 23, 24, 26
- ☐ **Test 1**: Passage III: 38, 40, 43, 45
- ☐ **Test 1**: Passage IV: 46, 49, 50, 52, 54, 60
- ☐ **Test 1**: Passage V: 62, 64, 71, 73, 74, 75

These practice problems should *not* be completed as a closed-book test. Do *not* time yourself. While you complete these problems, review the lessons from this chapter (summarized on the previous page). These practice problems offer you a chance to learn and master the techniques you've learned, in the context of real ACT passages and questions. If you have trouble identifying the best technique to use on a problem, see the Techniques Reference information (Chapter VI) for the sample passages.

PRACTICE TEST

30- and 40-hour programs: Now is a good time to take **Test 4** in the ACT book. We recommend that you review the Timing chapter first, especially if you've had trouble finishing past tests; make sure you have a timing plan in place. Also, don't forget to correct any missed questions after you grade the test (see below). If you have time after you have completed and corrected Test 4, take **Test 5**.

TEST CORRECTIONS

After each practice test is graded, you should correct Rhetorical Skills problems that you missed or left blank. As explained before, there are three steps to correcting the practice tests:

1. The Rhetorical Skills questions for each test are listed below (the brackets show individual passages). Go back to your answer sheet for the corresponding test and circle the question numbers below that you missed (or guessed on, if you kept track of your guesses).

   □ **Test 2**: [5, 6, 8, 13, 14, 15], [18, 24, 27, 28, 29, 30], [35, 37, 39, 45], [48, 50, 53, 56, 58], [65, 69, 70]

   □ **Test 3**: [4, 6, 7, 14, 15], [20, 23, 25, 30], [32, 33, 38, 39, 43], [47, 48, 55, 56, 57, 60], [65, 66, 69, 73, 75]

   □ **Test 4**: [5, 9, 13, 15], [17, 18, 24, 28, 29, 30], [41, 42, 43, 44, 45], [46, 47, 51, 52, 54, 56, 58], [71, 74, 75]

   □ **Test 5**: [2, 5, 6, 11, 13, 15], [17, 22, 25, 30], [35, 36, 37, 44, 45], [49, 54, 55, 57, 60], [62, 63, 68, 70, 73, 74, 75]

2. Correct the problems in *The Real ACT Study Guide*. As you correct the problems, go back to the tutorial and review the techniques. The idea is to: (1) identify techniques that have given you trouble, (2) go back to the tutorial so you can review and strengthen these techniques, and (3) apply these techniques to the specific problems on which you struggled.

3. If you have trouble identifying the best technique to use on a problem, see the Techniques Reference information in Chapter VI, starting on page 138.

V
TIMING

This chapter will cover techniques that will help you finish the English Test *in time*.

1. TIMES

GENERAL APPROACH

The questions on the English Test are generally *not* arranged in order of difficulty. In addition, the last of the five passages may be just as easy as the first passage. **Thus, it is important to get through all five passages.** (This does *not* necessarily mean that you'll spend time answering every question—you may have to guess on some, as we'll explain shortly.)

TIMES

The test is **45-minutes** long, and there are **5 passages**. Thus, you should plan to spend no more than **9 minutes per passage** (9 + 9 + 9 + 9 + 9 = 45 minutes).

DEADLINES

As taught in the Reading section, *deadlines* help you avoid falling behind as you take the test. Imagine that you start the test at "time 0." Since you have 9 minutes for each passage, your fist deadline will occur after 9 minutes, your second deadline after 18 minutes, and so on:

English Deadlines

Start Test	**0 minutes**
Finish Passage I	**9 minutes**
Finish Passage II	**18 minutes**
Finish Passage III	**27 minutes**
Finish Passage IV	**36 minutes**
Finish Passage V	**<45 minutes***

*Remember, you should never leave questions blank when you're done with the test. At the end of the test, with the last 30 seconds or so, quickly guess on any unanswered questions.

USING A STOPWATCH

As you take practice tests, we recommend using a stopwatch to keep track of your times. Start your watch at the beginning of the test, and stick to the deadlines above. Note: Practice timing when you take *practice* tests, *not* when you take the real ACT. The ACT folks do not allow any beeping noises during testing, so they probably won't let you use a stopwatch. The important thing is to get a feel for your timing when you *practice* so you know how quickly you need to work during the real test.

MOVING FASTER THAN THE DEADLINES

Unlike the Reading and Science tests, where most students struggle to keep up with the deadlines, the English test tends to be easier to stay on time. In fact, many students find they can move considerable faster than the deadlines. While moving a *little* faster than the deadlines is fine, we do not recommend getting more than a few minutes ahead. As long as you are staying within the deadlines, working slowly and carefully is better than rushing through the test, potentially making careless mistakes along the way.

WORK UP TO IT

Because it is important to get through all five passages, you might have to skip questions, especially at first, to stick to the 9-minute deadlines. Rhetorical Skills questions are usually harder than Usage/Mechanics ones, so the Rhetorical Skills questions are the ones to skip (especially if you're following the **20-hour program**, in which you probably won't get to the Rhetorical Skills chapter). First, review the methods for identifying the two types of questions:

USAGE/MECHANICS:

Usage/Mechanics questions generally lack a written question next to the question number—the question is *implied*. In other words, you will only see the answer choices.

RHETORICAL SKILLS:

Rhetorical Skills questions, unlike Usage/Mechanics questions, generally have a written question next to the question number. In addition, the answer choices tend to be longer than those on Usage/Mechanics questions.

If necessary, go to page 87 to see examples of Usage/Mechanics and Rhetorical Skills questions.

STEP 1: ANSWER ALL USAGE/MECHANICS QUESTIONS FOR A PASSAGE

As you go through a particular passage, answer all of the Usage/Mechanics questions. Most of the passages have 15 questions, and on average 10 of them will be Usage/Mechanics ones. Skip the Rhetorical Skills questions (on average, there will be 5 Rhetorical Skills questions per passage). This will ensure that you complete most of the easier questions for a passage. Watch the clock. You need to answer these 10 (or so) questions in less than 9 minutes.

STEP 2: ANSWER RHETORICAL SKILLS QUESTIONS FOR THE PASSAGE

If you have time left over for the passage that you're working on, go back and start answering Rhetorical Skills questions that you left blank. Tackle as many of these as you can. If a question has you stumped, guess. When you reach the deadline for that passage, even if you haven't answered all of the Rhetorical Skills questions, move on quickly to the next passage.

––––––––––

FIRST TIME THROUGH

It is usually to your advantage to answer each question as you get to it, rather than having to go back for a second pass of the Rhetorical Skills questions as described above, so push yourself. Your goal is to eventually be able to answer all the questions, including the Rhetorical Skills ones, as you work your way through the passage *the first time*. This is the preferred approach because relevant parts of the passage will be fresh in your mind as you tackle each question. But if you are not able to finish each passage in 9 minutes, follow the two steps above.

2. TIMING SUMMARY

- Spend no more than **9 minutes** on each of the 5 passages (9 + 9 + 9 + 9 + 9 = 45 min.).
- Stick to the *deadlines* below while you take practice tests:

English Deadlines

Start Test	**0 minutes**
Finish Passage I	**9 minutes**
Finish Passage II	**18 minutes**
Finish Passage III	**27 minutes**
Finish Passage IV	**36 minutes**
Finish Passage V	**<45 minutes**

- If you have trouble sticking to the 9-minute deadlines, take the following steps for *each passage*:
  - **Step 1:** Just answer the Usage/Mechanics questions (skip the Rhetorical Skills questions) for a passage.
  - **Step 2:** Answer Rhetorical Skills questions for that passage with any extra time, before moving on to the next passage.

VI
ACT PRACTICE TESTS: TECHNIQUES REFERENCE

Eliminating answer choices is an important part of tackling the ACT English questions. Recognizing errors in the answer choices also gives you a good idea of what technique or techniques are being tested on a particular question. The following pages show the recommended KlassTutoring techniques for each question in *The Real ACT Prep Guide*, 3rd Edition*.

 For each problem on the following pages, the given technique or techniques apply to *all incorrect answer choices*, unless labeled otherwise. For example, look at Question 1 below

    1.   Run-ons/Pronouns (Agreement) (B)

Here's what this means: <u>All three</u> incorrect answer choices have Run-on errors. *In addition*, answer choice B (and <u>only B</u>) has a Pronoun Agreement error. Here's a similar example:

    2.   Run-ons (A & C)/Pronouns (Agreement) (B)

Now, <u>only A and C</u> have Run-on errors, and <u>only B</u> has a Pronoun Agreement error.

Do not look at these techniques until you have attempted the problems on your own. One of the most important ACT skills you can develop is the ability to determine what technique or techniques apply to a given problem. Review the magnifying glass information in this tutorial, and make sure you've tried to determine techniques on your own before you use the information in this chapter.

*ACT is a registered trademark of ACT, Inc., which was not involved in the production of and does not endorse this book.

1. ACT PRACTICE TEST 1

1. Run-ons/Pronouns (Agreement) (B)*

2. Fragments/-*ING* (F)

3. Pronouns (Case) (B & C)/Run-ons (D)

4. Transitions

5. Main Ideas: Keyword = "Ligia"; watch out for off-topic information.

6. Apostrophes and Confused Words

7. Punctuation

8. Main Ideas: Watch out for off-topic information.

9. Wordy (A)/Redundancies (B & C)

10. Vocabulary

11. Paired Conjunctions: We expect "but also;" only B comes close.

12. Passive Voice

13. Verb Tense

14. Verb Tense

15. Main Ideas/Answer the Question: The answer must capture a "positive tone" and have something to do with Ligia.

16. Punctuation

17. Verb Tense

18. Punctuation

19. Adjectives and Adverbs

20. Wordy/Redundancies

21. Organization: Clue words = "threatening" ("signs") in Sentence 5 and "the threats" in Sentence 4.

22. Subject-Verb Agreement

23. Main Ideas: Keyword = "paneling;" B is probably false; the paneling is not described as "wood paneling."

24. Main Ideas (Topic Sentences): Focus on the main idea of Paragraph 3: "machines."

25. More Confused Words

26. Meaning Questions

27. Fragments (A & B)/Subject-Verb Agreement (C)

28. -*ING*/Wordy (G)

29. Subject-Verb Agreement (A & D)/ -*ING* (C)

30. Fragments

31. Apostrophes and Confused Words

32. Punctuation

33. Pronouns (Agreement) (A & B)/Fragment (D)

34. Passive Voice

35. Redundancies (A & B)/Vocabulary (C)

36. Misplaced Words (Improper Modifiers)

37. Redundancies

38. Main Ideas: Keywords = "sales" of "Glory Foods"

39. Punctuation

40. Meaning Questions

41. -*ING* (B & C)/Senseless (D)

42. Misplaced Words

43. Main Ideas: Keywords = the "company's name"; details about the movie are off-topic.

44. Verb Tense

45. Organization: Clue word = "Williams" in Paragraph 2.

46. Main Ideas: Keyword = "pinball"; "movies" are off-topic)

47. Subject Verb Agreement (A & C)/Verb Tense (D)

48. Fragments

49. Organization: Focus on the transition "on the other hand"; also, "Some machines" (Sentence 5) are clue words.

50. Main Ideas: Watch out for off-topic information.

51. Pronouns (Agreement): See "you" in previous sentence.

*See note on how to read these technique references on the previous page.

52. Transitions

53. Punctuation

54. Main Ideas (Topic Sentences): Keywords = "chance" (Sentence 6) and "each game is different" (Sentence 7).

55. Redundancies/Wordy

56. Verb Tense (G)/Pronouns (Agreement) (H & J)

57. Punctuation/Fragments (C & D)

58. Redundancies/Wordy

59. Adjectives and Adverbs

60. Meaning Questions

61. Punctuation

62. Transitions/Run-ons: The comma requires a FANBOYS conjunction, such as *and*.

63. Punctuation

64. Parallelism (F)/Main Ideas (Topic Sentences) (H & J): Keywords = "these viruses" and "these bombs."

65. Wordy (B)/-*ING* (C & D)

66. Redundancies/Wordy

67. Subject-Verb Agreement

68. -*ING* (F & H)/Fragments (J)

69. Punctuation

70. Idiom (H & J)/Adjectives and Adverbs (G)

71. Answer the Question: "the second recommendation"

72. Misplaced Words

73. Organization: Clue words = "Names like these"

74. Style

75. Main Ideas: The essay does not focus on "programming a computer virus.

2. ACT PRACTICE TEST 2

1. Run-ons (B)/-*ING* (C & D)

2. Punctuation

3. Verb Tense

4. Wordy (F & G)/Transitions (J): The conjunction "so" is illogical.

5. Main Ideas: Keyword = "remote control"

6. Transitions

7. Punctuation

8. Transitions

9. Pronouns (Ambiguous)/Nonsense (D)

10. Punctuation (G)/Fragments (H & J)

11. Misplaced Words (Awkward)

12. -*ING* (G & H)/Verb Tense (J)

13. Main Ideas: Grandpa feels *positively* toward the remote control; B-D are negative.

14. Organization: Clue words = "He programs" and "grandchild"

15. Main Ideas (Topic Sentences)

16. Comparisons (G)/Senseless (H & J): The word "liveliest" (or "most lively") only works with a singular *form*, not "forms."

17. Apostrophes and Confused Words

18. Main Ideas: Keywords = history of "Tejano music"

19. Punctuation

20. Fragments (F)/Punctuation (H & J)

21. Pronouns (Ambiguous) (A)/-*ING* (C & D)

22. Idiom (Prepositional)

23. Parallelism (A-C)/Run-ons (A)/Paired Conjunctions (B)/-*ING* (C)

24. Meaning Questions

25. Fragments (A & C)/Wordy (B)

26. Punctuation

27. Organization: Clue words = "She became widely known"

28. Main Ideas: Keywords = "Tejano music"

29. Style (A & C are too informal)/Wordy (B)

30. Main Idea (of the Passage)

31. Fragments

32. Apostrophes and Confused Words

33. Verb Tense

34. Redundancies/-*ING* (H)

35. Meaning Questions

36. Punctuation

37. Meaning Questions

38. Fragments/-*ING* (J)

39. Transitions

40. Vocabulary

41. Apostrophes and Confused Words

42. Misplaced Words

43. Redundancies

44. Vocabulary: The word "halt" often refers to a *temporary* stop.

45. Main Idea (of the Passage)

46. Idiom (Prepositional)

47. Comparisons (A & B)/Pronouns (B & D)

48. Answer the Question: "unity of the people."

49. Idiom (Prepositional)

50. Meaning Questions

51. Misplaced Words: The word "them" should refer to "other Miami," not the pictures./Wordy (B & D)

52. Punctuation

53. Organization: Clue word = "rooms" (in the third sentence)

54. Noun Agreement (F & J): See "rooms" above./Pronouns (Agreement and Ambiguous) (G)

55. Transitions (A): The conjunction "and" is illogical./Run-ons (B & C)

56. Main Ideas: Keywords = "no reservation lands"

57. Run-ons (B & C): Note that there is no comma before the FANBOYS conjunction "and."/Wordy (C)/-*ING* (D)

58. Transitions

59. Fragments/-*ING* (A)

60. Idiom (Common Mistakes): See the "like/as" rule.

61. Fragments: Only A prevents the second part of the sentence from becoming a fragment. Note: Questions 61 & 62 are Interrelated Questions.

62. Pronouns (Agreement) (F & G): The word "itself" refers to "howling"—both singular./Idiom (Prepositional) (J)

63. Fragments/-*ING* (C)

64. Run-ons (F & G)/Fragments (H)

65. Transitions

66. -*ING*/Wordy (G & H)/Passive Voice (J)

67. Vocabulary

68. Redundancies

69. Answer the Question

70. Transitions

71. Parallelism

72. Punctuation

73. Misplaced Words (Misplaced Modifiers)

74. Subject-Verb Agreement (F-H)/Wordy (G & H)/-*ING* (G)

75. Punctuation

3. ACT PRACTICE TEST 3

1. -*ING*/Wordy

2. Subject-Verb Agreement/-*ING* (J)

3. Run-ons

4. Main Ideas (Topic Sentences): The keyword in Paragraph 4 is "offerings," referring to "hundreds of manuscripts."

5. Punctuation

6. Answer the Question: "contrast"

7. Main Ideas: The "typesetting" is off-topic here.

8. Comparisons (G)/Adjectives and Adverbs (H & J)

9. Redundancies

10. Apostrophes and Confused Words

11. Idiom: Hopefully your ear hears the awkward idiom in the incorrect answer choices./-*ING* (A)

12. Punctuation

13. Apostrophes and Confused Words

14. Main Ideas (F & G): The "snow" is off-topic./Wordy (H)

15. Main Ideas: The quantity of material is off-topic here; see Paragraph 5.

16. Redundancies

17. -*ING* (B & D)/Fragments (C)

18. Adjectives and Adverbs/-*ING* (J)

19. Idiom (Common Mistakes): see "of → have" rule.

20. Main Ideas (Topic Sentences): Keyword = "wolves"

21. Punctuation

22. Punctuation/-*ING* (J)

23. Meaning Questions: Which answer offers the most direct evidence of wolves?

24. Parallelism

25. Main Ideas (Topic Sentences): The keywords for Paragraph 4 are "endangered species."

26. Idiom (Prepositional)

27. Punctuation

28. Verb Tense/-*ING* (F)

29. Idiom (Prepositional)

30. Organization: Clue words in Paragraph 2, Sentence 2 = "animals killed by wolves"

31. Run-ons (A & B)/Fragments (C)

32. Answer the Question: "did not feel prepared"

33. Transitions

34. Wordy

35. Passive Voice (A)/Fragments (B)/Misplaced Words (Misplaced Modifiers) (D)

36. Apostrophes and Confused Words

37. Pronouns (Agreement) (A & B)/Apostrophes and Confused Words (C)

38. Main Ideas (Topic Sentences): The keywords in Sentence 6 are "music education."

39. Main Ideas (A-C are off-topic)

40. Fragments (G & H)/Run-ons (J)

41. Redundancies

42. Verb Tense (G & H)/-*ING* & Fragment (J)

43. Transitions (A)/Wordy (B & D)/Idiom (B & D)

44. Parallelism/-*ING* (G & H)

45. Misplaced Words (A & B)/Wordy (D)

46. Misplaced Words (F & H)/Verb Tense (G)

47. Answer the Question: "clearest examples"

48. Transitions

49. Redundancies

50. Pronouns (Agreement)/Verb Tense (H & J)

51. Comparisons

52. -*ING* (F)/Transitions (G)/Fragments (J)

53. Run-ons (A & D)/ Apostrophes and Confused Words (C & D)

54. Punctuation

55. Main Ideas: Keywords = "This expressway" (Sentence 1)

56. Main Ideas (Topic Sentences): Keywords = "alternate... routes"

57. Transitions

58. Verb Tense (F & J)/Punctuation (G & J)

59. Redundancies

60. Main Ideas: Watch out for off-topic answer choices.

61. *-ING* (A)/Fragments (A & D)/Verb Tense (B)

62. Verb Tense

63. Punctuation

64. Idiom (Prepositional)

65. Organization: Clue word = "gardens"

66. Main Ideas (Topic Sentences): Keywords = "Many farmers and agronomists"

67. Redundancies: See the word "recent."

68. Subject-Verb Agreement

69. Main Ideas (Topic Sentences): The next paragraph should discuss the Iroquois farming "method" and contrast the "hidden costs" of the previous paragraph.

70. Verb Tense

71. *-ING*/Transitions (A): The conjunction "because" is illogical.

72. Run-ons (J)

73. Main Ideas: Only C ties into the "Iroquois."

74. Punctuation

75. Main Idea (of the Passage): See the title of the essay.

4. ACT PRACTICE TEST 4

1. Punctuation

2. Vocabulary

3. Run-on (A)/Punctuation (C)/-*ING* (D)

4. Fragments

5. Meaning Questions

6. Misplaced Words

7. Verb Tense

8. Pronouns (Ambiguous)

9. Transitions

10. Punctuation (G)/Apostrophes and Confused Words (H & J)

11. Fragments (A & D)/Run-ons (B)

12. Redundancies

13. Meaning Questions/Answer the Question: "emphasize the women's main accomplishment"

14. Misplaced Words

15. Meaning Questions

16. Run-ons: Remember, the word "however" is not a FANBOYS conjunction.

17. Transitions

18. Answer the Question: Note use of colors and fruit.

19. Misplaced Words (Improper Modifiers)

20. Punctuation

21. Punctuation/Run-ons (A & D)

22. Run-ons

23. Subject-Verb Agreement: The subject is "bins."

24. Answer the Question: "most specific"

25. Verb Tense (B & C)/Pronouns (Agreement) (D)

26. Fragments/-*ING* (H)

27. Punctuation

28. Organization: Clue word = "the grass"

29. Meaning Questions

30. Organization: Clue word = "the shop"

31. Apostrophes and Confused Words

32. Misplaced Words (F)/Wordy (G)/Redundancies (J)

33. Comparisons: Watch out for the word "then" incorrectly used in a comparison.

34. Punctuation/Fragments (F)

35. Pronouns (Ambiguous) (A & C)/Misplaced Words (D)

36. Run-ons/Punctuation (G)/Apostrophes and Confused Words (J)

37. Run-ons/-*ING* (D)

38. Run-ons (G)/Transitions (H)/-*ING* (J)

39. Subject-Verb Agreement

40. -*ING* (F & G)/Verb Tense (H)

41. Main Ideas: Keywords = "useful to humans"

42. Meaning Questions

43. Main Ideas: Keywords at beginning = "common misconceptions"

44. Meaning Questions

45. Main Ideas: The "extinction" is discussed in only one paragraph.

46. Answer the Question: "Free Speech Movement"

47. Main Ideas: Information about "Mississippi" is off topic.

48. Punctuation/Fragments (J)

49. Style (A): The word "stuff" is too casual./Fragments (C)/Pronouns (Ambiguous) (D)

50. Run-ons (G)/Nonsense (H & J)

51. Main Ideas: Keywords = "Free Speech Movement" (Sentence 3) and "Savio" (Sentence 4)

52. Answer the Question: "succeeded"/Vocabulary

53. Vocabulary

54. Transitions

55. Nonsense

56. Main Ideas

57. Wordy (B & C)/Verb Tense (C & D)

58. Transitions

59. Fragments (A & D)/Punctuation (A)/Run-ons (C)

60. Punctuation

61. Apostrophes and Confused Words (A & C)/Punctuation (B & C)

62. Vocabulary

63. Parallelism/Passive Voice

64. Fragments

65. Pronouns (Agreement)

66. Redundancies

67. Nonsense: The "plane crash" was not delivering anything.

68. Redundancies

69. Punctuation

70. Misplaced Words

71. Organization: Clue word = "them," referring to "projects"

72. Adjectives and Adverbs

73. Idiom (Prepositional) (B & C)/A and B also test commonly confused words (*principal* and *principle*); see the Apostrophes and Confused Words section.

74. Answer the Question: "summarize key points"

75. Organization: Clue word = "this honor"

5. ACT PRACTICE TEST 5

1. Punctuation (A & B)/Fragments (D)

2. Answer the Question: "grandmother's interests"

3. Redundancies

4. Fragments (F & G)/Run-ons (H)

5. Main Ideas: Keywords = "Miami time"

6. Punctuation (F)/Transitions (H & J)

7. Wordy

8. Verb Tense: See "Recently"

9. Subject-Verb Agreement (A & B)/Nonsense (D)

10. Punctuation

11. Organization: Clue word: "there," referring to "clearing"

12. Parallelism

13. Transitions

14. Comparisons: Watch out for the word "then" incorrectly used in a comparison.

15. Main Idea (of Passage): Main keyword of essay = "Miami Time"

16. Run-ons

17. Transitions

18. Misplaced Words

19. Apostrophes and Confused Words (A & B)/Pronouns (Agreement) (D)

20. Punctuation

21. Misplaced Words

22. Transitions

23. Apostrophes and Confused Words

24. Subject-Verb Agreement

25. Answer the Question: See keywords: "unity of purpose" (Sentence 2)

26. Redundancies

27. Misplaced Words (Improper Modifiers)

28. Punctuation

29. Run-ons

30. Meaning Questions/Main Ideas: Keywords = "women's accomplishments" and "shared vision"

31. Subject-Verb Agreement

32. Fragments (G)/Nonsense (H & J)

33. Pronouns (Agreement)/Apostrophes and Confused Words (D)

34. Punctuation

35. Organization: Clue word = "undaunted"; see "the public preferred…"

36. Main Ideas: Keywords = "special effects"

37. Answer the Question: "skill and inventiveness"

38. Adjectives and Adverbs

39. Redundancies

40. Wordy

41. Run-ons

42. Verb Tense (F & H)/Idiom (Common Mistakes) (G)

43. Vocabulary

44. Main Ideas/Answer the Question: "science fiction"

45. Main Idea (of Passage): Keywords = "Méliès" and "film world"

46. Verb Tense(F & H)/Idiom (H & J): The phrase "out of style" is a common idiom.

47. Idiom (Common Mistakes) (A & C)/Verb Tense (D)

48. Punctuation (F & G)/Apostrophes and Confused Words (G & H)

49. Answer the Question: "specific information"/Style (A)/Idiom (Common Mistakes (D)

50. Punctuation

51. Pronouns (Ambiguous)

52. Fragments (F & H)/-*ING* (H)/Verb Tense (J)

53. Punctuation

54. Answer the Question: "variety of settings" and "Liana's interest"

55. Main Ideas: Keyword = "Nancy Drew," not the "series"

56. Parallelism

57. Transitions

58. Parallelism/-*ING* (G & H)

59. Run-ons (A & B)/-*ING* (D)

60. Main Ideas: Keywords = "the stories themselves"

61. Idiom: The phrase "from… to…" is a common idiom.

62. Answer the Question: The words "ill will and danger" = "spine-tingling" in H.

63. Main Ideas: Eliminate off-topic answer choices.

64. Verb Tense/Idiom (Common Mistakes) (F)

65. Run-ons (A)/Wordy (B)/Nonsense (D)

66. Run-ons

67. Punctuation

68. Main Ideas: Keyword = "cost"

69. Nonsense

70. Answer the Question: What are "Mars Rovers"?

71. Redundancies (A & C)/Wordy (B)

72. Redundancies (F & H)/Adjectives and Adverbs ("age" is not an adjective) (G)

73. Transitions

74. Transitions

75. Main Ideas: Keyword = "cost"

6. ACT PRACTICE PROBLEMS

Sample Passage I:

1. Redundancies

2. Wordy

3. Run-On

4. Fragment (F)/Wordy (G)/-ING (H)

5. Punctuation

6. Misplaced Words (Improper Modifiers)

7. Punctuation

8. Verb Tense: Tense should be *present* (see previous sentence).

9. Apostrophes and Confused Words

10. Main Ideas: Keywords = "waila," "history," and "influence"

11. Misplaced Words

12. Verb Tense (F & G)/-ING (G)/Passive Voice and Senseless (H)

13. Main Ideas: Keywords = "O'odham," "waila," and instruments (in general); note: a saxophone is a "woodwind" instrument.

14. Fragments/Punctuation

15. Organization: Clue words = "Those same German influences"

Sample Passage II:

16. Vocabulary

17. Punctuation (A & C)/Fragments (C & D)

18. Main Ideas: Keywords = "difference" (see 16) in the ways a person's age is computed.

19. Vocabulary

20. Meaning Questions

21. Transitions

22. Idiom (Prepositional)

23. Apostrophes and Confused Words (B & C)/Punctuation (D)

24. Pronouns (Agreement)

25. Fragments

26. Answer the Question: "positive attitude"

27. Pronouns (Case)

28. Meaning Questions

29. Redundancies

30. Vocabulary

Sample Passage III:

31. Answer the Question (A & D): "illustrate the term *dress code*"/Subject-Verb Agreement (B & D): "types" does not agree with "was" (B) or "is" (D).

32. Idiom (F): The word "inefficient" is awkward when followed by a preposition./Style (G & H)

33. Main Ideas: Keywords: "Kevin's case"

34. Punctuation

35. -ING/Idioms (Prepositional)

36. Punctuation

37. Main Ideas: Keyword = the "court" and "clothing" (watch out for off-topic answer choices)

38. Apostrophes and Confused Words

39. Pronouns (Case)

40. Transitions

41. Fragments (A & B)/-ING (D): The word "having" is usually incorrect.

42. Answer the Question: "convey the importance of the case"

43. Punctuation

44. Idioms (Prepositional)

45. Meaning Questions: Look for false answer choices.

VII
ENGLISH ANSWERS

The following answers are to all lesson problems, homework problems, and quizzes.

VERB TENSE

1. **D.** Note the word "today."
2. **J.** Tense should be the same as "were" earlier in the sentence.
3. **D.** Use the recently-to-present tense ("has…").
4. **G.** The tense is set as past by "learned" and "competed."
5. **D.** Use the same tense as "will ensure," the future tense.

Homework:

1. **B.** The tense is set as present by the verb "peeks."
2. **G.** The research paper has not yet been finished. The word "will" makes the verb phrase a future tense.
3. **B.** Use the past tense of "come."
4. **G.** Use past-of-the-past since Ken wrote before the rocket launched.
5. **A.** The verb "fell" sets the tense as past.

SUBJECT-VERB AGREEMENT

1. **A.** The subject is "Each" (singular). Remember to cross off prepositional phrases.
2. **H.** The subject is "Mike" (singular); note the "or." Remember to cross off modifying phrases.
3. **A.** The subject is "team" (singular).
4. **F.** The subject is "One" (singular).
5. **B.** The subject, "boats" (plural), comes after the verb.

Homework:

1. **D.** The subject is "Either" (singular).
2. **H.** The subject is "Everyone" (singular).
3. **C.** The subject is "audience" (singular).
4. **G.** The subject is "Every" (singular).
5. **C.** The subject is "feeling" (singular). Note that "got" sets the tense as past, so B is incorrect.

PRONOUNS

1. **B.** The case should be object. Note that "Dorothy and he" follows a preposition ("for").
2. **H.** Again, note the preposition "about." The case should be object.
3. **B.** The word "students" (plural) must match the number of the pronoun.
4. **G.** The subject "Nobody" (singular) must match the number of the pronouns.
5. **C.** Words such as "company" and "staff" are singular. The correct pronoun is "it."

Homework:

1. **A.** Remove the noun "seniors" to hear that "We" is the correct choice. There is no need for a comma.
2. **G.** The pronoun follows a preposition "to" so must be the object case "her." G has the correct tense as well.
3. **D.** The subject "Anyone" is singular.
4. **G.** The pronoun should stay consistent with the one earlier in the sentence "you."
5. **B.** With no clear group in the sentence, the pronoun "their" (a possessive pronoun) is ambiguous. B is the simplest way to correct the error.

PARALLELISM

1. **B.** The words "watching" and "finishing" are parallel in form.
2. **H.** The verbs "hides" and "looks" should be parallel.
3. **C.** The words "financial comfort" (adjective-noun) are parallel to "creative freedom."

Homework:

1. **B.** The word "become," on its own, is the simplest way to stay parallel to "learn."
2. **F.** The word "taking" is parallel to "driving."
3. **A.** This is not the same question as Number 3 (above). Look carefully at what is underlined. The phrase "being creatively free" ("being"-adverb-adjective) is parallel to "being financially comfortable.

PUNCTUATION

1. **B.** A comma should separate the dependent clause from the following independent clause.
2. **J.** Commas should separate the modifying phrase from the rest of the sentence. Notice that this phrase could be removed from the sentence.
3. **C.** A comma must precede a conjunction (such as "but") between two independent clauses.
4. **J.** When the dependent clause follows the independent clause, a comma is unnecessary.
5. **A.** The word "however" should be separated from the rest of the sentence with commas, similar to a modifying phrase. Listen to the correct sound of the pauses.

Homework:
1. **B.** The phrase "friendly as always" is a modifying phrase.
2. **F.** The comma correctly separates the dependent clause from the following independent clause.
3. **B.** Separate the modifying phrase from the rest of the sentence with commas.
4. **H.** A semicolon correctly separates the two independent clauses.
5. **A.** Don't forget to "listen" to the pauses when you see commas.

FRAGMENTS LESSON PROBLEMS

1. **C.** In the original sentence, the subject "The Problems of Philosophy" lacks a verb. The word *often* begins a modifying phrase. Remove the phrase to hear the error. C corrects the error.
2. **F.** The sentence is not a fragment. The subject of the independent clause, "scientists," has the verb "warned." The other answer choices create fragments (H and J) or a run-on (G).
3. **B.** The word "who" introduces a pronoun phrase; the original sentence lacks a verb for the subject "Hedy Lamarr." B corrects the error.
4. **H.** A semicolon must separate two independent clauses (the first phrase is not an independent clause). Change the semicolon to a comma to correct the error.
5. **A.** The sentence is correct. Remove the modifying phrase to hear that it's fine.

Homework:
1. **B.** The subject of the "that" clause, "climbing trees," must have a verb, as in B.
2. **G.** The subject "people" needs a verb, as in G. Remember, words in the -ing form—on their own—do not function as verbs.
3. **B.** Only B avoids a fragment. Remove all pronoun and modifying phrases to hear the correct sentence: "The so-called wind car was designed by…"
4. **F.** Since the first clause is not independent, only F is not a fragment.
5. **B.** The subject of the "that" clause, "ghost stories," must have a verb, as in B.

RUN-ONS

1. **C.** The word "because" turns the second clause into a dependent clause (no comma needed).
2. **G.** A semicolon is used to separate the two independent clauses.
3. **C.** In B, two independent clauses are correctly separated with a period.
4. **G.** In G, the two independent clauses are not properly separated with a comma/FANBOYS conjunction, semicolon, or period.
5. **A.** The semicolon correctly separates two independent clauses. The other answer choices are run-ons.

Homework:
1. **C.** The semicolon correctly separates two complete sentences. Make sure to read to the end of the sentence.
2. **H.** H turns the second independent clause ("this unconformity…") into a modifying phrase, one that adds information to the first part of the sentence. If necessary, use process of elimination to eliminate the other answer choices, all of which incorrectly link two independent clauses.
3. **A.** The two independent clauses are correctly separated with a comma and a FANBOYS conjunction.
4. **F.** The word "because" correctly makes the second clause a dependent clause.

5. **D.** The transition words "in other words" cannot be used in the same way as a FANBOYS conjunction. The semicolon in D correctly separates two independent sentences.

MISPLACED WORDS LESSON PROBLEMS

1. **B.** The underlined phrase must clearly relates to the use of the phone card, not the "fine dinner."
2. **J.** Keep "Corporations" and "smaller companies" close to avoid any ambiguity in the comparison. The original sentence suggests that "graduates with advanced degrees" and "smaller companies" are being compared. J best corrects the error.
3. **B.** The modifying phrase at the beginning of the sentence must modify "Sean." Notice that only B begins with "Sean."
4. **H.** Only H begins with the word "Chrissie," who is the person referred to in the modifying phrase. Note that in J, "Chrissie's A" is not the same as "Chrissie."

Homework:
1. **D.** The graffiti is obviously not in the last chapter of the book. D best removes the ambiguity.
2. **J.** Who heard the CD of the performance? The word "we" should immediately follow the modifying phrase. J is a better answer choice than H, which is wordy.
3. **C.** This answer choices removes any awkwardness or ambiguity. D has unnecessary commas.
4. **G.** Who had the "strength and endurance"? "Greg Lemond" must be the first words following the modifying phrase. (J is a fragment, lacking an independent clause.)

REDUNDANCIES

1. **D.** Innovations are, by definition, new.
2. **G.**
3. **B.** To sway is to move back and forth (by definition). B is the most succinct answer choice.
4. **H.**

Homework:
1. **D.** Remember, on Redundancy questions, if one of the answer choices is an OMIT one, it's probably correct.
2. **J.** The word "concluded" is redundant with "the last sentence of the book."
3. **A.** Careful—D is the shortest answer choice, but fastest and nimblest are not the same. To be nimble is to be light or easy in movement, not just fast. The best answer is A.
4. **H.** Insurmountable means unclimbable.

APOSTROPHES AND CONFUSED WORDS

1. **C.** There is only one shell ("it"). A possessive is correct (note the noun "shape" following "shells").
2. **F.** The word "its," the possessive of "it" (referring to the book), is correct.
3. **B.** The word "its" should be a possessive, as in B. The original sentence is a fragment.
4. **F.** Expand "they're" to **they are**—the sentence sounds correct.

Homework:
1. **A.** The contraction "It's" is correct (It is…). D is not idiomatically correct.
2. **F.** The "regions" belong to the "country," so the possessive in F is correct.
3. **D.** Expand the contraction "You're" (**You are**) in D to hear its correctness.
4. **J.** The "long necks" belong to the "Giraffes." Since "Giraffes" is plural (see the word "them"), add an apostrophe. Watch for added errors in other answer choices (H).

IDIOM

Prepositional Idiom Homework:
1. **A.** The original sentence is correct.
2. **F.** The running back would not fight **for** the opposing tacklers; he might fight **through** them.
3. **A.** The most appropriate preposition to follow "famous" in this context is "for."
4. **H.** The correct idiom is "independent of."

5. **B.** Using the word "through" in this instance is not idiomatically correct. One doesn't go **through** land (unless one is in a tunnel).

Common Mistakes Homework:
1. **C.** The word "that" should follow "reason" in this case. C is clearly more succinct than B.
2. **J.** The phrase "help noticing" is preferable to "help but notice."
3. **C.** Use "regardless" in place of "irregardless."
4. **F.** In a comparison, follow "more for" with "than."
5. **B.** B best corrects the error. The word "nor" should be used with the word "neither" (not "not").

ADJECTIVES AND ADVERBS

1. **D.** The word "carefully," an adverb, describes "how" tax returns are checked.
2. **G.** The adverb "rapidly" modifies the verb "moved." G is better than J, which is wordy.

Homework:
1. **B.** The adverb "typically" modifies the adjective "brilliant," which modifies the noun "dissertations." D is incorrect. The "dissertation" is certainly not "typical" (as in D).
2. **F.** The adjective "really" modifies the adjective "good."

COMPARISONS

1. **B.** Watch out for incorrect double comparisons ("more" + "longer").
2. **G.** Since there are probably more than two athletes on the team, the correct adjective is "fastest" (with -est).
3. **A.** For more than two people, "most intelligent" is the correct form.

Homework:
1. **A.** Since there are only two twins, the correct word is "more." A is better than D.
2. **J.** There are only two choices ("the high road or the low road"), so the correct word is "better." Watch out for double comparisons.
3. **C.** The term "more than happy" is an idiomatic expression. Since no comparison is given— "you and your friends" are not compared to "I"—A and B are incorrect. D is wordy.

ILLOGICAL COMPARISONS

1. **C.** Compare "students" to "students." Note that the two compared items in C, unlike those in D, are parallel in construction ("Our school's students...the average school's students").
2. **H.** The original sentence compares "history" to "islands." H corrects the error—the words "those" refers to the "histories" (plural) of the other islands.

Homework:
1. **A.** The comparison between "eating fish" and "eating other meats" is clear and correct.
2. **G.** Compare "score" to "score," and make sure the items are parallel ("Daniel's score" is parallel to "his score").

NOUN AGREEEMENT

1. **D.** The word "places" (plural) agrees with "bookstores" (plural).
2. **G.** The word "readers" (plural) agrees with "students" (plural).

Homework:
1. **C.** The word "boxes" (plural) agrees with there being more than one type of cookie. D introduces a redundancy error.
2. **J.** The words "vibraphone" and "instrument" are both singular.

PAIRED CONJUNCTIONS LESSON PROBLEMS

1. **H.** The words "but also" are the best choice to follow "not only." G is a run-on because the word "it" becomes the subject of an independent clause (and there is no comma before "but")—review run-ons if necessary.
2. **B.** The word "and" should follow "both." Note that the words "also" in C and "too" in D are redundant since the word "Both" already makes clear that two items are being discussed.

Homework:
1. **B.** "Neither...nor" is correct.
2. **G.** The "as" in G completes the comparison.
3. **C.** The word "as" should follow "not so much."

MORE CONFUSED WORDS

Homework:
1. **D.** Use "among" because there are **more than two** employees.
2. **G.** Since Matt is going from the outside to the inside, use "into."
3. **C.** When possible, use "as if" (or "as though") as a substitute for "like."
4. **F.** The original sentence is correct since there are more than two members.

VOCABULARY

1. **B.** The word "borrow" means the opposite of "lend."

NONSENSE

1. **D.** Removing the underlined portion leaves a sentence that doesn't make sense. Hopefully you hear the awkwardness. Learning did not "come before."

Homework:
1. **B.** It is the **raid** that Brown hoped would lead to a rebellion. It doesn't make sense that a place ("Harper's Ferry") would lead to rebellion, as suggested in A and C. D is particularly awkward.

GRAMMAR QUIZ 1 (SECTIONS 1-4)

1. **D.** (Verb Tense) The word "Played" and the year "1989" tell you to use the simple past tense.
2. **G.** (Pronouns - Case) Note the preceding preposition ("to"). The case should be object ("her").
3. **D.** (Subject-Verb Agreement) The subject is "Everyone" (singular).
4. **G.** (Verb Tense) The tense is set as present by "reads" and more importantly "has."
5. **A.** (Parallelism) The word "Enjoying" is parallel to "working." A is better than D, which is wordy.
6. **J.** (Pronoun - Agreement) The pronoun must agree with the singular subject "country."
7. **D.** (Subject-Verb Agreement) The subject is "number" (singular). All other answer choices are plural. Don't forget to cross off prepositional phrases to help identify the subject of the sentence.
8. **G.** (Parallelism) To stay parallel, the word "kind" earlier in the sentence should be repeated in the underlined portion.

GRAMMAR QUIZ 2 (SECTIONS 5-8)

1. **D.** (Punctuation) No punctuation is needed.
2. **F.** (Misplaced Words) The order of the words in the original sentence is correct.
3. **B.** (Fragments) Only B removes the "that" clause. All other answer choices are fragments.
4. **G.** (Misplaced Words) This one is tricky. It's not the "doctor's research papers" that was considered an expert. It was the **doctor**. Only G begins with the word "doctor."
5. **D.** (Punctuation) The dependent clause ("as though...") follows the independent clause; there is no need for a comma.
6. **J.** (Fragment) The subject "One" lacks a verb in the original sentence. J adds the verb "is."
7. **B.** (Run-ons) B is a run-on, missing a comma before the FANBOYS conjunction.

8. **G.** *(Fragments) The word "working" is not an active verb for the subject "lawyer." G corrects the error and is the correct tense, matching the present tense of "suggests."*
9. **D.** *(Run-ons) Only D connects two independent clauses correctly—in this case, with a comma and a FANBOYS conjunction ("but"). Remember, "then" is not a FANBOYS conjunction.*
10. **G.** *(Punctuation) Note that the secondary modifying phrase ("as…himself") could be removed from the primary modifying phrase ("or…boss"), and the primary modifying phrase can be removed from the independent clause. These are good indicators of the need for commas.*

GRAMMAR QUIZ 3 (SECTIONS 9-11)

1. **D.** *(Apostrophes and Confused Words) "It's" is a contraction for **It is**. Make sure you expand contractions so you know they work: "It is hot enough…"*
2. **H.** *(Redundancies) The time is clearly "nearly 20 minutes"—saying so is redundant.*
3. **B.** *(Idiom) The words "to make" are the best idiomatic choice in this case.*
4. **F.** *(Apostrophes and Confused Words) The word "puppy's" is a singular possessive (of "first steps").*
5. **C.** *(Apostrophes and Confused Words) The word "there's" is a contraction of **there is**.*
6. **J.** *(Idiom) The word "latter" (or former) should only be used with **two** items. J is the best correction.*
7. **B.** *(Redundancies) The words "excited" and "invigorated" are near synonyms.*
8. **H.** *(Idiom) The words "confused by" are idiomatically correct.*

GRAMMAR QUIZ 4 (SECTIONS 1-15)

1. **B.** *(Noun Agreement) "Elephants" (plural) and "creatures" (plural) must match in number.*
2. **G.** *(Adjectives and Adverbs) The word "lazily" describes how the raft floated, so it should be an adverb, as in G.*
3. **D.** *(More Confused Words) Use "fewer" when the items can be counted.*
4. **H.** *(Idiom) The correct preposition to follow "opposed" is "to."*
5. **B.** *(Pronouns - Ambiguous) The pronoun "it" could refer to "evidence," "the paper," or "a cellular tower." The pronoun "they" could refer to the "Researchers" or the "evidence and… paper." Only B removes the ambiguity.*
6. **J.** *(Punctuation) Since a comma is used to close the modifying phrase ending with "Animals," one should be used to open it. The word "or" is idiomatically correct here.*
7. **C.** *(Subject-Verb Agreement) The subject is "Each" (singular).*
8. **F.** *(Apostrophes and Confused Words) The word "family's" is a singular possessive (of "migration")—in other words: the migration of the Joad family.*
9. **D.** *(Redundancies) A "custom" is "usual," "regular," and "routine."*
10. **G.** *(Paired Conjunctions) The word "and" should follow "both."*
11. **A.** *(Verb Tense) The tense should be past ("last season's").*
12. **G.** *(Fragments) To avoid a fragment, remove the "that" clause.*
13. **D.** *(Pronouns - Case) Use **who** or **whom**, not **which**, for people. The subject case ("who") is correct here since the "citizens" are performing the action. Also, using a comma (and, thus, creating a pronoun phrase) would create a fragment.*
14. **G.** *(Illogical Comparisons / Parallelism) Compare apples to apples ("party" to "party"). Also, note that only G maintains parallel construction ("Last year's… party" and "this year's party").*
15. **B.** *(Comparisons) Since there are **two** people, use a word in the -er form ("faster").*

PART 2

MATH

I
MATH INTRODUCTION AND BASIC CONCEPTS

This chapter will introduce the ACT Math Test, including test layout and timing strategy. It will also cover the use of your calculator and other basic mathematical concepts and terminologies.

1. INTRODUCTION

The Math section is divided into nine chapters:

    I.   Introduction and Basic Concepts

    II.   Arithmetic

    III.   Algebra

    IV.   Geometry

    V.   Functions

    VI.   Trigonometry

    VII.   Math Odds and Ends

    VIII.   ACT Practice Tests: Techniques Reference

    IX.   Math Answers

The primary purpose of this part of the tutorial is to teach you *how* to use mathematical techniques. However, while knowing *how* to apply these techniques is obviously important, knowing *when* to use the techniques is perhaps just as important. You may be an expert at a particular technique, but if you come across a problem on the ACT and do not *use* this technique, then your mastery of the technique may not help you. For this reason, the tutorial also focuses on *identifying* the correct technique to use on a particular problem. Throughout the tutorial, look for the magnifying glass for information about identifying techniques.

TEST LAYOUT

The Math Test includes:

- 60 multiple-choice questions (5 answer choices each)
- Total test time = 60 minutes

TIMING STRATEGY

Generally speaking, the ACT Math Test gets harder as you go. However, you will likely find several relatively-easy questions near the end of the test and several relatively-difficult questions near the beginning. (The order-of-difficulty pattern of the ACT is certainly not as clear-cut as that of the SAT.) Use the following strategy:

STEP 1

As you work your way through the test, plan to leave some questions blank—even if some of these questions occur early in the test. (Don't forget to leave the answer choice bubbles blank as well!) Don't get bogged down on problems that you find especially difficult. Just skip them and keep moving. Stay aggressive and try to get to the last question of the test, even if you have to skip many questions to get there. Because the questions *generally* get harder as you go, the further into the test you get, the more questions you'll likely have to skip. Review our approach to skipping questions in the "Guessing on the ACT" section (in the Introduction).

STEP 2

After you get to the end of the test, with whatever time you have left, go back to the questions you left blank, starting from the beginning. If, for a particular question, you have no idea how to tackle it, take a guess and move on to the next one. (Remember, you don't lose points on the ACT, so you should answer every question, even if you have to guess.)

STEP 3

Make sure you leave yourself about 30 seconds at the end of the test to guess on any remaining questions.

As you learn the techniques in this tutorial and get better at identifying problems that use these techniques, you'll get better at choosing which problems to tackle your first time through. Taking real practice tests will definitely help you develop a timing strategy that works for *you*.

QUESTIONS THAT LOOK HARD ARE OFTEN <u>NOT</u> HARD

Don't assume that just because a question looks hard you should skip it. Some of the hardest-looking questions are often the easiest. There are two types of questions that typically scare away students:

1. Questions with lots of words
2. Questions with long formulas

Stay aggressive on these problems. They may not be too difficult, and getting them correct will certainly give you an edge over other students who will likely skip them or guess. It's worth noting, however, that questions with lots of words often take longer to complete than shorter questions, so as you get into the later (and potentially harder) parts of the test, these long, wordy questions may be good ones to skip and come back to if you have time.

HAPPY FACE TOPICS

As in the English section of the tutorial, topics that are indicated with the symbol below may be a review for many students. You may choose to move quickly through this material or (for advanced students) skip it altogether and go straight to the lesson problems. If you struggle on any lesson problems, go back and review the relevant material.

☺

2. CALCULATORS ☺

We recommend that you use a calculator on the ACT. Since functions and their graphs are part of the test, a graphing calculator is highly recommended. Most graphing calculators are fine; **calculators with built-in computer algebra systems, however, are not permitted**. (The most common of these is the Texas Instrument TI-89.) For more information about permitted calculators, go to the ACT website (http://www.actstudent.org/faq/answers/calculator.html).

Many students make careless mistakes because they try to solve difficult computations in their heads. Other students, on the other hand, tend to use calculators for all computations, even the easy ones, costing them valuable seconds on the test. **Keep in mind that the ACT does not require the use of a calculator.** If you find that you're using one on every problem, you might be slowing yourself down. Find a good balance. Don't use your calculator for 2 × 1, but if you have a tendency to make careless mistakes, *do* use it for 20 × 100.

Make sure you are comfortable with your calculator. Bring it to all of your tutoring lessons and use it on your homework assignments and practice tests.

> Your calculator can be used to solve problems involving *fractions*, *radicals*, *scientific notation*, and the π symbol.

If you are not comfortable with any of the above numerical forms, just use your calculator to simplify the problem into one of *decimal numbers*. Of course, you will likely have to convert the answer choices to decimals so you can compare them to the answer you found with your calculator. Make sure to stay accurate. Always round decimals to at least four decimal places to the right of the decimal point. For example:

$$\tfrac{1}{3} \neq 0.3 \Rightarrow \tfrac{1}{3} = 0.3333 \text{ (close enough)}$$

FRACTIONS AND YOUR CALCULATOR

It will be very helpful to learn how to use the **fraction key** that is found on most calculators. This will allow you to maintain perfect accuracy and check answer choices more quickly (when they are in fraction form). Check your calculator's manual to see how to enter fractions or convert decimals into fractions, or ask a tutor for assistance.

MIXED FRACTIONS

Mixed fractions include a whole number and a fraction, for example:

$$2\frac{3}{4}$$

To enter a mixed fraction into your calculator, think about how you *say* the number:

$$2\frac{3}{4} \equiv \text{"two \textbf{and} three-fourths"}$$

You probably know that the word "and" is used to describe addition ("1 *and* 1 is 2"). So to enter a mixed number into your calculator, use addition:

$$2\frac{3}{4} \rightarrow 2 + \frac{3}{4}$$

ORDER OF OPERATION

Most calculators follow the standard *order of operation* rules. You should be familiar with these rules for tackling more difficult algebra problems. Remember *PEMDAS*: (1) parentheses, (2) exponents, (3) multiplication/division (in order from left to right), and (4) addition/subtraction (in order from left to right).

CALCULATOR LESSON PROBLEMS

Try the following problems using *only* your calculator. The point of these problems is to become comfortable with your calculator. Do not worry about topics such as fractions, scientific notation, and radical simplification. You only need to know how to plug these numbers into your calculator. Answers to lesson and homework problems for this chapter start on page 460, which you may want to mark for future reference.

1. $-2^2 =$

2. $(-2)^2 =$

3. $\dfrac{317 + 257}{2} =$

4. $254 - 550 \div 25 =$

5. $2 \times (16 - 3)^2 =$

6. $2\tfrac{3}{4} + 3\tfrac{3}{8} =$

7. $\tfrac{3}{4} \times \tfrac{2}{3} =$

8. $\tfrac{3}{4} \div \tfrac{2}{3} =$

    A. $\tfrac{1}{2}$
    B. $\tfrac{7}{8}$
    C. 1
    D. $1\tfrac{1}{8}$
    E. $1\tfrac{3}{8}$

9. $\dfrac{\tfrac{1}{2} + \tfrac{2}{3}}{\tfrac{3}{4} + \tfrac{4}{5}} =$

    F. $\tfrac{70}{93}$
    G. $1\tfrac{1}{2}$
    H. $2\tfrac{17}{90}$
    J. $2\tfrac{16}{45}$
    K. 3

10. $125{,}000 \times 200{,}000 =$

    A. $25{,}000$
    B. $250{,}000$
    C. 2.5×10^8
    D. 2.5×10^{10}
    E. 2.5×10^{12}

Make sure to use a calculator on this problem:

11. $\sqrt{108} + \sqrt{48} =$

    F. $\sqrt{13}$
    G. $2\sqrt{39}$
    H. $\sqrt{156}$
    J. $6\sqrt{3}$
    K. $10\sqrt{3}$

3. BASIC CONCEPTS

TERMINOLOGY ☺

The following are some commonly misunderstood terms that show up on the ACT:

Integer — positive or negative whole number or zero.

...-3, -2, -1, 0, 1, 2, 3...

Zero — remember, zero is an integer. Zero is also an *even* number, but it is not a *positive* or a *negative* number—think of it as *neutral*.

Real Number — Any number that is not *imaginary*. If you don't know what imaginary numbers are (yet), don't worry about it; we'll cover imaginary numbers in Chapter VII. At this point, assume *all* numbers are real numbers.

Rational Number — Any number that can be written as an integer or a *fraction* of integers.

Examples: -4, $21\!\!/\!\!93$, $\dfrac{\sqrt{16}}{\sqrt{25}}$ (because it equals $\tfrac{4}{5}$)

Irrational Number — Any number that can *not* be written as an integer or a fraction of integers.

Examples: π, $\sqrt{2}$, $\sqrt{22}$ (any radical that cannot be simplified to a whole number)

Factor (or **divisor**) — any of the numbers multiplied together to form a *product*. For example:

$2 \times 3 = 6$ ← 2 and 3 are *factors* (or *divisors*) of the *product* 6.

Multiples — the multiples of a number are simply the products of that number and integers. For example: the multiples of 3 are 3, 6, 9, 12, 15, ...

Prime number — number *greater than one* whose only integer factors are one and itself. For example: The number 11 is only divisible by 11 and 1; it is therefore a *prime number*.

ABSOLUTE VALUE ☺

The ACT loves absolute value problems. Simply put, the absolute value of a number is the positive form of that number. Just get rid of the negative sign, if there is one.

$$|-20| = 20$$
$$|3 - 6| = |-3| = 3$$

BASIC OPERATIONS ☺

It may be helpful to memorize the rules below. If you ever forget one of these rules, just make up some numbers and use your calculator:

- even + even or even − even = even
- odd + odd or odd − odd = even
- odd + even or odd − even = odd

- even × even = even
- odd × odd = odd
- odd × even = even

- positive × positive or positive ÷ positive = positive
- negative × negative or negative ÷ negative = positive
- positive × negative or positive ÷ negative = negative

- (positive or negative real number)^2 = positive
- (positive real number)^3 = positive
- (negative real number)^3 = negative

A NOTE TO SELF STUDY STUDENTS ABOUT EX PROBLEMS

Example problems are indicated with an EX symbol:

You will see an italicized solution following each example. In the Math section of this tutorial, the solutions display the correct application of a mathematical technique or method. Make sure you understand how the given technique was used to solve the problem. The steps of the methods will generally be shown with circled numbers in the solution. You do *not* need to solve these example problems on your own. You will be able to practice the techniques on the hundreds of lesson, homework, and practice problems at the end of lessons and chapters.

FACTOR TABLE

When you are asked to find the *positive integer factors* (sometimes simply called the *positive factors*) of a number, use a *factor table*.

> Look for the words *positive integer factors (or divisors)* or *positive factors (or divisors)*.

1. Start with 1 in the first column and the original number in the second column of a table.
2. If the original number is even, mentally increase the number in the first column by 1. If the original number is odd, mentally increase the number in the first column by 2 (only odd numbers are divisors of odd numbers).
3. Is the new number a factor of the original number? Hint: you may want to use your calculator. If it is, place it in a new row in column one, and write the quotient (the number displayed on your calculator) in column 2.
4. Repeat steps 2 and 3 until the number in column one exceeds the number in column 2. When done, the numbers in the table will be the positive factors of the original number.

(EX) What are the positive integer factors of 66?

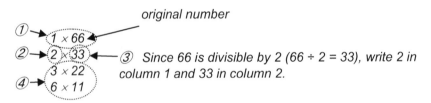

→ The positive integer factors of 66 are **1, 2, 3, 6, 11, 22, 33,** and **66**.

FACTOR TREE

When you are asked to find the *prime factors* of a number, use a *factor tree*. This is different from a factor table, so make sure you read carefully for the mention of *prime* factors.

> Look for the words *prime factors (or prime divisors)*.

1. Write the original number in your work space.
2. Think of a prime number that divides evenly into the original number. Write this prime number and its quotient as *branches* below the original number. Circle or underline the prime number.

3. Repeat step 2 with the quotient branch.

4. When all branches end with prime numbers, those prime numbers are the prime factors of the original number.

(EX) What are the prime factors of 66?

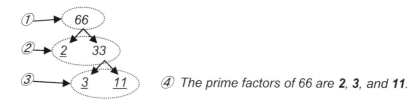

④ *The prime factors of 66 are **2**, **3**, and **11**.*

GREATEST COMMON FACTORS

Remember, a *factor* is a number that is part of a product of another number. For example, previously, we learned that 2 and 3 are factors of 6. Sometimes you may be asked to find the *greatest common factor* (GCF) of two or more numbers. Usually you can simply check the answer choices (starting with the biggest number) and use your calculator, but if that doesn't work, use the following method:

1. Find the prime factors of all numbers in question.

2. Look for any prime factors that are common to <u>all</u> of the original numbers.

3. Multiply these prime factors together to find the GCF.

(EX) What is the greatest common factor of 52 and 78?

① *Use factor trees to find the prime factors of each number:*
52 = 2 × 13 × 13
78 = 2 × 3 × 13
② *The common factors for 52 and 78 are: 2 and 13.*
③ *2 × 13 = 26 → The GCF of 52 and 78 is **26**.*

LEAST COMMON MULTIPLES

The *least common multiple* (LCM) is the smallest number that is a multiple of a given set of other numbers. One trick is to use trial and error. Just check multiples of the *largest* number in the set until you find one that is also a multiple of the other number(s). The concept is best explained with an example:

(EX) What is the least common multiple of 3 and 5?

Is 5 a multiple of 3? Nope. ✗
Is 10 a multiple of 3? Nope. ✗
Is 15 a multiple of 3? Yes. ✓
*→ So **15** is the LCM of 3 and 5.*

You can also often just check the answer choices. Make sure to start with the *smallest* number, as more than one answer will often be a multiple of the numbers in question, but only one will be the *least* common multiple.

For harder LCM problems, or if the methods above don't work, use the following method:

1. Find the prime factors of all numbers in question.
2. For each prime factor, count the greatest number of times this factor shows up for any one of the original numbers.
3. Multiply each prime factor by the greatest number of times the factor shows up, and multiply these products. **Caution**: Do not simply multiply all of the prime factors. This will give you a common multiple, but not the *least* common multiple.

(EX) What is the least common multiple of 52 and 78?

    ① *Use factor trees to find the prime factors of each number:*
       52 = 2 × 13 × 13
       78 = 2 × 3 × 13
    ② *The greatest number of times that 2 shows up is **once** (for both 52 and 78). The greatest number for 3 is also **once** (for 78). The greatest number for 13 is **twice** (for 52).*
    ③ *(2 × 1) × (3 × 1) × (13 × 2) = 156* → *The LCM of 52 and 78 is **156**.*

ADDING AND SUBTRACTING FRACTIONS

Usually, if you're comfortable using your calculator, dealing with fractions is a snap. The one exception involves problems that require you to find a *common denominator* (the *denominator* is the bottom number in a fraction). A *common denominator* is simply a *common multiple* of all the denominators. You'll usually be asked to find the *least* common denominator. Just use one of the methods above for finding the LCM.

BASIC CONCEPTS LESSON PROBLEMS

1. Circle all integers: 203   2.03 π 0   -2 $\frac{2}{3}$ 4.0

2. Circle all rational numbers: $\sqrt{18}$ $\sqrt{9}$ π $\frac{7}{8}$ 1.2 $\frac{1}{3}$

3. What are the prime numbers between 1 and 10?

4. $|4-5|-|5-4| =$

5. $|2(-3)-(-2)(-3)| =$

6. If $|x| = 4$, what are all possible values of x?

7. What are the positive integer factors of 42?

8. What are the prime factors of 42?

9. What is the least common denominator of $\dfrac{1}{3}$ and $\dfrac{1}{7}$?

10. What is the least common denominator of $\dfrac{1}{3}$, $\dfrac{1}{7}$, and $\dfrac{1}{14}$?

4. BASIC CONCEPTS PROBLEMS

PRACTICE PROBLEMS

The following worksheet tests techniques taught in this chapter. It is very important to look back to the lessons in this chapter and review the techniques while completing these problems. Try to determine which technique relates to each problem and apply the methods taught in the tutorial. Do not time yourself on these problems. The problems are provided to give you an opportunity to practice, and hopefully master, the techniques in this tutorial before you apply them on real ACTs in a timed setting.

☐   Basic Concepts Worksheet

Note: Test 1 in the ACT book, which we will use for extra practice problems in upcoming chapters, does not contain any Basic Concepts problems.

TEST CORRECTIONS

Practice tests will be assigned as you work your way through the tutorial (you should have already taken Test 2). After each practice test is graded, you should correct Basic Concepts problems that you missed or left blank. There are three steps to correcting the practice tests:

1.   The Basic Concepts questions for each test are listed below. Go back to your answer sheet for the corresponding test and circle the question numbers below that you missed (or guessed on, if you kept track of your guesses). (Note: As you can see below, there are not many problems that exclusively test techniques from this chapter. However, you will have to use these techniques *in combination* with techniques taught in later chapters.)

   ☐   **Test 2**: 40, 44

   ☐   **Test 3**: 9

   ☐   **Test 4**: 12, 55

   ☐   **Test 5**: 5, 11*, 26 (*Note: Question 11 is not completely covered by tutorial.)

2.   Correct the problems in *The Real ACT Study Guide*. As you correct the problems, go back to the tutorial and review the techniques. The idea is to: (1) identify techniques that have given you trouble, (2) go back to the tutorial so you can review and strengthen these techniques, and (3) apply these techniques to the specific problems on which you struggled.

3.   If you have trouble identifying the best technique to use on a problem, see the Techniques Reference information in Chapter VIII, starting on page 453.

BASIC CONCEPTS WORKSHEET

Problem numbers represent the *approximate* level of difficulty for each problem (out of 60). For more on order of difficulty, review page 161.

1. $|-2-4| =$

    A. −6
    B. −2
    C. 2
    D. 4
    E. 6

7. What is the least common denominator for adding the fractions $\frac{2}{3}$, $\frac{6}{7}$, and $\frac{11}{12}$?

    F. 36
    G. 84
    H. 126
    J. 168
    K. 252

10. What is the largest prime number that is a factor of both 35 and 77?

    A. 7
    B. 11
    C. 35
    D. 385
    E. 2,695

21. What is the least common multiple of 9, 105, and 210?

    F. 210
    G. 630
    H. 945
    J. 22,050
    K. 198,450

31. Which of the following is equal to $-\left(\dfrac{\frac{2}{5}-\frac{2}{3}}{\frac{2}{5}+\frac{2}{3}}\right)$?

    A. $-\dfrac{1}{2}$

    B. $-\dfrac{1}{4}$

    C. $\dfrac{1}{4}$

    D. $\dfrac{1}{2}$

    E. 1

Continued ➜

37. What is the correct ordering of $\dfrac{5}{6}$, $\dfrac{6}{7}$, and $\dfrac{7}{9}$ from least to greatest?

F. $\dfrac{5}{6} < \dfrac{6}{7} < \dfrac{7}{9}$

G. $\dfrac{6}{7} < \dfrac{5}{6} < \dfrac{7}{9}$

H. $\dfrac{6}{7} < \dfrac{7}{9} < \dfrac{5}{6}$

J. $\dfrac{7}{9} < \dfrac{5}{6} < \dfrac{6}{7}$

K. $\dfrac{7}{9} < \dfrac{6}{7} < \dfrac{5}{6}$

41. If $\dfrac{a}{10} - \dfrac{b}{55} = \dfrac{11a - 2b}{x}$ and a, b, and x are all integers greater than 1, then $x = ?$

A. 2
B. 55
C. 100
D. 110
E. 550

45. Which of the following is a rational number?

F. $\sqrt{\dfrac{1}{4}}$

G. $\sqrt{\dfrac{1}{2}}$

H. $\sqrt{2}$

J. $\sqrt{3}$

K. $\sqrt{8}$

46. $\dfrac{1}{\sqrt{2}} + \dfrac{1}{\sqrt{3}} = ?$

A. $\dfrac{1}{\sqrt{6}}$

B. $\dfrac{2}{\sqrt{5}}$

C. $\dfrac{2}{\sqrt{2} + \sqrt{3}}$

D. $\dfrac{\sqrt{2} + \sqrt{3}}{\sqrt{5}}$

E. $\dfrac{\sqrt{2} + \sqrt{3}}{\sqrt{6}}$

Continued ➜

47. For real numbers p and q, when is the equation $|p+q| = |-p-q|$ true?

    F. Always
    G. Only when $p = q$
    H. Only when $p = q = 0$
    J. Only when $p = 0$ or $q = 0$
    K. Never

50. If $x = ab$, $y = bc$, and $z = ac$, where a, b, and c are prime numbers, which of the following is the least common multiple of x, y and z?

    A. ab
    B. bc
    C. abc
    D. $(abc)^2$
    E. Cannot be determined
        from the information given

II

ARITHMETIC

The Arithmetic chapter covers topics and techniques that do not require complicated algebraic or geometric operations. You may have to use some simple algebra, such as solving for a single variable in a simple equation, but more complex algebra will be covered in Chapter III.

1. PERCENT PROBLEMS

PERCENT ↔ DECIMAL ☺

You must be able to quickly convert a number in percent form to a number in decimal form, and vice versa. This will always involve moving the decimal point *two places* to the right or to the left. An easy way to see which way to move the decimal point is to use 50%. You probably already know that 50% is equivalent to one half, or .50, so when you are working on a percent problem and can't remember which way to move the decimal point, just write:

$$50\% \leftrightarrow 0.50$$

You can easily see which way to move the decimal point:

50% → 0.50 for *percent to decimal* - move decimal point two places to the <u>left</u>.

0.50 → 50% for *decimal to percent* - move decimal point two places to the <u>right</u>.

When using your calculator on percent problems, remember that the calculator only "understands" *decimals* and will only give answers as *decimals*. You must convert percent to decimal before entering data into your calculator, and remember to convert decimal answers back to percent, if necessary.

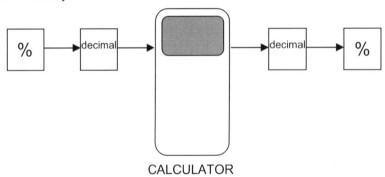

CALCULATOR

Answers to all lesson and homework problems in this chapter start on page 461.

1. 4.25 equals what percent?

2. 25% is equivalent to what fraction?

3. 220% is equivalent to what decimal?

4. $\frac{7}{8}$ equals what percent?

5. 0.0013 equals what percent?

A percent problem is easy to identify because it will display a % sign or the word *percent*.

OF/IS PERCENT PROBLEMS ☺

Of/Is problems require you to turn percent word problems into mathematical equations. Use the information in the following table.

word	operation
of *as big as*, *as old as*, *as fast as*, *etc.*	×
is *are*, *was*, *has*, *will be*, *equals*, *etc.*	=
what, what percent *what number*, *how much*, *etc.*	variable (*a, x*, etc.)

Of/Is problems are percent problems that do not involve *change*. In other words, no time passes and no values or variables change in the problem. **These problems are usually identifiable by the words *of* and *is* in the question.** For harder problems where the *of* or the *is* is not written, try creating an Of/Is sentence in your head.

(EX) 20% of 50 = **10**

(EX) 15% of what number is 60? *0.15 · x = 60* → *x = **400***

(EX) 18 is what percent of 20? *18 = x · 20* → *x = 0.90 = **90%***

(EX) Bill is 20. Fred is $\frac{3}{5}$ as old as Bill. How old is Fred? *B = 20, F = $\frac{3}{5}$ × 20 = **12***

Throughout this tutorial, you will notice question numbers that do not follow a consecutive numerical order. These problems use numbers from the ACT to represent the *approximate* level of difficulty for the problem. Remember, as discussed in the introduction, there are **60** questions on the ACT Math Test. **In general, the higher the number, the harder the problem.** See note about problem difficulty on page 161.

OF/IS PERCENT LESSON PROBLEMS

1. 25% of 25% of 32 is ?

    A. $\frac{1}{4}$
    B. $\frac{1}{2}$
    C. 1
    D. 2
    E. 4

5. During a 10%-Off sale at a store, if a shopper buys an item originally priced at $5.50, by how much is the item discounted?

    F. $0.50
    G. $0.55
    H. $1.50
    J. $4.95
    K. $5.40

25. If 40% of a number is 32, what is 50% of that number?

    A. 16
    B. 40
    C. 50
    D. 80
    E. 100

45. The volume of a cube with edge of length 1 inch is what percent of the volume of a cube with edge of length 2 inches?

    F. $12\frac{1}{2}$%
    G. 20%
    H. 25%
    J. 40%
    K. 50%

PART-OVER-WHOLE PERCENT PROBLEMS ☺

As the name implies, part over whole percent problems deal with finding a percent *of completeness* by comparing *part* of something to its *whole*.

> Like Of/Is problems, part-over-whole percent problems do not involve change (no time passes, and no values or variables change in the problem). **Look for part of something, and look for its whole.**

(EX) If you have traveled 200 miles of a 1000 mile trip, what percent of the trip have you completed?

$$\frac{part}{whole} = \frac{200}{1000} = .20 = \mathbf{20\%}$$

Try the following lesson problem:

3. If a 12-ounce can of soda currently contains 8 ounces of soda, how full is the can?

   A. $33^{1}/_{3}\%$
   B. 50%
   C. $66^{2}/_{3}\%$
   D. 75%
   E. 80%

PERCENT INCREASE/DECREASE

These problems deal with increasing or decreasing a value by a given percent. This involves finding a "percent of" something (see the Of/Is technique), and then adding or subtracting this value to the original value. Here's an example:

(EX) If a scarf normally costs $18, how much will it cost if the price is reduced 25%?

> *First, find the change in cost by calculating 25% **of** 18: 0.25 × 18 = 4.5*
> *Because this is a percent **decrease** problem, subtract this from the original value:*
> *18 − 4.5 = **$13.50***

A SHORTCUT

Some students prefer to tackle these percent increase/decrease problems in one step by finding the *multiplier* for a given percent change. The multiplier can be found by adding the percent change to 100% (for percent increase) or subtracting the percent change from 100% (for percent decrease), and converting the result to a decimal. For example, the multiplier for the example above is:

100% − 25% = 75% = **0.75**

Note that 18 × 0.75 gives you the answer ($13.50) in one step. If you're comfortable finding multipliers, this approach is faster. If you prefer the standard approach, that's fine.

! NEVER COMBINE PERCENT CHANGES

You must never combine percent changes. For example, you might assume that increasing a number by 20% and then increasing the result by 30% would be the same as increasing the original number by 50%, but this is not the case:

(EX) If the number 10 is increased by 20%, and then the result is increased by 30%, what is the final number?

$$10 \times 0.20 = 2 \rightarrow 10 + 2 = 12 \quad \textit{(Or, using a multiplier: 10} \times \textit{1.2 = 12)}$$

$$12 \times 0.30 = 3.6 \rightarrow 12 + 3.6 = \textbf{15.6} \quad \textit{(Or 12} \times \textit{1.3 = 15.6)}$$

$$\textit{Note: 10} \times \textit{0.50 = 5} \rightarrow \textit{10 + 5 = 15} \neq \textit{15.6}$$

Percent increase/decrease problems involve *change*, which obviously means a value or values in the problem change, sometimes over a period of time. The easiest way to identify these problems is to look for a **given percent change**—either a percent increase or a percent decrease.

PERCENT INCREASE/DECREASE LESSON PROBLEMS

6. A store marks up all items 10% of their wholesale cost. In dollars, how much would a radio sell for if its wholesale cost is $200?

A. 20
B. 180
C. 190
D. 210
E. 220

32. A book sold for $4.80 after a 20% discount was taken off the list price. What was the list price of the book?

F. $3.84
G. $5.00
H. $5.76
J. $6.00
K. $6.50

DIFFERENCE-OVER-ORIGINAL PERCENT PROBLEMS

Difference-over-original percent problems ask for the percent that a value or values have changed. These problems compare some new value to an older or *original* value. The *difference* is simply the new number subtracted from the original number.

(EX) A school had 1000 students in 1980. It now has 1200 students. What percent did the school's population change since 1980?

$$\frac{difference}{original} \frac{1200-1000}{1000} = \frac{200}{1000} = 0.20 = \textbf{20\%}$$

Try the following lesson problem:

34. When Bob started his job, he earned $7 per hour. At the end of 3 years, he earned $28 per hour. By what percent did his hourly rate increase?

   A. 3%
   B. 4%
   C. 25%
   D. 300%
   E. 400%

_____

Let's summarize the ways to identify each of the four percent techniques:

Of/Is: Look for the words "of" and "is."
Part-Over-Whole: Look for *part* of something and look for the *whole*.
Percent Increase/Decrease: The question *gives* you a percent change.
Difference-Over-Original: The question *asks you to find* a percent change.

PICK 100

Often, difficult percent problems will involve several percent changes. If no original number is given, it becomes easier to tackle these types of problems by *picking 100* as the original number. Pick 100, and after you've gone through the steps of the problem, compare your final answer to 100. (You can also pick 100 on other types of problems that do not have original numbers given. This will give you a number to work with and a place to start.)

Look for percent problems that have no original number given. Harder problems may have several percent changes.

Try the following lesson problem. Remember to pick 100 for your starting number (the number of workers in 1990):

53. The number of workers at a company increased 30 percent between 1990 and 2000. Employment increased 40 percent between 2000 and 2009. The employment in 2009 was what percent greater than in 1990?

    A. 30%
    B. 35%
    C. 70%
    D. 80%
    E. 82%

―――――

7. If $300 is deposited into a savings account that pays 4% interest per year, how much money will be in the account after one year?

    A. $304
    B. $312
    C. $340
    D. $420
    E. $430

9. If it rained 12 days in November and was clear the other 18 days, what percent of the days in November did it rain?

    F. 40%
    G. 50%
    H. $66^2/_3$%
    J. 75%
    K. 80%

19. John scored 80 points on test 1 and 92 points on test 2. What was the percent increase?

    A. 8%
    B. 12%
    C. 13%
    D. 15%
    E. 87%

28. At a company, 60 percent of the employees are women. If one-third of the women and one-half of the men drive to work, what percent of the employees do NOT drive to work?

  F. 20%
  G. 40%
  H. 60%
  J. 75%
  K. $83^{1}/_{3}$%

55. A positive number p is reduced by 25 percent to produce q. If q is increased by 50 percent to produce r, then r is:

  A. p decreased by 25 percent
  B. p decreased by 12.5 percent
  C. p increased by 12.5 percent
  D. p increased by 25 percent
  E. p increased by 75 percent

60. A machine takes m hours to close 50 boxes. After the machine is upgraded to a new design, it can close 90 boxes in $0.6m$ hours. By what percent did the machine's per-hour production rate increase after the upgrade?

  F. 40%
  G. 80%
  H. 180%
  J. 200%
  K. 300%

2. PROPORTIONS

A *proportion* is two equal *ratios*, or fractions, for example:

$$\frac{2}{3} = \frac{34}{51}$$

In proportion problems, solve unknown values by cross multiplying: ☺

(EX) If $\frac{2}{3} = \frac{62}{x}$, what is the value of *x*? $\frac{2}{3} \diagup\!\!\!\!\diagdown \frac{62}{x}$ → $2 \cdot x = 3 \cdot 62$ → **x = 93**

> Proportion problems have at least one *known relationship* between two items. Here are a few examples of *known relationships*:
>
> - 12 socks cost 4 dollars
> - 2 ounces of vanilla are needed to make 3 cakes
> - 20 miles per gallon
>
> Note that each known relationship includes *two* numbers (no unknowns).

Proportion problems are fairly straightforward to set up. Just use the following method:

1. Identify and underline the known relationship.
2. Write the **units** as a ratio (no numbers yet!). Leave space to the right of the units for the eventual numbers. You can think of this step as similar to setting up a table, with the "headings" (the units) to the left of each row.
3. Now, add the numbers, starting with the known relationship. The units on the top of each ratio must be the same, and the units on the bottom of each ratio must be the same (that's why we only write the units *once*, to the left of the proportion). Of course, use a variable (such as *x*) for the unknown.
4. Solve by cross multiplying.

(EX) If 5 dozen flowers cost $25, how much do 24 flowers cost?

① *Known relationship: "5 dozen flowers cost $25"*

② $\frac{dozen\,(flowers)}{\$} \underline{} = \underline{}$

    24 flowers = 2 dozen flowers

③ $\frac{dozen\,(flowers)}{\$} \frac{5}{25} = \frac{2}{x}$

④ *Cross multiply to find x:* $5 \cdot x = 2 \cdot 25$ → **x = 10 dollars**

MORE THAN ONE KNOWN RELATIONSHIP

More difficult problems may involve two or more known relationships. Set up a proportion for *each* known relationship. See the following example:

(EX) A florist must purchase 72 flowers to make 6 bouquets. If 8 flowers cost $20, how much would the florist spend to make 8 bouquets?

① *Known relationships (there are two of them): "72 flowers . . . make 6 bouquets" and "8 flowers cost $20"*

② *First, write the units for the two known relationships (as shown in the previous example—no numbers yet); you will have two proportions.*

③ *Then, plug in the given numbers. Solve the top proportion first:*

$$\frac{flowers}{bouquets} \; \frac{72}{6} = \frac{x}{8} \; \rightarrow \; ④ \; cross \; multiply: x = 96 \; flowers$$

$$\frac{flowers}{\$} \; \frac{8}{20} = \frac{96 \; (from \; above)}{y} \; \rightarrow \; ④ \; cross \; multiply: y = \mathbf{\$240}$$

LESSON PROBLEMS

12. If Bryan takes 6 minutes to light 15 candles, how many minutes would it take him working at the same rate to light 35 candles?

   A. 8
   B. 9
   C. 10
   D. 12
   E. 14

27. A bullet train takes 45 minutes to travel 300 kilometers. If it continues at the same rate, how many hours will it take the train to travel 1600 kilometers?

   F. 3
   G. 4
   H. 5
   J. 6
   K. 8

54. A 7-pound bag of apples costs 10 dollars and 5 pounds of apples are needed to make 2 apple pies. What is the dollar cost of apples needed to make 14 apple pies?

   A. 40
   B. 50
   C. 60
   D. 70
   E. 80

3. If cans of soda sell at the rate of 25 every 4 hours, how many cans of soda will be sold in 20 hours?

   A. 125
   B. 100
   C. 80
   D. 50
   E. 5

21. A tree casts a shadow 140 feet long. To determine the height of the tree, Craig stands next to the tree and has someone measure the length of his shadow. If Craig is 6 feet tall and casts a 14-foot shadow, what is the height of the tree?

   F. 12
   G. 36
   H. 60
   J. 132
   K. 140

43. Robot A can assemble 30 computer chips per hour and robot B can assemble 39 computer chips per hour. How many more minutes will it take robot A than robot B to assemble 26 computer chips?

   A. 12
   B. 15
   C. 20
   D. 34
   E. 52

3. RATIOS

BASIC RATIO PROBLEMS

Basic ratio problems can be recognized by numbers or variables separated by the word *to* or a colon (:), such as 2:3, 2 to 3, *x*:*y*, or *x* to *y*.

Each ratio symbol—the word "to" or a colon (":")—is equivalent to a *divided-by line*, so ratios can be rewritten as standard fractions. Use the following method for ratio problems:

1. First, get rid of all ratio signs by rewriting the ratios as fractions.
2. Use your calculator and your knowledge of proportions or algebra to solve.

The following examples illustrate basic ratio techniques:

(EX) What fraction is equivalent to the ratio 3:5 (or 3 to 5)? $\dfrac{3}{5}$

(EX) If the ratio of blue marbles to yellow marbles in a jar is 3:5, and there are 39 blue marbles in the jar, how many yellow marbles are in the jar?

$$\frac{blue}{yellow}\ \frac{3}{5} = \frac{39}{y} \quad \rightarrow \quad y = \mathbf{65}$$

(EX) What is the *fraction* of blue marbles in the jar described above?

$$\frac{part}{whole}\ \frac{39}{39+65} = \frac{\mathbf{3}}{\mathbf{8}}$$

*This problem is similar to a part-over-whole percent problem; just leave the answer in **fraction** form.*

RATIO SHARE PROBLEMS

Ratio share problems are different from basic ratio problems, even though their identification is similar.

Ratio share problems are also recognized by numbers or variables separated by the word *to* or a colon (:), but **they involve splitting some *whole* value or quantity into different *shares*.** Any problem with a ratio containing more than two terms, for example 2:3:4, is *definitely* a ratio share problem.

The method is straightforward and is best explained using the examples below:

1. Add up all the numbers in the ratio.
2. Remember, these problems typically involve some *whole* value (of dollars, eggs, students, etc.) that will be divided into shares. Divide this given whole value by the sum of the ratio numbers (from Step 1). This will give you the value of each "part."
3. To find each share, multiply the value from Step 2 (the "part") by the appropriate number in the original ratio.

(EX) If two friends split $700 dollars in a ratio of 3:4, how much does each friend get?

①$3 + 4 = 7$ → ② $\dfrac{\$700}{7} = \$100$ → ③ $\$100 \times 3 = $**$300**; $\$100 \times 4 = $**$400** (So one friend gets $300 and one friend gets $400.)

(EX) If three friends split $700 dollars in a ratio of 3:4:7, how much does each friend get?

①$3 + 4 + 7 = 14$ → ② $\dfrac{\$700}{14} = \$50$ → ③ $\$50 \times 3 = $**$150**; $\$50 \times 4 = $**$200**; $\$50 \times 7 = $

$350

(EX) A high school play is made up entirely of sophomores, juniors, and seniors. If the ratio of sophomores, juniors, and seniors in the play is 1:3:2, respectively, each of the following could be the number of students in the play EXCEPT

A. 12
B. 15
C. 18
D. 24
E. 30

As above, first add up the numbers in the ratio:

$1 + 3 + 2 = 6$

Next, notice that a "whole" value is not given in the question. These values are given in the answer choices. We must find the one that does not work. When you check B, note that you get a non-integer:

$\dfrac{15}{6} = 2.5$ → *But could we have halves of people? Of course not. The answer must be* **B**.

This leads us to a good shortcut for this type of problem: **The "whole" must be a multiple of the sum of the ratio numbers.** *Notice that only B (15) is* **not** *a multiple of 6. Thus, the answer is* **B**.

RATIOS LESSON PROBLEMS

14. If the ratio of x to y is 1 to 6, then the ratio of $15x$ to y is

 A. $\dfrac{5}{18}$

 B. $\dfrac{5}{6}$

 C. $\dfrac{5}{2}$

 D. 3

 E. $\dfrac{15}{2}$

23. Prize money for the top three finishers in a golf tournament is divided up in a ratio of 10:4:1. If the total prize money for the three top golfers is $75,000, how much does the first place golfer receive?

 F. $5,000
 G. $20,000
 H. $50,000
 J. $67,500
 K. $70,000

8. The ratio of n to 9 is equal to the ratio of 33 to 198. What is the value of n?

 A. $\dfrac{2}{3}$

 B. 1

 C. $1\frac{1}{2}$

 D. 3

 E. 54

35. Apple juice, grape juice, and orange juice are mixed by volume in the ratio of 5:4:1, respectively, to produce fruit punch. In order to make 10 gallons of punch, how many gallons of orange juice are needed?

 F. $\dfrac{1}{2}$

 G. 1
 H. 3
 J. 4
 K. 5

Continued ➜

46. A basket contains only red and green apples. If there are 20 apples in the basket, which of the following could NOT be the ratio of red to green apples?

A. $\dfrac{1}{2}$

B. $\dfrac{1}{3}$

C. $\dfrac{2}{3}$

D. $\dfrac{1}{9}$

E. $\dfrac{3}{2}$

4. AVERAGES, MEDIANS, & MODES

TERMINOLOGY ☺

Average or **arithmetic mean** – the sum of a set of values divided by the number of values in the set.

Median – the middle number in a set of increasing values. If the set has an even number of values, average the two middle numbers. **Don't forget the values must be in order before you can find the median.**

Mode – the value or values in a set of numbers that occur(s) the most frequently.

Average problems are easy to identify because you only need to look for the words *average*, *median*, or *mode*. Note: Some *rate* problems also have the word *average*, but these problems use another technique that we will discuss in the next section.

1. What is the median of the following numbers?

    2, 6, 0, 10, -5

2. What is the median and mode of the following numbers?

    2, 6, 0, 10, -5, 10

The table below shows the hourly wages for 11 workers at a small company. Two workers make $9 per hour, two workers make $10 per hour, and so on.

Hourly wage (in $)	# of workers
9	2
10	2
12	1
13	2
14	4

3. What is the average of the 5 wages?
4. What is the median of the 5 wages?
5. What is the average hourly wage of the 11 workers? (Hint: write all 11 workers' wages in a list.)

6. What is the median hourly wage of the 11 workers?

7. What is the mode of the workers' wages?

30. Spencer measures the noon temperature once a day for a week and records the following values: 62°, 70°, 80°, 72°, 72°, 65°, $x°$. If the median temperature for the seven days is 70°, then x could be any of the following EXCEPT

    A. 59
    B. 66
    C. 67
    D. 70
    E. 73

ANS → $A \times N = S$

The *ANS*wer to average problems can usually be found using *ANS*. This technique will help make harder average problems much easier, but it is also simple enough to use on easier problems. We know that the average (A) is the sum (S) of a set of values divided by the number (N) of values in the set:

$$A = \frac{S}{N}$$

By multiplying both sides by N, we can create the simple equation:

$$A \times N = S$$

Average x Number of items in set = Sum of the items in the set

Use the following technique for *ANS* problems:
1. Write $A \times N = S$ at the top of your workspace and work in the columns below each letter.
2. Read the problem carefully, and plug values into the *ANS* table. Make sure to keep *averages* under the A column, *numbers in set* under the N column, and *sums* under the S column. Remember, the S column is for the added sum of the items in the set.
3. Anytime two entries in a row are known, calculate to find the missing entry.

(EX) The average of five numbers is −10. What is the sum of these numbers?

     ① $\underline{A \times N = S}$
     ② −10 5 **−50** ← ③ −10 × 5 = −50

HARDER *ANS* PROBLEMS

Harder *ANS* problems typically deal with more than one group of numbers (each group with its own average). This will require you to use multiple rows in an *ANS* table (each group of numbers with its own row). You will also probably use a "Total Row" beneath the other rows. Here's the method:

1. Write *ANS* and plug values into the *ANS* table, as described before. Each group of numbers will get its own row. **Leave any unknowns blank.**

2. Remember, anytime two entries in a row are known, calculate or use algebra to find the missing entry.

3. We'll call the third row the "Total Row." The Total Row is the sums (or sometimes the differences) of the numbers in the *N* and *S* columns. Look for verbal clues to determine whether you should add or subtract the *N* and *S* columns. Whatever operation you perform on one of these columns, you will also perform on the other column. For example, if you add the *N* column, you will also add the *S* column.

(!) **NOTE: The entries in the *A* column should never be added or subtracted into the Total Row.** These *A* entries are only used to calculate missing information in their respective rows.

4. You should now have enough information to answer the question.

(EX) If the average age of 500 students at school A is 14 and the average age of 300 students at school B is 18, what is the average age of all the students at the two schools?

A. 14
B. 14.5
C. 15
D. 15.5
E. 16

     ① $\underline{A \times N = \quad S}$
     14 500 (7000) ← ②
     18 300 5400

     ③ A 800 12,400 → ④ A·800 = 12,400 → A = 15.5 **D.**

*Note: since we were finding the average of "all" students, we **added** the N and S columns into the Total Row.*

AVERAGES, MEDIANS, AND MODES LESSON PROBLEMS

10. If the average of x, y, and z is 20 and the average of p and q is 25, then $x+y+z+p+q=$?

   A. 22
   B. 22.5
   C. 45
   D. 60
   E. 110

22. An average of 14 people use a park's tennis courts each weekday and an average of 42 people use the courts each weekend day. What is the average daily use of the courts over the entire week?

   F. 20
   G. 22
   H. 25
   J. 26
   K. 27

50. If the average of six numbers is −2 and the average of four of the numbers is 2, what is the average of the other two numbers?

   A. −10
   B. −2
   C. $-\frac{2}{5}$
   D. 0
   E. $\frac{2}{5}$

24. Samara takes a logic test five times and scores 12, 10, x, 20, and 27 points. If the average of her five scores is 18, what is the median of the five scores?

   A. 10
   B. 15
   C. 18
   D. 20
   E. 21

32. A 20-year-old bank gave away an average of 152 toasters a year for the first 15 years of its existence. For the past five years, the bank did not give away any toasters. What was the average number of toasters given away per year over the bank's entire 20 years?

   F. 76
   G. 98
   H. 114
   J. 120
   K. 152

5. RATES, TIMES, & DISTANCES

RTD → R × T = D

You must be familiar with the following equation:

$$R \times T = D$$

Rate or speed ($\dfrac{distance}{time}$) x Time = Distance

Rate problems usually deal with some sort of travel over time and distance, such as: driving a car, flying an airplane, etc. However, any problem that deals with accomplishing something (not exclusively travel) over a period of time can be an *RTD* problem. For example, a problem dealing with *pages read per hour* or *machines made per day* could be an *RTD* problem. Note that the *D* column in these examples would be used for whatever is being accomplished over time (*pages read, machines made*).

> *RTD* problems will mention something that is accomplished over a period of *time*, usually travel. Look for key words like *rate*, *speed*, *pace*, or *velocity*, or look for any mention of *per time*, such as *per hour* or *per minute*. You will also notice the word *average*, but don't use *ANS* on *RTD* problems.

RTD problems are solved very similarly to *ANS* problems:

1. Write *RTD* and plug values into the *RTD* table, as we did with the *ANS* tables in the previous section. Leave any unknowns blank. Since *RTD* questions involve units (such as miles and hours), you might write the appropriate unit above each letter of the table. (Of course, make sure your inputs match the written units.)

2. Just as with *ANS* tables, anytime two entries in a row are known, calculate or use algebra to find the missing entry.

3. The Total Row for *RTD* problems (when needed) is typically the sums of the numbers in the *T* and *D* columns.

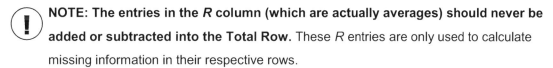 **NOTE: The entries in the R column (which are actually averages) should never be added or subtracted into the Total Row.** These *R* entries are only used to calculate missing information in their respective rows.

4. You should now have enough information to answer the question.

(EX) Kyle travels ⅔ of a 6-mile trip by bicycle, and the bicycle portion takes 15 minutes. What is

the average speed, in miles per hour, of the bicycle portion of the trip?

A. 8   *It is helpful to convert units **before** plugging numbers into the RTD table.*

B. 12   *Since the final answer should be in miles per hour, we'll use these units*

C. 16

D. 20   *below (15 min. = 0.25 hrs.). Note that this problem does not need a Total*

E. 24   *Row.*

① $R \times T = D$

    R 0.25 4 → ② $R \cdot 0.25 = 4$ → $R = 16$ *miles per hour* **C.**

RATES LESSON PROBLEMS

13. A car travels 48 miles in 45 minutes. What is the car's average speed in miles per hour?

    A. 52

    B. 56

    C. 60

    D. 64

    E. 68

50. Erica rides a bicycle from her home to her work 24 miles away at an average speed of 12

miles per hour. She returns home along the same route at an average speed of 8 miles per

hour. What was Erica's average speed in miles per hour for the entire trip?

    F. 9.2

    G. 9.6

    H. 9.8

    J. 10.0

    K. 10.5

26. A helicopter flies 360 miles in 3 hours. If it continues at this rate, how many hours will it

take the helicopter to travel 800 miles?

    A. $2^2/_9$

    B. $3^2/_3$

    C. $4^2/_9$

    D. $5^7/_9$

    E. $6^2/_3$

45. Hilary and Vivian begin a 5-mile walk at the same time. When Hilary finishes the walk,

Vivian is half a mile behind. If Hilary walked the 5 miles in 75 minutes, what was Vivian's

average speed in miles per hour for the portion of the walk that she has completed?

    F. 3.0

    G. 3.2

    H. 3.4

    J. 3.6

    K. 3.8

6. PATTERNS

Pattern problems deal with sequences of numbers or other items. These problems can take several different forms.

> Number pattern problems will either give you a long list of numbers or other items, or give you enough information to create a long list on your own. You may see the words *sequence* or *pattern*.

SHORT PATTERNS

Many pattern problems deal with a short sequence of numbers or items, often less than 20. There will usually be instructions that tell you how to find each number in the sequence. If you can find a pattern, great. This will generally help you solve the problem quickly. But if you can't find a pattern, follow the instructions and simply *count* to the term you're looking for. These problems usually don't take as long as you may expect. Here are some examples:

2. In the sequence below, each term after the first is obtained by finding the sum of <u>all</u> terms preceding the given term. If the pattern continues indefinitely, 256 will be which term of the sequence?

    1, 1, 2, 4, 8, 16, 32, …

   A. 7th
   B. 8th
   C. 9th
   D. 10th
   E. 11th

12. Each triangle in the pattern below is surrounded by 3 congruent rectangles. How many of these rectangles will there be if the pattern is repeated until there are 7 triangles?

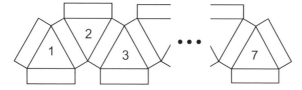

   F. 15
   G. 17
   H. 19
   J. 21
   K. 23

LONG PATTERNS

Long pattern problems will typically take too long to figure out "by hand." You need to find a pattern. Often, the best way to do this is to look at the results of the first three or four items given, and see if you can figure out an equation. This is best explained with an example:

(EX) Each triangle in the pattern below is surrounded by 3 congruent rectangles. How many of these rectangles will there be if the pattern is repeated until there are 31 triangles?

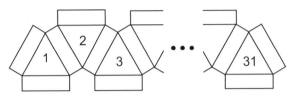

A. 63
B. 65
C. 67
D. 91
E. 93

Unlike the previous problem, you can't solve this one "by hand." Let's see if we can spot a pattern:

1 triangle = 3 rectangles. (Or to put or more simply: 1 → 3)
2 triangles = 5 rectangles (2 → 5)
3 triangles = 7 rectangles (3 → 7)

Do you see the pattern? To get the number of rectangles (r), multiply the number of triangles (t) by 2 and add 1: r = 2t + 1

→ *So the total number of rectangles is: 2·31 + 1 = 63* **A.**

Some students might notice another pattern: r = t + (t + 1); (1 + 2 = 3, 2 + 3 = 5, etc.). So if we have 31 triangles, there will be 31 + 32 = 63 rectangles.

REPEATING PATTERNS

Some long pattern problems have a *group* of numbers (or items) that repeats.

> Look for a group of numbers or items that repeats. Some examples: 1, 2, 3, 1, 2, 3…
> and ♠, ♣, ♥, ♦, ♠, ♣, ♥, ♦… Repeating decimal problems (such as 1.234 234 234…) often
> test this technique.

Use the method below with the following example problem:

1. Write out enough numbers or items so you can identify the group that is being repeated.
2. Count the number of items in the group. This is your repeating pattern.
3. If the *term-number* whose value you are being asked to find is divisible by the number of items in the pattern, then the term is equal to the *last item* in the pattern.
4. If the term-number whose value you are being asked to find is *not* divisible by the number of items in the pattern, then find a nearby term-number that *is* divisible, and count up or down to the term you're looking for.

100, 150, 200, 100, 150, 200, ...

(EX) How many numbers are repeated in the pattern above? **3** ← *step ② (the numbers are*
100, 150, and 200)

What is the 3rd term in the pattern? **200** ← *step ③*

What is the 6th term in the pattern? **200** ← *step ③*

What is the 30th term in the pattern? **200** ← *step ③*

What is the 32nd term in the pattern? **150** ← *step ④*

What is the 133rd term in the pattern? **100** ← *step ④ The 132nd term is 200 (since 132*

is divisible by 3); count up one term.

Try the following lesson problem:

26. In the pattern below, the numbers −2, −1, 0, 1, 2 repeat as shown.

    −2, −1, 0, 1, 2, −2, −1, 0, 1, 2, ...

    What is the 45th term in the pattern?

    A. −2
    B. −1
    C. 0
    D. 1
    E. 2

SPECIAL SEQUENCES

ARITHMETIC SEQUENCES

Arithmetic sequences are formed by taking a starting value and *adding* the same value over and
over again. For example:

  2, 8, 14, 20, 26, ... The starting value is 2, and the number added each time is 6. (2 + 6 = 8,
    8 + 6 = 14, and so on)

We can refer to terms in the sequence using a_n, where the n represents the nth term in the
sequence. In the example above, a_1 is the first term in the sequence (2), a_2 is the second term
in the sequence (8), and so on. The number that is added each time, in this case 6, is called
the *difference* and is represented by the variable *d.* There is no great trick for these problems,
so memorize the formula for an arithmetic sequence:

> FLASH
> CARDS

$$a_n = a_1 + (n - 1)d$$

Any sequence of numbers that has the same value *added* over and over again is an arithmetic sequence problem.

37. The nth term of a sequence is defined as $2 + (n - 1)2$. The 500th term is how much greater than the 499th term?

F. 1
G. 2
H. 4
J. 6
K. 8

GEOMETRIC SEQUENCES

Geometric sequences are similar to arithmetic sequences except they are formed by taking a starting value and *multiplying* the same value over and over again. The following are examples:

- 2, 8, 32, 128, ... The starting value is 2, and the number multiplied each time is 4.
  $(2 \times 4 = 8, 8 \times 4 = 32, \text{ and so on})$
- 2, 1, $\frac{1}{2}$, $\frac{1}{4}$, ... The starting value is 2, and the number multiplied each time is $\frac{1}{2}$.
- 2, -8, 32, -128, ...The starting value is 2, and the number multiplied each time is -4.

The number multiplied each time, called the *ratio*, is represented by the constant r. Memorize the formula for a geometric sequence:

$$a_n = a_1 r^{n-1}$$

Any sequence of numbers that has the same value *multiplied* over and over again is a geometric sequence problem.

44. The nth term of a sequence is defined as $4 \times (\frac{1}{2})^{n-1}$. What is the average of the 2nd, 3rd, and 4th terms in this sequence?

A. $\frac{7}{12}$
B. $\frac{7}{6}$
C. $\frac{7}{3}$
D. $\frac{7}{2}$
E. 2

ARITHMETIC AND GEOMETRIC SERIES

A *series* is the *sum* of the terms of a sequence. For most ACT series problems, you don't *have* to use a formula. Just add the terms, if there aren't too many, using your calculator, or look for clues in the answer choices. For example:

(EX) In an arithmetic series, each term is x more than the preceding term. For example, if the first term is 1, then the series is: $1 + (1 + x) + (1 + x + x) + ...$ If the first term of an arithmetic series is 5, the last term is 200, and the sum is 615, what are the first three terms of the series?

F. 5, 10, 20
G. 5, 20, 35
H. 5, 25, 45
J. 5, 25, 125
K. 5, 102.5, 200

You may think this problem is impossible if you don't know the formula for an arithmetic series. But look at the answer choices.
A: Not arithmetic (5 + 5 = 10, 10 + 5 ≠ 20) ✗
B: Could work
C: The difference between terms is 20. Notice that each term ends in 5. You'll never get to a term equaling 200 (the last term in the series). ✗
D: Not arithmetic ✗
E: This series is arithmetic, but notice that the third term is 200 (the last term in the series). Clearly, these numbers don't add to 615. ✗
➜ *Using process of elimination, the answer must be* **G**.

While there is usually a way to solve series questions without using formulas, knowing the formula for an arithmetic series of n terms (S_n) occasionally comes in handy:

$$\boxed{\text{FLASH CARDS}} \qquad S_n = n\left(\frac{a_1 + a_n}{2}\right)$$

(EX) Doug wants to build a structure by starting with one block, and adding one more block to each new row, so that each successive row of blocks has 1 more block than the level above it. If Doug wants to build a structure with 30 rows, how many blocks will he need?

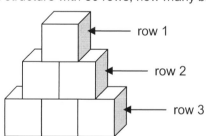

A. 30
B. 60
C. 240
D. 405
E. 465

Notice that you're really trying to find the sum of the integers from 1 to 30: $1 + 2 + ... + 30 = ?$

Use the formula ($a_1 = 1$, $a_{30} = 30$, $n = 30$):

$$S_{30} = 30\left[\frac{1 + 30}{2}\right] = 465 \quad \textbf{E.}$$

5. In the sequence below, each term after the first term is ⅕ of the term preceding it. What is the fifth term of this sequence?

        150, 30, 6 . . .

   A. −6
   B. 0
   C. ⁶⁄₂₅
   D. 1
   E. ⁶⁄₅

21. A number is a "perfect cube" if it is the cube of a positive integer. How many integers less than or equal to 1,000 are perfect cubes?

   F. 10
   G. 15
   H. 20
   J. 25
   K. 30

41. What is the 6th term of the geometric sequence $49\frac{1}{2}, 16\frac{1}{2}, 5\frac{1}{2}, \ldots$?

   A. $\dfrac{11}{162}$

   B. $\dfrac{11}{54}$

   C. $\dfrac{11}{18}$

   D. $1\frac{5}{6}$

   E. $4\frac{5}{6}$

45. The fraction $\dfrac{9}{7}$ is equivalent to the repeating decimal $1.\overline{285714}$. What is the 100th digit to the right of the decimal point?

   F. 1
   G. 2
   H. 4
   J. 5
   K. 7

58. The sum of the first n terms of an arithmetic series with first term a and nth term b is given by:

$$S_n = n\left(\frac{a+b}{2}\right).$$

If the common difference of the series is 3 and the sum of the first 7 terms is 49, what is the first term in the series?

   A. -7
   B. -2
   C. 2
   D. 7
   E. 14

60. The sum of the first 50 positive integers is 1,275. What is the sum of the first 100 positive integers?

   F. 2,550
   G. 3,775
   H. 5,050
   J. 6,250
   K. 6,275

7. EXPONENTS

RULES FOR EXPONENTS ☺

These problems involve an *exponent* (raised number) or a *root* ($\sqrt{\ }$).

Memorize the following exponential rules:

MULTIPLYING WHEN BASES ARE THE SAME

Remember, the bases must be the same.

$$a^m \times a^n = a^{m+n}$$ (EX) $p^2 \times p^3 = p^5$

DIVIDING WHEN BASES ARE THE SAME

$$a^m \div a^n = a^{m-n}$$ (EX) $p^3 \div p^2 = p^1 = p$

RAISING POWERS TO POWERS

Don't confuse this rule with the first rule above.

$$(a^m)^n = a^{mn}$$ (EX) $(p^2)^3 = p^6$

DISTRIBUTING EXPONENTS

Don't forget to distribute the outside exponent to *number* terms within the parentheses.

$$(ab)^m = a^m \times b^m$$ (EX) $(2p^2q^3)^2 = 2^2(p^2)^2(q^3)^2 = 4p^4q^6$

NEGATIVE EXPONENTS

$$a^{-m} = \frac{1}{a^m}$$

(EX) $p^2 \div p^3 = p^{-1} = \frac{1}{p} \neq -p$

THE ZERO EXPONENT

$$a^0 = 1$$

(EX) $(2x^2y^3)^0 = 1$

ROOTS AND FRACTIONAL EXPONENTS

Convert all roots to fractional exponents. The rules above also apply to these fractional exponents. Get comfortable plugging these into your calculator (use parentheses carefully).

$$\sqrt{a} = a^{\frac{1}{2}}$$

(EX) $\sqrt[3]{64} = 64^{\frac{1}{3}} = 4$ *(OK to use calculator)*

$$\sqrt[n]{a} = a^{\frac{1}{n}}$$

(EX) $\sqrt[3]{p^2} = p^x$, $x = \frac{2}{3}$ *since* $\sqrt[3]{p^2} = p^{\frac{2}{3}}$

$$\sqrt[n]{a^m} = a^{\frac{m}{n}}$$

(EX) $\sqrt[7]{2{,}187} = 2{,}187^{\frac{1}{7}} = 3$

COMPARE APPLES TO APPLES

Sometimes, you will be asked to compare the exponents of expressions with different bases, but that's like comparing apples and oranges. **The trick is to make the bases the same so you can easily compare the exponents** (compare apples to apples).

(EX) Which real number for x satisfies $2^x = 4^4$?

A. 2
B. 4
C. 6
D. 8
E. 10

First, find a number that you could use for each base in the equation.

Since 4 = 2², the number to use is 2. We can substitute 2² for 4:

$$2^x = (2^2)^4 \;\rightarrow\; 2^x = 2^8$$

Once the bases equal, you can set the exponents equal: x = 8 **D.**

SOLVING EXPONENTIAL EQUATIONS

To solve for a squared variable (such as x^2), use the method below. Look at the following example as you read each step:

1. Get the squared variable alone on one side of the equal sign.

2. Take the square root of each side of the equation.

3. Add a plus or minus sign (±). This is the most common mistake on these problems.

    You should generally expect *two* answers when you solve a squared variable.

(EX) If $x^2 = 121$, what is a possible value of $x + 11$?

A. 0
B. 11
C. 21
D. 133
E. 14,652

① The squared term is already alone on the left-hand side of the equation.

② Take the square root of both sides:

$$\sqrt{x^2} = \pm\sqrt{121} \;\rightarrow\; x = \pm 11 \;\leftarrow\; \text{③ Don't forget the } \pm$$

So $x + 11 = 11 + 11 = 22$ or $x + 11 = -11 + 11 = 0$. The answer is **A**.

Note: Rarely will you have to solve for a variable raised to a power greater than 2, but if you do, you can usually use the Pick Tricks (covered in the Algebra chapter).

COMMON MISTAKES

Watch out for these common mistakes. For practice, see if you can correctly simplify each one, or write "n/a" if the expression cannot be simplified:

	simplify?			simplify?
(EX) $(2pq)^2 \neq 2p^2q^2$	$4p^2q^2$	4.	$\sqrt{p^2 + q^2} \neq p + q$	
1. $p^2 + p^3 \neq p^5$		5.	$p^2 p^3 \neq p^6$	
2. $(p+q)^2 \neq p^2 + q^2$		6.	$\dfrac{p^2}{p^3} \neq p^{\frac{2}{3}}$	
3. $p^{-2} \neq -p^2$		7.	$2p^{-2} \neq \dfrac{1}{2p^2}$	

EXPONENTS LESSON PROBLEMS

1. $x^2 x^7 =$

2. $\dfrac{x^5}{x^2} =$

3. $(x^4)^5 =$

4. $(5xy)^2 =$

5. If $a^2 = 16$, then $a =$

6. $4^{\frac{3}{2}} =$

28. If $(2^t)^t = 2^{20}$ and $t > 0$, what is the value of t?

    A. $\sqrt{10}$

    B. $2\sqrt{5}$

    C. 10

    D. $4\sqrt{5}$

    E. 20

32. $(-2xy^3)^2(3x^3y) = ?$

    F. $-12x^6y^6$

    G. $-12x^5y^6$

    H. $-6x^5y^7$

    J. $12x^6y^6$

    K. $12x^5y^7$

37. For all real numbers x and y, which of the following expressions is equivalent to $x^{\frac{1}{2}}y^{\frac{2}{3}}$?

    A. $\sqrt{xy^3}$

    B. $\sqrt{x^2y^3}$

    C. $\sqrt[6]{x^3y^4}$

    D. $\sqrt[6]{x^2y^3}$

    E. $\sqrt[6]{x^{12}y^{18}}$

42. $3^{n+1} \cdot 3^2 = ?$

    F. 3^{2n+2}

    G. 3^{n+3}

    H. 9^{2n+2}

    J. 9^{n+3}

    K. $3^{n+1}+9$

51. If $9^x = \sqrt[3]{81}$, then what is the value of x?

    A. $\dfrac{1}{3}$

    B. $\dfrac{1}{2}$

    C. $\dfrac{2}{3}$

    D. 2

    E. 3

8. TABLES AND GRAPHS

Tables and graphs can have many different forms. There are two general steps to tackling these kinds of problems:

1. Carefully study and understand the table or graph *before* trying to answer the question.
2. Watch the problem number. A higher-numbered question may have a trap, so be careful.

Try the following lesson problems:

17. According to the graph below, Company X showed the greatest change in net income between which two consecutive years?

NET INCOME FOR COMPANY X, 1995-2000

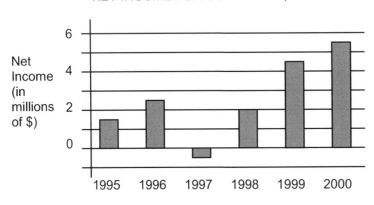

A. 1995 and 1996
B. 1996 and 1997
C. 1997 and 1998
D. 1998 and 1999
E. 1999 and 2000

42. How many <u>hours</u> will it take to clean all 40 streets in City A listed in the table below?

STREET CLEANING IN CITY A	
Number of Streets	Cleaning Time per Street
7	20 minutes
8	40 minutes
10	80 minutes
15	100 minutes

F. 4
G. 44
H. 46
J. 240
K. 2,760

17. The circle graph below represents all income for a sports stadium in 1999. If the stadium made $15,000 in beverage sales, what was the total dollar income of the stadium in 1999?

INCOME FOR STADIUM *A* IN 1999

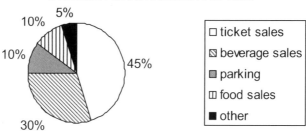

A. 19,500
B. 45,000
C. 50,000
D. 55,000
E. 60,000

28. Chris lives 6 miles from school. On a particular day, he walked for 2 miles, stopped for 5 minutes to talk with some friends, and then ran the rest of the way to school. Which of the following graphs could correctly represent his journey to school on this day?

F.
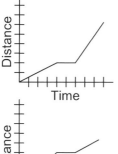

H.
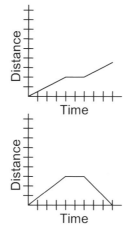

K.
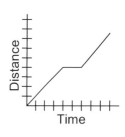

G.

J.

Use the following information to answer questions 39-42.

Wallace's Brick Company sells three different styles of bricks. The sale prices and number of bricks per pallet are given in the table below. The sale price is the amount a customer pays for one pallet of the indicated style.

Style of brick	Number of bricks per pallet	Sale price per pallet
A	75	$75.00
B	50	$80.00
C	30	$90.00

39. Which of the following is the sale price per brick for a Style B brick?

    A. $1.00
    B. $1.50
    C. $1.60
    D. $2.00
    E. $3.00

40. For a special sale, Wallace's Brick Company offers customers a 5% discount off the total sale price for any style of brick when at least 5 pallets are purchased. If a customer buys 8 pallets of Style C bricks, what is the sale price per pallet of these bricks?

    F. $85.00
    G. $85.50
    H. $95.00
    J. $680.00
    K. $684.00

41. If Conrad bought an equal number of Style A, B and C bricks, what is the minimum number of bricks of each style that he could have bought? (Note: customers may not purchase individual bricks at Wallace's Brick Company.)

    A. 5
    B. 75
    C. 100
    D. 125
    E. 150

42. Each month, Wallace's Brick Company must pay a fixed cost for each style of brick it manufactures, plus a constant production cost per brick. If the monthly fixed cost for Style A bricks is $75.00, and the production cost per Style A brick is $0.50, how much profit does the company make if it sells 40 pallets of Style A bricks in one month? (Note: Wallace's Brick Company does not offer any discounts this month.)

    F. $1,375
    G. $1,425
    H. $1,500
    J. $1,575
    K. $3,000

49. Volts Electric Car Company manufactures only compact and family cars, both of which are available as either all-electric or hybrid. On the basis of the information in the table below, how many family, all-electric cars will the company produce in 2011?

VOLTS ELECTRIC CAR COMPANY'S
SALES FOR 2011

	All-electric	Hybrid	Total
Compact	a	b	
Family		c	
Total			d

A. $a + b - c$
B. $d - (a + b)$
C. $d - (a - b - c)$
D. $d + (a - b - c)$
E. $d - a - b - c$

9. ARITHMETIC WORD PROBLEMS

As you may have noticed, most problems on the ACT are *word* problems (they all contain words), but some problems have more words than others. Arithmetic word problems, which can take several different forms, usually involve basic calculations. You'll likely have to use your calculator. (Word problems that involve *algebra*, where you'll have to solve for unknowns (variables), will be discussed in the next chapter.)

As you tackle arithmetic word problems, read carefully, and keep track of the information. It's often a good idea to write down and label information as you read the question. Also, keep in mind that these problems are usually not as difficult as they look. Let's look at an example:

(EX) 10. A museum parking lot charges $3.00 for the first hour and $1.25 for each additional hour after the first, or any portion thereof. If Tom has only a $20 bill, how much change should he expect if he parked for 4½ hours?

A. $8.00
B. $8.25
C. $10.00
D. $12.00
E. $12.63

First, write down what you know:

Parking rate = $3/hour + $1.25 each additional hour

Tom has $20. He parks for 4½ hours.

Now, calculate Tom's parking: Since he parked for 4.5 hours, his rate is $3 (for the first hour) + $1.25 × 3 (for the next 3 hours) + $1.25 (for the 30-minute portion of the next hour) = $8.00

Finally, calculate his change: $20 − $8 = $12.00 **D.**

12. A rental car company owns 45 small cars and 25 large cars. There are 3 small cars and 7 large cars that are currently being repaired and are out of commission. If the company rents 80% of its available cars, how many cars does it rent?

A. 22
B. 42
C. 48
D. 56
E. 60

10. ARITHMETIC PROBLEMS

PRACTICE PROBLEMS

The following worksheets and practice problems (from Test 1 in *The Real ACT Prep Guide*, 3rd Edition) test techniques taught in this chapter. It is very important to look back to the lessons in this chapter and review the techniques while completing these problems. Try to determine which technique relates to each problem and apply the methods taught in the tutorial. Do not time yourself on these problems. The problems are provided to give you an opportunity to practice, and hopefully master, the techniques in this tutorial before you apply them on real ACTs in a timed setting.

- ☐ Arithmetic Worksheet 1
- ☐ Arithmetic Worksheet 2
- ☐ **Test 1**: 1, 2, 3, 4, 5, 14, 15, 19, 29, 42, 44, 49, 53 (see Step 3 under "Test Corrections" below)

You might choose to space the above assignments out over the course of your studies. See the "Schedules" section in the introduction for more details about programs.

TEST CORRECTIONS

After each practice test is graded, you should correct Arithmetic problems that you missed or left blank. There are three steps to correcting the practice tests:

1. The Arithmetic questions for each test are listed below. Go back to your answer sheet for the corresponding test and circle the question numbers below that you missed (or guessed on, if you kept track of your guesses).
   - ☐ **Test 2**: 1, 2, 3, 4, 9, 15, 29, 34, 37, 39, 53, 60
   - ☐ **Test 3**: 1, 3, 11, 14, 18, 25, 31, 40, 44, 47, 56, 59, 60
   - ☐ **Test 4**: 1, 4, 28, 29, 32, 33, 34, 35, 50, 51, 52, 56
   - ☐ **Test 5**: 2, 4, 10, 12, 21, 28, 32, 37, 39, 50, 52

2. Correct the problems in *The Real ACT Study Guide*. As you correct the problems, go back to the tutorial and review the techniques. The idea is to: (1) identify techniques that have given you trouble, (2) go back to the tutorial so you can review and strengthen these techniques, and (3) apply these techniques to the specific problems on which you struggled.

3. If you have trouble identifying the best technique to use on a problem, see the Techniques Reference information in Chapter VIII, starting on page 453.

ARITHMETIC WORKSHEET 1

Problem numbers represent the *approximate* level of difficulty for each problem (out of 60).

6. In a table, Luther recorded the number of minutes he watched television over the course of a week during his summer vacation, as shown below. What was the mean number of minutes he watched television per day for this week?

Day	Mon.	Tues.	Wed.	Thurs.	Fri.	Sat.	Sun.
Minutes	20	120	100	0	140	240	360

   A. 100
   B. 120
   C. 140
   D. 163 ⅓
   E. 180

7. The ratio of two numbers is 4:5. If one of the numbers is 80, what is a possible value of the other number?

   F. 64
   G. 74
   H. 84
   J. 94
   K. 104

17. If 20% of *x* equals 1, what is 50% of *x*?

   A. 0.5
   B. 1
   C. 1.5
   D. 2
   E. 2.5

Continued ➔

18. The mayoral election results for the 54,000 voting residents of Vonnegut City are shown below. If the information in the table were converted into a circle (or pie) graph, then what would be the measure of the central angle of the sector for the candidate named Pilgrim?

Candidate	Number of voters
Pilgrim	20,400
Rumfoord	17,100
Trout	10,500
Hoover	5,280
Hoenikker	720

F. 130°
G. 132°
H. 134°
J. 136°
K. 224°

24. Two trains leave a station at the same time on two sets of straight parallel tracks. Train A heads east at an average speed of 50 kilometers per hour. Train B heads west at an average speed of 70 kilometers per hour. How many minutes after the trains leave the station will they be 30 kilometers apart?

A. 60
B. 45
C. 30
D. 20
E. 15

Continued →

25. If, for all x, $\left(x^{3a-1}\right)^2 = \left(x^4\right)^{\frac{1}{2}}$, then $a = ?$

    F. $\dfrac{1}{3}$

    G. $\dfrac{1}{2}$

    H. $\dfrac{2}{3}$

    J. $\dfrac{3}{4}$

    K. 2

26. A new car loses 20% of its value after a year of ownership. Which of the following gives the cost, after one year, of a car that cost $20,000 new?

    A. $20,000 - 20$
    B. $20,000(0.20)$
    C. $20,000 - 20,000(0.02)$
    D. $20,000 - 20,000(0.20)$
    E. $20,000 - 20,000(20)$

44. The distance the earth travels around the sun in a year is about 5.80×10^8 miles. Approximately how many miles does the earth travel in the 30-day month of November (assume 365 days in one year)?

    F. $(30)(365)(5.80 \times 10^8)$

    G. $\dfrac{(30)(5.80 \times 10^8)}{365}$

    H. $\dfrac{(365)(5.80 \times 10^8)}{30}$

    J. $\dfrac{5.80 \times 10^8}{(30)(365)}$

    K. $\dfrac{365}{(30)(5.80 \times 10^8)}$

47. Rachel needs to average 80.0 points on 5 equally weighted gymnastics tests if she hopes to be invited to an upcoming tournament. If she has taken 4 of the tests, and her average score is 75.5, how many points must she score on the 5th test to get invited to the tournament?

    A. 92
    B. 94
    C. 96
    D. 98
    E. 100

Continued ➔

50. The first and second terms in an arithmetic sequence are p and $p + q$, in that order. What is the 1000th term of the sequence?

F. $999(p + q)$
G. $1,000(p + q)$
H. $p + 998q$
J. $p + 999q$
K. $p + 1,000q$

52. At Wright High School, 80% of the students of the graduating class plan to go to four-year universities. Of the remaining graduating class members, 90% plan to go to community colleges. What percent of the graduating class do NOT plan to go to a four-year university or a community college?

A. 1%
B. 2%
C. 10%
D. 20%
E. 98%

59. A scientist measures the lengths of the back legs of lizards from two different islands. She measures 200 lizards from Island A and 250 lizards from Island B. If the average back-leg length of the lizards from Island A is 5 centimeters and the average back-leg length of the lizards from Island B is 4 centimeters, to the nearest tenth of a centimeter, what is the average back-leg length of all 450 lizards?

F. 4.3
G. 4.4
H. 4.5
J. 4.6
K. 4.7

ARITHMETIC WORKSHEET 2

Problem numbers represent the *approximate* level of difficulty for each problem (out of 60).

8. The product of $(3x^2y^3)(4x^5y^4)$ is equivalent to:

    A. $7x^7y^7$
    B. $12x^7y^7$
    C. $7x^{10}y^{12}$
    D. $12x^{10}y^{12}$
    E. $12xy^7$

9. The average of 24 numbers is −2. If each of the numbers is increased by 2, what is the average of the 24 new numbers?

    F. −1.0
    G. −0.5
    H. 0.0
    J. 0.5
    K. 1.5

15. The distance from Town A to Town B is 20 miles, the distance from Town B to Town C is 15 miles, and the distance from Town C to Town D is 5 miles. An automobile starts at Town A, travels through Towns B and C, and stops at Town D. If the total time for the trip is 1 hour, what is the automobile's average speed, in miles per hour?

    A. 20
    B. 30
    C. 40
    D. 50
    E. 60

22. Pedro copied a map of the world onto a square sheet of paper with a side of 11 inches. He measures the distance from Los Angeles to the Panama Canal as 2 inches. If he enlarges the map so it fits on a square poster board that has a side of 40 inches, what is the new distance, to the nearest inch, between Los Angeles and the Panama Canal?

    F. 7
    G. 8
    H. 9
    J. 10
    K. 11

Continued ➔

23. The recipe for rice pilaf calls for 2 parts vegetable broth to 3 parts rice to 4 parts water. If you want to make 8 cups of rice pilaf, how many cups of vegetable broth will you need?

A. $\dfrac{8}{9}$

B. $1\dfrac{7}{9}$

C. $2\dfrac{2}{3}$

D. $3\dfrac{5}{9}$

E. 16

28. The graph below shows the number of books sold at Read-A-Lot's 5 bookstores. According to the graph, what was the average number of books sold per bookstore for Read-A-Lot?

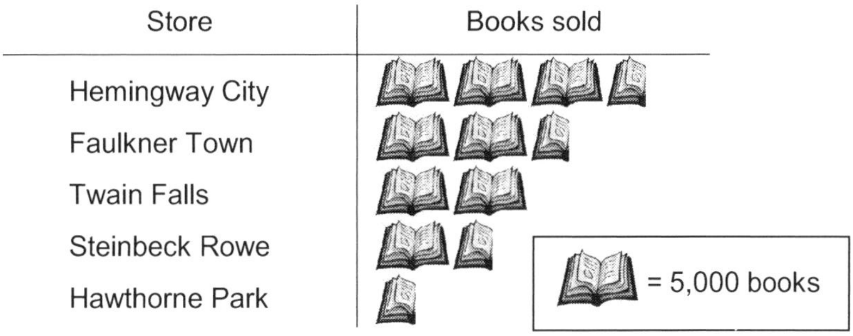

Store	Books sold
Hemingway City	
Faulkner Town	
Twain Falls	
Steinbeck Rowe	
Hawthorne Park	

= 5,000 books

F. 5,000
G. 7,500
H. 10,000
J. 17,500
K. 50,000

29. The number 0.2 is 1,000 times as large as what number?

A. 0.0002
B. 0.002
C. 0.02
D. 200
E. 2,000

Continued ➜

33. The table below shows the number of three point shots hit by Team A in each of its 25 games during a tournament. What is the average number of three-point shots hit by Team A per game?

Total number of 3-point shots in a game	Number of games with this total
0	1
1	0
2	2
3	4
4	8
5	2
6	5
7	2
8	1

F. 3.6
G. 3.8
H. 4.0
J. 4.2
K. 4.4

49. In the real numbers, what is the solution of the equation $8^a = 4^{2a+1}$?

A. −8
B. −6
C. −4
D. −2
E. 0

53. Greg decides to collect bottle caps each day during a family vacation. On his first day, he collects 10 bottle caps. His goal is to collect 1 more bottle cap on each successive day than he collected the day before. If Greg meets, but does not exceed, his goal, and if the vacation lasts 24 days, how many bottle caps in all will Greg collect?

F. 483
G. 484
H. 516
J. 517
K. 518

Continued ➔

58. Marc is trying to increase his weight for an upcoming wrestling match. After each training session, Marc's weight increases 2%. If Marc has two training sessions, by what percent does his weight increase?

A. 2.02%
B. 4%
C. 4.04%
D. 8%
E. 8.08%

60. The sum of the first n terms of a geometric series with first term a and common ratio $r \neq 1$ is given by $\dfrac{a(r^n - 1)}{r - 1}$. The sum of a given geometric series is $-1,100$, there are 5 terms in the series, and the common ratio is -2. What is the second term of the series?

F. -100
G. 0
H. 1
J. 100
K. 200

III

ALGEBRA

This is the most important chapter in the Math section of the tutorial, not only because algebra is such an important part of the ACT, but also because a number of *tricks* (called *The Pick Tricks*) will be taught that will allow supposedly difficult, high-numbered problems to be solved with relative ease. If your time is limited, or if you're following the **20- or 30-hour programs**, just cover the first three sections. The Pick Tricks (Section 3) will allow you to solve most of the problems covered in the last few sections of this chapter.

1. ESSENTIAL ALGEBRA

EQUALITIES ☺

If you've come this far, you probably already have a grasp of the basic algebraic operations that allow you to solve simple equalities. If not, the Working with Variables lesson on page 228 might help you get started, or find a good Algebra 1 book and review. For problems 1-10, solve for a. Answers to all lesson and homework problems in this chapter start on page 470.

1. $3a = -54$

2. $10a - 4 = 6$

3. $4 - 5a = 14$

4. $3a + 6 = 4\frac{1}{2}a$

5. $3a - 4 = 2a + 2$

6. $2(a - 6) = -4$

7. $\frac{2}{3}(9 - a) = \frac{1}{2}a - 8$

8. $\dfrac{1}{a + 2} = \dfrac{3}{5}$

9. $\dfrac{1}{2a + 2} = \dfrac{3}{a + 11}$

10. $a = b - 2$ and $b = 2a$, solve for a

INEQUALITIES ☺

If you can solve equalities like the ones on the previous page, then solving *inequalities* shouldn't be a problem. Just treat the inequality sign ($<, >, \leq, \geq$) as if it were an equal sign, but you must remember one important rule:

When multiplying or dividing both sides of an inequality by a negative number, the inequality sign changes direction. For example:

$$-2a \geq 14 \;\rightarrow\; \frac{-2a}{-2} \leq \frac{14}{-2} \;\rightarrow\; a \leq -7$$

inequality sign changes direction

Solve for *a*:

1. $4a < 120$

2. $-\frac{1}{2}a + 6 \leq 8$

RADICALS ☺

Radical were introduced in the Exponents lesson. To solve radical equations:

1. Isolate the radical expression so it is alone on one side of the equal sign.
2. Square both sides.

(EX) If $2\sqrt{a} = 12$, then $a =$

$$\sqrt{a} = 6 \;\rightarrow\; a = \mathbf{36}$$

Solve for *a*:

1. $2\sqrt{a} - 5 = 11$

2. $2\sqrt{a - 5} = 8$

WORKING WITH VARIABLES ☺

Some ACT problems will ask you to perform operations on variables. You should be comfortable with the following three rules:

- **Distributive property**: $a(b + c) = ab + ac$

- **Combine like terms**, for example: $2x^2 + 5x^2 = 7x^2$

- **Canceling terms**, for example: $\dfrac{8ab}{4b} = \dfrac{2 \cdot 4ab}{4b} = 2a$

 Caution: You can only cancel terms that are *factors* of the whole top and the whole bottom of a fraction. In other words, if a term is part of an addition or subtraction expression, you can *not* cancel it. This is a very common mistake. For example:

$$\frac{8 + ab}{4b} \neq \frac{2 \cdot 4 + ab}{4b}$$

Try the following lesson problem:

4. $m^2 - 22m + 11 - 12m^2 + 11m$ is equivalent to:

  A. 11
  B. $-22m^6 + 11$
  C. $-22m^2 + 11$
  D. $-11m^2 - 11m + 11$
  E. $-11m^2 + 11m + 11$

———

(HW)

ESSENTIAL ALGEBRA HOMEWORK

2. What is the value of the expression $a \cdot \sqrt{a} \cdot \sqrt{a + 3}$ for $a = 1$?

  A. 6
  B. 5
  C. 4
  D. 3
  E. 2

8. If $50(4x) = 200$, then $4x =$

  F. $\dfrac{1}{4}$

  G. 1

  H. 2

  J. 4

  K. 50

14. For what value of x is $p = 2$ a solution to the equation $x - 3 = px - 1$?

    A. −6
    B. −3
    C. −2
    D. 0
    E. 3

20. If $a = x + y$ and $b = x - y$, which of the following equals $(a + b) - (a - b)$?

    F. $2x$
    G. $2y$
    H. $2x - 2y$
    J. $2y - 2x$
    K. $x - y$

2. ALGEBRAIC WORD PROBLEMS

We talked about arithmetic word problems in the previous chapter. What we call *algebraic* word problems are ones that require one of the following:

1. Plugging numbers into a given equation.
2. Coming up with your own equation or equations.

Of course, you will likely have to use some of the algebraic techniques from the previous lesson to get a final answer.

GIVEN EQUATIONS

Sometimes the equation you need is conveniently given in the problem. You will usually simply plug numbers into the equation. These problems may look difficult (because they are wordy or have difficult-looking equations), but they tend to be easier than they look. Try the following problem:

30. The surface area, S, of a sphere is determined by the formula $S = 4\pi r^2$, where r is the radius of the sphere. What is the surface area, in square inches, of a sphere with diameter 6 inches long?

    A. 24π
    B. 36π
    C. 48π
    D. 60π
    E. 144π

If you thought the problem above was fairly straightforward, great! Notice that it's a number 30 (out of 60). Stay aggressive on these problems, especially the wordier ones, and you'll gain valuable points on problems that other students tend to skip or guess on.

CREATE YOUR OWN EQUATION(S)

Some questions *do* require you to make up your own equations and sometimes your own variables for these equations. The following table will help:

Word	Operation
product, of, multiplied, times	$\times$
sum of, more than, older than, farther than, greater than, added	$+$
difference, less than, younger than, fewer, subtracted	$-$
quotient, per, for, divided	$\div$
square	x^2
cube	x^3

32. When the square of the product of x and 4 is subtracted from the square of the difference of x and 4, the result is 0. Which of the following equations will allow you to solve for x?

    A. $(x - 4)^2 - (4x)^2 = 0$
    B. $(x - 4)^2 - 4x^2 = 0$
    C. $(4x)^2 - (x - 4)^2 = 0$
    D. $4x^2 - (x - 4)^2 = 0$
    E. $4x^2 - (x - 4) = 0$

A COMMON ALGEBRAIC WORD PROBLEM

You will likely come across a two-unknown/two-equation algebraic word problem similar to the one below. The example below covers the steps:

(EX) 40. The Bakerville Library held a charity event. Tickets for library members cost $5, and tickets for nonmembers cost $15. If an amount of $2,500 was collected from the 200 guests who paid admission, how many guests were members?

A. 15
B. 25
C. 50
D. 75
E. 150

First, choose variables for the number of members and the number of nonmembers: m = # of members, n = # of nonmembers.

Next, write your two equations:
Since the tickets cost $5 for members and $15 for nonmembers, we can write: 5m + 15n = 2,500.
Since there were 200 guests, we can write: m + n = 200.

Finally, solve the two equations. We'll use substitution, but you could also use the simultaneous equation method taught later in this chapter:
n = 200 − m → 5m + 15n = 5m + 15(200 − m) = 2,500
→ 5m + 3,000 − 15m = 2,500 → −10m = −500 → m = 50 C.

11. You have been hired to make sales calls for a small company. For each day of calling, you make $50 plus a fixed amount for each call you make. Currently you earn $140 per day for making 60 calls. If you increased the number of calls per day by 20, what would be your new daily earnings?

    A. $170
    B. $165
    C. $160
    D. $155
    E. $150

17. Four times a number is four more than two times the number. What is the number?

    F. −2
    G. 0
    H. 2
    J. 4
    K. 8

56. Nick purchased a box that contained red, blue, and yellow straws. There were ⅓ as many red straws as there were blue straws. If ⅓ of the straws were blue and 20 of the straws were yellow, how many straws were in the box?

    A. 12
    B. 24
    C. 36
    D. 48
    E. 60

3. THE PICK TRICKS

The two most important techniques in this tutorial are called *Pick Numbers* and *Pick Answers*—collectively called the *Pick Tricks*. These techniques make problems easier, often by eliminating difficult algebra. In addition, the Pick Tricks may allow you to solve a problem that would otherwise require a specific mathematical approach that you are not familiar with. **How** **important are the Pick Tricks? On average, nearly 1 out of every 3 problems on the ACT Math Test can be solved using a Pick Trick!**

That doesn't mean you'll have to use the Pick Tricks on 20 problems per test. Most problems that can be solved with Pick Tricks can also be solved using more traditional mathematical approaches. However, you should learn these techniques. Because the Pick Tricks make problems *easier*, they will benefit all levels of students. And the Pick Tricks are tools that can get you out of jams. The next several pages will ensure that you are comfortable using these tools.

PICK NUMBERS

The Pick Numbers technique allows variables (or unknowns) to be replaced with actual numbers that you pick. There are four types of Pick Numbers problems:

- Type 1: Variables in the answer choices
- Type 2: Variables in the question only
- Type 3: No variables
- Type 4: Guess and check

We'll discuss each one on the following pages.

PICK NUMBERS TYPE 1: VARIABLES IN THE ANSWER CHOICES

The first type of Pick Trick is the easiest to identify and the most straightforward and systematic to solve. Simply look for problems with **variable *expressions* in the answer choices**, for example:

  A. $x - 3$
  B. $x - 2$
  C. $x - 1$
  D. x
  E. $x + 1$

Note: For most problems with equal signs (=) or inequalities (<,>...) in the answer choices, this technique will not work. Make sure the answer choices are variable *expressions* (not equations or inequalities).

The following is a step-by-step method for solving these types of problems:

1. **Pick numbers for variables found in the answer choices.** The numbers 0 and 1 are usually not good choices. If there is more than one variable, pick *different* numbers for each variable. Write your picked numbers somewhere close to the answer choices—you will have to plug them in later. Draw a *box* around the numbers so they are easy to keep track of.

2. **Answer the question using an appropriate technique.** Remember, the variables should now be read as the numbers you picked in step 1, thereby simplifying the problem. Once you've solved the problem, *circle* or *underline* the answer.

3. **Plug your picked numbers into *each* of the answer choices.** You must plug in the number values that you picked in step 1. Cross out any answer choices that don't match your circled or underlined answer from step 2. **YOU MUST CHECK EVERY ANSWER CHOICE!** If only one answer equals your circled answer from step 2, you're done. Occasionally, more than one answer choice works, and you will have to go back to step 1 and pick new numbers to complete the elimination process. Once an answer choice has been eliminated, you do not have to check it again.

(EX) If a pen costs p cents, how many pens can be purchased for $4.00?

  A. $4p$

  B. $400p$

  C. $p/4$

  D. $4/p$

  E. $400/p$

① $\boxed{p = 2}$

② $\dfrac{pen}{cents}\dfrac{1}{2} = \dfrac{x}{400} \rightarrow x = \underline{200}$

③ Plug $p = 2$ into the answer choices. Make sure to **check every** **answer choice,** and **cross off** the incorrect ones. The answer is **E.**

Try the following lesson problems:

33. The expression $(a + b + 1)(a - b)$ is equivalent to: ?

    A. $a^2 - b^2$
    B. $a^2 - b^2 - b$
    C. $a^2 - b^2 + b$
    D. $a^2 + a - b^2 - b$
    E. $a^2 + a - b^2 + b$

42. If m and n are consecutive even integers and $m > n > 0$, how many integers are greater than $m + n$ and less than $m \times n$?

    F. 1
    G. 2
    H. $m - n$
    J. $n^2 - 3$
    K. $m^2 - n^2$

A note on Pick Numbers (Type 1) identification:

> As mentioned on the previous page, you should look for variable *expressions* in the answer choices (no equations or inequalities), but if every answer choice begins with the same variable and an equal sign (see example below), then you can still use Pick Numbers (Type 1):
>
> **A.** $y = x - 3$
> **B.** $y = x - 2$
> **C.** $y = x - 1$
> **D.** $y = x$
> **E.** $y = x + 1$
>
> Since the "$y =$" could have been the last words in the question, we can look at the answer choices as just variable expressions ($x - 3$, $x - 2$, etc.). In other words, pick a number for x, and follow the steps described above.

PICK NUMBERS TYPE 2: VARIABLES IN THE QUESTION ONLY

These problems have **variables in the question** and **no variables in the answer choices**. This means the answer choices are actual numbers.

Picking numbers for some or all of the variables in the question may lead you to the correct answer. You must read the question carefully to avoid picking numbers that break the specific rules of the problem. **You will usually not pick numbers for *every* variable.** Use the following method:

1. Start with the easiest equation or expression in the problem and pick a number for *one* of the variables.
2. Solve for as many other variables as possible.
3. If necessary, pick numbers for additional variables (that could not be solved in step 2) until you have enough information to solve the problem.

Remember to read the problem carefully. To avoid picking numbers for too many variables, make sure all of the specific rules for the problem are being followed.

(EX) If $a(b - c) = 6$ and $ab = 12$, what is the value of ac?

A. −6
B. 2
C. 3
D. 4
E. 6

Start with the second equation because it is simpler:

① *Pick a = 3*

② $3 \cdot b = 12$ → $b = 4$ → $3(4 - c) = 6$ → $c = 2$

③ $ac = 3 \cdot 2 = 6$ *E.*

Try the following lesson problem:

50. If $\dfrac{a}{b} = \dfrac{2}{3}$ and $\dfrac{b}{c} = \dfrac{2}{5}$, then $\dfrac{a}{c} = ?$

A. $\frac{4}{15}$
B. $\frac{3}{10}$
C. $\frac{2}{5}$
D. $\frac{2}{3}$
E. $\frac{5}{3}$

PICK NUMBERS TYPE 3: NO VARIABLES

Picking numbers when there are no variables allows you to create an example problem with your own numbers. This will give you a place to start and something to work with. The number 100 is sometimes a convenient number to pick, as we've already seen in some of the percent problems in chapter II.

These problems are harder to identify because *many* types of problems do not involve variables. If you are ever stuck on what seems to be a difficult problem with **no variables**, you may be able to use this technique.

(EX) Last week, Bill scored 10 fewer points than Fred in a game, and today, Bill scored 2 more points than Fred. Which of the following must be true about Bill's point total for the two games compared to Fred's?

A. Bill scored 1/5 of what Fred scored
B. Bill scored 5 times of what Fred scored
C. Bill scored 8 points more than Fred
D. Bill scored 8 points fewer than Fred
E. Bill scored 12 points fewer than Fred

Pick any numbers that satisfy the constraints above:
Game 1: Bill = 10, Fred = 20
Game 2: Bill = 12, Fred = 10
→ Combined: Bill = 22, Fred = 30
➜ 30 − 22 = 8 (Bill scored 8 fewer points)
D.

Try the following lesson problem:

31. When the perimeter of a square doubles, then the square's area increases by what percent?

A. 50%
B. 100%
C. 200%
D. 300%
E. 400%

PICK NUMBERS TYPE 4: GUESS AND CHECK

Sometimes when you Pick Numbers (Type 2), something doesn't work. For example, if you pick a number and end up with 2 = 3, you know something's wrong. Or perhaps you know the answer is supposed to be an integer and you keep getting fractions. You may have to *guess* numbers and *check* to see if you're getting closer to the correct answer. Use the following general method:

1. Pick a number or numbers for variables, as with the Pick Numbers (Type 2) technique. You will usually *not* pick numbers for every variable. This is your *guess*.

2. *Check* to see if your picked number or numbers lead you to the correct answer. **Always keep track of your results. You need to make sure that, when you pick new numbers, you're getting closer to the correct answer. You will often want to use a table to keep track of your picked numbers and their results.**

3. Continue picking numbers until you find the correct answer. Sometimes you might have to pick decimals, fractions, or negative numbers (not all problems on the ACT deal only with positive integers).

This technique works on many types of difficult, high-numbered problems. Often, they involve one or more equations that you cannot easily solve.

(EX) If $xy = 91$ and $x + y = 20$, then $x^2y + xy^2 = ?$

A. 111
B. 1,820
C. 1,919
D. 2,000
E. 2,091

Start with the second equation, since it looks easier than the first, and pick (guess) a number for x. We'll use a table to keep track of the results. Remember, x + y = 20, so once you pick for x, solve for y:

x	y	xy
10	10	$10 \cdot 10 = 100 > 91$ *(too big)*
11	9	$11 \cdot 9 = 99 > 91$ *(still too big, but getting closer!)*
13	7	$13 \cdot 7 = 91$ ✓

➔ $x^2y + xy^2 = 13^2 \cdot 7 + 13 \cdot 7^2 = 1,820$ **B.**

Non-Pick Trick Shortcut: The trick is to recognize that the two expressions (xy) and (x + y) multiply to form the expression in question $(x^2y + xy^2)$: $(xy)(x + y) = x^2y + xy^2$. If you substitute the given values for xy and x + y, you have $(91)(20) = x^2y + xy^2$ ➔ So $x^2y + xy^2 = 1,820$.

Try the following lesson problem:

50. If $7x + 3y = 29$, where x and y are positive integers, what is the value of $x + y$?

A. 3
B. 7
C. 8
D. 10
E. 17

PICK ANSWERS

If the answer choices are actual numbers, you may be able to *pick answers* to make the problem easier to solve. This tip is especially useful on harder problems or problems that have you stumped. Essentially, this technique allows you to solve a problem by picking answers and *working backwards*.

Before picking answers, you must identify the *barebones question*. This is the question in its simplest form and describes exactly what the problem is asking. Barebones questions are usually very simple, such as: "...what is the value of *x*?" or "...what was the price of the book?"

> These problems generally have **numbers as answer choices** (no variables). **Usually, the barebones question is very simple and involves at most one variable**. If you are ever stuck on a high-numbered problem, consider picking answers.

The method is as follows:

1. **Identify and underline the barebones question**, as described above.
2. **Answer this question by picking one of the answer choices.** Since the answers are often in ascending order, you should usually start with the middle answer choice (C or H). This may allow you to eliminate answers more quickly. If some answer choices appear easier to check than others, however, you can check these first.
3. **Look at the rest of the question to see if the answer you picked makes sense.** Essentially, you are creating an *if-then* question: *If* the answer to the barebones question is C (for example), *then* are the parameters of the problem possible? **Once you find the answer that works, stop—you do *not* have to check all the answers for picking answer problems.**

(EX) If Ed and Lorena divide a deck of 52 cards so that Lorena has 8 fewer cards than Ed, how many cards does Lorena receive?

A. 18
B. 22
C. 26
D. 30
E. 34

① The barebones question is "How many cards does Lorena receive?" Answer this question, starting with C:

② Pick C: L = 26

③ If Lorena has 26 cards, how many cards does Ed have?

E = 26 + 8 = 34

Is this possible? The total number of cards is 26 + 34 > 52, so the original number was too big. Eliminate C, D, and E.

Pick B: L = 22 → E = 22 + 8 = 30 → 22 + 30 = 52 ✓ **B.**

Try the following lesson problems:

29. Ryan had *d* dollars when he took Amy on a date. He spent one-fourth of his money on flowers and two-thirds of his <u>remaining</u> money on dinner. If he only spent money for flowers and dinner, and he is left with 35 dollars at the end of the night, what is the value of *d*?

    A. 70
    B. 140
    C. 160
    D. 180
    E. 210

41. Raymond has 8 buckets and 22 rocks. Each bucket can hold at most 5 rocks. What is the greatest possible number of buckets that can contain 5 rocks if NONE of the buckets are empty?

    F. 0
    G. 1
    H. 2
    J. 3
    K. 4

PICK ANSWERS → PICK NUMBERS

There are several ways you can combine the Pick Tricks. Sometimes, when each answer choice represents a *range* of values, you can pick an answer choice, and then test a number that lies in the range of that answer choice. First make sure you can identify these problems:

> Pick Answers → Pick Numbers problems tend to be high-numbered problems. The answer choices usually have a range of values. Here are some examples of what the answer choices might look like:
>
> **A.** $x > 0$
>
> **A.** x is an even number
>
> **A.**
>
> 0   2

The following method will help you approach Pick Answers → Pick Numbers problems:

1. Pick an answer choice.

2. Pick a number that falls in the range of that answer choice. The number you pick should also fall in the range of some (but not all) of the other answer choices. (This will ensure that you can eliminate at least some of the answer choices.)

3. Check that number against the parameters of the problem and eliminate answer choices. **The key is to eliminate answer choices. If a number you check *works*, eliminate answer choices that do *not* contain that number. If a number you check *fails*, eliminate answer choices that *do* contain that number.**

4. Repeat the steps until you have eliminated four of the answer choices.

(EX) If $\dfrac{x-5}{2}$ is an integer, then x must be: ?

A. a negative integer
B. a positive integer
C. a multiple of 5
D. an even integer
E. an odd integer

① *Start with answer choice A ("Pick" A):*
② *Pick a number that is part of A: $x = -2$ (Note: −2 is also part of D, so we're really checking two answer choices; this is good!)*
③ *When you plug $x = -2$ into the equation, you get −3.5 (not an integer)* ✗ → *Eliminate all answer choices that contain −2 (A and D).*

① *Now, move on to another answer choice. Pick B:*
② *Pick $x = 3$ (Note: 3 is also part of E, so again we're checking two answer choices.)*
③ *When you plug $x = 3$ into the equation, you get 1 (an integer)* ✓ → *Eliminate any answer choices that do not contain 3 (C). So we're left with B and E. Let's check E:*

① *Pick E:*
② *Make sure to pick a number that is in E but not in B (so we can eliminate one of the answer choices). Pick $x = -3$*
③ *When you plug $x = -3$ into the equation, you get −4, which is an integer* ✓ → *Eliminate B. The answer must be **E.***

Try the following lesson problem:

57. If $x \geq 0$, which of the following is the solution set of $\left| x^2 - 10 \right| \leq 6$?

    A. $0 \leq x \leq 2$

    B. $0 \leq x \leq 4$

    C. $1 \leq x \leq 4$

    D. $2 \leq x \leq 4$

    E. $2 \leq x \leq 8$

PICK NUMBERS → PICK ANSWERS

As the name implies, with these problems, you will first pick a number and then check the answer choices with your picked number. See the following example:

(EX) On a roller coaster ride at an amusement park, riders must be greater than 4 feet tall but less than 6 feet tall. If x represents the allowable height of a rider, in feet, which of the following represents all of the possible values of x?

A. $\left| x + 6 \right| < 4$	*Pick a number between 4 and 6 and eliminate answer choices that*
B. $\left| x - 6 \right| = 4$	*don't work with your number:*
C. $\left| x - 5 \right| < 1$	*Pick x = 5 → Eliminate A, B, D, and E. The answer must be* **C**.
D. $\left| x - 5 \right| > 1$	*Note: We got lucky this time, but sometimes the original number you*
E. $\left| x - 5 \right| = 1$	*pick does not eliminate all four incorrect answer choices. You might*
	have to pick additional numbers.

Try the following lesson problem:

53. If $(x - 3)$ is a factor of $2x^2 - 4x - k$, what is the value of k?

    A. 2
    B. 3
    C. 4
    D. 5
    E. 6

PICK TRICK HOMEWORK

Use at least one of the Pick Tricks on each of the following problems. Yes, you may know how to solve some of these problems using more "traditional" techniques, but remember that the goal of this section is to get comfortable with the *Pick Tricks*, so you can use them—when you choose to—on the ACT.

21. Six people visit Anna's blog every x seconds. At this rate, how many people will visit her blog in y minutes?

   A. $10xy$

   B. $10x/y$

   C. $10y/x$

   D. $360x/y$

   E. $360y/x$

23. If $a = b$, $c = d$, and $e = f$, which of the following equations must be true?

   F. $a + b = e + f$
   G. $a + c = d + e$
   H. $a + d = a + f$
   J. $a + d = b + c$
   K. $a + c = b - d$

31. If m and n are positive integers, what is the least value of m for which $\dfrac{2m}{11} = n^2$?

   A.   1
   B.   2
   C.   11
   D.   22
   E.   44

Continued ➜

34. If $3^x = 8$, then $3^{2x} = ?$

   F. 4
   G. 16
   H. 24
   J. 40
   K. 64

35. Anna, Tanya, and Stephanie decide to split the buried treasure that they find so that Anna receives $\frac{3}{5}$ of the treasure, Tanya receives $\frac{1}{3}$ of the treasure, and Stephanie receives the rest. What is the ratio of Anna's share to Tanya's share to Stephanie's share?

   A. 15:5:3
   B. 9:5:1
   C. 9:3:1
   D. 5:3:1
   E. 3:2:1

37. Max can sweep his patio in x minutes. What fraction of the task remains if he sweeps his patio steadily for y minutes, where $y < x$?

   F. $\dfrac{x+y}{y}$

   G. $\dfrac{x+y}{x}$

   H. $\dfrac{x+y}{x-y}$

   J. $\dfrac{x-y}{x}$

   K. $\dfrac{x-y}{y}$

38. Which of the following is the solution set for the inequality below?

$$|x+2| > 6$$

   A. $x < -6$ or $x > 6$
   B. $x < -8$ or $x > 4$
   C. $x < 4$ or $x > 8$
   D. $x < -8$ and $x > 4$
   E. $x < 4$ and $x > 8$

Continued ➔

42. Joshua is ½ as old as Keith and ¼ as old as Sean. If the average of all three ages is 21, how old is Keith now?

    F. 3
    G. 9
    H. 12
    J. 18
    K. 36

43. A business is owned by 3 men and 1 woman, each of whom has an equal share. If one of the men sells $\frac{1}{3}$ of his share to the woman, and another man keeps $\frac{1}{3}$ of his shares and sells the rest to the woman, what fraction of the business will the woman own?

    A. $\frac{5}{12}$
    B. $\frac{1}{2}$
    C. $\frac{3}{4}$
    D. $\frac{11}{12}$
    E. $1\frac{1}{4}$

48. Which of the following defines the solution set for the the system of inequalities below?

$$-2x + 3 > -1$$
$$2x - 3 > -7$$

    F. $x > -2$
    G. $x < 2$
    H. $-4 < x < 4$
    J. $-2 < x < 2$
    K. $-2 < x < 4$

51. Jody played a video game three times and improved his score by the same percent each time. If he scored 600 points the first time and 864 points the third time, what was the percent change after each game?

    A. 13.2%
    B. 20%
    C. 22%
    D. 26.4%
    E. 44%

Continued ➜

56. For every dollar that a software company raises the price of a computer program, it sells 1,000 fewer programs. The company normally sells 5,000 programs a day at a cost of $75.50 per program. If the company raises the price d dollars, which of the following expressions represents the number of programs sold per day?

   F. $75.50 - d$
   G. $5,000(75.50 - d)$
   H. $5,000 - 1,000(75.50 - d)$
   J. $5,000 - 1,000d$
   K. $75.50(5,000 - 1,000d)$

———

All programs: At this point, jump to the end of this chapter and complete Algebra Worksheets 1 and 2 and relevant test corrections for Test 2. (Remember, Test 1 is for practice problems.) Then move on to the Geometry chapter.

Note: If you are in the **40-hour program**, you will eventually cover the next several Algebra lessons (see Tutoring Schedules in the Introduction). If you are in the **20- or 30-hour programs**, you will skip these lessons. However, most problems covered by the next several lessons can be solved using The Pick Tricks, so learn them well!

4. SIMULTANEOUS EQUATIONS

SIMULTANEOUS EQUATIONS

You should be comfortable solving two linear equations with two unknowns. A *linear equation* has the form $ax + by = c$, where a, b, and c are numbers, called *coefficients*.

Coefficient – a number or constant that multiplies a variable (for example, in the expression $2x$, the coefficient is 2).

When there are two linear equations and two unknowns, the equations can be solved *simultaneously*.

To identify these problems, look for *two* linear equations with *two* unknowns.

Use the following method:
1. Stack the equations (one above the other)—make sure that the variables line up vertically.
2. If necessary, multiply one or both of the equations by a constant (or constants) so that one of the variables has the same coefficient in each equation.
3. Add or subtract the equations to eliminate this variable.
4. Solve for the remaining variable using algebra.
5. Plug this value into one of the original equations to find the other variable.

Solve for x and y:

(EX) $x + 2y = 8$ and $x - 2y = -4$

$$x + 2y = 8$$
$$\underline{-(x - 2y = -4)}$$
$$4y = 12 \rightarrow y = 3$$
$$\rightarrow x + 2 \cdot 3 = 8 \rightarrow x = 2$$

2. $100x + y = 25$ and $200x + y = 45$

1. $2x + 2y = 8$ and $3x - 2y = 2$

3. $5x - 5y = -10$ and $2x + 3y = 16$

Here's a tricky lesson problem that tests simultaneous equations (hint: use RTD):

60. Pam rode her bike to work in the morning at an average speed of 10 miles per hour. After work, she discovered that she had a flat tire, so she walked home along the same route at an average speed of 2 miles per hour. If Pam spent a total of 3 hours commuting to and from work, what was the total distance in miles that Pam traveled to and from work?

    F. 2
    G. 3
    H. 5
    J. 10
    K. 12

23. If $2x - 2y = 12$ and $x + 3y = -6$, what is the value of y?

    A. -3
    B. -1
    C. 1
    D. 3
    E. 6

52. What is the 17th term of the arithmetic sequence in which the 5th term is 6 and the 9th term is 13?

    F. 20
    G. 27
    H. 29
    J. 34
    K. 39

5. FACTORING

There are only three types of *factoring* you need to be familiar with for the ACT:

1. Common factors
2. Factoring quadratics
3. Difference of two squares

COMMON FACTORS ☺

First, some terminology:

Term – a product of numbers and/or variables, such as $4x$ or $\frac{1}{2}x^2$

Expression – one or more terms added or subtracted together, such as $4x + \frac{1}{2}x^2$

If you are solving a difficult equation, always check to see if you can pull a common factor out of every term of an expression. This may sound complicated, but the method is actually fairly straightforward and is best displayed with examples:

Factor the following expressions:

(EX) $\frac{1}{2}x^2 + 4x = x(\frac{1}{2}x + 4)$

1. $20q^2 - 40q =$

(EX) $12a^3b - 6a^2b^2 = 6a^2b(2a - b)$

2. $2x^2y + 3xy^2 =$

> Look for difficult equations that have common factors in every term on one side of the equal sign.

SOLVING EQUATIONS BY FACTORING

Factoring will often help you solve an otherwise difficult equation. First, remember that whenever the product of two expressions equals zero, either the first expression equals zero or the second expression equals zero (or they both do). This is called the *Zero Product Theorem*:

If $a \cdot b = 0$, then $a = 0$ or $b = 0$

For example, if $x(\frac{1}{2}x + 4) = 0$, then $x = 0$ or $(\frac{1}{2}x + 4) = 0$. If you solve the second equation for x, you'll get $x = -8$. So the solutions are: $x = 0$ or $x = -8$.

The following method is useful on many *common factor* problems:

1. For most of these problems, add or subtract terms so that one expression equals zero (all terms on one side of the equal sign).
2. Factor out common factors.
3. Set each new expression equal to zero and solve (as explained by the Zero Product Theorem). These solutions are sometimes called "zeros" because the original expression equals zero when any of the solutions are plugged in.

(EX) If $x^2 + 9x = 0$, then what is the <u>sum</u> of the possible values of x?

    A. −9   *① The expression already is equal to zero.*
    B. −3
    C. 0   *② x(x + 9) = 0*
    D. 3
    E. 9   *③ x = 0 or x = −9 → 0 + (−9) = −9 **A.***

Try the following lesson problem:

29. If $x^2 = 4x$, which of the following is a possible value of $x - 4$?

    A. −4
    B. −2
    C. 2
    D. 4
    E. 8

FACTORING QUADRATICS ☺

Quadratics usually take the form $ax^2 + bx + c = 0$, where a, b, and c are numbers. In general, on the ACT, a will equal 1, which is fortunate because it makes solving the quadratic much easier.

If you are unfamiliar with factoring quadratics, read over the following method carefully:

1. Set the quadratic equal to zero with the *x-squared term* (x^2) first and the *number term* (no *x*) last.

2. Find two numbers that *multiply* to the number term. If necessary, use a *factor table* to find the pairs of factors (see Basic Mathematical Concepts), but don't forget about negative numbers, as well.

3. The factor pair from step 2 that *adds* to the coefficient of the *x-term* is the correct pair.

4. Write the quadratic in a factored form (see example).

5. Solve for *x* using the Zero Product Theorem.

(EX) Factor $x^2 - 7x + 10 = 0$ and solve for *x*.

      ① The equation already equals zero.

      ② Find the factors of 10 (the number term): 1·10, 2·5, −1·−10, −2·−5

      ③ The fourth pair above adds to −7 (the x-term coefficient).

      ④ A quadratic in factored form looks something like this:

      (x + ?)(x + ?) = 0. The factored quadratic is (x − 2)(x − 5) = 0

      *⑤ x = **2** or x = **5***

Factor the following quadratics and solve for *x*.

1. $x^2 + 5x = -6$

2. $x^2 - 12x + 12 = -8$

3. $x^2 + 4x = 21$

4. $x^2 + 22x - 23 = 0$

THE QUADRATIC FORMULA

On rare occasion a question may show up that requires you to use the *quadratic formula*. This formula allows you to find the solutions of a quadratic equation of the form $ax^2 + bx + c = 0$. We recommend you memorize the formula:

$$\boxed{\textit{FLASH CARDS}} \quad x = \frac{-b \pm \sqrt{b^2 - 4ac}}{2a}$$

The expression within the square root ($b^2 - 4ac$, called the *discriminant*) offers some useful information:

- If $b^2 > 4ac$, then the quadratic equation has 2 *real* solutions (since you'll be taking the square root of a positive number).
- If $b^2 = 4ac$, then the quadratic equation has 1 real solution ($b^2 - 4ac = 0$).
- If $b^2 < 4ac$, then the quadratic equation has 2 *imaginary* solutions (since you'll be taking the square root of a negative number—we'll cover imaginary numbers in the Odds and Ends chapter).

DIFFERENCE OF TWO SQUARES ☺

A *square* is just a number or variable (or term) that has been squared. Some examples of squares are: 16 (square of 4), x^2 (square of x), and $36y^4$ (square of $6y^2$). Expressions that are a *difference* (subtraction) of two squares can be factored using the following formula:

$$a^2 - b^2 = (a + b)(a - b)$$

 To identify these problems, look for an expression that is a difference of squared items. Note that these squared items can be numbers, variables, terms, or expressions.

(EX) If $(x - 4)^2 - (4x)^2 = 0$, what is the <u>product</u> of the possible values for x?

A. $-\dfrac{7}{15}$

B. $-\dfrac{8}{15}$

C. $-\dfrac{11}{15}$

D. $-\dfrac{16}{15}$

E. $-\dfrac{17}{15}$

We've seen this equation before (see number 32 in the Algebraic Word Problems section). This question asks for the product of the possible values of x, so we can't pick answers (the barebones question is not simple enough).

The equation is a difference of two squares: $(x - 4)^2$ and $(4x)^2$, so we can write: $[(x - 4) + 4x][(x - 4) - 4x] = 0$

→ *By the Zero Product Theorem: $(x - 4) + 4x = 0$ or $(x - 4) - 4x = 0$*

→ $5x - 4 = 0 \rightarrow x = \dfrac{4}{5}$ *or* $-3x - 4 = 0 \rightarrow x = -\dfrac{4}{3}$

→ $\dfrac{4}{5} \cdot \left(-\dfrac{4}{3}\right) = -\dfrac{16}{15}$ **D.**

FACTORING HOMEWORK

15. Which of the following has both $x = 3$ and $x = -4$ as solutions?

    A. $(x - 3)(x + 4) = 0$
    B. $(x + 3)(x - 4) = 0$
    C. $(x - 3)(x - 4) = 0$
    D. $x + 3 = x - 4$
    E. $x - 3 = x + 4$

46. If $a^2 - ka + 6 = (a - 3)(a - 2)$, then $k = ?$

    F. 1
    G. 3
    H. 5
    J. 6
    K. 7

53. Which of the following is a quadratic equation that has $\dfrac{1}{3}$ as its only solution?

    A. $9x^2 - 6x + 1 = 0$
    B. $9x^2 + 6x + 1 = 0$
    C. $9x^2 - 6x - 1 = 0$
    D. $9x^2 + 1 = 0$
    E. $9x^2 - 1 = 0$

6. QUADRATICS

FOIL ☺

There are three specific quadratic equations you must memorize. The *difference of squares* one was covered in the previous section. All three are easy to derive if you are comfortable using *FOIL* (multiply *F*irst terms, *O*uter terms, *I*nner terms, and *L*ast terms and add these products). For example:

$$(x + y)^2 = (x + y)(x + y) = x^2 + xy + xy + y^2 = x^2 + 2xy + y^2$$

THE THREE QUADRATIC EQUATIONS

FLASH CARDS

1. $(x + y)(x - y) = x^2 - y^2$
2. $(x + y)^2 = x^2 + 2xy + y^2$
3. $(x - y)^2 = x^2 - 2xy + y^2$

To identify these problems, look for any of the elements of the three equations:
$(x + y)$, $(x - y)$, $(x + y)^2$, $(x - y)^2$, $x^2 + 2xy + y^2$, $x^2 - 2xy + y^2$, $2xy$, etc.

Use the following method to tackle these problems:

1. **Identify which of the three quadratic equations above is being tested.** Look for clues; for example, if you see the expressions $(x + y)$ and $(x - y)$, you know that the first equation above is being tested.

2. **Write the appropriate equation as it appears above.** Enter no numbers at this point.

3. **Beneath the equation, write all given numerical values.**

4. You should be able to solve for the variable, term, or expression in question.

(EX) If $m - n = 5$ and $m + n = 7$, then $m^2 - n^2 =$

A. 12   ① *Use quadratic equation number 1.*

B. 25

C. 35   ② $(m - n)(m + n) = m^2 - n^2$

D. 49

E. 74   ③ $(5) \times (7) = m^2 - n^2$ → ④ $m^2 - n^2 = 35$ **C.**

Try the following lesson problem:

44. If $a + b = 5$ and $2ab = 5$, then $a^2 + b^2 =$

    A. 0
    B. 5
    C. 10
    D. 20
    E. 25

1. Use *FOIL* to derive quadratic equation number 3 on the previous page:

    $(x - y)^2 = x^2 - 2xy + y^2$. Show your work:

6. The expression $(3x - 2)(x + 7)$ is equivalent to: ?

    A. $3x^2 - 14$
    B. $3x^2 + 5$
    C. $3x^2 + 23x - 14$
    D. $3x^2 + 19x - 14$
    E. $3x^2 + 19x + 14$

38. If $x^2 - y^2 = 20$ and $x - y = 5$, what is the value $x + y$?

    F. 5
    G. 4
    H. 0
    J. −4
    K. −5

7. ALGEBRA PROBLEMS

PRACTICE PROBLEMS

The following worksheets and practice problems (from Test 1 in *The Real ACT Prep Guide*, 3rd Edition) test techniques taught in this chapter. It is very important to look back to the lessons in this chapter and review the techniques while completing these problems. Try to determine which technique relates to each problem and apply the methods taught in the tutorial. Do not time yourself on these problems. The problems are provided to give you an opportunity to practice, and hopefully master, the techniques in this tutorial before you apply them on real ACTs in a timed setting.

- ☐ Algebra Worksheet 1
- ☐ Algebra Worksheet 2
- ☐ Algebra Worksheet 3
- ☐ Algebra Worksheet 4
- ☐ **Test 1**: 7, 8, 9, 10, 11, 16, 21, 23, 26, 32, 34, 36, 43[40], 51, 59 (see Step 3 under "Test Corrections" below)

[40] Questions marked with a "40" are covered by the **40-hour program**.

You might choose to space the above assignments out over the course of your studies. See the "Schedules" section in the introduction for more details about programs.

TEST CORRECTIONS

After each practice test is graded, you should correct Algebra problems that you missed or left blank. There are three steps to correcting the practice tests:

1. The Algebra questions for each test are listed below. Go back to your answer sheet for the corresponding test and circle the question numbers below that you missed (or guessed on, if you kept track of your guesses).

    - ☐ **Test 2**: 5, 8, 10, 11, 12, 18, 22, 26, 27, 28, 36, 41, 46, 49, 56, 58
    - ☐ **Test 3**: 2, 6, 7, 10, 12, 16, 20, 23, 24, 26, 27, 33, 34, 36, 52, 54, 55, 56, 57
    - ☐ **Test 4**: 2, 3, 7, 8, 9, 13, 18, 19, 21, 22, 23[40], 27, 30, 31, 36, 40, 48, 59
    - ☐ **Test 5**: 1, 6, 7, 9, 14, 19, 24[40], 25, 34, 40, 41, 45, 47, 49

    [40] Questions marked with a "40" are covered by the **40-hour program**.

2. Correct the problems in *The Real ACT Study Guide*. As you correct the problems, go back to the tutorial and review the techniques. The idea is to: (1) identify techniques that have given you trouble, (2) go back to the tutorial so you can review and strengthen these techniques, and (3) apply these techniques to the specific problems on which you struggled.

3. If you have trouble identifying the best technique to use on a problem, see the Techniques Reference information in Chapter VIII, starting on page 453.

ALGEBRA WORKSHEET 1

Problem numbers represent the *approximate* level of difficulty for each problem (out of 60).

4. For what value of x is the equation $3(2x - 4) = 2x - 16$?

    A. 0
    B. −1
    C. −3
    D. −4
    E. −18

10. If a, b, and c are all nonzero real numbers and $a + b = c$, which of the following equations is always true?

    F. $a = b - c$
    G. $a = b + c$
    H. $a = -(c - b)$
    J. $-a = c - b$
    K. $-a = b - c$

12. If x is a positive real number and $\dfrac{3}{x} \le \dfrac{1}{3}$, what is the smallest possible value of x ?

    A. $\dfrac{1}{9}$

    B. $\dfrac{1}{3}$

    C. 1

    D. 3

    E. 9

20. If $x^3 + x^2 = 0$, which of the following is the <u>sum</u> of the possible values of x?

    F. −3
    G. −2
    H. −1
    J. 0
    K. 1

Continued ➔

30. The formula used to calculate the current value of an investment is $A = P(1 + r)^n$, where A is the current value, P is the investment amount, r is the rate of interest for 1 compounding period, and n is the number of compounding periods that have passed. Which of the following, to the nearest dollar, is the value after 10 years of a $5,000 investment at a 6% annual interest compounded yearly?

A. $\$\dfrac{(1.06)^{10}}{5,000}$

B. $\$\dfrac{5,000}{(1.06)^{10}}$

C. $\$\dfrac{5,000}{(1.06)(10)}$

D. $\$5,000(1.06)^{10}$

E. $\$5,000(1.6)^{10}$

36. Which of the following is equivalent to the identity $-3x + 6 < -6x$?

F. $x < -\frac{2}{3}$

G. $x < 2$

H. $x > 2$

J. $x < -2$

K. $x > -2$

41. A circle in the standard (x,y) coordinate plane has center $(0,2)$ and radius 2 units. Which of the following equations represents the circle?

A. $x^2 + (y - 2)^2 = 2$

B. $x^2 + (y + 2)^2 = 2$

C. $x^2 - (y - 2)^2 = 4$

D. $x^2 + (y - 2)^2 = 4$

E. $x^2 + (y + 2)^2 = 4$

Continued ➔

42. For all $x > 4$, $\dfrac{x^2 - 4x}{x^2 + 4x - 32} = ?$

    F. $\dfrac{-x}{x+8}$

    G. $\dfrac{x}{x+8}$

    H. $\dfrac{-1}{x+8}$

    J. $\dfrac{-1}{32}$

    K. $\dfrac{1}{32}$

60. If x and y are real numbers and $x - y = 10$, what is the smallest possible value for xy ?

    A. -25
    B. -21
    C. 0
    D. 1
    E. 11

ALGEBRA WORKSHEET 2

Problem numbers represent the *approximate* level of difficulty for each problem (out of 60).

14. Which of the following is equivalent to $\dfrac{x+x}{x}$?

   A. 2
   B. x
   C. $2x$
   D. x^2
   E. $2x^2$

29. At a fair, red tickets are good for rides and blue tickets are good for carnival games. Red tickets cost r dollars and blue tickets cost b dollars. The difference between the cost of 5 red tickets and 10 blue tickets is $15. Which of the following equations could be used to find possible costs for the two types of tickets?

   F. $r - b = 15$
   G. $\dfrac{5r}{10b} = 15$
   H. $|5r + 10b| = 15$
   J. $|5r - 10b| = 15$
   K. $|10r - 5b| = 15$

31. If $a - b = 4$ and $a^2 + b^2 = 26$, what is the value of ab?

   A. -10
   B. -5
   C. 1
   D. 5
   E. 25

32. A boat sits in still water off the coast of an island with two lighthouses. The light from the first lighthouse is visible every 21 seconds and the light from the second lighthouse is visible every 60 seconds. If the captain of the boat sees the lights from both lighthouses at the same time, how many seconds will pass before he again sees the lights at the same time?

   F. 120
   G. 210
   H. 420
   J. 840
   K. 1,260

Continued ➔

33. If $\sqrt{x-3} - 3 = 3$, then $x = ?$

   A. 3
   B. 7
   C. 36
   D. 39
   E. 42

45. A rectangle is twice as long as it is wide. If the sides are both tripled, then the area of the new rectangle is how many times greater than the area of the original rectangle?

   F. 3
   G. 6
   H. 9
   J. 12
   K. 15

54. Which of the following inequalities is represented by the graph below?

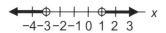

   A. $|x+3| > 1$
   B. $|x+1| < 3$
   C. $|x+1| > 3$
   D. $|x+1| > 2$
   E. $|x+1| < 2$

58. Let x be a positive 2-digit number with a tens digit a and units digit b. If y is the 2-digit number formed by reversing the digits of x, which of the following is equal to $x + y$?

   F. $11|a-b|$
   G. $11|b-a|$
   H. $a + b$
   J. $11(a + b)$
   K. $121(a + b)$

59. For all real numbers x and y, if the sum of 10 and x is y, which of the following expressions represents the product of 10 and x in terms of y?

   A. $10y$
   B. $10y + 100$
   C. $10y - 100$
   D. $y + 100$
   E. $y - 100$

ALGEBRA WORKSHEET 3

Problem numbers represent the *approximate* level of difficulty for each problem (out of 60).

8. If $q = -10$, then $-q^2 + q - 100 = ?$

    A. -210
    B. -200
    C. -190
    D. 110
    E. 210

9. The five consecutive integers below add up to 115.

    $$x - 3,\ x - 2,\ x - 1,\ x,\ x + 1$$

    What is the value of x?

    F. 21
    G. 22
    H. 23
    J. 24
    K. 25

24. A car rental company charges $25.00 per day to rent a car plus 25¢ per mile driven. Which of the following expressions represents the cost to drive a rented car m miles per day for d days?

    A. $\$25.00(d + m)$
    B. $\$25.00d(1 + m)$
    C. $\$25.00d + \$0.25m$
    D. $\$25.00d + \$0.25md$
    E. $\$25.00d + \$0.25(m + d)$

35. If $x - y = -8$, then $\sqrt{2y - 2x} = ?$

    F. $2\sqrt{2}$

    G. $4\sqrt{2}$

    H. 4

    J. 8

    K. 16

Continued ➔

38. If $a^2 - b^2 = 16$ and $a^2 + b = 28$, then what is a possible value of a?

   A. 3
   B. 4
   C. 5
   D. 6
   E. 7

48. If $4a^2 - 25b^2 = 0$, what is the <u>sum</u> of the possible values of a in terms of b?

   F. $-\frac{5}{2}b$

   G. $-\frac{2}{5}b$

   H. 0

   J. $\frac{2}{5}b$

   K. $\frac{5}{2}b$

53. Which of the following is the graph in the standard (x,y) coordinate plane of the points that satisfy the inequality $|x| \geq 10$?

A.
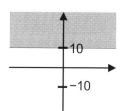

D.
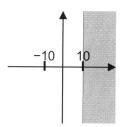

B.
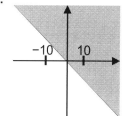

E.
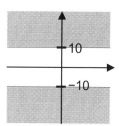

C.
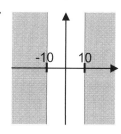

Continued ➜

54. A company wants to buy phones for its employees. Employee executives will get smart phones at a cost of $250 each and regular employees will get flip phones at a cost of $50 each. If the company spends $4,000 on a total 40 phones, and every employee gets a phone, how many more regular employees than executives work at the company?

    F. 20
    G. 25
    H. 30
    J. 35
    K. 40

57. If $\dfrac{a}{a^2+1} + \dfrac{1}{a^2+1} = \dfrac{5}{b}$ for integers a and b and $a > 1$, what is a possible value of b?

    A. 2
    B. 4
    C. 5
    D. 17
    E. 85

40-hour program: Now is a good time to go to the Odds and Ends chapter and complete the tutorial.

ALGEBRA WORKSHEET 4

Problem numbers represent the *approximate* level of difficulty for each problem (out of 60).

5. The total cost to hire a web service company is $50.00 for each day plus 75¢ for each customer click on a keyword. What is the total cost to hire this company for 30 days if a total of 2,500 keywords are clicked?

    A. $(50)(30) + $(0.75)(2,500)
    B. $(50)(30) + $(75)(2,500)
    C. $(50)(2,500) + $(0.75)(30)
    D. $(50)(2,500) + $(75)(2,500)
    E. $(50)(30)(2,500)(0.75)

15. What binomial must be subtracted from $2x^2 + 7x - 14$ so that the difference is $x^2 - 14$?

    F. $x^2 - 14x$
    G. $x^2 + 7$
    H. $x^2 - 7$
    J. $x^2 + 7x$
    K. $x^2 - 7x$

24. Which of the following is equivalent to $a(a + a) - a(a + a - 1)$?

    A. $-a$
    B. $-4a^2 + a$
    C. $-4a^2 - a$
    D. $-2a^2 - a$
    E. a

25. If $(m - n)^2 = 4$ and $2mn = 16$, what is the value of $m^2 + n^2$?

    F. -12
    G. 12
    H. 20
    J. 44
    K. 64

Continued ➔

26. Which of the following gives all the solutions of $x^2 - 2x = 35$?

    A. −5 and 7
    B. −7 and 5
    C. −2 and 0
    D. 0 and 2
    E. 0 only

32. If two numbers are both divisible by 3, which of the following numbers must be a factor of the product of the two numbers?

    F. 6
    G. 9
    H. 12
    J. 15
    K. 18

55. Patrick's basketball team has won 8 of its first 16 games. What is the minimum number of additional games his team must play to raise its win percentage to 80%?

    A. 4
    B. 8
    C. 16
    D. 24
    E. 40

Continued ➔

57. When graphed in the standard (x,y) coordinate plane, the lines $2x - 2y = 30$ and $x - 5y = 7$ intersect at what point?

    F. (16, 2)
    G. (2, 16)
    H. (17, 2)
    J. (2, 17)
    K. (30, 7)

59. There are 270 questions on a high-school entrance exam. To achieve a maximum scaled score of 100, the school scales the exam so that a student's score equals $\frac{1}{3}C + 10$, where C is the number of correct answers. If a student can take the exam twice, how many additional questions must a student answer correctly on the second exam in order to raise her initial score by 20 points?

    A. 30
    B. 45
    C. 60
    D. 75
    E. 90

IV
GEOMETRY

This chapter will cover all relevant geometry topics. Preparing for geometry problems is a matter of familiarizing yourself with the geometry formulas and rules that are tested on the ACT and completing practice problems.

1. GEOMETRY INTRODUCTION

NO REFERENCE INFORMATION

The ACT (unlike the SAT) does *not* provide geometry reference information. You need to memorize the formulas that are discussed in the following sections. For any formulas you don't know, make flash cards.

GEOMETRY FIGURES

While the ACT says that figures are NOT necessarily drawn to scale, we have found that the figures are *almost always* drawn perfectly to scale. Feel free to use the figures to check the likelihood of your answers or to make educated guesses.

MEASURE THE DRAWING

DISTANCES

Here's a great trick that you can use if you're ever stuck on a difficult or time-consuming problem that gives at least one distance (see the following example):

1.   Use the edge of your answer sheet, starting at a corner, to mark a distance given in the drawing. If the distance is relatively long, divide the distance into smaller parts (hint: you can find half the distance by folding the given distance in half).

2.   Your answer sheet is now a ruler. Use it to measure the distance in question.

(EX) In the figure below, $AB = 5$. If the perimeter of the rectangle is 10 less than twice the square of AB, what is the *area* of the rectangle?

A. 2
B. 25
C. 50
D. 70
E. 75

① *Using the figure above, mark the distance AB = 5 on a piece of paper (on a real test, you could use your answer sheet).*

② *Measure BC. You'll see that BC is about 3 AB's, so BC ≈ 15.*

➔ *Area = AB·BC ≈ 5·15 = 75* **E.**

Caution: This approach works best when there is only <u>one</u> answer choice close to your measured value. (If there was an answer choice of 74 or 76 in the example above, we would be less confident of our answer.)

ANGLES

You can also "measure the drawing" by estimating angles. Hopefully you can (roughly) recognize 30°, 45°, 60°, and 90° angles. (You can always use the corner of your answer sheet to see 90°. If you're really fancy, you can fold any corner exactly in half, and now you have a 45° angle—but don't crease your answer sheet.) See if you can solve the following problem by "measuring the angle."

55. In the figure below, *D*, *E*, and *F* are the midpoints of the sides of △*ABC*. If the measure of ∠*BAC* is 20°, and the measure of ∠*ABC* is 45°, what is the measure of ∠*EFD*?

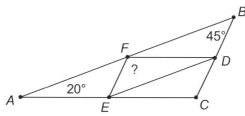

A. 15°
B. 75°
C. 95°
D. 115°
E. 145°

Try "measuring the drawing" for the following problem:

57. Triangle △*ABC* is shown in the figure below. Which of the following is the length of $\overline{BC}$?

(Note: For a triangle with sides of length *a*, *b*, and *c* and opposite angles ∠*A*, ∠*B*, and ∠*C*, respectively, the law of sines states $\frac{\sin\angle A}{a} = \frac{\sin\angle B}{b} = \frac{\sin\angle C}{c}$ and the law of cosines states $c^2 = a^2 + b^2 - 2ab\cos\angle C$.)

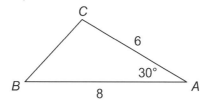

A. $6\sin 30°$

B. $\dfrac{\sin 30°}{6}$

C. $\sqrt{6^2 + 8^2}$

D. $\sqrt{8^2 - 6^2}$

E. $\sqrt{6^2 + 8^2 - 2(6)(8)\cos 30°}$

2. AREA AND PERIMETER

Memorize the following formulas. Make flash cards if necessary.

AREA OF A RECTANGLE ☺

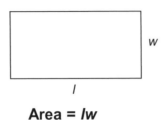

Area = *lw*

AREA OF A TRIANGLE ☺

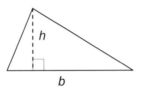

$$A = \frac{1}{2}bh$$

Finding the area of a triangle can be difficult. The base, *b*, can be *any* side of the triangle, not just the lowest and, oftentimes, horizontal side. The height is defined as the *perpendicular distance* from the corner *opposite the base* to the *line containing the base*. The following method will help you find the height of a triangle relative to a given base:

1. **Identify the base.** Note that the base is a *line segment*.

2. **Identify the corner opposite this base.** This is the corner that is *not* an endpoint of the base's line segment.

3. **With your pencil starting on this corner, draw a perpendicular line to the line containing the base.** Sometimes, the height line will intersect the actual base, as in the first example below. Other times, you may have to extend the base's line segment because the height falls *outside* the triangle, as in the second example below. Note that this does not change the length of the base, which is bound by the endpoints of the triangle.

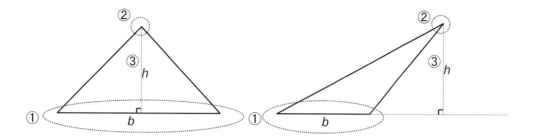

In each drawing below, sketch the height relative to the given base. Note that the bases are different from above. Answers to all lesson and homework problems in this chapter start on page 482.

1.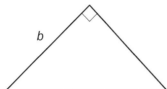

2.

AREA AND CIRCUMFERENCE OF A CIRCLE ☺

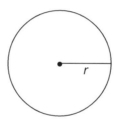

$$A = \pi r^2$$
Circumference $= 2\pi r$

We call the "perimeter" of a circle its *circumference*. If you're worried about remembering which formula is which above, it might help to know that measures of area have "square" units (for example, the size of a house is measured in *square* feet). Thus, the formula for area is the one with the r^2.

AREA OF A PARALLELOGRAM

A *parallelogram* is a four-sided shape (a *quadrilateral*) that has *parallel* and *congruent* (equal-length) opposite sides.

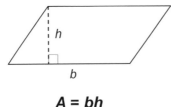

$$A = bh$$

AREA OF A TRAPEZOID

A *trapezoid* is a quadrilateral that has *two* parallel sides.

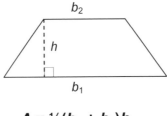

$$A = \tfrac{1}{2}(b_1 + b_2)h$$

PERIMETER

The *perimeter* of a shape is the sum of the measures of each side.

SHADED REGION PROBLEMS

There are two ways to solve shaded region area problems:

1. **Area Cutting**: Cut the shaded region into simpler shapes whose areas you can find, and add up these areas:

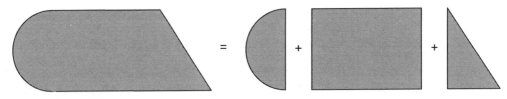

2. **Area Subtracting:** Subtract the areas of known shapes from the total area of the entire figure so that you're left with the shaded area.

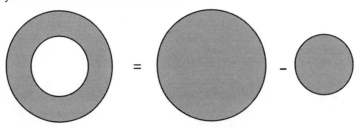

AREA AND PERIMETER LESSON PROBLEMS

5. The figure below is composed of square *ACDF* and equilateral triangles △*ABC* and △*DEF*. The length of *AF* is 5 inches. What is the perimeter, in inches, of *ABCDEF*?

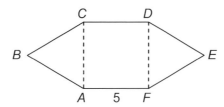

    A. 20
    B. 25
    C. 30
    D. 35
    E. 40

7. If the rectangle below has a perimeter of 20, what is the area of the rectangle?

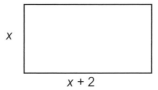

    F. 16
    G. 24
    H. 36
    J. 40
    K. 49

25. A parallelogram, with dimensions in inches, is shown in the diagram below. What is the area, in square inches, of the parallelogram?

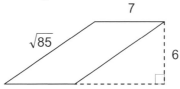

    A. $42\sqrt{85}$
    B. $7\sqrt{85}$
    C. $6\sqrt{85}$
    D. 42
    E. 21

40. The figure below is made up of a square with side of length 8 and two semicircles with diameters of length 3. What is the area of the shaded region?

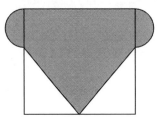

F. $24 + \frac{9}{4}\pi$

G. $24 + \frac{9}{2}\pi$

H. $44 + \frac{9}{4}\pi$

J. $44 + 9\pi$

K. $64 + 9\pi$

48. The eight equal semicircles below are placed so that they exactly cover the sides of the square. If the perimeter of the square is 32, what is the area of one of the semicircles?

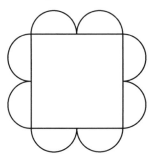

A. 2π

B. 4π

C. 8π

D. 16π

E. 32π

10. In the figure below, the large square is divided into two smaller squares and two rectangles (shaded). If the perimeters of the two smaller squares are 8 and 24, respectively, what is the sum of the perimeters of the two shaded rectangles?

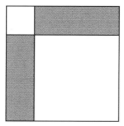

   A. 12
   B. 16
   C. 24
   D. 32
   E. 36

29. The equilateral triangle below is formed by connecting the centers of three tangent circles. If the perimeter of the triangle is 12, what is the sum of the circumferences of the three circles?

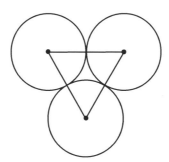

   F. 4π
   G. 8π
   H. 12π
   J. 18π
   K. 24π

Note: the problem above uses the word "**tangent**," which means *touching at exactly one point*. Notice that each circle above touches each of the other circles at exactly one point. The circles are, thus, *tangent* to one another.

Continued ➔

43. Square *ABCD* has side of length 8. The width of the border between squares *ABCD* and *EFGH* is 2. What is the area of the shaded region?

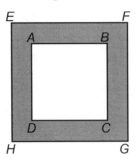

A. 36
B. 40
C. 48
D. 80
E. 100

46. In the figure below, O is the center of the circle of diameter 12. What is the area of △*AOB* ?

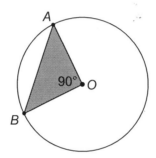

F. 36
G. 18
H. 15
J. 12
K. 6

Continued →

52. In the figure below, points *A, B, C, D, E, and F* are equally spaced on line segment *AF*. If the sum of the areas of the three circles is 18π, what is the radius of the smaller circle?

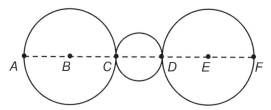

A. 1

B. $\sqrt{2}$

C. 2

D. $2\sqrt{2}$

E. 3

53. The area of circle *O* is *x* square inches, and the circumference of circle *O* is *y* inches. If *x = y*, what is the radius of the circle?

F. 1

G. 2

H. 3

J. 4

K. 5

Continued ➜

58. In the figure below, *ABCD* is a rectangle inscribed in the semicircle with center *O*. If *AD* = 5 and the semicircle has an area of 84.5π, what is the length of segment *AB*?

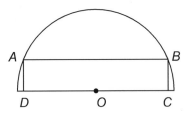

A. 12
B. 13
C. 24
D. 26
E. 28

3. TRIANGLES

In addition to finding the area of a triangle, as discussed in the previous section, there are a number of other topics related to triangles:

TYPES OF TRIANGLES ☺

Isosceles triangles have two equal sides (and two equal angles).

Equilateral triangles have three equal sides (and three equal angles, each measuring **60°**).

RIGHT TRIANGLES ☺

PYTHAGOREAN THEOREM

Memorize the *Pythagorean Theorem*. Make sure the *c* side is the *hypotenuse*, which is the longest side and always opposite the right angle.

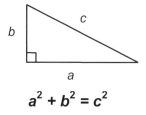

$$a^2 + b^2 = c^2$$

You can use the Pythagorean Theorem with *right* triangles when you know *two* of the three sides.

SPECIAL RIGHT TRIANGLES

30-60-90 AND 45-45-90 TRIANGLES

Memorize the relationships for the two special right triangles, the *isosceles-right (45°-45°-90°)* and *30°-60°-90°* triangles.

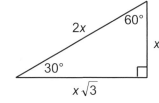

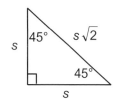

3-4-5 AND 5-12-13 TRIANGLES

These right triangles with integer sides show up frequently. You can save time if you have them memorized. You might also see multiples of these sides, such as 6-8-10.

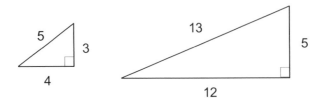

SIMILAR TRIANGLES ☺

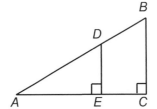

$\triangle ABC$ is similar to $\triangle ADE$

Similar triangles can be identified because they have equal angles. There are two relationships to remember:

1. **The ratio of any two sides of one triangle is equal to that of any two *related* sides of a similar triangle.** For example, in the triangle above:

    $$\frac{AB}{AC} = \frac{AD}{AE}$$

    Try the number 1 below, based on the triangles above:

    1. $\dfrac{DE}{AE} =$

2. **The ratio of *equivalent* sides of similar triangles remains constant.**

    $$\frac{AD}{AB} = \frac{AE}{AC} = \frac{DE}{BC} = k \text{ , where } k \text{ is some constant.}$$

To identify similar triangle problems, look for triangles that have equal angles. Usually, on the ACT, triangles that *appear* similar are indeed similar, but if you can, try to identify angles.

ANGLE-SIDE RELATIONSHIPS

In any triangle, the largest angle is opposite the longest side; the smallest angle is opposite the shortest side; and so on. Similarly, if two angles are equal, then their opposite sides are equal.

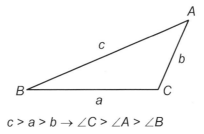

$$c > a > b \rightarrow \angle C > \angle A > \angle B$$

THIRD SIDE RULE

In any triangle, the sum of the two shortest sides must be greater than the longest side.

If a, b, and c are the lengths of sides of a triangle and $a \leq b \leq c$, then:

$$\boxed{\text{FLASH CARDS}} \; a + b > c$$

To illustrate the point, imagine sticks of different lengths. In the first example below, where the sum of the two shortest sides is *larger* than the third side, a triangle can obviously be constructed. In the second example, where the sum of the two shortest sides is *smaller* than the third side, the triangle is incomplete. You may want to make a flash card to remember this rule.

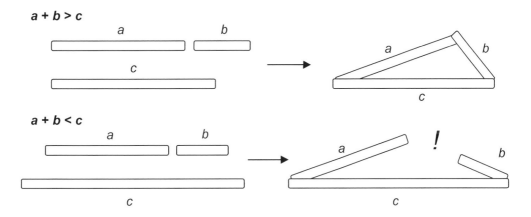

CONGRUENT TRIANGLES

Occasionally, a problem may require you to recognize *congruent triangles*. Two congruent triangles have the exact same size and shape. If you've covered congruent triangles in school, then the following rules should be a review. If you haven't covered congruent triangles, you might skip the following rules—rest assured that these types of problems are not common on the ACT.

RULES FOR CONGRUENT TRIANGLES

- **Side-Side-Side (SSS)**: If all sides of one triangle are congruent to those of another triangle, then the triangles are congruent.
- **Side-Angle-Side (SAS)**: If two sides and the included angle of one triangle are congruent to those of another triangle, then the triangles are congruent.
- **Angle-Side-Angle (ASA)**: If two angles and the included side of one triangle are congruent to those of another triangle, then the triangles are congruent.
- **Angle-Angle-Side (AAS)**: If two angles and the adjacent side of one triangle are congruent to those of another triangle, then the triangles are congruent.
- **Hypotenuse-Leg (HL)**: For right triangles, if the hypotenuse and one leg of one right triangle are congruent to those of another right triangle, then the triangles are congruent.

TRIANGLE PROBLEMS WITH NO TRIANGLES

Many geometry problems on the ACT are triangle problems even though there is no triangle given. Remember that drawing a triangle, usually a right triangle, can often help you solve a problem. Question 58 in the previous section is a good example of this. We will see many more of these types of problems.

TRIANGLE LESSON PROBLEMS

In the following triangles, find the lengths of all sides. The answers can be expressed as "unsimplified" radicals or as decimals:

1.

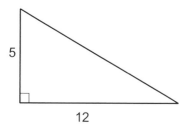

2.

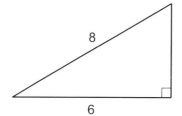

3.

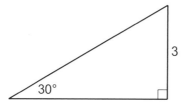

4.

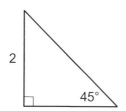

5.

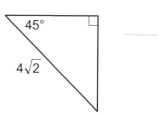

6.

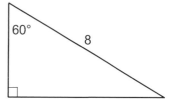

7.

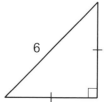

8.

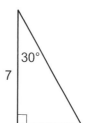

8. In the right triangle shown below, which of the following statements is true about side *AB*?

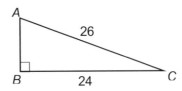

A. $AB = 26 - 24$
B. $AB = 26^2 - 24^2$
C. $AB^2 = 26^2 + 24^2$
D. $AB^2 = 24^2 - 26^2$
E. $AB^2 = 26^2 - 24^2$

20. If the area of the triangle below is 54, what is the length of the hypotenuse?

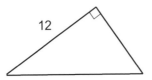

F. 9
G. 13
H. 15
J. 18
K. 21

29. If the area of a square is 50, how long is the longest straight line that can be drawn between any two points of the square?

A. 5
B. $5\sqrt{2}$
C. 10
D. 25
E. $25\sqrt{2}$

41. If an equilateral triangle with a perimeter of 6 is inscribed in a rectangle, as shown in the figure below, what is the area of the rectangle?

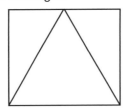

F. $\sqrt{3}$
G. 3
H. $2\sqrt{3}$
J. 4
K. $3\sqrt{3}$

17. Given the equilateral triangle below, what is the value of x?

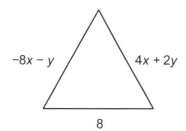

$-8x - y$ $4x + 2y$

8

    A. −2
    B. −1
    C. 0
    D. 1
    E. 2

40. In the figure below, AB and DE are each perpendicular to AE. If $AB = 2$, $DE = 4$, and $CD = 10$, what is the length of AE?

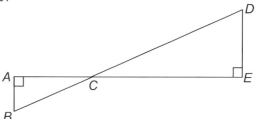

    F. $\sqrt{21}$
    G. $2\sqrt{21}$
    H. 5
    J. $3\sqrt{21}$
    K. 15

Continued ➜

44. What is the <u>perimeter</u> of the figure shown below?

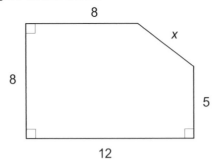

A. 33
B. 36
C. 38
D. 40
E. 42

45. In △ABC below, AB > AC. Which of the following must be true?

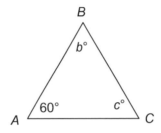

F. BC > AB
G. BC = AB
H. b = c
J. c = 70
K. b < 60

48. A triangle has sides of length 4 and 5. If the third side is an integer, what is the shortest possible length for this side?

A. 1
B. 2
C. 3
D. 5
E. 8

4. ANGLES

Let's see what you know. Fill in the missing information below. Answers are on page 486.

LINE

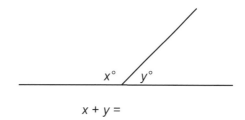

$$x + y =$$

TRIANGLE

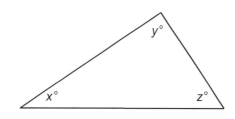

$$x + y + z =$$

CIRCLE

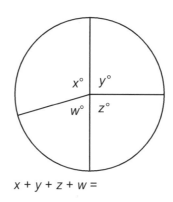

$$x + y + z + w =$$

RIGHT ANGLE

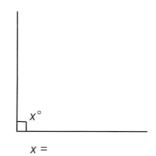

$$x =$$

VERTICAL ANGLES

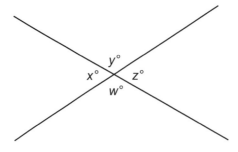

If x = 50°, then:

z =

y =

w =

PARALLEL LINES

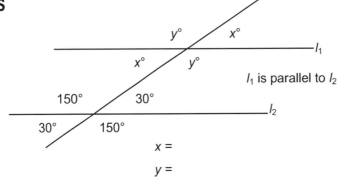

l_1 is parallel to l_2

x =

y =

LINE TANGENT TO A CIRCLE

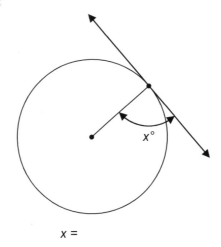

x =

SUM OF INTERIOR ANGLES

There is a simple method for finding the sum of the interior angles for any polygon of four or more sides:

1. Start at one vertex (corner) of the polygon.
2. From this one vertex, draw straight lines to all other (non-adjacent) vertices.
3. Count the number of triangles and multiply by 180°.

QUADRILATERAL

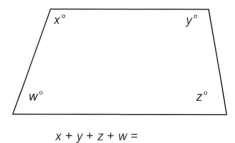

$$x + y + z + w =$$

OTHER POLYGONS

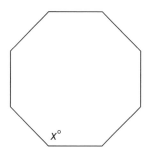

1. What is the sum of the interior angles of the polygon above?

2. If the above polygon is a *regular polygon* (all sides and angles are equal), what is the value of x?

COMPLEMENTARY/SUPPLEMENTARY ANGLES

Memorize these terms:

- If two angles add up to 90°, they are called *complementary* angles.
- If two angles add up to 180°, they are called *supplementary* angles.

ANGLE BISECTOR

As the name implies, an *angle bisector* is a line that divides an angle into two equal angles. Segment *BD* is the angle bisector of ∠*ABC*, below:

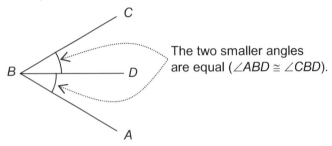

The two smaller angles are equal (∠*ABD* ≅ ∠*CBD*).

THE ISOSCELES TRAPEZOID

An *isosceles trapezoid* has two congruent, non-parallel sides (just like an isosceles triangle) and two sets of equal base angles (in the diagram below, *AB* = *CD*, ∠*BAD* = ∠*CDA*, and ∠*ABC* = ∠*DCB*). The ACT likes isosceles trapezoid problems, so you should memorize the angle relations below:

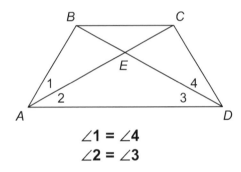

$$\angle 1 = \angle 4$$
$$\angle 2 = \angle 3$$

The top base angles follow the same pattern of equality as the bottom base angles. Knowing this, you can see that △*AED* and △*BEC* are both isosceles. In addition, because *AD* ∥ *BC*, a simple proof shows that these two triangles are *similar*. Finally, △*ABE* and △*DCE* are congruent (by the SAS or ASA property). To summarize:

- △*AED* and △*BEC* are both **isosceles triangles**; they are also **similar** to each other.
- △*ABE* and △*DCE* are **congruent**.

As you can see, there's a lot to know about isosceles trapezoids. If you ever forget some of this information, remember that the figures are generally drawn to scale on the ACT. **Most of the above properties are visually apparent, so trust your eyes.**

ANGLES LESSON PROBLEMS

3. In the figure below, what is the value of *x*?

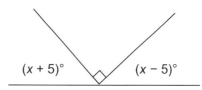

- **A.** 0
- **B.** 30
- **C.** 45
- **D.** 60
- **E.** 90

30. In the figure below, what is the value of *a* + *b* + *c* + *d* + 2*e*?

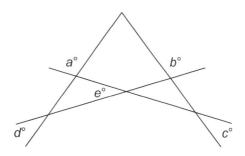

- **F.** 90
- **G.** 180
- **H.** 360
- **J.** 450
- **K.** 540

32. If lines *m* and *n* are parallel in the figure below, *a* + *g* must equal which of the following?

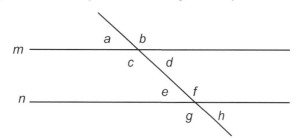

- **A.** *a* + *d*
- **B.** 3*e*
- **C.** *b* + 2*h* − *d*
- **D.** *c* + 2*e* − *g*
- **E.** *d* + 2*h* + 60°

48. In triangle *PQR* below, what is the value of *y* in terms of *x*?

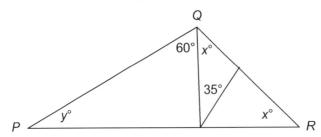

F. *x*
G. 2*x*
H. 100 − 2*x*
J. 120 − 2*x*
K. 140 − 2*x*

7. In the right triangle below, what is the value of *x*?

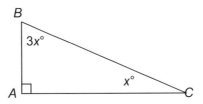

A. $22\frac{1}{2}$
B. 30
C. 45
D. $67\frac{1}{2}$
E. 90

28. In the figure below, what is the value of *y*?

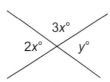

F. 36
G. 45
H. 60
J. 72
K. 80

50. In the figure below, lines *l* and *m* are parallel. What is *y* in terms of *x*?

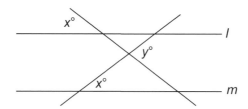

   F. *x*
   G. ¾ *x*
   H. 2*x*
   J. 180 − *x*
   K. 180 − 2*x*

51. Pentagon *ABCDE* below has equal angles and equal sides. If *O* is the center of the pentagon, what is the degree measure of ∠*AOB* (not drawn)?

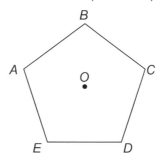

   A. 45°
   B. 60°
   C. 72°
   D. 108°
   E. 540°

5. COORDINATES

The coordinate plane consists of two perpendicular axes called the *x*-axis and the *y*-axis. The *x*-axis is horizontal and the *y*-axis is vertical.

POINTS

The most common mistake on simple coordinate problems is to confuse the *x* and *y* coordinates of *points*. **Remember, the *x*-coordinate is always the *first* coordinate of a point, and the *y*-coordinate is always the *second* coordinate of a point.** Identify the coordinates of the following points:

1. *A* =
2. *B* =
3. *C* =
4. *D* =
5. *E* =

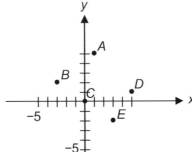

HORIZONTAL AND VERTICAL DISTANCES ☺

The coordinate plane allows you to easily find horizontal and vertical distances between points, just by knowing the points' *x* and *y* coordinates.

1. **To find the *horizontal* distance between two points, find the *positive difference* between the points' *x*-coordinates.** In other words, *subtract* the *x*-coordinates and take the *absolute value* of the result.

2. **To find the *vertical* distance between two points, find the *positive difference* between the points' *y*-coordinates.** In other words, *subtract* the *y*-coordinates and take the *absolute value* of the result.

Try the following lesson problem:

17. On the standard (x,y) coordinate plane shown below, Matt wants to draw a rectangle (not shown) that has two of its vertices at points (3,9) and (−1,3). If two sides of the rectangle are parallel to the x-axis, what is the perimeter of the rectangle?

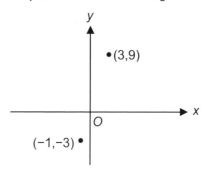

A. 8

B. $4\sqrt{10}$

C. 16

D. $8\sqrt{10}$

E. 32

SLANTED DISTANCES BETWEEN POINTS

If you need to find the straight-line distance between two points that do *not* lie on a vertical or horizontal line, you have two options:

1. THE PYTHAGOREAN THEOREM REVISITED

If you draw a right triangle, with the hypotenuse connecting the two points in question, you can use the Pythagorean Theorem to find the distance between the points, as shown below:

(EX) In the standard (x,y) coordinate plane, what is the distance between the points (−1,−1) and (2,3)?

A. $\sqrt{7}$
B. 3
C. 4
D. 5
E. 25

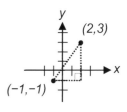

First, sketch the points on a coordinate plane.

Then draw a right triangle, with the hypotenuse connecting the two points, as shown:

Calculate the lengths of the two legs: bottom leg = 3, right leg = 4.

Finally, use the Pythagorean Theorem to find the distance (c) between the two points: $a^2 + b^2 = c^2$
*→ $3^2 + 4^2 = c^2$ → $25 = c^2$ → $c = 5$ (It's a 3-4-5 Δ.) **D.***

2. THE DISTANCE FORMULA

The other option is the *distance formula*. The distance between two points with coordinates (x_1, y_1) and (x_2, y_2) is:

$$\boxed{\text{FLASH CARDS}} \quad d = \sqrt{(x_1 - x_2)^2 + (y_1 - y_2)^2}$$

For the example above, $d = \sqrt{(-1-2)^2 + (-1-3)^2} = \sqrt{9+16} = \sqrt{25} = 5$, which agrees with our answer using the Pythagorean Theorem approach. (You might be interested to know that the distance formula actually derives from the Pythagorean Theorem. The calculations are the same. It's not surprising that you'll get the same answer using either approach.)

———

For finding slanted distances between points, we recommend the first approach (using the Pythagorean Theorem) because you don't have to memorize a new formula and there are fewer chances of careless calculator mistakes. However, both approaches work.

MIDPOINT

You may have to find the coordinates of the *midpoint* between two points. The formula is straightforward. The *x* coordinate of the midpoint is the average of the *x* coordinates of the two endpoints. Similarly, the *y* coordinate of the midpoint is the average of the *y* coordinates of the two endpoints:

$$\boxed{\text{FLASH CARDS}} \quad \text{Midpoint} = \left(\frac{x_1 + x_2}{2}, \frac{y_1 + y_2}{2} \right)$$

COORDINATE PLANE MODELING

Some problems will require you to set up a two-dimensional problem using a coordinate plane. Once you have the problem drawn onto a coordinate plane, you should be able to use the previous rules to answer the question. For example:

(EX) An architect places an overlay of the standard (x,y) coordinate plane on the blueprint of a house to find the length of a diagonal pathway. If one end of the pathway lies at (0,0) and the other end lies at (6,2), what is the unit length of the pathway?

A. $\sqrt{8}$

Sketch the pathway on a coordinate plane and draw a right triangle:

B. 6

C. $\sqrt{40}$

$d^2 = 6^2 + 2^2 = 36 + 4 = 40 \rightarrow d = \sqrt{40}$ **C.**

D. 8

E. 10

You could also use the distance formula.

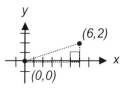

COORDINATES LESSON PROBLEMS

5. In the standard (x,y) coordinate plane below, both circles are centered at point O and $OA = AB$. If the coordinates of A are $(0,-6)$, what are the coordinates of C?

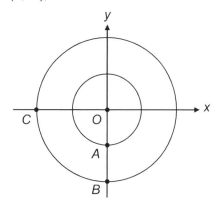

A. $(-6,0)$
B. $(-12,0)$
C. $(0,-12)$
D. $(0,-6)$
E. $(0,12)$

17. In the standard (x,y) coordinate plane, what are the coordinates of the midpoint of a line segment with endpoints at $(-2,-6)$ and $(2,5)$?

F. $(0,-11)$
G. $(0,-5.5)$
H. $(0,-0.5)$
J. $(0,-1)$
K. $(-1,0)$

11. In the standard (x,y) coordinate plane below, $\triangle ABC$ is an isosceles right triangle. Which of the following are the coordinates of point A?

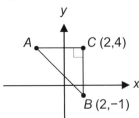

    A. (4,−3.5)
    B. (4,−3)
    C. (−2,4)
    D. (−2.5,4)
    E. (−3,4)

39. Point A has coordinates $(−2,−3)$ and point B has coordinates $(6,9)$. If point C is the midpoint of $\overline{AB}$ and D is the midpoint of $\overline{AC}$, then what are coordinates of point D?

    F. (−4,−6)
    G. (−2,−3)
    H. (2,−3)
    J. (−2,3)
    K. (0,0)

59. In the standard (x,y) coordinate plane, what is the area of the triangle shown below?

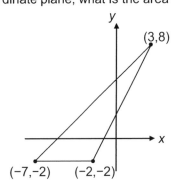

    A. 10
    B. 15
    C. 25
    D. 50
    E. 100

6. LINES

There are several different types of problems that deal with lines. First, let's look at some general definitions:

TERMINOLOGY

LINE

A *line* is perfectly straight and extends infinitely in both directions. Line *AB* can be notated as $\overleftrightarrow{AB}$:

LINE SEGMENT

A *line segment* is a section of a line, having two endpoints. Segment *AB* can be notated as $\overline{AB}$:

RAY

A *ray* has one endpoint and extends infinitely in one direction. Ray *AB* can be notated as $\overrightarrow{AB}$:

ONE-DIMENSIONAL LINE PROBLEMS

One-dimensional line problems include *number line* problems and *line segment* problems. You won't have to worry about vertical distances or slanted lines with these problems—the lines will generally be *horizontal*, like the *x*-axis of a standard coordinate plane.

> One-dimensional line problems tend to deal with horizontal lines (no vertical or slanted lines).

NUMBER LINES

Number line problems usually have tick marks. The tick marks may *not* always be a distance of *1* apart, but the marks will be equally spaced. Number lines generally increase to the right. As taught in the Coordinates section, to find the distance between two points, find the *positive difference* between them. In other words, *subtract* the endpoints and find the *absolute value* of the result.

Try the following lesson problem:

6. The marks on the number line below are equally spaced. What is the distance between points *A* and *B*?

A. $\dfrac{1}{5}$

B. $\dfrac{4}{5}$

C. 1

D. $\dfrac{6}{5}$

E. 6

LINE SEGMENTS

On some number line problems, there won't be any tick marks. These problems tend to deal with *line segments*. The Pick Tricks often prove useful on these types of problems.

(EX) On line segment *AB*, if point *C* lies one third of the distance from *A* to *B* and point *D* is the midpoint of *AC*, what is $\dfrac{DB}{AB}$?

A. $\dfrac{1}{3}$

B. $\dfrac{1}{2}$

C. $\dfrac{2}{3}$

D. $\dfrac{3}{4}$

E. $\dfrac{5}{6}$

This problem is easier if you pick a number for one of the distances, as shown below:

Pick # ⟶ 2   2   8

A   D   C   B

→ $\dfrac{DB}{AB} = \dfrac{10}{12} = \dfrac{5}{6}$ **E.**

Try the following one-dimensional line problem:

48. The antennas for two radio stations lie 250 miles apart on a straight highway. The radio signal for station A can be received within a radius of 200 miles in all directions from its antenna, and the radio signal for station B can be received within a radius of 100 miles in all directions from its antenna. For how many miles along the highway can the radio signals of *both* stations be received?

   A. 50
   B. 75
   C. 100
   D. 125
   E. 150

SLOPE OF A LINE

Memorize the formula for the slope of a line in a coordinate plane:

$$\boxed{\begin{array}{c}FLASH \\ CARDS\end{array}} \quad m = \frac{y_1 - y_2}{x_1 - x_2} \quad \begin{array}{l}\leftarrow (rise) \\ \leftarrow (run)\end{array}$$

Make sure the difference of the *y* coordinates (the "rise") is in the *numerator* and the difference of the *x* coordinates (the "run") is in the *denominator*. The order of the points does not matter as long as the order in the numerator is the same as that in the denominator.

SOME IMPORTANT CHARACTERISTICS OF SLOPE

- Lines with a *positive* slope angle up to the right, and lines with a *negative* slope angle up to the left:

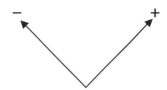

- Vertical lines have an *undefined* slope, and horizontal lines have a slope of *zero*:

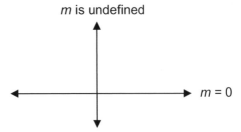

- The greater the absolute value of the slope, the steeper the line:

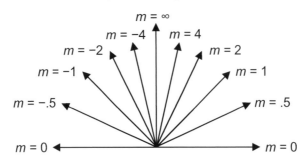

USING SLOPE TO FIND UNKNOWN COORDINATES

These problems will ask you to solve for an unknown *coordinate* of a point on a line. If there are two missing coordinates, you should pick a number for one of the coordinates, and then follow the method below.

Use the method below. An example follows.

1. **Find the slope of the line.** If the line appears to go through the origin, then point (0,0) can be used as one of the points on the line.

2. **Use the equation for slope with one of the known points and the point with the missing coordinate.** Set the equation equal to the slope found in step 1.

3. **Use algebra to find the missing coordinate.**

(EX) In the standard (x,y) coordinate plane below, the three points lie on the same line. What is the value of b?

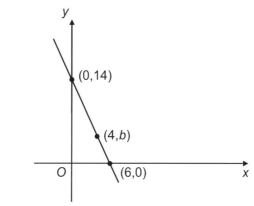

A. $3\frac{3}{4}$
B. 4
C. $4\frac{1}{4}$
D. $4\frac{1}{3}$
E. $4\frac{2}{3}$

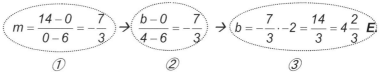

$$m = \frac{14-0}{0-6} = -\frac{7}{3} \quad \rightarrow \quad \frac{b-0}{4-6} = -\frac{7}{3} \quad \rightarrow \quad b = -\frac{7}{3} \cdot -2 = \frac{14}{3} = 4\frac{2}{3} \; \textbf{E.}$$

① ② ③

SLOPE OF PARALLEL AND PERPENDICULAR LINES

For the following examples, the slope of line a is m_a, and the slope of line b is m_b.

When two lines are parallel, their slopes are *equal*:

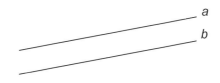

FLASH CARDS

Line a is parallel to line b.

$$m_a = m_b$$

When two lines are perpendicular, use the following formula:

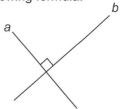

FLASH CARDS

$$m_a = -\frac{1}{m_b} \quad \text{(or vice versa)}$$

Try the following slope lesson problem:

17. The standard (x,y) coordinate plane has four quadrants, as labeled below. If a line has one point in quadrant II and another point in quadrant IV, which of the following gives the possible values of the slope of the line? (Note: the points do not lie on the x-axis or y-axis.)

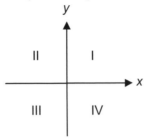

A. Any negative real number
B. 0
C. Any positive real number
D. No real numbers
E. Cannot be determined from the information given

EQUATION OF A LINE

THE SLOPE-INTERCEPT EQUATION

The most common equation of a line found on the ACT is called the *slope-intercept* equation. This equation is convenient because, at a glance, it gives you the *slope* of the line and the place where the line crosses the *y-axis* of the coordinate plane (called the *y-intercept*).

> *FLASH CARDS*
>
> $$y = mx + b$$
> Slope-intercept equation of a line

In the equation above, *m* is the slope, *b* is the y-intercept, and *x* and *y* are the variables. The variables x and y are the coordinates of points on the line—for example, if you know an x coordinate of a point, you could use the equation to find the y coordinate.

OTHER LINEAR EQUATIONS → THE SLOPE-INTERCEPT FORM

If the equation for a line is not in the slope-intercept form, use basic number operations to rearrange the equation so that y is alone on the left side of the equal sign. See the following example:

(EX) What is the y-intercept of the line defined by the equation $(y + 2) = 2(x - 1)$?

> *The line is not in slope-intercept form. Use the distributive property to get rid of the parentheses from the x side of the equation, and then isolate the y:*
>
> $y + 2 = 2x - 2$ → $y = 2x - 2 - 2$ → $y = 2x - 4$ → y-intercept = **−4**

FINDING THE SLOPE-INTERCEPT EQUATION

When you are given the y-intercept and the slope of a line, finding the slope-intercept equation is straightforward. Just plug values for m and b into the slope-intercept equation above.

You can also find the slope-intercept equation when you are given:

1. **A point on the line and the slope of the line**

   OR

2. **Two points on the line**

Use the following method:

1. Identify or calculate the slope of the line (m).
2. Plug the x and y values of a given point and the slope (m) from step 1 into the slope-intercept equation.
3. Solve for b.
4. Rewrite the equation with x and y as variables: $y = mx + b$.

(EX) What is the slope-intercept equation of the line that goes through the point (2,0) and has a slope of 3?

> ① *The slope is given as 3. The slope-intercept equation is:*
>
> $y = 3x + b$.
>
> ② *Plug x = 2 and y = 0 into the equation:* $y = 3x + b$ → $0 = 3 \cdot 2 + b$
>
> ③ $b = -6$
>
> ④ $y = 3x - 6$

THE LINE $y = x$

This line shows up frequently. The slope of the line is 1 and the y-intercept is 0. The equation ($y = x$) makes clear that for each point on the line, the x-coordinate equals the y-coordinate (for example: (1,1), (−20,−20), etc.). Note that the line makes a 45° angle with the x-axis (assuming the x and y scales are the same, as they usually are). See the following figure:

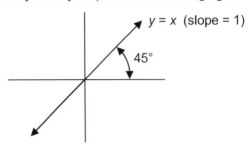

WHERE'S THE x? WHERE'S THE y?

Equations that involve only the x variable are vertical lines. Equations that involve only the y variable are horizontal lines. Write the equations for the following lines:

(EX) Line A: $x = -6$

1. Line B:

2. Line C:

3. Line D:

4. Line E:

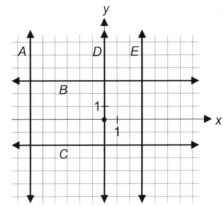

_____

Try the following line equation lesson problems:

10. The point $(2,p)$ lies on the line with equation $y - 3 = 2(x - 4)$. What is the value of p?

    A. −1
    B. 0
    C. 1
    D. 2
    E. 3

37. In the figure below, if line *l* has a slope of $\frac{3}{2}$, what is the *y*-intercept of *l*?

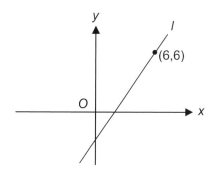

F. −1

G. $-\frac{3}{2}$

H. −2

J. −3

K. −6

INTERSECTING LINES

Equations that define lines are called *linear* equations. When you have two linear equations, the "solution" can be found algebraically using methods taught in the Algebra chapter (using Substitution or the Simultaneous Equations technique). But what does this solution mean? Graphically speaking, the solution (when there is one) is the *point of intersection* of the two lines. For example:

(EX) When graphed in the standard (*x*,*y*) coordinate plane, the lines *y* = 5 and *y* = 5*x* − 5 intersect at what point?

A. (0,5)

B. (0,−5)

C. (1,5)

D. (2,−5)

E. (2,5)

Do not graph these line problems! Just solve the equations, either by stacking the equations as taught in the Simultaneous Equations lesson, or by substitution, which is convenient here:

y = 5 → 5 = 5x − 5 → 10 = 5x → x = 2 → Plug x = 2 into the second equation, or just look at the first equation: y = 5. So the point of intersection is (2,5). **E.**

INFINITE SOLUTIONS

When would two lines have an infinite number of solutions?—when the two lines are in fact *the same line*. In other words, if the equations of both lines are simplified to point-intercept forms (*y* = *mx* + *b*), the slopes will be the same and the *y*-intercepts will be the same.

- Infinite solutions: **Same slopes, same *y*-intercepts**

NO SOLUTIONS

When would two lines have no solutions?—when the two lines are *parallel*. The lines never cross. In other words, if both equations are simplified to point-intercept forms, the slopes will be the same but the y-intercepts will be *different*.

- No solutions: **Same slopes, different y-intercepts**

You may want to make flash cards to help memorize the rules above.

Try the following lesson problem:

42. For which of the following values of k will the system of equations below have <u>no</u> solutions?

$$y = 2x + 20$$
$$y = kx + 40$$

- A. -10
- B. -2
- C. 0
- D. 2
- E. 10

———————

LINES HOMEWORK

4. If R is the midpoint of segment QS below, then $x = ?$

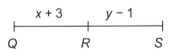

- A. $y - 4$
- B. $y - 3$
- C. $y - 2$
- D. $y - 1$
- E. y

Continued ➜

10. If point C is the midpoint of segment AB and point D is the midpoint of segment CB, which of the following is NOT true?

   F. $AC - CD = DB$
   G. $CB < AD$
   H. $AB - CD = AD$
   J. $CB < AC$
   K. $3DB = AD$

32. In the figure below, line l passes through the origin. What is the value of $\dfrac{b}{a}$?

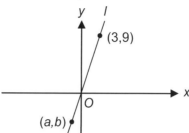

   A. -3
   B. $-\frac{1}{3}$
   C. $\frac{1}{3}$
   D. $\frac{2}{3}$
   E. 3

53. In the standard (x,y) coordinate plane below, line b is perpendicular to line a. Which of the following is the equation for line a?

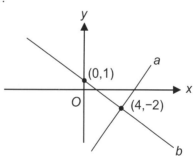

   F. $y = -\frac{3}{4}x + 1$
   G. $y = \frac{3}{4}x - \frac{10}{3}$
   H. $y = -\frac{3}{4}x - \frac{22}{3}$
   J. $y = \frac{4}{3}x - \frac{10}{3}$
   K. $y = \frac{4}{3}x - \frac{22}{3}$

Continued ➔

56. The marks on the number line below are equally spaced. What is the value of *A*?

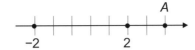

A. $\dfrac{4}{5}$

B. $1\dfrac{3}{5}$

C. $3\dfrac{3}{5}$

D. 4

E. $4\dfrac{1}{5}$

20-hour program: Jump to the end of this chapter and complete relevant questions from Geometry Worksheets 1 and 2 and relevant test corrections for Test 2. Then move on to the Functions chapter.

7. MORE CIRCLES

We have already discussed the area and circumference of a circle. We have also looked at the sum of the degrees in a circle (360°). There are a few more topics that have to do with circles.

EQUATION OF A CIRCLE

The equation of a circle in the standard (x,y) coordinate plane is shown below. While most equation-of-circle problems can be solved using the Pick Tricks (for example, see Algebra Worksheet 1, #41), you'll save time by memorizing the equation:

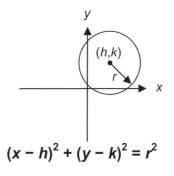

$$(x - h)^2 + (y - k)^2 = r^2$$

To identify circle equation problems, make sure you can identify the equation of a circle in its standard form. You'll either see the equation in the question or in the answer choices.

(EX) In the (x,y) coordinate plane, what is the radius of the circle defined by the equation:

$(x + 2)^2 + (y + 2)^2 = 25$?

A. 2
B. 5
C. 10
D. 25
E. 50

Once you know the equation, this problem is not difficult. Just remember that the number on the right hand side (25) is the radius **squared**:

$r^2 = 25 \rightarrow r = 5$ **B.**

It's unlikely that you'll have to know the equations of other conic sections (parabolas, ellipses, and hyperbolas). If you've covered these in school, however, you may want to review your notes, just in case one of these problems shows up. Even if you're *not* familiar with these equations, you can hopefully use the Pick Tricks or your graphing calculator to get out of a jam.

SECTORS OF CIRCLES

A *sector* of a circle is like a piece of pizza. Below are the three most common measurements we can use to evaluate the size of a sector:

1. **Angle** – this is the measure of $\angle AOB$ in the figure below. It is sometimes called the "**measure of arc *AB***" or the "**central angle**" to arc *AB*.

2. **Arc length** – this is the actual curved distance from point *A* to point *B* along the circle.

3. **Area** – this is the area between line segments *AO* and *BO* and arc *AB* (shaded below).

We can write each of these measurements as a *part over whole* ratio, where the *part* is relating to the sector of the circle and the *whole* is relating to the entire circle. The trick to sector problems is to realize that each of these ratios is *equal*:

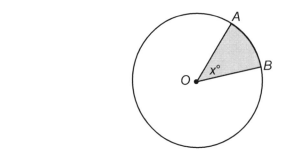

$$\frac{\text{part (sector)}}{\text{whole (circle)}} \rightarrow \frac{x}{360°} = \frac{\text{length of arc } \textit{AB}}{\text{circumference of circle}} = \frac{\text{area of sector } \textit{AOB}}{\text{area of circle}}$$

Look for circles with sectors, but don't confuse these problems with circle-graphs (pie-graphs), which also have sectors drawn.

The method below should be used for circle sector problems. An example follows.

1. **Identify which *two* of the three measurements of the sector are mentioned in the problem.** Remember, the three measurements are *degrees*, *arc length*, and *area*. Usually, only *two* of them will be tested in a problem.

2. **Set up a proportion problem with the two appropriate ratios above, and solve for the missing information.** Keep in mind that if the radius (or diameter) of the circle is given, then you can calculate the circumference or area of the circle.

(EX) If the area of circle *O* below is 240 in^2 and the area of sector *AOB* is 20 in^2, what is the value of *x*?

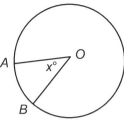

A. 25
B. 30
C. 35
D. 40
E. 45

① *The two measurements are **degrees** and **area**.*

degrees   area

② $\dfrac{x}{360} = \dfrac{20}{240}$ → *x = 30* **B.**

SECTORS OF CIRCLES: OTHER MEASURMENTS

We've looked at the *areas*, *arc lengths*, and *angles* of sectors, but there are other ways sectors can be measured, including:

- Minutes (or hours) on a clock (think of the sector formed by the sweep of a hand)
- Volume or weight of a disk
- Any quantity (population, dollars, etc.) on a pie graph

Just remember that the part-over-whole ratios of any two measurements will always equal.

REVOLUTION PROBLEMS

These problems have to do with a rolling circle or wheel. When a circle rolls *one* revolution without slipping, it will travel a distance equal to the *circumference* ($2\pi r$) of the circle. This is a *known relationship* that you must memorize. You will use this known relationship as part of a proportion problem:

$$\frac{\text{revolutions}}{\text{distance (units)}} \rightarrow \frac{1}{2\pi r \text{ (circumference)}} = \frac{\text{total revolutions}}{\text{total distance}}$$

(EX) A wheel with circumference of 10 inches rolls a distance of 40 inches without slipping. How many revolutions did the wheel make?

A. 4
B. 8
C. 10
D. 40
E. 400

$\dfrac{\text{revolutions}}{\text{inches}} \dfrac{1}{10} = \dfrac{x}{40}$ → *x = 4 revolutions* **A.**

MORE CIRCLES LESSON PROBLEMS

32. If the length of arc *AB* in the circle below with center *O* is 5 and angle *AOB* is 120°, what is the circumference of the circle?

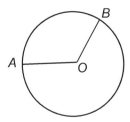

    A. 10
    B. 15
    C. 5π
    D. 10π
    E. 100

41. Which of the following equations represents a circle in the standard (*x,y*) coordinate plane that has center (3,5) and radius $\sqrt{5}$ units?

    F. $(x-3)^2 + (y-5)^2 = 5$
    G. $(x+3)^2 + (y+5)^2 = 5$
    H. $(x-3)^2 + (y-5)^2 = \sqrt{5}$
    J. $(x+3)^2 + (y+5)^2 = \sqrt{5}$
    K. $(x-3)^2 - (y-5)^2 = \sqrt{5}$

51. A device measures distance by counting the revolutions of a wheel with a diameter of 6 inches. What is the distance, in feet, if the device measures 1000 revolutions?

    A. 200π
    B. 400π
    C. 500π
    D. 1000π
    E. 6000π

18. Each of the 200 students at George Washington High School voted for his or her favorite American president. The results of the poll are given in the table below.

President	Number of Voters
George Washington	60
Abraham Lincoln	58
Thomas Jefferson	35
Franklin D. Roosevelt	17
Other	30

If the information in the table were converted into a circle graph (pie chart), then the central angle of the sector that voted for George Washington would measure how many degrees?

   A. 60°
   B. 100°
   C. 108°
   D. 110°
   E. 252°

35. In circle *O* below, *x* = 36. What is the area of sector *AOB*?

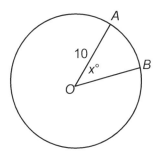

   F. 2π
   G. 10
   H. 20
   J. 10π
   K. 100π

Continued ➔

50. Which of the following is an equation of the circle in the standard (x,y) coordinate plane shown below?

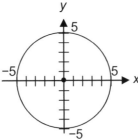

A. $x^2 - y^2 = 25$
B. $x^2 + y^2 = 25$
C. $x^2 + y^2 = 5$
D. $(x + y)^2 = 5$
E. $x + y = 5$

56. Kevin had a bicycle with 30-inch diameter wheels. He decided to replace the front wheel with a 20-inch diameter wheel. If he traveled 300 feet on the modified bicycle, how many more full revolutions did the front wheel make than the back wheel?

F. 19
G. 20
H. 21
J. 22
K. 60

8. SOLIDS AND VOLUME

Solids are shapes that occupy three dimensions, such as cubes, cylinders, or rectangular boxes. Most solids problems are *volume* problems that deal with rectangular solids or cubes. Though less common, some problems will require you to know the formula for the volume of a cylinder.

Volume – the amount of space occupied by a solid or a substance.

Surface area – the sum of the areas of all the faces of a solid.

RECTANGULAR SOLIDS

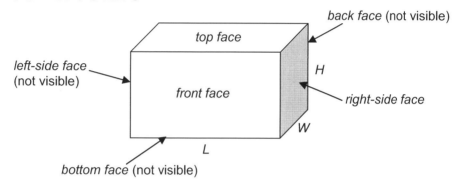

$$V = L \cdot W \cdot H$$

To find surface area, notice that there are 3 different rectangular faces (the 3 faces you can see above), and each one has an opposite rectangular face of the exact same size. For example, the front face (visible above) is the exact same size as the back face (*not* visible above). This can help you find the formula for surface area. Don't memorize this. Just make sure you understand how we found it:

$$SA = 2LH + 2LW + 2WH$$

Try the following lesson problems, based on the rectangular solid below:

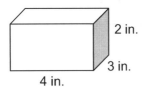

2 in.

3 in.

4 in.

1. What is the area of the front face?

2. What is the area of the top face?

3. What is the area of the right-side face?

4. What is the total surface area of the box?

5. What is the volume of the box?

CUBES

Since all sides of a cube are the same length, the formulas for volume and surface area are simplified:

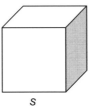

s

$$V = s^3$$
$$SA = 6s^2$$

SURFACE AREA → VOLUME

You might need to find the *volume* of a cube when the *surface area* is given. Consider a cube with a surface area of 600 in^2:

1. What is the area of one face?

2. What is the length of an edge?

3. What is the volume of the cube?

The above example illustrates the following method for finding the volume of a cube when the surface area is given:

1. *Divide* the surface area by 6 to find the area of one face.

2. Take the *square root* of this area to find the length of a side.

3. *Cube* this length to find the volume of the cube.

DIAGONALS OF RECTANGULAR SOLIDS

You may be asked to calculate the length of a rectangular solid's *diagonal*, which is a segment that connects a pair of opposite vertices. The formula is below.

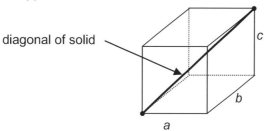

diagonal of solid

$$\text{diagonal} = \sqrt{a^2 + b^2 + c^2}$$

FLASH CARDS

Note that a *cube*, where $a = b = c$, uses the same formula.

If you're interested, here's the proof for the general formula:

1. Let e = the diagonal of the bottom face and d = diagonal of the solid.
2. Triangle 1: Use the Pythagorean Theorem to find e: $e = \sqrt{a^2 + b^2}$
3. Triangle 2: Use the Pythagorean Theorem again to find d:
   $d = \sqrt{e^2 + c^2}$ → $e^2 = a^2 + b^2$ → $d = \sqrt{a^2 + b^2 + c^2}$

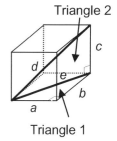

Triangle 2

Triangle 1

VOLUME OF PRISMS

A *prism* is a three-dimensional shape that has the same cross section along its entire length. Prisms have two *bases*, one at each end. Below is a prism with a triangular cross section:

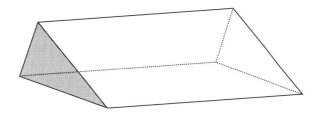

Below is a prism with a circular cross section (a cylinder):

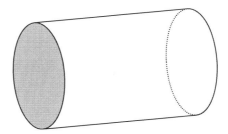

The volume of any prism is:

$$V = \text{Area of base} \times \text{Length of prism}$$

Try the following lesson problem:

47. The figure below shows the elliptical cross section of a 20 foot long storage tank. If the area of the cross section is found to be 18π square feet, what is the volume, in cubic feet, of the tank?

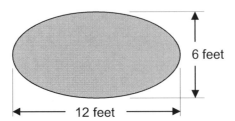

    A. 1440
    B. 1240
    C. 405π
    D. 360π
    E. 180π

VOLUME FITTING (AND AREA FITTING) PROBLEMS

Some volume problems will ask you to find the volume or number of small solids (usually cubes) that can *fit* into a larger volume or solid. These problems are very similar to *area fitting* problems, so we'll talk about area problems too (yes, we know we're in the "Solids and Volume" section; bear with us).

> Area fitting problems will ask how many shapes can fit into a larger shape. Volume fitting problems will ask how many solids can fit into a larger solid.

The method for area and volume fitting problems is straightforward:

1. For area fitting problems, find the *areas* of the large shape and the small shape. For volume fitting problems, find the *volumes* of the large solid and the small solid.
2. Divide the large area or volume by the small area or volume.

$$\text{Number of } \textit{small areas} \text{ that will fit into the } \textit{larger area} = \frac{\textbf{Large Area}}{\textbf{Small Area}}$$

$$\text{Number of } \textit{small volumes} \text{ that will fit into the } \textit{larger volume} = \frac{\textbf{Large Volume}}{\textbf{Small Volume}}$$

(EX) How many 24 inch × 24 inch square tiles are needed to cover the 20 foot × 30 foot floor shown below?

20'

30'

A. 50
B. 100
C. 150
D. 200
E. 600

Divide the area of the floor by the area of one tile (don't forget to make sure your units are the same—we'll use feet below):

$$\frac{20 \cdot 30}{2 \cdot 2} = 150 \text{ tiles } \boldsymbol{C.}$$

Try the following lesson problem:

48. A cylindrical cup has a radius of 2 inches and a height of 6 inches. A cylindrical water jug has a radius of 10 inches and a height of 12 inches. If the jug is full of water, how many cups of water can be filled before the jug is empty?

   A. 5
   B. 20
   C. 35
   D. 50
   E. 65

———————

11. Elisa has two boxes, each with lengths 10 inches, widths 8 inches, and heights 6 inches. If she wants to ship these boxes in a third, larger box with length 20 inches, width 10 inches, and height 8 inches, how much additional space, in cubic inches, will be left in the larger box?

   A. 600
   B. 640
   C. 680
   D. 720
   E. 1120

29. If cube A has an edge of length 2 centimeters and cube B has an edge of length 3 centimeters, what is the ratio of the volume of cube A to the volume of cube B?

   F. 3:2
   G. 8:27
   H. 5:9
   J. 4:9
   K. 2:3

32. A steel worker is going to pour 300 cubic inches of molten steel into the rectangular mold shown below. If the molten steel is spread evenly over the entire base of the mold, what will be the approximate height, in inches, of the molten steel?

6 inches

5 inches

30 inches

- A. 0.5
- B. 1
- C. 2
- D. 4
- E. 6

54. Soap cubes, each with a total surface area of 54 square centimeters, are stacked in a cube box. If the box has a volume of 729 cubic centimeters, what is the maximum number of soap cubes that can fit in the box?

- F. 13
- G. 27
- H. 100
- J. 192
- K. 8304

9. GEOMETRY PROBLEMS

PRACTICE PROBLEMS

The following worksheets and practice problems (from Test 1 in *The Real ACT Prep Guide*, 3rd Edition) test techniques taught in this chapter. It is very important to look back to the lessons in this chapter and review the techniques while completing these problems. Try to determine which technique relates to each problem and apply the methods taught in the tutorial. Do not time yourself on these problems. The problems are provided to give you an opportunity to practice, and hopefully master, the techniques in this tutorial before you apply them on real ACTs in a timed setting.

- ☐ Geometry Worksheet 1
- ☐ Geometry Worksheet 2
- ☐ Geometry Worksheet 3
- ☐ Geometry Worksheet 4
- ☐ **Test 1**: 6, 17, 20, 22, 25, 27^{30}, 30, 31, 33, 35, 37, 38, 39, 40, 41, 45, 46, 47, 52*, 55
  (see Step 3 under "Test Corrections" below)

[30] Questions marked with a "30" are covered by the **30- and 40-hour programs**.
*Not entirely covered by tutorial.

You might choose to space the above assignments out over the course of your studies. See the "Schedules" section in the introduction for more details about programs.

TEST CORRECTIONS

After each practice test is graded, you should correct Geometry problems that you missed or left blank. There are three steps to correcting the practice tests:

1. The Geometry questions for each test are listed below. Go back to your answer sheet for the corresponding test and circle the question numbers below that you missed (or guessed on, if you kept track of your guesses).

   - ☐ **Test 2**: 6, 7, 13^{30}, 14, 16, 17, 19, 21, 25, 30, 31, 33, 38, 43, 47, 48, 50, 51, 52, 57
   - ☐ **Test 3**: 4, 8, 15, 17, 21, 28, 30, 32, 35, 38, 39^{30}, 41, 42^{30}, 43^{30}, 45^{30},
   - ☐ **Test 4**: 6, 10, 14, 15, 17, 20, 24, 26, 38, 39, 43^{30}, 44, 45, 46^{30}, 57, 60^{30}
   - ☐ **Test 5**: 8, 13, 15^{30}, 16^{30}*, 17, 18, 22, 23, 29, 30, 31, 33, 35, 36^{30}, 38, 42, 44, 54, 55^{30}, 59

[30] Questions marked with a "30" are covered by the **30- and 40-hour programs**.
*Not entirely covered by tutorial.

2. Correct the problems in *The Real ACT Study Guide*. As you correct the problems, go back to the tutorial and review the techniques. The idea is to: (1) identify techniques that have given you trouble, (2) go back to the tutorial so you can review and strengthen these techniques, and (3) apply these techniques to the specific problems on which you struggled.

3. If you have trouble identifying the best technique to use on a problem, see the Techniques Reference information in Chapter VIII, starting on page 453.

GEOMETRY WORKSHEET 1*

Problem numbers represent the *approximate* level of difficulty for each problem (out of 60).
*20-hour program: You may choose to skip 50 and 56.

12. In the figure below, Z is on line AB and $AB \parallel XY$. Which of the following is NOT true?

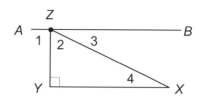

    A. $m\angle 3 = m\angle 4$
    B. $m\angle 3 + m\angle 4 = 90°$
    C. $m\angle 1 = 90°$
    D. $m\angle 2 + m\angle 3 = 90°$
    E. $m\angle 1 + m\angle 2 + m\angle 4 = 180°$

23. The coordinates of point A are (p,q), with $p \neq 0$ and $q \neq 0$. If $p = -q$, then A must be located in which of the 4 quadrants of the standard (x,y) coordinate plane labeled below?

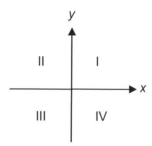

    F. I only
    G. II only
    H. I or III only
    J. I or IV only
    K. II or IV only

Continued ➔

25. You want to build a square garden that will be fenced on all four sides. If you have enough material to build 30 feet of fence, what can be the maximum area, to the nearest square foot, of your garden?

   A. 225
   B. 128
   C. 64
   D. 60
   E. 56

27. A rope is stretched straight from the top of a 50 foot vertical tower to a point on the ground 120 feet from the base of the tower. Assuming the ground is level, how long, in feet, is the rope?

   F. 125
   G. 130
   H. 135
   J. 140
   K. 145

31. Which of the following lines has the largest slope?

   A. $y = 2x + 2$
   B. $y = 2x + 4$
   C. $y = 4x + 2$
   D. $2y = 4x + 4$
   E. $2y = 6x + 2$

44. In right triangle ABC below, points A, D, and C are collinear and line segment BD bisects $\angle ABC$. If the measure of $\angle ACB$ is 35°, as shown, what is the measure of $\angle BDC$?

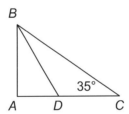

   F. 110°
   G. 112.5°
   H. 115°
   J. 117.5°
   K. 120°

Continued ➜

46. In △ABC shown below, $\overline{DE}$ is parallel to $\overline{AC}$. The length of $\overline{AB}$ is 8 inches, the length of $\overline{BC}$ is 9 inches, and the length of $\overline{DE}$ is 4 inches. If points D and E are the midpoints of $\overline{AB}$ and $\overline{BC}$, respectively, which of the following is the length, in inches, of $\overline{AC}$?

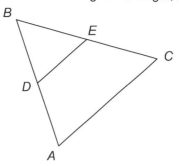

A. 8
B. 8½
C. 9
D. 9½
E. 10

50. As shown below, a clock has a minute hand with a tip that is 6 inches from the center of the clock. To the nearest inch, how far does the tip of the minute hand travel between 12:05 PM and 12:30 PM?

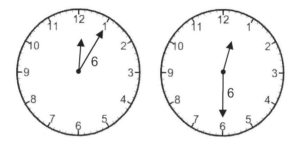

F. 12
G. 13
H. 14
J. 15
K. 16

Continued ➔

51. The area of trapezoid *ABCD*, shown below, is 108 square inches. If the lengths of the bases are 14 and 22, what is the height, *h*, in inches, of the trapezoid?

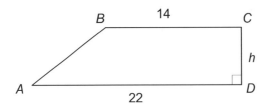

A. 5½
B. 6
C. 6½
D. 7
E. 7½

56. Which of the following is an equation of the circle in the standard (*x,y*) coordinate plane shown below?

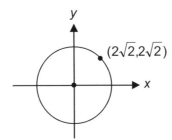

F. $x^2 + y^2 = 16$
G. $x^2 + y^2 = 8$
H. $x^2 + y^2 = 4$
J. $x^2 + y^2 = 4\sqrt{2}$
K. $x^2 + y^2 = 2\sqrt{2}$

PRACTICE TEST

30- and 40-hour programs: Now is a good time to take **Test 3** in the ACT book. (You should have already taken Test 2, and Test 1 is being used for practice problems.) If you have any questions about taking these tests, review "Taking Practice Tests" in this tutorial's introduction.

GEOMETRY WORKSHEET 2*

Problem numbers represent the *approximate* level of difficulty for each problem (out of 60).
***20-hour program:** You may choose to skip 58.

6. On a number line, if point A has coordinate −5 and point B has coordinate 3, what is the coordinate of the point that is ¾ of the way from A to B?

    A. −1
    B. 0
    C. 1
    D. 3
    E. 6

12. In the triangle shown below, what is the sum of a, b, and c?

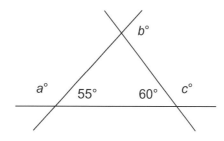

    F. 375
    G. 360
    H. 245
    J. 180
    K. Cannot be
        determined
        from the given
        information

25. In the figure below, ΔI is similar to ΔII, with lengths given in inches. What is the perimeter of ΔII?

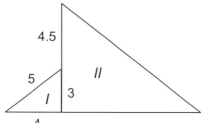

    A. 23.5
    B. 26
    C. 28.5
    D. 30
    E. 36

Continued ➜

26. In the circle with center O shown below, which of following statements is NOT true?

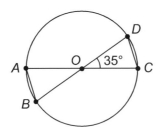

F. $AO = DO$
G. $AB = DC$
H. measure of arc $ABD = 215°$
J. $\angle AOD = 145°$
K. $\angle ABO = 70°$

33. The figure below shows square XYZO, with vertices X and Z lying on circle O. If the area of the square is 25 square centimeters, what is the area, in square centimeters, of the circle?

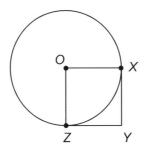

A. 25π
B. 50π
C. 100π
D. 250π
E. 625π

Continued →

41. What is the distance in the standard (x,y) coordinate plane between the points $(-12,-5)$ and $(12,5)$?

    F. $\sqrt{13}$
    G. $\sqrt{26}$
    H. 13
    J. 26
    K. 34

56. In the standard (x,y) coordinate plane, lines a and b intersect at point $(-2,3)$ and lines a and c intersect at point $(-2,-2)$. Which of the following is an equation for line a?

    A. $y = -2x - 6$
    B. $y = -2x - 1$
    C. $y = -2x + 3$
    D. $x = -2$
    E. Cannot be determined from the information given

Continued ➜

58. The cross section of a 10 foot long trough used for watering cattle is an equilateral triangle. If the trough is filled with water to a depth of 6 inches, as shown below, what is the volume, in cubic inches, of water in the trough?

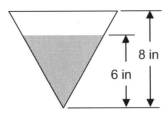

8 in

6 in

F. $320\sqrt{3}$

G. $360\sqrt{3}$

H. $640\sqrt{3}$

J. $720\sqrt{3}$

K. $1{,}440\sqrt{3}$

60. In $\triangle ABC$ below, the measure of $\angle A$ is 45° and the measure $\angle C$ is 30°. What is the perimeter of the triangle?

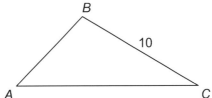

B

10

A

C

A. $5+5\sqrt{3}$

B. $10+5\sqrt{2}+5\sqrt{3}$

C. $15+5\sqrt{5}$

D. $10+10\sqrt{3}$

E. $15+5\sqrt{2}+5\sqrt{3}$

GEOMETRY WORKSHEET 3*

Problem numbers represent the *approximate* level of difficulty for each problem (out of 60).
*20-hour program: You may choose to skip 52.

2. Chuck wants to determine the height of a wall. He props a 10-foot long ladder against the wall, so that the top of the ladder meets the top of the wall and the base of the ladder is 2 feet from the base of the wall, as shown below. What is the height, in feet, of the wall?

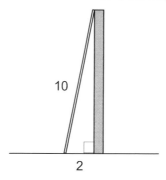

- **A.** 8
- **B.** 9
- **C.** $\sqrt{96}$
- **D.** $\sqrt{104}$
- **E.** $\sqrt{112}$

7. In the figure below, $l_1 \parallel l_2$ and $l_3 \parallel l_4$. What is the measure, in degrees, of angle x?

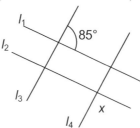

- **F.** 85
- **G.** 95
- **H.** 100
- **J.** 105
- **K.** Cannot be determined from the given information

Continued ➔

26. In the figure below, vertex E of $\triangle ADE$ lies on square $ABCD$. What is the ratio of the area of $\triangle ADE$ to the area of square $ABCD$?

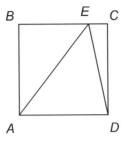

A. 1:2
B. 3:4
C. 1:1
D. 2:1
E. Cannot be
   determined
   from the given
   information

35. Which of the following could be the equation for the graph of the line shown in the standard (x,y) coordinate plane below?

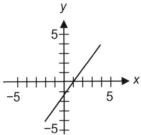

A. $y = -\frac{4}{3}$

B. $y = -\frac{4}{3}x + \frac{4}{3}$

C. $y = -\frac{4}{3}x - \frac{4}{3}$

D. $y = \frac{4}{3}x - \frac{4}{3}$

E. $y = \frac{4}{3}x$

Continued ➔

47. The target below is made up of three circles with the same center. The radius of the small circle is one-third of the radius of the middle circle and one-fifth of the radius of the large circle. If the radius of the small circle is 2, what is the area of the shaded region?

    F. 36π
    G. 64π
    H. 68π
    J. 72π
    K. 100π

48. In the circle below, O is the center. Chord $\overline{AB}$ is 8 inches long and line segment $\overline{OC}$ is 3 inches long. What is the circumference of the circle?

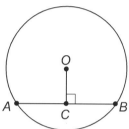

    A. 5π
    B. 7π
    C. 8π
    D. 9π
    E. 10π

Continued ➜

52. The circle below is inscribed in a square with sides of length 4 units. What is the perimeter, in units, of the shaded region shown below?

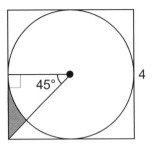

A. $2 + \dfrac{\pi}{2}$

B. $2\sqrt{2} + \dfrac{\pi}{2}$

C. $2\sqrt{3} + \dfrac{\pi}{2}$

D. $4\sqrt{2} + 2\pi$

E. $4\sqrt{3} + 2\pi$

55. In the standard (x,y) coordinate plane, point M with coordinates $(4,1)$ is the midpoint of line segment AB. If B has coordinates (p,q), what are the coordinates of A, in terms of p and q?

F. $(8 + p, 2 + q)$
G. $(8 - p, 2 - q)$
H. $(p - 8, q - 2)$
J. $(4 - p, 1 - q)$
K. $(p - 4, q - 1)$

Continued ➔

58. In hexagon *ABCDEF* below, ∠*A* is given. What is the measure of angles *B* + *C* + *D* + *E* + *F*?

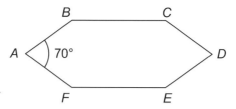

    A. 630°
    B. 650°
    C. 670°
    D. 700°
    E. 720°

GEOMETRY WORKSHEET 4*

Problem numbers represent the *approximate* level of difficulty for each problem (out of 60).
*20-hour program: You may choose to skip 14.

14. A rectangular water tank 4 ft wide, 8 ft long, and 10 ft high is filled to 20% of capacity. How many additional cubic feet of water must be added to the tank so that it is 30% full?

   A. 32
   B. 64
   C. 96
   D. 160
   E. 256

24. The lengths of corresponding sides of two similar right triangles are in the ratio 3 to 4. If the hypotenuse of the larger triangle is 10 centimeters, then how long, in centimeters, is the length of the hypotenuse of the smaller triangle?

   F. 5
   G. $6\frac{2}{3}$
   H. $7\frac{1}{2}$
   J. 10
   K. $13\frac{1}{3}$

27. In the figure below, square *ABCD* has sides of length 5 inches, and the four right triangles are congruent. What is the area of the shaded region?

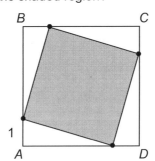

   A. 25
   B. 17
   C. $\sqrt{17}$
   D. 8
   E. 2

Continued ➔

30. Thomas finds the treasure map shown below. The treasure is buried exactly halfway between points *A* and *B*. If he overlays a standard (*x*,*y*) coordinate plan onto the map, with the origin at the bottom left corner, he finds that the coordinates of points *A* and *B* are (2, 3) and (8,9), respectively. What are the coordinates of the buried treasure?

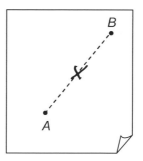

F. (4,5.5)
G. (4,6)
H. (5,5.5)
J. (5,6)
K. (10,12)

44. Trapezoid *PQRS* below is isosceles, with side lengths indicated and diagonals intersecting at *T*. What is the ratio of the length of segment *QT* to the length of segment *PT*?

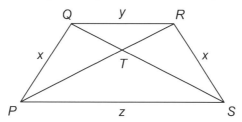

A. $\dfrac{x}{z}$

B. $\dfrac{y}{z}$

C. $\dfrac{y}{x}$

D. $\dfrac{x}{y}$

E. $\dfrac{z}{y}$

Continued ➜

45. In the figure below, segment *AB* is tangent to circle *C* and has a length of 12. If circle *C* has a radius of 4, what is the area of △*ABC*?

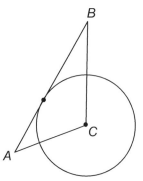

F. 12
G. 18
H. 24
J. 30
K. 36

49. Mary measures the distance around the perimeter of a circular track as 100 feet. What is the area, in square feet, enclosed by the circular track?

A. $\dfrac{10,000}{\pi}$

B. $\dfrac{2,500}{\pi}$

C. $\dfrac{1,000}{\pi}$

D. $\dfrac{50}{\pi}$

E. 100π

50. Points *A*, *B*, and *C* lie on the same line. If the length of *AB* is 6 and the length of *BC* is 3, what are the possible unit lengths for *AC*?

F. 3 only
G. 9 only
H. 3 and 9 only
J. Any number less than 2 or greater than 8
K. Any number greater than 2 or less than 8

Continued ➜

60. In the figure below, if *OA* has length $2b$, what is the slope of the segment?

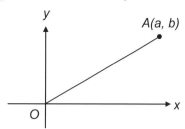

A. $\frac{1}{2}$

B. $\frac{\sqrt{3}}{3}$

C. 1

D. $\sqrt{3}$

E. Cannot be determined from the information given

V

FUNCTIONS

This chapter will cover all relevant topics related to functions, including their graphs.

1. FUNCTION BASICS

It is important to be familiar with basic function notation. A function is typically notated with a letter (often *f*) and parentheses containing a variable, number, or expression. The letter is the "name" of the function. Whatever is inside the parentheses is the *input* of the function. It may be helpful to think of a function as a *rule* that tells you how to find an *output* for any given input. For example:

$$f(x) = 2x + 3$$

The function above is called "the function *f*." The variable inside the parentheses, *x*, represents the input. The rule for this function is: "multiply the input by 2 and then add 3." Several examples are below.

> Look for the function notation, such as $f(x)$, $g(a)$, $P(2)$, etc. When functions are represented graphically, they may only contain the letter of the function without the parentheses (*f*, *g*, *P*, etc). Not surprisingly, the word "function" will also help you identify these problems.

We'll use $f(x) = 2x + 3$ for the following examples:

EX $f(2) = 2·2 + 3 = 7$

EX $f(\frac{a-3}{2}) = 2(\frac{a-3}{2}) + 3 = a - 3 + 3 = a$

EX $f(2 + 3) = f(5) = 2·5 + 3 = 13$

EX $f(g(x)) = 2[g(x)] + 3$

EX $f(a) = 2a + 3$

EX If $f(x) = -1$, what is the value of *x*?

$2x + 3 = -1 \rightarrow x = -2$

Use the following general method for function problems. The steps are illustrated in the example following the method.

1. **Identify the function rule.** It will usually be represented as an equation (as above), but functions can also be represented by graphs or tables. In all cases, the function will give you a *rule* that will allow you to find outputs for given inputs.
2. **Find another expression or equation that contains the function found in step 1.**
3. **Write the problem without the function notation by following the rule of the function.** The trick is to get rid of the function notation so you can solve using basic algebra.
4. Use basic math or algebra to answer the question.

$\textcircled{EX}$ Let the function g be defined by $g(x) = x + 3$. If $g(m) = 2m$, what is the value of m?

- **A.** 6
- **B.** 5
- **C.** 4
- **D.** 3
- **E.** 2

① The function rule is $g(x) = x + 3$

② The other equation is $g(m) = 2m$. (This equation also contains the function, g.)

③ We want to get rid of the $g(m)$ part of the equation above so we can use algebra. Using the function rule found in step 1 ($g(x) = x + 3$), we can write $g(m) = m + 3$. Substitute this into the second equation, found in step 2: $m + 3 = 2m$.

*④ Use algebra to solve for m: $3 = 2m - m$ → $m = 3$ **D.***

Try the following lesson problems. Answers to all lesson and homework problems in this chapter start on page 498. **Note:** The following problems are part of a *multi-question set*. Typically, for these multi-question sets: **regardless of the number, the first one will usually be easy, but the last one will usually be hard**. Watch out for these problems on the ACT.

Questions 23-25 refer to the following functions f and g.

$f(n) = n^2$

$g(n) = n^2 - n$

23. $f(6) - f(-6) =$

- **A.** −6
- **B.** 0
- **C.** 6
- **D.** 36
- **E.** 46

24. Which of the following is equivalent to $g(m + 1)$?

- **F.** $f(m) + 1$
- **G.** $f(m) + 3$
- **H.** $f(m) + m$
- **J.** $g(m) + 1$
- **K.** $g(m) + m$

25. Which of the following in an expression for $f(g(x))$?

- **A.** $x^4 + 2x^3 + x^2$
- **B.** $x^4 - 2x^3 + x^2$
- **C.** $x^4 - 2x^3 - x^2$
- **D.** $x^4 + x^2$
- **E.** $x^4 - x^2$

19. For the function $f(x) = -2x^3 - 3x^2 + 4$, what is the value of $f(-2)$?

    A. 8
    B. 4
    C. 0
    D. −12
    E. −24

21. A function h of the variables p and q is defined as $h(p,q) = p^p - q^q$. What is the value of $h(5,4)$?

    F. 1
    G. 9
    H. 399
    J. 2,869
    K. 3,125

51. Let the function g be defined by $g(x) = x + 4$. If $\frac{1}{2}g(\sqrt{a}) = 4$, what is the value of a?

    A. 4
    B. 6
    C. 16
    D. 36
    E. 64

Continued ➔

55. According to the table below, if $a = g(3)$, what is the value of $h(a)$?

x	g(x)	h(x)
0	3	4
1	1	3
2	2	2
3	0	1

F. 0
G. 1
H. 2
J. 3
K. 4

2. GRAPHS OF FUNCTIONS

The function $f(x)$ can be represented graphically on a coordinate plane. The x-axis represents the values of x (the inputs of the function) and the y-axis represents the values of $f(x)$ (the outputs of the function). There are several characteristics of these graphs that you should be comfortable with; they will be taught using the following graph of $f(x)$:

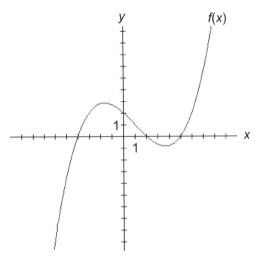

The following examples are based on the graph of $f(x)$ above:

(EX) $f(-2) \approx 3$

(EX) $f(1) \approx 1$

(EX) If $x < 0$ and $f(x) = 2$, then $x \approx -3$

(EX) For what values of x is $f(x) = 0$? $x = -4, 2, 5$

(EX) If $x = 0$, then $f(x) = 2$

(EX) What are the values of x for which $f(x)$ is positive? $-4 < x < 2$ and $x > 5$

(EX) What are the values of x for which $f(x)$ is negative? $x < -4$ and $2 < x < 5$

(EX) What are the approximate values of x for which $f(x)$ is increasing? $x < -2$ and $x > 3.5$

(EX) What are the approximate values of x for which $f(x)$ is decreasing? $-2 < x < 3.5$

Try the following lesson problems:

25. The graph of $f(x)$ in the standard (x,y) coordinate plane is shown below. What is the approximate x-coordinate for the point on the curve with y-coordinate -1?

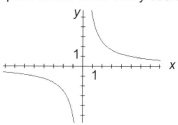

    A.   −25
    B.   −5
    C.   −1
    D.   0
    E.   5

52. Point A lies on the graph of $f(x)$ in the standard (x,y) coordinate plane shown below. What is the value of a?

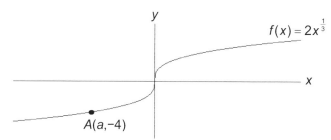

    F.   −4
    G.   −7
    H.   −7.5
    J.   −8
    K.   −8.5

ZEROS/ROOTS OF A FUNCTION

The points where a function crosses (or touches) the **x-axis** are called *zeros* or *roots* of that function. These points are easy enough to see graphically. For example, on the graph at the beginning of this section, the zeros (or roots) are −4, 2 and 5. Make sure you focus on the *x*-axis (not the *y*-axis).

EVEN AND ODD FUNCTIONS

An *even function* is one where $f(x) = f(-x)$. Below is an example of an even function. Notice that the right and left sides of the function (on either side of the y-axis) are mirror images of each other; in other words, the part of the graph to the right of the y-axis is *reflected* across the y-axis:

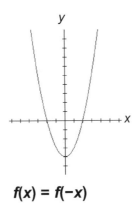

$$f(x) = f(-x)$$

An *odd function* is one where $f(x) = -f(-x)$. Below is an example of an odd function. Notice that the right and left sides of the function (on either side of the y-axis) are *upside-down* mirror images of each other; in other words, the part of the graph to the right of the y-axis is *rotated* *180°* about the origin:

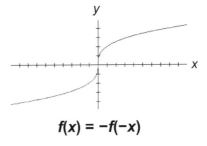

$$f(x) = -f(-x)$$

Try the following lesson problem:

50. The graph of $f(x) = 4\sin(0.5x)$ in the standard (x,y) coordinate plane is shown below. Which of the following is true?

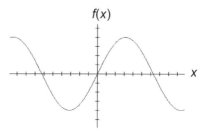

A. $f(x)$ is an even function
B. $f(x)$ is an odd function
C. $f(x)$ is neither even nor odd
D. $f(x)$ is symmetrical about the x axis
E. $f(x)$ is symmetrical about the y axis

GRAPHING CALCULATOR

If you have a graphing calculator, make sure you are comfortable using its graphing features. If you don't have a graphing calculator, don't worry—no problems on the ACT *require* you to graph functions. When the specific algebraic function is not given, your calculator's graphing features will generally *not* help you. But if the function *is* given, don't be shy. (Note: make sure to review the calculator guidelines on the ACT website. See the Calculators lesson in Chapter I.)

AXIS INTERCEPTS

You can find the x and y intercepts of a function using algebra.

1.   To find the y-intercept, let $x = 0$. Solve for y.
2.   To find the x-intercept(s), let $y = 0$. Solve for x.

Try the following lesson problem:

48. What is the y-intercept of the quadratic function f given by $f(x) = ax^2 + bx + c$ where a, b, and c are different positive integers?

A. a
B. a/c
C. b
D. b/c
E. c

SYMMETRY

When a function is symmetrical across an axis or a line, it appears to have a mirror image reflected across that axis or line. The quadratic function is a common function that is symmetrical across some vertical line. In the figure below, the line of symmetry is $x = 2$.

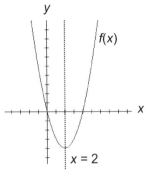

(EX) The figure above shows a quadratic function f. The vertex of f is $(2,-4)$. If two points (not shown) on f are $(-2,12)$ and $(a,12)$ and $a > 0$, what is the value for a?

A. 12
B. 6
C. 4
D. 2
E. 0

The function f is symmetrical across the line x = 2. Since the y-coordinates of the two points are the same, the two points will have the same horizontal distance from the line of symmetry. The first point is 4 horizontal units from the line, so "a" must be 2 + 4 = 6. ***B.***

————————

35. Based on the graph of the function *f* below, what are the values of *x* for which *f(x)* is negative?

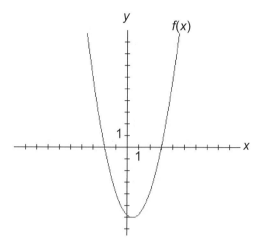

A. $-6 < x < 0$

B. $-\frac{7}{2} \le x < -2$

C. $-\frac{7}{2} \le x < -2$ or $3 < x \le \frac{9}{2}$

D. $-2 < x < 3$

E. $-2 < x < 0$

54. *ABCD* is a rectangle with one side on the *x*-axis and point *A* on the graph of *f(x)*, as shown in the figure below. If $f(x) = \sqrt{x} + 2$, what is the area of *ABCD*?

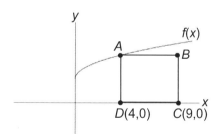

F. 10

G. 18

H. $6\sqrt{10}$

J. 20

K. $10\sqrt{6}$

58. The graph of $f(x)$ is shown below. Which of the following is the graph of $|f(x)|$?

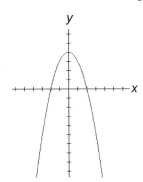

A.

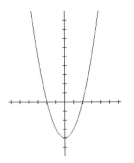

D.

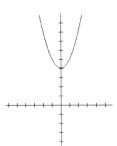

B.

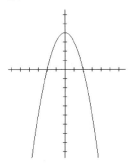

E.

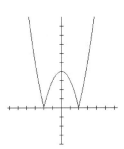

C.

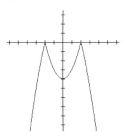

_____

20- & 30-hour programs: Jump to the end of this chapter and complete relevant questions from Functions Worksheet 1 and relevant test corrections for Test 2. Then move on to the Trigonometry chapter.

3. TRANSFORMATIONS

Some questions may ask you to identify the effects of a *transformation* on the graph of a function. There are several types of transformations, including movements (translations), reflections, stretches, contractions, and rotations.

REFLECTIONS

As mentioned in the previous section, a *reflection* creates a mirror image of a shape across a line (called the *line of reflection*). For example, $\triangle A'B'C'$ is the reflection of $\triangle ABC$ across line *l* below:

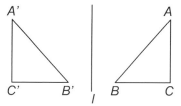

ROTATIONS

A *rotation* spins a shape around some given point. Rotation problems tend to use degrees to tell you how much to spin the shape. For example, point *A'* below is a 90° clockwise rotation of point *A* around the point (0,0):

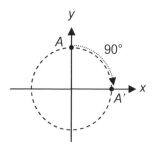

ALGEBRAIC TRANSFORMATIONS

Sometimes, instead of *visually* transforming a graph, as in the examples above, you may have to transform a graph by making changes to the function's *algebraic expression*. If you've covered this in school, the following offers a good review of the material. If you have not yet covered this, you might want to skip this part of the lesson. These algebraic transformations are not common on the ACT.

TRANSFORMATION RULES FOR MOVING (OR TRANSLATING) A FUNCTION

- $f(x) + a$ → moves graph UP *a* units
- $f(x) - a$ → moves graph DOWN *a* units
- $f(x + a)$ → moves graph to the LEFT *a* units
- $f(x - a)$ → moves graph to the RIGHT *a* units

TRANSFORMATION RULES FOR REFLECTING A FUNCTION

- $-f(x)$ → reflects graph across *x*-axis
- $f(-x)$ → reflects graph across *y*-axis

TRANSFORMATION RULES FOR STRETCHING/CONTRACTING A FUNCTION

- $af(x)$, where $a > 1$ → STRETCHES the graph vertically
- $af(x)$, where $0 < a < 1$ → CONTRACTS the graph vertically
- $f(ax)$, where $a > 1$ → CONTRACTS the graph horizontally
- $f(ax)$, where $0 < a < 1$ → STRETCHES the graph horizontally

USE A TEST FUNCTION

Instead of memorizing the rules above, you may choose to test the rules, while taking the ACT, using a standard function (such as $f(x) = \sqrt{x}$) and your graphing calculator. First, you must be familiar with the graph of $f(x) = \sqrt{x}$:

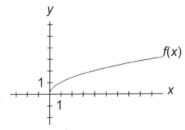

Use your calculator to check any of the rules above. Pick a small number for *a* if one is not given. For example, to check the transformation $g(x + 3)$ for some function *g*, check the graph $f(x + 3) = \sqrt{x + 3}$ on your calculator:

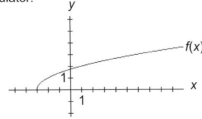

Since $f(x)$ moved to the left 3 spaces, the graph of function g will also move to the left 3 spaces.

Note: *Horizontal* stretches and contractions are easier to see if you use a function such as $f(x) = x^2$.

Transformation questions involve the *movement* (or *translation*), *reflection*, *rotation*, *stretch*, or *contraction* of a graph of a function. *Algebraic* transformations ask about the change in the graph of a function when that function is algebraically changed in some way.

Try the following lesson problem:

58. The graph of $f(x)$ is shown below. Which of the following could be the graph of $-f(x-1)$?

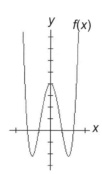

A.

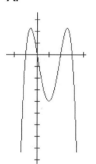

C.

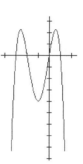

E.

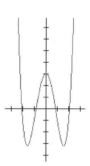

B.

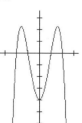

D.

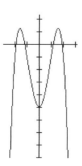

14. In the standard (x,y) coordinate plane, $\triangle ABC$ has vertices $(-2,-2)$, $(-1,4)$, and $(2,3)$. Suppose $\triangle ABC$ is transposed 1 unit to the right and 2 units up to form $\triangle A'B'C'$. Which of the following shows the coordinates for the vertices of $\triangle A'B'C'$?

   A. $(0,-1)$, $(0,6)$, $(4,5)$
   B. $(0,-1)$, $(1,5)$, $(4,5)$
   C. $(-1,0)$, $(1,6)$, $(3,1)$
   D. $(-1,0)$, $(0,6)$, $(3,5)$
   E. $(-1,0)$, $(1,6)$, $(3,5)$

60. The figures below show the graphs of f and g. The function f is defined by $f(x) = x^2 + 2x + 3$. The function g is defined by $g(x) = f(x + h) + k$, where h and k are constants. What is the value of $h - k$?

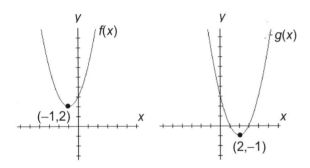

   F. -6
   G. -3
   H. 0
   J. 3
   K. 6

4. DOMAIN AND RANGE

DOMAIN

The *domain* of a function $f(x)$ is the set of *inputs* that may be put into a function without violating any laws of math. In other words, the domain is all allowable values of x.

> These problems may mention the word *domain*. They may also ask for the values of x for which $f(x)$ is a real number, or, alternatively, they may ask for the values of x for which $f(x)$ is "undefined."

There are two rules used for finding the domain of a function:

1. **The denominator of a fraction cannot equal zero.**

2. **It is impossible to take the square root (or any *even* root) of a negative number.**

The following rules are used to find the domain of a function:

1. **If there is a variable in the denominator of a fraction, set the entire denominator *not-equal* ($\neq$) to zero.** Solve for the variable. Any values of the variable that make the denominator zero are *not* part of the function's domain.

    (EX) What is the domain of $f(x) = \dfrac{25}{x - 25}$? $x - 25 \neq 0 \;\rightarrow\; \boldsymbol{x \neq 25}$

2. **If there is a variable under an <u>even</u> root ($\sqrt{\ }, \sqrt[4]{\ }, \sqrt[6]{\ }$, etc.), set the entire expression under the root *greater than or equal* ($\geq$) to zero.** Solve for the variable. These values are the domain of the function. (Note: if the root is *odd*, then negative numbers are allowed.)

    (EX) What is the domain of $f(x) = \sqrt{x - 25}$? $x - 25 \geq 0 \;\rightarrow\; \boldsymbol{x \geq 25}$

3. **If there is a variable under an even root that is in the denominator of a fraction, set the entire expression under the root *greater than* (>) zero.** Solve for the variable. These values are the domain of the function.

    (EX) What is the domain of $f(x) = \dfrac{25}{\sqrt{x - 25}}$? $x - 25 > 0 \;\rightarrow\; \boldsymbol{x > 25}$

Try the following lesson problem:

27. For the function f, defined below, what are the values of x for which $f(x)$ is a real number?

$$f(x) = \frac{5}{\sqrt{x+4}}$$

- A. $x = -4$
- B. $x = 0$
- C. $x \geq -4$
- D. $x \geq 0$
- E. $x > -4$

RANGE

The *range* of a function $f(x)$ is the set of values that can be *produced* by the function. In other words, the range is all possible values of $f(x)$, the *outputs* of the function. These outputs are the y values in the (x,y) coordinate plane. Range questions are not very common on the ACT, and the method for finding range is not as straightforward as that of domain. You should, however, be able to recognize the range of a function by looking at the function's graph. Don't forget, you may use your graphing calculator if the function is given.

Try the following lesson problem:

42. What is the range of the function f shown below?

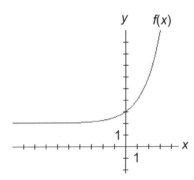

- A. All real numbers
- B. $f(x) \geq 0$
- C. $f(x) > 2$
- D. $f(x) \geq 3$
- E. $f(x) < 3$

42. What is the domain of the function f, defined below?

$$f(x) = (x+2)^{\frac{1}{4}}$$

   A. All real numbers

   B. $x \geq -2$

   C. $x \geq 0$

   D. $x \geq \frac{1}{4}$

   E. $x \geq 2$

5. FUNCTIONS AS MODELS

Functions are often used to *model* real life situations. These problems are very similar to some of the problems we've already seen in the Algebraic Word Problems section. They often look difficult because they are wordy and may contain complicated-sounding formulas, but they are usually much easier than the look. Typically, you'll only have to plug in a few values to find your answer.

 Be aggressive on Functions as Models questions. They usually turn out to be easier than they look.

 These questions provide a function or formula that models some real life situation. The functions may appear complicated, and the questions are often wordy.

(EX) The position, p, of a rolling bowling ball on a bowling alley is given by the function $p(t) = vt$, where v is the initial velocity of the ball, in feet per second, t is time, in seconds, and p is the distance, in feet, from the start of the alley where the ball is thrown. If a bowling alley is 63 feet long and a bowling ball is rolled at an initial velocity of 10½ feet per second, how long, in seconds, will it take for the bowling ball to reach the pins?

A. 5
B. 6
C. 7
D. 8
E. 9

Yes, these problems can be wordy, but the function above is clearly defined. Just plug in the values given in the problem:

First, plug in v: v = 10.5 → p(t) = 10.5·t

We're trying to find a value for t, given a value for p. Let T be the time it takes the bowling ball to travel p = 63 feet:

*p(T) = 10.5·T = 63 → T = 6 seconds **B.***

Try the following lesson problem:

34. Dennis deposited $1000 into a savings account that paid 2% interest per year. The amount of money in the account n years from the original deposit is given by the function M, where

$$M(n) = 1000\left(\tfrac{51}{50}\right)^n.$$

Approximately how much money will be in the account, in dollars, after 10 years?

A. 1002
B. 1200
C. 1219
D. 1220
E. 10,200

24. If the profit, in dollars, of a small company is given by the function P, where $P(x) = 100\sqrt{x}$, and x is the number of products sold, how many products must the company sell to make a profit of $10,000?

   A. 10
   B. 1,000
   C. 1×10^4
   D. 1×10^6
   E. 1×10^8

36. The volume, V, of a cone is determined by the formula $V = \frac{1}{3}Bh$, where B is the area of the base of the cone and h is the height of the cone. What is the volume, in cubic centimeters, of a cone with a base area of 60 square centimeters and a height of 10 centimeters?

   F. 200
   G. 300
   H. 400
   J. 500
   K. 600

6. FUNCTIONS PROBLEMS

PRACTICE PROBLEMS

The following worksheets and practice problems (from Test 1 in *The Real ACT Prep Guide*, 3rd Edition) test techniques taught in this chapter. It is very important to look back to the lessons in this chapter and review the techniques while completing these problems. Try to determine which technique relates to each problem and apply the methods taught in the tutorial. Do not time yourself on these problems. The problems are provided to give you an opportunity to practice, and hopefully master, the techniques in this tutorial before you apply them on real ACTs in a timed setting.

- □ Functions Worksheet 1
- □ Functions Worksheet 2
- □ **Test 1**: 56, 57, 58[40] (see Step 3 under "Test Corrections" below)

[40] Questions marked with a "40" are covered by the **40-hour programs**.

You might choose to space the above assignments out over the course of your studies. See the "Schedules" section in the introduction for more details about programs.

TEST CORRECTIONS

After each practice test is graded, you should correct Functions problems that you missed or left blank. There are three steps to correcting the practice tests:

1. The Functions questions for each test are listed below. Go back to your answer sheet for the corresponding test and circle the question numbers below that you missed (or guessed on, if you kept track of your guesses).

   - □ **Test 2**: 23, 32, 54
   - □ **Test 3**: 19[40], 48[40], 50[40]
   - □ **Test 4**: 11, 25, 42, 47
   - □ **Test 5**: 3, 48[40], 57[40], 60

   [40] Questions marked with a "40" are covered by the **40-hour programs**.

2. Correct the problems in *The Real ACT Study Guide*. As you correct the problems, go back to the tutorial and review the techniques. The idea is to: (1) identify techniques that have given you trouble, (2) go back to the tutorial so you can review and strengthen these techniques, and (3) apply these techniques to the specific problems on which you struggled.

3. If you have trouble identifying the best technique to use on a problem, see the Techniques Reference information in Chapter VIII, starting on page 453.

FUNCTIONS WORKSHEET 1*

Problem numbers represent the *approximate* level of difficulty for each problem (out of 60).
*20- & 30-hour programs: You may choose to skip 12, 43, and 44.

12. Point P lies in the standard (x,y) coordinate plane and has coordinates $(2,2)$. Suppose point P is translated 4 units to the left, then translated 4 units down, and then reflected across the y axis, forming point P'. What are the coordinates of P'?

    A. $(2,2)$
    B. $(2,-2)$
    C. $(-2,2)$
    D. $(-2,-2)$
    E. $(0,-4)$

14. If $f(x) = 2x^2 + x$ and $g(x) = 5x$, what is the value of $f(2) \times g(2)$?

    F. 1
    G. 10
    H. 20
    J. 100
    K. 1,000

20. The graph of $f(x)$ is shown on a standard (x,y) coordinate plane below. Which of the following is NOT a zero of $f(x)$?

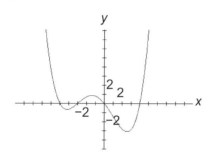

    A. -5
    B. -3
    C. 0
    D. 4
    E. 6

Continued ➔

36. Let the function f be defined by $f(x) = \left| x^2 - 6 \right|$. When $f(x) = 5$, what is one possible value of $x - 6$?

    F.   −25
    G.   −7
    H.   −6
    J.   −1
    K.   0

43. For a certain pipe, the velocity, v, of water flow is given by the formula $v = 50\sqrt{\dfrac{h^2 d}{1 + 71d}}$ where h is the head length coefficient of the pipe and d is the diameter of the pipe. What is the velocity, in feet per second, of water flow for a 1 foot diameter pipe of this type if the head length coefficient is 12 feet per second?

    A.   30
    B.   40
    C.   50
    D. $50\sqrt{2}$
    E. $50\sqrt{5}$

44. The graphs of $f(x)$ and $nf(x)$ are shown in the standard (x,y) coordinate plane below, where n is a constant. What is a possible value of n?

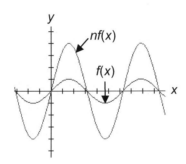

    F.   −4
    G.   −1
    H.   0
    J. $\dfrac{1}{4}$
    K.   4

Continued →

55. If $f(x) = ax^{\frac{1}{3}}$ and point A lies on the graph of $f(x)$ below, what is the value of a?

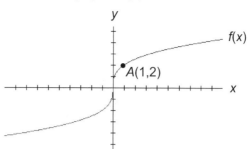

A. $\dfrac{1}{3}$

B. $\dfrac{1}{2}$

C. 2

D. 4

E. 6

57. Which of the following functions in standard (x,y) coordinate planes is an even function?

F.

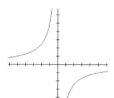

H.

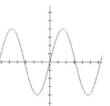

K.

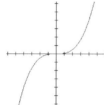

G.

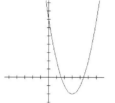

J.

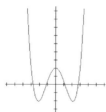

FUNCTIONS WORKSHEET 2*

Problem numbers represent the *approximate* level of difficulty for each problem (out of 60).
***20- & 30-hour programs:** You may choose to skip 19, 34, and 52.*

16. The graph of $f(x)$ in the standard (x,y) coordinate plane is shown below. For what value or values of x, if any, is $f(x) = 4$?

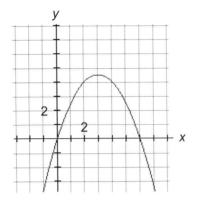

   A. 0 and 6 only
   B. 2 only
   C. 4 only
   D. 2 and 4 only
   E. No real values

19. For which value or values of x is the expression $\dfrac{(x-4)}{(x+3)(x-2)}$ undefined?

   F. 4 only
   G. −3 only
   H. −3 and 2 only
   J. 3 and −2 only
   K. −3, 2, and 4

32. If $f(x) = 2x + 5$ and $g(x) = x^2$, what is the value of $g[f(x)]$?

   A. $4x^2 + 25$
   B. $4x^2 + 20x + 25$
   C. $2x^2 + 20x + 25$
   D. $2x^2 + 10x + 5$
   E. $2x^2 + 5$

Continued ➔

34. To study population growth, a biologist released 70 frogs on an island. The population, p, of frogs on the island is given by the function $p(t) = 300t^{\frac{3}{4}} + 70$, where t is the number of days after the frogs were released. According to this function, how many frogs will be on the island after 1 year (1 year = 365 days)?

F. $300(1)^{\frac{3}{4}} + 70$

G. $300^{\frac{3}{4}} + 70$

H. $300(365)^{\frac{3}{4}} + 70$

J. $365^{\frac{3}{4}} + 70$

K. $(300 \cdot 365)^{\frac{3}{4}} + 70$

44. The graph of $f(x)$ in the standard (x,y) coordinate plane is shown below. For what real values of x, if any, is $f(x) < 0$?

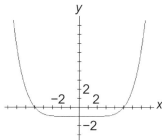

A. $-5 < x < 5$
B. $x > -1$
C. $x < -1$
D. $x < -5$ or $x > 5$
E. No real values

49. If $f(x) = 2x^2$, then what is the value of $\dfrac{f(x+h) - f(x)}{h}$?

F. $4x + 2h$
G. $2x + 4h$
H. $4x^2 + 2h$
J. $2x^2 + 2h$
K. $2x^2 + 4h$

Continued ➔

52. In the standard (x,y) coordinate-plane, the equation of line l is $y = -3x - 4$. If line m is the reflection of line l across the y-axis, what is the equation of line m?

A. $y = -3x + 4$
B. $y = 3x + 4$
C. $y = 3x - 4$
D. $y = \frac{3}{4}x - 4$
E. $y = \frac{3}{4}x + 4$

58. In the figure below, $ABCD$ is a square centered on the y-axis. If points B and C lie on the graph $y = ax^4$ where a is a constant, what is the value of a?

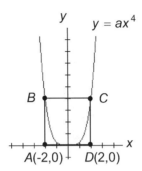

F. 4
G. 2
H. 1
J. $\dfrac{1}{2}$
K. $\dfrac{1}{4}$

VI
TRIGONOMETRY

This chapter covers what you need to know about trigonometry (we'll call it "trig" for short). If you haven't covered trig yet in school, then you might just go over Section 1: Basic Trigonometry. This section covers about half of the trig you'll see on the ACT. If you're looking to maximize your score, or if you've covered trig in school and feel pretty comfortable with it, then tackle the whole chapter.

1. BASIC TRIGONOMETRY

Basic trigonometry, or *trig*, is the study of the relations between the angles and the sides of *right triangles*. Look at the triangle below:

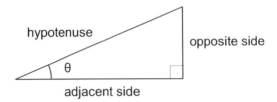

In a right triangle, each trig function of an angle is a ratio of 2 of the sides of the triangle. Notice that relative to each angle (such as the angle θ—pronounced "THEY-tuh"—in the figure above), there is an *opposite* side, an *adjacent* side, and the *hypotenuse*. Note that the hypotenuse is always the longest side of the triangle and is always opposite the right angle. **Don't confuse the hypotenuse with one of the other sides.** Let's get started with an important word:

SOHCAHTOA

Memorize this acronym. It will help you remember the basic trig functions:

SOH: The **Sine** (*sin* for short) of an angle is the ratio of the **Opposite** side to the **Hypotenuse**:

$$\sin\theta = \frac{\text{opposite}}{\text{hypotenuse}} = \frac{O}{H}$$

CAH: The **Cosine** (*cos* for short) of an angle is the ratio of the **Adjacent** side to the **Hypotenuse**:

$$\cos\theta = \frac{\text{adjacent}}{\text{hypotenuse}} = \frac{A}{H}$$

TOA: The **Tangent** (*tan* for short) of an angle is the ratio of the **Opposite** side to the **Adjacent** side:

$$\tan\theta = \frac{\text{opposite}}{\text{adjacent}} = \frac{O}{A}$$

NO NEED FOR A CALCULATOR

You can use your calculator to find the values of trig functions (look for the SIN, COS, and TAN keys), but you'll never actually *have* to use it. The ACT does not require the use of a calculator. If you know how to use your calculator with trig, great—but if you don't, don't worry about it.

(EX) In the right triangle below, what is the value of cos θ?

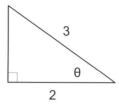

A. $\dfrac{2}{3}$

B. $\dfrac{3}{2}$

C. $\dfrac{\sqrt{5}}{3}$

D. $\dfrac{\sqrt{5}}{2}$

E. $\sqrt{5}$

From SOHCAHTOA, use the CAH:

cos = adjacent side over hypotenuse = $\dfrac{A}{H}$

→ *The side adjacent to θ is 2, and the hypotenuse is 3.*

→ *cos θ =* $\dfrac{A}{H} = \dfrac{2}{3}$ **A.**

FINDING MISSING INFORMATION

The power of trig is that it allows us to find the missing sides of any right triangle when we know just *one* of the sides. In the past, we could only do this with the two special right triangles (30-60-90 and 45-45-90). So trig is an important tool. Let's put it to work:

(EX) Side *BC* of △*ABC* below is 10 inches long. If the sin of ∠*A* is $\frac{5}{13}$, how long, in inches, is the hypotenuse of the triangle?

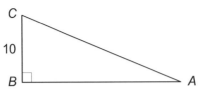

A. 12
B. 13
C. 24
D. 26
E. 28

Here's where we see the power of trig. We only know one side of the triangle, but because we know the sine of ∠A, we can find another side.

First, write the trig equation for sine. Remember that we know the opposite side (O = 10) of angle A: $\sin A = \dfrac{O}{H} = \dfrac{10}{H}$

Since sin A is given, we can write the following equation:

$\sin A = \dfrac{5}{13} = \dfrac{10}{H}$ → *Cross multiply: 5·H = 13·10* → *H = 26* **D.**

THE SPECIAL RIGHT TRIANGLES, REVISITED

Remember these?

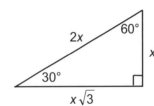 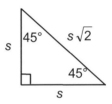

Sometimes, you will be asked for the trig functions of the special angles: 30°, 45°, and 60°. If you have the two special right triangles memorized, you can quickly find these trig values. First, let *x* = *s* = 1, above, so you have the following triangles:

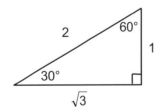 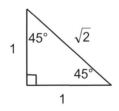

Now, just by looking at these triangles, you can find the trig functions of important angles. Try filling in the information in the following table. Answers to all lesson and homework problems in this chapter start on page 501.

	30°	45°	60°
sin			
cos			
tan			

Note: Unless you're comfortable working with radicals, some of these functions can be tricky. It's probably not that important to stay in radical form. Just use decimals if you'd like. If you do want to stay in radical form, that's great—it might save time when you look at answer choices. Below is how you would find sin 45°, for example:

$$\sin 45° = \frac{O}{A} = \frac{1}{\sqrt{2}} = \frac{1}{\sqrt{2}}\frac{\sqrt{2}}{\sqrt{2}} = \frac{\sqrt{2}}{2}$$

As you can see, it can get a little tricky. You can either memorize the values, or just use decimals.

———

BASIC TRIGONOMETRY LESSON PROBLEMS

43. What is the value of tan θ in the triangle shown below?

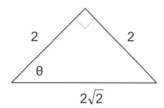

A. $2 + 2\sqrt{2}$
B. 2
C. $\sqrt{2}$
D. 1
E. $\dfrac{1}{\sqrt{2}}$

58. Henry wants to measure the length of the pond shown below. If the length of leg *YZ* of △*XYZ* is 50 feet and the measure of ∠*X* is 20°, which of following expresses the length of the pond?

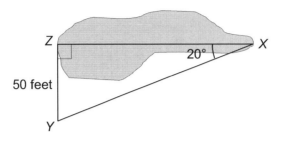

F. $\dfrac{50}{\sin 20°}$

G. $\dfrac{50}{\cos 20°}$

H. $\dfrac{50}{\tan 20°}$

J. 50 sin 20°

K. 50 tan 20°

30. In the right triangle pictured below, *x*, *y*, and *z* are the lengths of its sides, as shown. What is the value of cos θ?

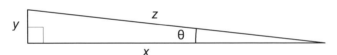

A. $\dfrac{x}{y}$

B. $\dfrac{y}{x}$

C. $\dfrac{x}{z}$

D. $\dfrac{y}{z}$

E. $\dfrac{z}{y}$

60. Right triangle *ABC* is shown below. Which of the following is equal to sin α − cos β?

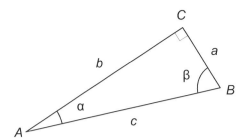

F. 0

G. 1

H. $\dfrac{a-b}{c}$

J. $\dfrac{a-c}{b}$

K. $\dfrac{a}{c} - \dfrac{a}{b}$

20-hour program: Jump to the end of this chapter and complete relevant questions from Trigonometry Worksheet 1 and relevant test corrections for Test 2.

2. TRIG AND THE UNIT CIRCLE

We can analyze trig functions for the angles of right triangles, but what if we're dealing with angles that wouldn't fit into a right triangle? For example, what's the cosine of 120°? This angle could not be part of a right triangle—it's too big—but it *does* have a cosine. That's where the unit circle comes in.

THE UNIT CIRCLE

THE FOUR QUADRANTS

The unit circle has a radius equal to 1 and is centered at the origin of a standard (*x,y*) coordinate plane. The *x* and *y* axes divide the circle into four quadrants, labeled I, II, III, and IV below. **Notice that the top right quadrant is I, and the subsequent quadrants are numbered *counterclockwise*.**

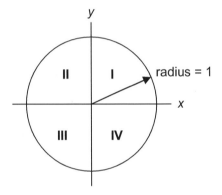

ANGLES

The circle is used to display the measures of angles. Like the quadrants, the angles are measured *counterclockwise* from the positive side of the *x*-axis. The example below shows the angle 120°. The line where the angle ends is called the *terminal side* of the angle:

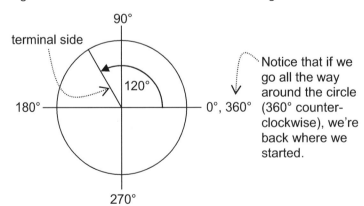

REFERENCE TRIANGLE

If you draw a *vertical* line to the *x* axis from the end of the angle's terminal side, you create what is called a *reference triangle*. This is a right triangle. Remember, the unit circle has a radius of 1, so the hypotenuse of this right triangle is 1. **Make sure you always draw a *vertical* line to the *x*-axis.**

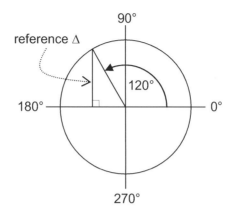

REFERENCE ANGLE

Let's enlarge the triangle. Can you calculate the measure of the angle between the *x*-axis and the terminal side? This is an important angle. It's called the *reference angle*.

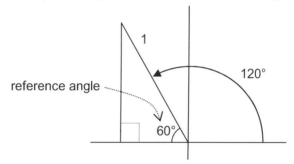

The reason for looking at these reference triangles and reference angles is that they allow us to find trig functions of larger angles. Remember our original question? What's the cosine of 120°? We couldn't figure that out because 120° isn't part of a right triangle, but the reference angle for 120°, which we found to be 60°, *is* part of a right triangle. So:

$$\cos 120° \overset{?}{=} \cos 60°$$

Not quite. We have to think about one more thing:

THE QUADRANTS AND THE TRIG FUNCTIONS

Reference angles and triangles will give us the *absolute value* of a trig function, but we need to know whether the trig function is positive or negative. That's where the four quadrants and the acronym *ASTC* come in to play:

Starting in Quadrant I and moving counterclockwise (as usual), we write *ASTC*. There are several ways to memorize this acronym. The most popular is "All Students Take Calculus." Feel free to think of your own. Just remember to move in a *counterclockwise* direction from Quadrant I.

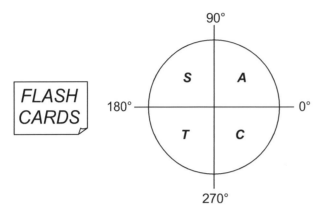

Each letter tells us something important about the trig functions in that letter's quadrant:

- *A*: All trig functions are positive in Quadrant I.
- *S*: Sine only is positive in Quadrant II.
- *T*: Tangent only is positive in Quadrant III.
- *C*: Cosine only is positive in Quadrant IV.

USING THE UNIT CIRCLE TO FIND TRIG FUNCTIONS: SUMMARY

Finally, we can answer the original question. What is the cosine of 120°? The reference angle tells us that the absolute value of cos 120° is equal to cos 60°. But we're in Quadrant II, so cosine must be *negative*. So we have:

$$\cos 120° = -\cos 60°$$

If you remember the special right triangles, you can find that $\cos 60° = \dfrac{1}{2}$, so:

$$\cos 120° = -\cos 60° = -\dfrac{1}{2}, \text{ and we're done!}$$

Here's a summary of the method:

1. Draw the angle in question on a unit circle.
2. Draw the reference triangle and identify the reference angle.
3. Consider the sign of the trig function (positive or negative) by using the *ASTC* acronym.
4. Find the trig function of the reference angle, and apply the correct sign from step 3.

There are a few ways you can identify these trig problems. Some problems will have a drawing of a unit circle. Otherwise, look for a reference to one of the quadrants—such as the degree inequality shown in the example below—or look for large angles (> 90°) that wouldn't fit into a right triangle.

Here's how the ACT will typically test trig and the unit circle:

(EX) If $180° \leq x \leq 270°$ and $\sin x = -\dfrac{4}{5}$, then $\cos x = $?

A. $-\dfrac{3}{5}$

B. $-\dfrac{4}{5}$

C. $-\dfrac{3}{4}$

D. $\dfrac{3}{5}$

E. $\dfrac{3}{4}$

First of all, what quadrant are we in? The inequality $180° \leq x \leq 270°$ means we're in Quadrant III. This is the "T" quadrant. Tangent is positive; both sine and cosine are negative.

Now, let's sketch the unit circle with a reference triangle drawn in. We don't know what angle x is, so don't worry about it. Just make sure you're triangle is in the correct quadrant:

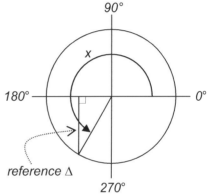

The sine of x is given. This means we know the reference angle's opposite side and hypotenuse. (The hypotenuse is 1 in a unit circle, but it's usually easier to use the numbers given in the ratio):

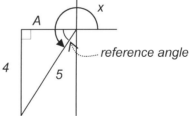

The Pythagorean Theorem tells us that $A = 3$ (or recognize the 3-4-5 $\triangle$). To find the cos x, find the cosine of the reference angle, and don't forget to add a negative sign because cosine is negative in Quadrant III:

$$\cos x = -\dfrac{A}{H} = -\dfrac{3}{5} \quad \textbf{A.}$$

COORDINATES

An interesting thing about the points along the unit circle is that they can tell you the sine and cosine of an angle. **Each x coordinate is the *cosine* of the related angle, and each y coordinate is the *sine* of the related angle.**

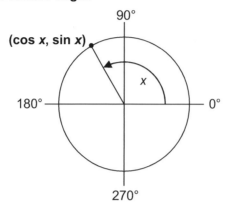

FOUR IMPORTANT POINTS

The most useful reason for memorizing the relationship above (cos x, sin x) is that you can find the trig functions for angles that don't have reference triangles, namely (0°, 90°, 180°, and 270°):

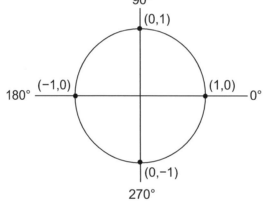

cos 0° = 1, sin 0° = 0
cos 90° = 0, sin 90° = 1
cos 180° = −1, sin 180° = 0
cos 270° = 0, sin 270° = −1

You shouldn't have to memorize these values. Just use the unit circle, and remember that cos x is the x coordinate and sin x is the y coordinate.

DEGREES AND RADIANS

Up until now, we've only worked with degrees when measuring an angle. Sometimes, the ACT will use alternate units of measurement called *radians*. Radians may look and sound complicated, but if you memorize the following proportion, you can always switch back and forth.

$$\boxed{\begin{array}{c} FLASH \\ CARDS \end{array}} \quad \frac{\text{degrees}}{180°} = \frac{\text{radians}}{\pi}$$

Let's use this proportion to find a few important radian measures:

(EX) What is the radian measure of 90°?

> *Plug 90 into the "degrees" place in the proportion, and solve for radians (rads):*
>
> $$\frac{90°}{180°} = \frac{rads}{\pi} \quad \rightarrow \quad rads = \frac{\pi}{2}$$

1. What is the radian measure of 180°?

2. What is the radian measure of 270°?

3. What is the radian measure of 360°?

Warning: Most calculators have separate modes for *radians* and *degrees*. For example, if you have your calculator set to radians, you can type radian measures into your calculator without having to first convert them to degrees. Just make sure you have your calculator set correctly. If you're in radian mode and you type in degrees, your answers will be incorrect.

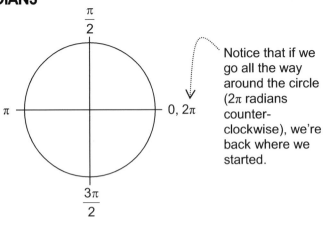

Notice that if we go all the way around the circle (2π radians counter-clockwise), we're back where we started.

UNIT CIRCLE LESSON PROBLEMS

51. If $\tan x \approx 0.577$, which of the following could be true about x?

    A. $90° \leq x \leq 135°$
    B. $135° \leq x \leq 180°$
    C. $180° \leq x \leq 225°$
    D. $270° \leq x \leq 315°$
    E. $315° \leq x \leq 360°$

57. If $\sin \theta = -\dfrac{5}{13}$, and $\dfrac{3\pi}{2} \leq \theta \leq 2\pi$, then $\tan \theta = $?

    F. $\dfrac{12}{13}$

    G. $-\dfrac{13}{12}$

    H. $-\dfrac{12}{5}$

    J. $-\dfrac{12}{13}$

    K. $-\dfrac{5}{12}$

49. If cos $x = a$, where $\dfrac{\pi}{2} \le x \le \pi$, then what is sin x?

    A. $\dfrac{1}{a}$

    B. $-\dfrac{1}{a}$

    C. $-a$

    D. $\dfrac{1}{\sqrt{1-a^2}}$

    E. $\sqrt{1-a^2}$

54. If cos 30° = $\dfrac{\sqrt{3}}{2}$, what is cos 330° ?

    F. 1

    G. $\dfrac{\sqrt{3}}{2}$

    H. $\dfrac{1}{2}$

    J. $-\dfrac{1}{2}$

    K. $-\dfrac{\sqrt{3}}{2}$

30-hour program: Jump to the end of this chapter and complete relevant questions from Trig Worksheet 1 and relevant test corrections for Tests 2 and 3. Then move on to the Math Odds and Ends chapter.

3. GRAPHS OF SINE AND COSINE

You may have noticed that we've used the word *function* to refer to sine, cosine, and tangent. They are, indeed, functions, and like other functions, they can be graphed on a standard (*x,y*) coordinate plane. Our inputs, *x*, are the measure of angles (in degrees or radians). Our outputs, *y*, are the values of the trig function for those angles. It's a safe bet that you'll only have to worry about sine and cosine graphs on the ACT. Here's what they look like:

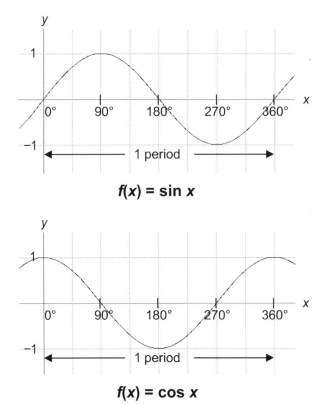

$$f(x) = \sin x$$

$$f(x) = \cos x$$

If you ever forget which graph is which, just type sin 0 (or cos 0) into your calculator to see which one goes through (0,0). Also, note that the graphs above are the graphs of points as you go around the *unit circle*. For example, the unit circle shows us that at $\theta = 180°$, $\cos \theta = -1$. You can see this point on the second graph above. This is an important connection to make.

The ACT is *not* going to expect you to memorize much about these graphs, but you should understand some of their basic features.

PERIOD

Trig functions are called *periodic functions* because they keep repeating. Notice that when the graph reaches 360°, it looks the same as it did at 0°. (If you think about the unit circle, which also begins repeating at 360°, this may not surprise you.) The *period* is the x distance that the function travels before it begins repeating again, as shown in the graphs above. For the standard functions of both sine and cosine:

$$\text{period} = 360° \text{ (or } 2\pi)$$

AMPLITUDE

The amplitude is the measure of the vertical distance from the *neutral axis* (usually the x-axis) to the function's highest (or lowest) point. Look back to the graphs. For both sin x and cos x, the function never goes higher than 1 (or lower than −1). For the standard functions of both sine and cosine:

$$\text{amplitude} = 1$$

RADIANS

In the graphs above, the units for the x-axis are *degrees*. More typically, graphs of trig functions will use *radians*, as shown below. If necessary, review degree to radian conversions in the Basic Trigonometry section.

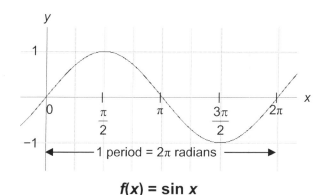

$$f(x) = \sin x$$

IMPORTANT POINTS

Notice some of the important points on the two graphs:

- $\sin 0 = \sin 2\pi = 0$, $\cos 0 = \cos 2\pi = 1$
- $\sin \dfrac{\pi}{2} = 1$, $\cos \dfrac{\pi}{2} = 0$
- $\sin \pi = 0$, $\cos \pi = -1$
- $\sin \dfrac{3\pi}{2} = -1$, $\cos \dfrac{3\pi}{2} = 0$

TRANSFORMATIONS

The ACT may ask you to *transform* a trig function. All of the transformation rules that you learned in Chapter V apply to trig functions. For example, if you multiply a trig function by a positive number greater than 1, as with $f(x) = 4\sin x$, the trig function will *stretch* vertically by a factor of that number (multiply by 4). Similarly, if you multiply the x part of the function by a number greater than 1, as with $f(x) = \sin 4x$, the function (and its period) will *contract* horizontally by a factor of that number (divide by 4). You might want to review the Transformations section.

Try the following lesson problem:

54. Which of the following displays the graph $y = 2 \sin x$?

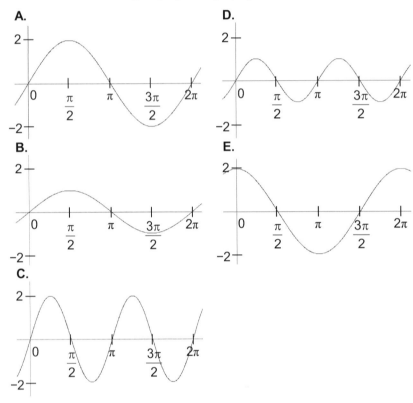

57. The following figure shows the graph of $y = \cos bx$, where b is a constant and the period of the function is equal to $\dfrac{2\pi}{b}$. What is the value of b?

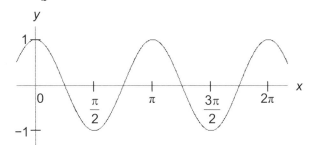

A. $\dfrac{1}{2}$

B. 2

C. π

D. 2π

E. 4π

4. THE LAWS OF SINES AND COSINES

So far, trigonometry works great with *right* triangles, but in the real world not all triangles are right. That's where the Law of Sines and the Law of Cosines come in.

THE LAW OF SINES

Notice that the letter we use for each side is the lowercase version of the angle opposite that side. This is standard notation. Here's the Law of Sines:

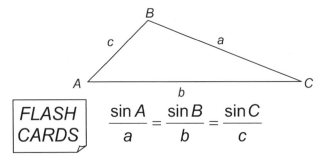

FLASH CARDS

$$\frac{\sin A}{a} = \frac{\sin B}{b} = \frac{\sin C}{c}$$

First of all, these problems deal with **non-right triangles**. The ACT will probably make it easy to recognize Law of Sines problems. They'll probably even mention the "Law of Sines." In general, the Law of Sines can be used when you know either 2 sides and 1 opposite angle (SSA) or 2 angles and 1 opposite side (SAA).

You probably agree that the Law of Sines is fairly easy to memorize. Here's how it works:

(EX) In △ABC below, which of the following expresses the length of side *AB*?

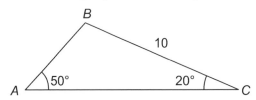

A. $\dfrac{10\sin 110°}{\sin 50°}$

B. $\dfrac{10\sin 110°}{\sin 20°}$

C. $\dfrac{10\sin 20°}{\sin 110°}$

D. $\dfrac{10\sin 20°}{\sin 50°}$

E. $\dfrac{10\sin 50°}{\sin 20°}$

Set up a Law of Sines proportion involving the given angles A and C, and the opposite sides (a and c, respectively; note that c = AB):

$$\frac{\sin A}{a} = \frac{\sin C}{c} \quad \rightarrow \quad \frac{\sin 50°}{10} = \frac{\sin 20°}{c} \quad \rightarrow \quad c\cdot\sin 50° = 10 \sin 20°$$

$$\rightarrow \quad c = \frac{10\sin 20°}{\sin 50°} \quad \textbf{D.}$$

THE LAW OF COSINES

The Law of Cosines is a little more complicated:

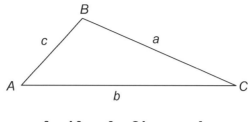

$$a^2 = b^2 + c^2 - 2bc \cos A$$

Notice a few things about this equation. The side on the left (a) will always match the angle on the right (A). The other two sides (b and c) form the rest of the right side of the equation. We only gave you one of the equations (the one for side a). The other two (for sides b and c) follow the same form. Here's the good news. **If the ACT tests the Law of Cosines, they will give you the equation!** So don't memorize it; just make sure you're comfortable using it. Here's an example:

(EX) In $\triangle ABC$ below, which of the following expressions gives the length of side AC? (Note: The Law of Cosines states that for any triangle with vertices A, B, and C and the sides opposite those vertices with lengths a, b, and c, respectively, $c^2 = a^2 + b^2 - 2ab \cos C$.)

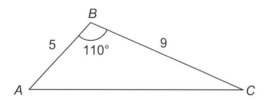

A. $\sqrt{16 \cos 110°}$

B. $\sqrt{106 \cos 110°}$

C. $\sqrt{14 - 90 \cos 110°}$

D. $\sqrt{106 - 90 \cos 110°}$

E. $\sqrt{106 - 45 \cos 110°}$

Notice that the general equation is given. Since we're trying to find AC (side b), use the following form of the equation:

$b^2 = a^2 + c^2 - 2ac \cos B$

Plug in the values for a, c, and B:

$b^2 = 81 + 25 - 2 \cdot 9 \cdot 5 \cos 110°$ → $b = \sqrt{106 - 90 \cos 110°}$ **D.**

Again, these problems deal with **non-right triangles**. As you can see, the ACT will give you the Law of Cosines equation, so you'll know when you're working on a Law of Cosines problem. In general, the Law of Cosines can be used when you know either 2 sides and the included angle (SAS) or all 3 sides (SSS)—hint: think of a "SASsy SSSnake."

Try the following lesson problem:

45. The radar screen below displays two approaching airplanes. Airplane A is 10 nautical miles from the control tower and bearing 45°, and airplane B is 15 nautical miles from the control tower and bearing 195°. Which of the following expressions would give the straight line distance, in nautical miles, between the 2 airplanes? (Note: The Law of Cosines states that for any triangle with vertices A, B, and C and the sides opposite those vertices with lengths a, b, and c, respectively, $c^2 = a^2 + b^2 - 2ab \cos C$.)

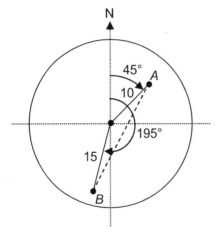

A. $\sqrt{15^2 + 10^2 - 2(15)(10)\cos 15°}$

B. $\sqrt{15^2 + 10^2 - 2(15)(10)\cos 45°}$

C. $\sqrt{15^2 + 10^2 - 2(15)(10)\cos 150°}$

D. $\sqrt{15^2 + 10^2 - 2(15)(10)\cos 195°}$

E. $\sqrt{15^2 + 10^2 - 2(15)(10)\cos 240°}$

45. In △*ABC* below, which of the following expressions gives the length of side *AC*? (Note: The Law of Sines states that, for any triangle, the ratios of the sines of the interior angles to the lengths of the sides opposite those angles are equal.)

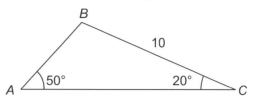

A. $\dfrac{10\sin 110°}{\sin 20°}$

B. $\dfrac{10\sin 110°}{\sin 50°}$

C. $\dfrac{10\sin 110°}{\sin 70°}$

D. $\dfrac{10\sin 20°}{\sin 50°}$

E. $\dfrac{10\sin 50°}{\sin 20°}$

5. TRIGONOMETRY ODDS AND ENDS

INVERSE TRIG FUNCTIONS

Thus far, trig functions have been expressed as a function of *angles*. Angles are the inputs of the functions, and we get out numbers, which we know are ratios of sides of a triangle. For example, in the triangle below, $\sin \theta = \dfrac{O}{H}$.

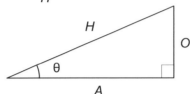

But what if we know the *sides* and want to find the *angle*? That's where we use inverse trig functions, which are notated with a raised −1. Below is the inverse function for sine:

$$\theta = \sin^{-1}\left(\frac{O}{H}\right)$$

It's a good idea to be able to put $\sin^{-1}\left(\dfrac{O}{H}\right)$ into words: "The $\sin^{-1}\left(\dfrac{O}{H}\right)$ is the angle whose sine is $\dfrac{O}{H}$." **The important thing to realize is that an inverse trig function gives you an *angle*.** Let's try an example:

(EX) For △*ABC* below, which of the following expressions gives the value of ∠*A*?

A. $\sin^{-1}\left(\dfrac{3}{5}\right)$

B. $\sin^{-1}\left(\dfrac{4}{5}\right)$

C. $\cos^{-1}\left(\dfrac{3}{5}\right)$

D. $\cos^{-1}\left(\dfrac{3}{4}\right)$

E. $\tan^{-1}\left(\dfrac{4}{3}\right)$

We know that the sin A = $\left(\dfrac{3}{5}\right)$, but the question is asking for ∠A, so use the inverse trig function:

∠A = sin$^{-1}\left(\dfrac{3}{5}\right)$ **A.**

In words: "∠A is the angle whose sine is $\left(\dfrac{3}{5}\right)$."

THE OTHER TRIG FUNCTIONS

You may come across 3 other trig functions: cosecant (csc), secant (sec), and cotangent (cot). Each one is simply the inverse of one of the other trig functions that we've already seen.

$$\csc x = \frac{1}{\sin x}$$

FLASH CARDS $\quad \sec x = \frac{1}{\cos x}$

$$\cot x = \frac{1}{\tan x}$$

Questions involving the other trig functions are not common, but if you're looking for the maximum score possible, memorize the names and equations above.

TRIG PROPERTIES

There are only two trig properties that you should memorize for the ACT.

FLASH CARDS $\quad \tan x = \dfrac{\sin x}{\cos x}$

$\sin^2 x + \cos^2 x = 1$

These trig properties questions tend to look more *algebraic* and less *geometric* than other kinds of trig questions. Notice that there is no triangle in the example below.

(EX) Which of the following is equivalent to (tan *x*)(cos *x*) ?

A. csc *x*
B. sec *x*
C. cot *x*
D. sin *x*
E. cos *x*

When you need to algebraically simplify a trig expression, simplify everything into an expression of sines and cosines. Hopefully, you'll be able to cancel terms:

$$(tan\ x)(cos\ x) = \frac{sin\ x}{cos\ x}cos\ x$$

→ *The cosines cancel, so you're left with sin x* **D.**

GIVEN FORMULAS

Some ACT problems will give you a trig formula. These formulas may look complicated, but typically you'll just have to plug in some numbers. Like other ACT problems that give you formulas, be aggressive. Many students are scared off by these problems, but you should find them easier than they look.

Try the following lesson problem:

48. In $\triangle ABC$ below, line segment AD is the angle bisector for $\angle A$. Which of the following gives the sin α ?

(Note: $\sin^2\left(\dfrac{x}{2}\right) = \dfrac{1}{2}(1-\cos x)$, for all x.)

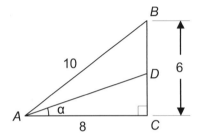

A. $\sqrt{\dfrac{1}{2}\left(1-\dfrac{3}{4}\right)}$

B. $\sqrt{\dfrac{1}{2}\left(1-\dfrac{3}{5}\right)}$

C. $\sqrt{\dfrac{1}{2}\left(1-\dfrac{4}{5}\right)}$

D. $\sqrt{\dfrac{1}{2}\left(1+\dfrac{3}{5}\right)}$

E. $\sqrt{\dfrac{1}{2}\left(1+\dfrac{4}{5}\right)}$

_____

TRIGONOMETRY ODDS AND ENDS HOMEWORK

45. Right triangle *ABC* is shown below, with lengths in centimeters. Which of the following expressions is the length, in centimeters, of the hypotenuse of the triangle?

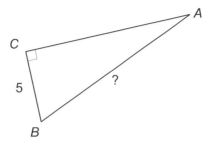

- **A.** 5 tan *A*
- **B.** 5 sin *A*
- **C.** 5 csc *A*
- **D.** 5 cos *A*
- **E.** 5 sec *A*

51. Which of the following is equivalent to the expression $(1 - \sin x)(1 + \sin x)$?

- **F.** $\cos^2 x$
- **G.** $\sin^2 x$
- **H.** 1
- **J.** $\cos x$
- **K.** $\sin x$

59. A line connects vertices A and C of Quadrilateral $ABCD$, below, forming two right triangles. Which of the following gives the degree measure of $\angle A$?

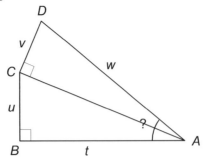

A. $\sin^{-1}\left(\dfrac{u}{t}\right) + \cos^{-1}\left(\dfrac{v}{w}\right)$

B. $\tan^{-1}\left(\dfrac{u}{t}\right) + \cos^{-1}\left(\dfrac{v}{w}\right)$

C. $\tan^{-1}\left(\dfrac{u}{t}\right) + \sin^{-1}\left(\dfrac{v}{w}\right)$

D. $\sin^{-1}\left(\dfrac{u}{t}\right) + \cos^{-1}\left(\dfrac{v}{w}\right)$

E. $\tan^{-1}\left(\dfrac{u}{t}\right) + \tan^{-1}\left(\dfrac{v}{w}\right)$

6. TRIGONOMETRY PROBLEMS

PRACTICE PROBLEMS

The following worksheets and practice problems (from Test 1 in *The Real ACT Prep Guide*, 3rd Edition) test techniques taught in this chapter. It is very important to look back to the lessons in this chapter and review the techniques while completing these problems. Try to determine which technique relates to each problem and apply the methods taught in the tutorial. Do not time yourself on these problems. The problems are provided to give you an opportunity to practice, and hopefully master, the techniques in this tutorial before you apply them on real ACTs in a timed setting.

- ☐ Trigonometry Worksheet 1
- ☐ Trigonometry Worksheet 2
- ☐ **Test 1**: 24, 28, 54^{30}, 60^{40} (see Step 3 under "Test Corrections" below)

^{30} Questions marked with a "30" are covered by the **30- and 40-hour programs**.
^{40} Questions marked with a "40" are covered by the **40-hour program**.

You might choose to space the above assignments out over the course of your studies. See the "Schedules" section in the introduction for more details about programs.

PRACTICE TEST

20-hour program: Now is a good time to take **Test 3** in the ACT book. If you have any questions about taking these tests, review "Taking Practice Tests" in this tutorial's introduction.

TEST CORRECTIONS

After each practice test is graded, you should correct Trigonometry problems that you missed or left blank. There are three steps to correcting the practice tests:

1. The Trigonometry questions for each test are listed below. Go back to your answer sheet for the corresponding test and circle the question numbers below that you missed (or guessed on, if you kept track of your guesses).
   - ☐ **Test 2**: 20, 35^{40}, 45^{40}, 55^{30}
   - ☐ **Test 3**: 37^{30}, 46, 49^{30}, 53^{40}, 58^{30}
   - ☐ **Test 4**: 37, 53^{40}, 54^{40}, 58^{30}
   - ☐ **Test 5**: 43, 46, 53^{40}, 58^{30}

   ^{30} Questions marked with a "30" are covered by the **30 (and 40-hour) programs**.
   ^{40} Questions marked with a "40" are covered by the **40-hour program**.

2. Correct the problems in *The Real ACT Study Guide*. As you correct the problems, go back to the tutorial and review the techniques. The idea is to: (1) identify techniques that have given you trouble, (2) go back to the tutorial so you can review and strengthen these techniques, and (3) apply these techniques to the specific problems on which you struggled.

3. If you have trouble identifying the best technique to use on a problem, see the Techniques Reference information in Chapter VIII, starting on page 453.

TRIGONOMETRY WORKSHEET 1*

Problem numbers represent the *approximate* level of difficulty for each problem (out of 60).
***20-hour program:** You may choose to only complete 23 and 48.
***30-hour program:** You may choose to *skip* 45 and 58.

23. In right triangle $\triangle ABC$ below, which of the following is equal to sin A?

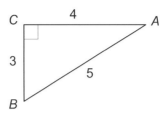

   A. sin B
   B. cos B
   C. tan B
   D. cos A
   E. tan A

45. The lengths of right triangle $\triangle ABC$ are shown below. What is the secant of $\angle A$ in terms of a, b, and c?

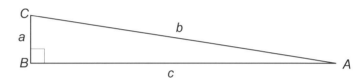

   F. $\dfrac{c}{b}$

   G. $\dfrac{b}{c}$

   H. $\dfrac{a}{b}$

   J. $\dfrac{b}{a}$

   K. $\dfrac{c}{a}$

Continued ➜

48. A vertical structure casts a shadow at an angle of 40° from the ground, as shown below. If the shadow ends 30 feet from the edge of the structure, how high, in feet, is the structure?

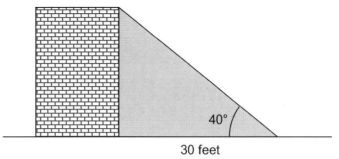

30 feet

A. 30 sin 40°
B. 30 tan 40°
C. 30 cos 40°
D. $\dfrac{30}{\sin 40°}$
E. $\dfrac{30}{\tan 40°}$

55. If 0° ≤ θ ≤ 90° and tan θ = 2, then sin θ = ?

F. −2
G. $\dfrac{1}{2}$
H. $\dfrac{\sqrt{5}}{2}$
J. $\sqrt{5}$
K. $\dfrac{2}{\sqrt{5}}$

Continued →

58. Which of the following equations is represented by the graph below?

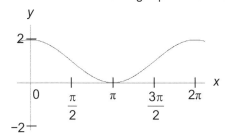

    A. $y = 2 \sin x$
    B. $y = 2 \cos x$
    C. $y = \sin x + 1$
    D. $y = \cos x + 1$
    E. $y = \cos 2x + 1$

40-hour program: Now is a good time to go back to the Algebra chapter and cover the remaining lessons, beginning with Simultaneous Equations.

TRIGONOMETRY WORKSHEET 2*

Problem numbers represent the *approximate* level of difficulty for each problem (out of 60).
20-hour program: You may choose to only complete 38 and 47.
30-hour program: You may choose to *skip* 58 and 60.

38. For right triangle $\triangle ABC$ below, what is the cos $\angle B$?

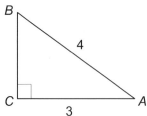

A. $\dfrac{3}{4}$

B. $\dfrac{4}{3}$

C. $\dfrac{4}{\sqrt{7}}$

D. $\dfrac{\sqrt{7}}{4}$

E. $\dfrac{\sqrt{7}}{3}$

47. In $\triangle ABC$, shown below, the length of side BC is 6 units, the length of side AC is 15 units, and sin $\gamma = 0.8$. What is the area, in square units, of $\triangle ABC$?

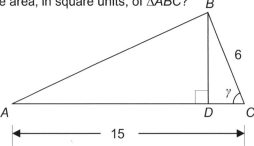

F. 80
G. 75
H. 72
J. 40
K. 36

Continued ➔

56. If $\pi \le \alpha \le \dfrac{3\pi}{2}$ and $\sin \alpha = -\dfrac{\sqrt{3}}{2}$, then $\tan \alpha = ?$

   A. $2\sqrt{3}$
   B. $\sqrt{3}$
   C. $\dfrac{\sqrt{3}}{2}$
   D. $-\dfrac{\sqrt{3}}{2}$
   E. $-\sqrt{3}$

58. If $\cos 40° = x$ and $\sin 40° = y$, what is $\cos 80°$ given that $\cos(2\theta) = \cos^2\theta - \sin^2\theta$?

   F. $x^2 - y^2$
   G. $x^2 + y^2$
   H. $y^2 - x^2$
   J. $x - y$
   K. $x + y$

Continued ➔

60. A manufacturing firm creates a steel triangular plate that fits into a triangular housing, as shown below. If the vertices are labeled A, B, and C, and the lengths of the sides of the triangular plate are 5 inches, 6 inches, and 7 inches, which of the following expressions gives the measure of the recess angle ($\angle A$)? (Note: The Law of Cosines states that for any triangle with vertices A, B, and C and the sides opposite those vertices with lengths a, b, and c, respectively, $c^2 = a^2 + b^2 - 2ab \cos C$.)

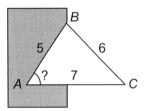

A. $\cos^{-1}\left(\dfrac{1}{5}\right)$

B. $\cos^{-1}\left(\dfrac{19}{35}\right)$

C. $\cos^{-1}\left(\dfrac{5}{7}\right)$

D. $\cos^{-1}\left(-\dfrac{1}{5}\right)$

E. $\cos^{-1}\left(-\dfrac{11}{7}\right)$

VII
MATH ODDS AND ENDS

This chapter covers a number of topics that occasionally show up on the ACT. Probability and Counting are the most common types of problems from this Chapter tested on the ACT, so you should definitely try to look at these sections. Some of the other topics are relatively difficult, and you might want to cover them only if you've studied them in school. In particular, these difficult topics include Complex Numbers, Logarithms, and Matrices.

1. PROBABILITY

BASIC PROBABILITY

Probability is a way of describing the mathematical likelihood of a particular event occurring. It is usually written as a fraction and is always a number between 0 and 1 ($0 \leq P \leq 1$). Memorize the following equation:

$$\text{Probability} = \frac{\textbf{Outcomes giving a desired result}}{\textbf{Total possible outcomes}}$$

Probability problems will include one of the following words: *probability, likelihood, chance,* or *odds.*

(EX) If a fair die is rolled one time, what is the probability of rolling a 6? $\frac{1}{6}$

(EX) If a fair die is rolled one time, what is the probability of rolling an even number? $\frac{1}{2}$

(EX) If a fair die is rolled one time, what is the probability of rolling a prime number? $\frac{1}{2}$ *(2, 3, and 5)*

Try the following lesson problem. Answers to all lesson and homework problems in this chapter start on page 507.

6. A box contains 30 marbles. If the chance of drawing a red marble from the bag is ⅔, how many marbles in the bag are <u>not</u> red?

    A. 5
    B. 10
    C. 15
    D. 20
    E. 25

PROBABILITY OF MULTIPLE EVENTS

These problems will ask you to find the probability of multiple events occurring together when the probability of each individual event can be found.

The following method can be used to find the probability of multiple events:

1. Find the probability of each event. **Important: Make sure to consider how the occurrence of one event may affect the probability of another event.**

2. *Multiply* the probabilities to find the probability of multiple events occurring together.

(EX) If the probability of winning a game of bingo is $\frac{1}{25}$, what is the probability of winning two games of bingo in a row?

A. $\frac{1}{625}$

B. $\frac{1}{125}$

C. $\frac{1}{50}$

D. $\frac{1}{25}$

E. $\frac{2}{25}$

① *The probability of each event is given as* $\frac{1}{25}$

② $P = \dfrac{1}{25} \cdot \dfrac{1}{25} = \dfrac{1}{625}$ **A.**

Notice that the events are **independent**. *The probability of winning the second game is the same as the probability of winning the first game.*

2. A bag contains 5 green marbles, 6 blue marbles, and 7 yellow marbles. If a marble is selected at random from the bag, what is the probability that the marble selected will be blue?

A. $\frac{5}{18}$

B. $\frac{1}{3}$

C. $\frac{7}{18}$

D. $\frac{1}{2}$

E. $\frac{6}{7}$

55. The target below is made up of three circles with the same center. The radius of the small circle is one-third of the radius of the middle circle and one-fifth of the radius of the large circle. If an archer hits the target, what is the probability that he hits the shaded region?

F. $\frac{1}{25}$

G. $\frac{17}{35}$

H. $\frac{3}{5}$

J. $\frac{17}{25}$

K. $\frac{26}{35}$

57. In a game, 100 cards are labeled 1-100. A player draws 2 cards at random, without returning the first card. If both cards have the same tens digit, the player is a winner. If the first card Grant draws is a 12, what is the probability that he will be a winner on the next draw?

A. $\frac{1}{8}$

B. $\frac{1}{9}$

C. $\frac{1}{10}$

D. $\frac{1}{11}$

E. $\frac{1}{99}$

2. PRINCIPLE OF COUNTING

The *principle of counting* allows you to figure out the number of different ways multiple **independent** events can occur together. When events are *independent*, the occurrence of one event does not affect the occurrence of another event. When one event can happen in m ways and a second event can happen in n ways, the total ways in which the two events can happen can be found by the expression: $m \times n$. If there are more than two events, simply multiply the number of ways that any additional events can occur.

> Counting problems will have **multiple events that are independent of each other**, as described above. The problems will ask you to find the number of ways that these events can occur together.

(EX) Mike has 5 dress shirts and 3 ties. How many different shirt-tie combinations are possible?

A. 8
B. 14
C. 15
D. 16
E. 17

There are 5 ways Mike can pick a shirt and 3 ways he can pick a tie:

$m \times n = 5 \times 3 = 15$ **C.**

Try the following lesson problem:

14. Luigi's Pizzeria is offering a 1-topping special. Each pizza can be ordered with 1 of 2 types of bread, 1 of 2 types of sauce, 1 of 3 types of cheese, and 1 of 8 toppings. How many types of 1-topping pizzas can you order?

A. 96
B. 94
C. 92
D. 15
E. 4

18. Company employees are given a two-digit ID code, AB, where A represents the 1st digit and B represents the 2nd digit. If $1 \le A \le 6$ and $1 \le B \le 6$, how many different codes are possible?

A. 12
B. 15
C. 25
D. 30
E. 36

3. COMPLEX NUMBERS

IMAGINARY NUMBERS (*i*)

Try finding $\sqrt{-25}$ using your calculator. You'll get an error message (unless your calculator is smarter than most). There is no *real number* solution to $\sqrt{-25}$, but there *is* what is called an *imaginary* solution, which uses the variable *i* to refer to $\sqrt{-1}$. First, make sure you are comfortable with the following property of radicals:

$$\sqrt{ab} = \sqrt{a}\sqrt{b}$$

Using this property, we can write:

$$\sqrt{-25} = \sqrt{25(-1)} = \sqrt{25}\sqrt{-1} = 5i$$

That's all *i* is—just a way for us to refer to the square roots of negative numbers.

WORKING WITH *i*

Notice what happens when we take some simple powers of *i*:

$$i^1 = i$$
$$i^2 = \left(\sqrt{-1}\right)^2 = -1$$
$$i^3 = i^2 \cdot i = (-1)(i) = -i$$
$$i^4 = i^2 \cdot i^2 = (-1)(-1) = 1$$

If we go on to find i^5, you'll see that the pattern begins to repeat:

$$i^5 = i \cdot i^4 = i \cdot 1 = i$$

This is an important pattern to memorize: $\{i, -1, -i, 1, i, -1, -i, 1...\}$. It allows us to find *i* to the power of large numbers, using the following rules:

1. If the power is divisible by 4, *i* to that power is 1.
2. If the power is NOT divisible by 4, find the nearest power that IS divisible by 4, and count up or down to the power in question.

Look at the following example:

(EX) What is the value of i^{45}?

    A. -1
    B. 0
    C. 1
    D. $-i$
    E. *i*

45 is not divisible by 4, but 44 is. $i^{44} = 1$. The next term in the pattern is i, so:

$i^{45} = i$ **E.**

ALGEBRA WITH *i*

Nearly all of the ACT problems that involve *i* have to do with basic algebraic operations. When you're solving equations with *i*, you can pretend that *i* is just like any other variable, but with one exception: **You must remember the power rules for *i*.** For example, if you get an i^2, you have to remember to turn it into −1. Simplify the following expressions:

1. $3i + 7i =$
2. $(3i)(7i) =$
3. $\dfrac{24i^5}{12i} =$
4. $(2 + i)(3 − i) =$
5. $(x − i)(2x + 2i) =$

> These problems will obviously include the variable *i*. The ACT tends to be nice enough to tell you that $i^2 = −1$, so look for that, too.

27. For $i^2 = −1$, what is the value of $2i^4 + 2i^2$?

    A. 4
    B. 3
    C. 2
    D. 1
    E. 0

COMPLEX NUMBERS

A complex number is the sum (or difference) of a real number and an imaginary number. If *a* and *b* are real numbers, a complex number takes the form:

$$a + bi$$

An example of a complex number is 3 + 5*i*. The real number part is 3; the imaginary part is 5*i*.

You should be able to convert an expression into a complex number, which, remember, has the form *a* + *bi*. You can use the algebra rules, as described before.

(EX) Which of the following is equivalent to $\dfrac{6+9i}{3}$?

    A. −1
    B. 2 + 3*i*
    C. 2 + 9*i*
    D. 9 + 12*i*
    E. 18 + 9*i*

$$\dfrac{6+9i}{3} = \dfrac{6}{3} + \dfrac{9i}{3} = 2 + 3i \quad \textbf{B.}$$

i IN THE DENOMINATOR

Problems that require you to simplify a fraction with *i* in the denominator are rarely found on the ACT, but in case one shows up, there are two tricks:

1. If *i* (or a term including *i, such as 3i*) is alone in the denominator, multiply the numerator and denominator by *i*. This will give you an i^2 in the denominator (and thus, because i^2 = −1, the *i* goes away). Now you can put the number in complex form, as in the example above.

2. If the denominator is a complex number, multiply the numerator and denominator by the *complex conjugate* of the complex number. The complex conjugate of a complex number is simply the complex number with the *i* term multiplied by −1. For example: 2 − 3*i* is the conjugate of 2 + 3*i*. Multiplying by a complex conjugate gets rid of the imaginary number when you FOIL the two expressions. Look at the example below:

(EX) Which of following is equivalent to $\dfrac{20}{6+2i}$?

A. 1 + *i*
B. 1 − *i*
C. 2 − *i*
D. 3 − *i*
E. 4 − *i*

Multiply the numerator and denominator by the complex conjugate (6 − 2i), and use FOIL in the denominator:

$$\frac{20}{6+2i}\cdot\frac{6-2i}{6-2i}=\frac{120-40i}{36-12i+12i-4i^2}=\frac{120-40i}{36-4(-1)}=\frac{120-40i}{40}=3-i \ \ \textbf{D.}$$

THE COMPLEX PLANE

If you're comfortable with the (*x,y*) coordinate plane, you should be fine with the *complex plane*. The *real* part of the complex number is graphed on the *horizontal axis* of the complex plane, and the *imaginary* part is graphed on the *vertical axis*. The complex number 3 + 5*i* is graphed below:

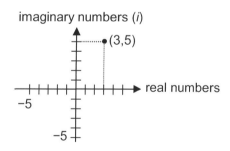

THE ABSOLUTE VALUE OF A COMPLEX NUMBER

If you can graph a complex number on the complex plane, and if you remember the Pythagorean Theorem, you should have no problem finding the *absolute value* of a complex number. Think of the absolute value as the "distance from the complex number to zero." (This is actually the same way we thought about absolute values in Chapter I.) Draw a line from the complex number "point" to the origin ("0") and find the length of the line. See the following example:

(EX) $|2 + 3i| = ?$

A. $\sqrt{5}$

B. $\sqrt{6}$

C. $\sqrt{10}$

D. $2\sqrt{3}$

E. $\sqrt{13}$

Graph 2 + 3i. Remember, the 2 is graphed on the horizontal real axis, and the 3 is graphed on the vertical imaginary axis.

Use the Pythagorean Theorem to find the distance to the origin (call this distance: c):

$2^2 + 3^2 = c^2 \rightarrow 13 = c^2 \rightarrow c = |2 + 3i| = \sqrt{13}$ ***E.***

Note: Once you understand the basic concept, you might recognize the shortcut: $|a + bi| = \sqrt{a^2 + b^2}$

———————

HW

46. For $i^2 = -1$, $(3 - 5i)^2 =$

A. $-16 - 30i$
B. -16
C. $9 + 25i$
D. $9 - 25i$
E. $9 - 30i$

58. For $i^2 = -1$, which of the following is equivalent to $\dfrac{5}{2 + i}$?

F. $10 - i$
G. $5 - i$
H. $4 - i$
J. $3 - i$
K. $2 - i$

60. Five complex numbers are graphed in the complex plane below. Which of the complex numbers has the greatest absolute value?

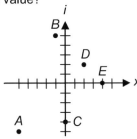

A. A
B. B
C. C
D. D
E. E

4. LOGARITHMS

The following rules should cover any logarithm problems that you may see.

DEFINITION OF LOGARITHM

Logarithms (or logs) are just tools that allow us to solve exponential equations. The basic definition is:

$$\boxed{\textit{FLASH CARDS}} \quad \log_a x = y \leftrightarrow a^y = x$$

The way you say this is: "the log of base *a* of *x* is *y*." Notice how the two equations compare:

$$\log_a x = y \leftrightarrow a^y = x$$

Perhaps the easiest thing to remember is that the "base," which is the lowered "*a*" following the word "log," is also the base in the exponential part of the equation.

Here's how you may be asked to use this equation:

(EX) Which of the following values of *x* satisfies $\log_x 27 = 3$?

   A. 3
   B. 6
   C. 9
   D. 12
   E. 13.5

Rewrite the log equation as a conventional exponential equation:

$\log_x 27 = 3 \rightarrow x^3 = 27$

What number cubed equals 27? The answer is 3 (if necessary, Pick Answers). **A.**

LOGARITHMIC PROPERTIES

The three following properties allow you to simplify logarithmic equations. Use flashcards to memorize them:

$$\boxed{\textit{FLASH CARDS}}$$

THE PRODUCT RULE

$$\log_x (ab) = \log_x a + \log_x b$$

THE QUOTIENT RULE

$$\log_x \left(\frac{a}{b} \right) = \log_x a - \log_x b$$

THE POWER RULE

$$\log_x a^b = b \log_x a$$

(EX) What is the value of the $\log_2 (AB)$ if $\log_2 A = 5$ and the $\log_2 B = 6$?

    A. 10   *Using the product rule, we can write $\log_2 (AB)$ as $\log_2 A + \log_2 B$. These*
    B. 11   *values are given, so:*
    C. 12   *$\log_2 (AB) = \log_2 A + \log_2 B = 5 + 6 = 11$* ***B.***
    D. 30
    E. 60

Try the following lesson problem:

51. If $\log_p a = q$, then $\log_p a^3 = $?

    A. $3q$
    B. $9q$
    C. q^3
    D. $3q^3$
    E. $9q^3$

LOG$_{10}$

When a log has a base of 10, you can write it without the base—the 10 is implied.

$$\log_{10} x = \log x$$

THE BASE-CHANGE RULE

This rule will probably only come in handy if you want to type logs into your calculator (something you would never *have* to do on the ACT, but something you might *choose* to do if you're stuck on a problem). Notice the "LOG" key on your calculator. Your calculator accepts logs that have a base of 10. So if you wanted to calculate, say, $\log_2 32$, you could use the base-change rule:

$$\log_a b = \frac{\log b}{\log a}$$

Notice that the number on top goes to the numerator and the base number goes to the denominator. This is what you might visually expect.

So what is $\log_2 32$? You can use your calculator:

$$\log_2 32 = \frac{\log 32}{\log 2} = \frac{1.505149978}{0.3010299957} = 5$$

LOGARITHMS HOMEWORK

31. What is the value of $\log_4 64$?

    A. 1
    B. 2
    C. 3
    D. 16
    E. 24

34. Which of the following values of x satisfies $\log_{2x} 4 = 2$?

    F. 16
    G. 8
    H. 4
    J. 2
    K. 1

58. If $\log_a 10 = A$ and $\log_a 5 = B$, then $\log_a 2 = $?

    A. $\dfrac{A}{B}$
    B. $A + B$
    C. $A - B$
    D. $2A - 4B$
    E. AB

5. MATRICES

Matrices problems generally take one of two forms. They either provide you information in a word problem, just as *tables* do, or they test *matrix operations*.

MATRICES AS TABLES

Matrices may look difficult, especially if you haven't spent much time working with them in school, but most matrices problems are really just table problems. Once you understand how the information is displayed, you can find your answer. Let's look at an example.

(EX) At a track meet, 10 points are awarded for a 1st place finish, 5 points are awarded for a 2nd place finish, and 2 points are awarded for a 3rd place finish. The matrices below show the number of 1st, 2nd, and 3rd place finishes for two schools: Richmond and Oakville. How many more points did Richmond score than Oakville in the track meet?

$$\begin{array}{ccc} \text{1st} & \text{2nd} & \text{3rd} \\ \end{array}$$
$$\text{Richmond} \begin{bmatrix} 4 & 5 & 2 \end{bmatrix} \quad \text{Oakville} \begin{bmatrix} 3 & 6 & 4 \end{bmatrix}$$

A. 1
B. 2
C. 3
D. 4
E. 5

The matrices simply provide you information, just as a table would. The math is straightforward. Remember: 10 points for 1st, 5 points for 2nd, and 2 points for 3rd:

Richmond: $4\cdot10 + 5\cdot5 + 2\cdot2 = 69$ points

Oakville: $3\cdot10 + 6\cdot5 + 4\cdot2 = 68$ points

➔ *$69 - 68 = 1$ A.*

Try the following lesson problem:

15. The Manatee Shirt Store sells four styles of a particular shirt (A, B, C, and D). The matrices below display the numbers of each style of shirt sold last month and the cost of each style of shirt. What was the total dollar amount that the store charged for these shirts last month?

$$\begin{array}{cccc} \text{A} & \text{B} & \text{C} & \text{D} \\ \end{array}$$
$$\begin{bmatrix} 10 & 15 & 5 & 20 \end{bmatrix} \qquad \begin{array}{c} \text{Cost} \\ \begin{array}{c} \text{A} \\ \text{B} \\ \text{C} \\ \text{D} \end{array} \begin{bmatrix} \$5.00 \\ \$10.00 \\ \$7.50 \\ \$12.50 \end{bmatrix} \end{array}$$

A. $477.50
B. $480.00
C. $482.50
D. $485.00
E. $487.50

MATRIX OPERATIONS

Sometimes you might have to add, subtract, or multiply matrices. Unlike the previous matrices problems, these *matrix operations* problems are usually *not* word problems.

ADDING AND SUBTRACTING MATRICES

You can only add or subtract matrices that are the same size. The process is straightforward. Simply add or subtract elements in the same position of each matrix. For example:

$$\begin{bmatrix} 5 & -2 \\ 3 & 6 \end{bmatrix} + \begin{bmatrix} 3 & 6 \\ -4 & 4 \end{bmatrix} = \begin{bmatrix} 5+3 & -2+6 \\ 3+(-4) & 6+4 \end{bmatrix} = \begin{bmatrix} 8 & 4 \\ -1 & 10 \end{bmatrix}$$

MULTIPLYING A MATRIX BY A NUMBER

This operation is also straightforward. Simply multiply each element in the matrix by the number in front. For example:

$$5\begin{bmatrix} 3 & -3 \\ 2 & 1 \end{bmatrix} = \begin{bmatrix} 5 \cdot 3 & 5 \cdot (-3) \\ 5 \cdot 2 & 5 \cdot 1 \end{bmatrix} = \begin{bmatrix} 15 & -15 \\ 10 & 5 \end{bmatrix}$$

MULTIPLYING MATRICES

Now that the easier stuff is out of the way, let's look at multiplying matrices. First, let's refer to the size of a matrix as $m \times n$, where m is the number of rows and n is the number of columns. Don't forget: the number that comes first refers to the number of *rows*.

There are two rules that you should know before we get into actually multiplying matrices:

Rule 1: To multiply two matrices, the number of *columns* in the first matrix must equal the number of *rows* in the second matrix. For example, we can multiply matrices A and B below:

$$A_{1 \times 2} = \begin{bmatrix} -1 & 2 \end{bmatrix} \qquad B_{2 \times 4} = \begin{bmatrix} 3 & 0 & -1 & 3 \\ -2 & 1 & 2 & 0 \end{bmatrix}$$

$$2 = 2$$

Rule 2: The product of two matrices will result in a matrix with the same number of rows as the first matrix and the same number of columns as the second matrix.

$$A_{1 \times 2} \times B_{2 \times 4} = C_{1 \times 4} = \begin{bmatrix} ? & ? & ? & ? \end{bmatrix}$$

So how do we actually multiply matrices? Most graphing calculators can perform matrix multiplication; you may want to learn how to do this; check your calculator's manual. If you don't have a graphing calculator, use the following method. Follow along with the example below:

1. Circle each row in the first matrix and circle each column in the second matrix (see the example below). Note that each row of the first matrix and each column of the second matrix must have the same number of elements (in this case, 2)—see rule 1 above.

2. Draw a blank matrix with the same number of rows as the first matrix and the same number of columns as the second matrix (see rule 2 above). This will become the final product matrix.

3. To find the first element in row 1 of the product matrix, multiply each element in row 1 of the first matrix by each related element of column 1 of the second matrix, and add these products together. This sounds confusing, but it's not that hard. See step 3 in the example below.

4. To find the second element in row 1 of the product matrix, multiply each element in row 1 of the first matrix by each related element of column 2 of the second matrix, and add these products together. Repeat these steps until you have constructed the product matrix.

(EX) What is the matrix product $\begin{bmatrix} -1 & 2 \end{bmatrix} \begin{bmatrix} 3 & 0 & -1 & 3 \\ -2 & 1 & 2 & 0 \end{bmatrix}$?

A. $\begin{bmatrix} -7 & 2 & 5 & -3 \end{bmatrix}$

B. $\begin{bmatrix} -3 & 0 & 1 & -3 \end{bmatrix}$

C. $\begin{bmatrix} -3 & 0 & 1 & -3 \\ -4 & 2 & 4 & 0 \end{bmatrix}$

D. $-\begin{bmatrix} 6 & 0 & -2 & 6 \\ -4 & 2 & 4 & 0 \end{bmatrix}$

E. -3

① Circle the row of the first matrix and the columns of the second matrix, as shown below. ② The product matrix will have 1 row and 4 columns.

$\begin{bmatrix} -1 & 2 \end{bmatrix} \begin{bmatrix} 3 & 0 & -1 & 3 \\ -2 & 1 & 2 & 0 \end{bmatrix} = ② \begin{bmatrix} ? & ? & ? & ? \end{bmatrix}$

③ To find the first element in row 1 of the product matrix, multiply each element in row 1 of the first matrix by each related element in column 1 of the second matrix, and add together: $-1\cdot3 + 2\cdot-2 = -3 - 4 = -7$

④ Here are the calculations for the other elements:

row 1, column 2: $-1\cdot0 +2\cdot1 = 2$

row 1, column 3: $-1\cdot(-1) +2\cdot2 = 5$

row 1, column 4: $-1\cdot3 +2\cdot0 = -3$

→ So the final product matrix is: $\begin{bmatrix} -7 & 2 & 5 & -3 \end{bmatrix}$ **A.**

Try the following lesson problem:

47. What is the matrix product of $\begin{bmatrix} 1 & 2 \\ 3 & 4 \end{bmatrix} \cdot \begin{bmatrix} -1 & -2 \\ -3 & -4 \end{bmatrix}$?

A. $\begin{bmatrix} 0 & 0 \\ 0 & 0 \end{bmatrix}$

B. $\begin{bmatrix} -7 & -10 \\ -15 & -22 \end{bmatrix}$

C. $\begin{bmatrix} 10 & -10 \end{bmatrix}$

D. $\begin{bmatrix} -7 & -10 & -15 & -22 \end{bmatrix}$

E. 0

34. Sell-U-Phone Company makes three types of phones (X, Y, and Z). The matrix below shows the number of phones of each type manufactured last week at two Sell-U-Phone factories (A and B).

$$\begin{array}{c} \\ A \\ B \end{array} \begin{array}{ccc} X & Y & Z \\ \begin{bmatrix} 500 & 300 & 160 \\ 600 & 0 & 900 \end{bmatrix} \end{array}$$

If a manufactured phone cannot be sold, it is called a "failure." Quality control at Sell-U-Phone provides estimates of the failure rate for each type of phone, as shown in the matrix below.

$$\begin{array}{c} X \\ Y \\ Z \end{array} \begin{bmatrix} 0.02 \\ 0.01 \\ 0.05 \end{bmatrix}$$

Based on the matrices, what is the estimate for the total number of failures at both factories last week?

A. 72
B. 74
C. 76
D. 78
E. 80

6. LOGIC

Logic problems are not common, but it's not a bad idea to be familiar with them. The best approach on logic problems is to keep track of information by writing it down. Also, be on the lookout for answer choices that are easy to eliminate. This will help you focus on the other answer choices.

 Logic problems will generally list two or more "logical statements." They will then ask which of the answer choices is true based on these statements. These problems are usually not too difficult, as reflected in the problem numbers.

Let's look at an example:

(EX) Consider the following three logical statements:

All squares are rectangles.
Quadrilateral *ABCD* is NOT a square.
Quadrilateral *EFGH* is a square.

Which of the following statements is necessarily true?

A. Quadrilateral *ABCD* is NOT a rectangle.
B. Quadrilateral *ABCD* is a square.
C. Quadrilateral *EFGH* is a rectangle.
D. Quadrilateral *EFGH* is NOT a rectangle.
E. Quadrilateral *EFGH* is NOT a square.

First, let's eliminate the easy ones. Notice that B and E both directly disagree with the given statements. Eliminate them.

Answer choice A may be the most difficult to eliminate, but just because ABCD is not a square does not mean that it couldn't be a rectangle. Many rectangles are not squares.

You can also eliminate D. EFGH must be a rectangle if it's a square.

*The answer is **C**. If EFGH is a square, then, as stated in the first given logic statement, it is also a rectangle.*

Try the following lesson problem:

2. Consider the following two logical statements to be true.

If Bob goes shopping at Al's Groceries, he buys a comic book.
Bob did NOT buy a comic book.

Which of the following statements is necessarily true?

A. Bob did NOT go shopping at Al's Groceries.
B. Bob went shopping at Al's Groceries.
C. Bob did NOT go shopping.
D. Bob went shopping at another store.
E. Bob bought a comic book at another store.

7. DIRECT AND INVERSE VARIATION

You should memorize two simple equations for *direct* and *inverse variation* problems.

DIRECT VARIATION

If two positive numbers are *directly proportional*, then as one number increases (or decreases) the other number also increases (or decreases). To help remember the following equation, notice that **d**irect variation and **d**ivision start with the same letter—the equation for direct variation shows that the **d**ivision of two numbers y/x will always equal a constant number k:

$$\frac{y}{x} = k$$

These problems usually mention the words *directly proportional*, but could also say: x and y are *in direct variation*, x and y are *in proportion*, or x *varies directly with* y.

INVERSE VARIATION

If two positive numbers are *inversely proportional*, then as one number increases the other number does the opposite—it decreases, or if one number decreases the other number increases. The equation for inverse variation shows that the *product* of two numbers xy will always equal a constant number k:

$$xy = k$$

These problems usually mention the words *inversely proportional*, but could also say x *varies indirectly with* y.

SOLVING VARIATION PROBLEMS

To solve these problems, you will usually be given initial values for x and y.

1. Using the correct equation above with the given values of x and y, solve for k.
2. Once you know the value for k, you can solve for y (for any given value of x) or solve for x (for any given value of y).

Ⓔ If *y* is directly proportional to *x* and *y* = –5 when *x* = 5, what is the value of *y* when *x* = 15?

A. 15
B. 5
C. 0
D. –5
E. –15

Direct variation:

① $\frac{y}{x} = \frac{-5}{5} = -1$ *(so k = –1)* → ② $\frac{y}{15} = -1$ → *y* = –15 **E.**

Note: *Since x is positive and y is negative, k < 0 and y **decreases** as x increases (the opposite of what you might expect in a **direct**-proportion problem). As you can see, just make sure to use the correct equation, and you will find the correct answer.*

Try the following lesson problem:

6. If *x* varies indirectly with *y* and *x* = 20 when *y* = 2, what is the value of *y* when *x* = –2?

A. –40
B. –20
C. –⅕
D. 10
E. 20

26. If *x* varies indirectly with *y²* and *x* = 200 when *y* = 2, what is the value of *y* when *x* = 8?

F. 50
G. 40
H. 30
J. 20
K. 10

38. If *x* is directly proportional to *y* and *x* = ½ when *y* = 4, what is the value of $\frac{y}{x}$ when *y* = 2 × 10⁸?

A. 2
B. 8
C. 2 × 10⁸
D. 4 × 10⁸
E. 8 × 10⁸

Continued ➜

51. The cost to use Sound Ideas Studios varies directly with the square root of the time the studio is used. If a band pays $60 for 36 minutes of studio time, how much would 15 hours of studio time cost?

    F. $1,500
    G. $640
    H. $300
    J. $144
    K. $12

8. SETS AND GROUPS

SETS

A *set* is a collection of items. These items are called *elements* or *members* of the set. A set is usually represented by brackets, for example:

set *A* = {1, 3, 4, 5, 7, 8, 9}
set *B* = {2, 4, 6, 8, 10}

VENN DIAGRAMS

You may be asked to find the *intersection* or the *union* of two or more sets. It may be helpful to look at sets as circles and the members of the sets as numbers inside the circles. These are called Venn diagrams.

Intersection – the common elements of the sets. The intersection of sets *A* and *B* above is {4, 8} since 4 and 8 are members in *both* sets:

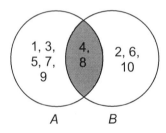

Union – consists of the elements that are in either set *or* in both sets (in other words—all the elements). The union of sets *A* and *B* above is {1, 2, 3, 4, 5, 6, 7, 8, 9, 10} since these 10 numbers are in either set (1, 2, 3, 5, 6, 7, 9, and 10) or in both sets (4 and 8):

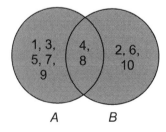

VENN DIAGRAMS: *NUMBERS* OF ELEMENTS

The Venn diagrams above display the actual elements of each region. For example, the intersection of sets *A* and *B* is made up of the numbers 4 and 8. Venn diagrams can also display the *number* of elements in each region. The Venn diagram for sets *A* and *B* is shown below:

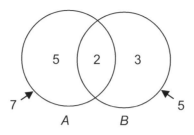

Make sure you are clear that each number represents the *number* of elements in that region. For example, there are 5 elements unique to set *A*, and 2 elements in set *A* *and* set *B* (the intersection). Thus, the total number of elements in set A is 7 (written outside the circle).

————

 To identify set problems, look for elements surrounded by brackets, such as {1, 2, 3}, or look for Venn diagrams.

Try the following lesson problem:

7. Sets *M* and *N* are shown below. How many numbers are in the intersection of sets *M* and *N*?

       set *M* = {all prime numbers less than 10}
       set *N* = {all odd numbers less than 10}

    A. 1
    B. 2
    C. 3
    D. 4
    E. 5

GROUPS

When you are asked to find the number of members of a particular group, you're probably dealing with a *groups* problem. Let's use a Venn diagram to visualize a typical group problem:

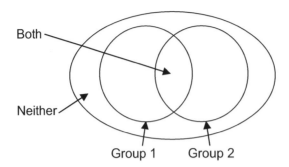

In the Venn diagram above, we have two groups that intersect (the intersection is labeled "Both"). Notice that we also have a region where members are not part of either group ("Neither"). You can create a simple equation from this Venn diagram:

> **FLASH CARDS** | **Total = Members of Group 1 + Members of Group 2 + Neither − Both**

Why did we subtract members in "Both" groups? Because when we counted Group 1 and Group 2, we ended up counting members in both groups twice, so subtract them once.

For groups problems, you can usually use either the equation above or a Venn diagram. If you ever see a problem with more than two groups, use a Venn diagram.

> These problems will usually involve two groups (generally of people). They ask about the number of members in *one*, *both*, or *none* of the groups.

(EX) If at a school of 200 students, 75 students take Spanish and 25 students take Latin. 10 of the students who take Latin also take Spanish, how many students are not taking Spanish or Latin?

A. 80
B. 90
C. 100
D. 110
E. 120

Total = Group 1 + Group 2 + Neither − Both

200 = 75 + 25 + Neither − 10

*→ Neither = 110 **D.***

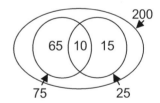

Try the following lesson problem:

52. At a school of 90 students, all of the students take Spanish, Latin, or both. If 75 students take Spanish and 25 students take Latin, how many students take Spanish or Latin but not both?

    A. 10
    B. 70
    C. 80
    D. 90
    E. 100

SETS AND GROUPS HOMEWORK

31. The figure below is a Venn diagram for sets X, Y, and Z. The number in each region indicates how many elements are in that region. If there are 20 elements common to sets X and Y, what is the value of a?

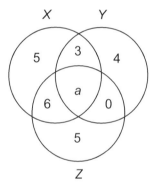

    A. 2
    B. 5
    C. 11
    D. 17
    E. 20

52. Of the 120 international students at a camp, 90 spoke Spanish and 40 spoke French. What is the least possible number of campers that could speak both Spanish and French?

    F. 0
    G. 10
    H. 40
    J. 50
    K. 80

58. Hot Rod Auto Body's employees perform the three basic tasks of auto body repair: body work, sanding, and painting. All employees can perform at least one of these tasks, and some can perform more than one. Using the information in the table below, how many people are employed at Hot Rod Auto Body?

Number of workers	Task(s)
5	body work
7	sanding
7	painting
2	both body work and sanding but not painting
0	both body work and painting but not sanding
1	both sanding and painting but not body work
1	body work, sanding, and painting

   A. 14
   B. 16
   C. 18
   D. 19
   E. 23

9. SYMBOL PROBLEMS

Symbol problems use unfamiliar symbols to represent some mathematical operation or expression. These problems are usually not as difficult as they look—they tend to be easier than the problem numbers indicate—so be confident and aggressive.

> Look for problems with unfamiliar symbols. These symbols will be clearly defined in the problem.

Use the following method:

1. **The first step is to make sure you completely understand the symbol's definition.** The symbol will always be *clearly defined* somewhere in the question. The definition will tell you what to do with one or more variables.

2. **Rewrite the problem *without* the symbol by following the rules of the symbol's definition.** The definition may tell you where to put the question's numbers or variables in a mathematical expression, or you may be asked to apply some operation on a number or variable.

3. Use basic math to answer the question.

The following examples display the most common type of symbol problem, where the symbol represents a mathematical *expression*:

For all numbers p and q, where $p \neq q$, $p \diamond q = \dfrac{p \times q}{p - q}$.

(EX) $3 \diamond 2 =$ $\qquad \dfrac{3 \cdot 2}{3 - 2} = 6$

(EX) $2 \diamond 3 =$ $\qquad \dfrac{2 \cdot 3}{2 - 3} = -6$

(EX) $q \diamond p =$ $\qquad \dfrac{q \times p}{q - p}$

(EX) $(x - y) \diamond (x + y) = \dfrac{(x - y) \cdot (x + y)}{(x - y) - (x + y)}$

(EX) $\bigcirc \diamond \square = \qquad \dfrac{\bigcirc \cdot \square}{\bigcirc - \square}$

(EX) If $2 \diamond b = -4$, what is the value of b?

$\qquad \dfrac{2b}{2 - b} = -4$

$\rightarrow 2b = -8 + 4b$

$\rightarrow -2b = -8$

$\rightarrow b = 4$

Try the following lesson problems:

> Use the following information to answer questions 13 and 14.

For all numbers p and q, where $p \neq q$, $p \diamondsuit q = \dfrac{p \times q}{p - q}$.

13. $(6 \diamondsuit 4) - (8 \diamondsuit 6) =$

    A. −24
    B. −12
    C. −4
    D. 12
    E. 24

The next question is an example of a *true-false* question. Always work on one *Roman numeral* (I, II, or III) at a time. As soon as you are able to eliminate a Roman numeral or determine that it is definitely true, eliminate answer choices accordingly. Sometimes, you will be able to eliminate enough answer choices to avoid checking all of the Roman numerals.

Remember that the following question relates to the symbol defined above:

14. If $p \neq 0$ and $q \neq 0$, which of the following is (are) necessarily true?

    I. $p \diamondsuit q = q \diamondsuit p$

    II. $\left(\dfrac{1}{p} \diamondsuit \dfrac{1}{q} \right)^{-1} = q - p$

    III. $(-p) \diamondsuit (-q) = -(p \diamondsuit q)$

    F. I only
    G. II only
    H. I and II only
    J. II and III only
    K. I, II, and III

The following example displays another type of symbol problem, where the symbol represents a mathematical *operation*:

(EX) Let $\underline{\underline{x}}$ be defined as the largest prime number that is a factor of *x*. What is the value of

$\underline{\underline{10}} \times \underline{\underline{16}}$?

A. 4

B. 10

C. 25

D. 40

E. 160

① *The symbol has to do with prime factors. You might want to review factor trees in Chapter 1.*

② *"Let $\underline{\underline{10}}$ be defined as the largest prime number that is a factor of 10".*

③ *The prime factors of 10 are 5 and 2.* → $\underline{\underline{10}}$ = 5

Repeat steps 2 and 3 for the number 16:

② *"Let $\underline{\underline{16}}$ be defined as the largest prime number that is a factor of 16".*

③ *The prime factors of 16 are 2, 2, 2, and 2.* → $\underline{\underline{16}}$ = 2

→ $\underline{\underline{10}} \times \underline{\underline{16}}$ = 5 × 2 = 10 **B.**

SYMBOLS IN THE ANSWER CHOICES

Some symbol problems are made more difficult by including the symbol in the answer choices. In these problems, make sure you apply the symbol to the numbers in the answer choices. Try the following lesson problem:

30. Let ♦*n* be defined for any positive integer *n* as the number obtained by adding the digits of *n*. For example, ♦5 = 5, ♦25 = 7, and ♦550 = 10. What is the value of ♦25 + ♦50?

A. ♦5

B. ♦7

C. ♦12

D. ♦66

E. 75

———————

6. For all integers n, where $n \neq -1$, let $n\heartsuit = \dfrac{n-1}{n+1}$. What is the value of $(-3)\heartsuit$?

   A. -2
   B. -1
   C. 0
   D. 1
   E. 2

38. Let $\Uparrow$ be defined by $a\Uparrow b = a^b$. If $x = 2\Uparrow p$, $y = 2\Uparrow q$, and $p + q = 5$, what is the value of xy?

   F. 7
   G. 10
   H. 25
   J. 32
   K. 128

10. CONSECUTIVE INTEGERS

Consecutive integers (for example: −2, −1, 0, 1, 2, 3) can be written algebraically as:

x, $x + 1$, $x + 2$...

Consecutive *even* or *odd* integers (for example: 2, 4, 6, 8 or 1, 3, 5, 7) can be written algebraically as:

x, $x + 2$, $x + 4$...

> These problems almost always include the words *consecutive integers, consecutive odd integers*, or *consecutive even integers*. Some problems may instead mention that terms are *one more than the preceding term* or *two more than the preceding term*. This is just another way of saying that terms are consecutive.

Usually on the ACT, you will *not* have to express consecutive integers algebraically. The following method is faster. The consecutive integers in these problems are usually given as a *sum*.

1. Divide the sum of the consecutive integers by the *number* of consecutive integers.
2. If there is an *odd* number of integers, this technique will give the actual middle integer. It is worth noting that this number is also the *average* and the *median* of the consecutive integers. (Look at the 1st example below.)
3. If there is an *even* number of integers, the above technique will give a value exactly *halfway between* the two middle integers. This is also the average and the median of the consecutive integers. Once you know this value, you can find the two middle consecutive integers. (Look at the 2nd example below.)
4. Once you know the middle integer or integers, count to the term in question. (Look at the last example.)

(EX) What is the middle integer of three consecutive even integers if the sum of these integers is 12?

① $\dfrac{12}{3} = 4$ → *②* The number 4 is the middle integer. → 2, **4**, 6

(EX) What are the two middle numbers of four consecutive integers if the sum of these integers is 26?

① $\dfrac{26}{4} = 6.5$ → *③* The number 6.5 is exactly halfway between the two middle integers, so the middle integers must be 6 and 7.

→ 5, **6**, **7**, 8

(EX) What is the largest of 5 consecutive odd integers if the sum of these integers is 75?

$①\ \dfrac{75}{5} = 15$ → $②$ *The number 15 is the middle integer.*

$④$ *Since there are 5 odd integers, we have* <u>11</u>, <u>13</u>, <u>15</u>, <u>17</u>, **<u>19</u>**

LESSON PROBLEMS

4. What is the smaller of 2 consecutive even integers if the sum of these integers is 290?

   A. 142
   B. 143
   C. 144
   D. 145
   E. 146

19. Which of the following is the sum of two consecutive integers?

   F. 90
   G. 91
   H. 92
   J. 94
   K. 100

31. A set of 20 consecutive integers has a sum of 50. If x is a member of this set, and if x is less than the median of the set, what is the greatest possible value of x?

   A. 0
   B. 2
   C. 3
   D. 19
   E. 24

11. GREATEST/LEAST POSSIBLE VALUES

Some problems may ask you to find the *greatest possible value* (GPV) or *least possible value* (LPV) of a number or group of numbers.

Look for the words *greatest* (or *maximum, biggest,* etc.) *possible value* or *least* (or *minimum, smallest,* etc.) *possible value.*

Be familiar with the following rules:

GREATEST AND LEAST VALUES

Students often forget that if a variable is negative (for example: $-x$), then the *greater* the value of x, the *lesser* the value of $-x$. Alternatively, the *lesser* the value of x, the *greater* the value of $-x$. Look at the following example:

(EX) If $-2 \le x \le 3$, what is the maximum value of $-2x$?

    A. −6
    B. 0
    C. 2
    D. 4
    E. 6

Since the variable is negative, the maximum value for −2x will occur when x is minimized (−2):

Maximum value of −2x = −2(−2) = 4 **D.**

GPV OF NUMBERS MULTIPLIED TOGETHER

Some problems ask you to find the GPV of a *product* of two numbers. These problems typically give you the *sum* of the numbers. The GPV of two numbers multiplied together will occur when the values of the two numbers are *equal or as close to each other as possible*. Look at the following example:

(EX) If the sum of two positive integers is 12, what is the greatest possible value of the product of the two integers?

    A. 12
    B. 32
    C. 35
    D. 36
    E. 144

$x + y = 12$

$x = 6, y = 6$ *(6 and 6 are as close as you can get!)*

$\rightarrow 6 \times 6 = 36$ **D.**

LPV OF NUMBERS MULTIPLIED TOGETHER

You might also see a problem that gives you the *difference* of two numbers and asks for the LPV of the *product* of the numbers. The LPV will occur when:

1. One value is negative and one value is positive (to get a negative product).
2. The *absolute* values of the two numbers are equal or as close to each other as possible.

For example:

(EX) What is the least possible value for the product of 2 integers that differ by 7?

A. −49
B. −12
C. −10
D. 0
E. 10

Let's call the two numbers x and y.

Think of some numbers that have a difference of 7. Remember, one of the numbers should be negative and one should be positive:

−1 and 6, −2 and 5, −3 and 4, etc.

Now, which pair of numbers has the closest absolute values?

Since |−4| = 4 and |3| = 3, this pair has the closest absolute values (they're only 1 apart).

*So x = 3 and y = −4 → 3 × −4 = −12 **B.***

Note: You could have also used the numbers x = 4 and y = −3. The answer is the same.

LESSON PROBLEMS

42. The sum of three positive integers is 40. If one of the integers is 11, what is the greatest possible value of the product of the other two integers?

A. 29
B. 200
C. 210
D. 225
E. 400

50. If x is a member of the set {−2, 0, 2} and y is a member of the set {−3, −1, 1, 3}, what is the greatest possible value of $x - y$?

F. 5
G. 4
H. 3
J. 2
K. 1

54. If $0 \le x \le 3$ and $-3 \le y \le 0$, what is the maximum value of $|2y - x|$?

    A. 12
    B. 9
    C. 6
    D. 3
    E. 0

60. If x and y are real numbers and $x - y = 10$, what is the smallest possible value for xy?

    F. −25
    G. −21
    H. 0
    J. 1
    K. 11

12. MATH ODDS AND ENDS PROBLEMS

PRACTICE PROBLEMS

The following worksheet and practice problems (from Test 1 in *The Real ACT Prep Guide*, 3rd Edition) test techniques taught in this chapter. It is very important to look back to the lessons in this chapter and review the techniques while completing these problems. Try to determine which technique relates to each problem and apply the methods taught in the tutorial. Do not time yourself on these problems. The problems are provided to give you an opportunity to practice, and hopefully master, the techniques in this tutorial before you apply them on real ACTs in a timed setting.

- ☐ Math Odds and Ends Worksheet
- ☐ **Test 1**: 12^{30}, 13^{40}, 18^{30}, 48^{40}, 50^{40} (see Step 3 under "Test Corrections" below)

[30] Questions marked with a "30" are covered by the **30- and 40-hour programs**.
[40] Questions marked with a "40" are covered by the **40-hour program**.

PRACTICE TEST

30- and 40-hour programs: Now is a good time to take **Test 4** in the ACT book. You've now covered most (if not all) of the topics tested on the ACT. Good luck! If you have time after you have completed and corrected Test 4, take **Test 5**.

TEST CORRECTIONS

After each practice test is graded, you should correct Math Odds and Ends problems that you missed or left blank. There are three steps to correcting the practice tests:

1. The Math Odds and Ends questions for each test are listed below. Go back to your answer sheet for the corresponding test and circle the question numbers below that you missed (or guessed on, if you kept track of your guesses).
   - ☐ **Test 2**: 24^{30}, 42^{40}, 59^{40}
   - ☐ **Test 3**: 5^{40}, 13^{30}, 22^{40}, 29^{40}, 51^{30}
   - ☐ **Test 4**: 5^{30}, 16^{40}, 41^{40}, 49^{40}
   - ☐ **Test 5**: 20^{40}, 27^{30}, 51^{40}, 56^{40}

[30] Questions marked with a "30" are covered by the **30- and 40-hour programs**.
[40] Questions marked with a "40" are covered by the **40-hour program**.

2. Correct the problems in *The Real ACT Study Guide*. As you correct the problems, go back to the tutorial and review the techniques. The idea is to: (1) identify techniques that have given you trouble, (2) go back to the tutorial so you can review and strengthen these techniques, and (3) apply these techniques to the specific problems on which you struggled.

3. If you have trouble identifying the best technique to use on a problem, see the Techniques Reference information in Chapter VIII, starting on page 453.

MATH ODDS AND ENDS WORKSHEET*

Problem numbers represent the *approximate* level of difficulty for each problem (out of 60).
*30-hour program: You may choose to only complete 7, 28, 47, and 55.

5. Consider the 3 statements below to be true.

    All lizards on Island A are blue-bellied lizards.
    Lizard X is a blue-bellied lizard.
    Lizard Y is a green-bellied lizard.

    Which of the following statements is necessarily true?

    A. Lizard X does NOT
       live on Island A.
    B. Lizard X lives on
       Island A.
    C. Lizard Y does NOT
       live on Island A.
    D. Lizard X and Lizard Y
       live on the same
       island.
    E. Lizard X and Lizard Y
       do NOT live on the
       same island.

7. If a player plays one game on a slot machine, the probability that she will win is 0.01. What

    is the probability that she will NOT win if she plays one game?

    F. 0.01
    G. 0.09
    H. 0.19
    J. 0.90
    K. 0.99

22. The annual membership fee at a country club varies indirectly with the number of years that

    you have been a member, up to the point where membership is free. If you pay $4,000 for

    your 2nd year of membership, how much will you pay for your 10th year of membership?

    A. $400
    B. $700
    C. $800
    D. $2,000
    E. $20,000

Continued ➔

28. Floyd starts at City A. He must pick up a package at City B and deliver the package to City C. If there are 7 possible routes between City A and City B and 8 possible routes between City B and City C, how many routes are possible for Floyd to travel from City A to City B to City C?

F.   15
G.   48
H.   52
J.   56
K.   150

30. Which of the following values of a satisfies $\log_a 1{,}000 = 3$?

A.   1
B.   10
C.   100
D.   1,000
E.   10,000

34. The integer 15 is to be expressed as a sum of n consecutive positive integers. Which of the following can NOT be a value for n?

F.   2
G.   3
H.   4
J.   5
K.   None of these

38. At a car repair shop, 10 of the cars have mechanical problems and 16 of the cars have electrical problems. If there are 20 cars at the shop and all of the cars have either mechanical problems, electrical problems, or both, how many cars have both mechanical and electrical problems?

A.   6
B.   8
C.   16
D.   20
E.   26

39. For $i^2 = -1$, what is the value of $(4 + i)(-3 - i)$?

F. $-7 - 7i$
G. $-11 - 7i$
H. $-11 - i$
J. $-12 - 7i$
K. $-12 - 8i$

Continued ➔

42. For all numbers where $a \neq -1$, let $a\uparrow = \dfrac{a}{a+1}$. If $a \neq 1$ and $a \neq 2$, then $(a-2)\uparrow \times (1-a)\uparrow = ?$

   A. 1

   B. $\dfrac{1}{a+1}$

   C. $\dfrac{a+1}{a-2}$

   D. $\dfrac{a-1}{2}$

   E. $-a^2 + 3a - 2$

45. What is the matrix product $\begin{bmatrix} x & y & z \end{bmatrix} \cdot \begin{bmatrix} 1 \\ 2 \\ 3 \end{bmatrix}$?

   F. $\begin{bmatrix} 6x + 6y + 6z \end{bmatrix}$

   G. $\begin{bmatrix} 3x + 2y + z \end{bmatrix}$

   H. $\begin{bmatrix} x + 2y + 3z \end{bmatrix}$

   J. $\begin{bmatrix} x \\ 2y \\ 3z \end{bmatrix}$

   K. $\begin{bmatrix} 6x \\ 6y \\ 6z \end{bmatrix}$

47. A kitchen drawer is filled with forks, spoons, and knives. The probability that a spoon is selected at random is $\frac{1}{2}$, and the probability that a knife is selected at random is $\frac{1}{6}$. If all of the forks are removed from the drawer, what is the probability of selecting a knife at random?

   A. $\frac{1}{6}$

   B. $\frac{1}{4}$

   C. $\frac{1}{3}$

   D. $\frac{1}{2}$

   E. $\frac{3}{4}$

Continued ➜

55. A bag contains exactly 7 blue marbles. If there are 21 marbles in the bag, what is the probability that the first three marbles drawn at random will be blue if the marbles are not replaced after they are drawn?

F. $\frac{1}{3}$

G. $\frac{1}{9}$

H. $\frac{1}{27}$

J. $\frac{1}{38}$

K. $\frac{1}{46}$

58. Which of the following values of x satisfies $\log_5 125^2 = 2x$?

A. 3
B. 5
C. 6
D. 15
E. 25

VIII
ACT PRACTICE TESTS: TECHNIQUES REFERENCE

The following pages show the recommended KlassTutoring techniques for the Math Test questions in *The Real ACT Prep Guide*, 3rd Edition*. Do not look at these techniques until you have attempted the problems on your own. One of the most important ACT skills you can develop is the ability to determine what technique or techniques to use on a given problem. Review the magnifying glass information in this tutorial, and make sure you've tried to determine techniques on your own before you use the information in this chapter.

*ACT is a registered trademark of ACT, Inc., which was not involved in the production of and does not endorse this book.

1. ACT PRACTICE TEST 1

1. Rates, Times, and Distances (RTD)

2. Exponents or Pick Numbers (Type 1)

3. Arithmetic Word Problems

4. Averages (ANS)

5. Percent Problems

6. Area and Perimeter

7. Essential Algebra or Pick Numbers (Type 1)

8. Essential Algebra

9. Pick Answers

10. Pick Numbers (Type 4)

11. Algebraic Word Problems

12. Probability

13. Matrices (as Tables)

14. Averages

15. Arithmetic Word Problems

16. Pick Numbers (Type 1) or Essential Algebra

17. Coordinates

18. Principle of Counting

19. Proportions

20. Triangles (Pythagorean Theorem)

21. Essential Algebra or Pick Numbers (Type 1)

22. Lines (Equation of)

23. Factoring or Pick Answers

24. Basic Trigonometry

25. Triangles (Pythagorean Theorem)

26. Algebraic Word Problems

27. Solids and Volume

28. Basic Trigonometry

29. Tables and Graphs/Ratios

30. Lines (One-Dimensional)/Pick Answers

31. Lines (Intersecting)

32. Pick Numbers (Type 1) or Essential Algebra

33. Area (of Parallelogram or Area Cutting)

34. Pick Numbers (Type 2)

35. Coordinates (Modeling/Midpoint)

36. Algebraic Word Problems

37. Triangles (Pythagorean Theorem)

38. Area

39. Triangles (Similar)

40. Angles (Parallel Lines)/Area(Def. of Trapezoid) or Pick Answers

41. Area and Perimeter

42. Percent (Of/Is): The problem uses *fractions* instead of percent.

43. Factoring/Pick Answers: Hint: the greatest common factor of the two expressions is xy^2; set equal to 45 and Pick Answers.

44. Percent (Of/Is)

45. Coordinates (Slanted Distances)

46. Ratios/Area

47. More Circles (Equation of) or Pick Numbers → Pick Answers

48. Complex Numbers

49. Patterns

50. Groups/Pick Answers

51. Pick Answers → Pick Numbers

52. General Geometry Problem: Hint: Just draw carefully.

53. Tables and Graphs

54. Trig and the Unit Circle

55. Coordinates/Pick Numbers → Pick Answers

56. Function Basics

57. Graphs of Functions (Graphing Calculator) or Pick Answers → Pick Numbers

58. Transformations

59. Pick Numbers → Pick Answers

60. Trig. Odds and Ends (Given Formulas) or Calculator (just find sin (π/12))

2. ACT PRACTICE TEST 2

1. Proportions
2. Proportions
3. Proportions
4. Averages (ANS)
5. Pick Numbers (Type 1)
6. Angles (Sum of Interior)
7. Triangles (Similar)
8. Algebraic Word Problems
9. Proportions
10. Essential Algebra or Pick Numbers (Type 2)
11. Algebraic Word Problems/Simultaneous Equations or Pick Answers
12. Essential Algebra
13. Solids and Volume (Area Fitting)
14. Angles (Triangle)
15. Ratios (Share Problems)
16. Lines (Equation of)
17. Angles (Parallel Lines/Triangles/Vertical Angles)
18. Pick Answers
19. Lines (Equation of)
20. Basic Trigonometry
21. Lines (Equation of/Slope)
22. Algebraic Word Problems/Pick Answers
23. Function Basics
24. Principle of Counting
25. Triangles (Similar)
26. Pick Answers
27. Algebraic Word Problems/Pick Answers
28. Essential Algebra or Pick Numbers (Type 1)
29. Averages (Medians)
30. Area (Shaded Regions)
31. Triangles (Special Right)
32. Function Basics

33. Triangles (Pythagorean Theorem)
34. Area/Tables and Graphs
35. Law of Sines and Cosines
36. Pick Numbers (Type 2)
37. Patterns (Arithmetic Sequences)
38. Area (of Parallelogram)
39. Calculator/Arithmetic Word Problems
40. Calculator
41. Essential Algebra/Quadratics (FOIL) or Pick Numbers (Type 1)
42. Matrices (Multiplication of)
43. Angles (Line)
44. Basic Concepts (Prime Numbers)
45. Trig Odds and Ends (Other Trig Functions)
46. Arithmetic Word Problems/Pick Answers
47. Area (Trapezoid/Shaded Regions) or Measure the Drawing (see Geometry Introduction)
48. Triangles (Pythagorean Theorem)
49. Pick Numbers (Type 4)
50. Angles/Triangles (Similar)
51. Area and Perimeter
52. Triangles (Pythagorean Theorem)/Area
53. Patterns (Arithmetic Series)
54. Graphs of Functions or Pick Answers → Pick Numbers
55. Trig and the Unit Circle or Trig Odds & Ends (Inverse)
56. Pick Numbers (Type 2)
57. More Circles (Equation of) or Pick Numbers → Pick Answers
58. Pick Numbers (Type 2)
59. Logarithms
60. Percent (Pick 100/Increase/Decrease & Difference-over-Original)

3. ACT PRACTICE TEST 3

1. Averages (ANS)
2. Essential Algebra
3. Proportions
4. Triangles (Pythagorean Theorem)
5. Logic
6. Pick Numbers (Type 1) or Alg. Word
7. Essential Algebra
8. Angles (Parallel Lines/Triangles/Line)
9. Basic Concepts (Adding Fractions)
10. Essential Algebra or Pick Numbers (Type 1)
11. Averages
12. Quadratics (FOIL) or Pick Numbers (Type 1)
13. Principle of Counting
14. Exponents (Solving Equations of)
15. Lines (One-Dimensional/Midpoint)
16. Essential Algebra: good calculator prob.
17. Lines (Intersecting) or Graphing Calculator
18. Pick Answers or Exponents (Compare Apples to Apples)
19. Transformations
20. Pick Numbers (Type 1)
21. Lines (One-Dimensional)
22. Symbols: Hint: Even if don't know what a "determinant" is, the question clearly defines it, as with all Symbols probs.
23. Pick Numbers (Type 3) or Alg. Word Problems
24. Algebraic Word Problems/Pick Numbers (Type 2)
25. Rates (RTD)
26. Pick Answers/Calculator (or use Algebra)
27. Pick Answers → Pick Numbers
28. Lines (Equations of)
29. Logarithms
30. Triangles (Congruent)/Angles (Triangle)
31. Exponents

32. Lines (One-Dim.)/Pick Numbers (Type 3)
33. Essential Algebra or Pick Answers → Pick Numbers
34. Algebraic Word Problems
35. Angles (Triangle/Line)
36. Pick Answers → Pick Numbers
37. Trig and the Unit Circle (Degrees and Radians)
38. Coordinates (Slanted Distances)
39. Solids and Volume
40. Proportions
41. Triangles (Pythagorean Theorem) or Measure the Drawing (see Geom. Intro.)
42. Solids and Volume (Surface Area)
43. More Circles (Sectors of)/Triangles/Pick Numbers (Type 3)
44. Proportions
45. Solids and Volume (Area Fitting)
46. Basic Trigonometry
47. Tables and Graphs
48. Lines (Slope)/Graphs of Functions (Zeros)/Domain and Range
49. Trig and the Unit Circle
50. Transformations
51. Area/Probability
52. Ratios/Pick Numbers (Type 2)
53. Graphs of Sine and Cosine
54. Pick Answers → Pick Numbers
55. Basic Concepts (Factors)/Pick Numbers → Pick Answers
56. Pick Numbers (Type 2)
57. Pick Numbers (Type 3)
58. Pick Numbers (Type 1)/Trig and the Unit Circle
59. Averages (ANS)
60. Percent (Increase/Decrease and Of/Is)

4. ACT PRACTICE TEST 4

1. Proportions

2. Algebraic Word Probs or Pick Answers

3. Essential Algebra

4. Arithmetic Word Problems

5. Probability

6. Area and Perimeter

7. Algebraic Word Problems

8. Essential Algebra or Pick Answers

9. Essential Algebra or Pick Answers

10. Triangles (Isosceles)/Angels (Tri./Line)

11. Function Basics

12. Basic Concepts (Hint: check answers)

13. Pick Numbers (Type 3) → Pick Answers

14. Area and Perimeter

15. Angles (Tri.)/Pick Numbers (Type 3)

16. Symbol Problems

17. Lines (Equation of)

18. Algebraic Word Problems

19. Algebraic Word Problems

20. Triangles (Pythagorean Theorem)

21. Pick Numbers (Type 1) or Essential Algebra

22. Simultaneous Eqns. or Pick Answers

23. Quadratics

24. Area and Perimeter

25. Function Basics/Lines (Slope): Hint: The slope will be *constant* for the linear function.

26. Lines (Equation of)

27. Factoring (Quads.) or Pick Numbers (Type 4)

28. Ratios

29. Averages, Medians and Modes

30. Algebraic Word Problems/Pick Answers or Factoring (Quadratics)

31. Algebraic Word Problems

32. Patterns: Hint: find the *ratio*, i.e. the expression, multiplied each time.

33. Ratios

34. Tables and Graphs

35. Averages

36. Pick Numbers (Type 1) or Factoring

37. Basic Trigonometry

38. Coordinates (Midpoint)

39. Coordinates (Slanted Distances)

40. Pick Answers → Pick Numbers/Basic Concepts (Terminology)

41. Complex Numbers

42. Pick Answers/Function Basics

43. Solids and Volume

44. Measure the Drawing (see Geom. Intro.) or Triangles (Sim.)/Pick #s (Type 3)

45. Triangles (Special Right) or Measure the Drawing (see Geom. Intro.)

46. More Circles (Equation of)/Area

47. Pick Numbers (Type 1)/Graphs of Functions

48. Pick Numbers (Type 1)

49. Logarithms or Calculator

50. Percent (Difference-over-Original)

51. Averages (ANS)

52. Percent (Increase/Decrease)

53. Graphs of Sine and Cosine

54. Trigonometry Odds and Ends or Geometry Intro. (Measure the Drawing)

55. Basic Concepts (Abs. Value) or Pick Ans.

56. Tables and Graphs

57. Proportions or More Circles (Sectors)

58. Trig and the Unit Circle

59. Exponents/Pick Numbers (Type 4)

60. Solids and Volume (Diagonals of Rectangular Solids)

5. ACT PRACTICE TEST 5

1. Essential Algebra or Pick Answers
2. Exponents or Pick Numbers (Type 1)
3. Function Basics
4. Tables and Graphs
5. Calculators: Hint: Not sure how to round? Choose the answer closest to the decimal.
6. Alg. Word Problems or Pick Answers
7. Essential Algebra or Pick Answers
8. Lines (Terminology)
9. Essential Algebra or Pick Answers
10. Averages (ANS)
11. (Basic Concepts)
12. Proportions
13. Coordinates/Percent (Part-over-Whole)
14. Pick Numbers (Type 1) or Essential Algebra (Working with Variables)
15. More Circles (Equation of)
16. (More Circles)
17. Lines (Equation of)
18. Pick Answers/Area and Perimeter
19. Pick Answers or Logarithms
20. Direct and Inverse Variation
21. Arithmetic Word Problems
22. Patterns (Arithmetic Sequence)/Angles (Triangle)/Pick Answers or Algebraic Word Problems
23. Angles (Line)
24. Simultaneous Equations
25. Essential Alg. (Working with Variables)
26. Basic Concepts (Basic Operations) or Pick Answers → Pick Numbers
27. Probability
28. Percent (Of/Is)
29. Lines (1-D Problems)
30. Triangles (Similar)
31. Coordinates (Slanted Distances)

32. Patterns (Series)/Calculators
33. Triangles (Third Side Rule)
34. Pick Numbers (Type 1)
35. Area and Perimeter
36. Solids and Volume (Area Fitting)
37. Arithmetic Word Problems/Percent (Of/Is)
38. Triangles (Isosceles)/Angles (Triangle)
39. Percent (Part-over-Whole)/Tables and Graphs
40. Algebraic Word Problems
41. Pick Numbers (Type 2)
42. Coordinates (Midpoint)
43. Basic Trigonometry
44. Area and Perimeter/Triangles (Equilateral)
45. Pick Numbers (Type 3): Hint: Pick numbers for unknown angles; remember: drawing is drawn to scale.
46. Basic Trigonometry
47. Pick Numbers (Type 1)
48. Transformations
49. Pick Answers
50. Averages (ANS)
51. Logic
52. Exponents or Pick Numbers → Pick Answers
53. Trigonometry Odds and Ends (Properties) or Pick Numbers (Type 1)
54. Lines (Slope or Equation of)
55. Solids and Volume
56. Pick Numbers (Type 2)/Logarithms
57. Transformations/Pick Numbers → Pick Answers
58. Trig and the Unit Circle
59. Area and Perimeter/Lines (Slope)
60. Pick Numbers (Type 1)/Function Basics: Hint: similar to a Symbol problem.

IX

MATH ANSWERS

The following answers are to all lesson, homework, and worksheet problems in the previous chapters.

CALCULATORS

1. **−4**
2. **4**
3. **287**
4. **232**
5. **338**
6. **6.125** (see mixed fractions)
7. **.5**
8. 1.125 **D.**
9. $^{70}\!/_{93}$ **F.**
10. **D.**
11. First, use your calculator to answer the original question: $\sqrt{108} + \sqrt{48} = 17.3205...$
   Then convert the answer choices to decimal numbers so you can compare them to your answer. Only **K** also equals 17.3205.

BASIC CONCEPTS

1. **203, 0, -2, 4.0**
2. $\sqrt{9} = 3$, $^{7}\!/_{8}$, **1.2**, $^{1}\!/_{3}$
3. **2, 3, 5, 7**
4. $\left|-1\right| - \left|1\right| = 1 - 1 = \mathbf{0}$
5. **12**
6. x = **4** or **−4**
7. 1×42
   2×21
   3×14
   6×7 The positive integer factors of 42 are **1**, **2**, **3**, **6**, **7**, **14**, **21**, and **42**.
8.   The prime factors of 42 are **2**, **3**, and **7**.
9. The least common denominator is **21** since 21 is the smallest number that both 3 and 7 divide evenly into.
10. Pick two of the denominators. It's probably faster to pick the two largest ones, 7 and 14. 14 is the least common multiple of 7 and 14, but 3 doesn't divide into 14. Check the next number divisible by 7 and 14: 28—still not divisible by 3. The next number, **42**, works: 3 × 14 = 42, 7 × 6 = 42, 14 × 3 = 42.

BASIC CONCEPTS WORKSHEET

1. Basic Concepts (Absolute Value)
   $\left|-2-4\right| = \left|-6\right| = 6$ **E.**

7. Basic Concepts (Adding and Subtracting Fractions)
   If you have trouble calculating the least common denominator, just check the answer choices (starting with the smallest one). The least common denominator is 84 since it is the smallest number that 3, 7, and 12 all divide evenly into. **G.**

10. Basic Concepts (Prime Numbers)
   Use factor trees to find the prime factors of 35 and 77:
   35 = 5 × 7, 77 = 7 × 11 → The largest prime number that is a factor of both 35 and 77 is 7.
   A.
   As with the previous problem, you could check the answer choices. Also, note that C, D, and E are not prime numbers since they are divisible by 5.

21. *Basic Concepts (LCM)*
    The fastest way to tackle this problem is to just check the answer choices, starting with the smallest number:
    F: 210 is not a multiple of 9. ✗
    G: 630 is a multiple of 9, 105, and 210. The answer is **G**.
31. *Calculators*
    Use your calculator. Either use parentheses carefully, as shown below, or calculate in steps. Don't forget the negative sign.

$$-\left(\frac{\frac{2}{5}-\frac{2}{3}}{\frac{2}{5}+\frac{2}{3}}\right)=-\left[\left(\frac{2}{5}-\frac{2}{3}\right)\div\left(\frac{2}{5}+\frac{2}{3}\right)\right]=\frac{1}{4}\quad\textbf{C.}$$

37. *Calculators*
    Use your calculator to find decimals of each fraction:

$$\frac{5}{6}\approx.833,\ \frac{6}{7}\approx.857,\ \frac{7}{9}\approx.778\ \rightarrow\ .778<.833<.857\ \rightarrow\ \frac{7}{9}<\frac{5}{6}<\frac{6}{7}\quad\textbf{J.}$$

41. *Basic Concepts (Adding and Subtracting Fractions)*
    The numerator on the right side of the equation may look tricky, but this is just a Subtracting Fractions problem. What's the least common denominator of the two fractions on the left? This will give you the value of x. The answer is 110 (10 × 11 = 110 and 55 × 2 = 110). **D.**
45. *Basic Concepts (Rational Numbers)*

    Only A can be reduced to a rational number (check using your calculator): $\sqrt{\frac{1}{4}}=\frac{1}{2}$ **F.**

46. *Calculator*
    Unless you're very comfortable working with radicals, just plug the values (carefully) into your calculator, and then check the answer choices:

    $\frac{1}{\sqrt{2}}+\frac{1}{\sqrt{3}}\approx1.285$ *Now check the answer choices. Only* **E** *will work:* $\frac{\sqrt{2}+\sqrt{3}}{\sqrt{6}}\approx1.285$

47. *Basic Concepts (Absolute Value)*
    This equation is true for all real numbers. Go ahead and plug in some values. For example, try p = 2 and q = 3. Once you see that the equation works, you can eliminate G-K. The answer is **F.**
50. *Basic Concepts (LCM)*
    Use the rules for finding the LCM. Notice that each prime number (a, b, and c) shows up at most one time for each of the original numbers (x, y, and z). So the LCM is: a × b × c. **C.**
    Note: Eventually you'll be able to use a technique called Pick Numbers (Type 1) to make this problem easier. We'll cover this in the Algebra chapter.

PERCENT PROBLEMS
1. **425%**
2. **¼**
3. **2.20**
4. **87.5%**
5. **0.13%**

OF/IS PERCENT PROBLEMS
1. *0.25 × 0.25 × 32 = 2* **D.**
5. *10% of 5.50 is* → *0.10 × 5.50 = 0.55* **G.**
25. *Let x be the number we're looking for.*
    0.40·x = 32 → *x = 32 ÷ 0.40 = 80* → *0.50·80 = 40* **B.**

45. volume of a cube = (length of edge)^3 ← *This will be covered in the Geometry chapter.*
    1^3 "is what percent of" 2^3 → $1^3 = x \cdot 2^3$ → $1 = x \cdot 8$ → $x = 12.5\%$ **F.**

PART-OVER-WHOLE PERCENT PROBLEMS

3. $^8/_{12} = 0.666... = 66\,^2/_3\,\%$ **C.**

PERCENT INCREASE/DECREASE

6. These solutions use multipliers: $100\% + 10\% = 110\% = 1.10$
    $200(1.10) = 220$ **E.**

32. For a 20% discount, the multiplier is: $100\% - 20\% = 80\% = 0.80$
    $x \cdot (0.80) = 4.80$ → $x = 4.80 \div 0.80 = \$6.00$ **J.**

    ↖   ↑
    original   final

DIFFERENCE-OVER-ORIGINAL PERCENT PROBLEMS

34. $\dfrac{28 - 7}{7} = \dfrac{21}{7} = 3\ = 300\%$ **D.**

PICK 100

53. Pick 100 for employment in 1990:

    $100(1.30) = 130$ → $130(1.40) = 182$ → $\dfrac{diff.}{orig.}\ \dfrac{182 - 100}{100} = \dfrac{82}{100} = 82\%$ **E.**

        ↑   ↑
    30% increase   40% increase

    Note: The answer is NOT 70%. This is a trap (30% + 40%).

Homework:

7. The multiplier for a 4% increase is 1.04 ($100\% + 4\% = 104\% = 1.04$). $300(1.04) = 312$ **B.**

9. $\dfrac{part}{whole}\ \dfrac{12}{30} = .4 = 40\%$ **F.**

19. $\dfrac{diff.}{orig.}\ \dfrac{92 - 80}{80} = \dfrac{12}{80} = 15\%$ **D.**

28. Pick 100 for the number of employees:
    60 women → $^1/_3 \cdot 60 = 20$ women drive to work; 40 men → $^1/_2 \cdot 40 = 20$ men drive to work

    → $100 - 40 = 60$ employees do **not** drive to work → $^{60}/_{100} = 60\%$ **H.**

55. The multiplier for a 25% decrease is 0.75. The multiplier for a 50% increase is 1.50.
    Pick 100 for p: $100(0.75) = 75$ → $75(1.50) = 112.50$

    $\dfrac{diff.}{orig.} = \dfrac{112.5 - 100}{100} = .125 = 12.5\%$ (increase) **C.**

60. This is a difficult problem. First find the rates by dividing machines by hours:

    rate before upgrade = $\dfrac{50}{m}$, rate after upgrade = $\dfrac{90}{.6m} = \dfrac{150}{m}$

    $\dfrac{diff.}{orig.} = \dfrac{\dfrac{150}{m} - \dfrac{50}{m}}{\dfrac{50}{m}} = \dfrac{\dfrac{150 - 50}{m}}{\dfrac{50}{m}} = \dfrac{\dfrac{100}{m}}{\dfrac{50}{m}}$ (continued)

→ multiply top and bottom by m: $\dfrac{m \cdot \frac{100}{m}}{m \cdot \frac{50}{m}} = \dfrac{100}{50} = 2 = 200\%$ **J.**

You may find the algebra above difficult. The easiest approach to this problem is to pick a number for m and use a technique called RTD. Make a note to come back to this problem after you cover Pick Numbers (Type 2), (make a note on page 236 in the Algebra chapter). The solution is below:

$m = 10$ ← *plug into the first row of RTD below as T.*

$\underline{R \ \ x \ \ T = D}$ *(boxes)*
$\quad$ 10 $\quad$ 50 $\quad$ → $R = 50 \div 10 = 5$
$\quad\ $ 6 $\quad$ 90 $\quad$ → $R = 90 \div 6 = 15$

$\dfrac{diff.}{orig.} = \dfrac{15 - 5}{5} = 2 = 200\%$ **J.**

PROPORTIONS

12. Known relationship: "6 minutes to light 15 candles"

$\dfrac{minutes}{candles} \dfrac{6}{15} = \dfrac{x}{35}$ → $x = 14$ minutes **E.**

27. Known relationship: "45 minutes to travel 300 kilometers"

$\dfrac{min.}{km} \dfrac{45}{300} = \dfrac{x}{1600}$ → $x = 240$ minutes → $\dfrac{240}{60} = 4$ hours **G.**

54. Known relationships (there are two): "7-pound bag of apples cost 10 dollars" and "5 pounds of apples are needed to make 2 apple pies"
Note: complete the second proportion before the first one.

$\dfrac{pounds}{\$} \dfrac{7}{10} = \dfrac{35 \text{ (from below)}}{y}$ → $y = 50$ dollars **B.**

$\dfrac{pounds}{pies} \dfrac{5}{2} = \dfrac{x}{14}$ → $x = 35$ pounds

Homework:

3. $\dfrac{cans}{hours} \dfrac{25}{4} = \dfrac{x}{20}$ → $x = 125$ cans **A.**

21. $\dfrac{object (ft.)}{shadow (ft.)} \dfrac{6}{14} = \dfrac{x}{140}$ → $x = 60$ **H.**

43. There are two known relationships: "30 chips per hour" and "39 chips per hour," so we need two proportions.

A: $\dfrac{chips}{hour} \dfrac{30}{1} = \dfrac{26}{a}$ → $a = .8666...$ hours → $.8666... \times 60 = 52$ minutes

B: $\dfrac{chips}{hour} \dfrac{39}{1} = \dfrac{26}{b}$ → $b = .6666...$ hours → $.6666... \times 60 = 40$ minutes

→ $52 - 40 = 12$ minutes **A.**

RATIOS

14. First, rewrite the ratios above as fractions: $\dfrac{x}{y} = \dfrac{1}{6}$, $\dfrac{15x}{y} = ?$

Rewrite $\dfrac{15x}{y}$ as $15 \cdot \dfrac{x}{y}$. Now, substitute $\dfrac{1}{6}$ for $\dfrac{x}{y}$: $15 \cdot \dfrac{x}{y} = 15 \cdot \dfrac{1}{6} = \dfrac{15}{6} = \dfrac{5}{2}$ **C.**

23. $10 + 4 + 1 = 15$ → $\dfrac{\$75,000}{15} = \$5,000$ → $10 \times \$5,000 = \$50,000$ **H.**

Homework:

8. $\dfrac{n}{9} = \dfrac{33}{198}$ ← $n = 1.5$ **C.**

35. $5 + 4 + 1 = 10$ ← $\dfrac{10 \text{ gallons}}{10} = 1 \text{ gallon}$ ← *Since orange juice gets only 1 "part": 1×1*

gallon = 1 gallon **G.**

46. *Use the shortcut described in the last example of the lesson: The whole (20) must be a multiple of the sum of the ratio numbers (the ratios are shown as fractions in the answer choices). Start with A: Sum of ratio numbers is $1 + 2 = 3$ ← $\dfrac{20}{3} = 6.666...$, which is not an integer, so 1:2 could not be the ratio. The answer is **A**. Notice that for all of the other answer choices, 20 is a multiple of the sum of the ratio numbers.*

AVERAGES, MEDIANS, & MODES

1. -5, 0, **2**, 6, 10

2. -5, 0, 2, 6, 10, 10 ← *median* = $\frac{2+6}{2}$ = **4**, *mode* = **10**

3. $\dfrac{9 + 10 + 12 + 13 + 14}{5}$ = **11.60**

4. **12**

5. $\dfrac{9 + 9 + 10 + 10 + 12 + 13 + 13 + 14 + 14 + 14 + 14}{11}$ = **12**

6. **13**

7. **14**

30. *Put the known values in order: 62, 65, 70, 72, 72, 80*
*Since 70 is the median, it must be the fourth (middle) number in the final list. So x must be less than or equal to 70. The answer is **E**.*

ANS → A × N = S

10. A x N = S
   20   3   60 → *60 is the sum of x, y, and z*
   25   2   50 → *50 is the sum of p and q*
         110 **E.**

22. A x N = S
   14   5   70 → *There are 5 weekdays in a week*
   42   2   84 → *There are 2 weekend days in a week*
   A   7 154 ← *A = 22* **G.**
         ↖ *"entire week"*

50. A x N = S
   −2 6 −12   *(Note: $6 - 4 = 2$, so we **subtract** the*
    2 4   8   *values in the S column as well.)*
    A 2 −20
       ↖ *"other **two** numbers"*
  ← *A = −10* **A.**

Homework:

24. A x N = S
   18   5   90 ← $12 + 10 + x + 20 + 27 = 90$ ← $x = 21$
Make sure to put the scores in increasing order:
     10, 12, 20, 21, 27
       ↖ *median* **D.**

32. $A \times N = S$

    152   15 2280

    <u>0   5   0</u>

    A   20 2280 → A = 114 **H.**

         ↖ *"20 years"*

RATES, TIMES, & DISTANCES

13. It may be helpful to convert units **before** plugging numbers into RTD: 45 min. → .75 hrs.

    <u>R x T = D</u>

    R   .75 48 → R = 64 **D.**

50. <u>R x T = D</u>   (Note: Distance is the same for both rows.)

    12 2   24

    <u>8   3   24</u>

    R   5   48 → R = 9.6 mph **G.**

Homework:

26. <u>R x T = D</u>   (Note: Rate is the same for both rows.)

    120 3   360 ← 360 ÷ 3 = 120

    120 x   800 → x = 6.6666... hours **E.**

45.   <u>R x T = D</u>   (Note: Time is the same for both rows.)

    H: 1.25 5

    V: x   1.25 4.5 → x = 3.6 miles per hour **J.**

PATTERNS

2. You may think that it will take a while to get to 256, but just looking at the answer choices tells you that it's at most the 11th term. Just calculate the numbers after 32 and count the terms: 1, 1, 2, 4, 8, 16, 32, … 64, 128, 256 → **D.** Note: Did you see the pattern? After the second term, each number is 2 times the previous number.

12. You could probably find a pattern here, but the easiest approach is to quickly draw the figure with all 7 triangles showing (see below), and count the rectangles. → The total number of rectangles is: 15 **F.**

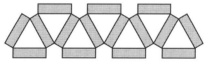

26. There are 5 repeated numbers in the pattern, and 45 is divisible by 5, so the 45th term is the last term in the pattern (2). **E.**

38. See if you can find a pattern. The first triangle is surrounded by 3 rectangles. The second triangle adds 2 new rectangles, as does the third triangle, and so on, up to the 20th. In other words, each of the 19 triangles after the first adds 2 rectangles. (You might want to quickly shade in the rectangles as you analyze the problem.)

    So the total number of rectangles is: 3 + (2 × 19) = 41 **H.**

37. Notice that the given expression is for an arithmetic sequence. The first term is 2, and the difference between any two terms is also 2. Thus, the difference between the 499th and 500th terms must be 2. **G.**

    You could also simply plug 500 and 499 into the formula (for n) and subtract, but this takes longer.

44. According to the formula, the first term is 4 and the ratio is ½.

    2nd term = 4 × (½)$^{2-1}$ = 4 × ½ = 2

    3rd term = 2 × ½ = 1 (since each term is ½ times the previous term)

    4th term = 1 × ½ = ½

    Average of 2, 1, and ½ is 1.1666... = $^{7}/_{6}$ (or convert answer choices to decimals) **B.**

    You could use the formula to find each number, but this takes longer.

Homework:

5. 150, 30, 6, $\frac{6}{5}$, $\frac{6}{25}$ → **C.**

21. *You may think that this problem will take forever—1,000 is a big number. Luckily, cubed numbers get big quickly. $1^3 = 1$, $2^3 = 8$, $3^3 = 27$ (see? we're already up to 27). You might skip ahead: $9^3 = 729$, $10^3 = 1,000$. We're done. There are 10 perfect cubes less than or equal to 1,000.* **F.**
    As you can see, there really isn't a trick to these types of problems, but they are generally not as difficult as they look.

41. *These numbers look hard, but just use your calculator to find the ratio r. Divide a_2 by a_1 (remember $a_1 \cdot r = a_2$): $r = 16\frac{1}{2} \div 49\frac{1}{2} = \frac{1}{3}$. Now, multiply the third term by r 3 times to find the 6th term:* $5\frac{1}{2} \times \frac{1}{3} \times \frac{1}{3} \times \frac{1}{3} = \frac{11}{54}$ **B.**

45. *This is a repeating pattern problem. There are 6 items in the pattern (2, 8, 5, 7, 1 and 4). Since the term number we're looking for (100) is not divisible by 6, find a term nearby that **is** divisible by 6: 96 is divisible by 6. So the 96th term is the last item in the pattern (4). Count four more terms to the 100th term: 4, 2, 8, 5, **7**. The answer is* **K.**

58. *First, plug in numbers for S_n and n to find a + b:*

$$S_n = n\left(\frac{a+b}{2}\right) \;\rightarrow\; 49 = 7\left(\frac{a+b}{2}\right) \;\rightarrow\; 7 = \frac{a+b}{2} \;\rightarrow\; a + b = 14$$

Now, using the equation for arithmetic sequences, define b (the 7th term) in terms of a:
$a_n = a_1 + (n - 1)d \rightarrow b = a + (7 - 1)3 \rightarrow b = a + 18$
Finally, substitute a + 18 for b in the equation found in the first step, and solve for a, the first term in the series: $a + b = 14 \rightarrow a + (a + 18) = 14 \rightarrow 2a = -4 \rightarrow a = -2$ **B.**

You could also Pick Answers and use your calculator.

60. *This question would clearly take too long to figure out "by hand" (adding the numbers using your calculator), so use the series equation (S_n) for an arithmetic series ($a_1 = 1$, $a_{30} = 100$, n = 100):* $S_{100} = 100\left[\dfrac{1 + 100}{2}\right] = 5,050$ **H.**

EXPONENTS

1. **n/a**
2. **$p^2 + 2pq + q^2$**
3. $\dfrac{1}{p^2}$
4. **n/a**
5. **p^5**
6. $p^{2-3} = p^{-1} = \dfrac{1}{p}$
7. $\dfrac{2}{p^2}$

EXPONENTS LESSON PROBLEMS

1. **x^9**
2. **x^3**
3. **x^{20}**
4. **$25x^2y^2$**
5. **$a = \pm 4$**
6. **8** *(use calculator)*

Homework:

28. $2^{t^2} = 2^{20} \rightarrow t^2 = 20 \rightarrow t = \sqrt{20} = 2\sqrt{5}$ *(t > 0)* **B.**
    (You could use a calculator to convert $\sqrt{20}$ into a decimal; don't forget the answer choices.)

32. *Start with the first part of the expression:* $(-2xy^3)^2 = (-2)^2 x^2 y^{3 \cdot 2} = 4x^2y^6$
    Next, combine like terms: $(4x^2y^6)(3x^3y) = 4 \cdot 3 \cdot x^2 \cdot x^3 \cdot y^6 \cdot y = 12x^5y^7$ **K.**

37. *By finding a common denominator for the exponential fractions, we can rewrite the expression with one root (a "6th root"):* $x^{\frac{1}{2}}y^{\frac{2}{3}} = x^{\frac{3}{6}}y^{\frac{4}{6}} = (x^3y^4)^{\frac{1}{6}} = \sqrt[6]{x^3y^4}$ **C.**

42. Review: multiplying when bases are the same. $3^{n+1} \cdot 3^2 = 3^{n+1+2} = 3^{n+3}$ **G.**
   If you struggled with this problem, you might want to come back to it after covering Pick Numbers (Type 1) in the Algebra chapter.

51. Compare apples to apples:
   $(3^2)^x = (3^4)^{\frac{1}{3}}$ $\rightarrow$ $3^{2x} = 3^{\frac{4}{3}}$ $\rightarrow$ $2x = \frac{4}{3}$ $\rightarrow$ $x = \frac{2}{3}$ **C.**

   OR:
   $9^x = (9^2)^{\frac{1}{3}} = 9^{\frac{2}{3}}$ $\rightarrow$ $x = \frac{2}{3}$ **C.**

TABLES AND GRAPHS

17. The greatest change is the loss between 1996 and 1997 (−$3 million). **B.**

42. Read the table carefully. The Cleaning Time is "**per street**."

   $7 \cdot 20 + 8 \cdot 40 + 10 \cdot 80 + 15 \cdot 100 = 2760$ minutes $\rightarrow$ $\dfrac{2760}{60} = 46$ hours **H.**

Homework:

17. A circle graph displays **percents** of something. Use the part over whole percent technique:

   $\dfrac{part}{whole}\ \dfrac{15{,}000}{whole} = .30$ $\rightarrow$ whole = 50,000 (total income) **C.**

   Or, you could use the Of/Is technique:
   15,000 is 30% of what? $\rightarrow$ $15{,}000 = .30 \cdot x$ $\rightarrow$ $x = 50{,}000$ (total income)

   Note: The central angle of each sector is always equal to the percent of that sector × 360°. For example, the 30% beverage sales sector will have a central angle of 0.30 × 360° = 108°. Some circle graph questions will require you to understand this percent-angle relationship.

28. It is important to recognize that the faster Chris walks (or runs), the steeper the graph (more distance is covered in less time). If Chris stops, the graph is a horizontal line (time continues but the distance remains the same). The correct answer is **F.**

39. Use the proportions technique: $\dfrac{bricks}{\$}\ \dfrac{50}{80} = \dfrac{1}{x}$ $\rightarrow$ $x = \$1.60$ **C.**

40. Note that the question asks for the sale price **per pallet**, not the total price for 8 pallets. Use the percent increase/decrease technique (we will use a multiplier of 0.95 for a 5% decrease): $90.00 × 0.95 = $85.50 **G.**

41. This problem is a Least Common Multiple problem. You must find the smallest number that is a multiple of the three brick quantities given for each pallet (30, 50 and 75). Just check the answer choices (starting with the smallest number). Among the answer choices, only 150 is a multiple of 30, 50 and 75. **E.**

42. First, calculate the cost of selling 40 pallets of Style A bricks: 40 x 75 = 3,000 bricks $\rightarrow$ cost = $75.00 (fixed cost) + 3,000 × $0.50 (per brick production cost) = $1,575
   Next, find the sale price for the 40 pallets: 40 × $75.00 = $3,000.
   Finally, subtract the costs from the sale price: $3,000 − $1,575 = $1,425 **G.**

49. Familiarize yourself with these types of tables. **Any time two entries in a row or column are known, you can find the missing item.**
   First, notice that the total number of Compact cars sold is a + b.
   Since the Total number of all cars is d, the total number of Family cars can be found:
   Family + Compact = Total $\rightarrow$ Family + (a + b) = d $\rightarrow$ Family = d − (a + b) = d − a − b
   Now, you can find the number of Family/All electric cars (let's call this "e"):
   $e + c = d − a − b$ $\rightarrow$ $e = d − a − b − c$ **E.**

   Note: The answer choices are tricky; you might want to Pick Numbers (Type 1) (to be covered in the Algebra chapter) at the beginning of the problem to avoid any algebraic mistakes. (continued)

*Shortcut: Notice that we have the total number of cars (d) and the number of cars in 3 of the 4 categories (a, b, and c). So the remaining, unknown category (Family/All-electric) must be d − a − b − c **E**.*

ARITHMETIC WORD PROBLEMS

12. *Small cars = 45 − 3 = 42, Large cars = 25 − 7 = 18 → Total available cars = 60*
    → *80% of 60 = 0.80 × 60 = 48* **C**.

ARITHMETIC WORKSHEET 1

6. *Averages*
   Add the numbers together and divide by 7.
   20 + 120 + 100 + 140 + 240 + 360 = 980 → 980 ÷ 7 = 140. **C**.

7. *Ratios*
   The question does not tell us whether 80 is the smaller number or the larger number. Set up proportions to test both possibilities:

   $\dfrac{4}{5} = \dfrac{80}{x}$ → *x = 100 This value is not an answer choice, so 80 must be the larger number:*

   $\dfrac{4}{5} = \dfrac{x}{80}$ → *x = 64* **F**.

17. *Percent (Of/Is)*
    20% of x equals 1 → 0.20·x = 1 → x = 1 ÷ 0.20 = 5
    50% of x → 0.50·5 = 2.5 **E**.

18. *Tables and Graphs/Percent (Part over Whole)*
    First, determine the percent or fraction of the voters who voted for Pilgrim:

    $\dfrac{part}{whole} \dfrac{20{,}400}{54{,}000} = \dfrac{17}{45} = .3777...$

    You might want to keep this in fraction form because the decimal is repeating.
    As described in the Tables and Graphs lesson, the central angle of a sector is equal to the percent of that sector × 360°. For example, a sector worth 50% of the total value would have 0.50 × 360° = 180°. So to find the degree measure of the central angle for Pilgrim, multiply the fraction (or decimal) above by 360°:

    $\dfrac{17}{45} \cdot 360° = 136°$ **J**.

24. *Rates (RTD)*
    We'll have to do some algebra here. Let t be the time.

R	x	T = D
50	t	50t
70	t	70t

    The total distance is 30 kilometers, so 50t + 70t = 30 → 120t = 30 → t = 0.25
    *What are the units? Go back to the question. The rates were given in kilometers per **hour**, so the time is 0.25 hours. Convert to minutes: 0.25 × 60 = 15 minutes* **E**.

    Note: In the next chapter you will learn a technique called Pick Answers. If you have trouble with the algebra above, you might want to come back to this problem after you learn this new technique.

25. *Exponents*
    Because the bases are the same (both x), once we've simplified the exponents, we can set them equal and solve for a:

    $\left(x^{3a-1}\right)^2 = \left(x^4\right)^{\frac{1}{2}}$ → $x^{2(3a-1)} = x^{\frac{1}{2}\cdot 4}$ → $x^{6a-2} = x^2$ → $6a - 2 = 2$ → $6a = 4$ → $a = \dfrac{2}{3}$

    H.

26. *Percent (Increase/Decrease)*
    Remember, 20% = 0.20
    To calculate the final value, you would subtract 20% of the original value from the original value, as in **D**.
44. *Proportions*
    Don't forget to write your units. Use days as your original units (note the answer choices):

    $$\frac{miles}{days} \frac{5.80 \times 10^8}{365} = \frac{x}{30} \;\rightarrow\; 365 \cdot x = 5.80 \times 10^8 \cdot 30 \;\rightarrow\; x = \frac{(30)(5.80 \times 10^8)}{365} \; miles \;\; \textbf{G.}$$

47. *Averages (ANS)*

    A x N = S
    80.0 5   400 ← *Put the bigger numbers on top for easy subtracting.*
    75.5 4   302
          1   98 ← *So, on her 1 remaining test, she must score 98 points.* **D.**

    In other words: she has 302 total points. She needs 400 total points to average 80.0, so she needs 98 points on the last test.
50. *Patterns (Arithmetic Sequence)*
    The difference (d) in the sequence is q. Use the formula for an arithmetic sequence:
    $a_n = a_1 + (n - 1)d \;\rightarrow\; a_{1,000} = p + (1,000 - 1)q = p + 999q$ **J.**

    If you have questions, review arithmetic sequences in the Patterns section.
52. *Percent (Pick 100, Of/Is, Part/Whole)*
    First, pick 100 as the number of graduating students. Then use the Of/Is technique.
    0.80 × 100 = 80 students (four-year university) → 20 students remaining
    0.90 × 20 = 18 students (community college) → 2 students remaining

    $\rightarrow \;\; \dfrac{part}{whole} \dfrac{2}{100} = 2\%$ **B.**

59. *Averages (ANS)*

	A	x N	= S
Island A:	5	200	1,000
Island B:	4	250	1,000
	A	450	2,000

    → *A = 2,000 ÷ 450 ≈ 4.4 centimeters* **G.**

ARITHMETIC WORKSHEET 2

8. *Exponents*
   $(3x^2y^3)(4x^5y^4) = 3 \cdot 4 \cdot x^2 \cdot x^5 \cdot y^3 \cdot y^4 = 12x^7y^7$ **B.**
9. *Averages (ANS)*

   A x N = S
   −2 24 −48
   Since each number is increased by 2, the total increase is 24 × 2 = 48.
   A x N = S
   A   24   0 ← −48 + 48
   → *A = 0 ÷ 24 = 0* **H.**
15. *Rates (RTD)*
    This problem is easier than it looks. Simply add up the total miles traveled (20 + 15 + 5 = 40 miles) and use RTD. Note that the units are already in miles and hours.
    R x T = D
    R   1   40 → *R = 40 mile per hour* **C.**
22. *Proportions*

    $\dfrac{inches\ (paper)}{inches\ (poster)} \dfrac{11}{40} = \dfrac{2}{x} \;\rightarrow\; 11 \cdot x = 40 \cdot 2 \;\rightarrow\; x \approx 7.27 \approx 7$ **F.**

23. *Ratios (Share Problems)*
The ratio of vegetable broth to rice to water is 2:3:4. Review the ratio share technique if necessary: $2 + 3 + 4 = 9$. → *The "whole" is 8 (cups), so each "part" = $\frac{8}{9}$* → *Since there are 2 parts vegetable broth:* $2 \cdot \frac{8}{9} = \frac{16}{9} = 1\frac{7}{9}$ **B.**

28. *Tables and Graphs/Averages*
Add up the total number of books and divide by 5:
Total books = 17,500 + 12,500 + 10,000 + 7,500 + 2,500 = 50,000
→ $50,000 \div 5 = 10,000$ **H.**

29. *Percent (Of/Is)*
There are no percents in this problem, but the words "as large as" function the same way as "of" in the Of/Is technique for percents—they mean multiplication. Let n be the number you're looking for: $0.2 = 1,000 \times n$ → $n = 0.2 \div 1,000$ → $n = 0.0002$ **A.**

33. *Averages*
First, make sure you understand the table. Team A scored 0 3-point shots in 1 game. Team A scored 1 3-point shot in 0 games. Team A scored 2 3-point shots in 2 games. And so on. You have to calculate the total number of 3-point shots in all 25 games:
$0 \cdot 1 + 1 \cdot 0 + 2 \cdot 2 + 3 \cdot 4 + 4 \cdot 8 + 5 \cdot 2 + 6 \cdot 5 + 7 \cdot 2 + 8 \cdot 1 = 110$ 3-point shots
→ *Remember, there were 25 games:* $110 \div 25 = 4.4$ **K.**

49. *Exponents*
You must "compare apples to apples" (get the bases the same).
Since $8 = 2^3$ and $4 = 2^2$, we can write: $8^a = 4^{2a+1}$ → $(2^3)^a = (2^2)^{2a+1}$ → $2^{3a} = 2^{4a+2}$
→ $3a = 4a + 2$ → $-a = 2$ → $a = -2$ **D.**

53. *Patterns (Arithmetic Series)*
Notice that the sequence for the bottle caps collected each day is arithmetic: 10, 11, 12… (the difference is 1)
So this is a series question: 10 + 11 + 12 + …. But since you shouldn't worry about memorizing series formulas, just plug the values into your calculator. Make sure you count 24 entries. It won't take as long as you may think. The sum is 516. **H.**

58. *Percent (Pick 100, increase/decrease, difference/original)*
First, pick 100 so you have a number to work with. (The following solution uses multipliers, but you can use the conventional percent increase/decrease approach):
$100 \times 1.02 = 102$ → $102 \times 1.02 = 104.04$
→ $\dfrac{\text{difference}}{\text{original}} \dfrac{104.04 - 100}{100} = \dfrac{4.04}{100} = 0.0404 = 4.04\%$ So his weight increased by 4.04%.
The answer is **C**.

Remember, do not combine percent changes:
The answer is **not** 4% (2% + 2%).

60. *Patterns (Geometric Series)*
Remember, these series questions often look harder than they are. In this case, the equation is given. Plug in the given information and find a, the first term:
$-1,100 = \dfrac{a(-2^5 - 1)}{-2 - 1} = \dfrac{a(-33)}{-3} = 11a$ → $a = -100$
Now, be careful! The question asks for the second term. Remember, the common ratio is −2, so $-100 \times -2 = 200$. **K.**

ESSENTIAL ALGEBRA
EQUALITIES

1. $a = -18$
2. $a = 1$

3. $a = -2$

4. $a = 4$

5. $a = 6$

6. $a - 6 = -2 \rightarrow a = 4$
7. $6 - \frac{2}{3}a = \frac{1}{2}a - 8$
   $14 = \frac{7}{6}a \rightarrow a = 12$
8. (cross multiply)
   $3a + 6 = 5 \rightarrow 3a = -1 \rightarrow a = -\frac{1}{3}$
9. (cross multiply)
   $a + 11 = 6a + 6 \rightarrow 5 = 5a \rightarrow a = 1$
10. (use substitution)
    $a = 2a - 2 \rightarrow -a = -2 \rightarrow a = 2$

INEQUALITIES

1. $a < 30$

2. $-\frac{1}{2}a \le 2 \rightarrow a \ge -4$

RADICAL EXPRESSIONS

1. $2\sqrt{a} = 16 \rightarrow \sqrt{a} = 8 \rightarrow a = 64$

2. $\sqrt{a-5} = 4 \rightarrow a - 5 = 16 \rightarrow a = 21$

WORKING WITH VARIABLES

4. Combine like terms:
   $m^2 - 12m^2 = -11m^2$, $-22m + 11m = -11m$
   $\rightarrow m^2 - 22m + 11 - 12m^2 + 11m = -11m^2 - 11m + 11$ **D.**

Homework:

2. Plug $a = 1$ into the expression:
   $a \cdot \sqrt{a} \cdot \sqrt{a+3} = 1 \cdot \sqrt{1} \cdot \sqrt{4} = 1 \cdot 1 \cdot 2 = 2$ **E.**

8. The shortcut to this problem is to divide both sides by 50. Do <u>not</u> multiply 50 and 4x:

   $50(4x) = 200 \rightarrow \dfrac{50(4x)}{50} = \dfrac{200}{50} \rightarrow 4x = 4$ **J.** Note: the question is asking for 4x, not x.

14. First, plug $p = 2$ into the equation: $x - 3 = 2x - 1$
    Then solve for x (combine like terms): $-3 + 1 = 2x - x \rightarrow -2 = x$ **C.**

20. First, use substitution to rewrite the question:
    $(a + b) - (a - b) = [(x + y) + (x - y)] - [(x + y) - (x - y)]$
    Now, combine like terms and simplify:
    $[(x + y) + (x - y)] - [(x + y) - (x - y)] = (2x + 0y) - (0x + 2y) = 2x - 2y$
    The answer is **H.**

    Shortcut: $(a + b) - (a - b) = 2b = 2(x - y) = 2x - 2y$ **H.**

ALGEBRAIC WORD PROBLEMS

30. First, notice that an equation is given. All you have to do is plug in the information. You don't need to know much about geometry to get this problem, but you should know that if the diameter is 6, the radius (r) is 3:
    $S = 4\pi r^2 = 4\pi 3^2 = 4 \cdot \pi \cdot 9 = 36\pi$ **B.**

32. Use the rules in the chart:
    "the square of the product of x and 4" = $(4x)^2$
    "the square of the difference of x and 4" = $(x - 4)^2$
    Subtract the first expression from the second expression and set equal to 0:
    $(x - 4)^2 - (4x)^2 = 0$ **A.**

Homework:

11. Let's say you make d dollars per call. Find an equation for the amount you earn per day (capital D) for c calls:
    $D = 50 + c \cdot d$ ← As you can see, the number of calls you make times the amount you make per call should be added to your base pay ($50). (continued)

Now, plug in the given information:

$140 = 50 + 60d$ → $90 = 60d$ → $d = 1.50$ (So you get $1.50/call)

→ The final D can be found: $D = 50 + (60 + 20)1.50 = 170$ **A.**

17. $4x = 2x + 4$ ← Note the position of the word "is" in the sentence. This helps you figure out where to put the equal sign.

$4x - 2x = 2x - 2x + 4$ → $2x = 4$ → $x = 2$ **H.**

56. Tackle this difficult problem one step at a time.

First, label your variables. Let r = number of red straws, b = number of blue straws, y = number of yellow straws, and t = total number of straws = $r + b + y$.

Now look at the words: "⅓ as many red straws as there were blue straws." There is no "is," so it's hard to know where to put the equal sign. Let's restate the phrase as: "number of red straws **is** ⅓ of the number of blue straws." Now we can write: $r = ⅓ \cdot b$

"⅓ of the straws were blue" → $b = ⅓ \cdot t$

"20 of the straws were yellow" → $y = 20$

Finally, put it all together. Your goal is to get one equation in terms of t (which is what you're looking for): $t = r + b + y = \dfrac{1}{3}b + \dfrac{1}{3}t + 20 = \dfrac{1}{3}\left(\dfrac{1}{3}t\right) + \dfrac{1}{3}t + 20 = \dfrac{4}{9}t + 20$

→ $t - \dfrac{4}{9}t = 20$ → $\dfrac{5}{9}t = 20$ → $t = 36$ **C.**

You could Pick Answers for this problem (see The Pick Tricks section). If the algebra is too difficult, come back to it after you learn the Pick Answers technique in the next section.

THE PICK TRICKS
PICK NUMBERS TYPE 1

33. First, pick numbers for a and b:

$\boxed{a = 3, b = 2}$

Plug these picked numbers into the original expression:

$(a + b + 1)(a - b) = (3 + 2 + 1)(3 - 2) = \underline{6}$

Last, **check every answer choice.** Only **D** equals 6: $3^2 + 3 - 2^2 - 2 = 6$ ✓

42. $\boxed{m = 4, n = 2}$ → How many integers are greater than $4 + 2 = 6$ and less than $4 \cdot 2 = 8$? There is only $\underline{1}$ integer (7). So plug in your picked numbers and look for 1. → Only G., H., and K. can be eliminated, so pick new numbers:

$\boxed{m = 6, n = 4}$ Since there is obviously more than 1 integer greater than 10 and less than 24, eliminate F. The answer must be **J.** Remember, **check every answer choice.**

PICK NUMBERS TYPE 2

50. Pick $a = 2$ (any number would work, but 2 is especially convenient)

$\dfrac{2}{b} = \dfrac{2}{3}$ → $b = 3$

$\dfrac{3}{c} = \dfrac{2}{5}$ → $c = \dfrac{15}{2}$ → $\dfrac{a}{c} = \dfrac{4}{15}$ **A.**

As always, if you are uncomfortable with fractions, you can convert them into decimals (including answer choices) using a calculator.

PICK NUMBERS TYPE 3

31. Original square: Pick side = 2, so perimeter = 8 and area = 4.

Final square: Perimeter doubles: $8 \times 2 = 16$ → side = $16 \div 4 = 4$ → area = $4 \times 4 = 16$

$\dfrac{\text{difference}}{\text{original}} \dfrac{16 - 4}{4} = \dfrac{12}{4} = 3 = 300\%$ **D.**

PICK NUMBERS TYPE 4

50. The equation suggests that x will be a small integer. ($x = 5$ is already too large since $7 \cdot 5 >$ 29).

Pick (guess) $x = 1$: $7 + 3y = 29$ → $3y = 22$ → y is not an integer ✘

Pick (guess) $x = 2$: $14 + 3y = 29$ → $3y = 15$ → $y = 5$ ✓

→ $x + y = 2 + 5 = 7$ **B.**

PICK ANSWERS

29. Barebones question: "what is the value of d?"

Pick C.: $d = 160$ → $\frac{1}{4} \times 160 = 40$ → $160 - 40 = 120$ left after flowers → $\frac{2}{3} \times 120 = 80$

→ $120 - 80 = 40$ left after dinner → $40 > 35$, so eliminate C., D., and E..

Pick B.: $d = 140$ → $\frac{1}{4} \times 140 = 35$ → $140 - 35 = 105$ left after flowers → $\frac{2}{3} \times 105 = 70$

→ $105 - 70 = 35$ left after dinner. ✓ **B.**

41. Barebones question: "What is the greatest possible number of buckets . . .?"

For this problem, since we're looking for the **greatest** possible number, start with K.

Pick K: 4 buckets each have 5 rocks. Does this work? If 4 buckets have 5 rocks each (20 rocks), there are only 2 rocks left (22 −20) for the other 4 buckets (so some of them would have to be empty). ✘

Pick J: 3 buckets each have 5 rocks (15 rocks). Now there are 7 rocks left (22 − 15) for the other 5 buckets, which works! ✓ **J.**

PICK ANSWERS → PICK NUMBERS

57. Look at the answer choices first, and pick a number that will eliminate at least two of them:

Pick A & B → Pick $x = 0$ → $|0 - 10|$ is not ≤ 6, so eliminate A and B.

Pick C → Pick $x = 1$ → $|1 - 10|$ is not ≤ 6, so eliminate C.

Only D and E remain. Can you think of a number that falls in one, but **not** both, of the answer choices? You have to look at E:

Pick E → Pick $x = 5$ (not in D) → $|25 - 10|$ is not ≤ 6, so eliminate E.

→ The remaining answer choice is **D.**

PICK NUMBERS → PICK ANSWERS

53. Pick $x = 5$:

This simplifies the problem considerably. After plugging 5 in for x, the question now reads: If 2 is a factor of $30 - k$, what is the value of k? Check the answer choices. You'll find that B and D can be eliminated (since 2 is not a factor of 27 or 25, respectively).

Pick $x = 6$:

New question: If 3 is a factor of $48 - k$, what is the value of k? Check the remaining answer choices. Only **E** works (3 is a factor of $48 - 6 = 42$).

PICK TRICK HOMEWORK:

21. Pick Numbers (Type 1)

$\boxed{x = 30, y = 2}$ → $\dfrac{people}{seconds} \dfrac{6}{30} = \dfrac{x}{120}$ (120 seconds = 2 minutes)

→ $b = \underline{24}$ → **E.** Remember, **check every answer choice**.

Note: the numbers used above are convenient, but any numbers will work. When you plug the numbers into the answer choices, remember to plug in the numbers that you picked in step 1.

23. Pick Numbers (Type 2)

$a = b = 2$, $c = d = 3$, $e = f = 4$ → Only **J** works with these numbers.

31. **Pick Answers**
The barebones question is "what is the least value of m?" Since you are looking for the **least** value of m, start with A:

A: $m = 1$ → $\frac{2}{11} = n^2$ (n is not an integer) ✗

B: $m = 2$ → $\frac{4}{11} = n^2$ (n is not an integer) ✗

C: $m = 11$ → $\frac{22}{11} = 2 = n^2$ (n is not an integer) ✗

D: $m = 22$ → $\frac{44}{11} = 4 = n^2$ → $n = 2$ (an integer) ✓ **D.**

34. **Pick Numbers (Type 4)**
This approach will especially help you if you're not comfortable with exponents or logs. Just pick (guess) a number for x. Remember to keep track of your results so you know if you're getting closer to the answer.
$x = 2$ → $3^2 = 9 > 8$ (but close)
$x = 1.8$ → $3^{1.8} = 7.225... < 8$ (so pick a number between 1.8 and 2)
$x = 1.9$ → $3^{1.9} = 8.064... \approx 8$ (close enough)
→ $3^{2x} = 3^{(2 \cdot 1.9)} = 65.022... \approx 64$ **K.** Note: 8.064 > 8, so it's not surprising that 65.022 > 64.

35. **Pick Numbers (Type 3)**
Pick a number for the value of the treasure (a good number will be divisible by both 3 and 5): treasure = 15 → Anna = $\frac{3}{5}$ x 15 = 9 → Tanya = $\frac{1}{3}$ × 15 = 5 → Stephanie = 15 − (9 + 5) = 15 − 14 = 1 → The ratio is 9:5:1 **B.**

37. **Pick Numbers (Type 1)**
Pick simple numbers. Let's say it takes him 20 minutes to sweep the patio and he's worked for 15 minutes. $\boxed{x = 20 \text{ and } y = 15}$. You can calculate that he has 5 minutes left, or ¼ of the task (review the part-over-whole percent technique if necessary). → When you plug in your picked numbers, only **J** equals ¼. Don't forget to check every answer choice.

38. **Pick Numbers → Pick Answers**
Pick a number that works in the inequality above, such as x = 5.
Now, plug x = 5 into the answer choices and eliminate accordingly. Keep in mind that "or" means **either** of the two inequalities can work, while "and" means they **both** must work. You should be able to eliminate A, C, D, and E. The answer is **B.**

42. **Pick Answers**
Barebones question: "how old is Keith now?"
Pick H: K = 12 (note: "as old as" means multiplication - see Of/Is technique) → J = ½·12 = 6 → 6 = ¼·S → S = 24
Average = 14 < 21, so eliminate H, G, and F.
Pick J: K = 18 → J = 9 → S = 36 → Average = 21 ✓ **J.**

43. **Pick Numbers (Type 3)**
Pick 60 for each person. ← Any number divisible by 3 is convenient.
Total = 60 × 4 = 240

The woman's share = 60 + 20 + 40 = 120 → $\frac{120}{240} = \frac{1}{2}$ **B.**

48. **Pick Answer → Pick Numbers**
First pick an answer choice, such as F, and pick a number that is true for F: x = 3 (note: x = 0 is true for every answer choice and is thus a bad pick). Since x = 3 fails when plugged into the first inequality above, eliminate answer choices that are true for x = 3: eliminate F, H, and K.
Now, pick a number that is true for G but not J (the alternative is not possible): x = −3. Since x = −3 fails when plugged into the second inequality above, eliminate G. The answer must be **J.**

51. *Pick Answers*
   The barebones question is "what was the percent change after each game?"
   Note: a 22% increase is equivalent to multiplying by 1.22—review Percent
      Increase/Decrease)
   Pick C: $600 \times 1.22 = 732$ → $732 \times 1.22 = 893 > 864$ (eliminate H-K)
   Pick B: $600 \times 1.20 = 720$ → $720 \times 1.20 = 864$ ✓ **B.**
56. *Pick Numbers (Type 1)*
   Pick an easy number for d: $\boxed{d = 2}$
   If the company normally sells 5,000 programs a day, and each dollar increase results in
   1,000 fewer sales, then increasing the price $2 will result in 2,000 fewer sales:
   $5,000 - 2,000 = \underline{3,000}$ programs → Only **J** works when you plug in d = 2.

   Note that you don't need the current price of the program ($75.50) to solve the problem.
   Sometimes, particularly on higher-numbered problems, you'll be given more information
   than you need.

SIMULTANEOUS EQUATIONS

1. $2x + 2y = 8$
   $\underline{+(3x - 2y = 2)}$
   $5x \quad\quad = 10$ → $x = 2$ → $2 \cdot 2 + 2y = 8$ → $y = 2$
2. $100x + y = 25$
   $\underline{-(200x + y = 45)}$
   $-100x \quad\quad = -20$ → $x = \frac{1}{5}$ → $100 \cdot \frac{1}{5} + y = 25$ → $y = 5$
3. $(5x - 5y = -10) \times 2$ → $10x - 10y = -20$
   $(2x + 3y = 16) \times 5$ → $\underline{-(10x + 15y = 80)}$
   $\quad\quad\quad\quad\quad\quad -25y = -100$ → $y = 4$ → $5x - 5 \cdot 4 = -10$ → $x = 2$
60. The first step to this problem is to use RTD to find the equations.
   Let's call x the time to work, y the time to home, and d the distance each way.
   $\underline{R \ \times \ T = D} \quad\quad$ (Note: Distance is the same for both rows.)
   $\underline{10 \ \times \ \ x \quad\quad d}$
   $\underline{2 \quad\quad y \quad\quad d}$
   $\quad\quad\quad 3$
   Using the information above, we can write three equations:
   $10x = d$, $2y = d$, and $x + y = 3$
   Use substitution to combine (1) and (2): $10x = 2y$ → $10x - 2y = 0$
   Finally solve for x using simultaneous equations:
   $10x - 2y = 0$ → $\quad\quad\quad 10x - 2y = 0$
   $\quad x + \ y = 3$ → $\times 2$ → $\underline{+(2x + 2y = 6)}$
   $\quad\quad\quad\quad\quad\quad\quad 12x \quad\quad = 6$ → $x = 0.5$ → $d = 5$ → $2d = 10$ **J.**
   Note: The above approach displays the Simultaneous Equation technique, but you can also
   Pick Answers.

Homework:
23. $2x - 2y = 12 \quad\quad\quad\quad\quad\quad$ → $2x - 2y = 12$
   $\quad x + 3y = -6$ → $2 \times (x + 3y = -6)$ = $2x + 6y = -12$

   Subtract the bottom equation from the top to get rid of x:
   $\quad 2x - 2y = 12$
   $\underline{-(2x + 6y = -12)}$
   $\quad\quad -8y = 24$ → $y = -3$ **A.**

52. First of all, recall that the formula for the nth term of an arithmetic sequence is:
$a_n = a_1 + (n − 1)d$. *(See the Patterns section).* So let's plug in what we know: 5th term (n = 5): $6 = a_1 + 4d$; 9th term (n = 9): $13 = a_1 + 8d$
Now, stack the terms and solve for d (for convenience, we'll put the second equation on top):

$$13 = a_1 + 8d$$
$$\underline{−(6 = a_1 + 4d)}$$
$$7 = \quad 4d \;\; → d = {}^7\!/_4$$

Plug in d to either equation to solve for a_1: $6 = a_1 + 4·{}^7\!/_4$ → $a_1 = −1$
Finally, use the formula above to find a_{17} (the 17th term):
$a_{17} = a_1 + (17 − 1)d = −1 + (16){}^7\!/_4 = 27$ **G.**

FACTORS
COMMON FACTORS
1. $20g^2 − 40q = 20q(q − 2)$
2. $2x^2y + 3xy^2 = xy(2x + 3y)$
29. $x^2 − 4x = 0$ → $x(x − 4) = 0$ → $x = 0$ or $x = 4$ → → $x − 4 = 0 − 4 = −4$ **A.**
   Note: $4 − 4 = 0$ is not an available answer choice.

FACTORING QUADRATICS
1. $x^2 + 5x +6 = 0$ → $(x + 2)(x + 3) = 0$ → $x = $ **−2 or −3**
2. $x^2 − 12x +20 = 0$ → $(x − 10)(x − 2) = 0$ → $x = $ **10 or 2**
3. $x^2 + 4x − 21 = 0$ → $(x + 7)(x − 3) = 0$ → $x = $ **−7 or 3**
4. $(x + 23)(x − 1) = 0$ → $x = $ **−23 or 1**
Homework:
15. This question illustrates the Zero Product Theorem. If 3 is a solution, then $(x − 3)$ is a factor, and if −4 is a solution, then $(x + 4)$ is a factor. The answer is **A.**

   You could also simply plug the given values of x into each equation and eliminate answer choices. A common mistake, however, is to plug x = 3 into the left side and x = −4 into the right side of an equation (see E). This is incorrect: x must equal 3 on **both** sides OR x must equal −4 on **both** sides—you can't have different values for x in the same equation **at the same time.**
46. −k must equal the sum of the two numbers in the factored form (see step 3 in *Factoring Quadratics*): $−k = (−3) + (−2)$ → $k = 5$ **H.**

   Alternate solution:
   Use FOIL to expand the right side of the equation: $(a − 3)(a − 2) = a^2 − 5a + 6$
   Compare this to the left side of the original equation: $a^2 − ka + 6 = a^2 − 5a + 6$
   Notice that the coefficients in front of the a^2 terms are equal (both 1) and the number terms are equal (both 6). Similarly, the coefficients in front of the a terms must also equal. So: $−k = −5$ → $k = 5$ **H.**
   This is a good general rule to keep in mind when you compare polynomials (multi-termed expressions).
53. You'll probably want to use the quadratic formula for this one. Since using the formula for every answer choice is time consuming, here is a shortcut:
   Since there is only **one** solution for the equation, the part of the quadratic formula following the ± must be 0, so $b^2 − 4ac = 0$. You can eliminate C, D, and E. Now you only need to use the quadratic formula for two answer choices (A and B). The answer is **A.**

QUADRATICS
44. Equation 2: $(a + b)^2 = a^2 + 2ab + b^2$ *(Remember: write the equation first.)*
   $$(5)^2 = a^2 + 5 + b^2$$
   → $25 = a^2 + b^2 + 5$ → $a^2 + b^2 = 25 − 5 = 20$ **D.**

Homework:

1. $(x - y)^2 = (x - y) \cdot (x - y) = x \cdot x + x \cdot (-y) + (-y) \cdot x + (-y) \cdot (-y) = x^2 - xy - xy + y^2 = \mathbf{x^2 - 2xy + y^2}$

6. *Use FOIL:*

   $(3x - 2)(x + 7) = 3x \cdot x + 3x \cdot 7 + (-2) \cdot x + (-2) \cdot 7 = 3x^2 + 21x - 2x - 14 = 3x^2 + 19x - 14$ **D.**

38. *Use Quadratic Equation 1:*

   $(x - y)(x + y) = x^2 - y^2$

   $(5) \quad (x + y) = (20) \quad \rightarrow \quad x + y = 20 \div 5 = 4$ **G.**

ALGEBRA WORKSHEET 1

4. *Essential Algebra*

   $3(2x - 4) = 2x - 16 \quad \rightarrow \quad 6x - 12 = 2x - 16 \quad \rightarrow \quad 6x - 2x = -16 + 12 \quad \rightarrow \quad 4x = -4 \quad \rightarrow \quad x = -1$ **B.**

10. *Pick Numbers (Type 2)*

   *Let $a = 2$ and $b = 3$. $\rightarrow$ $c = 5$ $\rightarrow$ Now check the answer choices. Only **K** works with the numbers above. You should probably check every answer choice.*

   Notice the equal signs in the answer choices. This is not a Pick Numbers (Type 1) problem—you could not pick numbers for all 3 variables (just 2 of them).

12. *Pick Answers*

   Even though the question asks for the "smallest possible value of x," you might still start with C (as opposed to the smaller A and B) since integers are easier to check.

   Pick C: $\dfrac{3}{1} = 3 \nleq \dfrac{1}{3}$ ✗ *It's not clear what direction to go, so check D (easier to plug in).*

   Pick D: $\dfrac{3}{3} = 1 \nleq \dfrac{1}{3}$ ✗ *We're still not there, but we're getting closer, so check E.*

   Pick E: $\dfrac{3}{9} = \dfrac{1}{3} \leq \dfrac{1}{3}$ ✔

   *At this point, since C and D did not work, E is probably the answer. If you have time, however, you might check A and B to be safe since they are both smaller than E. Indeed, the answer is **E.***

20. *Factoring*

   $x^2(x + 1) = 0 \quad \rightarrow \quad x = 0$ or -1 *(by the Zero Product Theorem)* $\rightarrow$ $0 + (-1) = -1$ **H.**

   *You could also Pick Numbers (Type 4). You probably know that $x = 0$ $(0 + 0 = 0)$. Guess some other numbers. It's apparent that x would have to be negative. The only other value that work is $x = -1$. The answer is **H.***

30. *Algebraic Word Problems*

   This problem sounds hard, particularly all the "compounding" talk. But remember: be aggressive on these word problems. You don't really need to know much about the equation. Just plug in values:

   $P = 5{,}000, r = 6\% = 0.06, n = 10$ $\rightarrow$ $A = P(1 + r)^n = 5{,}000(1 + 0.06)^{10} = 5{,}000(1.06)^{10}$ **D.**

36. *Essential Algebra*

   $-3x + 6 < -6x \quad \rightarrow \quad 6 < -6x + 3x \quad \rightarrow \quad 6 < -3x \quad \rightarrow \quad 6 \div -3 > x$ *(don't forget to change the inequality sign when you multiply/divide by a negative number)* $\rightarrow$ $-2 > x$ $\rightarrow$ $x < -2$ **J.**

   Note: You could also Pick Answers $\rightarrow$ Pick Numbers.

41. *Pick Numbers $\rightarrow$ Pick Answers*

   We know what you're thinking: What is this problem doing in the Algebra chapter? This problem is a good example of how the Pick Tricks can get you out of a jam. If you have some idea of a coordinate plane, you should be able to sketch the circle. Can you pick any obvious points on the graph of the circle? See the drawing below. (continued)

*Start with (0,0). Plug x = 0 and y = 0 into the answer choices. You can eliminate A-C. Next, check (0,4). Plug x = 0 and y = 4 into the remaining answer choices. Eliminate E. The answer must be **D**. Note that we didn't need to know anything about the equation of a circle to get this one correct. Not bad!*

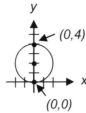

42. Pick Numbers (Type 1)

Make sure to pick a number greater than 4:

$$\boxed{x = 5} \;\rightarrow\; \frac{x^2 - 4x}{x^2 + 4x - 32} = \frac{25 - 20}{25 + 20 - 32} = \frac{5}{13}$$

➔ At a glance, you can see that **G** works when you plug in x = 5. Make sure to look at every answer choice.

Note: If you're comfortable factoring, you could factor the top and bottom and cancel like expressions.

60. Pick Numbers (Type 4 – Guess and Check)

Try some numbers that have a difference of 10. Remember, you're looking for the smallest value for xy: 10 and 0 might come to mind: 10·0 = 0 ➔ Eliminate D and E which are clearly greater than 0.

At this point, notice the negative numbers in the answer choices. Check some more numbers that have a difference of 10. You might recognize that the numbers must have opposite signs (one positive, one negative) to get a negative product. Remember to keep track of your results so you know you're heading in the right direction:

9 × −1 = −9 ➔ Smaller than 0!
6 × −4 = −24 ➔ Getting smaller!
5 × −5 = −25 ➔ That must be the answer. No answer choice is less. **A.**

ALGEBRA WORKSHEET 2

14. Essential Algebra (Working with Variables)

You could always Pick Numbers (Type 1), but if you're comfortable working with variables, the problem can be solved quickly: $\dfrac{x + x}{x} = \dfrac{2\cancel{x}}{\cancel{x}} = 2$ **A.**

29. Algebraic Word Problems

5 red tickets cost 5r dollars. 10 blue tickets cost 10b dollars. The difference between the costs is $15, but we don't know which is greater (5r or 10b). 5r − 10b could equal 15, or 10b − 5r could equal 15. Hence, the use of absolute values in the answer choices, which guarantees a positive answer (15), regardless of the order of the terms. **J.**

You might choose to Pick Numbers ➔ Pick Answers: Pick r = $5 ➔ 5 red tickets × $5 = $25. Since the difference is $15, the blue tickets must add to $40 or $10 ➔ Remember there are 10 blue tickets, so b = $4 (if they add to $40) or b = $1 (if they add to $10). Now find the answer that satisfies r = 5 and b = 4 or b = 1. Only **J** works.

31. Quadratics

Use Equation 3, with $a^2 + b^2$ written next to each other:

$(a - b)^2 = a^2 + b^2 - 2ab$

$(4)^2 = (26) - 2ab$ ➔ $-2ab = 16 - 26 = -10$ ➔ $ab = 5$ **D.**

Note: You could also Pick Numbers (Type 4). Start with the first (easier) equation. You might guess a = 5 and b = 1 on your first try.

32. *Pick Answers*

   *The first lighthouse is visible every 21 seconds (21, 42, ...) and the second lighthouse is visible every 60 seconds (60, 120, ...). So you need to find an answer choice that is divisible by **both** 21 and 60. Since you're looking for the **first** time that the lights shine together again, start with F:*
   Pick F: 120 is not divisible by 21. ✗
   Pick G: 210 is not divisible by 60. ✗
   *Pick H: 420 is divisible by both 21 and 60. ✓ The answer is **H**.*

33. *Essential Algebra (Radicals)*

   $$\sqrt{x-3} - 3 = 3 \;\to\; \sqrt{x-3} = 6 \;\to\; (\sqrt{x-3})^2 = 6^2 \;\to\; x - 3 = 36 \;\to\; x = 39 \;\textbf{D}.$$

   You could also Pick Answers. Notice the simple barebones question.

45. *Pick Numbers (Type 3)*

   Pick sides for the original rectangle that satisfy the problem: l = 2, w = 1 → area = 2 × 1 = 2
   Now, triple these sides and find the new area:
   new l = 2 × 3 = 6, new w = 1 × 3 = 3 → new area = 6 × 3 = 18
   *➜ 18 is 9 times greater than 2. **H**.*

54. *Pick Numbers → Pick Answers*

   Pick a number on the graph above, and check the answer choices. Start with an easy number, such as x = 2 → Eliminate B, C and E.
   *Pick x = −4 → Eliminate A. The answer must be **D**.*

58. *Pick Numbers (Type 1)*

   Make sure to only pick numbers for the variables in the answer choices:
   a = 2 and b = 3 → So x = 23 and y = 32. → 23 + 32 = 55
   *➜ Only **J** works. Make sure to check every answer choice.*

   Notice how relatively easy this problem becomes when you use a Pick Trick! Not bad for a number 58.

59. *Pick Numbers (Type 1)/Algebraic Word Problems*

   Only y is in the answer choices, so pick a number for y: y = 12 (Note that we picked a number that made x easy to calculate. This is convenient but not necessary.)
   Now solve for x: 10 + x = 12 → x = 2 → 10x = 10·2 = 20
   *➜ Only **C** equals 20 when you plug in your picked number for y. Don't forget to check every answer choice.*

ALGEBRA WORKSHEET 3

8. *Essential Algebra*

   Plug q = −10 into the equation (use parentheses if you type values into your calculator):
   *−(−10)^2 + (−10) − 100 = −100 − 10 − 100 = −210 **A**.*

9. *Essential Algebra*

   Each integer is represented by an expression. Set the sum of the five given expressions equal to 115 and solve for x:
   *x − 3 + x − 2 + x − 1 + x + x + 1 = 115 → 5x − 5 = 115 → 5x = 120 → x = 24 **J**.*

   You could also Pick Answers for this problem.

24. *Pick Numbers (Type 1)*

   Pick simple numbers: m = 3 and d = 2
   The daily cost is 2 × 25 = 50. Since 3 miles are driven each of 2 days, the total miles are 6, so the cost is 0.25 × 6 = 1.50.
   *The total cost is: 50 + 1.50 = 51.50. ➜ Only **D** works when you plug in your picked numbers.*
   If you're comfortable with Algebraic Word Problems, by all means find the expression. Picking numbers is probably the safe way to go, however.

35. *Pick Numbers (Type 2)*
   Pick a number for x and solve for y:
   $x = 2$ ➔ $2 - y = -8$ ➔ $-y = -10$ ➔ $y = 10$ ➔ So $\sqrt{2y - 2x} = \sqrt{20 - 4} = \sqrt{16} = 4$ **H.**

38. *Pick Answers*
   The barebones question is "what is a possible value of a?" Start with answer choice C.
   Solve for b using the second equation (which appears to be the easier equation) and then
   check the first equation.
   Pick C: $a = 5$ ➔ 2nd equation: $5^2 + b = 28$ ➔ $b = 28 - 25 = 3$
   ➔ 1st equation: $5^2 - 3^2 = 25 - 9 = 16$ ✓ The answer is **C.**

48. *Pick Numbers (Type 1)/Factoring*
   The problem is easier if you Pick Numbers (Type 1). Remember that when you use this
   technique, only pick numbers for variables in the answer choices (in this case, just b).
   $\boxed{b = 2}$ ➔ $4a^2 - 100 = 0$ ➔ Difference of squares: $(2a - 10)(2a + 10) = 0$
   ➔ $a = 5$ or -5 ➔ $5 + (-5) = \underline{0}$ ➔ **H.** Remember, check every answer choice.

   You could also solve $4a^2 - 100 = 0$ using exponential rules. Just don't forget that when you
   solve for a squared variable, you will get a positive **and** a negative answer:
   $4a^2 = 100$ ➔ $a^2 = 25$ ➔ $a = 5$ or -5 ➔ $5 + (-5) = \underline{0}$ ➔ **H.**

53. *Pick Answers* ➔ *Pick Numbers:*
   Yes, we know you haven't covered geometry yet, but remember that the Pick Tricks will
   often help you tackle problems that you might otherwise find exceptionally difficult. You
   might not know how to graph absolute value functions in 2 dimensions, but let's see if the
   Pick Tricks can help. Pick answer choice A ➔ Pick a number in the shaded region that
   does not fall in the shaded region of some of the other answer choices, such as (0, 20) (the
   first number is x and the second number is y). ➔ Since $|0| \not\geq 10$ we can eliminate answer
   choices that include (0, 20) in the shaded region. Eliminate A, B, and E.
   Now pick a number that falls in the shaded region of **one** of the remaining answer choices.
   Pick C ➔ Pick (−20, 0). Since $|-20| = 20 \geq 10$, the answer must be **C.**

54. *Algebraic Word Problems/Simultaneous Equations:*
   Note that we have two items (smart phones and flip phones). We know the total **number** of
   phones, and the total **cost** of these phones. This is a common type of algebraic word
   problem (see the Algebraic Word Problems section), so make sure you're comfortable
   setting up the equations. First, call the number of smart phones s and the number of flip
   phones f. The total cost of smart phones is 250s and the total cost of flip phones is 50f. We
   can write two equations (one for the number of phones and one for the cost of the phones):
   $s + f = 40$ and $250s + 50f = 4{,}000$.

   Solve these equations using the Simultaneous Equation method (or Pick Numbers-Type 4).
   You should get $s = 10$ and $f = 30$. ➔ So there must be 10 executives and 30 regular
   employees. ➔ $30 - 10 = 20$ **F.**

   You could also try Picking Answers, but for most students figuring out the number of each
   type of employee from the **difference** of these numbers (the answer choices) is tricky.

57. *Pick Numbers (Type 4):*
   First, simplify the equation: $\dfrac{a}{a^2 + 1} + \dfrac{1}{a^2 + 1} = \dfrac{a + 1}{a^2 + 1} = \dfrac{5}{b}$
   Now, we have two options. We could Pick Answers for b (note the simple barebones
   question and the numbers as answer choices). But if we pick a number for b (by picking an
   answer choice), a is difficult to solve.
   So the better option is to Pick Numbers (Type 4) for a. Remember, a > 1, and both a and b
   are integers.
   $a = 2$ ➔ $\dfrac{3}{5} = \dfrac{5}{b}$ ➔ b is not an integer ✗ (continued)

$a = 3 \rightarrow \dfrac{4}{10} = \dfrac{5}{b} \rightarrow$ b is not an integer ✗

$a = 4 \rightarrow \dfrac{5}{17} = \dfrac{5}{b} \rightarrow b = 17$ ✓ **D.**

ALGEBRA WORKSHEET 4

5. *Algebraic Word Problems*
   Let days be "d" and clicks be "c." The equation is: 50d + 0.75c. (75¢ = $0.75) Plug in the given numbers: 50·30 + 0.75·2,500 **A.**

15. *Pick Numbers (Type 1)*
    If you're comfortable working with polynomials, you'll probably get this one without having to use a Pick Trick. If not, picking a number for x will make the problem much easier:
    $\boxed{x = 2} \rightarrow 2x^2 + 7x - 14 = 2\cdot4 + 7\cdot2 - 14 = 8$ *and* $x^2 - 14 = 4 - 14 = -10$
    → *So what number must be subtracted from 8 to get −10? We're looking for* <u>18</u>*.*
    → *Only **J** equals 18 when you plug in x = 2. (Check every answer choice.)*

24. *Essential Algebra (Working with Variables)*
    You can either distribute first, or simplify the parenthetical expressions first, as shown in the solution: $a(a + a) - a(a + a - 1) = a(2a) - a(2a - 1) = 2a^2 - 2a^2 + a$
    Now, combine like terms: $2a^2 - 2a^2 + a = a$ **E.**

    You could also Pick Numbers (Type 1).

25. *Quadratics*
    Use Equation 3:
    $(m - n)^2 = m^2 - 2mn + n^2$
    $\quad (4) \quad = m^2 - 16 \quad + n^2 \rightarrow 4 + 16 = m^2 + n^2 \rightarrow m^2 + n^2 = 20$ **H.**

    You could also Pick Numbers (Type 4) for m and n. You might be surprised how quickly you can come up with the correct numbers.

26. *Factoring*
    First, subtract 35 from both sides so the expression equals 0:
    $x^2 - 2x - 35 = 0$
    Now, factor into the form (x − ?)(x +?). The two terms must multiply to −35 and add to −2. The numbers 5 and −7 work, so we have: $(x - 7)(x + 5) = 0$
    → *Now use the Zero Product Theorem: x = 7, x = −5* **A.**

    Note: If you'd rather not factor, just Pick Answers. Only A works when you plug the values into the equation.

32. *Pick Numbers (Type 3)*
    Let's pick numbers so we have something to work with. Make sure you pick numbers that satisfy the conditions given in the problem:
    Let one of the numbers equal 3 and the other number equal 6. The product is 18. F, G, and K all work, but we can eliminate H and J. Let's pick new numbers.
    *Let one of the numbers equal 3 and the other number equal 9. The product is 27. Only **G** is a factor of 27.*

55. *Pick Answers*
    *To find the **minimum** number of additional games, assume the team wins **all** of them.*
    Pick C: wins = 16 additional wins + 8 original wins = 24, played games = 16 additional games + 16 original games = 32 → *Use the Part/Whole percent technique to find the win percentage:*
    $\dfrac{\text{won}}{\text{played}} \dfrac{24}{32} = 0.75 < .80$ ✗ *So the team needs to play (win) more games.*
    Pick D: wins = 24 + 8 = 32, played games = 24 + 16 = 40 →
    $\dfrac{\text{won}}{\text{played}} \dfrac{32}{40} = 0.80 = 80\%$ ✓ *The answer is **D.***

57. **Simultaneous Equations**

Do not graph these lines. This is just a Simultaneous Equation problem. Find x and y to find the point of intersection.

$2x - 2y = 30$ $2x - 2y = 30$

$x - 5y = 7$ → ×2 → $-\underline{(2x - 10y = 14)}$

                                $8y = 16$ → $y = 2$

→ Plug $y = 2$ into the first original equation: $2x - 2·2 = 30$ → $x = 17$

➜ (17, 2) is the solution. **H.**

You could also Pick Answers. Only H works when the values are plugged into the first equation, so you actually don't have to check the second equation.

See the Lines section in Chapter IV for more about intersecting lines.

59. *Pick Numbers → Pick Answers:*

Pick an initial number for C: $C = 30$ → So the initial **score** is: ⅓·30 +10 = 20

The barebones question is: "how many <u>additional</u> questions must a student answer correctly… to raise her score by 20 points?" Answer the question starting with C:

Pick C: The new number of correct answers is: $C = 30 + 60 = 90$ → The new score = ⅓C + 10 = ⅓·90 +10 = 40 → So she raised her original score by 20 points. ✓ The answer is **C.**

MEASURE THE DRAWING

55. You can see that ∠EFD is greater than 90°, but how much greater? Place a sheet of paper along line segment FD, with the corner at vertex F. You might guess that ∠EFD ≈ 90° + 30° = 120°. The closest answer is **D.**

Homework:

57. The trick to this problem is to use the drawing to find a distance of 2: just mark distances of 6 and 8 on the edge of a sheet of paper; the difference is 2.

Next, using your sheet of paper as a ruler, check the length of BC. If you're careful, you should find that BC measures a little over 4.

Finally, use your calculator to check the answer choices. Only **E** is close (4.106. . .).

AREA AND PERIMETER

1 and 2. The first triangle is a right triangle, so the height is the length of a leg adjacent to the base, as shown below. On the second triangle, the base must be extended.

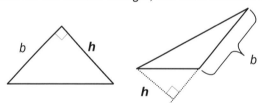

5. Since all four sides of a square are equal, we know that AC = CD = DF = AF = 5. As the name implies, the sides of an equilateral triangle are also equal, so AB = BC = AC = 5 and DE = EF = DF = 5. So all the sides are the same! Count up the sides (not the dotted lines) and multiply by 5: 6 × 5 = 30 **C.**

7. $(x) + (x + 2) + (x) + (x + 2) = 20$ → $4x + 4 = 20$ → $4x = 16$ → $x = 4$

→ Area = $(4)·(4 + 2) = 4·6 = 24$ **G.**

You could also pick numbers for x (guess and check), but this could take a while.

25. The area of a parallelogram is bh. The base is 7 (remember, opposite sides of a parallelogram are equal) and the height (which falls outside the parallelogram) is 6, so the area is: $A = 6·7 = 42.$ **D.**

40. Cut the shaded region within the square into a triangle and a rectangle (see figure). The triangle has a height of 5 and a base of 8 → Area = 20

The rectangle area = 8 × 3 = 24. (continued)

The area of one semicircle is $\frac{1}{2}\pi r^2 = \frac{1}{2}\pi(\frac{3}{2})^2 = \frac{9}{8}\pi$

The total area is: $20 + 24 + \frac{9}{8}\pi + \frac{9}{8}\pi = 44 + \frac{9}{4}\pi$ **H.**

Shortcut: If you find the area of the two semicircles first and recognize that this area is the second part of each answer choice, you can eliminate G, J, and K. The area of the square is 64, and the shaded part of the square is clearly more than half of the total area, so 24 is too small. The answer must be **H.**

Note: You could also subtract the areas of the two white triangles from the area of the square, and then add the two shaded semicircles.

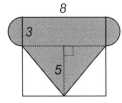

48. *Work carefully. Notice the high problem number.*
The length of each side of the square is $32 \div 4 = 8$ → *The diameter of a semicircle is* $8 \div 2 = 4$ → *The radius of a semicircle is* $4 \div 2 = 2$

→ *area* $= \dfrac{\pi r^2}{2} = \dfrac{\pi 2^2}{2} = \dfrac{4\pi}{2} = 2\pi$ **A.**

Homework:

10. *Perimeter of one shaded region* $= 2 + 2 + 6 + 6 = 16$ → $16 + 16 = 32$ **D.**

29. *side of triangle* $= 12 \div 3 = 4$ → *radius of one circle* $= \dfrac{4}{2} = 2$

→ *circumference of one circle* $= 2\pi r = 2\cdot 2 \cdot \pi = 4\pi$
→ $(4\pi)\cdot 3 = 12\pi$ **H.**

43. *Use the area subtracting method:*
AB = 8, EF = 8 + 2 + 2 = 12
→ *area of EFGH* $= 12^2 = 144$
→ *area of ABCD* $= 8^2 = 64$
→ $144 - 64 = 80$ **D.**

Note: you could also cut up the area into rectangles.

46. *The trick to this problem is to recognize that the triangle is a right triangle with both legs equal to the radius of the circle.* $\dfrac{1}{2}bh = \dfrac{1}{2}6\cdot 6 = 18$ **G.**

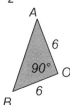

52. *Pick Answers*

Barebones question: *"what is the radius of the smaller circle?"*

Pick C: *r of small = 2* → *CD = BC = DE = r of large = 4* → *Total area of three circles= 4π + 16π + 16π = 36π > 18π* ✗ → *Eliminate C, D, and E.*

Pick A (easier than B): *r of small = 1* → *r of large = 2* → *Total area = π + 4π + 4π = 9π < 18π* ✗ → *Eliminate A. The answer must be **B**.*

53. $x = \pi r^2$ and $y = 2\pi r$

Since x = y, $\pi r^2 = 2\pi r$ → divide both sides by πr: $\dfrac{\pi r^2}{\pi r} = \dfrac{2\pi r}{\pi r}$ → r = 2 **G.**

You could also pick answers.

58. *There are three ways that you could solve this problem:*

(1) First, find the diameter of the circle:

Area of semicircle = $\dfrac{1}{2}\pi r^2 = 84.5\pi$ → solve for r: $r^2 = 169$ → r = 13 → diameter = 26.

*Now look at segment AB. Since we can be fairly sure that the drawing is drawn to scale (see the Geometry Introduction), the length of AB appears to be a little less than the diameter of the circle. If you look at the answer choices, D and E can be eliminated because they are not less than 26 (the diameter). The answer is clearly **C**.*

*(2) If you have trouble finding the radius (and diameter) of the circle, you could measure the drawing, as described in the Geometry Introduction. Use the drawing to mark a distance of 5 (AD) on a piece of paper and use this as a ruler to estimate the distance of AB. You should get close to 24. **C.***

(3) You will learn about the Pythagorean Theorem in the triangle section. Once you find the radius of the circle, create a right triangle and use the Pythagorean Theorem to find half the distance of AB (see the drawing below): $5^2 + b^2 = 13^2$ → b = 12 → 2·12 = 24 **C.**

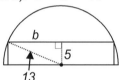

TRIANGLES
SIMILAR TRIANGLES

1. $\dfrac{DE}{AE} = \dfrac{BC}{AC}$

TRIANGLE LESSON PROBLEMS

1. *hypotenuse = 13*

2. *short leg* $= \sqrt{28} = 2\sqrt{7} \approx$ **5.29...**

3. *hypotenuse = 6, long leg* $= 3\sqrt{3} \approx$ **5.20...**

4. *leg = 2, hypotenuse* $= 2\sqrt{2} \approx$ **2.83...**

5. *legs = 4*

6. *short leg = 4, long leg* $= 4\sqrt{3} \approx$ **6.93...**

7. *legs* $= \dfrac{6}{\sqrt{2}} = 3\sqrt{2} \approx$ **4.24...**

8. *short leg* $= \dfrac{7}{\sqrt{3}} = \dfrac{7}{3}\sqrt{3} \approx$ **4.04...** *, hypotenuse* $= 2 \times \dfrac{7}{\sqrt{3}} = \dfrac{14}{\sqrt{3}} = \dfrac{14}{3}\sqrt{3} \approx$ **8.08...**

8. *Use the Pythagorean Theorem:* $AB^2 + BC^2 = AC^2$ → $AB^2 = AC^2 - BC^2$
→ $AB^2 = 26^2 - 24^2$ **(E)**

20. *The two legs of a right triangle can be used as the base and height since they are perpendicular to each other.*
    ½·12·b = 54 → b = 9
    Pythagorean Theorem:
    $9^2 + 12^2 = c^2$ → c = 15 **H.**

29. $x \cdot x = x^2 = 50$ → $x = \sqrt{50} = 5\sqrt{2}$ *(or use calc.)*
    $x^2 + x^2 = c^2$ → $50 + 50 = 100 = c^2$ → c = 10 **C.**

    You might also notice that the triangle is a 45-45-90, so c = $x \cdot \sqrt{2} = 5\sqrt{2}\sqrt{2} = 5 \cdot 2 = 10$ **C.**

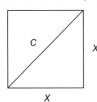

41. *The length of each side of the triangle is 2, and each angle of an equilateral triangle is 60°.*

    Notice the 30-60-90 triangle (see figure). The sides of the rectangle are: $\sqrt{3}$ *and 2.*

    → *Area of rectangle =* $\sqrt{3} \cdot 2 = 2\sqrt{3}$ **H.**

    As always, if you are uncomfortable with radicals, use a calculator to convert radicals into decimals (answer choices too).

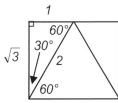

Homework:

17. *The triangle is equilateral, so −8x − y = 8 and 4x + 2y = 8. Since we are solving for x, let's eliminate y using simultaneous equations (or use substitution). First, multiply the first equation by 2:* 2 × (−8x − y = 8) = −16x − 2y = 16
    −16x − 2y = 16
    + (4x + 2y = 8)
    −12x   = 24 → x = −2 **A.**

    Note: you could also Pick Answers.

40. *First, find CE using the Pythagorean Theorem:* $4^2 + CE^2 = 10^2$ → $CE = \sqrt{84}$

    Now, △ABC is similar to △EDC (you may not be able to prove the angles are equal until you go through the Angles section, but remember that when triangles appear similar on the ACT, they usually are). We need to find AC:
    Since DE = 2 × AB, CE = 2 × AC:

    $\sqrt{84} = 2 \times AC$ → $AC = \dfrac{\sqrt{84}}{2}$ → $AE = AC + CE = \dfrac{\sqrt{84}}{2} + \sqrt{84} \approx 13.75$

    → *Check the answer choices with your calculator.* **J.**

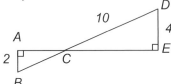

44. *This is a good example of a triangle problem that doesn't have an original triangle drawn. See the drawing. The missing side, x, can be found by using the Pythagorean Theorem:* $3^2 + 4^2 = x^2$ → $x = 5$ *(or you could have recognized the 3-4-5 triangle).* $P = 12 + 5 + 5 + 8 + 8 = 38$ **C.**

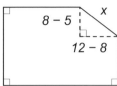

45. *Review the angle-side relationships.*
Since AB > AC, c > b → *Pick a number for angle c: c = 61* → *The sum of the angles of a triangle are 180°, so: b = 59. We also now know:*
AC < BC < AB (following the order of the sides' opposite angles: c > a > b).
Now look at the answer choices. All can be eliminated except for **K.**

You might note that J **could** *be true, but it's not* **necessarily** *true.*

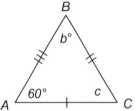

48. *Review the third side rule for a triangle:*
c + 4 must be > 5 → *Pick Answers (starting with A) if necessary):*
Pick A: c = 1 → $1 + 4 \not> 5$ ✗
Pick B: c = 2 → $2 + 4 > 5$ ✓ → *The answer is* **B.**

ANGLES

LINE: x + y = **180**
TRIANGLE: x + y + z = **180**
CIRCLE: x + y + z + w = **360**
RIGHT ANGLE: x = **90**
VERTICAL ANGLES: z = **50**, *y =* **130**, *w =* **130**
PARALLEL LINES: x = **30**, *y =* **150**
LINE TANGENT TO A CIRCLE: x = **90**

SUM OF INTERIOR ANGLES:

QUADRILATERAL: x + y + z + w = 2·180 = **360**

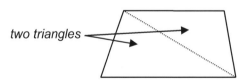

two triangles

OTHER POLYGONS:
1.   6·180 = **1080°**
2.   There are 8 congruent angles → 1080 ÷ 8 = **135**

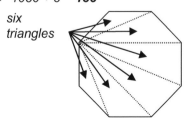

six triangles

ANGLES LESSON PROBLEMS

3. $(x + 5) + 90 + (x - 5) = 180$ → $2x + 90 = 180$ → $2x = 90$ → $x = 45$ **C.**
    Note: you could also pick answers

30. Use vertical angles to show that the angles above make up the angles of two triangles.
    → $2 \cdot 180 = 360$ **H.**
    You could also Pick Numbers (Type 2) for a, b, and c (or any three angles)—then solve for the other two.

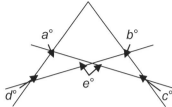

32. Use the figure to Pick Numbers (Type 1); write the numbers directly on the figure so they are easy to keep track of. $a = d = e = h = 40°$ → $b = c = f = g = 140°$ → $a + g = \underline{180°}$ → **C.**
    *Remember, **check every answer choice**.*

48. Pick Numbers (Type 1):
    $x = 50$ → The fastest approach is to look at the large triangle ($\triangle PQR$)—look at angles P, Q, and R. Notice that $y + (x + 60) + x = 180$ $y + (50 + 60) + 50 = 180$ → $y + 160 = 180$ → $y = \underline{20}$ → **J.**
    Make sure you check every answer choice when you use Pick Numbers (Type 1).

    To find y (after picking a number for x), you could also start at angle Q ($x + 60°$) and solve for all angles as you work your way around the triangle clockwise.

Homework:

7. If one angle of a triangle equals 90, the other two angles must add to 90:
    $3x + x = 90$ → $x = 22\frac{1}{2}$ **A.**

28. $5x = 180$ (straight line) → $x = 36$
    $y = 2x$ (vertical angles) → $y = 2 \cdot 36 = 72$ **J.**

    Note: you could also Pick Answers.

50. Pick Numbers (Type 1):
    $x = 40$ Look at the bottom triangle. The right base angle can be found because the lines are parellel (40).
    Once you know the two base angles of this triangle, you can find the top angle ($180 - (40 + 40) = 100$).
    Finally, y can be found by the straight-line angle rule: $y = 180 - 100 = \underline{80}$
    → Plug 40 into the answer choices. Only **H** works. Remember, **check every answer choice**.

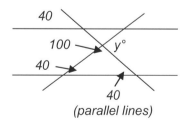

(parallel lines)

51. Since there are five "central angles" (∠AOB is one of them), you can divide 360° by five: 360° ÷ 5 = 72° **C.**

   Another approach: sum of interior ∠s = 3·180° = 540° → Each interior ∠ = 108° → ∠BAO = ∠ABO = 108° ÷ 2 = 54° → ∠AOB = 180° − 54°·2 = 180° − 108° = 72° (see drawing)

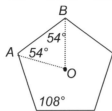

COORDINATES

1. A = **(1,5)**
2. B = **(−3,2)**
3. C = **(0,0)**
4. D = **(5,1)**
5. E = **(3,−2)**

17. horizontal sides: $|-1-3| = 4$; vertical sides: $|-3-9| = 12$

   → perimeter = 4 + 4 + 12 + 12 = 32 **E.**

5. OA = 6 → AB = 6 → OB = OC = 12 → The coordinates of point C are (−12,0) **B.**

17. Use the equation for midpoint: $M = \left(\dfrac{x_1 + x_2}{2}, \dfrac{y_1 + y_2}{2}\right) = \left(\dfrac{-2+2}{2}, \dfrac{-6+5}{2}\right) = (0,-0.5)$ **H.**

Homework:

11. Since the triangle is isosceles, AC = BC.
   BC = $|4 - (-1)| = 5$
   So the coordinates of A must be 5 units to the left of point C: x coordinate = 2 − 5 = −3; y coordinate is the same as that of point C. → (−3, 4) **E.**
   Check: AC = $|-3 - 2| = |-5| = 5$ ✓

39. First, using the midpoint formula, find the coordinates of C: $C = \left(\dfrac{-2+6}{2}, \dfrac{-3+9}{2}\right) = (2,3)$

   Now find the coordinates of D: $D = \left(\dfrac{-2+2}{2}, \dfrac{-3+3}{2}\right) = (0,0)$ → The answer is **K.**

59. This is one of those "leaning" triangles where the height is measured **outside** the triangle. See the figure.
   The base of the triangle is: $|-7 - (-2)| = |-5| = 5$
   The height of the triangle is: $|8 - (-2)| = |10| = 10$
   → ½bh = ½ · 5 · 10 = 25 **C.**

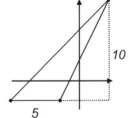

LINES

NUMBER LINES

6. Point A is at $-\frac{7}{5}$, Point B is at $-\frac{1}{5}$ → $\left|-\frac{7}{5} - \left(-\frac{1}{5}\right)\right| = \frac{6}{5}$ **D.**

   You could also calculate the "unit distance" (the distance between tick marks) and multiply this by the number of units between A and B: $\frac{1}{5} \times 6 = \frac{6}{5}$

LINE SEGMENTS

48. Sketch the highway with the two radio antennas, as shown. The length of highway where the two arrows overlap, labeled with an x, is where the radio signals from both stations can be heard. You can either use algebra or Pick Answers.

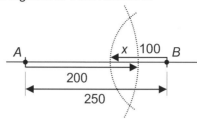

*Algebra: (200 − x) + (100 − x) + x = 250 → 300 − x = 250 → x = 50 **A**.*

SLOPE OF A LINE

17. The line will slant up to the left (from quadrant IV to quadrant II). Thus, the slope of the line will be negative. Feel free to sketch a few lines if you'd like. The answer is **A**.

EQUATION OF A LINE

1. Line B: **y = 3**
2. Line C: **y = −2**
3. Line D: **x = 0**
4. Line E: **x = 3**
10. Plug 2 in for x and p in for y: p − 3 = 2(2 − 4) → p = −1 **A**.
37. The slope of the line and a point on the line are given. Find the equation by plugging in the given values, and solve for b, the y-intercept.

$$y = mx + b \rightarrow 6 = \tfrac{3}{2} \cdot 6 + b \rightarrow 6 = 9 + b \rightarrow b = -3 \textbf{ J.}$$

INTERSECTING LINES

42. First, notice that the y-intercepts are different. So when the slopes are the same, the two lines will never cross and there will be no solutions. So k must equal 2. **D**.

Homework:

4. One-Dimensional Lines
Because R is the midpoint of QS, we know that QR = RS. You could solve algebraically by solving for x in the following equation:
x + 3 = y − 1 → x = y − 4 **A**.

If you'd prefer to avoid the algebra, you could Pick Numbers (Type 1) for y (the variable in the answer choices):
y = 4 → x + 3 = 4 − 1 → x = 0 → Only **A** works. Remember, **check every answer choice**.

10. One-Dimensional Lines
Remember, the Pick Tricks are often helpful on these segment problems. Pick a number for one of the segments, as shown. Only **J** is NOT true when the answer choices are checked:
CB = 4, AC = 4, → CB ≮ AC

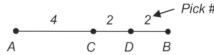

32. Slope

First, find the slope of the line (the line goes through the origin (0,0): $m = \dfrac{9-0}{3-0} = 3$

Now, Pick Numbers (Type 2) for a, and solve for b:

$a = -1 \;\rightarrow\; \dfrac{b-0}{-1-0} = 3 \;\rightarrow\; b = -3 \;\rightarrow\; \dfrac{b}{a} = 3$ **E.**

53. Equation of Lines and Slope

First, find the slopes of the two lines, starting with line b.

$m_b = \dfrac{-2-1}{4-0} = -\dfrac{3}{4} \;\rightarrow\; m_a = -\dfrac{1}{-\frac{3}{4}} = \dfrac{4}{3}$

Line a: $y = \dfrac{4}{3}x + b \;\rightarrow\;$ (plug in the known point) $-2 = \dfrac{4}{3} \cdot 4 + b \;\rightarrow\; b = \dfrac{-22}{3} \;\rightarrow$

$y = \dfrac{4}{3}x - \dfrac{22}{3}$ **K.**

56. Number Lines

The distance between −2 and 2 is 4, and there are 5 "spaces" between these two points, so

the distance between adjacent tick marks is: $\dfrac{4}{5}$. Point A is 2 spaces from 2 on the number

line, so $A = 2 + 2\left(\dfrac{4}{5}\right) = \dfrac{18}{5} = 3\dfrac{3}{5}$ **C.**

Note: As with many geometry problems with given figures, you could have "measured the drawing" (see the Geometry Introduction section).

MORE CIRCLES

32. The first ratio is for degrees; the second ratio is for arc length:

$\dfrac{120}{360} = \dfrac{5}{circumference} \;\rightarrow\; c = 15$ **B.**

41. Use the equation of a circle. Plug in: $h = 3$, $k = 5$, $r^2 = (\sqrt{5})^2 = 5$

$(x - h)^2 + (y - k)^2 = r^2 \;\rightarrow\; (x - 3)^2 + (y - 5)^2 = 5$ **F.**

51. This is a revolution problem: circumference (in feet) = 0.5π

$\dfrac{revs}{feet} \dfrac{1}{0.5\pi} = \dfrac{1000}{x} \;\rightarrow\; x = 500\pi$ **(C)**

Homework:

18. Measure the sector in "voters" (the first ratio) and "degrees" (the second ratio). Remember to put the sector measurements on top and the circle measurements on the bottom:

$\dfrac{60}{200} = \dfrac{x}{360} \;\rightarrow\; x = 108°$ **C.**

35. The first ratio is for degrees; the second ratio is for area:

$\dfrac{36}{360} = \dfrac{area\ of\ AOB}{\pi 10^2} \;\rightarrow\;$ area of AOB = 10π **J.**

50. The radius of the circle is 5 and the center is (0,0) (h = 0 and k = 0).
The equation is: $(x - 0)^2 + (y - 0)^2 = 5^2 \;\rightarrow\; x^2 + y^2 = 25$ **B.**

56. 30-inch wheel: $\dfrac{revolutions}{inches} \dfrac{1}{30\pi} = \dfrac{x}{300 \cdot 12} \;\rightarrow\; x \approx 38.2 \;\rightarrow\;$ 38 full revolutions

20-inch wheel: $\dfrac{revolutions}{inches} \dfrac{1}{20\pi} = \dfrac{x}{300 \cdot 12} \;\rightarrow\; x \approx 57.3 \;\rightarrow\;$ 57 full revolutions

$\rightarrow$ 57 − 38 = 19 revolutions **F.**

SOLIDS AND VOLUME

1. **8**
2. **12**

3. **6**

4. **52**

5. **24**

1. $600 \div 6 =$ **100**

2. $\sqrt{100} =$ **10**

3. $10^3 =$ **1000**

VOLUME OF PRISMS

47. The length and height of the cross section are not relevant here because the area is given (18π). Use the formula to find the volume: $V = A \times L = 18\pi \times 20 = 360\pi$ **D.**

VOLUME FITTING (AND AREA FITTING) PROBLEMS

48. Volume of jug $= \pi r^2 h = \pi \cdot 10^2 \cdot 12 = 1200\pi$ in^2
Volume of cup $= \pi \cdot 2^2 \cdot 6 = 24\pi$ in^2

$\rightarrow \dfrac{1200\pi}{24\pi} = 50$ cups of water **D.**

Homework:

11. Each small box: $10 \times 8 \times 6 = 480$ cubic inches
Large box: $20 \times 10 \times 8 = 1600$ cubic inches
$\rightarrow 1600 - (2 \times 480) = 1600 - 960 = 640$ cubic inches **B.**

29. Volume of cube A $= 2^3 = 8$
Volume of cube B $= 3^3 = 27$
$\rightarrow$ The ratio is 8:27 **G.**

32. The volume is given (300 cubic inches), as are the dimension of length (30 inches) and width (5 inches). The height of the mold is not used since the molten steel volume is less than the volume of the mold. $V = LWH$ $\rightarrow$ $300 = 30 \cdot 5 \cdot H$ $\rightarrow$ $H = 2$ inches **C.**

54. First, find the volume of the soap cubes:

Area of face $= \dfrac{54}{6} = 9$ $\rightarrow$ Length of side $= \sqrt{9} = 3$ $\rightarrow$ Volume $= 3^3 = 27$

$\dfrac{\text{volume of box}}{\text{volume of soap cube}} = \dfrac{729}{27} = 27$ **G.**

GEOMETRY WORKSHEET 1

12. Angles (Parallel Lines)
If it helps to see the parallel lines, extend line XY in both directions. Since the lines are parallel, alternate interior angles are equal: $\angle 3 = \angle 4$ and $\angle 1 = 90$. Eliminate A and C. Since angles 1, 2, and 3 form a straight line, $\angle 1 + \angle 2 + \angle 3 = 180$. Since $\angle 1 = 90$, $\angle 2 + \angle 3 = 180 - 90 = 90$. Eliminate D.
Since $\angle 3$ and $\angle 4$ are equal, $\angle 1 + \angle 2 + \angle 3 = \angle 1 + \angle 2 + \angle 4 = 180$. Eliminate E.
The answer is **B.**

23. Coordinates/Pick Numbers (Type 3)
Since $p = -q$, the coordinates must have opposite signs. Pick some numbers to see examples:
$p = 2$ $\rightarrow$ $q = -2$ (quadrant IV)
$p = -2$ $\rightarrow$ $q = 2$ (quadrant II)
$\rightarrow$ The answer is **K.**

25. Area and Perimeter
30 feet is the perimeter of the square. Since every side is the same, you can calculate the length of one side by dividing by 4:
One side $= 30 \div 4 = 7.5$
Area $= $ side $\times$ side $= 7.5 \cdot 7.5 = 56.25 \approx 56$ feet **E.**

27. Triangles (Pythagorean Theorem)

If it helps, draw a quick sketch of the triangle. Use the Pythagorean Theorem to solve for b:

$50^2 + 120^2 = b^2$ → $b^2 = 16{,}900$ → $b = 130$ **G.**

Note: The triangle is a multiple of 5-12-13.

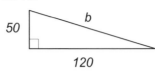

31. Lines (Equations of/Slope)

Don't be fooled by answer choice K. When you divide by 2 to put the equation in the standard slope-intercept form ($y = mx + b$), you'll see that the slope is 3 (not 6). Similarly, J has a slope of 2, not 4. The largest slope belongs to **C** ($m = 4$).

44. Angles (Triangles, Straight Lines)

First of all, do you know what **collinear** means? You might guess that it means lying on the same line (col-line-ar). The drawing confirms this.

Now, look at △ABC. Since it is a right triangle (given), $\angle ABC = 180 - 90 - 35 = 55$.

Since BD is a bisector of $\angle ABC$, $\angle ABD = \angle DBC = 55 \div 2 = 27.5$.

Now look at △BDC: Since the angles add up to 180, and since we know two of them, we can find $\angle BDC$:

$\angle BDC + \angle DBC + \angle C = 180$ → $\angle BDC + 27.5 + 35 = 180$ →

$\angle BDC = 180 - 27.5 - 35 = 117.5$ **J.**

46. Triangles (Similar)

Since $\overline{DE}$ is parallel to $\overline{AC}$, we know that △ABC ~ △DBE (review parallel lines in the angles lesson). So we can write the following equation for similar triangles:

$\dfrac{DB}{AB} = \dfrac{DE}{AC}$ → $\dfrac{4}{8} = \dfrac{4}{AC}$ → $AC = 8$ **A.**

50. More Circles (Sectors)

Notice that the minute hand sweeps a "25-minute sector" as it travels. In the proportion below, use minutes for the first ratio and arc length for the second ratio. Remember to keep sector measurements on top and circle measurements on the bottom (there are 60 minutes in a circle, and the arc length of the circle—the circumference—is 12π).

$\dfrac{25}{60} = \dfrac{x}{12\pi}$ → $x = 15.707963\ldots \approx 16$ inches **K.**

51. Area (Trapezoid)

The area of a trapezoid is: $A = \frac{1}{2}(b_1 + b_2)h$. Plug in values and solve for h:

$108 = \frac{1}{2}(14 + 22)h$ → $108 = 18h$ → $h = 6$ **B.**

Note: If you'd rather not use the formula for the area of a trapezoid (perhaps you forgot it), and if you're comfortable working with triangles, you can divide the figure into a triangle and a rectangle, and Pick Answers for h.

56. More Circles (Equations of)/Lines (Distances)

The challenge to this problem is finding the radius. Draw a right triangle with legs $2\sqrt{2}$ units long. Then use the Pythagorean Theorem: $(2\sqrt{2})^2 + (2\sqrt{2})^2 = r^2$ →

$2^2(\sqrt{2})^2 + 2^2(\sqrt{2})^2 = r^2$ → $4 \cdot 2 + 4 \cdot 2 = 16 = r^2$ → $r = 4$

The center is (0,0) ($h = 0$ and $k = 0$). The equation is: $(x - 0)^2 + (y - 0)^2 = 4^2$ → $x^2 + y^2 = 16$ **F.**

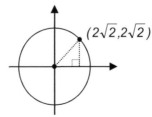

GEOMETRY WORKSHEET 2

6. *Lines (One-Dimensional)*
The distance between A and B is: $|{-5} - 3| = 8$ ➔ $\frac{3}{4} \cdot 8 = 6$ ➔ $-5 + 6 = 1$ **C.**

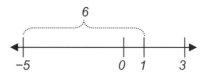

12. *Angles (Triangles/Straight Lines)*
First, since we know two of the angles of the triangle, we can find the third angle (at the top): 180 − 55 − 60 = 65
Since the sum of angles for a straight line is 180, we can find a, b, and c:
a = 180 − 55 = 125, b = 180 − 65 = 115, c = 180 − 60 = 120
➔ *125 + 115 + 120 = 360* **G.**

25. *Triangles (Similar)*
We know the length of the vertical side of ∆II: 3 + 4.5 = 7.5
Use proportions to find the lengths of the other sides of ∆II (call the slanted side x and the horizontal side y). Make sure to keep equivalent sides in the same fraction, and label the proportions so you keep ∆I on top and ∆II on the bottom:

$$\frac{\Delta I}{\Delta II} \frac{3}{7.5} = \frac{5}{x} \rightarrow x = 12.5, \quad \frac{\Delta I}{\Delta II} \frac{3}{7.5} = \frac{4}{y} \rightarrow y = 10$$

➔ *So the perimeter of ∆II is 7.5 + 10 + 12.5 = 30* **D.**

26. *Angles/Triangles*
The first things to notice are: (1) the two triangles are isosceles (because AO = BO = CO = DO = radius of circle) and (2) ∠AOB = ∠COD (vertical angles). From this, we know that the triangles are congruent (by SAS). At this point, eliminate F and G.
Look at ∠AOD. It forms a straight line angle with ∠DOC, so ∠AOD = 180 − 35 = 145. Eliminate J.
Finally, the degree measure of an arc is the measure of its corresponding central angle. Arc ABD is the arc that starts at A, goes through B, and ends at D. Just add the corresponding central angles: ∠AOB + ∠BOC + ∠COD = 35 + 145 + 35 = 215. Eliminate H.
➔ *The answer must be* **K.**

33. *Area*
Since the area of the square is given, you can find the length of a side:
A = side × side = side² ➔ 25 = side² ➔ side = 5
Notice that the side of the square equals the radius of the circle, so r = 5.
A = πr² = 25π **A.**

41. *Coordinates (Distances)*
Sketch the two points on a coordinate plane and connect the points with a right triangle. Then use the Pythagorean Theorem:
The length of the bottom leg is |−12 − 12| = 24, and the length of the right leg is |−5 − 5| = 10.
➔ *d² = 24² + 10² ➔ d² = 676 ➔ Take the square root of both sides: d = 26* **J.**

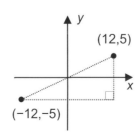

56. **Lines (Intersecting/Equations of)**
Since we know 2 points of intersection for line a, we know 2 **points** on line a. First calculate the slope:

$$m = \frac{3-(-2)}{-2-(-2)} = \frac{5}{0}$$ → But this is undefined! The line is vertical: x = ? Notice that the x coordinate of both points is −2, so the equation is x = −2 **D.**

58. **Solids and Volume/Triangles (Special Right)/Area**
From the Volume lesson, recall that the volume of a prism is the area of the base of the prism × the length of the prism. The length of the prism is given. We have to find the area of the shaded equilateral triangle.

See the figure. The height is given as 6. To find the base of the triangle (which in this case is the length of the top of the triangle), use the special right triangle rules. Because the shaded triangle is equilateral, with angles 60-60-60, the right triangle shown is a 30-60-90 triangle. The top leg, or half the base of the shaded triangle, is $\frac{6}{\sqrt{3}}$, so the base of the

shaded triangle is $\frac{12}{\sqrt{3}}$. The area of the triangle is: $\frac{1}{2}bh = \frac{1}{2} \cdot \frac{12}{\sqrt{3}} \cdot 6 = \frac{36}{\sqrt{3}} = \frac{36}{\sqrt{3}} \frac{\sqrt{3}}{\sqrt{3}} = 12\sqrt{3}$.

Finally, the volume of the water, using a length of 10 feet = 120 inches (multiply by 12 to covert feet to inches), is: $12\sqrt{3} \cdot 120 = 1,440\sqrt{3}$ **K.**

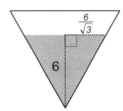

60. **Triangles (Special Right)**
This is a potentially difficult problem and a great test of the special right triangles. Draw a perpendicular line from B to segment AC. This creates a 45-45-90 triangle and a 30-60-90 triangle. See the figure.

Now, you can find the lengths of all sides. The answer is **E**. If you are not comfortable with radicals, work with decimals. Note: △ABC is **not** a 30-60-90 triangle.

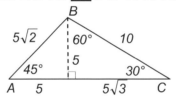

GEOMETRY WORKSHEET 3

2. **Triangles (Pythagorean Theorem)**
Since the triangle is a right triangle, you can use the Pythagorean Theorem to find the missing side (b): $2^2 + b^2 = 10^2$ → $b^2 = 100 − 4 = 96$ → $b = \sqrt{96}$ **C.**

7. **Angles (Parallel Lines/Straight Lines))**
The angles marked in the figure equal 85° (by parallel lines angle rules). As you can see, 85 + x = 180 (by straight line angle rules). → x = 95 **G.**

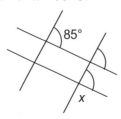

26. *Area*

   The height and base of △ADE is the same as the height and base of the square (see the drawing). The area of the square is bh. The area of the triangle is ½bh. So the ratio is ½:1 = 1:2 **A.**

35. *Lines (Equations of)*

   First of all, notice that the y-intercept appears to be a little less than −1: Eliminate B and E. Now, notice that the slope is positive (the line slants up to the right): Eliminate A (which has a slope of 0) and C. ➜ The answer must be **D.**

47. *Area (Shaded Regions)*

   Use the area subtracting method:
   Radius of small circle = 2 ➜ Radius of medium circle = 3·2 = 6
   ➜ Radius of large circle = 5·2 = 10
   To find the area of the shaded area, subtract the area of the middle circle from the area of the large circle, and add the area of the small circle. See the figure.
   Shaded area = $\pi(10)^2 - \pi(6)^2 + \pi(2)^2 = 68\pi$ **H.**

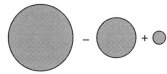

48. *Triangles*

   Here's another triangle problem with no triangles in the given figure. First note that C appears to be the midpoint of AB (indeed, many of these circle properties are self-evident). Next, draw line OB, a radius of the circle (see drawing). This creates a 3-4-5 triangle, so r = 5. Finally, the circumference is $2\pi r = 10\pi$. **E.**

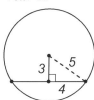

52. *Triangles (Special Right)/More Circles (Sectors)*

   Notice that the shaded region is bound by three sides. The side on the left is the easiest to find—it's just half of one side of the square: 2.
   The bottom side can be found by subtracting the radius of the circle (2) from ½ of the diagonal length of the square. The diagonal of the square forms a 45-45-90 triangle with legs of 4, so the diagonal = $4\sqrt{2}$. Divide by 2. ➜ $2\sqrt{2}$. So the bottom side of the shaded region is $2\sqrt{2} - 2$.
   Finally, the length of the top (or right) side of the shaded region can be found using a proportion (see the lesson on sectors in More Circles; radius = 2, circumference = 4π):

   $$\frac{sector}{circle}\frac{45}{360} = \frac{x}{4\pi} \quad ➜ \quad x = \frac{\pi}{2}$$

   Add the sides together: $P = 2 + (2\sqrt{2} - 2) + \dfrac{\pi}{2} = 2\sqrt{2} + \dfrac{\pi}{2}$ **B.**

55. Coordinates (Midpoint)

Let the coordinates of point A be (a,b), as shown in the figure. Solve for each coordinate of A separately, using the equation for the midpoint of a line. First, work on the x coordinate:

$$M_x = 4 = \frac{a+p}{2} \rightarrow a + p = 8 \rightarrow a = 8 - p$$

Now, look at the answer choices. The answer must be **G**! We're done!

If you'd prefer to work with numbers instead of variables, you could Pick Numbers (Type 1) for p and q.

58. Angles (Sum of Interior Angles)

Draw diagonals and count triangles, as explained in the Angles section: Since there are 4 triangles, the sum of the interior angles is 4·180 = 720.
To find the sum of angles B-F, subtract $m\angle A$ from 720: 720 − 70 = 650 **B**.

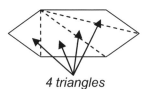

4 triangles

GEOMETRY WORKSHEET 4

14. Solids and Volume

Volume of tank = 4·8·10 = 320
320 × 20% = 64
320 × 30% = 96
→ 64 + x = 96 → x = 96 − 64 = 32 **A**.

You could also simply find 10% of the volume since this is the percent of the volume that you're adding: 320 × 10% = 32

24. Triangles (Similar)

Set up a proportion. Make sure to label the two triangles so you don't mix up the sides. Call h the length of the hypotenuse in question:

$$\frac{small\ \triangle}{big\ \triangle} \frac{3}{4} = \frac{h}{10} \rightarrow 30 = 4h \rightarrow h = 7.5\ \textbf{H}.$$

27. Area/Triangles (Pythagorean Theorem)

Since the short leg of each triangle is 1, the long leg must be 5 − 1 = 4. Use the Pythagorean Theorem to find the length (c) of the side of the shaded square:
$a^2 + b^2 = c^2 \rightarrow 1^2 + 4^2 = c^2 \rightarrow c^2 = 17$
You can stop here because you have to square the value of c to find the area of the shaded square ($A = c^2 = 17$). **B**.

30. Coordinates (Midpoint)

You must find the midpoint of the line segment AB. Use the formula:

$$M = \left(\frac{x_1 + x_2}{2}, \frac{y_1 + y_2}{2} \right) = \left(\frac{2+8}{2}, \frac{3+9}{2} \right) = (5,6)\ \textbf{J}.$$

44. Angles (Isosceles Trapezoids)/Triangles (Similar)/Ratios

This can be a tricky problem. You should be familiar with the angle relations of an isosceles trapezoid. See the Angles section.
Since segments QT and PT are sides of △QRT and △PTS, respectively, focus on these two triangles. Because the trapezoid is isosceles, the two triangles are similar isosceles triangles, as taught in the Angles section.
So, using the rules of similar triangles, the ratio of any side from △QRT to any equivalent side from △PTS will equal y to z (the given sides). The answer is **B**. (continued)

Note: You could Pick Numbers for the variables. You could also make a ruler and measure the drawing (after picking numbers). See the Geometry Introduction.

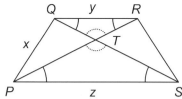

45. *Angles (Line Tangent to a Circle)*
    Since AB is tangent to the circle, it is perpendicular to the radius drawn from the point of tangent to the center of the circle (see the figure).
    The area = ½·12·4 = 24 **H.**

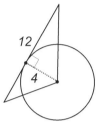

49. *Area and Perimeter*
    Since the circumference is given, use the formula for circumference to find r. Then you can calculate the area:

$$2\pi r = 100 \ \rightarrow \ r = \frac{50}{\pi}$$

$$A = \pi r^2 = \pi\left(\frac{50}{\pi}\right)^2 = \pi\frac{2{,}500}{\pi^2} = \frac{2{,}500}{\pi} \ \textbf{B.}$$

   If you're uncomfortable working with π, convert all numbers (including the answer choices) to decimals (find the π button on your calculator).

50. *Lines (One-Dimensional Problems)*
    Would this problem be a number 50 if 9 were the only answer? Probably not. Here's the trick: the points can be in two orders. The answer is **H.**

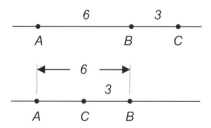

60. *Slope/Pick Numbers (Type 2)/Triangles*
    Create a triangle, as shown. Then pick a number (Type 2) for b:

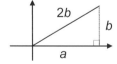

   $b = 2 \ \rightarrow$ *You now have 2 sides.* $\rightarrow$ *Use the Pythagorean Theorem:*
   $$2^2 + a^2 = (2\cdot2)^2 \ \rightarrow \ a = \sqrt{12}$$

   Now, find the slope: $m = \dfrac{2}{\sqrt{12}} \approx .577...$ *(continued)*

*Use your calculator to check the answer choices. The answer is **B**.*

Additional notes: If interested, here is the simplification of the radical:

$$m = \frac{2}{\sqrt{12}} = \frac{2}{2\sqrt{3}} = \frac{1}{\sqrt{3}} \cdot \frac{\sqrt{3}}{\sqrt{3}} = \frac{\sqrt{3}}{3}$$

Alternate solution: You might notice that the hypotenuse is twice the short leg—this is a 30-60-90 triangle: $a = \sqrt{3} \cdot b$ → *slope* $= \frac{\sqrt{3}}{3}$

FUNCTION BASICS

23. *The function rules for f are defined above the question:* $f(n) = n^2$
    $f(6) = 36$
    $f(-6) = 36$
    → $36 - 36 = 0$ **B**.

24. *To make this problem easier, Pick Numbers (Type 1):*
    $\boxed{m = 2}$ → $g(2 + 1) = g(3) = \underline{6}$ → *The answer is **H**. Don't forget to check all answer choices.*

    You could also use algebra to solve the problem. Simplify g(m + 1) and check the answer choices.

25. *This is a "composite function" problem. Just take it step by step, starting from the inside:*
    $g(x) = x^2 - x$ → $f(g(x)) = f(x^2 - x) = (x^2 - x)^2$
    Finally, use FOIL to find the correct answer:
    $(x^2 - x)^2 = (x^2 - x) \cdot (x^2 - x) = x^4 - x^3 - x^3 + x^2 = x^4 - 2x^3 + x^2$ **B**.

    You could also Pick Numbers (Type 1), which is probably the easier approach.

Homework:

19. *Plug x = −2 into the function:*
    $f(-2) = -2(-2)^3 - 3(-2)^2 + 4 = -2 \cdot -8 - 3 \cdot 4 + 4 = 16 - 12 + 4 = 8$ **A**.

21. *We're used to seeing functions with only one input (for example, f(x)), but don't let the extra input in this function scare you. The first number (5) takes the place of p (in the function's definition), and the second number (4) takes the place of q:* $h(5,4) = 5^5 - 4^4 = 3,125 - 256 = 2,869$ **J**.

51. *First, observe the function rule for g. It's a simple function—just add 4 to the input. Now look at the second equation in the question. Remember, the goal is to get rid of the function part of the equation,* $g(\sqrt{a})$. *The first step is to isolate this term by dividing both sides by ½ (or multiplying by 2):*

    $g(\sqrt{a}) = 8$

    Use the function rule (g(x) = x + 4) to simplify $g(\sqrt{a})$: $g(\sqrt{a}) = \sqrt{a} + 4$

    Now we've gotten rid of the function notation! Set this equal to 8 and solve for a:

    $\sqrt{a} + 4 = 8$ → $\sqrt{a} = 4$ → $a = 16$ **C**.

    You could also Pick Answers. Note the simple barebones questions and the numbers in the answer choices.

55. *Function rules will not always be given in an algebraic form. In this case, the rule is give with a table of values. Just like other table problems, make sure you understand the table before looking at the question. The table gives values of the functions g and h for 4 given inputs (0, 1, 2, and 3). For example, looking at the top row, g(0) = 3 and h(0) = 4. Now, let's answer the question: a = g(3) and the table tells us that g(3) = 0, so a = 0*
    → $h(a) = h(0) = 4$ **K**.

GRAPHS OF FUNCTIONS

25. *Find the point on the f(x) graph that has a y value of −1. If necessary, draw a horizontal line through y = −1. Where this line crosses the f(x) graph is the point (because y = −1 at this point). What is the x value at this point? It appears to be about −5. The answer is **B**.*

52. *Look at point A. The x coordinate is "a" and the y coordinate is −4. Remember, the graph of a function gives inputs (x's) and outputs (y's) of that function, so knowing the coordinates of point A tells us that f(a) = −4.*

    *Now solve algebraically by plugging "a" into the function rule, as discussed in the previous section: $f(a) = 2a^{\frac{1}{3}} = -4$ → $a^{\frac{1}{3}} = -2$ → $(a^{\frac{1}{3}})^3 = (-2)^3$ → a = −8 **J**.*

EVEN AND ODD FUNCTIONS

50. *The graph is odd. For all values of x, f(x) = −f(−x). For example, f(3) appears to be about 4. f(−3) appears to be about −4. The answer is **B**.*

AXIS INTERCEPTS

48. *Plug x = 0 into the equation to find the y-intercept: f(0) = a·0 + b·0 + c = c **E**.*

    Note: this might be a good problem on which to experiment with your graphing calculator, if you're planning to use one. Pick numbers for a, b, and c, and type the function into your calculator. Observe the y-intercept, and check the answer choices. Don't forget to check every answer choice.

Homework:

35. *The function is negative where it falls below the x axis, between the x values of −2 and 3. The answer is **D**.*

54. *We do not know the length of side AD, but we can find the y-coordinate of point A, which has an x-coordinate of 4. (Remember that point A lies on the function f(x).) Plug x = 4 into the given function: $f(4) = \sqrt{4} + 2 = 4$ → AD = 4*

    *The base of the rectangle is 5 (9 − 4 = 5), so the area can be found: Area = base × height = 5 × 4 = 20 **J**.*

58. *Since we are dealing with absolute value, all positive values of f(x) remain positive and all negative values become positive (reflect across the x-axis).*
    The positive part of f(x) is the region between x = −2 and 2. This "hump" remains unchanged. Only B and E retain this positive "hump."
    *The two section on either side, where x < −2 or x > 2, are both negative, so they will be reflected across the x axis, as seen in **E**.*

    Note: We'll talk more about reflections in the Transformations section.

TRANSFORMATIONS

58. *Start inside the parentheses. Since 1 is subtracted from x, move the graph 1 unit to the right.*
    *Now apply the negative sign in front of the function. This creates a reflection across the x-axis. **A** displays the resulting graph.*

Homework:

14. *To solve this kind of transformation problem, just perform the appropriate operation on each coordinate of △ABC. You should add 1 to each x coordinate and add 2 to each y coordinate. Check answer choices as you go:*
    (−2,−2) → (−1,0) → Eliminate A and B.
    *(−1,4) → (0,6) → Eliminate C and E. We're done! The answer must be **D**.*

60. *This is a question that relies so heavily on knowledge of the algebraic transformation rules that most students won't even try it. If you get it, great! You'll find yourself in a small company.*
    *The graphs moves 3 units to the right, so h = −3. The graph moves 3 units down, so k = −3. → h − k = −3 − (−3) = −3 + 3 = 0 **H**.*

DOMAIN AND RANGE

27. Use rule 3 from the domain lesson: $x + 4 > 0$ → $x > -4$ **E.**
42. The graph clearly appears greater than $y = 2$: $f(x) > 2$ **C.**

Homework:

42. Raising an expression by ¼ is the same as taking the fourth root. For an even root, use the second rule for domain: $x + 2 \geq 0$ → $x \geq -2$ **B.**

FUNCTIONS AS MODELS

34. Simply plug $n = 10$ into the given equation:

$M(10) = 1000(\frac{51}{50})^{10} \approx 1219$ **C.**

Homework:

24. For this problem, P is given, and you have to use algebra (or Pick Answers) to find x:

$10,000 = 100\sqrt{x}$ → $100 = \sqrt{x}$ → $x = 100^2 = 1 \times 10^4$ **C.**

36. This sounds like a geometry problem, but it's just like a modeling question. A formula is

given. Just plug in the values: $B = 60$ and $h = 10$ → $V = \frac{1}{3}60 \cdot 10 = 200$ **F.**

If the units confuse you, don't worry about them. Everything is in centimeters, so it should work out in the end. The ACT won't generally try to fool you with units.

Also, if you're comfortable with this type of problem, you might be surprised how high the number is. Again, these problems are often easier than they look (and that includes the problem numbers).

FUNCTIONS WORKSHEET 1

12. Transformations
    First, move P 4 units to the left: $(2,2)$ → $(-2,2)$
    Then move 4 units down: $(-2,2)$ → $(-2,-2)$
    Finally, reflect across the y axis (multiply the x coordinate by -1): $(-2,-2)$ → $(2,-2)$ The answer is **B**.

    If it helps, you might choose to sketch a quick graph so you can follow the transformations of P.

14. Function Basics
    $f(2) = 2 \cdot 2^2 + 2 = 10$, $g(2) = 5 \cdot 2 = 10$ → $f(2) \cdot g(2) = 10 \cdot 10 = 100$ **J.**

20. Graphs of Functions
    Zeros are the x values of points where the graph crosses the x axis (the y values will be 0). Of the answer choices, only $x = 6$ is not a zero. **E.**

36. Function Basics/Pick Answers
    Pick Answers for this problem.
    Note the barebones question: "what is one possible value of **x − 6**?" Start at H:
    Pick H: $x - 6 = -6$ → $x = 0$ → $f(0) = 6 \neq 5$ ✗
    Pick J: $x - 6 = -1$ → $x = 5$ → $f(5) = 19 \neq 5$ ✗ Notice that we got further away from 5, so go the other direction. Check G:
    Pick G: $x - 6 = -7$ → $x = -1$ → $f(-1) = 5$ ✓ The answer is **G**. Remember to stop when you find the correct answer.
    If you are comfortable solving equations with absolute values, the algebraic approach might

    be faster: $\left|x^2 - 6\right| = 5$ → $x^2 - 6 = 5$ or -5 → $x^2 = 11$ or 1 → $x = \pm\sqrt{11}$ or $x = \pm 1$

    → When $x = -1$, $x - 6 = -7$ **G.**

43. Functions as Models
    As difficult as this problem may sound, all you have to do is plug in $h = 12$ and $d = 1$:

    $v = 50\sqrt{\dfrac{h^2 d}{1+71d}} = 50\sqrt{\dfrac{12^2 \cdot 1}{1+71 \cdot 1}} = 50\sqrt{\dfrac{144}{72}} = 50\sqrt{2}$ **D.**

44. **Transformations**

*By looking at the graphs, you can see that the function f(x) is stretched vertically by multiplying by n. This would occur when n is greater than 1. The only answer choice that works is **K**.*

55. **Graphs of Functions**

The trick is to use the x and y coordinates of point A. Plugging these values into the function equation will allow us to solve for a: $f(x) = ax^{\frac{1}{3}}$ → $2 = a \cdot 1^{\frac{1}{3}}$ → $a = 2$ **C.**

57. **Graphs of Functions**

*The only graph where f(x) = f(−x) is **J**. Note that the side of the graph to the right of the y axis is a mirror image of the side of the graph to the left of the y axis.*

Note: F, H, and K are all odd functions. G is neither even nor odd.

FUNCTIONS WORKSHEET 2

16. **Graphs of Functions**

*Remember, the outputs of f(x) are the y values of the graph. So when the problem says f(x) = 4, it's saying y = 4. According to the graph, the function equals 4 at two places: (2,4) and (4,4). The two x values are 2 and 4. **D.***

19. **Domain**

*The expression will be undefined when the denominator equals 0. This occurs when x = −3 or x = 2. **H.***

32. **Function Basics**

*Function rules are given for f and g. The question asks for g[f(x)], which means take f(x) and plug it into the function g: g[f(x)] = g(2x + 5) = $(2x + 5)^2$ → Solve using FOIL: (2x + 5)(2x + 5) = $4x^2$ + 10x + 10x + 25 = $4x^2$ + 20x + 25 **B.***

34. **Functions as Models:** *Plug t = 365 into the function:* $p(365) = 300(365)^{\frac{3}{4}} + 70$ **H.**

44. **Graphs of Functions**

*The graphs dips below the x-axis between x = −5 and x = 5. Between these points, f(x) < 0. The answer is **A.***

49. **Function Basics/Pick Numbers (Type 1)**

This problem may look harder than it is. Just Pick Numbers for x and h:

$\boxed{x = 3, h = 4}$

→ $\dfrac{f(x+h)-f(x)}{h} = \dfrac{f(3+4)-f(3)}{4} = \dfrac{f(7)-f(3)}{4} = \dfrac{98-18}{4} = \underline{20}$ → **F.** *(Make sure to check every answer choice. If x = 2, both F and J work.)*

Below is a method for solving the problem without using a Pick Trick.
First find f(x + h). Don't forget to FOIL:
$f(x + h) = 2(x + h)^2 = 2(x^2 + xh + xh + h^2) = 2(x^2 + 2xh + h^2) = 2x^2 + 4xh + 2h^2$
f(x) is given in the question (f(x) = $2x^2$). So now put the pieces together:
$\dfrac{f(x+h)-f(x)}{h} = \dfrac{2x^2 + 4xh + 2h^2 - 2x^2}{h} = \dfrac{4xh + 2h^2}{h} = 4x + 2h$ **F.**

52. **Transformations**

You may be tempted to graph the line and its transformation, which might lead you to the correct answer, but an algebraic approach is faster.
When you reflect across the y-axis, you change all x values to −x. So change the x in the equation to −x:
y = −3(−x) − 4 → *y = 3x − 4 The answer is **C.***

58. **Graphs of Functions**

The trick is to find one of the points on the function. Plugging this point into the function equation will allow us to solve for a. Since ABCD is a square, you can find point C (or B): C = (2,4). Plug point C into the function equation: $4 = a \cdot 2^4$ → $4 = a \cdot 16$ → a = ¼ **K.**

BASIC TRIGONOMETRY

	30°	45°	60°
sin	$\dfrac{1}{2}$	$\dfrac{\sqrt{2}}{2}$	$\dfrac{\sqrt{3}}{2}$
cos	$\dfrac{\sqrt{3}}{2}$	$\dfrac{\sqrt{2}}{2}$	$\dfrac{1}{2}$
tan	$\dfrac{\sqrt{3}}{3}$	1	$\sqrt{3}$

43. First, write the equation for tan (use SOHCAHTOA to remember these relationships):

$$\tan\theta = \frac{O}{A}$$

The side opposite θ is 2, and the side adjacent to θ (not the hypotenuse) is also 2. So

$$\tan\theta = \frac{O}{A} = \frac{2}{2} = 1 \ \textbf{D.}$$

58. We're given ∠X (20°) and we know the opposite side, YZ (50). We're trying to find the length of the pond (XZ), which is the adjacent side to ∠X. What trig function incorporates the **opposite** side and the **adjacent** side? Tangent. So use the equation for tan:

$$\tan 20° = \frac{O}{A} = \frac{50}{XZ} \ \rightarrow \ \tan 20°{\cdot}XZ = 50 \ \rightarrow \ XZ = \frac{50}{\tan 20°} \ \textbf{H.}$$

Homework:

30. Use the ratio for cosine: $\cos\theta = \dfrac{A}{H} = \dfrac{x}{z} \ \textbf{C.}$

60. Use the known ratios for sin and cos. Make sure you recognize where the hypotenuse is on the triangle (it's side c). To be clear, the A below stands for "adjacent" (not vertex A of the triangle).

$$\sin\alpha = \frac{O}{H} = \frac{a}{c} \ \text{and} \ \cos\beta = \frac{A}{H} = \frac{a}{c} \ \rightarrow \ \sin\alpha - \cos\beta = \frac{a}{c} - \frac{a}{c} = 0 \ \textbf{F.}$$

Note 1: If you're comfortable with basic trig, you should find this problem straightforward, even though it's a number 60 out of 60.
Note 2: You could Pick Numbers (Type 1) for a, b, and c if you'd prefer to work with numbers.

TRIG AND THE UNIT CIRCLE
DEGREES AND RADIANS

1. $\dfrac{180°}{180°} = \dfrac{rads}{\pi} \ \rightarrow \ rads = \pi$

2. $\dfrac{270°}{180°} = \dfrac{rads}{\pi} \ \rightarrow \ rads = \dfrac{3\pi}{2}$

3. $\dfrac{360°}{180°} = \dfrac{rads}{\pi} \ \rightarrow \ rads = 2\pi$

UNIT CIRCLE LESSON PROBLEMS

51. Since the tan x is a positive number, x must be in either Quadrant I or Quadrant III (review the ASTC acronym). The only answer choice that falls into one of these quadrants is **C**.

57. *Draw the reference triangle in quadrant IV. We know two of the sides from the given ratio. Since we need the side adjacent to the reference angle (for tangent), use the Pythagorean Theorem to find A (or recognize the 5-12-13 △): A = 12*
    Now, find the tangent of the reference angle. Don't forget, tangent is **negative** *in Quadrant IV:*

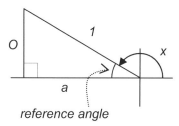

reference angle

$$\tan \theta = -\tan (\text{ref. } \angle) = -\frac{O}{A} = -\frac{5}{12} \quad \textbf{K.}$$

Homework:

49. *Draw the reference triangle in Quadrant II, as shown.*
    Use the Pythagorean Theorem to solve for the opposite side (O):

$$a^2 + O^2 = 1^2 \;\rightarrow\; O^2 = 1 - a^2 \;\rightarrow\; O = \sqrt{1 - a^2}$$

Find the sine of the reference angle. Remember, sine is positive in Quadrant II:

$$\sin x = \sin (\text{ref. } \angle) = \frac{O}{H} = \frac{\sqrt{1-a^2}}{1} = \sqrt{1-a^2} \quad \textbf{E.}$$

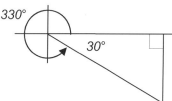

reference angle

54. *Draw the reference triangle. As you can see, the reference angle is 30°, and we're in Quadrant IV. Since cos 30° is given, we just need to worry about its sign (+ or −). Cosine is* **positive** *in Quadrant IV:*

$$\cos 330° = \cos 30° = \frac{\sqrt{3}}{2} \quad \textbf{G.}$$

GRAPHS OF SINE AND COSINE

54. *Your first step might be to eliminate E since it appears to be a graph of cosine.*
    Since sin x is multiplied by 2, the function sin x stretches vertically by a factor of 2. The amplitude = 1 × 2 = 2. The period (2π) remains unchanged. The answer is **A.**

Homework:

57. *This problem sounds tricky. The question seems to be asking about the period of the function. Notice that, according to the graph, the period is π.*

    The problem states that $\dfrac{2\pi}{b}$ *= period, so we can solve for b:* $\dfrac{2\pi}{b} = \pi \;\rightarrow\; 2\pi = b\pi \;\rightarrow\; b = 2$

    The answer is **B.**
    Note: If you're comfortable with transformations, you might notice that the graph displays a **contraction** *of cos x by a factor of 2 (cosine normally has a period of 2π). It's no surprise that b = 2.*

THE LAWS OF SINES AND COSINES

45. *This problem may sound confusing, but you don't need to know anything about reading radars. You just need to recognize the triangle formed by the 2 airplanes and the control tower, and then use the Law of Cosines. One thing to notice is that, unlike with the unit circle, the angle measures begin on the positive side of the vertical (N) axis and go clockwise. You should be able to calculate the measure of the large angle of the triangle:*

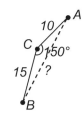

Large angle = 195° − 45° = 150°, as shown (for convenience, label the 3rd vertex C).

Now, use the Law of Cosines to solve for AB (which we'll call "c"):

$c^2 = a^2 + b^2 - 2ab \cos C$ → $c^2 = 15^2 + 10^2 - 2(15)(10)\cos 150°$

→ $c = \sqrt{15^2 + 10^2 - 2(15)(10)\cos 150°}$ **C.**

Homework:

45. *This question is similar to the earlier example, but now we need to find side AC (side b). This means we need the measure of the opposite angle to b, ∠B, which can be found easily:*

∠B = 180° − 50° − 20° = 110°

Set up a Law of Sines proportion involving angles B and A, and the opposite sides (b and a, respectively):

$\dfrac{\sin B}{b} = \dfrac{\sin A}{a}$ → $\dfrac{\sin 110°}{b} = \dfrac{\sin 50°}{10}$ → $b \cdot \sin 50° = 10 \sin 110°$ → $b = \dfrac{10 \sin 110°}{\sin 50°}$ **B.**

TRIGONOMETRY ODDS AND ENDS
GIVEN FORMULAS

48. *First of all, since AD is an angle bisector, ∠α = ½∠A.*
Now look at the given formula. It gives you a way to find the sine of an angle that is ½ of another angle. So use the formula; note that we can find cos A using △ABC:

$\sin^2 α = ½(1 - \cos A)$ → $\sin α = \sqrt{\dfrac{1}{2}(1 - \cos A)} = \sqrt{\dfrac{1}{2}\left(1 - \dfrac{8}{10}\right)} = \sqrt{\dfrac{1}{2}\left(1 - \dfrac{4}{5}\right)}$ **C.**

TRIGONOMETRY ODDS AND ENDS HOMEWORK:

45. *Look at the answer choices. This question may be testing the "other trig functions." Note that ∠A is in each answer choice. We're dealing with the opposite side to ∠A and the hypotenuse (c), so your first thought might be to use sine:*

$\sin A = \dfrac{5}{c}$ → $c \sin A = 5$ → $c = \dfrac{5}{\sin A}$ → *This answer choice is not available, so we're*

*probably dealing with sine's related function: **cosecant**.* $\csc A = \dfrac{c}{5}$ → $c = 5 \csc A$ **C.**

51. *This is a trig properties question. Note that there is no triangle given (or mentioned). There are only two properties to worry about. One involves tangent, which doesn't seem to have much to do with this problem. The other one is: $\sin^2 x + \cos^2 x = 1$.*
Let's see what we can do with the given expression. Start by using FOIL:
$(1 - \sin x)(1 + \sin x) = 1 + \sin x - \sin x - \sin^2 x = 1 - \sin^2 x$.
We have our $\sin^2 x$, but no $\cos^2 x$. However, you can rewrite the original property as follows:
$\sin^2 x + \cos^2 x = 1$ → $\cos^2 x = 1 - \sin^2 x$ ← *That's exactly what we we're looking for. The answer is **F**.*

Note: Assuming you can type trig functions into your calculator, Pick Numbers (Type 1) can be useful if you're not comfortable working with trig properties. Just pick a number for x, find a value for the given expression, and check the answer choices.

59. *To find the degree measure of an angle using trig, we need to use the inverse trig functions. Notice that $\angle A$ is made up of two smaller angles, one angle of $\triangle ABC$ and one angle of $\triangle ACD$. We need to find the measures of these two smaller angles, and then add them together.*

For $\triangle ABC$, we have the opposite side (u) and the adjacent side (t), so use tangent (call the small angle A_1): $\angle A_1 = \tan^{-1}\left(\dfrac{u}{t}\right)$

For $\triangle ACD$, we have the opposite side (v) and the hypotenuse (w), so use sine (call the small angle A_2): $\angle A_2 = \sin^{-1}\left(\dfrac{v}{w}\right)$

Add both angles together: $\angle A = \angle A_1 + \angle A_2 = \tan^{-1}\left(\dfrac{u}{t}\right) + \sin^{-1}\left(\dfrac{v}{w}\right)$ **C.**

TRIGONOMETRY WORKSHEET 1

23. *Basic Trigonometry*

$$\sin A = \frac{O}{H} = \frac{3}{5}$$

*Now, check the answer choices. Only **B** gives the same answer (as usual, A in the ratio below stands for "adjacent," **not** vertex A of the triangle):*

$$\cos B = \frac{A}{H} = \frac{3}{5}$$

45. *The Other Trig Functions*

If you know how to find secant (sec), then this problem is not difficult. The secant is the inverse of cosine. Cosine is the ratio of the adjacent side to the hypotenuse, so secant is the ratio of the hypotenuse to the adjacent side:

$$\sec A = \frac{b}{c} \quad \textbf{G.}$$

Do not be fooled by the labels in the drawing. Typically we label the hypotenuse "c." In this case, the hypotenuse, the side opposite the right angle, is labeled "b."

48. *Basic Trigonometry*

We can safely assume that the shaded triangle is a right triangle. We have the length of the side adjacent to the known angle, and we need the side opposite the known angle. Use the trig function that incorporates opposite and adjacent sides: tangent (let h be the height of the structure):

$$\tan 40° = \frac{O}{A} = \frac{h}{30} \quad \rightarrow \quad h = 30 \tan 40° \quad \textbf{B.}$$

55. *The Unit Circle*

Draw a reference triangle. Since we're in Quadrant I, the reference angle is the actual angle given (θ), and all trig functions are positive.

Knowing that $\tan \theta = 2$ (or $\frac{2}{1}$), we can write in lengths for the two legs of the right triangle. (Clearly, our triangle was not drawn to scale; that's fine.)

Use The Pythagorean Theorem to find H:

$$1^2 + 2^2 = H^2 \quad \rightarrow \quad H^2 = 5 \quad \rightarrow \quad H = \sqrt{5}$$

Now, find $\sin \theta$: $\sin \theta = \dfrac{O}{H} = \dfrac{2}{\sqrt{5}}$ **K.**

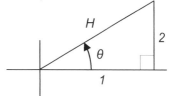

58. The Graphs of Sine and Cosine
Notice the general shape of the graph—it appears to be cosine (it starts at its maximum point, unlike sine, which starts at 0). Eliminate A and C.
You might think that the amplitude is 2, but look carefully. A regular cosine graph extends from −1 to 1 (for a range of 2). The graph here also has a range of 2, so it has **not** stretched vertically. Eliminate B.
The graph has moved **up** vertically by 1. Its lowest point is now 0 and its highest point is 2. And the period is 2π, which is the same as cos x. Eliminate E.
The equation for the graph is: $y = \cos x + 1$ **D.**

TRIGONOMETRY WORKSHEET 2

38. Basic Trigonometry
The cosine ratio involves the adjacent side and the hypotenuse. The hypotenuse is given, but notice that we only have the opposite side to $\angle B$. Use the Pythagorean Theorem to find BC:

$BC^2 + 3^2 = 4^2 \rightarrow BC^2 + 9 = 16 \rightarrow BC^2 = 7 \rightarrow BC = \sqrt{7}$

Now, use the cosine ratio (A = adjacent, H = hypotenuse):

$\cos B = \dfrac{A}{H} = \dfrac{BC}{4} = \dfrac{\sqrt{7}}{4}$ **D.**

Note: You might be comfortable with the 3-4-5 triangle, but remember that the 5 must be the **hypotenuse**. In this case, the given sides (3 and 4) might lead you to think that the missing side is 5. This is a trap.

47. Basic Trigonometry/Area
To find the area of $\triangle ABC$, we need to find its height (BD). Look at $\triangle BCD$. Since we know sin γ ("gamma"), we can set up an equation to find BD:

$\sin \gamma = \dfrac{O}{H} = \dfrac{BD}{6} = 0.8 \rightarrow BD = 4.8$

So the area of $\triangle ABC = \frac{1}{2}bh = \frac{1}{2} \cdot 15 \cdot 4.8 = 36$ **K.**

56. The Unit Circle
Draw a reference triangle with sides that work with the given ratio for sin α.
Keep in mind that since we're in Quadrant III, tangent will be **positive**.
Use The Pythagorean Theorem to find A:

$\sqrt{3}\,^2 + A^2 = 2^2 \rightarrow A^2 = 4 - 3 \rightarrow A = 1$

Finally, tan α = $\dfrac{O}{A} = \dfrac{\sqrt{3}}{1} = \sqrt{3}$ **B.**

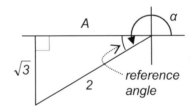

58. Trig Formulas
The formula to use is given. We need to find cos 80° = cos (2·40°):
cos (2·40°) = cos² 40° − sin² 40°
Conveniently enough, cos 40° and sin 40° are given (as x and y, respectively), so: cos² 40° − sin² 40° = x² − y²
$\rightarrow$ cos 80° = x² − y² **F.**

By the way, did you know that sin² x is equivalent to (sin x)² ? Now you do.

60. Law of Cosines/Inverse Trig Functions
Since you have all three sides, you can use the Law of Cosines. As expected, the equation is given. Just rewrite it for $\angle A$, and solve for cos A:
$a^2 = b^2 + c^2 - 2bc \cos A \rightarrow a^2 - b^2 - c^2 = -2bc \cos A$

$\rightarrow \cos A = -\dfrac{a^2 - b^2 - c^2}{2bc} = -\dfrac{36 - 49 - 25}{2(7)(5)} = \dfrac{38}{70} = \dfrac{19}{35}$ (continued)

If you're comfortable with inverse trig functions, you can solve for the angle:

➔ $A = \cos^{-1}\left(\dfrac{19}{35}\right)$ **B.**

If you have not looked over inverse trig functions, you could still probably make an educated guess. Only B includes the fraction above.

PROBABILITY

6. *Use the equation for probability: Probability* $(P) = \dfrac{2}{3} = \dfrac{red}{30}$ ➔ *red = 20*

   To find how many are NOT red, subtract: ➔ *30 − 20 = 10* **B.**

Homework:

2. $P = \dfrac{blue}{total} = \dfrac{6}{5+6+7} = \dfrac{6}{18} = \dfrac{1}{3}$ **B.**

55. *This problem is similar to the target problem from Geometry Worksheet 3. Now, we bring probability into the mix. First, Pick Numbers (Type 3):*
    Radius of small circle = 2 ➔ *Radius of medium circle = 3·2 = 6* ➔ *Radius of large circle = 5·2 = 10*
    Shaded area (see figure) = $\pi(10)^2 - \pi(6)^2 + \pi(2)^2 = 68\pi$
    Total area = $\pi(10)^2 = 100\pi$

    ➔ $P = \dfrac{68\pi}{100\pi} = \dfrac{17}{25}$ **J.**

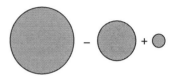

57. *Note that the second event is **dependent** on the first event. After Grant draws the first card (12), there are 99 cards remaining, and 9 of them (10, 11, 13, 14… 19) will make him a winner:*

    $P = \dfrac{9}{99} = \dfrac{1}{11}$ **D.**

PRINCIPLE OF COUNTING

14. *There are 2 types of bread, 2 types of sauce, 3 types of cheese, and 8 toppings. The number of options can be found from the Principle of Counting: 2·2·3·8 = 96* **A.**

Homework:

18. *There are 6 possibilities for A and 6 possibilities for B: $\underline{6}\cdot\underline{6} = 36$* **E.**

COMPLEX NUMBERS

1. ***10i***
2. $21i^2 = 21(-1) = \mathbf{-21}$
3. *FOIL: 2·3 − 2i + 3i − i² = 6 + i − (−1) =* **7 + i**
4. $\dfrac{24\,i^5}{12\,i} = 2i^4 = 2\cdot 1 = \mathbf{2}$
5. *FOIL: (x − i)(2x + 2i) = 2x² + 2xi − 2xi − 2i² = 2x² − 2(−1) =* **2x² + 2**
27. *Simplify the given expression: $i^4 = 1$ and $i^2 = -1$, so $2i^4 + 2i^2 = 2(1) + 2(-1) = 2 - 2 = 0$* **E.**

Homework:

46. *Use FOIL: (3 − 5i)(3 − 5i) = 9 − 15i − 15i + 25i² = 9 − 30i + 25(−1) = −16 − 30i* **A.**

58. To simplify, multiply numerator and denominator by the complex conjugate of $2 + i$ (which is $2 - i$): $\dfrac{5}{2+i} \cdot \dfrac{2-i}{2-i} = \dfrac{10-5i}{4-2i+2i-i^2} = \dfrac{10-5i}{4-i^2} = \dfrac{10-5i}{4-(-1)} = \dfrac{10-5i}{5} = 2 - i$ **K.**

60. This problem is not difficult if you're familiar with the absolute value of a complex number. It is the distance from the point that represents the complex number to the origin. In the figure, A is the farthest point from the origin, so the answer is **A.**

LOGARITHMS

51. The log in question can be rewritten using the power rule:
$log_p\, a^3 = 3\, log_p\, a$
Since $log_p\, a$ is given as q, we can write: $log_p\, a^3 = 3\, log_p\, a = 3q$ **A.**

Homework:

31. Let's say we're looking for the value x: $log_4\, 64 = x$
Rewrite this using the definition of a log:
$log_4\, 64 = x \rightarrow 4^x = 64 \rightarrow$ If necessary, take a guess for x, or Pick Answers.
$4^3 = 64$, so $x = 3$. **C.**

34. Rewrite the problem using the definition of a log:
$log_{2x}\, 4 = 2 \rightarrow (2x)^2 = 4$
Look at the answer choices. Only $x = 1$ works. **K.**

58. Why would we be given $log_a\, 10$ and $log_a\, 5$? How could we use these values to find $log_a\, 2$?
That's the trick to the problem. Notice that $10 \div 5 = 2$. So we can write: $log_a\, 2 = log_a\left(\frac{10}{5}\right)$
Now use the quotient rule: $log_a\left(\frac{10}{5}\right) = log_a\, 10 - log_a\, 5 = A - B$ **C.**
Note: You could also Pick Numbers (hint: pick 10 for a).

MATRICES

15. The first matrix gives the **quantity** of each style and the second matrix gives the **price** for each style. Multiply appropriately, and add up the total dollar amount. For example, the store sold 10 style-A shirts at a cost of $5 each, so the total for A is $10 \cdot 5 = \$50$.
$\rightarrow 10 \cdot 5 + 15 \cdot 10 + 5 \cdot 7.50 + 20 \cdot 12.50 = 487.50$ **E.**

47. $\begin{bmatrix} 1 & 2 \\ 3 & 4 \end{bmatrix}\begin{bmatrix} -1 & -2 \\ -3 & -4 \end{bmatrix} = \begin{bmatrix} ? & ? \\ ? & ? \end{bmatrix}$
row 1, column 1: $1 \cdot (-1) + 2 \cdot (-3) = -7$
row 1, column 2: $1 \cdot (-2) + 2 \cdot (-4) = -10$
row 2, column 1: $3 \cdot (-1) + 4 \cdot (-3) = -15$
row 2, column 2: $3 \cdot (-2) + 4 \cdot (-4) = -22$
$\rightarrow \begin{bmatrix} ? & ? \\ ? & ? \end{bmatrix} = \begin{bmatrix} -7 & -10 \\ -15 & -22 \end{bmatrix}$ **B.**

Homework:

34. First, add up the total number of each type of phone manufactured at the two factories:
$X = 500 + 600 = 1,100$, $Y = 300 + 0 = 300$, $Z = 160 + 900 = 1,060$
Now, apply the failure rates, given in the second matrix, for each phone:
$X = 1,100 \cdot 0.02 = 22$ failures, $Y = 300 \cdot 0.01 = 3$ failures, $Z = 1,060 \cdot 0.05 = 53$ failures
$\rightarrow$ The total number of failures $= 22 + 3 + 53 = 78$ **D.**

LOGIC

2. What do we know? If Bob goes shopping at Al's, he buys a comic book. The fact that he did NOT buy a comic book means that he did NOT go shopping at Al's. The answer is **A.** None of the other answer choices are definitely true.

DIRECT & INVERSE VARIATION

6. *Inverse variation:* $xy = 20 \cdot 2 = 40$ *(so k = 40)*
   Now, plug in x = −2: $-2 \cdot y = 40$ → $y = -20$ **B.**

26. *We're still going to use the inverse variation equation, but notice that the question says x varies indirectly with y², not y. So the equation is:* $xy^2 = k$ → $xy^2 = 200 \cdot 2^2 = 800$ *(so k = 800)*
    Now, plug in x = 8: $8 \cdot y^2 = 800$ → $y^2 = 100$ → $y = \pm 10$ → *The answer is* **K.**

Homework:

38. *Direct variation:*

    $$\frac{y}{x} = \frac{4}{1/2} = 8 \ \ (so \ k = 8) \ \rightarrow \ by \ definition, \ \frac{y}{x} \ always \ equals \ 8 \ \ \mathbf{B.}$$

    You could always plug in 2×10^8*, but this takes much longer:*

    $$\frac{2 \times 10^8}{x} = 8 \ \rightarrow \ x = 2.5 \times 10^7 \ \rightarrow \ \frac{y}{x} = \frac{2 \times 10^8}{2.5 \times 10^7} = 8 \ \checkmark$$

51. *Use the following direct variation equation. Let c = cost in dollars and t = time in minutes:*

    $$\frac{c}{\sqrt{t}} = k \ \rightarrow \ \frac{60}{\sqrt{36}} = \frac{60}{6} = 10 = k$$

    The original equation is given in minutes, so convert 15 hours into minutes and plug into the equation: $t = 15 \times 60 = 900$ *minutes* → $\dfrac{c}{\sqrt{900}} = 10$ → $\dfrac{c}{30} = 10$ → $c = \$300$ **H.**

SETS AND GROUPS

7. *set M = {2, **3**, **5**, **7**}*
   *set N = {...1, **3**, **5**, **7**, 9}*
   Three numbers are in both sets (the intersection of the sets): {3, 5, 7}. **C.**

52. *Since all of the students take Spanish, Latin, or both, "Neither" = 0.*
    Use the formula to find "Both:"
    $90 = 75 + 25 − Both$ → $Both = 10$
    10 students take both Spanish and Latin. Thus, 90 − 10 = 80 students take only one of the classes. **C.** *You could also use a Venn diagram.*

Homework:

31. *The number of elements common to sets X and Y is the same as the intersection of X and Y, which includes the region with 3 elements and the region with "a" elements: 3 + a = 20* → $a = 17$ **D.**

52. *This is a tricky problem. First, use the equation for groups. Then Pick Answers.*
    Total = Group 1 + Group 2 + Neither − Both
    $120 = 90 + 40 + N − B$ → $-10 = N − B$
    *Now, Pick Answers. It makes sense to start with F since we're looking for the **least** possible number of campers that are in both groups:*
    F: Both = 0 → $N = -10$ ✗ *(N must be ≥ 0 since it represents a number of students)*
    G: Both = 10 → $N = 0$ ✓ *So, at least 10 students speak Spanish <u>and</u> French.*
    The answer is **G.**

58. *Use a Venn diagram for this three-group problem, and input the given information (see figure). Note that the total number of employees for each group (5, 7, and 7) stays on the outside of the Venn diagram, as shown. You can use these totals to find the missing number for each group (body only = 5 − 3 = 2, sanding only = 7 − 4 = 3, and painting only = 7 − 2 = 5). Finally, add up all of the numbers in the Venn diagram. You should get 14.* **A.**

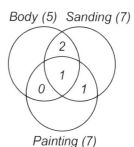

Body (5)   Sanding (7)

Painting (7)

SYMBOL PROBLEMS

13. Tackle this problem in two steps:

$$(6 \diamond 4) = \left(\frac{6 \cdot 4}{6 - 4}\right) = \frac{24}{2} = 12 \, , \, (8 \diamond 6) = \left(\frac{8 \cdot 6}{8 - 6}\right) = \frac{48}{2} = 24$$

→ $(6 \diamond 4) - (8 \diamond 6) = 12 - 24 = -12$ **B.**

14. In multi-question problems, it's not unusual for the problems to quickly get difficult. This problem is much harder than the previous one, even though it's only one number more.
Pick Numbers: $\boxed{p = 3, q = 2}$
I: $6 \neq -6$ ✗ *(Eliminate F, H, and K.)*
Since II is in both remaining answer choices, it must be true! So we only need to check III:
$(-p) \diamond (-q) = (-3) \diamond (-2) = -6, \, -(p \diamond q) = -(3 \diamond 2) = -6$ ✓
→ Both II and III are true. **J.**

Note: a full proof (but more difficult) method would be to simplify the expressions of each Roman numeral and solve algebraically.

30. $\blacklozenge 25 = 2 + 5 = 7, \, \blacklozenge 50 = 5 + 0 = 5$ → $\blacklozenge 25 + \blacklozenge 50 = 7 + 5 = 12$
So we're looking for 12. Don't forget to apply the symbol to the answer choices. Note that $\blacklozenge 12 = 1 + 2 = 3 \neq 12$. $\blacklozenge 66 = 12$ **D.**

6. $(-3) \heartsuit = \dfrac{-3 - 1}{-3 + 1} = \dfrac{-4}{-2} = 2$ **E.**

38. First, get rid of the symbols: $x = 2^p$ and $y = 2^q$
To make the problem easier, you might Pick Numbers (Type 2): $p = 3$ → $q = 5 - 3 = 2$
→ $xy = 2^3 \cdot 2^2 = 8 \cdot 4 = 32$ **J.**

CONSECUTIVE INTEGERS

4. $\dfrac{290}{2} = 145$ → 145 falls halfway between 144 and 146. **C.**

19. Check F: $\dfrac{90}{2} = 45$ → 45 is halfway between 44 and 46, but these are not consecutive integers. ✗

Check G: $\dfrac{91}{2} = 45.5$ → 45.5 is halfway between 45 and 46. This must be the correct answer: $45 + 46 = 91$ ✓ **G.**

Shortcut: Since we have 2 consecutive integers, the middle number will be a number with 5 in the tenths position (.5). Thus, the correct answer must be odd so that when it's divided by 2 we have a .5. There is only one odd answer choice. **G.**

Homework:

31. $\dfrac{50}{20} = 2.5$ → 2.5 is the median of the numbers, so 2 is the greatest possible integer that is less than the median. **B.**

GREATEST/LEAST POSSIBLE VALUES

42. $11 + x + y = 40$ → $x + y = 29$
Now, what two **integers**, having a sum of 29, are as close to each other as possible?
→ $x = 14, y = 15$ → $x \cdot y = 210$ **C.**

50. maximize x (since x is positive) → $x = 2$
minimize y (since y is negative) → $y = -3$
→ $x - y = 2 - (-3) = 2 + 3 = 5$ **F.**

Homework:

54. Since you are looking for the **absolute value** of the expression $2y - x$, you must consider both the LPV and GPV of the expression:

GPV of $2y - x$: maximize y and minimize x → $y = 0$, $x = 0$
→ $2y - x = 0 - 0 = 0$ → so $|2y - x| = |0| = 0$
LPV of $2y - x$: minimize y and maximize x → $y = -3$, $x = 3$
→ $2y - x = -6 - 3 = -9$ → so $|2y - x| = |-9| = 9$
→ So 9 is the GPV of $|2y - x|$. **B.**

60. You might recognize this problem from Algebra Worksheet 1. You used a Pick Trick then, but now use the techniques taught in this lesson.

Let x be the positive value and y be the negative value (remember, the numbers will have opposite signs).
What 2 numbers that have a difference of 10 have equal absolute values?
The difference of -5 and 5 is 10, and they have equal absolute values ($|5| = |-5| = 5$): → $x = 5$ and $y = -5$ → $-5 \times 5 = -25$ **F.**

MATH ODDS AND ENDS WORKSHEET

5. *Logic*
Here's what we know:
Lizard X could live on Island A because it is a blue-bellied lizard, but it could also live somewhere else (nowhere does it say that all blue-bellied lizards in the world live on Island A). Eliminate A and B.
The only thing we know is that Lizard Y definitely does not live on Island A because it does not have a blue belly (see the first statement). The answer is **C.**

Note: Lizards X and Y could live on the same island, but not Island A (so eliminate E), but they could also live on separate islands (eliminate D).

7. *Probability*
Assuming that she either wins or loses (no ties), the probability that she will win plus the probability that she will lose equals 1. Set up an equation and solve for P_{LOSE}:
$P_{WIN} + P_{LOSE} = 1$ → $P_{LOSE} = 1 - P_{WIN} = 1 - 0.01 = 0.99$ **K.**

22. *Inverse Variation*
Let c = cost in dollars and y = years. Use the equation for inverse variation:
$cy = k$ → $4,000 \cdot 2 = 8,000 = k$
Now, let $y = 10$: $c \cdot 10 = 8,000$ → $c = \$800$ **C.**

28. *Principle of Counting*
Using the Principle of Counting, multiply the number of routes for both portions of the trip:
$7 \cdot 8 = 56$ **J.**

30. *Logarithms*
Rewrite the log using the definition of a logarithm: $\log_a 1,000 = 3$ → $a^3 = 1,000$
Do you know the value for a? If not, Pick Answers. The answer is **B.** $10^3 = 1,000$ ($a = 10$)

34. *Consecutive Integers*
Check the answer choices:

Check F: $n = 2$ → $\dfrac{15}{2} = 7.5$ → 7.5 falls halfway between 2 consecutive integers (7 and 8) ✓

Check G: $n = 3$ → $\dfrac{15}{3} = 5$ → 5 is the middle of 3 consecutive integers (4, **5**, and 6) ✓

Check **H**: $n = 4$ → $\dfrac{15}{4} = 3.75$ → 3.75 does <u>not</u> fall exactly halfway between two integers.
✗ The answer must be **H.**

38. Groups

Use the formula for groups. Note that Neither (N) is 0:

Total = Group 1 + Group 2 + Neither − Both

20 = 10 + 16 − Both → 20 − 26 = −Both → Both = 6 **A.**

39. Complex Numbers

Use FOIL. Remember that $i^2 = -1$ (as given in the question):

$(4 + i)(-3 - i) = -12 - 4i - 3i - i^2 = -12 - 7i - (-1) = -11 - 7i$ **G.**

42. Symbols/Pick Numbers (Type 1)

$\boxed{a = 3}$ → $(3 - 2)\uparrow = (1)\uparrow = \frac{1}{2}$, $(1 - 3)\uparrow = (-2)\uparrow = \frac{-2}{-1} = 2$ → $\frac{1}{2} \times 2 = \underline{1}$

Eliminate B, C, and E. Since both A and D work, pick a new number:

$\boxed{a = 4}$ → $(4 - 2)\uparrow = (2)\uparrow = \frac{2}{3}$, $(1 - 4)\uparrow = (-3)\uparrow = \frac{-3}{-2} = \frac{3}{2}$ → $\frac{2}{3} \times \frac{3}{2} = \underline{1}$

Eliminate D. Only **A** works.

45. Matrices

The product matrix will have 1 row (as with the first matrix) and 1 column (as with the second matrix)—just 1 element. Follow the rules for matrix multiplication:

$$\begin{bmatrix} x & y & z \end{bmatrix} \cdot \begin{bmatrix} 1 \\ 2 \\ 3 \end{bmatrix} = \begin{bmatrix} x + 2y + 3z \end{bmatrix} \quad \textbf{H.}$$

Note: Do not view the product matrix above as having 3 columns. It has 1 column (and 1 row)—its 1 element is the sum of x, 2y, and 3z.

47. Probability/Pick Numbers (Type 3)

This problem is much easier if you pick a number for the total number of eating utensils, preferably one divisible by 2 and 6: Total utensils = 60

→ $P = \dfrac{1}{2} = \dfrac{spoons}{60}$ → spoons = 30

→ $P = \dfrac{1}{6} = \dfrac{knives}{60}$ → knives = 10

So there must be 20 forks (60 − 30 − 10). Remove the forks. There are 10 knives and 40 total remaining utensils: $P = \dfrac{knives}{total} = \dfrac{10}{40} = \dfrac{1}{4}$ **B.**

55. Probability

$P_1 = \frac{7}{21} = \frac{1}{3}$

→ (6 blue marbles left; 20 total marbles left) → $P_2 = \frac{6}{20} = \frac{3}{10}$

→ (5 blue marbles left; 19 total marbles left) → $P_3 = \frac{5}{19}$

Probability $= \frac{1}{3} \times \frac{3}{10} \times \frac{5}{19} = \frac{1}{38}$ **J.**

Notice that the events in this problem are **dependent**. The probability of event 2 is dependent on the outcome of event 1, and similarly the probability of event 3 is dependent on the outcomes of the previous events.

58. Logarithms

The ACT does not expect you to use your calculator (although you could if you're comfortable with the base-change rule).

The easiest approach is to first simplify the equation using the power rule:

$\log_5 125^2 = 2x$ → $2 \log_5 125 = 2x$ → Divide by 2: $\log_5 125 = x$

Now, apply the definition of a logarithm to create an exponential equation:

$\log_5 125 = x$ → $5^x = 125$

Guess values for x, or Pick Answers: $5^3 = 125$ → $x = 3$. **A.**

PART 3

READING

I
READING INTRODUCTION

The Reading section is divided into five chapters:

I.   Introduction

II. Reading Test Strategies

III. Timing

IV. Practice

V.   Reading Answers

TYPES OF QUESTIONS

The questions on the Reading Test are multiple choice, with four answer choices each.

TEST LAYOUT

The Reading Test includes:

- 40 questions
- 4 passages (10 questions each)
- A total test time of 35 minutes

TYPES OF PASSAGES

The test includes one passage (or occasionally a *double* passage) from each of the following:

- Prose Fiction (from a novel or short story)
- Social Science (including biography, history, political science, etc.)
- Humanities (including art, film, music, etc.)
- Natural Sciences (including chemistry, geology, technology, etc.)

The passages will generally be in the order shown above. There are some specific features of each type that you should expect (read over the following for homework):

PROSE FICTION

Some students find these passages more difficult to understand because they are often written in a stylized language. Furthermore, things are not always as they seem. Be on the lookout for literary tools such as *sarcasm*, *satire*, *metaphor*, and *irony* as you read fiction passages. These are ways that an author may say one thing but mean something else.

Sarcasm – a form of irony in which apparent praise conceals another, scornful meaning.

Satire – the use of witty and sometime humorous language to convey insults or scorn.

Metaphor – a figure of speech in which a word or phrase literally denoting one kind of object or idea is used in place of another to suggest a likeness or analogy between them (as in *drowning in money*).

Irony – a technique of indicating, as through character or plot development, an intention or attitude opposite to that which is actually or ostensibly stated.

Tones and emotions are particularly important in Prose Fiction passages. How does the author feel about the characters? How do the characters feel about the other characters in the passage? How do these emotions create mood in the passage?

SOCIAL SCIENCE

These passages are typically a result of gathered research. Be prepared to see dates, events, and names of people, places, and concepts. Things can get confusing, so make sure to keep track of the specific details. As discussed in the next chapter, you'll do a lot of marking up on the Social Science passages.

HUMANITIES

Humanities passages, unlike Prose Fiction passages, are *non*-fictional. They tend to be written in a straightforward prose. As in Prose Fiction passages, the author's tone is important. How does the author feel about the topic? How does the author feel about the people in the passage? Can you predict the author's likely response to some hypothetical situation or event?

NATURAL SCIENCE

These passages are often difficult to read because of technical-sounding language and concepts. You will very likely read about some scientific topic with which you are not familiar. And you can expect to see unfamiliar words. But don't worry about it! Stay aggressive. Because the questions are often based on concrete details in the passage, they are usually easier than those of other types of passages. You might find the reading a challenge, but that doesn't mean the questions will be—and you score points answering *questions*, not reading passages.

II
READING TEST STRATEGIES

This chapter will discuss the three main topics of the Reading Test:

1. Reading and marking up the passage (Section 1)
2. Using context (Section 2)
3. Answering the questions (Sections 3-9)

1. THE PASSAGE

READ THE INTRODUCTION (IF THERE IS ONE)

Each passage will include some brief text preceding the main body of the passage. Some important parts of these sections should be read before moving on:

- Confirm the passage type (Prose Fiction, Social Science, Humanities, Natural Science).
- Read the title of the book/article from which the passage is excerpted. This may give you a clue about the passage's main idea (especially on Social Science, Humanities, and Natural Science passages).
- Some passages may have a short sentence or two following the copyright information. This introductory information will assist you in understanding the context of the passage, so read it carefully.

READ THE PASSAGE

After reading the introduction, read the passage—and when we say read, we mean *read*. For most students, we do not recommend skimming.

 Do *not* read the questions first. Here's why:

1. Reading the passage is the best way to understand its *main idea* and *tone*. (More on main idea and tone soon.)
2. Most questions do *not* provide line numbers, so it is difficult to know where to look for information if you haven't read the passage.
3. The questions are generally *not* arranged in the order of the passage, again making it difficult to find information unless you've just read the passage.

EXCEPTIONS

Students who have ongoing difficulty finishing the Reading test may try *skimming* the passages. This gives students more time to answer the questions. Also, if a student is running out of time at the end of the test, going straight to the questions of the last passage might make sense. We will discuss both strategies in the Timing chapter (Chapter III).

WHAT TO DO WHILE YOU'RE READING

As you read, you should plan to mark up the passage. This will help you identify main ideas and tone and quickly find information when you start answering questions.

LOOK FOR TONE WORDS

Tone words are words that convey *feeling*, sometimes positive and sometimes negative. Some examples of tone words are: *stubborn*, *envious*, *irritated*, *pleased*, and *groundbreaking*. Tone words help you identify the attitude of the author or a character in the passage.

> **Darkly underline** tone words as you read.

CONTRAST SIGNALS

A great way to determine the author's tone is to look for *contrast signals*. Contrast signals are words that signal a change in the flow of a sentence. Examples:

although	even so	instead of	rather than
but	however	nevertheless	still
despite	in contrast	on the contrary	yet
even though	in spite of	on the other hand	

What comes *after* these words is usually something that the author feels is very important—this will help you determine his or her tone, not to mention the most important ideas in the passage.

> Draw a **box** around contrast signals as you read.

A NOTE TO SELF STUDY STUDENTS ABOUT "EX" PROBLEMS

Example problems are indicated with an EX symbol:

You will see a boxed solution following each example. For the following sections, try to answer the example question *before* looking at the solution. You may want to cover the solution with a sheet of paper so that you're not tempted to peek.

Let's try an example. Darkly underline tone words and draw a box around contrast signals in the following paragraph, and then try the example question:

> The result of this tedious and relentless attention to detail may seem well and good, but even the most accomplished editor has the tendency to lose the forest for trees, as the saying goes. Yes, of course one must take care, cross his *t*'s and dot his *i*'s. Let us not forget, however, *why* we do this—to bring about art from a tangle of letters and words.

(EX) According to the passage, the author expresses which of the following attitudes?

    A. Many editors today have become lax about crossing *t*'s and dotting *i*'s.
    B. Editors must do more than simply concern themselves with the details of writing.
    C. Editors must learn that creating artistic work is the sole domain of the writer.
    D. The best editors excel at looking at details and identifying mistakes in writing.

> Note the contrast signals: "but" in the second line and "however" in the third-to-last line. What follows these words suggests that all is **not** "well" and "good" in editors' "relentless attention to detail." As supported by the last sentence, the best answer is **B**.

FOCUS ON THE EASY STUFF

Don't worry about the hard stuff. Focus on the easy stuff. Every test will likely offer even the best readers with some challenging reading. The trick is to focus on the parts of these harder passages that you *do* understand. Don't get discouraged. Don't give up. Even if you finish a passage and only understood half of it (or less), that's better than giving up entirely.

> **Underline** the easy stuff while you read, particularly on harder passages. Search out clear statements that help you understand the passage.

Underline *the easy stuff* in the following paragraph, and then try the example question:

> One must wield his mighty sword against the manifest bureaucracy surrounding him, the sweeping malfeasance of our day. Do not bridle. Do not defer. But no shining shank or cutlass will do. No. Rather, put your pen to paper, and write, with anger, yes, and with resolve. Write.

(EX) One of the main points that the author seeks to make in the passage is that:

    A. when writing fails, one must turn to violent activism.
    B. the best writers hold their emotions in check when writing.
    C. the pen is mightier than the sword.
    D. any means of action is better than doing nothing when faced with injustice.

This paragraph is potentially confusing, using words such as "manifest," "bureaucracy," "malfeasance," "shank," and "cutlass." But did you find some easy stuff? Hopefully you underlined the last two sentences. The main idea of the paragraph probably has something to do with writing to express some anger or grievance. The pen is mighty (and mightier than the sword). The best answer is **C**.

CIRCLE IDENTIFIERS

Knowing where to look for information while you answer questions is probably the most important part of the Reading Test. As we said before, questions are typically out-of-order and usually do not have line numbers. You must use *clues* in the question (and sometimes the answer choices) to know where to find information in the passage. Since there is not enough time to skim the passage for every question, you must look for and **circle** *identifiers* while you read the passage. These will be words, almost always *nouns*, that stand out for a particular part of the passage. The following guidelines will help you find identifiers:

- **Proper Nouns**: The best identifiers are proper nouns, such as the name of a city, organization, book, movie, or person (just circle last names). These words will be *capitalized*.

- **Titles**: Identifiers may be the specific title or designation of a concepts or idea, such as *evolution* or *intelligent design*. These identifiers are often *not* capitalized.

- **Common Nouns**: Identifiers can also be common nouns, such as *truck* or *wallpaper*. You should circle common nouns that effectively relate to one small part of the passage (such as a single paragraph), especially if the passage doesn't have many proper nouns. You'll frequently circle common nouns on the Prose Fiction passages, which often lack many proper nouns.

WORDS OF CAUTION

- Do not circle **numbers** or **dates**. These are great identifiers, but they are fairly easy to spot without being circled.

- Do not circle words that aren't good identifiers. As discussed earlier, you might *underline* important words (such as tone words and "easy stuff"), but don't *circle* these words. **Save circles for identifiers only.**

- Do not circle words that show up too frequently, perhaps more than three or four times in a passage. For example, the word *airplane* is likely <u>not</u> a good identifier for a passage on *airplanes* because the word is probably used throughout the passage. Similarly, *George Washington* is <u>not</u> a good identifier for a passage that focuses on *George Washington*.

Circle identifiers in the following paragraph:

> The discovery of penicillin is popularly attributed to the Scottish scientist Alexander Fleming in 1928, but its use was reported far earlier. The use of blue mold from bread (presumably penicillin) as folk medicine to treat suppurating wounds dates back to Europe's Middle Ages. Much later, in 1875, the first published reference appears in the Royal Society publication by John Tyndall. An 1897 paper by Ernest Duchesne documented the potential positive side effects of penicillin. Between 1915 and 1927, Costa Rican doctor Picado Twight studied the inhibitory actions of penicillin in his home country, and eventually reported these to the world at the Paris Academy of Sciences. This all suggests that perhaps it is the *development* of penicillin as a medicine, not its *discovery*, that is Fleming's great achievement.

Focus on proper nouns and important words. You might circle the following words: blue mold, Middle Ages, Royal Society, Tyndall, Duchesne, Twight, and Paris Academy of Sciences. Note that "Fleming" is not a great identifier (even if you marked him as such) because he appears in different parts of the passage. Similarly, you may have been tempted to circle "penicillin," but you'll quickly realize that this word is used too frequently to be a good identifier.

OVER-CIRCLING?

Many students assume that if they circle too many words, they will have trouble finding relevant information for a given question. Of course, you don't want to circle words that are not good identifiers (rarely, for example, should you circle a non-noun), but every paragraph should have at least a few identifiers circled, especially words that have something to do *specifically* with that paragraph. You will be surprised how much this technique will help you quickly find information.

MAIN IDEAS

Passages often have one question that directly asks about the passage's main idea, so it's a good idea to consider the main idea while you read. If you identify a sentence or two that you believe may reflect the main idea—anything that you think is particularly important—put an asterisk (★) in the margin to the left of the sentence. This may help you find important information when you get to a main idea question.

FIRST AND LAST PARAGRAPHS

To identify main ideas, pay close attention to the first and especially the last paragraphs. (If the paragraphs are long, focus on the first couple sentences of the first paragraph and the last couple sentences of the last paragraph.) Often, just reading a few sentences will give you a good sense of the passage's main idea.

> Indicate potential main ideas with an asterisk (★) in the margin.

Below is a summary of what to mark up while you read a passage:

- Darkly underline tone words
- Box contrast signals
- Underline the easy stuff (especially main ideas)
- Circle identifiers
- Indicate main ideas with an asterisk

 Always remember that the most important of these markups is <u>circling identifiers</u>.

You will have plenty of opportunities to practice these markups on the following pages and on homework passages.

———

2. CONTEXT

ANSWER QUESTIONS USING <u>CONTEXT</u>

Context – the parts before or after a statement that can influence its meaning.

Answering questions using context is analogous to figuring out the meaning of an unknown word by using the context of the sentence in which the word is found. You must answer questions *contextually*, using the information in the passage. This simple-sounding rule is perhaps the most important one found in this tutorial:

 Make sure your answer to any question is clearly stated or supported by context.

ANSWER QUESTIONS <u>BEFORE</u> LOOKING AT THE ANSWER CHOICES

This is one of the best ways to answer questions contextually. This approach will force you to use the information in the passage to find your answer, and it will eliminate the temptation of picking answer choices that sound correct *out* of context.

Always answer the question before looking at the answer choices when the question provides:
1. **Line numbers**
2. **Identifiers**

THE EXCEPTION: BROAD OR GENERAL QUESTIONS

When the question is broad or if it covers a large part of the passage (such as a main idea question), you will have to look at the answer choices first and *then* use the context of the passage. See the following figure:

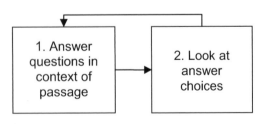

Questions with line numbers or identifiers

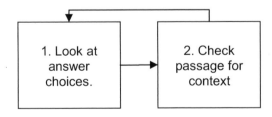

Broad questions and most main idea questions

Remember, regardless of whether you look at the answer choices before or after answering the question, you will still answer *all* questions using the context of the passage.

USE BRACKETS TO KEEP TRACK OF WHAT TO REREAD

If the question gives line numbers, draw a *bracket* to the left of the passage to keep track of what to reread. (This is faster than underlining and won't interfere with the underlines you may have already drawn.)

But keep in mind: you should be prepared to read several lines above and/or below the given line numbers to find your answer. If the specified lines are near the beginning of a paragraph, go back and start reading from the paragraph's first sentence. If the lines are near the end of a paragraph, you might read to the end of that paragraph. In short:

(!) The correct answer is often <u>not</u> found in the lines specified in the question.

3. ANSWERING THE QUESTIONS

READ THE QUESTIONS CAREFULLY

There are three main reasons why it is important to carefully read a given question before trying to answer it:

1. Often one or two answer choices are absolutely true according to the *passage* yet don't properly answer the *question*.

2. The question will often give clues (identifiers) that will help you know where to look in the passage to find your answer. (Of course, sometimes the question will give line numbers.)

3. Words in the question may help identify its *type* (as listed below). Different types of questions will be answered in different ways.

TYPES OF QUESTIONS

The ACT uses several different types of questions on the Reading test. The list below is roughly in order of most common to least:

- Direct (by far the most common type of question)
- Extended Reasoning
- Main Idea of Passage
- Main Idea of Section
- Tone
- Vocabulary
- Function
- Comparison
- Rhetorical Devices (rare)

We'll get into each of these question types on the following pages.

ANSWER CHOICES

ELIMINATING ANSWER CHOICES

Eliminating answer choices that you know are incorrect, particularly when you don't spot the correct answer right away, is an essential technique on the Reading test. We call this "Process of Elimination" (POE). Usually, anywhere from one to three answer choices can be eliminated using context. The following elimination methods, listed roughly in order of importance, will be covered on the following pages:

- Not Mentioned
- Tone
- Eye Catchers
- False
- Too Strong
- Every Word Counts

When we introduce an elimination method, you'll see the following symbol:

CAMOUFLAGED ANSWER CHOICES

The ACT likes to *camouflage* the correct answers with words that are different from, and often more *difficult* than, the words used in the passage. For lack of understanding, students are often tempted to eliminate these answer choices.

(!) **Just because the words in an answer choice are different from those in the passage, don't assume the answer choice is wrong. It may be *camouflaged*.**

———

4. DIRECT AND EXTENDED REASONING QUESTIONS

Now it's time to answer some questions. We'll use the abridged passages on the following pages to introduce each type of question. We'll also cover the methods for eliminating answer choices. **Note that real ACT passages will be longer, and will have 10 questions each.** We'll see plenty of these in the homework assignments and practice tests.

Remember that we'll be using *context* as we answer the questions, often by answering questions *before* we look at the answer choices (review the Context section if necessary).

Don't forget to mark up these passages while you read them:

- **Circle identifiers** ← most important!
- Darkly underline tone words
- Box contrast signals
- Underline the easy stuff (especially main ideas)
- Indicate main ideas with an asterisk

DIRECT QUESTIONS

Direct questions ask you to find information that is *explicitly stated* in the text. This doesn't mean these questions will necessarily be easy—the context may be difficult to understand, or the answer choices may be camouflaged—but these questions are usually easier than those that require you to *infer* something from the passage, such as Extended Reasoning questions (to be discussed soon).

Direct questions are probably easier to identify by *default*. Most of the other question types have clear keywords, for example words such as "main purpose" (Main Idea question) or "implies" (Extended Reasoning question). If a question does not seem to fit into another category, it's probably a Direct question.

Read the following passage. For this and future passages, you might want to tear out the page so you don't have to turn back to the passage when you start answering the questions.

Passage I

NATURAL SCIENCE: This passage is adapted from *The World of Trees* by Hugh Johnson (©2010).

Darwin could have been more specific. Not of all landscapes, but of most, he could have said: "trees form the chief embellishment." Of all plants they are the most prominent and the most permanent, the ones that set the scene and dictate the atmosphere. Trees define the character of a landscape, proclaim its climate, divulge
5 the properties of its soil—even confirm the preoccupation of its people.

I wrote the first edition of this book 37 years ago, in the excitement of discovering for the first time the beauty and diversity there is in trees, and dismay at seeing the principal and biggest trees around me suddenly dying. In 1973 Dutch elm disease had just arrived. Within five years it had destroyed the landscape where I had come to live,
10 in the east of England.

I remember a before-and-after sequence of two photographs in *Time* magazine. Before: main street in some New England town; all harmony; comely cream clapboard dappled with light from the crowns of an avenue of tremendous elms. After: the elms gone; comeliness has become nakedness. What was all proportion and peace is
15 desolate.

It was partly in impotent protest that I started this book. What, I asked, can we do and what should we plant to restore the serenity we had lost? Over time the question has answered itself: in East Anglia oaks, ashes, and willows now fill many of the spaces and delineate the devastated skyline. But as soon as I started to investigate, to visit
20 botanical gardens and get lost in forests, above all simply to look around me with an inquiring mind, I discovered a variety of beauty and meaning I had never suspected.

First, make sure you marked up the passage appropriately.

Did you circle identifiers? Proper nouns, such as "Darwin," "Dutch elm disease," and "England," are the most obvious identifiers, but you might have also circled common nouns such as "climate" (line 4), "soil" (line 5), "photographs" (line 11), and so on.

Did you underline tone words? Some examples include "excitement" (line 6), "beauty" (lines 7 and 21), "dismay" (line 7), and "devastated" (line 19) (there are several others).

Did you draw a box around the important contrast signal ("But") in line 19?

Start getting into the habit of quickly and efficiently marking up passages as you read. Make sure you practice this now, so that it becomes second nature when you start taking practice tests.

Let's try a Direct question:

1. In discussing the importance of trees in the first paragraph (lines 1-5), the author mentions that all of the following are true EXCEPT:

First of all, note that this question requires you to look for an answer choice that is *false*. These EXCEPT/NOT questions typically involve going back to the passage and eliminating answer choices that are *true*. We recommend you write a "not true" sign (ⓣ) next to the answer choices so you don't forget to eliminate *true* answer choices. Let's try that now with the answer choices below:

    A. trees live longer than other plants.
    B. trees characterize the general appearance of the land.
    C. trees alter the soil properties of the land.
    D. trees can verify the likely occupations of a region's inhabitants.

Solution:
Did you eliminate the three incorrect answer choices? All four are found *directly* in the passage: A: "most permanent" (line 3), B: "define the character of a landscape" (line 4), and D: "confirm the preoccupation of its people" (line 5). The answer is **C**. Not surprisingly, the answer choices are not written with the exact words of the passage; they are *camouflaged*.

Here's another Direct question:

2. The aspect of trees that the author finds most impressive is their:

The challenge to this question is finding the appropriate context in the passage (note that the question does not offer a good identifier). But do you remember the contrast signal that you boxed in line 19 ("But")? What follows is often important. Try to answer the question using this context (don't look at the answer choices yet).

Context:
The answer is found in the passage's last sentence: "I discovered a variety of beauty and meaning I had never suspected."

Can you identify the answer that best reflects this statement?

    F. resilience
    G. mystery
    H. size
    J. diversity

Solution:
The keyword in the passage is "variety" (line 21). The answer is **J**.

As stated earlier, direct questions are not necessarily easy. If the context is difficult, the question might be difficult:

3. According to the passage, when the author started writing his book, he was:

Once again, try to answer the question, using context, before you look at the answer choices.

Context:
The word "book" in the question is an identifier—you probably should have circled this word when you read the passage. It shows up in lines 6 and 16. The answer can be found in the latter line. The author started "this book" partly in "impotent protest."

If you're comfortable with the vocabulary here, the answer is straightforward. Otherwise, the answer may be difficult to find. Can you spot it?

    A. concerned that his book will not find a large readership.
    B. doubtful of his ability to effect real change with his writing.
    C. confident that his book will answer the questions related to the destruction of trees.
    D. encouraged by changes that he sees in botanical gardens and forests.

Solution:
The challenge to this problem is one of context. While the answer is found directly in the passage, many students are not comfortable with the word "impotent," which means: lacking power or ability. The best answer is **B**.

We talked about eliminating answer choices in the previous section. Let's take a minute to introduce two important methods for eliminating answer choices. All elimination methods will be indicated by the symbol below:

⊘ ELIMINATE ANSWER CHOICES THAT ARE NOT MENTIONED

This is probably the most commonly used elimination technique. Especially look for **specific references** in the answer choices that are not mentioned in the passage (answer choices that are vague or broad are more difficult to eliminate using this technique).

Look back to Question 3 above. Do you see an answer choice that can be eliminated using the Not Mentioned technique?

Eliminate:
A. concerned that his book will not find a large readership. [The author's "readership" is not mentioned]

WATCH OUT FOR EYE CATCHERS

Eye catchers are words or phrases that come directly from the passage but are not part of the correct answer. Students tend to be attracted to answer choices with eye catchers because they recognize these words or phrases from the passage. But, as discussed in the last section, correct answers will often *not* be written with the exact words of the passage (they may be *camouflaged*, as we saw in all three questions above). Before you select an answer choice with an eye catcher, be absolutely sure it answers the question correctly.

Go back to Question 3. Do you see any eye catchers in the incorrect answer choices?

Eliminate:
 C. confident that his book will answer the questions related to the destruction of trees. [Eye catcher: "the question" (line 17)]
 D. encouraged by changes that he sees in botanical gardens and forests. [Eye catchers: "botanical gardens" and "forests" (line 20)]

EXTENDED REASONING QUESTIONS

Extended Reasoning questions require you to go *beyond* the text to find the answers. This doesn't mean that you'll be making things up—you still must use context:

 Even when you must "extend your reasoning" beyond the text, the answers, as always, must be supported by context.

Extended Reasoning questions usually include one of the following words:
 * infer (as in: "it can logically be inferred" or "it is reasonable to infer")
 * most (as in: "most likely," "most strongly," or "most nearly means")
 * suggests
 * apparently
 * seems
 * implies

Let's try an Extended Reasoning question, based on the previous passage:

4. In describing the first photograph of a New England main street, the author suggests that:

Use the question's identifiers ("photograph," "New England," "main street") to find your context. Notice the word "harmony" in line 12. Whatever the author is saying (or suggesting), it is something good. Let's look at the answer choices. Can you identify one that is supported by the passage? Can you eliminate answer choices that, in full or in part, are not mentioned? Don't forget to watch out for eye catchers:

F.   some types of trees are more beautiful than others.
G.   trees are susceptible to different kinds of diseases.
H.   the streets of some towns are common photographic subjects.
J.   light plays an important role in the beauty of a scene.

Solution:
The only answer choice that is supported by the text is **J**. The key words are "dappled with light," something we know the author finds pleasing ("all harmony"). Note that the author doesn't explicitly say that light is important. It is *suggested*. This is the difference between an Extended Reasoning question and a Direct question.
Eliminate:
F.   some types of trees are more beautiful than others. [Not mentioned: "types of trees" (in this paragraph, only "elms" are mentioned)]
G.   trees are susceptible to different kinds of diseases. [Not mentioned: "different kinds of diseases"]
H.   the streets of some towns are common photographic subjects. [Eye catcher: "photographs" (line 11)]

MINIMIZE YOUR "EXTENDED REASONING"

The challenge to Extended Reasoning questions usually depends on how far reasoning must be extended. In other words, how clearly does the passage support the correct answer? How much do you have to "read into" things? A good rule of thumb:

 Go with the answer choice that requires the least amount of extended reasoning.

Also, don't be surprised if some questions that sound like Extended Reasoning questions (because of keywords in the question) are actually Direct questions, with clear and explicit supportive context. Don't make questions harder than they need to be. If an answer choices is clearly supported by context, go for it.

The previous question did not require significant expansion of the ideas in the passage. The following question might be more difficult:

5. In the context of the passage, Darwin most likely stated that:

Let's go back to the passage (the identifier is clearly "Darwin"). We know what Darwin "could have said: 'trees form the chief embellishment.'" What do you think he *actually* said?

Context:
Your identifiers should have brought you quickly to the first couple lines of the passage. You might be thinking: How do *I* know what Darwin said!? Look at the first sentence. The one thing we know is that, whatever Darwin said, it could have been "more specific." His actual words were thus probably more *general* than the words in the passage ("trees form the chief embellishment").

So Darwin said: "trees form the chief embellishment." Which answer choice offers a more *general* statement?

    A. plants are more important than trees in determining the character of a landscape.
    B. plants are the most conspicuous features of a landscape.
    C. plants and trees are only one of many types of organisms found on Earth.
    D. the classification of some plants can be difficult for scientists.

Solution:
The key hint to this question actually occurs in the sentence beginning in line 2 ("Of all plants . . ."). It is reasonable to assume that Darwin referred generally to "plants" (the author thinks he could have referred *specifically* to "trees"). Of course, the passage never states Darwin's actual words. We must read beyond the text (we must *extend our reasoning*). The answer is **B**.
Eliminate:
~~C.~~ plants and trees are only one of many types of organisms found on Earth. [Not mentioned: "types of organisms"]
~~D.~~ the classification of some plants can be difficult for scientists. [Not mentioned: "classification" of plants]

Important Note: You won't always eliminate every incorrect answer choice. For example, in Question 5 above we only eliminated *two* answer choices. This is not unusual. But every answer choice that you *can* eliminate makes it easier to identify the correct answer.

5. MAIN IDEA QUESTIONS

Main Idea questions ask about central ideas of the text. For example:

- What is the passage about?
- What is the principle argument expressed in the passage?
- What is the author's main purpose for writing the passage?
- What is the point of view from which the passage is told?

When you recognize a Main Idea question, watch out for answer choices that are absolutely *true*, according to the passage, but don't reflect the passage's main idea. Often, two or more answer choices will be supported by context, but only one will best capture the passage's main idea.

Main Idea questions usually include phrases such as:
- main point
- main purpose
- central idea
- principle aim

You might also see the words "best" or "primarily" in Main Idea questions, for example:
- Which answer is *best*?
- The passage (or paragraph) is *primarily* concerned with . . .

MAIN-IDEA-OF-SECTION QUESTIONS

Main Idea questions don't always focus on the entire passage. They may ask about just a *section* of a passage, such as a paragraph or even a single sentence. As usual, we will focus on context for these questions.

Read the following passage. As always, don't forget to mark up the passage while you read:

Passage II

HUMANITIES: This passage is adapted from *The Professor and the Madman* by Simon Winchester (©2005).

At the railway station a polished landau and a liveried coachman were waiting, and with James Murray aboard they clip-clopped back through the lanes of rural Berkshire. After twenty minutes or so the carriage turned up a long drive lined with tall poplars, drawing up eventually outside a huge and rather forbidding red-brick mansion. A
5 solemn servant showed the lexicographer upstairs, and into a book-lined study, where behind an immense mahogany desk stood a man of undoubted importance. Dr. Murray bowed gravely, and launched into the brief speech of greeting that he had so long rehearsed:

"A very good afternoon to you, sir. I am Dr. James Murray of the London
10 Philological Society, and Editor of the Oxford English Dictionary. It is indeed an honor and a pleasure to at long last make your acquaintance—for you must be, kind sir, my most assiduous helpmeet, Dr. W.C. Minor?"

There was a brief pause, a momentary air of mutual embarrassment. A clock ticked loudly. There were muffled footsteps in the hall. A distant clank of keys. And then the
15 man behind the desk cleared his throat, and he spoke:

"I regret, kind sir, that I am not. It is not at all as you suppose. I am in fact the Governor of the Broadmoor Criminal Lunatic Asylum. Dr. Minor is most certainly here. But he is an inmate. He has been a patient here for more than twenty years. He is our longest-staying resident."

Let's try a Main-Idea-of-Section question:

1. One of the main purposes of the first paragraph is to describe the "red-brick mansion" (line 4) as a place that is:

See the words "main purpose" in the question? This question asks about the description of the mansion, a description that may reflect the author's main idea of the first paragraph. Go back to the first paragraph and note some of its tone words, particularly ones that relate to the mansion.

Context:
Tone words often reflect main ideas. Note the following words: "solemn" (line 5), "immense" (line 6), "undoubted importance" (line 6), and "gravely" (line 7). The mansion itself is described as "huge" and "rather forbidding" (line 4).

Now look at the answer choices. You'll probably have more luck eliminating answer choices than spotting the correct one right away. Watch out for eye catchers. Can you narrow it down to one answer?

    A. natural and inviting.
    B. deceptive and solemn.
    C. immense and ancient.
    D. isolated and imposing.

BACK TO THE DRAWING BOARD

Sometimes, especially as you begin getting comfortable answering questions using context,
your contextual answer (the mansion is "huge" and "rather forbidding") does not lead you to the
correct answer (the mansion is "isolated" and "imposing"). Don't be afraid to go *back to the
drawing board*: return to the passage and reconsider the context, or attempt POE. The point is,
as we saw with the question above, you may not always spot the correct answer on your first try.

Also, if you're eliminating answer choices, don't go with the the fourth (remaining) answer
choice simply because you've eliminated the other three. Read all answer choices carefully
when using POE.

Here's another Main Idea question:

2. Which of the following best describes the interaction between Mr. Murray and the
   Governor of the asylum?

These main idea questions are sometimes difficult to answer before you look at the answer
choices. You might, however, already have a general idea of the interaction between Mr. Murray
and the Governor of the asylum (described in lines 9-19). Do you see the correct answer below?
Make sure the context of the passage supports your choice:

     F. They are embarrassed to be meeting after such a long time.
     G. They are pleased to finally be meeting each other.
     H. They speak to each other with polite formality.
     J. They speak to each other courteously but suspiciously.

⊘ ELIMINATE ANSWER CHOICES THAT ARE TOO STRONG

Answer choices that are too strong may take one of two forms:

EXTREME WORDS

The first type uses extreme words such as *always*, *only*, *never*, *without exception*, *completely*, or *perfectly*. These answer choices are usually incorrect.

EXAGGERATIONS

The second type uses words that go *too far* in describing someone or something. An author may be *disappointed* but not *devastated.* She may be *upset* but not *furious.* She may be *surprised* but not *shocked.* Watch out for answer choices that seem to overly exaggerate the attitude of an author or character in a passage—the ACT may be trying to trick you.

⊘ ELIMINATE ANSWER CHOICES THAT ARE FALSE

The ACT sometimes includes answer choices that are just plain *false*. Of course, make sure to eliminate these answer choices.

Look back to Question 2 above. Do you see any answer choices that can be eliminated using the Too Strong or False technique?

Eliminate:
- **F.** They are embarrassed to be meeting after such a long time. [False: Remember, Mr. Murray actually wants to meet *Dr. W.C. Minor*, the asylum's "longest-staying resident" (line 19).]
- **G.** They are pleased to finally be meeting each other. [False: see A above]
- **J.** They speak to each other courteously but suspiciously. [Too strong: "suspiciously"]

MAIN-IDEA-OF-PASSAGE QUESTIONS

Often, after reading a passage, you will have a feel for the passage's main idea. You may have also indicated some of the passage's main ideas with an asterisk (★) in the margin, as described earlier in the Passage section.

FIRST AND LAST PARAGRAPHS

If you're not sure about a passage's main idea, remember to focus on the first and last paragraphs. If the paragraphs are long, focus on the first couple sentences of the first paragraph and the last couple sentences of the last paragraph:

 To quickly find a passage's main idea, look at the *first* and *last* paragraphs.

NOT TOO BROAD, AND NOT TOO NARROW

Main-Idea-of-Passage questions often have answer choices that are too broad or too narrow:

1. **Too Broad**: These answer choices will usually fail to mention the specific person or topic discussed in the passage.

2. **Too Narrow**: These answer choices will usually only reflect *part* of the passage.

Let's try a Main-Idea-of-Passage question for the previous passage:

3. The passage is primarily concerned with:

What is the passage's main idea? Don't forget to focus on the last paragraph. Here are the answer choices:

  A. a meeting of two strangers in embarrassing circumstances.
  B. a surprising revelation of a man's true identity.
  C. an encounter of two adversaries.
  D. a humorous recounting of a case of mistaken identity.

Solution:
As is often the case with Main Idea questions, more than one of the answer choices are true (answer choices A and B are both supported by the passage), but only **B** captures the main idea of the passage, as emphasized in the last paragraph.
Eliminate:
~~C.~~ encounter of two adversaries. [Too strong: "adversaries"]

Did you notice that the answer choices for Question 3 were *broad*? You might have expected to see something about "Dr. James Murray" or "Dr. W.C. Minor," but instead the answer choices mention such vagaries as "two strangers" and "a man." Most ACT questions have specific answer choices, but don't be surprised to see some with answer choices that are broad.

⊘ EVERY WORD COUNTS

The ACT will sometimes include an answer choice that is *perfect*, except for just one or two words. Don't fall for this trap. Every word counts!

Go back to Question 3 above. Do you see an answer choice that is just one word away from being correct?

> **Eliminate:**
> ~~D.~~ humorous recounting of a case of mistaken identity. [Every Word Counts: "humorous"]

———

Now it's time to start practicing on real ACT passages. *The Real ACT Prep Guide*, 3rd Edition provides 7 practice passages, starting on page 91. Unfortunately, these passages do not each come with the expected 10 questions, so we made up our own questions, which can be found in the Questions section of Chapter IV (see page 596). For homework, complete **Passage I** (p. 91) in *The Real ACT Prep Guide*, 3rd Edition (and its questions). For convenience, we recommend tearing the passages out of the ACT book. Questions are on page 597.

MARK UP THE PASSAGE

Before tackling the first practice passage, review the Passage section. Make sure to review what to mark up while you read.

Remember to circle identifiers. These are the most important of the markups. It's essential that you practice circling identifiers quickly and effectively on these practice passages.

TIMING

For the homework passage above, don't worry about timing yet. Just focus on using the techniques you've learned so far. We'll discuss timing soon (see below).

———

All programs: Now that we've covered the first several sections of Reading Strategies, it's time to consider *timing*. Turn to and read the Timing chapter now (starting on page 583). When you've covered the timing strategies, continue with the next section on Tone.

6. TONE QUESTIONS

Tone is defined as a quality, feeling, or attitude expressed by a person, usually in speaking or in writing. Tone questions typically refer to the author of a passage, but they may also ask about characters in a passage, particularly those in prose fiction passages.

Tone questions often contain the following words:
- tone
- attitude
- characterized as

Also, be on the lookout for *tone words* in the answer choices. As described in the Passage section, tone words are words that convey positive or negative *feelings*.

⊘ ELIMINATE ANSWER CHOICES THAT CONTRADICT TONE

Since the answer-choice vocabulary is sometimes challenging on Tone questions, you might not spot the correct answer right away, but hopefully you can eliminate incorrect answers. Often one or more answer choices can be eliminated simply because they contradict tone (usually the author's tone).

Make sure to look for, and darkly underline, tone words (see the Passage section) as you read the following passage. In addition to tone words, you should continue to mark up the passage as usual, including circling identifiers.

SOCIAL SCIENCE: This passage is adapted from *Four Arguments for the Elimination of Television* by Jerry Mander (©1978).

The first really shocking burst of figures appeared in newspapers in the early 1970s.

It was reported that in the generation since 1945, 99 percent of the homes in the country had acquired at least one television set. On an average evening, more than 80
5 million people would be watching television. Thirty million of these would be watching the same program. In special instances, 100 million people would be watching the same program at the same time.

The average household had the set going more than six hours a day. If there was a child, the average was more than eight hours. The average person was watching for
10 nearly four hours daily. And so, allowing eight hours for sleep and eight hours for work, roughly half of the adult nonsleeping, nonworking time was spent watching television. Considering that these were average figures, they meant that half of the people in this country were watching television even more than that.

As these numbers sank in, I realized that there had been a strange change in the
15 way people received information, and even more in the way they were experiencing and understanding the world. In one generation, out of hundreds of thousands in human evolution, America had become the first culture to have substituted secondary, mediated versions of experience for direct experience of the world. Interpretations and representations of the world were being accepted as experience, and the difference
20 between the two was obscure to most of us.

Let's try a tone question for the previous passage:

1. Over the course of the author's research into television, the author apparently had a shift in feeling from:

Note the keyword "feeling" in the question (hence, it's a Tone question). How does the author feel at the beginning of the passage? How does the author's tone change in the last paragraph ("As these numbers sank in . . .")? Go back to the passage, and make sure to look for tone words.

Context:
The author initially refers to the "burst of figures" as "really shocking" (line 1). In the last paragraph, the author refers to the change in the way people receive information as "strange" (line 14). Television is presented as something that "obscure[s]" (line 20). His tone shifts from shock or surprise to something more strongly *negative*.

Do you see the correct answer below? Watch out for answer choices that are too strong (something commonly found on Tone questions):

- **A.** amazement to concern.
- **B.** surprise to curiosity.
- **C.** complacency to despair.
- **D.** apprehension to contentment.

Solution:
Only A and B reflect the author's tone in the first sentence ("really shocking"). The second part of B is not negative and can thus be eliminated. The answer choice best supported by the passage is **A**.
Eliminate:
- ~~B.~~ surprise to curiosity. [Tone: "curiosity" is not negative]
- ~~C.~~ complacency to despair. [Too Strong: "despair"]
- ~~D.~~ apprehension to contentment. [Tone: "contentment" is positive]

⊘ ELIMINATE DOUBLE ANSWER CHOICES ONE PART AT A TIME

When each answer choice includes two parts (as in the example above), try eliminating one part at a time. If you can eliminate any *half* of an answer choice (particularly the *easier* half), you can eliminate the whole thing.

In the example above, you can quickly eliminate B and D by looking at the second part of each answer choice, and if you're comfortable with the Too Strong elimination technique, you can also eliminate C by looking at the second part. You didn't actually have to worry about the first words of the answer choices at all!

Here's another Tone question:

2. The author would most likely characterize the way people were "experiencing and understanding the world" (lines 15-16) as:

Go back to the passage. How would you describe the author's tone in this paragraph? Do you see any other context that might come in handy?

Context:
We already know that the author's tone is negative: "strange" (line 14) and "obscure" (line 20) are the important tone words. You might also note the context in lines 16-18 ("In one generation . . ."); the author stresses that this "strange change" is a *recent* one.

Once again, the answers are "double answers":

    F. rapidly-changing and long-lasting.
    G. expected and disastrous.
    H. sudden and unfortunate.
    J. familiar and welcome.

Solution:
Answer choices F and H both reflect the context of lines 16-18. To say that the change occurred in one generation out of "hundreds of thousands in human evolution" is to say that the change was *sudden*. We also know that the author's tone is negative. The answer is **H**.
Eliminate:
F. rapidly-changing and long-lasting. [Not mentioned: "long-lasting"]
G. expected and disastrous. [False: "expected" / Too Strong: "disastrous"]
J. familiar and welcome. [Tone: "welcome" is not negative]

Questions continued on next page →

Let's try one more Tone question:

3. Regarding a culture's direct experience of the world, the author expresses which of the following attitudes?

If you circled "direct experience" as an identifier, you will see that the context is found in the last paragraph. Otherwise, you hopefully have a sense of where this topic was discussed in the passage. What is the author's tone toward "direct experience of the world" (line 18)?

> **Context:**
> The author is concerned because "secondary, mediated versions of experience" (that is, television) are taking the place of "direct experience." The author's attitude toward "direct experience" must be *positive*.

Note that the answer-choice vocabulary may not be easy for you. As we said earlier, vocabulary can be one of the main challenges of Tone questions. If you don't spot the correct answer, use POE:

A. Sorrow
B. Indifference
C. Resentment
D. Esteem

> **Solution:**
> The only answer that reflects the author's positive tone toward "direct experience" is **D**. The word *esteem* means: favorable opinion or judgment. All of the other answer choices can be eliminated because their tones are not positive.

For homework, complete **Passage III** (p. 93) in *The Real ACT Prep Guide*, 3rd Edition. Questions are on page 601.

TIMING

Don't forget to time yourself while you tackle this passage. You should have some idea of your timing plan now (review the Timing Summary on page 591). Make sure you record your *reading time* and your *total time*. Push yourself to move toward your next timing step.

7. VOCABULARY QUESTIONS

Vocabulary questions ask you to define a word or group of words using context. There are two steps to these problems:

1. **Define the original word.** Read the sentence from the passage that contains the word or phrase in question, and define the word or phrase **using context**. Even if you know (or think you know) what the word means, use *context*, not the dictionary in your head.

 Make sure to use context as you define the word. These questions usually deal with words that have several meanings, and the correct answer is almost *never* the most common of these definitions (so you must use context).

2. **Choose an answer and check.** Choose the answer that is closest to your definition. Substitute your answer for the original word, and read the original sentence. The correct answer should sound correct.

If you don't spot the correct answer, or if the context is difficult and you have trouble defining the word before looking at the answer choices, consider the following:

- **Awkwardness**: Try plugging the answer choices into the passage (in place of the word in question). When you read the passage with the answer choices plugged in, incorrect answer choices will often sound awkward or obviously wrong.
- **Tone**: If you know the word is, for example, *negative*, eliminate any words that sound *positive*.
- **Difficult Answer Choices**: It's OK to pick a difficult word as your answer, even if you don't know what the word means. POE is encouraged on Vocabulary questions. If you know the other words don't work perfectly, go with the remaining answer choice.
- **Word Familiarity**: If you're familiar with the word in question, consider possible definitions, especially if the context is difficult. This can help if you've narrowed it down to a couple answer choices that both seem to work.

Vocabulary questions will ask what a word "means" or "most nearly means."

Read the following passage:

Passage IV

PROSE FICTION: This passage is adapted from *Cold Mountain* by Charles Frazier (©1998).

At the first gesture of morning, flies began stirring. Inman's eyes and the long wound at his neck drew them, and the sound of their wings and the touch of their feet were soon more potent than a yardful of roosters in rousing a man to wake. So he came to yet one more day in the hospital ward. He flapped the flies away with his hands
5   and looked across the foot of his bed to an open triple-hung window. Ordinarily he could see to the red road and the oak tree and the low brick wall. And beyond them to a sweep of fields and flat piney woods that stretched to the western horizon. The view was a long one for the flatlands, the hospital having been built on the only swell within eyeshot. But it was too early yet for a vista. The window might as well have been
10   painted grey.
Had it not been too dim, Inman would have read to pass the time until breakfast, for the book he was reading had the effect of settling his mind. But he had burned up the last of his own candles reading to bring sleep the night before, and lamp oil was too scarce to be striking the hospital's lights for mere diversion. So he rose and dressed
15   and sat in a ladderback chair, putting the gloomy room of beds and their broken occupants behind him. He flapped again at the flies and looked out the window at the first smear of foggy dawn and waited for the world to begin shaping up outside.
The window was tall as a door, and he had imagined many times that it would open onto some other place and let him walk through and be there.

The following two Vocabulary questions are based on the passage above:

1.   As used in line 1, "gesture" most nearly means:

Using context, how would you define the word "gesture"?

Context:
You hopefully came up with a word such as "hint" or "sign."

Here are the answer choices. If you don't spot the correct answer, use POE:

    A. facial expression.
    B. movement.
    C. intimation.
    D. reminder.

Solution:
An "intimation" is a hint or suggestion. The answer is **C**. This may have been the most difficult word among the answer choices, so hopefully you were able to use POE. Note that A and B are more common definitions of "gesture" (think of a facial or hand gesture); not surprisingly, these answer choices are not correct.

Questions continued on next page →

Let's try one more Vocabulary question:

2. As used in line 17, "shaping up" most nearly means:

Once again, use context to define "shaping up."

Context:
Note that the world is "too dim" (line 11) to see clearly. The dawn is described as "foggy" (line 17). You might define "shaping up" as *appearing* or *becoming clear*.

Here are the answer choices:

F. adapting.
G. emerging.
H. fashioning.
J. exercising.

Solution:
The closest answer choice to our contextual definition is **G**. Note how the other answer choices, when plugged into the passage, sound awkward or nonsensical. Could the world begin *exercising*, for example? Probably not. This is a good way to eliminate answer choices whenever you're not sure of the correct answer. (Note: When you plug in answer choices, make sure you do so *exactly*, with every word—in this case both "shaping" and "up"—replaced.

The next two questions review Tone:

3. Inman's attitude toward the other occupants in the hospital ward is best described as one of:

We know this is a Tone question because of the word "attitude" in the question. Let's first try answering the question using context (did you circle "occupants" as an identifier?).

Context:
Inman put the room and its occupants "behind him" (line 16) and looked out the window. It seems he wanted to forget about his surroundings and focus on the world outside.

Here are the answer choices:

A. dread.
B. ambivalence.
C. detachment.
D. arrogance.

Solution:
Only **C** reflects the context of the passage ("putting the . . . occupants behind him"). There is no context to support the other two negative answer choices, A and D.

4. In the last paragraph (lines 18-19), the narrator's tone is best described as:

First, consider context.

Context:
The tone is clear. Inman wants to be in "some other place."

Now let's look at the answer choices. If the answer choice vocabulary is difficult for you, try POE:

  F. introspective.
  G. wistful.
  H. resolute.
  J. resigned.

Solution:
The best answer is **G**. The word *wistful* means: characterized by longing or yearning, often tinged with melancholy. Note that some of the other answer choices are possibly (perhaps even *probably*) true, but G is best supported by context (that is, by what we *know* from the passage).

TEST CORRECTIONS

Let's go back to Test 2 (which you should have already completed) in the ACT book and correct any questions that you missed. There are three steps to correcting the Reading practice tests:

1. Go back to your answer sheet to see which questions you missed (or guessed on, if you kept track of your guesses). Pay particular attention to the passages with the most incorrect answers.

2. Correct the problems in *The Real ACT Study Guide*. As you correct the problems, go back to the tutorial and review the techniques. The idea is to: (1) identify question types that have given you trouble, (2) go back to the tutorial so you can review and strengthen related techniques, and (3) apply these techniques to the specific problems on which you struggled.

3. If you have trouble finding context for a problem, see the Context Reference information in Chapter V, starting on page 615.

8. *FUNCTION QUESTIONS*

Function questions ask about the role (the function) of a sentence or paragraph in a passage. Some Function questions are clearly supported by the text (similar to Direct questions). Others require you to extend your reasoning (Extended Reasoning questions). Function questions will also often look like Main Idea questions; in fact, you'll often see Main Idea clue words (such as *best* or *primarily*) in the question. Clearly, the techniques we've covered so far will help you on Function questions.

FUNCTION QUESTIONS FOR PARAGRAPHS

The most common Function questions are concerned with the role of a particular paragraph in the passage, or the relationship between different paragraphs or sections. These questions can usually be answered by looking at the first sentence or two of the paragraph in question. Of course, it is helpful to be comfortable with details within the paragraph, but usually the answer can be found early in the paragraph.

 To solve Function questions relating to a paragraph, read the first couple sentences of the paragraph in question.

 The most important word in Function questions is, not surprisingly: "functions." You might also see the word "to," as in "in order to" or "to suggest that." The most common Function questions ask about how a paragraph functions in the passage.

Read the following passage. As usual, don't forget to mark up the passage (especially with identifiers).

NATURAL SCIENCE: This passage is adapted from *A Brief History of Time* by Stephen W. Hawking (©1988).

A well-known scientist (some say it was Bertrand Russell) once gave a public lecture on astronomy. He described how the earth orbits around the sun and how the sun, in turn, orbits around the center of a vast collection of stars called our galaxy. At the end of the lecture, a little old lady at the back of the room got up and said: "What
5 you have told us is rubbish. The world is really a flat plate supported on the back of a giant tortoise." The scientist gave a superior smile before replying, "What is the tortoise standing on?" "You're very clever, young man, very clever," said the old lady. "But it's turtles all the way down!"

Most people would find the picture of our universe as an infinite tower of tortoises
10 rather ridiculous, but why do we think we know better? What do we know about the universe, and how do we know it? Where did the universe come from, and where is it going? Did the universe have a beginning, and if so, what happened *before* then? What is the nature of time? Will it ever come to an end? Can we go back in time? Recent breakthroughs in physics, made possible in part by fantastic new technologies, suggest
15 answers to some of these longstanding questions. Someday these answers may seem as obvious to us as the earth orbiting the sun – or perhaps as ridiculous as a tower of tortoises. Only time (whatever that may be) will tell.

Let's take a moment and make sure you're marking up the passage effectively:

- **Tone words** (darkly underlined): well-known (line 1), rubbish (line 5), superior smile (line 6), ridiculous (lines 10 and 16)

- **Contrast signals** (boxed): But (line 8), but (line 10)

- **Identifiers** (circled): Russell, lecture, astronomy, earth, sun, galaxy, old lady, tortoise, time, breakthroughs, physics, technologies

Hopefully you had most of the above words marked accordingly. If not, you might want to go back and review the Passage section in Chapter II.

Now, on to the questions . . .

Here's a Function question:

1. The author refers to the scientist's superior smile primarily to suggest that:

Consider the author's reasons for mentioning the scientist's "superior smile" (line 6). What quality of the scientist is the author trying to convey? Make sure to use context.

Context:
Notice how the author contrasts the scientist and the "lady": The scientist is "well-known" (line 1) and describes the complex workings of the galaxy. The lady is "little" and "old" (line 4), and talks about tortoises. The "superior smile" likely supports the obvious differences between these two people.

Can you find the correct answer?

    A. the scientist believes he has cleverly found a flaw in the lady's theory.
    B. the scientist considers the woman's ideas counterintuitive to real scientific discourse.
    C. the scientist is genuinely interested in the woman's claim.
    D. the scientist's social standing is much higher than the woman's.

Solution:
Answer choice B is tempting (and probably true), but **A** is best supported by the context of the passage. The scientist's question is *rhetorical* (not intended to be answered)—he indeed thinks his question reveals a flaw in the lady's theory. A key word in the answer is "cleverly."
Eliminate:
~~C.~~ the scientist is genuinely interested in the woman's claim. [False: This answer choice is highly unlikely.]
~~D.~~ the scientist's social standing is much higher than the woman's. [Not Mentioned: "social standing"]

Questions continued on next page →

Here's another Function question. Note the word "to" in the question (a good way to identify these types of questions):

2. The author most likely mentions the "infinite tower of tortoises" (line 9) in order to:

As usual, let's explore context before looking at the answer choices. Make sure to consider the text that follows the quote in the question, and look out for contrast signals, such as "but."

Context:
Your first thought may have been that the tortoises were mentioned to diminish or even belittle the opinions of the old lady or those who think like her, but context suggests otherwise. The key words follow the contrast signal "but" in line 10: ". . . **but** why do we think we know better?"

Can you find the answer?

F. reveal a false impression of the nature of the universe.
G. examine recent changes in humans' knowledge of the cosmos.
H. display the humorous notions of some non-scientists about astronomy.
J. emphasize how little about the universe we actually know.

Solution:
Note the questions in lines 10-13. All of these questions reveal how little we really know about the universe. The answer is **J**. The incorrect answer choices for this question may not be easy to eliminate, so in this case it is important to use context to find the correct answer.

Questions continued on next page →

Here's a Function question that focuses on the function of *paragraphs*:

3. Which of the following statements best describes the way the two paragraphs function in the passage?

You might take a quick glance at the answer choices (below). Note that they are double answer choices. The question asks about the role of each paragraph. Generally speaking, how would you describe each paragraph? Consider main ideas.

Context:
The first paragraph recounts a story. The second paragraph is more complicated: we have several questions that suggest we don't know much about the universe, but the paragraph ends by saying that "answers to some of these longstanding questions" may be imminent.

Function questions sometimes have broad answer choices. Which one do you think best describes the organization of the passage? If you don't spot the correct answer, use POE (remember, this means Process of Elimination).

A. The first paragraph provides a humorous anecdote and the second paragraph introduces a subject.
B. The first paragraph recounts a personal story and the second paragraph provides a general overview of a subject.
C. The first paragraph describes a contentious conversation and the second paragraph details resulting actions.
D. The first paragraph gives a historical overview of a topic and the second paragraph summarizes the topic's current state.

Solution:
The best answer is **A**. The word "anecdote" means: a short account of a particular incident or event. If the answer was not apparent to you, the incorrect answer choices can be eliminated, as shown below:
Eliminate:
B. The first paragraph recounts a personal story and the second paragraph provides a general overview of a subject. [Every Word Counts: "personal"]
C. The first paragraph describes a contentious conversation and the second paragraph details resulting actions. [False: there is no "resulting action"]
D. The first paragraph gives a historical overview of a topic and the second paragraph summarizes the topic's current state. [False: there is no "historical overview"]

Questions continued on next page →

Let's try one more Function question for the previous passage:

4. The main function of the second paragraph (lines 9-17) is to present:

Take a quick glance at the answer choices. You can see that the question is asking about the general construction of the second paragraph. Think about how you might describe the second paragraph. Don't forget to eliminate double answers one part at a time:

F. a scientific study and its ramifications.
G. a statement followed by ironic questions.
H. questions followed by speculation.
J. questions followed by possible answers.

Solution:
The best approach to this question is probably POE. Let's start with the first parts of each answer choice. You probably eliminated F: there's clearly no scientific study. Now look at the second parts. Hopefully, after you're done eliminating, you're left with **H**. The "speculation" (the contemplation or consideration of some subject) is found in the last sentence of the passage: "Someday these answers may seem as obvious to us as the earth orbiting the sun . . ."
Eliminate:
F. a scientific study and its ramifications. [Not Mentioned: "scientific study"]
G. a statement followed by ironic questions. [Every Word Counts: "ironic"—the questions are meant to be taken seriously]
J. questions followed by possible answers. [Not Mentioned / Eye Catcher: "possible answers"—the passage mentions, but does not provide, possible answers.]

For homework, complete **Passage IV** (p. 94) in *The Real ACT Prep Guide*, 3rd Edition. Questions are on page 603.

REVIEW

Now might be a good time to review the techniques you've learned so far.

- Make sure you're effectively marking up the passage while you read, especially with **identifiers** (see the Passage section).
- Make sure you're using **context** while answering the questions (see the Context section). Are you answering most questions before looking at the answer choices?
- Review the question types and elimination techniques that we've covered so far (see the previous four sections).
- Review timing (see the Timing chapter). Are you pushing toward your next timing step (perhaps by strategically skipping some of the questions)? Don't forget to record your reading and total times for each passage.

PRACTICE TEST (all programs): After you finish the HW passage above, it is a good time to take **Test 3** (in the ACT book). (You should have already taken Test 2, and remember that Test 1 is used for extra practice passages.) Don't forget to correct any missed questions after you grade the test. See Test Corrections on page 554 for more on corrections.

20-hour program: You're now done with the 20-hour portion of the Reading section (after taking the test above). If you have extra time, you are encouraged to practice on additional reading passages (see the 30-hour Schedule in the Introduction).

30-hour program: You will not likely have time to cover the next section (Odds and Ends), but you should continue practicing the Reading techniques you've learned so far. See the Tutoring Schedule (Introduction) for additional practice passage homework assignments. You should plan to tackle at least one passage per week until you're done with the program.

9. ODDS AND ENDS

COMPARISON QUESTIONS

Comparison questions ask you to compare two short passages. Usually these questions focus on *contrasts*, but some questions ask you to find *similarities* in two otherwise different opinions. Before we get into these types of questions, note that:

 Double passages on the ACT do not show up on every test.

In the past, double passages were quite rare, but they have been showing up on recent tests more and more often, so it's a good idea to be prepared for them.

DOUBLE PASSAGES: ORDER

Double passages will be followed by 10 questions divided into 3 sets: one set for Passage A, one set for Passage B, and one set for both passages. For these double passages, go in the following order:

1. Read Passage A and answer the questions for this passage only.
2. Read Passage B and answer the questions for this passage only.
3. Finally, move on to the questions for both passages (where you'll see the Comparison questions).

 Do note read Passage B until you have answered the questions for Passage A.

FOCUS ON THE CORRECT PASSAGE

When you get to the Comparison questions, the first step is to underline (in the question) which passage to focus on. You will likely see information from *both* passages in the answer choices, so be careful. For example, in the question below, which passage should you focus on?

> In the response to the claims made in lines 2-3 of Passage A, the author of Passage B would most likely assert that . . .

Hopefully you underlined *Passage B*. Yes, of course you must consider the "claims" made in Passage A, but you should focus on the *opinion* of the Passage-B author.

Note: Some double passages include two passages written by the same author. You should still make sure to focus on the correct passage.

Comparison questions (which show up on double passages) mention *both* passages (and, often, the authors of the passages) in the question. For example:
- Unlike Passage A, Passage B . . .
- The author of Passage A would most likely respond to the author of Passage B . . .
- Which statement characterizes the differences between the authors of Passage A and Passage B . . .
- Both passages . . .

While typically, as explained above, you will read one passage and then answer questions for that one passage, before moving on to the next passage, the questions that follow Passage VI below are Comparison questions, so go ahead and read *both* passages now. (Pretend that you already answered the questions related to each passage individually.)

Passage VI

SOCIAL SCIENCE: Passage A is adapted from *Violence in the Black Imagination: Essays and Documents* by Ronald T. Takaki (©1972). Passage B is adapted from the biography *Frederick Douglass* by Jon Sterngass (©2009).

Passage A

Violence against the oppressor was a question Frederick Douglass faced with profound ambivalence. Committed to Garrisonian abolitionism during the 1840's, Douglass sincerely hoped the abolitionist movement could successfully appeal to men's sense of right and emancipation could be achieved nonviolently. As a moral suasionist,
5 Douglass denounced Henry Highland Garnet's bold address to the slaves advocating a war to the knife against the slaveholding class. "There was," Douglass protested, "too much physical force both in the address and remarks of Garnet." But at the same time Douglass believed slave violence against the master class could have crucial psychological and political meaning for the wretched, for the oppressed. The
10 ambivalence Douglass felt toward violence was very personal: It was deeply rooted in his years of childhood and early manhood, in his relationships with gentlewomen like his slaveholding mistress Sophia Auld, and in his racial ties to both white and black.

Passage B

Douglass had never been a real pacifist, even when he followed Garrison. Douglass took pride in having fought Edward Covey. He doubted the effectiveness of
15 Garrison's tactic of "moral persuasion" as a weapon for slaves. Douglass' arguments against violence were usually practical: The white masters had the guns, and the black slaves who fought against them would be killed. He wrote, "I never see much use in fighting, unless there is a reasonable probability of whipping somebody."

Let's try some Comparison questions for the passage above:

1. Both author's would likely agree that Frederick Douglass:

This question is broad, so let's look at the answer choices. Since you're looking for an answer that is true for both passages, eliminate answer choices that are true for only one of the passages.

    A. fought for emancipation using William Lloyd Garrison's tactic of "moral persuasion."
    B. considered violence a viable tool for emancipation in some instances.
    C. always thought that emancipation could be achieved nonviolently.
    D. was steadfast in his ideas about violence and emancipation.

Solution:
Only **B** is true for both passages. See lines 7-9 in Passage A ("But at the same time . . ."), and line 13 ("Douglass had never been a real pacifist") and elsewhere in Passage B. The last sentence of Passage B states that Douglass *did* believe violence was a viable tool when there was "a reasonable probability of whipping somebody."
Eliminate:
A̶. fought for emancipation using William Lloyd Garrison's tactic of "moral persuasion." [False: Passage B (lines 14-15)]
C̶. always thought that emancipation could be achieved nonviolently. [False: both passages (lines 7-10, 13, 17-18)/Too Strong: "always"]
D̶. was steadfast in his ideas about violence and emancipation. [False: Passage A (lines 9-10—"ambivalence")]

Questions continued on next page →

Try the following Comparison question. Underline the author (or passage) that you should focus on:

2. In response to the claim made in line 13 of Passage B, the author of Passage A would most likely assert that:

The answer will reflect the opinions of the author of Passage A, but first go back to Passage B and make sure you understand the claim made in line 13. How would the author of Passage A respond to this claim?

> **Context:**
> Did you see the "most likely" in the question? This could be a Main Idea question. The following two quotes sums up the main idea of Passage A: "Douglass sincerely hoped the abolitionist movement could successfully appeal to men's sense of right and emancipation could be achieved nonviolently" (lines 3-4). "But at the same time Douglass believed slave violence against the master class could have crucial psychological and political meaning . . ." (lines 7-9).

Now look at the answer choices. Do you see one that expresses the main idea of Passage A?

- F. Douglass's views on violence were complex and multifaceted.
- G. Garrison and Douglass both considered violence a last resort in the battle for emancipation.
- H. Douglass always disagreed with Garrison's views as an abolitionist.
- J. Douglass dismissed violence as an ineffective means to achieve an end.

> **Solution:**
> Douglass, as presented in Passage A, was both against violence and for it (indeed, a *complex* view). Note the word "ambivalence" in lines 2 and 10. Passage B presents Douglass as *never* having been a "real pacifist" (line 13). The best answer is **F**. You may have chosen to use POE on this one:
> **Eliminate:**
> G. Garrison and Douglass both considered violence a last resort in the battle for emancipation. [False: Garrisonian abolitionism is portrayed as nonviolent (lines 2-4).]
> H. Douglass always disagreed with Garrison's views as an abolitionist. [False: line 2]
> J. Douglass dismissed violence as an ineffective means to achieve an end. [False: lines 7-9]

Questions continued on next page →

Here's another Comparison question:

3. Which of the following aspects of Frederick Douglass is addressed in Passage A but not in Passage B?

The answer to this question will reflect the context of Passage A (again, don't forget to focus on the correct passage when answering these Comparison questions). The question is broad, so here are the answer choices. Eliminate answer choices that are either addressed in Passage B or not addressed in either passage:

A. Douglass's opinions about Garrison's principles of abolition
B. Douglass's reasons for his stance against violence
C. Douglass's race
D. The specific steps that Douglass felt should be taken before violence was acceptable

---

Solution:
After eliminating answer choices, you are hopefully left with **C**. Passage A discusses Douglass's race in line 12 (". . . his racial ties to both white and black"). There is no mention of Douglass's race in Passage B. The connection to Douglass's race in Passage A, however, is subtle (requiring some "extended reasoning"), so try POE:

Eliminate:
A. Douglass's opinions about Garrison's principles of abolition [Passage B: lines 14-15]
B. Douglass's reasons for his stance against violence [Passage B: lines 15-18]
D. The specific steps that Douglass felt should be taken before violence was acceptable [Not Mentioned in either passage: "specific steps"]

Questions continued on next page →

Here's one more Comparison question:

4. Which statement best characterizes the different ways in which the authors of Passage A and Passage B approach Frederick Douglass and his ideas?

We have another broad question, so look at the answer choices. Note that they are double answers, so eliminate answer choices one part at a time:

F. The first speculates on the origin of Douglass's ideas, while the second examines their results.
G. The first alludes to those who influenced Douglass, while the second presents Douglass's ideas as uniquely his own.
H. The first stresses the evolution of Douglass's ideas, while the second examines his background as an abolitionist.
J. The first emphasizes the ambiguity of Douglass's ideas, while the second focuses on their explicitness.

Solution:
Probably the best way to answer this question is to use POE. Hopefully you're left with **J** after eliminating parts of answer choices. The first part of J is clear: see "ambivalence" in lines 2 and 10 of Passage A. The second part may be more difficult to confirm, but the first sentence of Passage B does make an explicit (fully or clearly expressed) statement: "Douglass had never been a real pacifist . . ."

Eliminate:
F. The first speculates on the origin of Douglass's ideas, while the second examines their results. [Not Mentioned (Passage B): "results"]
G. The first alludes to those who influenced Douglass, while the second presents Douglass's ideas as uniquely his own. [Not Mentioned (Passage B): "Douglass's ideas [were] uniquely his own"]
H. The first stresses the evolution of Douglass's ideas, while the second examines his background as an abolitionist. [Not Mentioned (Passage B): Douglass's "background as an abolitionist" / You might also note that there is no mention of the "evolution" of Douglass's ideas in Passage A. His ideas, as far as the passage states, had always been ambivalent—see lines 7-8 (". . . at the same time . . .").

If you're following the **40-hour program**, see the Tutoring Schedule (Introduction) for additional practice passage homework assignments. You should plan to tackle at least one passage per week until you're done with the program.

RHETORICAL DEVICES

Rhetorical devices are specific tools that authors use to make their writing more effective. Questions that ask about rhetorical devices are not common on the ACT, but, like comparison questions (double passages), they have shown up on some recent tests. Here's how to identify these questions:

> Look for questions, and especially answer choices, that include rhetorical devices (such as metaphors, irony, allusions, etc.). As you get comfortable with the terms below, these questions will become easy to spot.

The following terms are the most common rhetorical devices that you may see on the ACT. Hopefully, many of these will be review for you. Carefully read them over for homework. For any terms that you're not familiar with, make flashcards to help you study them.

For now, just skim through the list, and perhaps read a few of the terms that are unfamiliar to you. Then move on to the following passage. You can turn back to these terms as you answer the questions.

allegory

A story that, in addition to maintaining its own narrative, may be applied to another, parallel situation. The novel *Animal Farm*, by George Orwell, in which the animals on the farm represent different sections of Russian society, is an example of allegory.

allusion

A symbol or allegory that refers to other works or sources. Common allusions include the Bible, Greco-Roman mythology, classic literature, and history. "She was almost ready to go, standing before the hall mirror, putting on her hat, and he, his hands behind him, appeared pinned to the door frame, waiting like Saint Sebastian for the arrows to begin piercing him."
—Flannery O'Connor. The allusion is to Saint Sebastian, a religious martyr.

analogy

A comparison of two things that are alike in some way. "He that voluntarily continues ignorance is guilty of all the crimes which ignorance produces, as to him that should extinguish the tapers [candles] of a lighthouse might justly be imputed the calamities of shipwrecks."
—Samuel Johnson

anecdote

A short, usually personal, account of a particular incident or event. (See Question 3 in the Function Questions section.)

connotation

What a word suggests (rather than its literal meaning). Consider the title of Elie Wiesel's Holocaust work: *Night*. Certainly the novel/memoir is not literally about "night."

dialogue

Conversation between two or more people. Dialogue is a common tool of fiction writers, but may be found in other forms. The first paragraph of the passage in the Function Questions section contains dialogue (between a "well-known scientist" and a "little old lady").

figure of speech

A word or phrase used in a nonliteral sense. Both metaphors and similes (these terms are defined below) are common examples of figures of speech.

flashback

A device in which an author recounts or "fills in" what has happened earlier. In John Milton's *Paradise Lost*, the novel opens with Satan already defeated in his battle with the Lord. Earlier events in the story are brought in later by flashback.

foreshadow

An intentional inciting of our anticipation for future events. The Russian writer Anton Chekhov wrote: "One must not put a loaded rifle on the stage if no one is thinking of firing it." The so-called "Chekhov's gun" foreshadows events to come.

imagery

Refers to words that trigger mental pictures (images) in the reader's mind of any of the five senses. "They arrive at dawn in their geography of hats. A dark field of figures, stalks in motion, bending towards the docklands." —Colum McCann

irony

A figure of speech in which the intended meaning of the words is different from the actual meaning. Guy Montag, the protagonist of Ray Bradbury's *Fahrenheit 451*, a man who starts fires, is ironically called a "fireman." Irony also may describe an outcome contrary to what might have been expected, such as a traffic cop losing his job because of unpaid parking tickets.

metaphor

A statement where one thing is something else, when in fact, literally, it is not. "Thus a mind that is free from passion is a very citadel." —Marcus Aurelius

omniscient narrator

A narrator who can see into the minds of all (or at least some) characters. See "point of view" below.

overstatement

An exaggeration for effect. Also called *hyperbole*. "I'll love you till the ocean / Is folded and hung up to dry." —W.H. Auden

parable

A brief story intending to teach a lesson or moral. The New Testament is replete with parables.

personification

The attribution of human characteristics to animals or inanimate objects. "Only the champion daisy trees were serene. After all, they were part of a rain forest already two thousand years old and scheduled for eternity, so they ignored the men and continued to rock the diamondbacks that slept in their arms. It took the river to persuade them that indeed the world was altered." — Toni Morrison

point of view

The "voice" of the text, i.e. the speaker who is narrating the story to the reader. The two most common points of view are *first-person*, where the narrator is a character in the text (typically includes "I"), and *third-person*, where the narrator reports events but does not take part in them.

> Example of *first-person* point of view: "It began at three o'clock one October afternoon as I sat in the grand stand at the fall trotting and pacing meet at Sandusky, Ohio." —Sherwood Anderson.

> Example of *third-person* point of view: "Eva and Carol took off their shoes and socks and waded in. The water was so cold it sent pain up their legs, like blue electric sparks shooting through their veins, but they went on, pulling their skirts high, tight behind and bunched so they could hold them in front." —Alice Monroe

satire

A literary tool designed to expose human follies and vices. In *Gulliver's Travels* by Jonathan Swift, the author introduces two fictional political parties, which are distinguished by the relative high or low boot heels of each party's members. Swift is satirizing the trivial differences and minor disputes between the two English political parties of his time.

simile

A figure of speech in which two unlike things are compared. A simile displays an *alikeness* between two things, using the words "like" or "as." "Elderly American ladies leaning on their canes listed toward me like towers of Pisa." —Vladimir Nabokov

symbolism

A literary tool in which one thing may be understood as something else, usually something bigger or more significant. The most obvious symbol in *Lord of the Flies*, by William Golding, is the conch shell. The conch shell, used to summon the boys to meetings and keep order during those meetings, represents order and civilization. By the end of the novel, the shell is destroyed, symbolically reflecting the demise of civilized instincts for most of the boys on the island.

understatement

To say something is less important or less significant than it really is. "I have to have this operation. It isn't very serious. I have this tiny little tumor on the brain." —J.D. Salinger

————

Now let's take a look at a passage that employs several rhetorical devices. Don't forget to circle identifiers while you read:

Passage VII

HUMANITIES: This passage is adapted from the memoir *Pilgrim at Tinker Creek* by Annie Dillard (©1998).

I used to have a cat, an old fighting tom, who would jump through the open window by my bed in the middle of the night and land on my chest. I'd half awaken. He'd stick his skull under my nose and purr, stinking of urine and blood. Some nights he kneaded my bare chest, powerfully, arching his back, as if sharpening his claws, or pummeling a
5 mother for milk. And some mornings I'd wake in daylight to find my body covered with paw prints in blood; I looked as though I'd been painted with roses.
It was hot, so hot the mirror felt warm. I washed before the mirror in a daze; my twisted summer sleep still hung about me like sea kelp. What blood was this, and what roses? It could have been the rose of union, the blood of murder, or the rose of beauty
10 bare and the blood of some unspeakable sacrifice or birth. The sign on my body could have been an emblem or a stain, the keys to the kingdom or the mark of Cain. I never knew. I never knew as I washed, and the blood streaked, faded, and finally disappeared, whether I'd purified myself or ruined the blood sign of the Passover. We wake, if we ever wake at all, to mystery, rumors of death, beauty, violence. . . . "Seem
15 like we're just set down here," a woman said to me recently, "and don't nobody know why."

Here is a question that tests rhetorical devices:

1. The author uses all of the following in the passage EXCEPT:

A glance at the answer choices confirms that this is a question that focuses on rhetorical devices. Can you identify the device *not* used in the passage?

    A. metaphor.
    B. allusion.
    C. direct quotation.
    D. satire.

Solution:
Remember that EXCEPT/NOT questions typically require you to eliminate answer choices. If you're comfortable with the rhetorical devices defined in this section, you should be able to eliminate the three incorrect answers. The answer is **D**. The author does not use satire in the passage.
Eliminate:
A. metaphor. [see lines 9-11; some writers would consider the *similes* in line 6 ("roses") and line 8 ("sea kelp") to be "metaphorical" as well.]
B. allusion. [". . . the keys to the kingdom or the mark of Cain" (line 11); ". . . blood sign of the Passover" (line 13)—these are Biblical allusions.]
C. direct quotation. [see lines 14-16]

The following questions review a few of the question types we've discussed so far:

2. It can reasonably be inferred that the author considers sea kelp something that is:

This is an Extended Reasoning question. Use context (did you circle "sea kelp"?). How would you describe the sea kelp? The answer choices are below:

    F. disorienting.
    G. entangling.
    H. floating.
    J. obstructing.

Solution:
The key word is "daze" (line 7). Watch out for answer choices that take the twisting effect of sea kelp literally: G and perhaps J. The best answer is **F**.

Questions continued on next page →

3. In the second paragraph (lines 7-16), the author is primarily concerned with:

Note the word "primarily" in the question. This is a Main Idea question (for a section of the passage). The meaning of the second paragraph is not easy. You might take a look at the answer choices (below), and look back to the passage for contextual support:

- **A.** the mysterious nature of sleep.
- **B.** the obvious differences between two ideas.
- **C.** new interpretations of an old discovery.
- **D.** possible meanings of a sign.

Solution:
The second paragraph includes a question in lines 8-9 ("What blood was this, and what roses?"). The next several lines offer possible answers to this question. The best answer is **D**.
Eliminate:
- A. the mysterious nature of sleep. [not the *primary* idea of the paragraph]
- B. the obvious differences between two ideas. [False: The question in lines 8-9 suggests that any differences are not "obvious," and in any case, there are more than "two ideas" presented.]
- C. new interpretations of an old discovery. [Not Mentioned: "new interpretations"]

Questions continued on next page →

4. The passage as whole could best be described as:

This is another Main Idea question, in this case one for the entire passage. Take a quick look at the answer choices below. You'll see from some of the key words ("flashback," "foreshadow," "ironic," and "analogy") that this question is also testing rhetorical devices.

We mentioned earlier that authors tend to work *toward* their most important points. You might focus on the end of the last paragraph as you look for context. Here are the answer choices:

F. a flashback to a traumatic event.
G. a foreshadow of a terrible crime.
H. an ironic investigation into consciousness.
J. an analogy to the nature of being.

Solution:
These Main Idea questions can be difficult, especially if the passage is challenging. We already know (from the previous question) that this passage has something to do with the interpretation of the blood roses. Look at the woman's statement at the end of the passage: "'Seem like we're just set down here . . . and don't nobody know why.'" At first glance, this quote may seem off topic, but of course, since it's at the end of the passage, it could very well be the passage's main point. The author is likely concerned with why we're "here." A sensible interpretation of the passage is that it provides an analogy between the mystery of the blood roses and the mystery of life. The best answer is **J**.

Eliminate:
F. a flashback to a traumatic event. [Too Strong: "traumatic" / False: The passage as a whole is not a flashback.]
G. a foreshadow of a terrible crime. [Not Mentioned: "terrible crime"]
H. an ironic investigation into consciousness. [False: There is no evidence that the narrator is being "ironic."]

DIFFICULT PASSAGES

Many ACTs will include at least one especially difficult passage. As you work on these passages, we remind you to:

FOCUS ON THE EASY STUFF

 If the passage is hard to understand or phrases or whole sentences confuse you, focus on the parts you *do* understand. Don't get discouraged. Read through the passage, diligently circle your identifiers, and focus on the easy stuff. Many of the questions, perhaps most of them, will focus on the parts of the passage that you *do* understand.

STAY OPEN-MINDED

This is an important tip, especially on difficult passages. As you know by now, for most questions we recommend you try answering the question using context *before* looking at the answer choices. But what happens if you go back to the passage and simply don't understand the relevant context? You shouldn't necessarily give up on the question. Start looking at the answer choices, and stay *open-minded*. If an answer choice is supported by context, even if it answers the question in a way you hadn't anticipated, it is probably the correct answer.

Many students will find the following passage difficult. Remember, just get through it. Circle identifiers and focus on the easy stuff.

SOCIAL SCIENCE: This passage is adapted from the biography *Beyond the Hundredth Meridian* by Wallace Stegner (©1992)

The tourist and the nature lover occupied a good large corner of Clarence Edward Dutton. He never quite made up his mind whether he was literary traveler or sober scientific analyst: the temptations were essentially equal. He escaped his dilemma by being both, and in his reports a rich and embroidered nineteenth-century traveler's
5 prose flows around bastions of geological fact as some of the lava coulees on the Uinkaret flow around gables of sedimentary strata. The literary tendency is progressive; it is apparent in *The Geology of the High Plateaus of Utah* (1880) and dominant in *The Tertiary History of the Grand Canyon* (1882). With hardly an apology, Dutton forsook the "sever ascetic style" of science when he came to deal with the Grand Canyon. The
10 Grand Canyon was beyond the reach of superlatives, it compelled effusion of a kind. The result is a scientific monograph of great geological importance which contains whole chapters as ebullient as the writing of John Muir, and deviates constantly into speculations so far from geological that they sound more like Ruskin than Lyell.

By now you are hopefully getting comfortable identifying question types. You should also have a sense of when to look back to the passage for context *before* looking at the answer choices, and when not to. For the following questions, the answer choices will immediately follow the questions (which of course is how the questions look on the ACT). Just remember that for most questions, you should look for context *before* looking at the answer choices. Don't let the placement of the answer choices tempt you to peek.

1. The primary purpose of the passage is to:

   A. point out the differences in two works of scientific writing.
   B. caution against combining literary and scientific writing styles.
   C. discuss the dualistic nature of a scientist's writing.
   D. examine the background and success of a scientist.

This is a Main Idea question. If you grasped the main idea while you were reading, you probably identified the correct answer. If not, then read through the answer choices and decide which one is best supported by the passage. As stated at the beginning of this section, you may have to be open-minded while reading the answer choices (especially if you weren't comfortable with the context).

Solution:
Remember that we often look to the first couple sentences and/or the last couple sentences of a passage to find its main idea. In this case, the information can be found in the second sentence: "He never quite made up his mind whether he was literary traveler or sober scientific analyst." Once you understand this dichotomy, the rest of the passage comes into focus. Compare "'sever ascetic style'" (line 9) (scientific writing) to "effusion" (line 11) (literary writing) and "great geological importance" (line 11) (scientific writing) to "speculations so far from geological" (line 13) (literary writing). The best answer is **C**. Note that D is tempting (the passage discusses, at least in passing, Dutton's background and success), but this answer choice does not capture the main idea of the passage: Dutton's writing style.

Eliminate:
A̶. point out the differences in two works of scientific writing. [Eye Catcher: lines 7-8]
B̶. caution against combining literary and scientific writing styles. [Tone: The author does not "caution" in the passage; his tone is more analytical and informative.]

Questions continued on next page →

2. As it is used in line 2, the word "sober" most nearly means:

    F. grave.
    G. not intoxicated.
    H. quiet.
    J. dispassionate.

Solution:
On Vocabulary questions, remember to define the word before looking at the answer choices. This question examines one of the two styles of Dutton's writing: the "scientific" style. Some of the key words from the passage for this style are: "scientific analyst" (line 3) and "fact" (line 5). Perhaps more important are the words that support the opposite style (the "literary" one): "rich and embroidered" (line 4) and "effusion" (unrestrained expression of feelings, line 11). The best answer is **J**. Note that *not intoxicated* (G) is probably the most common definition for "sober"; not surprisingly, this is not the correct answer.
Eliminate:
F. grave. [Too Strong: "grave" is too negative.]

---

3. The language in lines 3-6 ("He escaped . . . strata") is particularly notable for its:

    A. humorous allusions.
    B. noted understatement.
    C. abstract language.
    D. metaphorical prose.

Solution:
As stated in the previous section, questions that test *rhetorical devices* can be identified by looking at the answer choices. You might reread the lines and think about possible rhetorical devices before looking at the answer choices (in detail). The prose is referred to as "embroidered" and as something that "flows." These are examples of metaphorical writing. The answer is **D**.
Eliminate:
A. humorous allusions. [False: The author may, in a sense, use "allusion" (to the "lava coulees"), but the allusions are certainly not "humorous."]
B. noted understatement. [False: "understatement"]
C. abstract language. [False: The language is clear and concrete. Do not confuse abstract language with metaphorical language.]

Questions continued on next page →

4. The author presents Dutton's decision to write in a literary manner between 1880 and 1882 as something that:

    F. expanded markedly.
    G. became apparent for the first time.
    H. grew inconsistently.
    J. had wide-ranging influence.

Solution:
This is a Direct question. Note that the dates in the question are great identifiers. Dutton's "literary tendency" is described as "progressive" (line 7). It goes from "apparent" (line 7) to "dominant" (line 8). The best answer is **F**.

Eliminate:
~~G.~~ became apparent for the first time. [Not Mentioned: "for the first time"]
~~H.~~ grew inconsistently. [This answer choice is probably false: see solution above.]
~~J.~~ had wide-ranging influence. [Not Mentioned: "influence"]

---

5. The author's attitude toward Dutton's writing about the Grand Canyon is best described as one of:

    A. condescension.
    B. indifference.
    C. ambiguity.
    D. understanding.

Solution:
This is a Tone question, and not an easy one. The author's attitude is not clearly stated in the passage. As usual, go back to the passage, particularly lines 8-14 (where Dutton's writing about the Grand Canyon is discussed), and see if you get a sense of the author's tone. The main clue for this question is found in lines 10-11: "The Grand Canyon was beyond the reach of superlatives, it compelled effusion of a kind." The author seems to understand why Dutton "forsook the 'sever ascetic style' of science." The best answer is **D**.

Eliminate:
~~A.~~ condescension. [Tone: Even if the author's tone were interpreted as negative, "condescension" is too strong.]
Answer choices B and C can be difficult to eliminate. First B: The author's tone seems generally *positive* toward Dutton's writing, especially in lines 4-6. The author does not feel "indifference." The more difficult answer choice to eliminate is C. Indeed, the last sentence could be interpreted as tonally ambiguous ("great geological importance" is clearly positive; deviating into "speculations" sounds negative), but the author does not make clear that he feels negativity toward Dutton's writing, and if anything, as stated above, he hints at a generally positive tone. We do not have enough contextual support to choose C. As we mentioned in the Extended Reasoning section, if none of the answers are explicitly supported by the text, go with the one that requires the *least* amount of extended reasoning, in this case: D.

Questions continued on next page →

6. The author most likely mentions Muir and Ruskin in order to:

    F. give examples of writers who influenced the work of Dutton.
    G. compare Dutton to scientists known more for their informative scientific writing.
    H. argue that Dutton's writing is more like that of literary writers than science writers.
    J. provide well-known authors whose styles of writing are similar to that of Dutton.

Solution:
This is a Function question. Why does the author mention Muir and Ruskin? The most likely answer is that these authors have similar styles to that of Dutton. Note the comparing words: "as ebullient as the writing of John Muir" and "they sound more like Ruskin." The best answer is **J**. The fact that the author did not go into any detail about these writers suggests that they are "well-known" (at least as far as the author is concerned).

Eliminate:
F. give examples of writers who influenced the work of Dutton. [Not Mentioned: "influenced"]
G. compare Dutton to scientists known more for their informative scientific writing. [False: The author suggests that Ruskin, at least, is more literary than scientific ("far from geological").]
H. argue that Dutton's writing is more like that of literary writers than science writers. [Too Strong: The author makes clear that Dutton's writing is literary, but his writing is still of "great geological importance" (line 11). Without choosing one style over the other, the author posits that Dutton's writing is both literary *and* scientific. See lines 3-4.]

III
TIMING

This chapter will cover techniques that will help you finish the Reading Test _in time_.

1. TIMES

GENERAL APPROACH

Most students agree that one of the most difficult parts of the Reading Test is the minimal time allotted to complete it. The test is **35 minutes** long. If your goal is to get to every passage and answer every question, you only have **8 minutes and 45 seconds** per passage. So it's important to develop a timing approach to the Reading Test that maximizes your score.

Since different students work and read at different speeds, there is no "right" timing plan for all students. Some students may only have time to tackle the first three passages. Other students might finish the first three passages but find they run out of time on the fourth. The ultimate goal of course is to finish all four passages, but you may have to work up to it. We'll describe several timing steps below.

DEADLINES

Deadlines will help you avoid falling behind as you take the test. They give you an idea of when you need to finish up one passage and move on to the next. Start the test at "time 00:00." The first deadline will occur when you should finish Passage I and move on to Passage II. The next deadline is for Passage II (move on to Passage III). And so on. We'll provide deadlines for each timing step below.

STEP 1: FIRST THREE PASSAGES

If you tackle just the first three passages, you have about **11:30** (11 minutes and 30 seconds) per passage. Notice that 11:30 × 3 = 34:30; you will have 30 seconds at the end of the test to guess on any remaining questions. Here are the deadlines for Step 1:

Reading Deadlines: Step 1	
Start test	**00:00 (min:sec)**
Finish Passage I	**11:30**
Finish Passage II	**23:00**
Finish Passage III	**34:30***
Finish test	**35:00**

*Remember, you should never leave questions blank when you're done with the test. At the end of the test, with the last 30 seconds or so, quickly guess on any unanswered questions.

Make sure you are comfortable with what these deadlines mean. You should finish Passage I and start Passage II at the 11:30 mark (11 minutes and 30 seconds). You should finish Passage II and start Passage III 11 minutes and 30 seconds later, at the 23:00 mark. And you should finish Passage III and start guessing at the 34:30 mark.

READING TIMES FOR STEP 1

You should expect to *read* each passage (before you look at the answer choices) in **4 to 5 minutes**. Why the range? Because you'll likely find some passages easier (and faster) to read than others. Just make sure you don't spend *more* than 5 minutes reading a passage.

STEP 2: FIRST THREE PASSAGES, AND THEN SOME

If you can get through the first three passages with about 5 minutes left, you won't have time to *read* the last passage, but you can still attempt some of its questions. Answer the following questions, in the order shown:

- Questions with line numbers
- Questions with obvious identifiers (numbers, words in italics, proper nouns)
- Main Idea questions (if you have time to read the first and last paragraphs)

There may only be a few of these, but you'll have a good chance of getting them correct if you go back and use the context of the passage, even though you haven't read the whole passage. Set a goal of about **10 minutes for each of the first three passages**, which leaves **5 minutes** to answer some questions for the last passage and guess on any remaining questions. Here are the deadlines for Step 2:

Reading Deadlines: Step 2	
Start Test	**00:00 (min:sec)**
Finish Passage I	**10:00**
Finish Passage II	**20:00**
Finish Passage III	**30:00**
Finish Passage IV	**35:00**

Of course, the more time you have for Passage IV, the more questions you'll likely have time to answer, so push yourself to move quickly through the first three passages.

READING TIMES FOR STEP 2

You should expect to read each passage (Passages I-III) in **3:30 to 4:30 (minutes:seconds).**

STEP 3: ALL FOUR PASSAGES

As stated before, if you plan to tackle every question, you have 8 minutes and 45 seconds per passage. To be safe, let's round this down to **8:30**. Will each passage take you the exact same time? Probably not. Harder passages will take longer than easier ones. Your times will probably vary, but the 8:30 number should give you a general idea of how long to take for each passage, and you'll have a minute of cushion, in case you start to fall behind. Here are the deadlines for Step 3:

Reading Deadlines: Step 3	
Start Test	00:00 min:sec
Finish Passage I	08:30
Finish Passage II	17:00
Finish Passage III	25:30
Finish Passage IV	34:00+*

*You can fall up to a minute behind for this timing plan.

Not all students will reach this final step. That's fine. You may find that Step 1 or Step 2 is right for you. Experiment with the practice passages and tests in the ACT book, and push yourself to do the best that you can. We'll talk about ways to move faster on Reading questions in the next section.

READING TIMES FOR STEP 3

You should expect to read each passage in **3 to 4 minutes**.

USING A STOPWATCH

As you take practice tests and complete practice passages, use a stopwatch to keep track of your times. Start your watch at the beginning of the test (or passage), and stick to the deadlines. Note: Practice timing when you take *practice* tests, *not* when you take the real ACT. The ACT folks do not allow any beeping noises during testing, so they probably won't let you use a stopwatch (unless it's silent). The important thing is to get a feel for your timing when you *practice* so you know how quickly you need to work during the real test.

MOVING FASTER THAN THE DEADLINES

Remember that these times are all *deadlines*—you don't *have* to take this long. If you move faster than these times, great (especially for Steps 1 and 2). Don't slow down! You might need the extra time for one of the later passages. The deadlines just ensure that you won't fall behind.

GUESSING

As stated before, you should never leave questions blank when you're done with the test. Before you finish, make sure you guess on any unanswered questions. Keep your eye on the clock so you don't run out of time.

2. HOW TO GET FASTER

There are two ways to get faster on the Reading test: (1) answer the questions faster (Time Savers) and (2) read the passages faster (Skimming). We'll start with the questions.

TIME SAVERS

For each passage, you'll hopefully be able to answer 2-4 questions *fairly quickly*, compared to the other questions. We call these "fast" questions *Time Savers*.

DIRECT HITS

In the last chapter, we talked about eliminating answer choices to find the correct answers, but at no time did we say you *have* to look at every answer choice. Sometimes, you'll spot an answer choice that sounds perfect. This could be a *direct hit*. Go for it and move on. This can be a good way to save time.

Caution: Make sure you don't fall into traps. For example, you may think you've spotted a direct hit because the answer choice contains words from the passage, but the answer choice may be an *eye catcher*. If you find that you miss a number of your direct hits, you'll have to be more careful, and perhaps review the other answer choices.

MEMORY QUESTIONS

Do the answers come from information in the passage? Yes. Must you *always* look back to the passage to find your answers? No. Sometimes you'll read a question and have a pretty good idea of the answer without having to go back and review the passage. If you can answer a couple questions from *memory*, you'll save yourself some time.

Caution: If you miss memory questions, then the time savings didn't do you much good. Through practice, you'll get better at *retaining* information while you read. This may take a while, so if you don't answer many memory questions at first, that's OK. It's something to work toward.

MAIN IDEA QUESTIONS

If you feel comfortable with a passage's main idea, answer any Main Idea questions quickly, without looking back to the passage. Or, at most, quickly glance at any sentences you marked as main ideas while you were reading, or quickly look over the topic sentences of the first and last paragraphs (which often include information about the main idea). In any case, answer these questions quickly. If you *don't* feel comfortable with a passage's main idea, take a guess and move on.

ANSWER EASIER QUESTIONS FIRST

Here's a very important rule:

 You can answer the questions in any order you'd like!

The idea is to skip the harder questions, and tackle the easier ones, on your first pass. Thus, if you run out of time and need to move on to the next passage, you've answered the easiest questions. Of course, if you have time after you finish the easier questions, go back and answer skipped questions (the more questions you skip on your first pass, the more time you should have to go back). Below are the types of questions to consider skipping on your first pass:

- **Extended Reasoning questions**: Look for keywords in the question such as "it is reasonable to infer." These questions are often more difficult than others and should thus be skipped if time is an issue.
- **EXCEPT/NOT questions**: These questions aren't necessarily harder than others, but they often take longer to answer. Consider skipping them, but if you have time, come back to them before moving to the next passage, especially if the identifiers are good.
- **Paragraph questions**: If a question asks about a whole paragraph, especially a long paragraph, it might be a good question to skip. Rereading an entire paragraph takes time.
- **Poor identifiers**: If a question and its answer choices lack good identifiers, consider skipping the question. Students often spend too much time looking for information in the passage, even if the question sounds easy. Skip it and come back to it if you have time.

You should also skip any questions that seem difficult to you or test a part of the passage that you found confusing. Again, the idea is to answer the easier questions first, and answer the harder questions only if you have time. Don't feel bad about skipping questions. Order the questions in a way that works best for you.

SKIMMING

Improving your actual *reading* times is something that will happen naturally from practice (and you'll be doing plenty of practice in this tutorial). Make sure you push yourself while you're reading. Make your markups (identifiers, etc.) quickly, and don't let your mind wander. Hopefully, over time, your reading speed will increase (your eventual goal is 3-4 minutes per passage). But what if you've been practicing awhile, and you just can't get your reading times fast enough to get through the whole test? You might try *skimming*. Here's how to do it:

1. If the first paragraph is short (less than about 10 lines), read it. Otherwise, just read the first couple sentences and skim the rest of the paragraph.

2. **While skimming, look for and circle identifiers.** You may find this challenging at first, since you're not actually *reading*, but with practice you'll hopefully be able to spot most of the good identifiers.

3. Read the first sentence or two of each paragraph, and then *skim* the rest of the paragraph. Keep circling identifiers.

4. If the last paragraph is short (less than about 10 lines), read it. Otherwise, just read the first couple sentences, skim the middle sentences, and then read the last sentence or two. The last couple sentences of a passage are often important.

SKIMMING TIME

With practice, you should be able to get through the passage in **less than 2 minutes**. If you have trouble staying under 2 minutes, try skimming more; you might have to sacrifice reading some of the topic sentences. Circle your identifiers quickly, and keep moving. Make sure you don't get held up anywhere in the passage.

ANSWERING THE QUESTIONS

The whole point of this approach is to give you more time for the questions. You'll likely have to skip some of the harder Main Idea or Extended Reasoning questions, or questions with poor identifiers, but hopefully the extra time will allow you to get through all four passages and answer most of the easier questions. Experiment with this approach and see if your scores increase.

3. TIMING SUMMARY

- Stick to *deadlines* while you take practice tests, as outlined below. If you have trouble completing all 4 passages, *step up to it*:

- **Step 1:** 3 passages—11:30 (min:sec) per passage

  - Reading time per passage: **4 to 5 minutes**

Reading Deadlines: Step 1	
Start test	**00:00 (min:sec)**
Finish Passage I	**11:30**
Finish Passage II	**23:00**
Finish Passage III	**34:30**
Finish test	**35:00**

- **Step 2:** 3 passages, and then some—10 minutes for the first 3 passages; 5 minutes for the last passage (don't read the last passage; line-number questions only)

  - Reading time per passage: **3:30 to 4:30 (minutes:seconds)**

Reading Deadlines: Step 2	
Start Test	**00:00 (min:sec)**
Finish Passage I	**10:00**
Finish Passage II	**20:00**
Finish Passage III	**30:00**
Finish Passage IV	**35:00**

- **Step 3:** All 4 passages

  - Reading time per passage: **3 to 4 minutes**

Reading Deadlines: Step 3	
Start Test	**00:00 min:sec**
Finish Passage I	**08:30**
Finish Passage II	**17:00**
Finish Passage III	**25:30**
Finish Passage IV	**34:00+**

- Look for 2-4 (or more) *Time Savers* per passage:
  - Direct Hits
  - Memory Questions
  - Main Idea Questions
  - Skipped Questions
- If, after practicing, you're still having trouble finishing in time, try *skimming* to get through the passages faster: **less than 2 minutes** per passage.

For homework, complete **Passage II** (p. 92) in *The Real ACT Prep Guide*, 3rd Edition. For convenience, we recommend tearing the passages out of the ACT book. Questions are on page 599.

TIMING

Use a stopwatch as you answer the questions. Take note of: (1) how long you took to read the passage and (2) how long you took to finish answering the questions. From this information, decide what timing step to start on. As you practice, push yourself to move to the next step.

Don't forget to look for Time Savers as you answer the questions; your eventual goal is to find 2 to 4 of them for each passage.

Keep in mind that it may take a while before you can consistently finish all four passages in time (Step 3). Don't try to get there too quickly. Through practice and perseverance—in combination with the techniques and approaches taught in this tutorial—you will be able to maximize your score.

––––––––––

All programs: If you're following one of our standard programs, turn back to Tone Questions in the previous chapter.

IV
PRACTICE

This chapter includes practice assignments for the Reading Test.

1. *READING QUESTIONS*

PRACTICE PROBLEMS

We use passages from *The Real ACT Prep Guide*, 3rd Edition for homework practice. As stated earlier, these passages do not each come with the expected 10 questions, so we made up our own questions, which are found in the next section. If you have time, also try the practice passages from Test 1 in the ACT book. See the Tutoring Schedules section in the Introduction for more on when to tackle these passages for different programs. (Page numbers for Passages I-VII below are from the *The Real ACT Prep Guide*, 3rd Edition.)

- ☐ Questions for Sample Passage I (page 91)
- ☐ Questions for Sample Passage II (page 92)
- ☐ Questions for Sample Passage III (page 93)
- ☐ Questions for Sample Passage IV (page 94)
- ☐ Questions for Sample Passage V (page 95)
- ☐ Questions for Sample Passage VI (page 96)
- ☐ Questions for Sample Passage VII (page 97)
- ☐ **Test 1**: Passage I
- ☐ **Test 1**: Passage II
- ☐ **Test 1**: Passage III
- ☐ **Test 1**: Passage IV
- ☐ KlassTutoring bonus passage (see page 611)

EXTRA PRACTICE

You are encouraged to take an additional real ACT:

1. Ask your school counselor for the most recent "Preparing for the ACT" booklet. This free booklet contains one practice ACT (with 4 passages).
2. Go to: http://www.actstudent.org/testprep/index.html and download a PDF file of the above booklet, which can be viewed in and printed from Adobe Reader or any other free PDF reader.

READ

Perhaps the best way to raise your Reading Test scores is to read as much as possible.
Read material that is hard to understand at first. Choose a variety of reading materials, such as
novels, newspapers, and even poetry. While the previous techniques are certainly helpful and
will begin to compensate for less-than-great reading skills, no instruction can completely take
the place of a solid reading background. For this reason, *reading* is a significant part of
improving your Reading scores.

2. QUESTIONS FOR ACT PASSAGES

This section includes questions for the 7 practice passages in *The Real ACT Prep Guide*, 3rd Edition (starting on page 91). For convenience, we recommend you tear out the passages from the ACT book (or, if you prefer, tear out the questions from this tutorial) so you can place the passages next to the questions while you answer them. Answers and solutions start on page 622.

QUESTIONS FOR PASSAGE I

1. Based on the passage, which of the following statements best describes the overall attitudes of the narrator and Eugene at the time of their first meeting?
   - A. Eugene is interested but embarrassed, while the narrator is direct but nervous.
   - B. Eugene is disinterested and snobbish, while the narrator is eager and optimistic.
   - C. Eugene is attentive but shy, while the narrator is confident but reserved.
   - D. Eugene is talkative and direct, while the narrator is brave but apprehensive.

2. According to the passage, when the narrator spoke to Eugene for the first time:
   - F. Eugene had been unaware of the narrator.
   - G. Eugene and the narrator had spent time together on the fire escape.
   - H. Eugene had noticed but never spoken to the narrator.
   - J. Eugene was not interested in having a relationship with the narrator.

3. According to the passage, the narrator describes the "old couple" as:
   - A. often arguing and distant with each other.
   - B. typical examples of the immigrant experience in America.
   - C. possible models for her own relationship with Eugene.
   - D. eager to have the narrator become part of their family.

4. Which of the following questions can NOT be answered using information given in the passage?
   - F. Has the narrator ever walked around in her neighbor's (the old couple's/Eugene's) house?
   - G. What activity do the narrator and Eugene both enjoy?
   - H. What makes the old couple's house different from the other houses on the block?
   - J. Other than teaching, what careers is the narrator interested in pursuing?

5. The narrator compares her father's desire to move to a new house to:
   - A. a romantic attraction.
   - B. a fairy tale.
   - C. an impossible dream.
   - D. a career-oriented desire.

6. Which of the following statements about Eugene's father is best supported by the passage?
   - F. He is largely absent from the rest of the family.
   - G. He does not live at the house but visits on weekends.
   - H. He is focused on his career in America but is eager to return to his homeland.
   - J. He feels mutual hostility toward Eugene and Eugene's mother.

7. The main function of the last two paragraphs (lines 67-87) is to:
   - A. provide background information about the narrator's family in order to highlight the narrator's own unique and changing perspective.
   - B. give information about the narrator's family in order to contrast the narrator's and Eugene's parents.
   - C. describe the narrator's family in order to show how the narrator's friendship with Eugene affected the other members of her family.
   - D. portray the desires and dreams of the narrator's parents in order to show how her parents' hopes changed over time.

8. The narrator's words, "I began to think of the present more than of the future" (lines 80-81), most likely mean that her friendship with Eugene led her to:
   - F. shift some of her focus away from education and career plans and to the developing relationship.
   - G. consider her own career interests rather than those her parents thought most important.
   - H. delay her plans of visiting Puerto Rico in favor of continuing to prepare for college and her future career.
   - J. want to spend time with him rather than helping her parents prepare to visit Puerto Rico.

Continued →

9. According to the passage, which of the following does NOT describe one of the narrator's feelings about her "secret" (line 64) viewings of Eugene?

A. The narrator is concerned that Eugene will discover her secret arrangement.

B. The narrator feels dishonest about not telling Eugene that she can see him.

C. The narrator is happier now that she knows what books Eugene reads.

D. The narrator is happy to share time with Eugene, even if he is not aware that she can see him.

10. It can reasonably be inferred that the phrase "'to run into him'" (line 46) is in quotes because:

F. the narrator felt lucky to meet Eugene in a part of the school away from her locker.

G. the words are not to be taken literally.

H. the narrator's intention all along was to meet Eugene.

J. the narrator had not expected to meet Eugene.

Solutions are found on page 622.

QUESTIONS FOR PASSAGE II

1. The main conflict in the passage could best be expressed as:
   A. the tension between Frank and Mama.
   B. the bitterness expressed between the narrator and her mother.
   C. the narrator's desire to break her ties with her direct family.
   D. the narrator's struggle to connect her past to her future.

2. Which of the following best describes the narrator's decision to leave home?
   F. It was made suddenly, after the narrator lost her indis.
   G. It was a decision that all members of the reservation eventually have to make.
   H. It began as just a thought and eventually led to physical journey.
   J. It was one the narrator made as a small child.

3. It can reasonably be inferred from the passage that Frank "darts a glance" at the narrator, and "then stares at his feet and frowns" (lines 77-78) because he:
   A. desires an intimate connection with the narrator's mother.
   B. is concerned that the narrator's positive connection with her mother will induce her to return home.
   C. is anxious to go back downstairs to close up the store.
   D. nostalgically recollects his own life as a boy on the reservation.

4. It can reasonably be inferred from the passage that Mama's voice "suddenly hurts" (lines 73-74) because the narrator:
   F. is angry that her mother wants her to return home.
   G. is unhappy because of her own physical appearance.
   H. is torn between her yearning to be a young girl again and her desire to live on her own.
   J. wants to return home but must obey her mother's wishes that she stay with Frank.

5. Which of the following is NOT listed in the passage as a characteristic of the narrator's indis?
   A. It symbolizes the narrator's desire to leave her reservation land.
   B. It contains colorful beads.
   C. It is intended to serve the narrator for her entire life.
   D. It is partially made from the narrator's birth chord.

6. As described in the passage, which of the following might best reflect any positive feelings the narrator has about leaving home:
   F. Mama's voice
   G. Grandma Roy's singing drum
   H. Frank's bakery shop
   J. The narrator's posters and photos

7. The narrator implies that because she lost her indis, she:
   A. clung more desperately to her family.
   B. eventually left her home.
   C. had to remember every detail of it.
   D. developed animosity toward her family.

8. It can reasonably be inferred from the passage that the narrator's mother and Frank:
   F. are old friends who have grown distant over time.
   G. disagree over the narrator's choice of where to live.
   H. desire each other but cannot live together.
   J. were once married and now jointly care for the narrator.

9. According to the passage, when the narrator's mother finds out that the narrator is leaving home, the mother:
   A. anxiously begins making plans for the narrator.
   B. reluctantly gives in to the narrator's decision to make her own choices.
   C. discourages the narrator to leave by requiring her to live with her grandmas.
   D. happily accepts the narrator's decision because the mother can now reconnect with Frank.

Continued →

10. Which of the following best describes the way the eleventh paragraph (lines 73-76) functions in the passage?
    F. It suggests a change in attitude of the narrator's mother regarding the narrator's desire to leave home.
    G. It foreshadows the narrator's eventual return to the reservation.
    H. It reveals the narrator's lack of interest in returning to her home.
    J. It reveals the narrator's ambivalence about leaving home.

Solutions are found on page 624.

QUESTIONS FOR PASSAGE III

1. According to the passage, ER changed from a pacifist and isolationist to one who:
   A. supported military strength and multi-national cooperation.
   B. encouraged war to fight fascism and communism in Europe.
   C. encouraged military build up to help the United States avoid foreign entanglements.
   D. fought openly with socialists and radicals.

2. According to the passage, as First Lady, ER was the first to accomplish all of the following EXCEPT:
   F. the reversals of assumptions about race.
   G. the development of a New Deal for women.
   H. the organization of a parallel administration.
   J. the editing and co-publishing of a newspaper for women.

3. According to the last paragraph, the author would likely agree with which of the following statements about ER's vision and ideals?
   A. ER only tackled political issues when she knew that she could successfully influence their outcomes.
   B. ER worked with agitators and activists to bring about justice and peace.
   C. ER took on presidential responsibilities so she could determine White House policy.
   D. ER considered herself a role model who could single-handedly bring about change.

4. To improve the social issues discussed in lines 46-47, ER would likely encourage:
   F. direct and focused action.
   G. the development of complex theories that went to the root causes of the problems.
   H. violent and unequivocal revolution.
   J. government repeal of existing laws.

5. According to the passage, ER believed that people should:
   A. work separately to bring about progressive policies in the government.
   B. form a relationship with the government as modeled by the White House.
   C. work together to demand government change.
   D. communicate with the government through radio broadcasts and other formal channels.

6. As portrayed in the passage, ER could best be described as:
   F. outwardly controversial but quietly compromising.
   G. politically courageous and socially involved.
   H. morally sound and deeply conservative.
   J. fearlessly driven but reservedly moderate.

7. Which of the following best describes FDR's feelings toward ER?
   A. He fought bitterly with her and rejected her ideas outright.
   B. He admired her as a wife and supported her as a writer.
   C. He admired her influence but disagreed with many of her policies.
   D. He depended on her integrity and supported her social movements.

8. According to the passage, the women who "battled on the margins of national politics since the 1880s" (lines 34-35) moved to the forefront of the nation's agenda after FDR's election because:
   F. FDR's social policies closely mirrored those of the women.
   G. the women could now organize groups that would agitate and inspire community action.
   H. issues such as public health, universal education, and community centers were ones that concerned the women for decades.
   J. ER had direct influence on White House policy and action.

Continued →

9. It can reasonably be inferred from the passage that the New Deal was a response to:
   A. the Depression.
   B. the triumph of fascism and communism in Europe and Asia.
   C. international isolation.
   D. racism.

10. The statement "no other First Lady has actually rushed for her pen to jab her husband's public decisions" (lines 79-80) most nearly means:
   F. ER used her writing to openly reject FDR's policies.
   G. ER used her writing to illuminate the positive points of FDR's public decisions.
   H. ER hoped to privately change FDR's ideas and convictions.
   J. ER wrote down her disagreements with FDR because she could not confront him directly.

Solutions are found on page 626.

QUESTIONS FOR PASSAGE IV

1. The main purpose of the passage could best be described as an effort to:
   A. describe the accelerated pace of learning for infants between four and seven months of life.
   B. raise questions about whether organisms deprived of important life experiences develop normal perceptual abilities.
   C. explain the interaction between nature and experience in the development of perceptual abilities.
   D. discount the importance of research concerned with physical skills and attributes in expanding our knowledge of the growth of the mind.

2. The parenthetical comment in lines 48-49 most likely serves to:
   F. explain a difficult term.
   G. question a controversial opinion.
   H. describe the reasoning behind a claim.
   J. add distinct but unrelated information.

3. According to the passage, synaptic connections are formed:
   A. primarily from automatic chemical instructions.
   B. rapidly throughout a human's lifetime.
   C. from a combination of chemical and experiential influence.
   D. entirely from the stimulus of experience.

4. According to some brain researchers, sensory development from experience has an "offsetting advantage" (lines 80-81) because:
   F. most organisms fail to have the proper experiences at the right time.
   G. perceptual abilities that arise from experience are more specific than those that could arise from natural physical changes in the brain.
   H. brain structures of organisms develop similarly regardless of the organisms' sensory experiences.
   J. most essential experiences occur after the physical structure of the brain has developed.

5. The main function of the fourth paragraph (lines 21-35) in relation to the fifth paragraph (lines 36-53) is to:
   A. explain the method for determining what infants see.
   B. introduce psychologist Robert Fantz as a major contributor to the nature versus nurture debate.
   C. confirm that by two months old, an infant can distinguish major differences in the appearance of objects.
   D. display the development of an infants' vision.

6. It is reasonable to infer from the passage that one-month-old babies can perform which of the following actions?
   F. Notice the difference between a pale yellow rattle and a bright yellow rattle.
   G. Recognize siblings as individuals.
   H. Look from their mother's face to their father's face and back to their mother again.
   J. Follow a slow-moving butterfly from a mobile hanging above their bed.

7. According to the passage, research on the development of perceptual abilities has been focused on early infancy because:
   A. perceptual abilities evolve more quickly for infants than for children or adults.
   B. infants lack physical skills and physical attributes.
   C. scientists assume that infants learn more quickly than children or adults.
   D. perceptual abilities of infants are easier to measure than those of children or adults.

8. The author uses the term "nurture" (line 7) to refer to:
   F. the development of perceptual abilities due to the physical growth of the brain.
   G. the development of perceptual abilities that are learned.
   H. a controversial topic that is largely discounted by today's scientists.
   J. physical skills and physical attributes of infants.

Continued →

9. The main function of the sixth paragraph (lines 54-60) in relation to the passage as a whole is most likely to:
   A. shift the discussion from nurture to nature as the driving force behind the perceptual development of infants.
   B. shift the discussion from the outward nature of perceptive ability in infants to the inward physical development of the brain.
   C. conclude the author's discussion of perceptive development in infants so he can focus on older children.
   D. provide evidence to support the findings in the fifth paragraph.

10. Based on the passage, which of the following statements best supports the claim that experience plays an important role in perceptual development?
   F. By the time a human is twelve, the brain has an estimated hundred trillion synapses.
   G. Mice reared in the dark develop fewer dendritic spines than mice reared in the light.
   H. A human's brain triples in size during the first two years of life.
   J. Some of the synaptic connections are made automatically by chemical guidance.

Solutions are found on page 628.

QUESTIONS FOR PASSAGE V

1. It can reasonably be inferred from the passage that the author's grandparents "might smile at the laziness of Tom Sawyer" (lines 12-13) because:
   A. they know that there is a time for play and a time for work.
   B. later in life, Tom Sawyer helped his family and neighbors and did much that was useful.
   C. they recognize that young people are not yet expected to understand the importance of hard work.
   D. they consider Tom Sawyer a humorous case of someone who taught by word and example.

2. As it is used in line 34, the word *humanity* most nearly means:
   F. obligation to care for one's elders.
   G. right to maximize one's productivity.
   H. desire to accomplish as much as possible in the shortest time.
   J. obligation to live simply, honestly, and conservingly.

3. In the last paragraph, the author emphasizes the distinction between which of the following terms?
   A. acquiring and inquiring
   B. inquiring and learning
   C. money and salvation
   D. tomorrow and a hundred years from tomorrow

4. All of the following details compromise the ideas discussed in lines 39-42 EXCEPT:
   F. glittering goodies in stores.
   G. luxurious imagery on television.
   H. the universe as a gift.
   J. winning the lottery.

5. The author suggests that many people do not like their jobs because:
   A. new machines make their work more complicated.
   B. there are many layers of supervision.
   C. their jobs are rigidly controlled.
   D. they are forced to use tools that could easily be replaced with machines.

6. According to the passage, which of the following describes the essential difference between a bread-maker and a bread pan?
   F. The bread pan was used by previous generations while the bread maker is used today.
   G. The bread-maker came on the market in recent years while the bread pan has been around for much longer.
   H. The bread-maker is more complicated than a bread pan.
   J. The bread-maker diminishes the human role in performing a task while the bread pan extends the human role.

7. The "false dichotomy" described in line 66 could best be described as a:
   A. failure to recognize the differences in two distinct ideas.
   B. use of two different ideas to answer a question that can only be answered with one of them.
   C. dissociation of two ideas that are actually closely related.
   D. combination of two different ideas to explain a concept.

8. The phrase "work ethic" (line 25) is described in the passage as:
   F. something the author understood conceptually before he heard the term used.
   G. a phrase whose meaning is more powerful now than ever before.
   H. something bosses, politicians, managers, and officials might strive for.
   J. a phrase that is no longer used in a world where profit is more important than hard work.

9. The author indicates that the most important reason for appreciating hard work is that it:
   A. gives the worker pleasure in exercising a skill.
   B. benefits the world.
   C. allows people to practice their faith.
   D. usually leads to financial security.

Continued →

10. In the third paragraph (lines 24-42), the author mentions but does NOT agree with the point of view of which of the following?
   F. Those who believe that work is a kind of celebration.
   G. The manager who wants his employees to be more profitable.
   H. Those who believe that "the creation is a sacred gift."
   J. One who fixes rather than replaces what is broken.

Solutions are found on page 630.

QUESTIONS FOR PASSAGE VI

1. Which of the following best describes the overall structure of the passage?
   A. An analysis of the specific features of lightning is followed by a more general discussion of the types of lightning.
   B. A discussion of the specific features of lightning is discussed first globally and then locally.
   C. A discussion of the characteristics of lightning is followed by an analysis of the effects of lightning.
   D. A discussion of the damaging effects of lightning is followed by a discussion of the causes of lightning.

2. According to the passage, which of the following would likely NOT be considered a secondary effect of lightning?
   F. A tree weakened by lightning falls during a wind storm.
   G. The branches of a large tree are damaged after being struck by lightning.
   H. A tree in a scorch area succumbs to insect infestation.
   J. A tree is killed in a forest fire started by a direct lightning strike.

3. The *process of "electrocution"* in line 62 could best be described as:
   A. limited to trees.
   B. infestation by insects.
   C. a secondary effect of lightning.
   D. a product of physiological trauma caused by lightning.

4. As it is described in the first paragraph, which of the following is NOT true about thunderstorms?
   F. They produce 100 cloud-to-ground discharges per second.
   G. They occur at a rate of over 8 million per day.
   H. They produce lightning bolts with various levels of energy.
   J. Nearly 75% of the lightning energy they produce is lost to heat.

5. One of the most important points of the third paragraph (lines 41-61) is that:
   A. researchers in Arizona and Arkansas measure tree mortality by volume.
   B. rates of tree mortality only capture one aspect of lightning-related damage.
   C. pine trees are more susceptible to lightning-related damage than other kinds of trees.
   D. pine tree forests experience fewer lightning strikes than other types of habitats.

6. According to the passage, electrical potential discharges as lightning when:
   F. two charged regions move very close together.
   G. the change in electrical potential across a distance is great.
   H. an electrical potential is suddenly reversed.
   J. the earth is properly charged.

7. It can reasonably be inferred from the third paragraph (lines 41-61) that if lightning did not fix atmospheric nitrogen, then:
   A. nitrogen would be left in the atmosphere due to lack of rain fall.
   B. less nitrogen would fall to the earth surface.
   C. less electrical current would be conducted by the air.
   D. fewer lightning bolts would strike the earth.

8. According to the passage, which of the following best describes the differences between the two types of lightning discharge patterns?
   F. One has greater currents and longer durations.
   G. One has lesser currents but longer durations.
   H. One has longer duration and higher voltage.
   J. One has intense current that is more likely to start fires.

Continued →

9. It can reasonably be inferred from the passage that tropical landscapes:
   A. are susceptible to lightning fires that produce mosaic patterns.
   B. have climates that prevent lightning fires.
   C. display mosaic patterns even when lightning is not present.
   D. are the only type of terrestrial environment that is not susceptible to lightning fires.

10. The author states that thunderstorms are an "electromagnetic as well as a thermodynamic necessity" (lines 15-16) because:
   F. they replenish the earth's electrical charge.
   G. they produce more than 8 million discharges per day.
   H. most of the energy associated with thunderstorms is lost to heat.
   J. most pine forests would die off without the beneficial effects of lightning strikes.

Solutions are found on page 631.

QUESTIONS FOR PASSAGE VII

1. One of the main points of the passage is that:
   A. without water from small comets entering the atmosphere, the earth would have dried up long ago.
   B. sometimes important scientific discoveries come from research into seemingly unrelated subjects.
   C. the scientific community has a tendency to reject radical new scientific ideas.
   D. the small-comet theory is now embraced by most physicists.

2. According to the passage, which of the following best describes Frank's reaction to the "new evidence" in line 17?
   F. He was not surprised that his theory was finally embraced.
   G. He was happy to put a difficult ordeal behind him.
   H. He openly celebrated the success of his theory.
   J. He immediately went to work on a new, equally-radical theory.

3. It can reasonably be inferred from the passage that Frank had trouble publishing his small-comet theory in physics journals because:
   A. Frank's colleagues typically viewed him as an unstable scientist.
   B. the small-comet theory challenged a commonly-held idea of human evolution.
   C. Frank had not looked into other possible reasons for the patterns of dark spots on the satellite images.
   D. scientists had always believed that the earth's water supply was in some way replenished from space.

4. In order to emphasize the significance of the amount of water vapor produced by the comets, the author states that one must consider the:
   F. number of comets bombarding the earth per hour.
   G. size of each comet.
   H. amount of time that the comets have been bombarding the earth.
   J. amount of water carried by each comet.

5. According to the passage, the idea of the small-comet theory originated during research originally intended to study:
   A. the electrical nature of sunspots.
   B. the source of water entering the earth's atmosphere.
   C. transmission static in the Dynamics Explorer 1 satellite.
   D. dark specks in satellite images.

6. The words of Richard Zare in the fifth paragraph (lines 34-40) best describe a scientist as one who:
   F. must strictly adhere to the theories of past scientists.
   G. cannot possibly accomplish research because of dueling notions of scientific discovery.
   H. must steadfastly believe in his or her own theories in order to challenge resistance from scientific peers.
   J. searches for but must diligently question new ideas.

7. According to the passage, Frank and Sigwarth suggested that the dark spots on the satellite images were water because:
   A. this was the most logical explanation for the existence of the earth's oceans.
   B. they could find no other likely explanation for the spots.
   C. their study of sunspots suggested a high likelihood of water in comets.
   D. the chemical make up of the spots suggested the existence of water.

8. According to the passage, Frank's research on small comets has:
   F. proven that small, water-bearing comets enter the earth's atmosphere with regularity.
   G. encouraged scientists to study the small-comet theory.
   H. discouraged future scientists from tackling controversial subjects.
   J. proven that the earth's oceans are a direct result of water-bearing comets entering the earth's atmosphere.

Continued →

9. According to the tenth paragraph (lines 79-86), scientists began to accept Frank's ideas in part because:

   A. the small-comet theory explained the existence of water in our atmosphere better than any other theory.

   B. new images allowed the small comets to be seen more clearly.

   C. the images of small comets were taken from space rather than from land.

   D. new views of small comets unequivocally confirmed the small-comet theory.

10. The author most likely regards the choice of the word *ducked* in line 5 as:

   F. an amusing play on words.

   G. a scholarly word in keeping with the formal mood of the passage.

   H. a word that reflects the technical language of scientific papers.

   J. a word to be taken literally.

Solutions are found on page 633.

KLASSTUTORING BONUS PASSAGE

By now, you should be comfortable marking up the passage as you read. The mark ups for the following passage (next page) are shown below. You might not indicate all of them (and you may mark some words not shown below), but if you notice significant deviation, go back and review the Passage section (Chapter II).

TONE WORDS

You might have darkly underlined the following tone words: "abuse," "abusers", etc. (lines 18, 24, 106), "misleading" and "misled" (lines 20, 27, 79, 88), "unfortunate" (line 25), "bad" (line 26), "dreaded" (line 28), "inappropriate" (lines 44, 53), "dupe" (line 95), "terror" (lines 103), "half truths and lies" (line 106-107), and "daze" (line 108).

CONTRAST SIGNALS

There are just a few of these. The word "but" is found in lines 88, 98, 99.

IDENTIFIERS

As stated earlier, Natural Science passages and Social Science passages tend to have more identifiers than Prose Fiction and Humanities passages:

¶
1: Lang, drunken man, lamppost, sports fan and politician, business owner and real estate agent
2: bad samples, self-selected survey, Midwest restaurant chain
3: inappropriate samples, Lombard, research students, coal miners, firemen, and test pilots
4: small samples, student suspensions, Children's Defense Fund
5: Loaded questions, Washington, Glines Canyon Dam, Elwha River, farmer
6: partial pictures, car company
7: precise number dupe, car, laser beams, micrometer, accuracy
8: Huff, *How to Lie with Statistics*

MAIN IDEAS

You may have noticed some important sentences (not surprisingly in the first and last paragraphs) that reflect the passage's main idea: (1) "The number of ways [the abuse of statistics] can occur is an unfortunate statistic in itself" (last sentence of Paragraph 1) and (2) "We must understand the practices of statistical abusers to protect ourselves from their half truths and lies" (lines 104-107).

NATURAL SCIENCE: This passage is adapted from *Slippery Statistics* by Kire Salks (© 2007 Pull Press).

There was this statistician who, when driving his car, would always accelerate quickly before coming to an intersection, drive straight through it as quickly as he could, and then slow down again on the other side. He explained the practice to an understandably unnerved passenger: "Well, statistically speaking, one is far more likely to have an accident in an intersection, so I make sure to spend as little time there as possible." When I tell this joke to my first-semester students, it is always met with the usual laughter, perhaps as much directed at my willingness to poke fun at my profession as the joke itself. In the words of historian Andrew Lang, some people use statistics "as a drunken man uses lampposts—for support rather than illumination." The abuse of statistics, that is, the presentation of data in ways that are intentionally or innocently misleading, is employed in equal measure by the sports fan and the politician, the business owner and the real estate agent. The number of ways these abuses can occur is an unfortunate statistic in itself.

The use of bad samples is a significant source of misleading data. The culprit is typically the dreaded self-selected survey, one in which the respondent decides whether to be included or not. The problem with these surveys is that most of us choose to ignore them. Typically, only people with strong opinions choose to respond, so the responses are generally not representative of the population as a whole. A survey at a Midwest restaurant chain found that over 70% of the respondents were dissatisfied with their service. When upper management considers that less than 1% of the restaurant chain's customers actually chose to take the survey, it may not be particularly alarmed. Very likely, most of the customers were content.

Another example includes inappropriate samples. Swiss physician H.C. Lombard once looked at the life expectancy of several professions, including research students, by analyzing the ages at the time of death. He found that research students, with an average of only 20.7 years, had the earliest age of death of all professions, lower than coal miners, firemen, or test pilots. How could this be? The problem is that the sample is inappropriate. Most research students happen to be relatively young, including the few who happened to die during the study. Being a research student is not more dangerous than being a policeman—it just means that *if* you die, you'll probably be young.

Careless statisticians often employ small samples. In a study designed to emphasize the prevalence of student suspensions in one small city, the Children's Defense Fund found that among students who were suspended at least once, 67% of them were suspended at least three times. What the study failed to mention was that only three students were part of the sample.

Loaded questions can influence survey participants. For example, in a recent survey of eligible voters in Washington, 47% of the respondents felt that the "Glines Canyon Dam should be removed." When the words "to restore stocks of Pacific Salmon" were added to the survey, the number jumped to 86%. Needless to say, the farmer who would like the dam to stay put might prefer the first survey question.

Consumers are often misled by partial pictures. A car company once famously quipped: "ninety percent of the cars we've ever made are still on the road." Understandably, consumers might believe that this company's cars could last a lifetime. What the consumers were not told was that nearly 90% of the company's cars were sold in the past three years. The claim was correct, technically, but clearly misleading. All we really know is that most of the cars sold in the *past three years* are still on the road. Not much of a claim at all.

A colleague of mine once exclaimed that "92.6 percent of all statistics are made up." This is an example of the precise number dupe. If I told you that my car is 14.53125 feet long, you might believe that I studiously measured it using laser beams and a micrometer. But I could just as well have used a household ruler. My number is precise, but not necessarily accurate.

In Darrell Huff's classic book *How to Lie with Statistics*, he states: "There is terror in numbers." This terror can translate to a blind acceptance of the so-called experts. We must understand the practices of statistical abusers to protect ourselves from their half truths and lies. Huff sought to break through "the daze that follows the collision of statistics with the human mind." Only through our edification and skepticism can we find real statistical truth.

1. The main purpose of the passage can best be described as an effort to:
   A. warn students about the perils of trying to lie with statistics.
   B. humorously discuss the challenges of learning statistics in school.
   C. list the negative consequences of statistical manipulation.
   D. explain a number of ways that statistics can be misleading.

2. The author questions the accuracy of which of the following claims?
   F. At a Midwest restaurant chain, 70% of the respondents to a survey were dissatisfied with their service.
   G. The average age of death for research students is 20.7 years.
   H. In a small region in America, 67% of the students who were suspended once were suspended at least three times.
   J. The length of the author's car is 14.53125 feet.

3. It can reasonably be inferred from the passage that the author lists the professions of "coal miners, firemen, and test pilots" (lines 51-52) because these professions:
   A. are typically considered dangerous.
   B. have lower rates of death than research students.
   C. are professions that most students will find difficult to prepare for.
   D. are professions that rarely employ young people.

4. According to the author, which of the following will lead to finding "real statistical truth" (lines 110-111)?
   F. blind acceptance and authority
   G. study and belief
   H. education and suspicion
   J. learning and gullibility

5. As it is used in line 81, the word *quipped* most nearly means:
   A. deceptively announced
   B. strongly disagreed
   C. oddly advertised
   D. dishonestly joked

6. In the context of the passage, the author refers to self-selected surveys as "dreaded" (line 28) because:
   F. these surveys are often time-consuming to complete.
   G. a small percentage of people choose to ignore the surveys.
   H. most of the participants have strong feelings about their service.
   J. the results often show that customers are dissatisfied.

7. According to the passage, the author states that those who mislead others with statistical data:
   A. are usually well intentioned statisticians.
   B. are more concerned with illuminating the truth than supporting their causes.
   C. may not always know what they are doing.
   D. always intend to dupe the public.

8. Which of the following statements best reflects the main point, as expressed in the passage, of Andrew Lang?
   F. A drunken man is more concerned about support than illumination.
   G. Statistics are often used to illuminate the truth.
   H. Many people use statistics to further their own causes.
   J. Statisticians who abuse statistics are more concerned about their professions than about illuminating the truth.

Continued →

9. The passage discusses all of the following types of statistical abuses EXCEPT:
    A. loaded questions.
    B. enlarged sample sizes.
    C. partial pictures.
    D. the precise number dupe.

10. Which of the following would the author most likely agree intentionally misled the public using statistics?
    F. the sports fan and the politician
    G. the Midwest restaurant chain and H.C. Lombard
    H. The Children's Defense Fund and the car company
    J. the author's colleague and Darrell Huff

Solutions are found on page 635.

V

ACT PRACTICE TESTS: CONTEXT REFERENCE

As we discussed in Chapter II, the most important technique for Reading questions is the use of *context*. The answers must be clearly stated or supported by *the text*. If you miss a Reading question, the first step is to find the part of the passage that contains the information or evidence that will lead you to the correct answer. The following pages display the pertinent line numbers for each question. When necessary, clarifying words or phrases are sometimes included.

For EXCEPT/NOT questions, we'll often list the line numbers for the *incorrect* answer choices.

Of course, finding the context is only part of it. You have to *understand* the context, not to mention the language in the questions and the answer choices. If you still have trouble with a question even after you have found the appropriate context in the passage, check the solutions in the ACT book.

Note that on the following pages we generally only refer to context related to *correct* answers. Of course, you may often choose to use context to *eliminate* answer choices. This is encouraged, especially when you are not sure of the correct answer. Again, the solutions in the ACT book may be helpful.

1. ACT PRACTICE TEST 1

Passage I:

1. Lines 9-10, 70

2. 23-24: "strong-willed," "dragon-lady nails"; 93-99: "caring"

3. A: 68-71; B: 85 (False); C: 65-68; D. 72

4. 5-6

5. 97: "But you don't have to…"

6. 19-20

7. 56-58

8. 1, 70

9. 75

10. 87

Passage II:

11. 58-61

12. 34-41

13. 62-65

14. 78-79

15. 8-10

16. 18: "limited"

17. 48: "personal gossip"

18. 52-53

19. 56-61

20. 59-60

Passage III:

21. 32-33, 39-44, 45-47, 88-89

22. 3-5, 26-28: Note: Calcutta is *not* in England.

23. 44-47, also 88-89

24. 66: "immigration and accommodation"

25. 6: "never seen"; 27: "unglimpsed"

26. 28-32: Try Process of Elimination.

27. 53-54: "inner life"

28. 54-55

29. 10-13: Note camouflage: "sovereign" = "independent"

30. 76-79: "history"

Passage IV:

31. 13-15

32. 59-61

33. 61-63

34. 79-80, 81-83

35. 29-30

36. 31-33

37. 45-46

38. 47-48

39. 75: Note identifiers in the answer choices.

40. 81: "People"

2. ACT PRACTICE TEST 2

Passage I:

1. 53-61

2. 29-38, 69-74

3. 36-37

4. F: 14-15, G: 18, J: 71-73

5. Evidence for "respect" in D: "skills" (31), "slick" (35), "grace" (36). Evidence for "nostalgia" in D: "vast" and "prosperous" (20), "voluptuous" (24).

6. 29-31

7. 65-68

8. 62-63

9. 33-38: "mating dance"

10. 56-59

Passage II:

11. 75-87

12. 70-74, 83-87

13. 4: "justification of revolution"; 3: "statement of human rights"

14. 21-28: Try Process of Elimination, and watch out for Eye Catchers.

15. 32-35

16. 67-74

17. 19-20

18. 29-32

19. 45-48

20. 75-79: "imminent American defeat"

Passage III:

21. 8-10, 56-67, 82-91, etc.

22. 46: "visionary"; 70: "eloquently"; 78: "provocative insight"

23. 8-10

24. 28-29

25. 62-67

26. 18-24

27. 40-42

28. 43-49

29. 46: "visionary"; 49: "fantastic"; 51: "insight and added perspective"

30. In G, see lines 79-80 for "familiarity" and line 78 for "change."

Passage IV:

31. 5-9: "admiring lectures"

32. 42-44, 47

33. 5

34. 10-14

35. 15-16: Note camouflage: "illumination" = "source of light"

36. 14, 16: Try Process of Elimination.

37. 11-12: Try Process of Elimination.

38. 37-38

39. 41-42

40. 66-68: one "camera," one "lens"

3. ACT PRACTICE TEST 3

Passage I:

1. A: 18-19, 55-57; B: 28-35, 36-38; D: 37-38, 14-15

2. F: 1 ("fourteenth summer"), 91-92; G: "connects": 12, 46-47; "limits": 32-35, 59; H: 61-69, 75-77

3. 65-68, 74-77

4. 63-64

5. 1-6

6. 7-8: "center of his own universe"

7. 12-13: Note camouflage: "presence of love" = "warm emotions"

8. 25-27

9. 29-30

10. 58-60

Passage II:

11. A: 29; C: 32; D: 41-44

12. 1-2: "To keep our system from collapsing on itself"

13. 14-16, etc.

14. 3, 5-8

15. 31-34

16. 58-61

17. 65-71

18. 47-48

19. 48-51

20. 56-57

Passage III:

21. 27-29

22. 85-87

23. 1-5

24. 36-38, 43-44

25. 60-61

26. 80-87: "'It could be so different'"

27. 30-33: "the 'final' version," as opposed to "a radical departure" (line 36)

28. 52-55

29. 61-64

30. 77-80: "at its best"

Passage IV:

31. See Paragraph 3: "Some have proposed..." "Others have hypothesized..." etc., and Paragraph 6: "...some researches are questioning..."

32. 3-8, 14

33. 3-16

34. 8-10

35. 19-23: The "apocalypse" (23) refers to "something that stripped nearly all of its atmosphere" (19-20).

36. 34-38

37. 40-41

38. 71-81

39. 32

40. 59-62

4. ACT PRACTICE TEST 4

Passage I:

1. 26-28

2. 62: Use Process of Elimination if necessary.

3. 10-12

4. 35-37

5. 26-28

6. 35-37

7. 75-77: Note camouflage: "bedrock" = "foundation"

8. 40-41

9. 65-67

10. 78-79

Passage II:

11. Last paragraph, especially 90-91

12. 87-88: "The goal should be…"

13. In D, "solutions": 84-87, 90-91; "a problem": 6-10

14. G: 17-18; H: 73-74; J: last paragraph

15. A: 43-44; C: 46-47; D: 45-46

16. 74-79

17. 38-39

18. 51: "in the middle"

19. 64-66

20. 67: Note camouflage: "mixed uses" = "various types of development"

Passage III:

21. 25-27, 61-63, 67-70

22. 7-9: "…a sniff as he turned away…"

23. 38-51

24. 58-61

25. 57-58: "…this book led to the particulars, and that's what I wanted…"

26. 81-91: Use Process of Elimination if necessary.

27. 25

28. 57: "particulars"; 63: "individuals"

29. 25-26, 52-54

30. 70-71

Passage IV:

31. **12-14**, 34-40, 52-56, 74-75, 84-87

32. 69-73

33. 48-49

34. 46-48

35. 77-80

36. 66-73

37. 15-17

38. 31-32

39. 58-61

40. G: 84-85; H: 86; J: 85

5. ACT PRACTICE TEST 5

Passage I:

1. 17-20, 89-90

2. 17-18, 35, 70, etc.

3. A: 14-15; C: 31-33; D: 15-20, 34-36

4. F: 75-76, 80-81; G: 81, J; 25-26

5. 35-36

6. 75-78

7. 2-3 "…roars…"

8. F: 6; H: 6; J: 6

9. 30

10. 89-95: The language suggests she was literally "consumed."

Passage II:

11. 1-4

12. F: 30-32; G: 29-30; H: 25-28

13. 38-39: "…now he is not so sure."

14. 43-49

15. 63-67

16. 68-69: Note that the tone is negative toward the models: "'…false sense of integrity and purity…'" (72-73).

17. 84-86

18. 5-6: "virtually"

19. 19-22

20. 84-86

Passage III:

21. A: 31, 61, etc.; B: 8-15, etc.; D: 25-30, 69-73, 84-87

22. To place the events in time, see the following lines: F: 3; G: 44; H: 47; J: 51. (We can assume that the "music traveled to New York" *after* the Asian Underground.)

23. 55-57

24. 66-68: Consider tone.

25. 77-81: He's not an "expert on it."

26. 10-12

27. 21-24

28. 33-34, 36: "make a difference in the world"

29. 41-43

30. 61-63

Passage IV:

31. 32-33

32. 1-2: "thrilled," "in a tizzy"

33. 83-90

34. 26, 73

35. 26-27

36. 28-32: "miniscule"

37. 36-41: "fantastic," "never seen anything like these," "remarkable"

38. 44-46

39. 50-52: Careful! It is the man's *girlfriend*, not the man, who loves marine biology. The man, presumably, loves the *girlfriend*.

40. 76-82

VI
READING ANSWERS

The following are answers to all lesson, practice, and homework problems.

PASSAGE I SOLUTIONS

1.   Eugene "smiled" (line 55), was "blushing deeply" (lines 56-57), is "shy" (line 57), and "liked me" (line 57). He seems interested in the narrator but is embarrassed. The narrator "blurted out" (line 54), so she is direct, but her "stomach was doing somersaults" (line 52), so she is also nervous. The answer is **A**. Remember that you can eliminate double answers one part at a time.
Eliminate:
B.   False—Eugene is not "disinterested" and "snobbish." Notice the contrast signal "But" (line 53).
C.   False—the narrator is not "reserved;" she "blurted out" her greeting and did most of the talking.
D.   False—Eugene is not talkative; the narrator says: "I did most of the talking that day. He nodded and smiled a lot" (lines 57-58).

2.   The narrator states that in the library, "he first seemed to notice me, but did not speak" (lines 49-50). Soon after, the narrator "decided to approach him directly" (line 51). The answer is **H**.
Eliminate:
F.   False—see above.
G.   False—when the narrator says: "I kept him company on my fire escape" (line 42), she means that she *watched* him from the fire escape. They were not physically together. Remember, the words in prose passages are often not to be taken literally (see Prose Fiction in the Reading Introduction).
J.   This is not mentioned, and it's probably false: "he smiled" (line 55).

3.   The challenge to this problem is finding the information in the passage. Most of the discussion of the "old couple" is in Paragraph 1. However, the correct answer is not found in this paragraph. Look at the last paragraph: "...I wanted to sit at the kitchen table with Eugene like two adults, like the old man and his wife had done..." (lines 84-86). This supports **C**.
Eliminate:
A.   The word "often" makes this answer choice too strong. The author mentions that they argue but does not mention how often. Do not assume things.
B.   There is no mention that the old man and woman are immigrants.
D.   False—the narrator "had become part of their family, without their knowing it" (lines 11-12). The old couple was not familiar with the narrator, and would thus not be eager to have her become part of the family.

4.   Eliminate answer choices by finding answers in the passage to each question. Only **J** cannot be eliminated.
Eliminate:
F.   The narrator has never been into the house: "I wanted to see the other rooms where the old people had lived, and where the boy spent his time" (lines 82-84).
G.   Books are mentioned in lines 65-66 and 87.
H.   See lines 4-6.

5. The father's desire to move to a new house is discussed in lines 69-70. The next line compares the parents' "dreams" (we can infer that these dreams include the new house) to "fairy tales." The best answer (a direct hit), is **B**.
Eliminate:
A. False—the narrator, not her parents, may have a "romantic attraction."
C. Eye Catcher: "dream." The use of the word "impossible" makes this answer too strong. The father's "good job" (line 68) certainly makes a move to Passaic, if we interpret the dream as that, seem possible.
D. False—the parents' dreams are more focused on *place* ("Passaic," "Puerto Rico") than career.

6. The narrator says: "...the father was gone before I got up in the morning and was never there at dinner time" (lines 33-35). Even on weekends, when the narrator did see the father, he (like his wife) was "hidden behind a section of the newspaper" (line 37). The best answer is **F**.
Eliminate:
G. False—the father was gone before the narrator got up in the morning, implying the father *does* live in the house.
H. There is no mention that the father is eager to return to his homeland. Don't confuse the father with the residents of El Building.
J. The father may be distant, but "hostility" is too strong and is not supported by the passage.

7. This is a broad question. Let's get a feel for what these paragraphs are about. Notice the contrast signal "But" at the beginning of the last paragraph. What follows is probably important: "But after meeting Eugene I began to think of the present more than of the future." The narrator's aspirations have changed. Only **A** touches on this change. The fact that her perspective is "unique" is supported by the sentence beginning: "As for me..." (line 78).
Eliminate:
B. False—the parents of Eugene and the narrator are never contrasted.
C. There is no mention of how the narrator affects her parents in any way.
D. False—it's the narrator's, not her parents', hopes that have changed.

8. This is a potential direct hit. First, the narrator says: "I was going to go to college and become a teacher" (lines 78-79). Then she says: "But after meeting Eugene I began to think of the present more than of the future" (lines 80-81). She then talks about her maturing relationship with Eugene. **F** is the perfect answer. Hopefully you don't have to eliminate answer choices on this one.

9. Review Paragraph 5. Only **A** is not supported by the passage.
Eliminate:
B. "I felt dishonest..." (line 63)
C. "I liked my secret sharing... especially now that I knew what he was reading." (lines 63-65)
D. "I liked my secret sharing..." (lines 63-64)

10. The narrator says that she met Eugene after "much maneuvering" (line 46). She did not really "run into him," which implies a chance or random meeting—her meeting was *intentional*. The quotes humorously make light of the narrator's choice of words. The best answer is **H**. Watch out for G, which is true, but doesn't answer the question.
Eliminate:
F. False—the narrator planned to meet Eugene; the meeting wasn't "lucky."
G. True enough—the words "to run into him" are not to be taken literally—however, the words are not in quotes for this reason. The better answer is H.
J. False—see F.

PASSAGE II SOLUTIONS

1. This is similar to a main idea question. To determine the "main conflict" you must have a general understanding of the whole passage. While the passage clearly discusses a conflict of place (home versus away), as best exemplified by the sentence: "In spite of how I want to curl up in my city corner, I picture everything back home" (lines 82-83), the conflict is also rooted in past versus future: Past: "I've wondered about the meaning of my spirit name" (line 22); "I want to... be a small child again" (lines 74-75). Future: "I began to wander from home" (lines 11-12); "my city corner" (lines 82-83). The best answer is **D**.
Eliminate:
A. There may be tension between Frank and Mama, but this is not the main conflict of the passage, a passage that primarily reflects the experiences of the narrator.
B. The narrator's mother is not happy about the narrator's leaving home, but "bitterness" is too strong a word.
C. False—the narrator wants to leave home but does not want to "break her ties" with her family, as evidenced by the phone call to Mama soon after arriving at Frank's shop.

2. After the narrator lost her indis, she "thought nothing of it, at first and for many years, but slowly over time the absence... it will tell. I began to wander from home, first in my thoughts, then my feet took after..." (lines 10-13). The answer is **H**.
Eliminate:
F. False
G. There is no mention in the passage that all members have to make this decision. In fact, the implication is that members are supposed to be buried on the reservation land (line 8).
J. False—the narrator leaves "at the age of eighteen" (line 13).

3. Frank "can't drag himself away from the magnetic field" of the narrator's mother's voice (lines 68-69). We know the mother loves frank "too much" (line 36). It seems Frank has similar feelings toward the mother. The best answer is **A**. Note that this answer explains much of Frank's behavior "he lingers" (line 67) and he is "folding and refolding" the towel (lines 71-72).
Eliminate:
B. There is no mention that Frank is concerned about the narrator returning home.
C. Watch out for eye catchers. Closing up the store is discussed in lines 66 but is off topic here.
D. There is no mention of Frank's time as a boy on the reservation.

4. Go back to the passage and read carefully. The narrator states: "I want to curl next to her and be a small girl again" (lines 74-75). The best answer is **H**.
Eliminate:
F. False—the narrator is not "angry." Nor does she feel negatively about a return home, as is apparent in the quote above.
G. This may be true, in a sense—"My body feels too big..." (lines 75-76)—but the main point is the narrator's wish to reconnect with her past and her home. G is not the best answer choice.
J. False—the mother wants the narrator to "come back" (line 81), not stay with Frank.

5. Eliminate answer choices that are mentioned in the passage (remember, you're looking for the one that is NOT mentioned). Only **A** is not mentioned. As discussed in lines 1-8, the indis symbolizes a life-long connection to the reservation, not a desire to leave it.
Eliminate:
B. True—lines 3-5
C. True—lines 7-8
D. True—line 1

6.   Notice the positive tone words that the narrator uses when she arrives at Frank's shop: "cheerful" (line 40), "good bakery smells" (lines 40-41), "lemony light" (line 42), "He greets me with gentle pleasure" (line 46). These words suggest that the narrator is (at least temporarily) happy to be at this new place, away from the reservation. The answer is **H**. All of the other answer choices have to do with the narrator's longing to return home.

7.   If you got Question 2 correct, you'll probably get this one, too. Review lines 11-19, which describe how, after the narrator lost her indis, she eventually decided to leave her home. The answer is **B**.
Eliminate:
A.   False—she decides to leave her mother, so she definitely didn't cling to her family.
C.   There is no mention that she had to remember every detail of the indis after losing it.
D.   False—she decides to leave her mother, but the word "animosity" is too strong and is disproved by the information in the last two paragraphs.

8.   Review the explanation to number 3. Both Frank and the narrator's mother have feelings for each other. Frank is described as "the man [the narrator's mother] loves too much to live with" (lines 36-37). The best answer is **H**.
Eliminate:
F.   Frank and the mother are probably old friends, but it is unlikely they have grown "distant" (too strong a word). Not only do they have strong feelings for each other, but also Frank is the first non-family member the mother contacts regarding the narrator's leaving home. This does not suggest a distant relationship.
G.   Frank's opinion about where the narrator should live is not discussed.
J.   There is no mention that Frank and the mother were once married.

9.   The passage states: "In a panic, once she knew I was setting out, not staying home, Mama tried to call up my grandmas and ask if I could live at their apartment in the city" (lines 27-30). The best answer is **A**.
Eliminate:
B.   False—while Mama *does* allow the narrator to leave, she apparently does not want the narrator to make all of her own choices.
C.   False—Mama let's the narrator leave *and* would like her to live with her grandmas.
D.   False—Frank was not Mama's first choice, so this answer choice is unlikely. In addition, evidence suggests that Mama was not happy about the narrator leaving home; read the last paragraph.

10. Review the explanations to Questions 4 and 6. This eleventh paragraph shifts the focus from the narrator's contentment in the bakery shop to her longing to revisit her past ("I want to...be a small girl again"). The best answer is **J**.
Eliminate:
F.   False—the mother continues to want the narrator to return home. There is no change in the mother's attitude.
G.   False—in the time covered by the passage, the narrator does not return to the reservation.
H.   False—the narrator is clearly interested in returning home: "I want to curl next to her..." (line 74).

PASSAGE III SOLUTIONS

1. The passage states: "She departed, however, from pacifist and isolationist positions and encouraged military preparedness, collective security, and ever-widening alliances" (lines 71-74). The answer is **A**.
Eliminate:
B. There is no mention that she encouraged "war," just "military preparedness" and "security." The words "fascism and communism" are good examples of eye catchers (line 52).
C. False—"ever-widening alliances" signals a shift from isolationism and toward involvement with foreign countries.
D. False—ER "was not afraid of socialism—and she courted radicals" (lines 50-51). Once again, don't get fooled by eye catchers.

2. Read the fourth paragraph ("As First Lady, [ER] did things that had never been done before…"). Eliminate true answer choices. The correct answer is **J**. There is no question that ER edited and co-published a newspaper for women (see lines 16-18), but there is no mention that she was the *first* to do this.

3. The last paragraph emphasizes two aspects of ER: (1) she was not an "isolated individualist" (line 86)—in other words, she worked with others—and (2) "she refused to withdraw from controversy" (lines 89-90) or "defeat" (line 92). You may have more luck eliminating answer choices for this question. The best answer is **B**.
Eliminate:
A. False—ER tackled issues "[a]gainst great odds" (line 88) and was not always successful in her endeavors.
C. This is not mentioned; being active politically, questioning the president, and even running a "parallel administration" (line 23) are not the same as taking on presidential responsibilities.
D. False—the key word here is "single-handedly." ER did *not* work alone but sought "alliances" and "community" (line 87).

4. ER "demanded action" (line 49). The answer is **F**.
Eliminate:
G. False—"She was uninterested in complex theories" (lines 48-49).
H. False—"She feared violent revolution" (lines 49-50).
J. This answer choice is not mentioned.

5. "Her abiding conviction, however, was that nothing good would happen to promote the people's interest unless the people themselves organized to demand government responses. A people's movement required active citizen participation…" (lines 55-59). The best answer is **C**.
Eliminate:
A. False—ER stresses "active citizen participation."
B. There is no mention of a relationship "modeled by the White House."
D. There is no mention of "radio broadcasts…" in the part of the passage dealing with the relationship between people and government (Paragraph 8). Don't be fooled by eye catchers.

6. This is a broad question and one that requires a good general idea of how ER is portrayed. Remember, eliminate double answer one part at a time. If you don't see the right answer, a process of elimination will help. ER was politically courageous: "Against great odds, and under terrific pressure, she refused to withdraw from controversy" (lines 88-90). ER's social involvement is discussed throughout the passage, especially in Paragraphs 4-7. The best answer is **G**.
Eliminate:
F. There is no mention that ER is "quietly compromising."
H. False—ER is not "deeply conservative." She actively, and radically, seeks change.
J. False—ER is not "reservedly moderate." See H.

7. Make sure to read the question carefully. We are looking for FDR's feelings toward ER (not the other way around). "FDR admired his wife, appreciated her strengths, and depended on her integrity" (lines 6-8). We also know that FDR and his wife "often disagreed" (line 10) on many issues. The best answer is **C**.
Eliminate:
A. This answer is too strong. There is no mention that they "fought bitterly."
B. There is no mention that FDR supported ER's writing; in fact, it's quite likely that he did *not*, considering that ER "wrote to disagree with her husband" (line 78).
D. This is a classic eye catcher. Yes, he "depended on her integrity" (line 8), but he very likely disagreed with many of her social movements.

8. After FDR was elected, "Now [the women's] views were brought directly into the White House" (lines 39-40). Only **J** ties into this direct connection to the White House, thanks to ER.
Eliminate:
F. False—FDR's policies were often different from ER's and the women's.
G. False—the passage implies that the women had been organizing groups for action long before FDR was elected.
H. This is true but does not answer the question. Remember to read questions carefully.

9. Hopefully, your identifiers are helping you find information quickly. "New Deal" is a good identifier. "Between 1933 and 1938, while the Depression raged and the New Deal unfolded…" (lines 63-64). The best answer, the only one with any support from the passage, is **A**. If the Depression is raging, it's not a stretch to assume that the New Deal is a response to this. All of the other answers are eye catchers (see lines 52-53 for B, lines 66-67 for C, and line 66 for D).

10. ER "wrote to disagree with her husband" (line 78). The best answer is **F**.
Eliminate:
G. False
H. False—her writings were not private; they were "published" (line 75).
J. There is no mention that ER could not confront FDR directly.

PASSAGE IV SOLUTIONS

1. You may have found this passage difficult. On difficult passages, focus on the specific detail questions first. Since this is a main idea question, it's not a bad one to skip (at least at first) until you've answered the other questions. The main purpose of the passage is glimpsed in the first paragraph where the author asks: "How much [of the development of perceptual abilities] is due to nature and how much to nurture . . . ?" (lines 6-8). The author states that a combination of nurture and nature play a role in development: "Some of the synaptic connections are made automatically by chemical guidance [nature], but others are made by the stimulus of experience [nurture/learning]" (lines 64-67). And finally, the author confirms the role of experience (nurture): "...we catch the first glimpse of how mind is constructed out of matter by experience" (lines 88-89). The best answer is **C**.
Eliminate:
A. This is not the main focus of the entire passage. On main idea questions, remember to avoid answer choices that are true but don't reflect the main idea of the whole passage.
B. Similar to A, this is not the main focus of the passage.
D. The author suggests this answer choice is true in Paragraph 1 ("Much maturation research is concerned with physical skills and physical attributes, and adds little to our knowledge of the growth of the mind"), but again this answer choice does not reflect the purpose of the passage.

2. The author claims that four-month olds "begin to recognize the meaning of what they see" (lines 47-48). The parenthetical comment, which immediately follows the statement, explains the reasoning behind the claim: since infants "look longer" at a normal face than one with scrambled features, infants must (according to the author) "recognize the meaning" of what they see. The best answer is **H**.
Eliminate:
F. False—there is no "difficult term."
G. False—the parenthetical comment does not question anything.
J. False—the information is certainly related.

3. Hopefully your identifiers ("synaptic connections") helped you zero in on the right part of the passage. The passage states: "Some of the synaptic connections are made automatically by chemical guidance, but others are made by the stimulus of experience" (lines 64-67). This is also ties into the main point of the passage. The best answer is **C**.
Eliminate:
A. There is no mention that the connections are formed "primarily" from chemical guidance, or "instructions."
B. False—the passage implies that synaptic connections occur rapidly during infancy and young age, "during the period of rapid dendrite growth" (lines 67-68).
D. False—see the quoted sentence in the explanation above.

4. The passage states that essential experiences "fine-tune the brain structure so as to provide far more specific perceptual powers than could result from genetic control of synapse formations" (lines 82-85). The key word is "specific." The answer is **G**. Note the camouflage: "genetic control of synapse formation" is replaced with "natural physical changes in the brain." Both refer to changes in the brain *not* based on experience.
Eliminate:
F. False—"the essential experiences are almost always available at the right time" (lines 81-82).
H. Evidence in the passage suggests this answer choice is false (see Question 3 and Paragraph 7), but in any case, it does not answer the question.
J. False—the author stresses that experiences help determine the physical structure of the brain. Again, review Question 3 and Paragraph 7.

5. The fourth paragraph answers the question asked in the third paragraph: "Since we cannot ask [infants] what they see, how can we find out?" Once we understand the *method* for determining what infants see, we are prepared for a specific look at *what* infants see, in the fifth paragraph. The answer is **A**.
Eliminate:
B. Watch out for the eye catcher. There is no mention that Robert Fantz is a major contributor to the nature versus nurture debate.
C. This is not the main point of the paragraph.
D. False—the fifth, not the fourth, paragraph discusses this development.

6. Even though the answer choices are not specifically mentioned in the passage, use the context in the passage diligently to find your answer. One-month-old babies "begin to track slowly moving objects" (line 40). The best answer is **J**.
Eliminate:
F. The "levels of brightness" (line 43) are perceived by the second month.
G. Recognizing "family members" (line 45) occurs by three months.
H. See G.

7. Hopefully your identifiers led you to the second paragraph: "The work has been focused on early infancy, when perceptual abilities evolve rapidly" (lines 9-10). This is a potential direct hit. The answer is **A**.
Eliminate:
B. This is not mentioned in the passage.
C. False—scientists assume that new abilities in infants arise "not from learning but from maturation of the optic nervous structures…" (lines 13-14).
D. False—the effects are *not* easier to measure for infants, as discussed in Paragraphs 3 and 4.

8. The author elaborates on the term *nurture* in the first paragraph, explaining that "in developmental terms," it is synonymous with "learning" (lines 7-8). The answer is **G**.
Eliminate:
F. False—*nurture* has to do with *experience* and *learning*, not specifically the natural physical growth of the brain.
H. False—if you understand the similarities of *nurture*, *learning*, and *experience*, then the last sentence of the passage makes clear that nurture is *not* discounted by today's scientists.
J. This is an eye catcher (first sentence). It does not refer specifically to the term *nurture*.

9. The fifth paragraph discussed the apparent perceptual developments of infants. The sixth paragraph begins to discuss how the brain physically changes to produce these developmental changes (see the first sentence of Paragraph 6, lines 54-56). The best answer is **B**.
Eliminate:
A. False—there is no evidence to suggest a shift from nurture to nature.
C. False—the author continues to discuss infants (line 57) and does not focus on older children specifically (even though one is *mentioned* in line 61).
D. False—no evidence is given to support the findings in the fifth paragraph, which are taken to be true.

10. Which answer choice suggests that experience affects perceptual development? In **G**, the *experiences* of mice living in the dark affects their ability to see: "they never attain normal vision" (line 73).
Eliminate:
F. These synapses may be (and likely are) partially a result of experiences, but G is certainly the stronger answer choice.
H. This is a physical change, one not clearly based on experience.
J. This answer choice refers to synaptic connections that are *not* created by experience (note the "but" in line 66).

PASSAGE V SOLUTIONS

1.   This is a potential direct hit. The passage states that the grandparents "would remind you that Tom was a child" (lines 14-15). In other words, his laziness could be explained by his age. The best answer is **C**.
Eliminate:
A.   This answer choice is not mentioned in the passage.
B.   Again, not mentioned in the passage.
D.   False—the grandparents, not Tom Sawyer, "taught by word and example" (lines 19-20). Watch out for eye catchers.

2.   The passage describes fulfilling ones "humanity" as the belief that "creation is a sacred gift, and that by working we express our gratitude and celebrate our powers" (lines 37-39). The passage goes on to say: "To honor that gift, we should live simply, honestly, conservingly…" (lines 39-40). The answer is **J**. Notice that correct answers are not always camouflaged, as we see here—the answer uses words exactly as they are used in the passage.
Eliminate:
F.   Probably true, but not mentioned in the passage.
G.   False—the author states "As I understand it, a regard for the… virtue of work has nothing to do with productivity…" (lines 31-33)
H.   False—see G.

3.   The first sentence gives it away: "…the purpose of life is not to acquire but to *in*quire" (lines 81-82). The answer is **A**, a direct hit. Watch out for eye catchers. All of the other answer choices contain words from the passage.

4.   This is a straightforward detail question if you can find the information. The ideas in lines 39-42 are referred to in the next paragraph ("Those values are under assault…"). Only **H** is not listed as something that threatens ("compromises") these values.
Eliminate:
F.   line 45
G.   lines 45-46
J.   line 49

5.   The information that answers this question is in Paragraph 1: "When the freedom and craft have been squeezed out of work it becomes toil…" (lines 3-5). The key word is "freedom." The best answer is **C**.
Eliminate:
A.   This answer choice is not mentioned in the passage.
B.   False—read the passage carefully. The passage implies that the many "layers of supervision" (lines 7-8) are a *result* of the drudgery of a job, not the *reason* behind the drudgery. In other words, the work becomes "toil," people hate their jobs, and thus, layers of supervision are needed to keep people working ("keep the wheels spinning" (line 8)).
D.   False—the passage implies that workers are forced to use *machines*, not tools, and this is why the work becomes "toil."

6.   The passage clearly describes the difference: "…a tool extends human skills, a machine replaces them" (lines 2-3). The best answer, which is camouflaged, is **J**.
Eliminate:
F.   This answer choice is not mentioned in the passage.
G.   Again, not mentioned in the passage.
H.   Once again, not mentioned in the passage.

7. The passage states "work is how we act out that faith" (line 68). The ideas of work and faith are closely related. This idea is also supported by the quote beginning on line 73. The "false dichotomy" is that these two closely related ideas are considered separate. The answer is **C**.
Eliminate:
A. False—the failure is recognizing a difference where there isn't one.
B. False—the question is answered with both ideas, not one of them.
D. False—this is not the "false dichotomy." It actually comes close to describing the views of the author—"salvation" is gained by both faith and work, not one or the other; the author would obviously not consider his own views "false."

8. The passage states: "I knew this cluster of values by experience long before I heard it referred to as the work ethic" (lines 24-25). The answer is **F**.
Eliminate:
G. False—the phrase has "lost its edge" (line 26).
H. False—the phrase is something bosses, etc. *use* (verbally); it is not likely something that these people strive for. The idea of work ethic is *positive*. The author views the bosses, etc. *negatively*. Always remember the author's *tone*.
J. False—the author thinks the phrase is used too often (lines 25-27).

9. Perhaps you boxed the contrast signal, "But," in line 56. What follows is something the author feels is very important (more important than what came before). Some of the answer choices are reasons for appreciating hard work, but **C** is the most important—*faith* is the "chief reason" (line 57).

10. It is important to have a sense of the author's tone for this question. The bosses and politicians are described as "cynical," a negative word. The author disagrees with their opinions. The answer is **G**. All of the other answer choices include people who share the author's beliefs.

PASSAGE VI SOLUTIONS

1. Read the first sentences of each of the first three paragraphs: "Lightning affects electrical equilibrium on the earth" (lines 1-2), "Two types of discharge patterns are commonly identified..." (lines 25-26), and "The consequences of lightning are complex" (line 41). The passage first discusses lightning in technical terms and then discusses the effects ("consequences") of lightning. The answer is **C**.
Eliminate:
A. False—the second part of the passage discusses the *effects*, not the "types," of lightning,
B. False—the "specific features" of lightning are discussed in the first part of the passage. The second part of the passage discusses local ("Arizona," "Arkansas") *effects*, not "features," of lightning.
D. False—the "damaging effects" of lightning are discussed in the second half of the passage; the "causes" are discussed in the first part.

2. The passage defines "direct injury" as "primarily the mechanical destruction of branches and bole" (lines 56-57). Examples given of secondary effects include: "insects, wind, and mistletoe" (lines 58-59) as well as "fire" (line 61). The answer is **G**.

3. If you read lines 69-70, you'll see that this is a potential direct hit. Keep in mind that answers may be camouflaged, but often the answers use the same words as the passage, as we see in **D**.
Eliminate:
A. False—"Nor is the process limited to trees" (lines 64-65)
B. False—lines 66-70 suggests that "electrocution" sites are no longer attributed to infestation by insects (although they were in the past).
C. False—*insect infestation* and *diseases* may be "secondary effect[s]" (line 68), but the passage contrasts these conditions with "electrocution" (the implication is, thus, that "electrocution" is a primary effect).

4. Eliminate answers that are true. This can be a tricky one. If you read carefully, you'll see that thunderstorms produce 8 million *discharges* per day. The thunderstorms themselves do not occur 8 million times per day. The answer is **G**.
Eliminate:
F. line 19
H. lines 21-22
J. lines 23-24

5. This is similar to a main idea question ("most important points"). Because it is broad, as main idea questions usually are, you'll probably have to look at the answer choices before trying to answer the question. If necessary, eliminate incorrect answer choices. First notice that the mortality rates given in lines 51-55 describe only "direct injury" (line 56) (not secondary effects). The passage states: "the other major causes of mortality—insects, wind, and mistletoe—are likely secondary effects..." (lines 58-59). This information should lead you to **B**.
Eliminate:
A. This is not an important point of the paragraph. On main idea questions, remember to watch out for true answer choices that don't reflect main points of the passage.
C. This is not mentioned in the passage.
D. Again, this is not mentioned in the passage.

6. Hopefully, your identifiers ("electrical potential") led you to the first paragraph: "electricity moves back according to the gradient [change in potential with distance]. During a thunderstorm, the gradient becomes very steep..." (lines 4-6). The answer, **G**, is camouflaged ("gradient" = "change in electrical potential" and "steep" = "great").
Eliminate:
F. This is not mentioned in the passage. The only thing the passage states is that oppositely-charged regions must have a steep gradient.
H. There is no mention of a *reversal* of electrical potential in the passage.
J. False—the passage suggests that one possible cause of lightning is the fact that the earth is *not* properly charged (lines 10-16).

7. The passage states: "Lightning helps to fix atmospheric nitrogen into a form that rain can bring to earth" (lines 45-46). Answer choice **B** is a direct hit.
Eliminate:
A. There is no mention of a lack of rain fall. Make sure to read this answer choice carefully—the first part is correct.
C. This is not mentioned in the passage.
D. This, too, is not mentioned.

8.   The words "discharge patterns" hopefully lead you to the second paragraph. Take note of the characteristics of the two types: (1) cold stroke—"intense current but of short duration" (line 27), "has mechanical or explosive effects" (line 30), and (2) hot stroke—"lesser currents of longer duration" (lines 28-29), "more apt to start fires (line 31). From this information, you can see that **G** describes the hot stroke. All of the other answer choices include an element from each of the two types of discharge patterns.

9.   The passage states: "Except in tropical rain forests and on ice-mantled land masses, lightning fire has occurred . . ." (lines72-73). In other words, lightning fires do not occur in tropical landscapes (probably because of climate). The answer is **B**.
Eliminate:
A.   False—see above.
C.   False—the mosaic patterns are caused by "lightning bombardment" (line 76).
D.   False—"ice-mantled land masses" are also not susceptible to lightning fires (lines 72-73).

10.   Go back to the passage. The word "thus" (line 15) suggests that the answer to the question will be found before the given quote. Lines 10-15 explain that lightning replenishes the earth's electrical charge. The answer is **F**.
Eliminate:
F.   This is true but doesn't answer the question.
H.   Again, a true answer choice, but it doesn't answer the question.
J.   Off topic for this part of the passage.

PASSAGE VII SOLUTIONS

1.   Certainly, an important part of the passage is Louis Frank and his work on the small-comet theory, but the author also discusses the general nature of scientific research. The Frank example is used to illustrate points made in the fourth and fifth paragraphs that "scientists are...loath to embrace radically new ideas..." (lines 32-33). The last sentence of the passage suggests the tenuousness of new scientific ideas: "Had [Frank] been a researcher of lesser standing, his theory probably would have died long ago." The best answer is **C**.
Eliminate:
A.   This is a minor and, more importantly, unproven point in the passage (lines 10, 59-66, 87-89)
B.   True, but not a main point in the passage.
D.   False—"it has not been proved" (line 87).

2.   The passage states: "Frank seemed relieved that part of a long ordeal was ending" (lines 20-21). The answer is **G**.
Eliminate:
F.   False—he was not "anticipating glory" (line 20).
H.   False—he was not "gloating" (line 20).
J.   This is not mentioned in the passage.

3.   A physics journal is discussed in line 71. In that paragraph, Frank's research is described as suggesting "a fundamentally different picture of human evolution... than is commonly presented by scientists" (lines 68-70). The answer is **B**.
Eliminate:
A.   This is an eye catcher (line 12). It is perhaps partially correct, but it is not the best answer choice.
C.   False—"Try as they did, the scientists couldn't find any plausible explanation..." (lines 53-54).
D.   False—the "intimate interaction between Earth and space" was "fundamentally different" (lines 67-68) from the common views of scientists.

4.   The author states: "That may not seem like much, but when talking about a planet billions of years old, it adds up" (lines 64-66). The answer is **H**. All of the other answer choices are eye catchers. Each one ties into the fact that an inch of water is added every 10,000 years, which "may not seem like much."

5.   Look at the sixth paragraph: "It was in the early 1980s when the small-comet theory started…" (lines 41-50). In this paragraph, Frank and Sigwarth were researching "the electrical phenomena that accompany sunspots" (lines 46-47). The answer is **A**. This should be a direct hit. Don't let the other answer choices fool you. None of them were subjects of Frank's and Sigwarth's *original* research.

6.   Zare says that if a scientist "believe[s] nothing" (line 38), he or she won't make progress. He also cautions against "believ[ing] too much" (line 39). This idea of *balance* in a scientist's work is reflected in answer choice **J**.
Eliminate:
F.   False—"You have to… question beliefs" (lines 36-37).
G.   Wrong tone—it is unlikely that the chairman of the National Science Board would portray a scientist as one who cannot "accomplish research."
H.   False—Zare warns against believing too much.

7.   Even though Frank and Sigwarth tried to find other explanations, the existence of water was "the most likely answer" (lines 57-58). The answer is **B**.
Eliminate:
A.   There is no mention in the passage that the existence of the earth's oceans influenced Frank's and Sigwarth's research into the dark spots. It was likely the other way around: the research into the dark spots (and the discovery of the likelihood of water) led Frank and Sigwarth to hypothesize possible sources of the oceans.
C.   False—as far as we know from the passage, the study of sunspots led to the *discovery* of the dark spots, but the research of these topics was otherwise unrelated.
D.   The chemical make up of the spots is not mentioned in the passage. In addition, if the chemical make up could be analyzed, there wouldn't be much of a controversy.

8.   This question is broad, so check out the answer choices before searching for context. The passage states: "…Frank's evidence opens the matter up to study" (lines 89-90). The answer is **G**.
Eliminate:
F.   False—"it has not been proved that they are comets" (lines 87-88). The word "comet" is important here. Don't forget, every word counts.
H.   This is not mentioned in the passage.
J.   False—"it has not been proved… that they have anything to do with the oceans" (lines 87-89).

9.   The images from new equipment designed by Frank and Sigwarth "caused even harsh critics of the small-comet theory to concede that some water-bearing objects appear to be entering Earth's atmosphere with regularity" (lines 84-86). The answer is **B**.
Eliminate:
A.   There is no mention of this answer choice.
C.   False—the original images were also taken from space (via satellite).
D.   False—as discussed in the last paragraph of the passage, the theory was not proved.

10. The author writes in a relatively casual manner throughout. Nowhere is this more apparent than in the first paragraph. The word "ducked" humorously reflects the use of the words "cosmic snowballs" (lines 3-5). Get it? The answer is **F**.
Eliminate:
G. False—"ducked" is not a scholarly word.
H. The passage is not particularly technical, especially when compared to other Natural Science passages. In any case, the word "ducked" is not a technical word.
J. False—the word is *not* to be taken literally. One assumes that Frank did not physically duck to avoid the controversy.

KLASSTUTORING BONUS PASSAGE SOLUTIONS

1. Remember to identify main ideas as you read the passage. You may have marked two places. In the first paragraph: "The number of ways these abuses can occur is an unfortunate statistic in itself." And in the last paragraph: "We must understand the practices of statistical abusers to protect ourselves from their half truths and lies." The main purpose of the passage is to display a "number of ways" that statistics are abused; this will hopefully allow us to "protect ourselves." The best answer is **D**.
Eliminate:
A. No mention: "perils of trying to lie with statistics"
B. No mention: "the challenges of learning statistics"
C. No mention: "negative consequences" (at least not in detail)

2. The second-to-last paragraph discusses "accuracy" (a possible identifier). The author claims: "My number is precise, but not necessarily accurate." The author is referring to the length of his car (14.53125 feet). The answer is **J**. The other answer choices are *misleading*, but not necessarily inaccurate (in fact, we can assume these numbers *are* accurate).

3. Don't forget to try to answer questions *before* looking at the answer choices. The author asks the rhetorical question: "How could this be?" (lines 52-53). It is, no doubt, surprising that the age of death is lower for research students than for these other professions. Why?—because these other professions are *dangerous*; we would expect them to have relatively young ages of death. The answer is **A**. Note that the passage never explicitly states that these other professions are dangerous. We had to make an *inference* from the information given in the passage.
Eliminate:
B. No mention: "rates of death"
C. No mention: "difficult to prepare for"
D. No mention: "rarely employ young people"

4. The passage states: "Only through our edification and skepticism can we find real statistical truth" (lines 109-111). The best answer is **H**— "edification" is camouflaged with "education" and "skepticism" is camouflaged with "suspicion." Note that you can eliminate answer choices using just the second words (which correspond to the easier word from the passage: "skepticism"):
F. No mention: "authority"
G. False: "belief"
J. False: "gullibility"

5. Define the word "quipped" using context (before looking at the answer choices). You might come up with a simple definition such as *stated* or *claimed*. Keep in mind that the car company's claims were "clearly misleading" (line 88)—consider this negative tone as you look at the answer choices. The words "advertised" (C) and "dishonestly" (D) may be tempting, but the best answer is **A**. The car company made a deceptive announcement.

6. The context immediately following the mention of "self-selected surveys" indicates that the surveys are *voluntary*. This may have something to do with why the author considers them "dreaded." The author says: "Typically, only people with strong opinions choose to respond, so the responses are generally not representative of the population as a whole" (lines 32-35). The best answer is **H**.
Eliminate:
F. No mention: "time-consuming"
G. False: a small percentage of people choose to *take*, not ignore, the survey.
J. Eye catcher: "dissatisfied." The fact that the respondents in the example were generally dissatisfied is probably not what the author felt was "dreaded" about the survey. The author would likely be just as concerned if the majority of the respondents were *satisfied* with their service.

7. The author states: "The abuse of statistics, that is, the presentation of data in ways that are intentionally or innocently misleading…" (lines 18-23). The key word is "innocently." Sometimes, abusers do not intend to mislead others—they are *innocent*, or don't know what they're doing. The answer is **C**. This question is probably easier to tackled using POE (see below).
Eliminate:
A. Tone: "well intentioned." The author would not feel *positively* about those who mislead others with statistics.
B. Tone: "illuminating the truth" is positive (see A).
D. Too strong: "always." The word "always" suggests that this answer choice is too strong. Unless you can find very clear evidence in the passage, you can probably eliminate it.

8. The quote uses a "drunken man" as a metaphor for a person who abuses statistics. Lang's point is that some people use statistics to *support* their cause rather than to *illuminate* the truth. The best answer is **H**. Watch out for eye catchers (see below).
Eliminate:
F. Eye catchers: "drunken man," "support," and "illumination"
G. Eye catcher: "illuminate"
J. Eye catchers: "Statisticians" (the subject of much of the passage up to this point), "abuse" (line 18), and "illuminating"

9. This question tests your identifiers. After eliminating answer choices, you should be left with **B** (the word "samples," discussed in Paragraphs 2-4, is a potential eye catcher).
Eliminate:
A. "Loaded questions" (line 69)
C. "partial pictures" (lines 79-80)
D. "the precise number dupe" (lines 94-95)

10. The passage suggests that the Children's Defense Fund wanted to "emphasize the widespread prevalence of student suspensions" (lines 61-63). The passage also suggests that the car company's claim was "misleading" (line 88) consumers, probably to sell more cars. The answer is **H**. You might try eliminating *parts* of the answer choices on this one (see below). Eliminate:

F. The key word in the question is "intentionally." Go back and review the answer to Question 7. The author states: "The abuse of statistics, that is, the presentation of data in ways that are intentionally or innocently misleading, is employed in equal measure by the sports fan and the politician…" (lines 18-23). The sports fan and the politician may not *intentionally* mislead the public.

G. Certainly "the Midwest restaurant chain" wasn't trying to mislead anyone when the results of its survey showed that people were dissatisfied.

J. Darrell Huff wrote a book about statistical lies—he "sought to break through 'the daze that follows the collision of statistics with the human mind'" (lines 107-109). He wasn't trying to mislead anyone.

PART 4

SCIENCE

I
SCIENCE INTRODUCTION

The Science section is divided into seven chapters:

   I.   Introduction

   II.   Data Representation

   III.   Research Summaries

   IV.   Conflicting Viewpoints

   V.   Timing

   VI.   Science Answers

TEST LAYOUT / TYPES OF PASSAGES

The questions on the Science Test are multiple choice, with four answer choices each. You will see three types of passages (Data Representation, Research Summaries, and Conflicting Viewpoints).

The Science Test will *likely** include:

- 2-3 Data Representation passages (12-16 total questions)
- 3 Research Summaries passages (18-22 total questions)
- 1 Conflicting Viewpoints passage (6-8 questions)

*In recent years, the ACT has been inconsistent with both the number passages of each type and the number of *questions* per passage. The ranges above reflect this uncertainty. The important thing is to know what kind of passage you're working on. We'll get into identifying passage types on the following pages. In the Timing chapter (Chapter V), we'll discuss how to get through the test in time.

DATA REPRESENTATION

These passages present information using tables, graphs, and other diagrams. The questions ask you to interpret the given information.

RESEARCH SUMMARIES

These passages present descriptions of scientific experiments or studies, along with tables and graphs showing the results. Some of the questions will ask you to evaluate the methods used in the experiment. Most of the questions ask you to interpret the results presented in tables and graphs, just like the Data Representation questions.

CONFLICTING VIEWPOINTS

These passages present usually two viewpoints (occasionally more) on a given topic. The questions test your understanding of the topic and each viewpoint. Some questions will ask you to compare the viewpoints. Conflicting Viewpoints passages tend to have more words and fewer tables and graphs.

WHAT IF I DON'T KNOW ANY SCIENCE!?

Don't worry. For the most part, this test does *not* directly test science. The information you need is found in the *passages*. The Science Test is similar to the Reading Test in that you must answer questions using *context*, that is, the information given in the passage. In other words, don't worry about what you know (or what you *don't* know) about science. Just worry about the information given on the test.

As stated, the Science and Reading Tests are similar in *approach*, but they are very different in *appearance*. If you've seen a Science Test, then you probably already know the following:

The Science Test looks hard! In fact, it looks *very* hard!

But here's the good news: **The Science Test is not as hard as it looks. Not even close.** Most of it (well over half) involves interpreting graphs and tables, something you may already be comfortable with from your math classes (in fact, it's something you'll cover in the Geometry chapter of this tutorial's Math section). Yes, you're going to see some scary-looking figures. Yes, you're going to read about topics you've never heard of. And yes, you're going to come across countless scientific words that you've never seen before. But don't let the unfamiliarity of the material scare you!

You don't actually need to be an expert chemist or physicist to do well on the Science Test. Look past the intimidating material, and you'll realize that the questions don't expect you to be a scientist with a college degree. The sooner you overcome your fear of the test and confidently and aggressively attack each passage, the sooner your score will rise. The following chapters will help you dig beneath the imposing façade of the Science Test.

FAMILIARITY LEADS TO SUCCESS

As you've no doubt seen by now, much of this tutorial is filled with *techniques* that can be directly applied to ACT problems. While the Science Test certainly requires the use of some techniques, probably the most important part of preparing for the Science Test is becoming *familiar* with the test. The goal of this part of the tutorial is to expose you to many different kinds of Science passages and questions and then to encourage you to tackle real passages in the ACT book and elsewhere. We have found that the more passages a student attempts, the more familiar—and, thus, the more *comfortable*—she becomes with the test. And familiarity and comfort lead to higher scores.

II

DATA REPRESENTATION

Most of this chapter discusses the analysis of graphs and other diagrams, which happens to be the most important part of the Science Test. Once you finish this chapter, you'll be ready to tackle well over half of the questions on the test.

1. *DATA REPRESENTATION INTRO*

As stated before, Data Representation passages present information using tables, graphs, and other diagrams. The questions ask you to interpret the given information.

> The following clues should help you identify Data Representation passages:
> - Each passage typically includes **5-6** questions (usually 5).
> - These passages are heavy on figures, especially tables and graphs.
> - Data Representation passages typically do NOT include multiple "studies," "experiments," "activities," etc.
> - Data Representation passages typically do NOT include in-depth descriptions of the actual experiments.

To get a feel for what these passages look like, go ahead and check out some of the Data Representation passages in the ACT book. You should notice the following:

1. A short introduction.

2. One or more graphs, tables, or other diagrams.

3. Usually, each figure has a brief explanation, found either in the introduction or in a separate paragraph preceding the figure.

SKIM THE PASSAGE

You will not have time to read and understand the entire passage. (We'll talk more about timing in Chapter V.) You should, however, expect to *skim* the passage before you start answering the questions. Do not read every word, and do not expect to understand much of the passage, at least not in any depth. You just want to get some idea (perhaps just a *vague* idea) of what the passage is about. Here's what to look for:

1. If the introduction is short, go ahead and read it. Otherwise, skim it.
   - Circle *identifiers*. As taught in the Reading section, identifiers are important words that you may have to locate later, when you start answering questions. These may be words that describe something *specific* in the passage, including the scientific words that the ACT puts in *italics*.
   - Underline *definitions*, when given, of any terms.
   - Circle any *numbers*. These numbers might show up in a question.

2. As you go through the passage, skim any other paragraphs. Look for, and circle, identifiers, underline any definitions, and circle any numbers.

3. The most important step is to get a general idea of how information is presented in the figures (graphs, tables, etc.). In particular, read the *labels* and *units* for each figure. **Most of your "skim time" should be spent looking at figures.**

4.   Look for labels (and units) that are *repeated* in separate figures. Circle these labels and, if not too inconvenient, connect them with a line.

We'll talk about how long to take skimming the passage in the Timing Chapter.

VARIABLES

Whether you're looking at a graph or a table, the labels (along the axes of a graph or in the column headings of a table) are *variables*. You must understand the two types of variables:

INDEPENDENT VARIABLES

An *independent variable* is a value that *determines* the value or values of other variables. The person conducting the experiment typically varies, or changes, independent variables to see what effect they have on another variable (the dependent variable). Scientists generally have some *control* over independent variables. Independent variables usually (but not always!) show up on the horizontal axis of a graph (the exception is when the independent variable is a *vertical* measurement, such as with height, altitude, or depth).

DEPENDENT VARIABLES

A dependent variable is a value that is *determined by* the value of another variable. The values of dependent variables are typically the *results* of an experiment.

Let's look at a simple example:

The figure below shows the average snow depth, in inches, at a popular California ski resort.

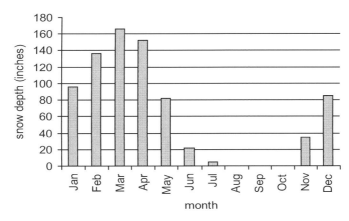

This type of graph is called a *bar graph*. Can you identify the variables? Which one is the independent invariable? Which one is the dependent variable? [Answer the questions before looking at the solution.]

The variables were *snow depth* and *months*. The *independent* variables were months. This was an arbitrary system of measure that we could control. For example, we could have used weeks, or years. The choice was ours. We based our measurements of snow depth off of this time duration, asking the question: How much snow fell in this month? The snow depth was our dependent variable. The snow depth values were the *results* of the data. We obviously didn't have control of these values (we can't control the weather).

Let's look at one more example, more typical of what you'll see on the ACT:

Under the right circumstances, light can be used to free electrons from the surface of a solid. This process is called *photoelectric emission*. A material that can exhibit this phenomenon is said to be *photoemissive*. The electrons that are ejected from the surface are called *photoelectrons*. The kinetic energy of photoelectrons depends on the frequency of the light and the kind of metal. Figure 1 shows how the kinetic energy varies for a range of light frequencies for potassium.

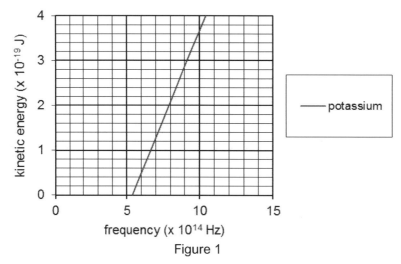

Figure 1

Yes, this may sound complicated. But remember: don't worry about understanding the information in the introduction. Just skim it. Circle some of the key words. The most important thing is to focus on the graph. This is called a *line graph*. Look at the labels and units. Can you identify the independent and dependent variables?

The frequency of the light *determines* the kinetic energy. For example, when we shine a light of 10×10^{14} Hz on potassium, the graph tells us that the kinetic energy of the ejected electrons is 3.6×10^{-19} J. Thus, the independent variable—the one we control—is *frequency* and the dependent variable is *kinetic energy*. Note: not surprisingly, the independent variable is the horizontal axis.

LINE GRAPHS

Since we're on the subject of line graphs, you should be familiar with *linear*, *exponential*, and *parabolic* graphs. We'll see more of these in the coming sections.

Linear graphs display a simple straight line:

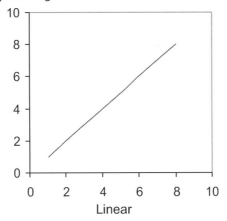

Linear

Exponential graphs display a curve that either gets steeper (as below) or shallower.

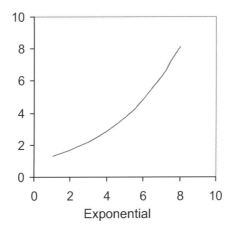

Exponential

Parabolic graphs may open up or down. Notice that these graphs have a minimum point (as below) or a maximum point (if the parabola opens down):

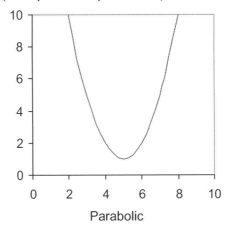

Parabolic

2. GRAPH BASICS

DIRECT QUESTIONS

Most questions on the Science Test directly test the material found in graphs or tables. We'll call these *direct questions*. Let's look at an example, using the previous graph:

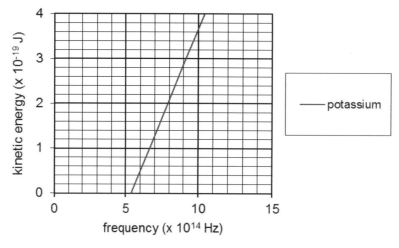

Figure 1

A NOTE TO SELF-STUDY STUDENTS ABOUT "EX" PROBLEMS

Example problems are indicated with an EX symbol:

You will see a boxed solution following each example. The solutions display various approaches to the questions found on the Science Test. Make sure you understand these solutions. You do *not* need to solve these example problems on your own (in other words, feel free to look ahead at the solutions for these example problems).

UNDERLINE IMPORTANT PARTS OF THE QUESTION

When you read a question on the Science Test, underline the following information:

- Any figures or tables mentioned in the question (such as "Figure 1" or "Table 2")
- Numbers and, more importantly, the <u>units</u> for these numbers
- Materials (in this example, there is only one—"potassium"—but you'll often see more)

(EX) According to Figure 1, the photoelectric kinetic energy for potassium in a light frequency of 10×10^{14} Hz is closest to:

A. 3.0×10^{-19} J.
B. 3.3×10^{-19} J.
C. 3.6×10^{-19} J.
D. 3.9×10^{-19} J.

Focus on the labels of the graph. Frequency is along the bottom (the *x*-axis). Kinetic energy is along the side (the *y*-axis). Look what's given in the question. The value 10×10^{14} Hz is a frequency. The corresponding kinetic energy, according to the given line, is 3.6×10^{-19} J, so the answer is **C**. (Note that the vertical grid lines are spaced 0.2×10^{-19} J apart.)

RESTATE THE QUESTION

Direct questions can get harder by the way they are worded. Sometimes you need to restate the question in a way that makes sense. Look at the following example:

(EX) A student wants to determine if a metal sample is potassium. If she uses a light frequency of 7×10^{14} Hz, what photoelectric kinetic energy should she expect to measure if the metal is potassium?

A. 1.2×10^{-19} J
B. 1.6×10^{-19} J
C. 2.0×10^{-19} J
D. 2.4×10^{-19} J

This question may sound harder than the previous one, but it's not that different. Restate the question to make it simpler: "What is the photoelectric kinetic energy for potassium in a light frequency of 7×10^{14} Hz?" Using the graph, you should get 1.2×10^{-19} J. The answer is **A**.

————

Try the following direct question. Answers to lesson and practice problems in this chapter start on pg. 770:

1. Based on the data in Figure 1, which of the following frequencies of light would potassium emit no photoelectric kinetic energy?

A. 5.4×10^{14} Hz
B. 6.6×10^{14} Hz
C. 7.8×10^{14} Hz
D. 9.0×10^{14} Hz

EXTRAPOLATION

To extrapolate is to estimate a value *outside* the observed or tabulated range. (Interpolation, where you will estimate values *between* known values, is more common on table problems; we will cover this technique later, when we cover tables.) Look at the following example. Note that a new material (titanium) has been introduced in Figure 2:

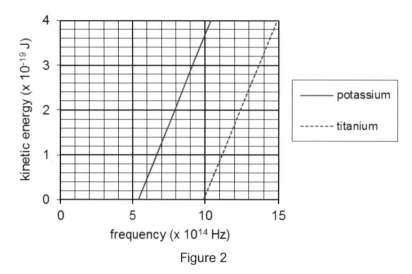

Figure 2

(EX) Based on the information in Figure 2, a sample of titanium exposed to a light with frequency 20×10^{14} Hz will exhibit photoelectric kinetic energy:

A. between 3.0×10^{-19} and 3.5×10^{-19} J.
B. between 3.5×10^{-19} and 4.0×10^{-19} J.
C. between 4.0×10^{-19} and 4.5×10^{-19} J.
D. over 4.5×10^{-19} J.

The highest frequency given for titanium is 15×10^{14} Hz. Just extend the line (make sure to look at "titanium") and estimate its kinetic energy for a frequency of 20×10^{14} Hz. The value will clearly be over 4.5×10^{-19} J (in fact, it appears to be around 8×10^{-19} J). The answer is **D**. See the following graph.

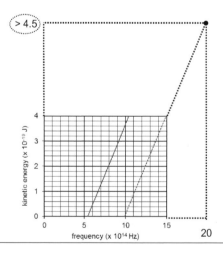

Try the following lesson problem. Notice that Figure 3 below now shows *three* different metals:

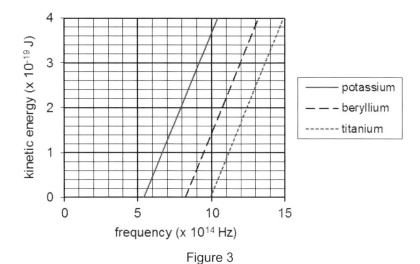

Figure 3

2. A scientist wants to determine whether a sample of metal is potassium, beryllium, or titanium. The scientist exposes the sample to light at a frequency of 12×10^{14} Hz and measures a photoelectric kinetic energy emission of 5.2×10^{-19} J. Based on the information in Figure 3, the sample is most likely:

A. potassium only.
B. beryllium only.
C. titanium only.
D. potassium or beryllium only.

Passage I

Binary fission is the process by which a single cell of bacteria divides into two cells. The rate of exponential growth of a bacterial culture is expressed as *generation time*, which is defined as the time required for the bacterial population to double. Table 1 displays a variety of bacteria at optimal growth temperatures and the resulting generation times.

Table 1			
Bacterium	Growth medium	Temperature (°C)	Generation time (min)
Escherichia coli	glucose-salts	37	17
Bacillus megaterium	sucrose-salts	34	25
Streptococcus lactis	milk	37	26
Streptococcus lactis	lactose broth	37	48
Staphylococcus aureus	heart infusion broth	30	29
Lactobacillus acidophilus	milk	35	82
Rhizobium japonicum	mannitol-salts	25	403
Mycobacterium tuberculosis	synthetic	37	862
Treponema pallidum	rabbit testes	31	1980

The *bacterial growth curve* consists of four characteristic phases, as shown in Figure 1.

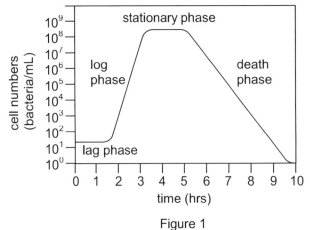

Figure 1

1. Based on the data in Table 1, if *Streptococcus lactis* was placed in a test tube containing a growth medium at 37°C, the generation time would most likely be:

   A. less than 20 min.
   B. between 20 and 25 min.
   C. between 25 and 50 min.
   D. greater than 50 min.

2. The initial population of the bacteria displayed in Figure 1 is closest to:

   F. 1 bacteria/mL.
   G. 10 bacteria/mL.
   H. 20 bacteria/mL.
   J. 100 bacteria/mL.

3. According to Table 1, which of the following combinations of bacteria and growth medium, at 37°C, would take closest to 30 minutes to double its population?

   A. *Escherichia coli* in glucose-salts
   B. *Mycobacterium tuberculosis* in a synthetic medium
   C. *Staphylococcus aureus* in heart infusion broth
   D. *Streptococcus lactis* in milk

4. According to the passage, if the temperatures of the growth mediums had been increased, the generation times for the bacterium in Table 1 would most likely have:

   F. increased, because the temperatures would no longer be optimal.
   G. increased, because temperature and generation times are always directly proportional.
   H. decreased, because temperature and generation times are always inversely proportional.
   J. decreased, because bacteria grow faster in hotter environments.

5. Which of the following hypotheses about bacterial growth is supported by Figure 1?

   A. Bacteria population will return to its initial population at the end of the death phase.
   B. Bacteria population begins to increase immediately after transfer to a new growth medium.
   C. Bacterial cells do not grow in volume or mass immediately after transfer to a new growth medium.
   D. Bacterial fission does not begin immediately after transfer to a new growth medium.

3. NEW INFORMATION

Sometimes, a question will add information that is not found in the passage.

NEW MATERIALS

Many questions add some new item or material, one that is not found in the passage. Look at the following example:

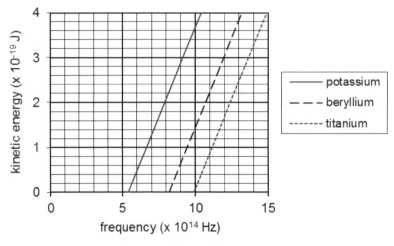

Figure 3

(EX) A student tested a sample of magnesium in a light frequency of 10×10^{14} Hz and found that the emitted photoelectric kinetic energy was 2.0×10^{-19} J. Based on Figure 3, which of the following correctly lists the 4 metals by their photoelectric kinetic energy at 10×10^{14} Hz from *least* to *greatest*?

A. titanium, magnesium, beryllium, potassium
B. titanium, beryllium, magnesium, potassium
C. potassium, magnesium, beryllium, titanium
D. potassium, beryllium, titanium, magnesium

Magnesium is not found on the graph. The question states that at 10×10^{14} Hz, the photoelectric kinetic energy of Magnesium is 2.0×10^{-19} J. Mark this point on the graph. As you move up the graph at 10×10^{14} Hz (from lower to higher kinetic energy), you'll get the following order: titanium, beryllium, magnesium, potassium. The answer is **B**. See the following graph.

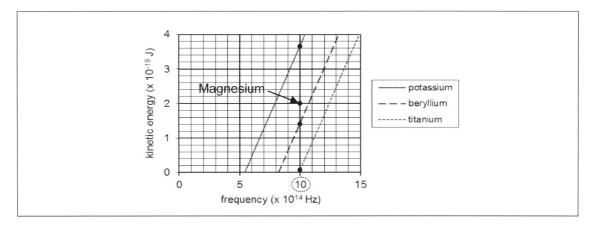

NEW DEFINITIONS

Another way the ACT may throw new information into a question is by introducing a new term or formula. Before we look at an example, a quick lesson on *yes or no* questions:

YES OR NO QUESTIONS

Glance at the answer choices for the following question. Two are *Yes's* and two are *No's*. After you read one of these types of questions, first decide whether the answer is *yes* or *no*, and eliminate answer choices accordingly. Then you can focus on only two answer choices. Now, to the question…

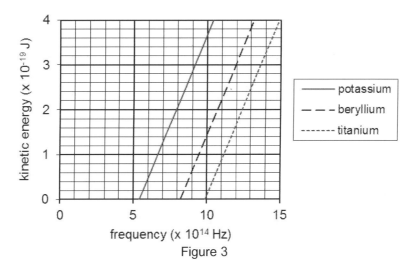

Figure 3

(EX) The slope of a line in the frequency-kinetic energy graph is defined as the ratio of the change in kinetic energy to the corresponding change in frequency. The value of the slope for a given material is called *Planck's Number*. Based on the information in Figure 3, would one be justified in concluding that Planck's Number is constant for potassium, beryllium, and titanium?

   A. Yes, because all three lines start at a kinetic energy of 0 J.
   B. Yes, because the slopes of all three lines are equal.
   C. No, because the frequency ranges of all three lines are different.
   D. No, because the information provided is insufficient to determine Planck's Number.

New information can be disorienting, but as usual, the bark of these problems tends to be worse than the bite. Planck's Number, which sounds complicated, is just the slope of a line. If you're comfortable with slope (an important part of the ACT Math Test), then you can see that all three lines have the same slope. Thus, Planck's Number is constant for these three materials. Eliminate the "no" answers: C and D. Only **B** gives the correct reason.

––––––––

Try the following lesson problem. Figure 3 is reprinted below:

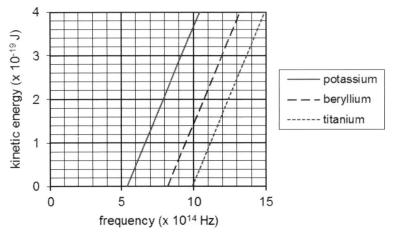

Figure 3

3. A *metal alloy* is a material composed of two or more metals. A student hypothesizes that a metal alloy will have a higher photoelectric kinetic energy emission rate at a given light frequency than the greater of the kinetic energy emission rates of the composite metals tested separately. To test the hypothesis, the student uses a titanium-beryllium sample, exposed to light at a frequency of 11×10^{14} Hz, and measures 1.2×10^{-19} J of emitted kinetic energy. Does the data in Figure 3 support the student's hypothesis?

A. Yes, because the emitted kinetic energy is greater than the sum of the kinetic energies emitted by each material separately.
B. Yes, because the emitted kinetic energy is greater than the kinetic energy emitted by titanium separately.
C. No, because the emitted kinetic energy is less than the kinetic energy emitted by beryllium separately.
D. No, because the emitted kinetic energy is less than the sum of the kinetic energies emitted by each material separately.

THE SECOND PARTS OF ANSWER CHOICES

Yes/No questions, as described above, are examples of questions that have answer choices each containing *two parts*. The second parts of these answer choices, through process of elimination, can often lead you easily to the correct answer, even when the question is confusing.

We've hidden the passage and the question in the following example, but see if you can guess the correct answer using process of elimination:

    A. lower, because the average temperature decreased as the comet approached the sun.
    B. lower, because the average temperature increased as the comet approached the sun.
    C. higher, because the average temperature decreased as the comet approached the sun.
    D. higher, because the average temperature did not change as the comet approached the sun.

You can be pretty sure that temperature will *increase* as a comet approaches the sun. The only sensible answer is **B** (even though we have no idea what the question was actually asking).

Feel free to use the second parts of answer choices to your advantage, especially for questions that sound difficult otherwise.

4. TRENDS

It is important that you recognize *trends* as you analyze data on the ACT. Think about what happens to one variable as another variable changes. As one variable increases, does the other also increase? Does it decrease? Does it stay the same? Does it go up and then down? Down and then up? And so on.

! **Keep track of trends using arrows (↑ or ↓).** For example, we can see in Figure 3 that as frequency increases, kinetic energy also increases, so write: *F*↑ *K*↑ (you can abbreviate however you'd like). Arrows will especially help when you're dealing with more than two variables. Let's try an example. Note the addition of "threshold frequency" below:

The *threshold frequency* of a metal is defined as the maximum frequency of light that emits no photoelectric kinetic energy.

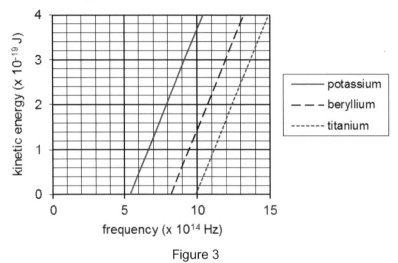

Figure 3

(EX) Figure 3 shows that the photoelectric kinetic energy increases:

    A. more slowly for metals with higher threshold frequencies.
    B. more quickly for metals with higher threshold frequencies.
    C. at the same rate for different metals as frequency decreases.
    D. at the same rate for different metals as frequency increases.

What is the relationship between frequency and kinetic energy? Do you see a trend? The graph clearly shows that as frequency *increases*, kinetic energy also *increases*. Use arrows: *F*↑ *K*↑. Now look at the answer choices. Remember the previous example? The rates of change for kinetic energy (as displayed by the lines' slopes) are constant for all three metals. You can eliminate A and B. (We never needed to use the "threshold frequency"; it was just there to throw you off.) The answer is **D**.

5. MAKE CONNECTIONS

On a single question, you may have to use information from different parts of the passage.

MULTIPLE FIGURES

Most of these connections problems deal with using *multiple figures* (graphs, tables, etc.). If you recall in the introduction, one of the things to look for in multiple figures is *repeated* labels (and units). Make sure to circle these labels and connect them with a line. These connections are the key to questions that require you to look at more than one figure. Let's add a figure to the example on photoelectric emission. Which label is repeated in both figures?

Figure 3 shows how the kinetic energy varies for a range of light frequencies for three types of metals.

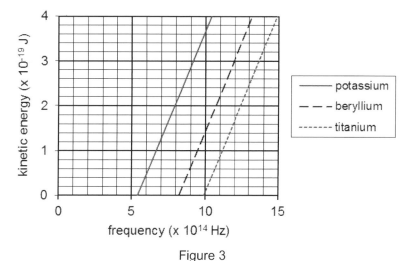

Figure 3

Light is visible if it falls in the *visible frequency spectrum*. Table 1 shows the frequency of six visible colors.

Table 1		
Color	Frequency (x 10^{14} Hz)	Wavelength (nm)
red	4.3-4.8	700-635
orange	4.8-5.1	635-590
yellow	5.1-5.4	590-560
green	5.4-6.1	560-490
blue	6.1-6.7	490-450
violet	6.7-7.5	450-400

The label "frequency" is found in both Figure 3 and Table 1? This is your repeated label.

Let's look at an example:

(EX) According to Figure 3 and Table 1, photoelectric emission occurs in the visible light spectrum for which of the following metals?

   A. potassium and beryllium
   B. potassium only
   C. beryllium only
   D. titanium only

The first step is to look at the range of the visible light spectrum and indicate this range on Figure 3. According to the table, the range is 4.3×10^{14}-7.5×10^{14} Hz. This range is shown below:

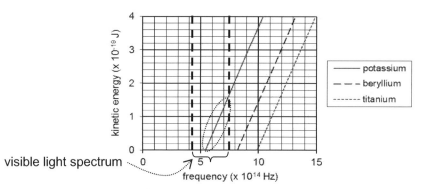

According to the graph, only potassium has photoelectric emission in the visible light spectrum. The answer is **B**.

Sometimes, new figures will be introduced in the questions or the answer choices:

(EX) Based on the information in Figure 3 and the table below, which of the following statements best describes the relationship, if any, between a material's atomic number and its emitted photoelectric kinetic energy at a light frequency of 10×10^{14} Hz?

Material	Atomic number
beryllium	4
potassium	19
titanium	22

   A. As the atomic number increases, the kinetic energy increases.
   B. As the atomic number increases, the kinetic energy decreases.
   C. As the atomic number increases, the kinetic energy does not change.
   D. There is no apparent relationship between a material's atomic number and its emitted photoelectric kinetic energy.

Pay attention to the order of the materials in the table. Beryllium has the lowest atomic number, but its kinetic energy at 10×10^{14} Hz is between the other two materials. Apparently, there is no relationship between a material's atomic number and its emitted kinetic energy at a given frequency. The answer is **D**. This is another example of a trend question.

Try the following lesson problem, which uses the same data as the previous examples. The information is reprinted below:

Figure 3 shows how the kinetic energy varies for a range of light frequencies for three types of metals.

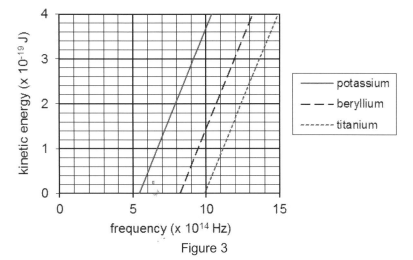

Figure 3

Light is visible if it falls in the *visible frequency spectrum*. Table 1 shows the frequency of six visible colors.

Table 1		
Color	Frequency $(x\ 10^{14}\ Hz)$	Wavelength (nm)
red	4.3-4.8	700-635
orange	4.8-5.1	635-590
yellow	5.1-5.4	590-560
green	5.4-6.1	560-490
blue	6.1-6.7	490-450
violet	6.7-7.5	450-400

4. Based on the data, which of the following best describes the change in emitted kinetic energy as light wavelength increases?

   A. The emitted kinetic energy increases.
   B. The emitted kinetic energy decreases.
   C. The emitted kinetic energy remains constant for a given material.
   D. The information provided is insufficient to determine the relationship between wavelength and kinetic energy.

MAKING CONNECTIONS WITH THE TEXT

Don't forget about the *text*. While most of the questions refer specifically (and entirely) to figures, sometimes you must pull information from the text as well. If you ever find yourself stuck or believe that the figures don't provide enough information to answer a question, skim the text, especially the passage's introduction.

Page intentionally left blank.

Passage II

A solid object will either sink or float in a liquid, depending on the relative densities of the object and the liquid. A fraction of a floating object will extend above the surface of the liquid.

Table 1 lists 6 objects and their densities, in grams per cubic centimeter (g/cm^3), at 15°C.

Table 1	
Object	Density (g/cm^3)
Balsa wood	0.12
Cedar wood	0.33
Birch wood	0.55
Ash wood	0.61
Polyethylene	0.92
Polystyrene	0.97

Table 2 lists 4 liquids and their densities, in g/cm^3, at 15°C.

Table 2	
Object	Density (g/cm^3)
Ethanol	0.79
Water	0.99
Benzene	1.23
Mercury	13.6

Each object in Table 1 was placed in containers containing the liquids in Table 2, and the fraction of each object extending above the liquid's surface was recorded. The results are shown in Figure 1.

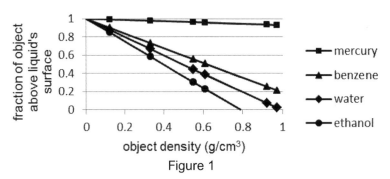

Figure 1

1. According to Figure 1, as object density increased, the fraction of the object that extended above each of the liquid's surface:

   A. decreased only.
   B. increased only.
   C. varied, but with no general trend.
   D. remained the same.

2. According to Table 1 and Figure 1, the fraction of polystyrene extending above the surface of benzene was closest to which of the following values?

   F. 0.1
   G. 0.2
   H. 0.3
   J. 0.4

3. The density of water varies with temperature. A scientist noticed that the fraction of a sample of birch wood extending above the surface of water decreased as the temperature of the water was increased from 15°C to 80°C. Based on the information provided in the the passage, as the temperature of the water increased from 15°C to 80°C, did the density of water increase or decrease?

   A. Decrease, because as the density of water decreases, the fraction of an object extending above the surface increases.
   B. Increase, because as the density of water increases, the fraction of an object extending above the surface decreases.
   C. Decrease, because as the density of water decreases, the fraction of an object extending above the surface also decreases.
   D. Increase, because as the density of water increases, the fraction of an object extending above the surface also increases.

4. According to Table 1 and Figure 1, which object(s) sank when placed in a container of ethanol at 15°C?

   F. balsa wood
   G. polyethylene only
   H. polystyrene only
   J. polyethylene and polystyrene

5. A scientist tests a sample of cedar wood in an unknown liquid at 15°C and finds that the fraction of the wood extending above the surface is 0.8. According to the passage, the density of the unknown liquid was most likely:

   A. less than 0.79 g/cm^3.
   B. between 0.79 g/cm^3 and 1.23 g/cm^3.
   C. between 1.23 g/cm^3 and 13.6 g/cm^3.
   D. greater than 13.6 g/cm^3.

6. TABLES

Of course, graphs aren't the only figures that show up on the test. We've already seen tables in some of the previous examples. Tables can be more difficult to read than graphs because you don't have the advantage of a visual representation. We will cover a number of topics that are commonly associated with tables.

INTERPOLATION

As mentioned earlier, *interpolation* involves estimating values *between* known values. **When interpolating with a table, draw a horizontal line between the values in question.** This will help you avoid making a careless mistake. We'll do this in the following example:

    Atmospheric pressure reflects the average density and thus the weight of the column of air above a given level. The pressure at a point on the earth's surface must be greater than the pressure at any height above it because of differences in the weight of the air. A *pressure gradient* is the vertical difference in pressure between two points.

    Table 1 shows the percent of sea-level density and atmospheric pressure (in kilopascals) at various altitudes.

Table 1		
Altitude ($\times 10^3$ m)	Percent of sea-level density	Atmospheric pressure (kPa)
0	100	101
10	70	65
20	42	38
30	25	22
40	20	13
50	14	10
60	10	7

The following formula gives the *air density* (*d*) in kg/m³ at −40°C for pressure (*P*) in kPa:

$$d = \frac{P}{84.108}$$

(EX) According to Table 1, the density of air at about what altitude is 50% of the density of air at sea level?

    A. 8,000 meters
    B. 17,000 meters
    C. 30,000 meters
    D. 50,000 meters

Did you underline "density" and "altitude" in the question? Focus on the first two columns. We must interpolate because 50% is not found in the second column. The density of air at 10,000 meters is 70% of the density of air at sea level, and the density of air at 20,000 meters is 42% of the density of air at sea level. So the altitude must be between 10,000 and 20,000 meters. Note where we drew the dotted line, below.

Table 1		
Altitude (× 10³ m)	Percent of sea-level density	Atmospheric pressure (kPa)
0	100	101
10	70	65
20	42	38
30	25	22
40	20	13
50	14	10
60	10	7

The answer must be **B**.

GRAPHS FROM TABLES

Some problems will ask you to visually interpret the information in a table. There are two ways to tackle these problems:

1. Check values from the table and eliminate answer choices accordingly.
2. Find the differences between adjacent vertical values in a table. This will give you an idea of the general shape of the graph.

(EX) According to the information in Table 1, a plot of atmospheric pressure versus altitude is best represented by which of the following graphs?

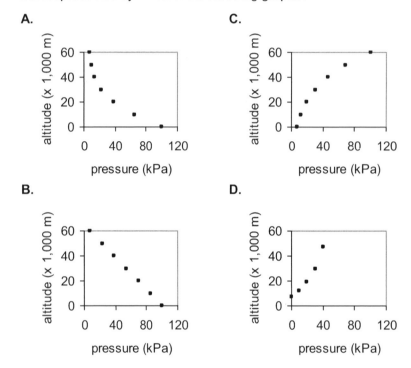

Solution 1: First, determine the general trend. You can see that as altitude increases, pressure (the third column) decreases ($A\uparrow P\downarrow$). You can eliminate C and D. Now simply check a point or two. For example, according to the table, when the altitude is 30,000 meters, the pressure is 22 kPa. In answer choice B, the pressure appears to be well over 40 kPa at 30,000 meters. The answer must be **A**.

Solution 2: You could also calculate the *differences* between values in the pressure column to determine whether the relationship is exponential (as in A) or linear (as in B). It's OK to just estimate (you won't have a calculator, as we'll discuss soon). Write the differences next to the table to the right of the numbers. Do you see how they start large ($101 - 65 = 36$) and get small ($10 - 7 = 3$)? The rate of change is slowing down as atmosphere increases. This means that the relationship is *exponential*. (The differences would be roughly equal if the relationship were linear.) The answer is **A**.

Try the following lesson problem. The information below is the same as that for the previous examples, but now we've added a second table:

Atmospheric pressure reflects the average density and thus the weight of the column of air above a given level. The pressure at a point on the earth's surface must be greater than the pressure at any height above it because of differences in the weight of the air. A *pressure gradient* is the vertical difference in pressure between two points.

Table 1 shows the percent of sea-level density and atmospheric pressure (in kilopascals) at various altitudes.

Table 1		
Altitude ($\times 10^3$ m)	Percent of sea-level density	Atmospheric pressure (kPa)
0	100	101
10	70	65
20	42	38
30	25	22
40	20	13
50	14	10
60	10	7

The following formula gives the *air density* (*d*) in kg/m³ at −40°C for pressure (*P*) in kPa:

$$d = \frac{P}{84.108}$$

The maximum migratory altitude of birds in clear weather is determined primarily by atmospheric pressure. Table 2 shows the maximum migratory altitude of various types of birds.

Table 2	
Bird type	Maximum migratory altitude ($\times 10^3$ m)
Swifts and swallows	1
Robins and crows	5
Most songbirds	10
Ducks and geese	16
Eagles, vultures, and hawks	22

5. Based on the information provided, the minimum atmospheric air pressure in which vultures can migrate is about:

A. 41 kPa.
B. 35 kPa.
C. 22 kPa.
D. 11 kPa.

KEEP IT EASY

Science questions often sound much harder than they are. Consider the previous question. The question tells us what bird to focus on (vultures). From Table 2, we can see that vultures correspond to an attitude of 22×10^3 m. Take this information to Table 1, and we find a corresponding pressure of about 35 kPa (by interpolation). Without worrying about "maximum altitudes" or "minimum air pressures," we can take our chances on B.

STAY FOCUSED

This is a good time to remind you to *stay focused*. These passages tend to give you a lot of information, most of which you won't use for any one question:

Most information is not used on any one problem!

Look at the lesson problem you just completed. It had nothing to do with air density. So the middle column of Table 1 and the given formula are not used for this question. Put this unneeded information out of your mind and focus on the information you *do* need.

Some information in the passage, in fact, you won't use on *any* of the problems. This is one of the main reasons why you should *skim* the passage instead of reading it. Otherwise, you might spend 5 minutes trying to understand something that's never actually tested:

Some information is not used on *any* problems!

Notice, for example, that a *pressure gradient* was defined in the passage introduction, but this term never came up in any of the questions. Aren't you glad you didn't worry about it too much? Just make sure you circle terms like this, just in case they do show up.

7. CALCULATIONS AND MATH

While the Science test is definitely not a math test, you may be asked to perform some relatively basic mathematical operations. Review the following topics from the Math section of this tutorial (all topics are found in the Arithmetic section):

- Percent
- Proportions
- Ratios
- Averages
- Rates (RTD)
- Tables and Graphs

You should also be prepared to make some calculations. **You are NOT permitted to use a calculator on the Science Test of the ACT, so don't expect any of the calculations to be too difficult.** The following examples are based on the table introduced in the previous section:

Table 1 shows the percent of sea-level density and atmospheric pressure (in kilopascals) at various altitudes.

Table 1		
Altitude ($\times 10^3$ m)	Percent of sea-level density	Atmospheric pressure (kPa)
0	100	101
10	70	65
20	42	38
30	25	22
40	20	13
50	14	10
60	10	7

The following formula gives the *air density* (d) in kg/m³ at $-40°C$ for pressure (P) in kPa:

$$d = \frac{P}{84.108}$$

6. Based on Table 1, the ratio of the atmospheric pressure at sea level to the atmospheric pressure at 50×10^3 meters is closest to which of the following?

    A. 100:1
    B. 10:1
    C. 1:10
    D. 1:50

The following is an example problem that requires *calculations*. See if you can follow along with the solution. Most students find this question challenging:

(EX) Using the information in the passage, which of the following expressions could be used to calculate the density at sea level, in kg/m³, if the temperature at an altitude of 30,000 meters is −40°C?

    A. $\dfrac{22}{(84.108)}$

    B. $\dfrac{(0.25)(22)}{(84.108)}$

    C. $\dfrac{22}{(0.25)(84.108)}$

    D. $\dfrac{25}{0.25}$

We'll take this question step-by-step. First, read the question carefully. Note that we're trying to find the "density at sea level," not the density at the given altitude (30,000 meters). Why does the question give you a temperature of −40°C? Remember when we said to circle numbers that show up in the text? The equation for density given in the passage is only valid at −40°C. So now we know, according to the question, that this equation is valid at 30,000 meters (but not necessarily at sea level!).

Again, we're trying to find the density at sea level. Note that air densities are *not* given in the table, only the *percent* of sea-level density. We must use the given formula to calculate density. But the formula only works at 30,000 meters (where the temperature is −40°C). The pressure is 22 kPa. So let's find the density at this altitude:

$$d = \frac{22}{84.108}$$

Now, according to the table, at 30,000 meters this density is 25% (0.25) of the density at sea level (let's call the density at sea level: d_o). If you've covered the percent section in the math part of this tutorial (the Of/Is technique), you should be able to create an equation:

$$d = \frac{22}{84.108} = 0.25d_o$$

Finally, solve for d_o:

$$d = \frac{22}{84.108} = 0.25d_o \quad \leftarrow \text{ divide both sides by 0.25:}$$

$$d_o = \frac{22}{(0.25)(84.108)} \quad \text{The answer is } \mathbf{C}.$$

Again, the previous question was a tough one, so don't worry if you found it difficult. The important thing to remember from this section is that, on the Science test, you will have to occasionally use your math skills, set up equations, and make some calculations.

8. COMBINING GRAPHS

MORE THAN TWO AXIS LABELS

Take a look at the graphs below. Do you see the common label?

Figure 1 shows the average temperature (in degrees Celsius) at various altitudes.

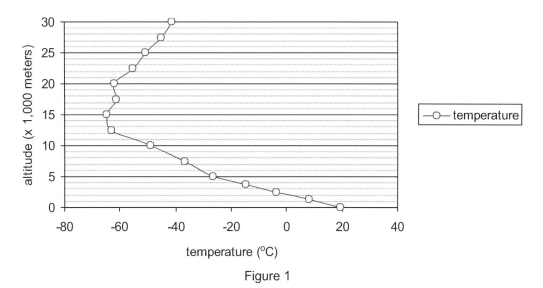

Figure 1

Figure 2 shows the average wind speed (in knots) at various altitudes.

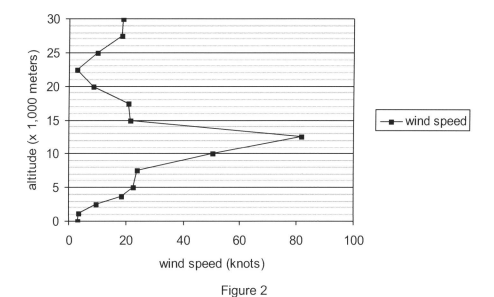

Figure 2

The ACT may combine these two graphs into one, using "altitude" as the common label. Use the information below for the following example:

The *troposphere* is the lowest layer of the atmosphere, ranging in elevation from sea level (0 meters) to a height of 10,000-12,000 meters above sea level.

The figure shows average temperature (in degrees Celsius) and wind speed (in knots) at various altitudes.

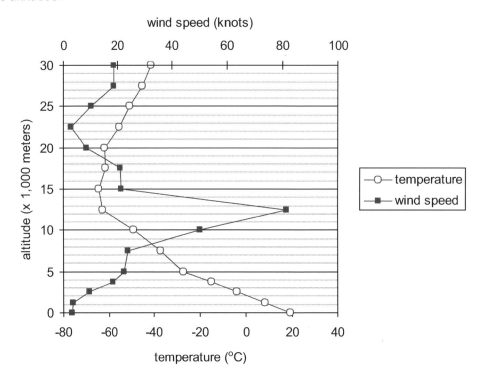

(EX) Based on the information provided, which of the following best describes the behavior of temperature and wind speed within the troposphere?

    A. As altitude increases, both temperature and wind speed increase.
    B. As altitude increases, both temperature and wind speed decrease.
    C. As altitude increases, temperature increases and wind speed decreases.
    D. As altitude increases, temperature decreases and wind speed increases.

The first thing you might note is that the altitude variable is multiplied by 1,000. So, for example, the number 5 on the *y*-axis is really 5,000. The next thing to note is that the temperature axis is at the bottom of the graph and the wind speed axis is at the top. Now, remember that the question focuses on the troposphere, which has a maximum altitude between 10,000 and 12,000 meters above sea level (as stated in the introduction). Look at one variable at a time. Temperature, which uses the circle symbols, decreases as altitude approaches 12,000 meters. Wind speed, which uses square symbols, increases as altitude approaches 12,000 meters. (Don't forget to use arrows: $A\uparrow T\downarrow W\uparrow$). The answer is **D**.

Try the following problem, based on the previous figure:

7. A scientist wants to estimate the height of a weather balloon. If instruments on the balloon measure a temperature of −62° C and a wind speed of 8 knots, then the balloon's altitude is most likely:

    A. 2,000-4,000 meters above sea level.
    B. 12,000-14,000 meters above sea level.
    C. 19,000-21,000 meters above sea level.
    D. 25,000-27,000 meters above sea level.

MULTIPLE TRIALS OR EXPERIMENTS

Another way extra variables can be tested is by showing multiple trials or experiments on the same graph, essentially combining multiple graphs—one for each trial or experiment—into one. For example, the following graph adds the variable "location" (Chicago, Anchorage, and Las Vegas) to the variables "altitude" and "temperature":

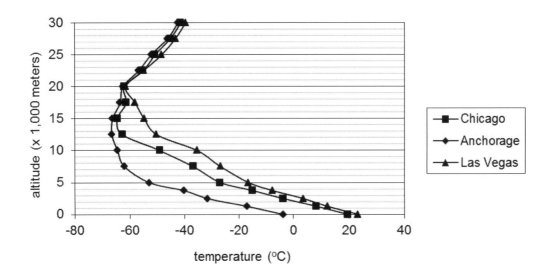

Try the following lesson problem:

8. According to the figure above, at what altitude is the temperature above all three cities approximately equal?

   A. 0 meters above sea level.
   B. 5,000 meters above sea level.
   C. 15,000 meters above sea level.
   D. 20,000 meters above sea level.

Page intentionally left blank.

Passage III

A *bomb calorimeter* is a device used for determining heats of combustion by igniting a sample in oxygen in a sealed vessel submerged in water. Each bomb calorimeter has a constant *heat capacity* (C_{cal}), measured in kilojoules per degree Celsius (KJ/°C). The heat of the reaction (q_r), measured in kilojoules (kJ), is calculated by multiplying the heat capacity of the bomb calorimeter by the change in temperature of the water surrounding the sealed vessel (ΔT):

$$q_r = C_{cal} \times \Delta T$$

Table 1 shows the heat released for various chemical compounds when burned in a bomb calorimeter. Table 2 shows the heat released when different amounts of octane were burned.

Table 1					
Chemical compound	Molecular formula	Mass (g)	ΔT (°C)	Heat released (kJ)	Molar mass (g/mol)
Sucrose	$C_{12}H_{22}O_{12}$	1.0	12.0	18.0	342.2965
Hydrazine	N_2H_4	1.0	13.9	20.9	32.0452
Methanol	CH_3OH	1.0	15.2	22.8	32.0419
Ethanol	C_2H_5OH	1.0	19.7	29.6	46.0684
Benzene	C_6H_6	1.0	28.1	42.2	78.1118
Octane	C_8H_{18}	1.0	31.7	47.6	114.2285

Table 2	
Amount of octane (g)	Heat released (kJ)
0.5	23.8
1.5	71.4
3.0	142.8
6.0	285.6

1. Based on the information in Table 2, the heat released from the burning of 4.0 grams of octane in a bomb calorimeter would be closest to which of the following?

    A. 100 kJ
    B. 200 kJ
    C. 300 kJ
    D. 400 kJ

2. Which of the following graphs best illustrates the relationship between the change in water temperature and the heat released of the chemical compounds listed in Table 1?

F.

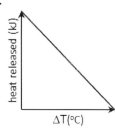

G.

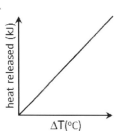

H.

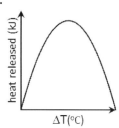

J.

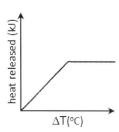

3. Using the results of the burning of 1.0 gram of sucrose in a bomb calorimeter, as shown in Table 1, which of the following could be used to calculate the heat capacity of the bomb calorimeter used in the experiments?

A. $C_{cal} = 18.0 \text{ kJ} + 12.0°C$
B. $C_{cal} = 18.0 \text{ kJ} - 12.0°C$
C. $C_{cal} = 18.0 \text{ kJ} \times 12.0°C$
D. $C_{cal} = 18.0 \text{ kJ} \div 12.0°C$

4. Based on the information in Tables 1 and 2, if 3.0 grams of methanol had been burned in a bomb calorimeter, the heat released would be closest to:

F. 23 kJ.
G. 68 kJ.
H. 106 kJ.
J. 143 kJ.

5. If a substance with a molar mass of 148.16 g/mol is burned in a bomb calorimeter, the change in temperature would be closest to which of the following?

A. Less than 28°C
B. Between 28°C and 32°C
C. Greater than 32°C
D. Cannot be determined from the given information

All programs: Now that we've covered the first several sections of the Data Representation chapter, it's time to consider *timing*. Turn to and read the Timing chapter now (starting on page 751). When you've covered the timing strategies, continue with the next section (Data Representation Odds and Ends).

9. DATA REPRESENTATION ODDS AND ENDS

DESCRIPTIONS AND HEADINGS

When a passage provides a number of similar figures, especially tables, pay close attention to the written descriptions for each figure, or the headings of each table. Underline any numerical values given, and note how these values may change from figure to figure. These values will likely show up in some of the questions.

In the example passage on the next page, what important part of the headings changes from table to table?

Consider the following reversible reaction:

$$N_2 + 3H_2 \rightleftharpoons 2NH_3$$

At chemical equilibrium, the formation of ammonia gas (NH_3) occurs at the same rate as the formation of nitrogen (N_2) and hydrogen (H_2) gasses.

The *equilibrium constant* is given by the following equation, where brackets represent the concentration (mol/L) of the reactant or product:

$$K_{eq} = \frac{[NH_3]^2}{[N_2][H_2]^3}$$

The tables below show the data collected while varying either temperature or initial reactant concentrations.

Table 1							
Temperature = 360°C							
Trial	Initial [N_2] (mol/L)	Initial [H_2] (mol/L)	Initial [NH_3] (mol/L)	Final [N_2] (mol/L)	Final [H_2] (mol/L)	Final [NH_3] (mol/L)	K_{eq}
1	0.50	1.50	0	0.100	0.300	0.800	237.0
2	1.00	3.00	0	0.146	0.438	1.708	237.0
3	1.50	4.50	0	0.182	0.545	2.637	237.0

Table 2							
Temperature = 380°C							
Trial	Initial [N_2] (mol/L)	Initial [H_2] (mol/L)	Initial [NH_3] (mol/L)	Final [N_2] (mol/L)	Final [H_2] (mol/L)	Final [NH_3] (mol/L)	K_{eq}
4	0.50	1.50	0	0.104	0.311	0.793	201.4
5	1.00	3.00	0	0.156	0.455	1.697	201.4
6	1.50	4.50	0	0.189	0.566	2.623	201.4

Table 3							
Temperature = 400°C							
Trial	Initial [N_2] (mol/L)	Initial [H_2] (mol/L)	Initial [NH_3] (mol/L)	Final [N_2] (mol/L)	Final [H_2] (mol/L)	Final [NH_3] (mol/L)	K_{eq}
7	0.50	1.50	0	0.108	0.325	0.784	165.8
8	1.00	3.00	0	0.159	0.476	1.683	165.8
9	1.50	4.50	0	0.197	0.592	2.605	165.8

(EX) Based on the data in the passage, as temperature increased the value of the equilibrium constant:

    A. decreased only.
    B. increased only.
    C. remained the same.
    D. varied, but with no general trend.

Note that each subsequent table displays data for an increased temperature ($360°C$, $380°C$, and $400°C$). The equilibrium constant (K_{eq}) decreases (237.0 to 201.4 to 165.8) as temperature increases ($T{\uparrow}K_{eq}{\downarrow}$). The answer is **A**.

When an equation is given in the passage, there's a good chance you'll be tested on calculations (review the Calculations and Math section if necessary). Try the following lesson problem:

9. A scientist reacted nitrogen and hydrogen to produce ammonia gas in two separate trials, Trial A and Trial B, and found that, compared to Trial A, the final concentration of nitrogen increased in Trial B, but the final concentration of hydrogen and the equilibrium constant did not change. What must be true about the final concentration of ammonia gas in Trial B compared to that in Trial A?

    A. The concentration of NH_3 did not change.
    B. The concentration of NH_3 cannot be determined.
    C. The concentration of NH_3 decreased.
    D. The concentration of NH_3 increased.

LEARN

Sometimes the ACT will ask a question that you cannot answer *directly* from the information given in the passage. The question may require you to *learn* from the given data. For example:

(EX) When hydrogen gas (H_2) reacts with chlorine gas (Cl_2), the following reversible reaction occurs:

$$H_2 + Cl_2 \rightleftharpoons 2HCl$$

When 1.0 mol/L of H_2 reacts with 1.0 mol/L of Cl_2 at 300°C, the equilibrium constant is found to be 4.0×10^{31}. Based on the data in the passage, if 3.0 mol/L of H_2 reacts with 3.0 mol/L of Cl_2 at 300°C, the equilibrium constant will be:

A. less than 4.0×10^{31}.
B. 4.0×10^{31}.
C. 12.0×10^{31}.
D. greater than 12.0×10^{31}.

You might think there's no way to answer this question because, quite simply, the passage does not provide data for the reaction of hydrogen and chlorine gasses. But you can *learn* something generally about the relationship of reactant concentrations, equilibrium constants, and temperatures from the data given in the passage. Look at Tables 1-3: It's safe to say that reactant concentrations have *no effect* on equilibrium constants (only temperature does). Thus, since the temperature remained constant in the question (300°C), the equilibrium constant will also remain unchanged. The answer is **B**.

RATIOS

Sometimes you must consider the *ratios* of values. Consider a mixture of lemonade. It is not the amount of water, lemon juice, and sugar that determines the taste but rather the *ratio* of these ingredients. If the ratios are the same, a glass taken from a gallon of lemonade will taste the same as a glass taken from 100 gallons. Any time materials are mixed together, consider the importance of ratios.

Let's add some new information to the passage at the beginning of this section and try one more lesson problem. We'll consider ratios as we tackle it:

A scientist assumes that a temperature, T_c, exists where the given chemical reaction becomes *irreversible*, as shown below:

$$N_2 + 3H_2 \rightarrow 2NH_3$$

The scientist uses a computer simulator and records the following information:

Table 4							
Temperature = T_c							
Trial	Initial [N_2] (mol/L)	Initial [H_2] (mol/L)	Initial [NH_3] (mol/L)	Final [N_2] (mol/L)	Final [H_2] (mol/L)	Final [NH_3] (mol/L)	K_{eq}
10	1.00	3.00	0	0	0	2.00	∞
11	1.50	3.00	0	0.50	0	2.00	∞
12	2.00	3.00	0	1.00	0	2.00	∞
13	1.00	3.50	0	0	0.50	2.00	∞
14	1.00	4.00	0	0	1.00	2.00	∞

10. Based on Table 4, if a scientist started with 2.0 mol/L of N_2 and 6.0 mol/L of H_2, then the final concentration of H_2 would be closest to:

   A. 0 mol/L.
   B. 0.50 mol/L.
   C. 1.00 mol/L.
   D. 3.00 mol/L.

OTHER FIGURES

Not all figures on the ACT are line graphs or tables. Here's an example that incorporates an illustration and a bar graph.

To measure the concentrations of hydrocarbon pollutants near or within the Cook Wetlands, soil samples were taken at four locations, as shown in Figure 1.

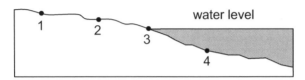

Figure 1

The concentrations of pollutants, measured as parts-per-million by total weight of the sample, are shown in Figure 2.

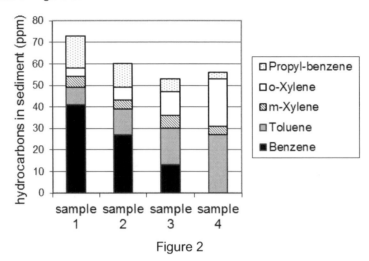

Figure 2

Try the following lesson problems:

11. According to the data, which hydrocarbon pollutant or pollutants showed an increase in concentration as the sample locations decreased in elevation?

    A. Propyl-benzene only
    B. Propyl-benzene and Benzene only
    C. o-Xylene and Toluene only
    D. m-Xylene, o-Xylene, and Toluene only

12. If a fifth sample was taken in water deeper than that of sample 4, based on the data, which of the following hydrocarbon pollutants would most likely NOT be found in concentrations greater than 10 ppm?

    F. Benzene only
    G. Benzene and Propyl-benzene only
    H. Benzene, Propyl-benzene, and m-Xylene only
    J. o-Xylene and Toluene only

―――――

You've now seen a number of different kinds of figures, but you should expect to see other types as you work your way through the practice problems and practice tests found in this tutorial and in the ACT book. Hopefully you're starting to feel prepared to tackle whatever may be thrown your way, no matter how strange or complicated it may look.

RESEARCH SUMMARIES AND CONFLICTING VIEWPOINTS PASSAGES

If you're following the **20-hour program**, you probably won't have time to cover the other two types of passages found on the Science Test (Research Summaries and Conflicting Viewpoints), but you should still plan to tackle these problems when you take the test:

- **Research Summaries:** About 75% of the Research Summaries questions are very similar to Data Representation ones (because they test graphs, tables, and other figures). You may not get to the Research Summaries chapter, but now that you've completed the Data Representation chapter, you should feel comfortable tackling most of the Research Summaries questions.

- **Conflicting Viewpoints:** The Conflicting Viewpoints passages tend to be less about tables, graphs, and numbers and more about *reading*, so you can tackle them as you would the passages on the Reading Test. Even though you probably won't have time to cover the Conflicting Viewpoints chapter, you'll hopefully get some of the easier questions correct.

TIMING

You should have covered the Timing chapter by now. Make sure to time yourself on all future homework assignments. You can always review the timing summary on page 756.

Page intentionally left blank.

Passage IV

Contaminated water from a coal mine had been detected flowing into the Vesey River. Engineers constructed two artificial marshes to help reduce the amounts of iron and manganese in the water and to reduce the water's acidity (see Figure 1).

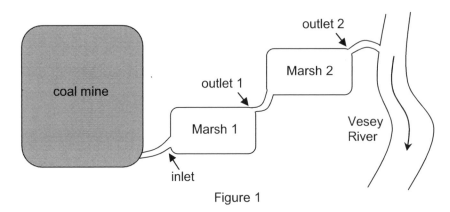

Figure 1

Measurements were taken at the inlet of Marsh 1 (I) and the outlets of both marshes (O1 and O2). Table 1 shows precipitation in centimeters (cm), flow rate in liters per minute (L/min), pH, and the content of iron and manganese in milligrams per liter (mg/L) over 5 days.

Table 1												
Day	Precipitation (cm)	Flow rate (L/min)			pH			Iron (mg/L)			Manganese (mg/L)		
		I	O1	O2	I	O1	O2	I	O1	O2	I	O1	O2
1	0	100	95	90	5.3	6.0	6.4	95	45	5.1	6.4	6.4	6.3
2	3.5	105	300	405	5.3	6.8	7.5	95	60	24.3	6.4	4.2	0.9
3	0.1	130	195	265	5.4	6.4	7.0	85	42	11.2	6.2	5.2	4.1
4	0	145	140	135	5.3	6.1	6.5	80	41	7.4	6.0	5.8	5.8
5	0	130	100	95	5.4	6.0	6.4	90	44	5.5	6.3	6.1	6.0

Table 2 shows the allowed contaminant levels for water. The given pH value is the minimum allowed. The given iron and manganese values are the maximum allowed.

Table 2		
Allowed contaminant levels		
pH	Iron (mg/L)	Manganese (mg/L)
6.0	3.5	2.0

1. According to Tables 1 and 2, which day, if any, was the water leaving Outlet 2 within acceptable contaminant levels?

   A. Day 1
   B. Day 2
   C. Day 3
   D. None of the days

2. Which of the following statements about Outlet 1 and Outlet 2 flow rates is supported by the information in Table 1?

    F. The flow rates increased during the heavy rain and returned to their Day 1 values the day after the heavy rain.

    G. The flow rates increased during the heavy rain and gradually decreased during the days after the rain.

    H. The flow rates increased both the day of the heavy rain and the day after the heavy rain.

    J. The flow rates did not change during the heavy rain.

3. According to the information in the passage, which of the following actions would best reduce the iron levels in the water that is released into the Vesey River?

    A. Removing the first marsh
    B. Removing the second marsh
    C. Adding a third marsh
    D. Increasing the inlet flow rate

4. According to Tables 1 and 2, did the marshes effectively bring pH measurements to within allowable contaminant levels prior to water entering the Vesey River?

    F. Yes; the water's acidity was higher than the allowed level at Outlet 2 for all 5 days.

    G. No; the water's acidity was higher than the allowed level at Outlet 2 for all 5 days.

    H. Yes; the water's acidity was lower than the allowed level at Outlet 2 for all 5 days.

    J. No; the water's acidity was lower than the allowed level at Outlet 2 for all 5 days.

5. A copper mine utilizes two marshes in an identical arrangement to those shown in Figure 1. Based on the information in the passage, which of the following are likely values for the content of manganese in milligrams per liter (mg/L) on a day of no precipitation?

	Inlet	Outlet 1	Outlet 2
A.	8.5	8.5	8.4
B.	8.5	5.3	2.1
C.	8.5	9.4	10.5
D.	8.5	8.4	0.5

10. DATA REPRESENTATION PROBLEMS

PRACTICE PROBLEMS

The Real ACT Prep Guide, 3rd Edition offers 1 Data Representation practice passage with 5 questions, starting on page 100, and 3 additional passages (that we'll use for practice) from Test 1. Additional Data Representation passages can be found on the following pages. Make sure you practice these passages timed. See the Schedules in the Introduction for more information about when to tackle practice passages.

☐ Sample Passage I* (page 100 of *The Real ACT Prep Guide*, 3rd Edition)

☐ KlassTutoring Sample Passages (following pages)

☐ **Test 1**: Passage II*

☐ **Test 1**: Passage IV*

☐ **Test 1**: Passage V*

*See Step 3 under "Test Corrections" below.

PRACTICE TEST

All programs: Now is a good time to take **Test 3** in the ACT book (you should have already taken Test 2, and remember that Test 1 will be used for extra practice problems). Also, even though we haven't covered Research Summaries and Conflicting Viewpoints, still plan to tackle these questions, especially the Research Summaries questions that test graphs, tables, and other figures; these questions tend to use the same techniques as Data Representation questions. And finally, don't forget to correct any missed questions after you grade the test (see below).

TEST CORRECTIONS

After each practice test is graded, you should correct Data Representation problems that you missed or left blank. There are three steps to correcting the practice tests:

1. The Data Representation questions for each test are listed below (the brackets show individual passages). Go back to your answer sheet for the corresponding test and circle the question numbers below that you missed (or guessed on, if you kept track of your guesses).

   □ **Test 2**: [1, 2, 3, 4, 5], [18, 19, 20, 21, 22], [36, 37, 38, 39, 40]

   □ **Test 3**: [1, 2, 3, 4, 5], [6, 7, 8, 9, 10], [36, 37, 38, 39, 40]

   □ **Test 4**: [1, 2, 3, 4, 5], [6, 7, 8, 9, 10], [36, 37, 38, 39, 40]

   □ **Test 5**: [1, 2, 3, 4, 5], [13, 14, 15, 16, 17], [18, 19, 20, 21, 22]

2. Correct the problems in *The Real ACT Study Guide*. As you correct the problems, go back to the tutorial and review the techniques. The idea is to: (1) identify techniques that have given you trouble, (2) go back to the tutorial so you can review and strengthen these techniques, and (3) apply these techniques to the specific problems on which you struggled.

3. If you have trouble identifying the best technique to use on a problem, see the Techniques Reference information in Chapter VI, starting on page 757.

DATA REPRESENTATION PASSAGES

Passage I

Enzymes are proteins that increase the rates of chemical reactions. In enzymatic reactions, molecules called *substrates* are converted into different molecules called *products*. The *relative activity rate* describes the rate by which a reaction increases due to the influence of an enzyme, in terms of 100 arbitrary units. Figures 1-3 show the effects of temperature, Ph, and substrate concentration on the relative activity rate for constant concentrations of Enzymes A and B. Figure 4 shows the effects of enzyme concentrations of Enzymes A and B on the relative activity rate.

The *pH scale* measures how *acidic* or *basic* a substance is. The pH scale ranges from 0 to 14. A pH of 7 is neutral. The lower a pH, the more acidic the substance.

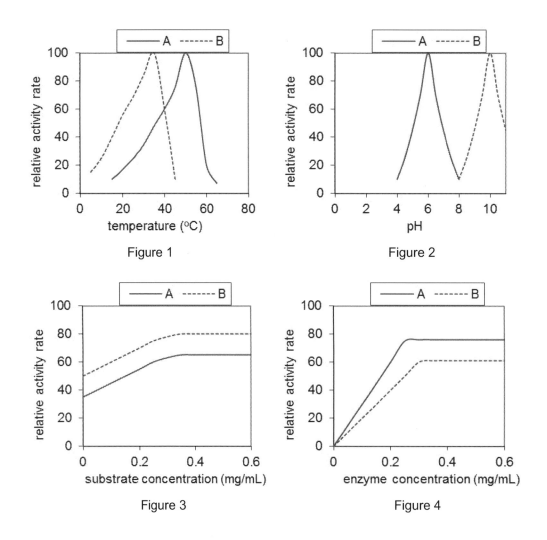

Figure 1

Figure 2

Figure 3

Figure 4

1. According to Figure 1, Enzyme A has the fastest activity rate of reaction at a temperature closest to:

   A. 35°C.
   B. 50°C.
   C. 65°C.
   D. 100°C.

2. Based on the data in Figure 2, which of the following is the best estimate for the relative activity rate for Enzyme B at a pH of 12?

F. 10
G. 30
H. 50
J. 70

3. A scientist claims that the relative activity rates of Enzymes A and B are dependent on the concentration of the substrate at concentrations below 0.3 mg/mL. Does the information in Figure 3 support the scientist's claim?

A. Yes, because the activity rates of Enzymes A and B do not change at concentrations above about 0.3 mg/mL.
B. Yes, because the activity rates of Enzymes A and B increase as concentrations increase below a concentration of about 0.3 mg/mL.
C. No, because the activity rates of Enzymes A and B do not change at concentrations above about 0.3 mg/mL.
D. No, because there is no relationship between the activity rates of Enzymes A and B.

4. The table below shows the relative activity rates for the enzyme Aspergillus at various pH readings.

pH	Relative activity rate
6	11
7	44
8	100
9	45
10	10

Based on the table and Figure 2, one could conclude that Aspergillus is most effective at a pH that is:

F. more acidic than the most effective pH readings for Enzymes A and B.
G. less acidic than the most effective pH readings for Enzymes A and B.
H. more acidic than the most effective pH reading for Enzyme A only.
J. less acidic than the most effective pH reading for Enzyme A only.

5. According to Figures 1 and 4, which of the following conditions will give the greatest relative activity rate for Enzyme B?

A. 0.5 mg/mL of Enzyme B at 60°C
B. 0.4 mg/mL of Enzyme B at 50°C
C. 0.3 mg/mL of Enzyme B at 35°C
D. 0.2 mg/mL of Enzyme B at 20°C

Passage II

A chain is released from rest with its lower end touching a scale (see Figure 1). While the chain is falling, its *momentary length* (*x*) is the length of the chain on the scale pan, and its *momentary weight* is the weight of this momentary length. The scale measures all weights and forces in newtons (N) (a *newton* is the force required to accelerate a 1-kilogram mass at a rate of 1.0 m/sec^2).

Various chains were released from rest and allowed to fall on a scale. The masses, lengths, momentary lengths, momentary weights, and forces are shown in Tables 1-3.

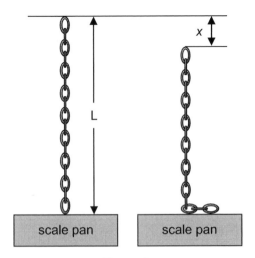

Figure 1

Table 1				
Mass of chain = 0.50 kg				
Trial	L (m)	x (m)	Momentary weight (N)	Force on scale pan (N)
1	1.0	0.2	0.98	2.94
2	1.0	0.4	1.96	5.89
3	1.0	0.6	2.94	8.83
4	1.0	0.8	3.92	11.77

Table 2				
Mass of chain = 0.75 kg				
Trial	L (m)	x (m)	Momentary weight (N)	Force on scale pan (N)
5	1.0	0.2	1.47	4.41
6	1.0	0.4	2.94	8.83
7	1.0	0.6	4.41	13.24
8	1.0	0.8	5.89	17.66

Table 3				
Mass of chain = 1.00 kg				
Trial	L (m)	x (m)	Momentary weight (N)	Force on scale pan (N)
9	0.5	0.1	1.96	5.89
10	1.0	0.2	1.96	5.89
11	1.5	0.5	3.27	9.81
12	2.0	0.5	2.45	7.36

1. A scientist hypothesizes that doubling the mass of a chain while keeping the length and the momentary length of the chain constant will double the force on the scale pan. Which of the following trials best supports this hypothesis?

    A. Trials 1 and 10
    B. Trials 1 and 9
    C. Trials 1 and 2
    D. Trials 9 and 10

2. Based on the information provided in the passage, if a 1.0-meter long chain with a mass of 0.25 kg is dropped onto a scale, the momentary weight on the pan if $x = 0.2$ m would be closest to:

   F. 0.50 N.
   G. 0.75 N.
   H. 1.0 N.
   J. 1.5 N.

3. Based on the information in Table 3 for a 1.00-kg chain, as the momentary weight of the chain on the scale pan increased:

   A. the momentary length of the chain increased.
   B. the momentary length of the chain decreased.
   C. the ratio of the momentary length to the length of the chain increased.
   D. the ratio of the momentary length to the length of the chain decreased.

4. For each trial, after the chain was released, the length of the chain that had not yet come in contact with the scale pan equaled:

   F. $L + x$
   G. $L - x$.
   H. $x - L$.
   J. x.

5. According to the data in the passage, which of the following graphs best represents the relationship between a chain's momentary weight and its force on a scale pan?

   A.
   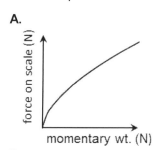

   C.
   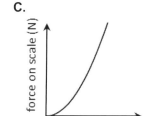

   B.
   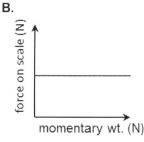

   D.
   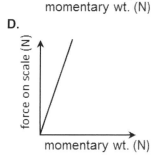

Passage III

An atom is made up of three primary particles: *protons* and *neutrons*, which are found in the atom's *nucleus*, and *electrons*, which move in orbits (see Figure 1) around the nucleus. Protons are positively charged particles, neutrons are uncharged particles, and electrons are negatively charged particles.

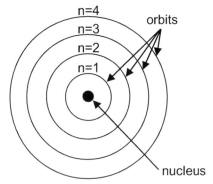

Figure 1 (Figure is NOT drawn to scale)

For three atoms containing only one electron, the energy (I, in electron volts, or eV) that is required to remove an electron and the energy (E, in eV) of a photon emitted when an electron falls from its initial orbit to the n = 1 orbit are shown in Figure 2.

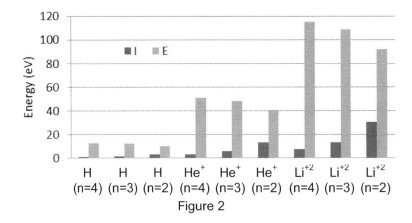

Figure 2

Table 1 contains data for the three atoms shown in Figure 2, including the number of protons (Z), the initial orbit (n), and the radius of the orbit (r).

Table 1			
Element	Z	n	r ($\times 10^{-8}$ cm)
H	1	4	8.5
H	1	3	4.8
H	1	2	2.1
He^+	2	4	4.2
He^+	2	3	2.4
He^+	2	2	1.1
Li^{+2}	3	4	2.8
Li^{+2}	3	3	1.6
Li^{+2}	3	2	0.7

1. According to Figure 2, as the value of n decreases for a given element, the values of I and E do which of the following?

	I	E
A.	increases only	increases only
B.	increases only	decreases only
C.	decreases only	decreases only
D.	decreases only	increases only

2. Based on the information in Figure 2, if n = 5, the value of E for the element He^+ would be closest to:

   F. less than 5.0 eV.
   G. between 5.0 and 40 eV.
   H. between 40 and 50 eV.
   J. greater than 50 eV.

3. According to Table 1 and the information provided in the passage, an atom has a net positive charge when:

   A. Z is greater than n.
   B. Z is less than n.
   C. Z is greater than the number of electrons.
   D. n is less than the number of electrons.

4. According to Figure 2 and Table 1, a photon with the most energy will be emitted when an electron falls from an orbit of what radius and from what element?

   F. 2.8×10^{-8} cm in Li^{+2}.
   G. 0.7×10^{-8} cm in Li^{+2}.
   H. 8.5×10^{-8} cm in H.
   J. 2.1×10^{-8} cm in H.

5. For a given value of n, the relationship between I and E for all single-electron elements can be approximated by the equation: I × c = E, where c is a constant. Given this information, and the information in the passage, for the single-electron element Be^{+3} with n = 2, if I = 54.2 eV, the value for E would be closest to:

   A. less than 50 eV.
   B. between 50 eV and 100 eV.
   C. between 100 and 150 eV.
   D. greater than 150 eV.

III

RESEARCH SUMMARIES

Research Summaries passages present descriptions of scientific experiments or studies, along with tables and graphs showing the results. Some of the questions will ask you to evaluate the methods used in the experiment. Most of the questions ask you to interpret the results presented in tables and graphs, just like the Data Representation questions.

1. *RESEARCH SUMMARIES INTRO*

The last chapter showed us that Data Representation passages display *results* of experiments or investigations. Research Summaries passages display results too, but they also discuss the *experimental methods* used to obtain these results. This is the major difference between Research Summaries and Data Representation passages.

> The following clues should help you identify Research Summaries passages:
> - Research Summaries passages typically include "studies," "experiments," "activities," etc. These will be indicated with italicized headings within the passage.
> - Each passage typically has **6-7** questions (usually 6).
> - Besides tables and graphs showing results, you may also see figures that display equipment or other parts of the actual experiment.

To get a feel for what these passages look like, check out some of the Research Summaries passages in the ACT book. You should notice the following:

1. A short introduction, which usually explains the *purpose* of the experiments.

2. Two or more *experiments* (sometimes called *studies*, *activities*, etc.). Each experiment includes two things:

   - A description of the experimental method, often supported by a figure.

   - The results of the experiment, usually supported by graphs or tables.

IDENTIFY THE PURPOSE OF THE RESEARCH

What was the researcher's goal? What was she trying to find out? For most Research Summaries passages, the *purpose* of the study will answer these questions. The purpose describes *why* the research was performed. It is generally found in the introduction. Underline it. The purpose is usually pretty easy to understand and will give you a good head start toward understanding the passage. It may directly help answer some of the questions, too.

SKIM THE PASSAGE IN PARTS

Just as with the Data Representation passages, you should expect to *skim* the passage to get some idea of what the passage is about (review page 646 to know what to look for while you skim). *Unlike* the Data Representation passages, however, we do not recommend skimming the *whole* passage right away. Here's why: **Many, if not most, of the questions on Research Summaries passages relate to only *one* of the experiments.** Why skim the whole passage, which can be confusing, when for many of the questions you can focus on just one part of the passage? Tackle the Research Summaries passage using the following method:

ONE EXPERIMENT AT A TIME

1. Before you read the introduction, quickly look through the questions. Nearly every question has a clue about what experiment or experiments are being tested. Look for obvious words, such as "in Experiment 1" or "according to Study 2." Don't forget to also look at the answer choices, which often have clues as well. **Next to each question number, write the number of the experiment that is tested.** If two (or more) experiments are tested by a question, write both (or all) of the numbers (for example, write "1-2"). If you're not sure about a question, just leave it unmarked. This whole process should take only about 15-20 seconds.

2. **Skim the intro.** Don't forget to underline the purpose. Also, as you would with a Data Representation passage, circle any *identifiers* and underline any *definitions* of terms.

3. **Skim the experiments one by one**, answering appropriate questions after each experiment.

EXCEPTIONS

You may indicate that a question pertains to only *one* experiment when in fact it requires information from another experiment. If you're careful with step 1 (above), this shouldn't happen often, but if you ever feel as though you don't have enough information to answer a question, skip it, and come back to it after you've skimmed the other experiments.

A WORD OF WARNING

Since you will be answering the questions out of order, be very careful not to make mistakes when you fill in the bubbles. **Always match the question number in your test booklet to the question number on the answer sheet.**

Note: The above approach should help you focus your attention on the relevant information in the passage and, hopefully, make these passages seem less daunting. Some students, however, are more comfortable first skimming all of the experiments and then tackling the questions (in order). We recommend you try the one-experiment-at-a-time method above—it might take a few tries to get used to it—but if it continues to feel uncomfortable after a few passages, go ahead and skim the whole passage before starting the questions.

2. DATA REPRESENTATION REVISITED

Great news! **About 75% of the questions on the Research Summaries passages are very similar to those on the Data Representation passages.** Questions will ask you to interpret data displayed in graphs, tables, and other figures. At this point, you should feel pretty comfortable with these kinds of questions, so be aggressive. Even if you are challenged by the other types of Research Summaries questions (ones that focus on experimental *methods* rather than *results*), most of the questions should feel very similar to the ones you saw in the last chapter.

UNDERLINE IMPORTANT PARTS OF THE QUESTION

We talked about this in the Data Representation section. You should underline the names of any figures and tables (Figure 1, Table 1, etc.), numbers and units, and any specific materials or test subjects, but now you must pay close attention to specific *experiments* (or *studies*, *activities*, etc.) mentioned in the question. Make sure to stay focused.

———————

Look at the Research Summaries passage on the next page. For now, just read through Experiment 1. You might want to tear this page out so you can refer to the passage for future questions in this chapter.

Temperature plays an important role in plant growth. Three experiments were performed to measure the effects of temperature on corn and soybean plants. The experiments were performed concurrently in the same part of an open-air laboratory.

Experiment 1

A scientist planted 50 pots with 10 corn seeds each. In quantities of 10, pots were inserted into each of 5 temperature chambers. The temperature chambers were designed to maintain a constant temperature while allowing free exposure to sunlight and air. After 40 days, the plants were uprooted, oven-dried, and weighed. The experiment was also performed with soybean seeds. The results are shown in Table 1.

Table 1		
Temperature (°C)	Average mass of plants (g)	
	corn	soybean
0	0.0	0.9
10	5.1	2.8
20	12.2	6.5
30	12.8	2.2
40	5.8	1.0

Experiment 2

The *thermoperiod* is the range of daily temperature. The temperature of each chamber of Experiment 2 varied over 24 hours as shown in the figure below.

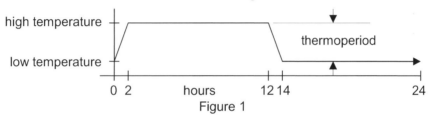

Figure 1

A scientist planted 70 pots with 10 corn seeds each. In quantities of 10, pots were inserted into each of 7 temperature chambers. Each temperature chamber had a low temperature of 20°C and was designed to allow free exposure to sunlight and air. After 40 days, the plants were uprooted, oven-dried, and weighed. The experiment was also performed with soybean seeds. The results are shown in Table 2.

Table 2		
Thermoperiod (°C)	Average mass of plants (g)	
	corn	soybean
0.0	12.2	6.5
2.5	14.8	7.5
5.0	18.2	9.4
7.5	22.5	12.4
10.0	28.0	14.8
12.5	34.1	13.1
15.0	37.0	12.0

Experiment 3

A scientist planted 10 corn seeds in each of 10 pots located in a location open to direct sunlight. The weights of the plants were measured after 40 days. The experiment was also performed with soybean seeds. During the 40 days, the average low temperature was 11.1°C and the average thermoperiod was 14.0°C. The results are shown in Table 3.

Table 3	
Average mass of plants (g)	
corn	soybean
35.8	12.7

(EX) The results of Experiment 1 indicate that, compared to corn plants, soybean plants likely thrive at a:

A. lower temperature because the weight of soybean plants is less than the weight of corn plants at all temperatures.
B. lower temperature because the temperature that yields the highest mass for soybean plants is lower than the temperature that yields the highest mass for corn plants.
C. higher temperature because the weight of soybean plants is greater than the weight of corn plants at 0°C.
D. higher temperature because the temperature that yields the highest mass for soybean plants is higher than the temperature that yields the highest mass for corn plants.

*Did you skim the whole passage? Hopefully not. This question only asks about Experiment 1. According to Table 1, soybean plants reach their maximum weight at about 20°C and corn plants reach their maximum weight closer to 30°C. The answer is **B**.*

You'll have to read up through Experiment 2 for the following question. Answers to all lesson problems in this chapter start on page 774:

1. Based on the results of Experiment 2, if corn and soybean plants had been grown in a thermoperiod of 17.0°C, the average mass, in grams, of the plants would most likely be:

	corn	soybean
F.	less than 37.0	less than 12.0
G.	greater than 37.0	greater than 12.0
H.	less than 37.0	greater than 12.0
J.	greater than 37.0	less than 12.0

3. RESEARCH METHODS

TERMINOLOGY

In addition to the terms defined in the previous chapter (*independent* and *dependent variables*), you should be familiar with the following terms:

Hypothesis – a statement that explains a set of facts or principles, usually forming a basis for possible experiments to confirm its viability. A hypothesis is *not* yet proven.

Control – a group—sometimes called the *control group*—in a scientific experiment where the factor being tested is not applied. The control group serves as a standard for comparison against another group where the factor *is* applied. For example, if a drug tablet is tested on a group of subjects, another group—the control group—would receive drug-*free* tablets. Note: do not confuse the *control group* with a *controlled variable* (an independent variable).

Constant variable – a "variable" that is not changed throughout a series of experiments.

The example and lesson problems below pertain to Experiment 3 (so skim it now):

(EX) Which of the following sets of plants served as the control group in the experiments?

    A. The plants in the 0°C chamber of Experiment 1
    B. The plants in the 0°C chamber of Experiment 2
    C. The plants in Experiment 3
    D. There were no sets of plants that served as the control in the experiments.

The control group for these experiments was one where the temperature and thermoperiod mirrored natural conditions—in other words, temperature was not controlled. Remember, the purpose of the experiments was to measure the effects of temperature on corn and soybean plants. It makes sense to have some plants that were not subjected to *controlled* temperatures or thermoperiods. The plants in Experiment 3 served this purpose: **C**.

---

2.   Which of the following factors was NOT directly controlled by the scientist in Experiment 2?

    A. The low temperature of the thermoperiod.
    B. The high temperature of the thermoperiod.
    C. The number of seeds planted in each pot.
    D. The amount of sunlight received by the plants.

THE EXPERIMENTAL METHOD

Most method questions ask about how the experiments were carried out. These questions often ask about *variables*. Why are some things varied and others held constant. For example, in the study of temperature and plants it was important to keep the soil concentrations constant in all experiments. Why? Because the study was testing the effects of *temperature*, not soil concentrations. Knowing what to vary (and, just as important, what *not* to) is one of the keys to conducting an effective experiment:

 Vary what is being tested, and keep constant what is not.

Here's an example.

(EX) The experiments were performed concurrently in the same laboratory to ensure:

- **A.** identical planting methods for all samples.
- **B.** identical soil concentrations for all samples.
- **C.** that the plants were tested in an ideal growing season and location.
- **D.** identical sunlight and air conditions, other than temperature, for all samples.

> Since the effects of planting methods (A), soil concentrations (B), and sunlight and air conditions (other than temperature) (D) were not being tested, it was important to keep them the same for all experiments. Only **D**, however, would require concurrent experiments (done at the same time) in the same laboratory.

BASIC METHOD QUESTIONS

Some questions simply ask about how the experiment was set up, or why it was set up in a particular way. Here's an example:

3. Which of the following temperature chambers presumably had the same variable effect on the corn and soybean plants?

- **A.** The 0°C chambers of Experiments 1 and 2.
- **B.** The 10°C chambers of Experiments 1 and 2.
- **C.** The 20°C chamber of Experiment 1 and the 0.0°C chamber of Experiment 2.
- **D.** The 0°C chamber of Experiment 1 and the 10.0°C chamber of Experiment 2.

MISTAKES

Some method questions focus on experimental *mistakes*. Typically, you'll be asked how a mistake might have affected the results.

(EX) In comparing the results of the three experiments, which of the following, if it had occurred, would probably have caused an error in interpreting these results?

    A. The eggs of an insect considered harmless to corn and soybean plants were found on some of the plants.
    B. The temperature chambers were found to reflect some incoming light.
    C. The weather conditions were cloudy for most of the 40 days of the experiments.
    D. The equipment used to control temperature in Experiment 1 was different from the equipment used in Experiment 2.

> Other than temperature (the variable tested in the experiments), all variables (water, soil, sunlight, etc.) should be kept constant from one experiment to the next. However, if the level of sunlight varied between Experiments 1 & 2 and Experiment 3, then Experiment 3 would no longer be a good control group. The best answer is **B**.

Try the following question:

4. If the goal of Experiment 2 was to find the ideal thermoperiod for corn plants and soybean plants, did the scientist meet this goal?

    A. Yes, because the data shows the ideal thermoperiods for both corn plants and soybean plants.
    B. Yes, because the data shows that as thermoperiod increases, plant mass also increases.
    C. No, because the corn plants were not tested at high enough thermoperiods to find the maximum mass.
    D. No, because the soybean plants were not tested at high enough thermoperiods to find the maximum mass.

EQUIPMENT

Some questions focus on the *equipment* or *materials* used in the experiment. Usually, there is a scientific reason for the choice of equipment. These questions can usually be answered with a general scientific knowledge. Look at the following example:

(EX) The scientist in Experiment 1 likely used temperature chambers that allowed for free exposure to sunlight and air because:

 A. the plants in Experiment 1 were part of a control group.
 B. a transparent enclosure allowed for visual monitoring of the plants.
 C. plants would otherwise overheat at some of the temperatures tested in Experiment 1.
 D. plants require sunlight and carbon dioxide for photosynthesis to take place.

Answer choice A is false, but the other answer choices sound possible. Think about what you know about plants. Why would they need free exposure to sunlight and air? The correct answer is **D**. This is an example of a question whose answer is not explicitly found in the passage (a "science sense" question). If you know the answer for a question like this, great. If not, take a guess.

CHANGES TO EQUIPMENT OR CONDITIONS

Some method problems focus on *changes* to the equipment or materials used in the experiment. They ask how changes might affect the results of the experiment. Again, you can often answer these questions using a general understanding of science.

Try the following question:

5. If the plants used in Experiments 1 and 2 had been grown in an enclosure with artificial lighting, which of the following changes in procedure would be necessary?

 A. The lighting brightness would have to be measured and labeled in Tables 1 and 2.
 B. The lighting brightness would have to be varied depending on the temperature of the temperature chambers.
 C. The plants in Experiment 3 would also have to be grown in an enclosure with artificial lighting.
 D. The plants in Experiment 3 would have to be shaded when the artificial lighting is turned off.

LABORATORY EQUIPMENT

Some questions require you to identify types of equipment used in the experiment. You might want to review some of the typical laboratory apparatuses, including:

graduated container or beaker – a glass container marked with units of measurement.

test tube – a hollow cylinder of thin glass with one end closed.

flask – a bottle, usually of glass, having a rounded body and a narrow neck.

stopper – a plug, cork, or other piece for closing a bottle, tube, drain, or the like.

valve – any device for halting or controlling the flow of a liquid, gas, or other material through a passage.

syringe – a small device consisting of a glass tube, narrowed at its outlet, and fitted with a piston for drawing in a quantity of fluid or gas or for ejecting fluid or gas in a stream.

plunger – another name for the piston of a syringe.

dropper – a glass tube with a hollow rubber bulb at one end and a small opening at the other, for drawing in a liquid and expelling it in drops

If you have trouble visualizing any of the above equipment, you can find pictures online. Note that any less-common equipment introduced in a passage will be described for you.

4. SCIENCE SENSE & SCIENCE KNOWLEDGE

SCIENCE SENSE

Some questions require a general understanding of science. In other words, the answers may not always be found directly in the passage, but if you have a good "science sense," the answer is usually clear. Here are some examples:

- Why would a scientist wait several minutes before analyzing the results of a chemical reaction?

  (To make sure the reaction has run to completion.)

- Why would a scale be *tared* (reset to zero) after a container is placed on it but before a substance is added to it?

  (To measure the weight of the substance alone, without the weight of the container.)

- Why are many subjects tested rather than just one?

  (To increase the accuracy of the results.)

If you can answer these questions, you're ahead of the game. Look at the following example:

(EX) Which of the following statements most likely describes an important reason for oven-drying the corn and soybean plants before weighing them?

- **A.** To test any variations in water storage of the plants.
- **B.** To remove any water found in the plants.
- **C.** To test the effects of high heat on the plants.
- **D.** To compare the effects of very high temperatures and relatively low temperatures on the plants.

The answer to this question is not found in the passage, but let's use some "science sense." Why might a scientist oven-*dry* a plant (the key word here is dry)? Probably to remove water or other moisture. (Perhaps there are variations in water storage/consumption from plant to plant and the scientist wanted to discount these variations in his measurements.) Be careful of A: The scientist did not test any variations in water storage (no pre-drying measurements were taken). The answer is **B**.

SCIENCE KNOWLEDGE

You will in fact come across some problems that require specific knowledge of science. Some tests won't have any of these types of questions; other tests may have up to perhaps three or four.

It's beyond the scope of this tutorial to get into the nitty gritty of all branches of science (we'd probably quadruple the size of the book). So if you're looking for the highest score possible, you might want to review some of the basic scientific principles in your science books. Here are some topics that have shown up on recent ACTs:

- Chemistry:
  - Balancing a chemical equation (this is an important one; review the basics)
  - General behavior of gasses, liquids, and solids
  - Atomic structure
- Physics:
  - Newton's Laws of motion
  - Fluid mechanics
- Biology:
  - Cellular biology

Let's look at an example, similar to the previous question, that requires scientific knowledge:

(EX) The plants in the experiments were oven-dried to remove water. Prior to oven-drying, most of the water would likely be found in which of the following cell structures?

A. Mitochondrion
B. Chloroplast
C. Ribosome
D. Vacuole

This question clearly requires more than just "science sense." You must have some knowledge of cellular biology. If you're familiar with the functions of some of the cell structures, you might try a process of elimination (you might know, for example, that chloroplasts handle photosynthesis, not water storage). But, unless you're a cell pro, you'll probably have to take a guess. The answer is **D**. A vacuole is an organelle that stores water (and other liquids) and usually occupies a large part of a cell's volume.

————

RESEARCH SUMMARIES SUMMARY

The following outline summarizes the approaches to Research Summaries passages:

- Work on one experiment at a time.
  - Next to each question, write the experiment number or numbers tested by that question before you start skimming the passage.
  - Underline the purpose in the introduction.
- About 75% of the Research Summaries questions test information found in tables, graphs, and other figures, just like the Data Representation questions.
- Memorize terms that have to do with experimental methods (*hypothesis*, *control*, *constant variable*). You might also review *independent (controlled) variables* and *dependent variables* (see Chapter II).
- Be familiar with standard experimental methods, including likely consequences of procedural *mistakes*.
- Be familiar with experimental equipment.
  - Some questions focus on *changes* to the equipment or materials used in the experiment.
  - Review the common types of laboratory equipment.
- You may see a few questions that (seemingly) require scientific knowledge. Stay aggressive, and try to use "science sense" and guess wisely if necessary.

CONFLICTING VIEWPOINTS PASSAGES

If you're following the **30-hour program**, you probably won't have time to cover the next chapter (Conflicting Viewpoints), but now that you've completed the Research Summaries chapter, you'll be ready to tackle at least 32 of the 40 questions on the Science test. You should still plan to tackle the Conflicting Viewpoints questions when you take the test. As stated before, you can approach them as you would the passages on the Reading Test. These Conflicting Viewpoints passages tend to be less about tables, graphs, and numbers and more about *reading*. So give them a try. You'll hopefully get some of the easier ones correct.

5. RESEARCH SUMMARIES PROBLEMS

PRACTICE PROBLEMS

The Real ACT Prep Guide, 3rd Edition offers 1 Research Summaries practice passage with 5 questions, starting on page 105, and 3 additional passages (that we'll use for practice) from Test 1. Additional Research Summaries passages (with the expected 6 questions) can be found on the following pages. Make sure you practice these passages timed. See the Schedules in the Introduction for more information about when to tackle practice passages.

- ☐ Sample Passage II* (page 105 of *The Real ACT Prep Guide*, 3rd Edition)
- ☐ KlassTutoring Sample Passage (following pages)
- ☐ **Test 1**: Passage I*
- ☐ **Test 1**: Passage III*
- ☐ **Test 1**: Passage VII*

*See Step 3 under "Test Corrections" below.

PRACTICE TEST

30-hour program: Now is a good time to take **Test 4** in the ACT book. You might want to first review the Timing chapter. Make sure you have a timing strategy in place before you take the test. Also, even though we haven't covered the Conflicting Viewpoints chapter, still plan to tackle these questions if time permits. You may have to guess on some them, but hopefully you can answer the more straightforward questions. And finally, don't forget to correct any missed questions after you grade the test (see below). If you have time after you have completed and corrected Test 4, take **Test 5**.

TEST CORRECTIONS

After each practice test is graded, you should correct Research Summaries problems that you missed or left blank. There are three steps to correcting the practice tests:

1. The Research Summaries questions for each test are listed below (the brackets show individual passages). Go back to your answer sheet for the corresponding test and circle the question numbers below that you missed (or guessed on, if you kept track of your guesses).

    □ **Test 2**: [6, 7, 8, 9, 10, 11], [12, 13, 14, 15, 16], [17; 23, 24, 25, 26, 27, 28]

    □ **Test 3**: [11, 12, 13, 14, 15, 16], [17, 18, 19, 20, 21, 22], [30, 31, 32, 33, 34, 35]

    □ **Test 4**: [11, 12, 13, 14, 15, 16], [17, 18, 19, 20, 21, 22], [30, 31, 32, 33, 34, 35]

    □ **Test 5**: [23, 24, 25, 26, 27, 28], [29, 30, 31, 32, 33, 34], [35, 36, 37, 38, 39, 40]

2. Correct the problems in *The Real ACT Study Guide*. As you correct the problems, go back to the tutorial and review the techniques. The idea is to: (1) identify techniques that have given you trouble, (2) go back to the tutorial so you can review and strengthen these techniques, and (3) apply these techniques to the specific problems on which you struggled.

3. If you have trouble identifying the best technique to use on a problem, see the Techniques Reference information in Chapter VI, starting on page 757.

RESEARCH SUMMARY PASSAGES

Passage I

Supercooled *sodium acetate* (CH_3COONa) is used in heating pads. A liquid is *supercooled* when it has been cooled below its freezing point without solidifying. When the supercooled liquid is disturbed with a seed crystal, it begins solidifying. The process is *exothermic* (heat is released). Students conducted the following experiments to study the formation and affects of CH_3COONa:

Experiment 1

CH_3COONa is produced when sodium bicarbonate ($NaHCO_3$) and acetic acid (CH_3COOH) are mixed together at a high temperature. Water (H_2O) and carbon dioxide (CO_2) are byproducts of the reaction. Students mixed 1.0 mol of $NaHCO_3$ and 2.0 mol of CH_3COOH in a graduated cylinder. The mixture was heated until boiling occurred. Once water vapor no longer was present, the cylinder was removed from the heat and the composition was analyzed. The procedure was repeated with different quantities of liquids, and the results were recorded in Table 1.

Table 1				
	Quantity (mol)			
Trial	Initial $NaHCO_3$	Initial CH_3COOH	Final $NaHCO_3$	Final CH_3COOH
1	1.0	2.0	0.0	1.0
2	1.0	1.5	0.0	0.5
3	1.5	2.0	0.0	0.5
4	2.0	1.0	1.0	0.0
5	2.0	1.5	0.5	0.0
6	2.0	2.0	0.0	0.0

Based on the data, the following equation was suggested:

$$NaHCO_3 + CH_3COOH + heat \rightarrow CH_3COONa + H_2O + CO_2$$

Experiment 2

The students poured 100 g of liquid CH_3COONa into a large Petri dish, placed the dish into an ice bath, and supercooled the liquid to a temperature T_c. The *velocity of crystallization* is the speed that crystallization expands from the point where a seed crystal is used to initiate the solidification process. Using a high-speed camera, the students measured the velocity of crystallization for various supercooled temperatures. The maximum temperature achieved was also recorded (Table 2).

Table 2		
T_c (°C)	Velocity of crystallization (mm/sec)	Maximum temperature (°C)
40	20	42.8
35	23	42.2
30	26	43.0
25	30	42.5
20	32	42.7

Experiment 3

The students placed 100 g of supercooled liquid CH_3COONa at 30°C in a Petri dish and introduced a seed crystal to begin the solidification process. They measured the maximum temperature achieved, the time to reach the maximum temperature, and the time until the CH_3COONa returned to 30°C. The procedure was repeated for different quantities of liquid CH_3COONa (see Table 3).

Table 3			
CH_3COONa (g)	Maximum temperature (°C)	Time to reach max temp. (sec)	Time to return to 30°C (sec)
100	42.5	42.4	183.9
150	43.5	46.3	191.5
200	43.2	51.0	198.0
250	42.3	54.5	206.2
300	42.9	58.2	212.0

1. Based on the results of Experiment 2, one can reasonably conclude that as the supercooled temperature (T_c) increased, the velocity of crystallization:

   A. decreased only.
   B. increased only.
   C. decreased, then stayed the same.
   D. stayed the same.

2. Based on the results of Experiments 2 and 3, which of the following variables affected the maximum temperature of CH_3COONa?

   F. Supercooled temperature of CH_3COONa
   G. Velocity of crystallization
   H. Weight of CH_3COONa
   J. None of the variables

3. The students measured the temperature of the CH_3COONa by taking the average reading of two thermometers, one at the center of the Petri dish where the seed crystal was introduced and one at the edge of the Petri dish. Based on the results of Experiments 2 and 3, at which mass and supercooled temperature of CH_3COONa would the temperatures of the two thermometers likely show the greatest variation 5 seconds after the solidification process had begun?

   A. 40°C and 300 g
   B. 20°C and 300 g
   C. 40°C and 100 g
   D. 20°C and 100 g

Continued ←

4. Based on the results of Experiment 3, which of the following graphs best represents the likely temperature differences between 50 g and 500 g of supercooled CH_3COONa at 30°C when a seed crystal is introduced?

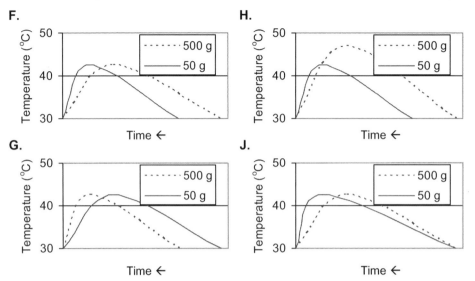

F.

H.

G.

J.

5. Based on the results of Experiment 1, if 3.0 mol of $NaHCO_3$ completely reacted with 3.5 mol CH_3COOH, what amount of $NaHCO_3$ would remain unreacted?

  A. 0.0 mol
  B. 0.5 mol
  C. 3.0 mol
  D. 3.5 mol

6. In Experiment 1, the students wanted to heat the solution until all H_2O and CO_2 had been removed, leaving pure CH_3COONa. Which of the following is the most likely reason why the students heated until no evidence of water vapor was present but did not measure the presence, if any, of CO_2?

  F. CO_2 has a significantly lower freezing point than H_2O.
  G. CO_2 has a significantly higher freezing point than H_2O.
  H. CO_2 has a significantly lower boiling point than H_2O.
  J. CO_2 has a significantly higher boiling point than H_2O.

Page intentionally left blank.

Passage II

A *top* is a cylindrical or conoidal device that spins on a tapering point. When a top spins, the rotating axis may display a rotational motion, called *precession*, around a line perpendicular to the surface at the point of contact with the top (see Figure 1). The following experiments were performed to study precession.

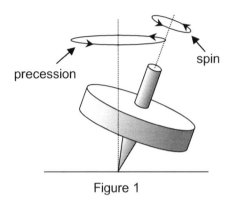

Figure 1

Experiment 1

Scientists used an electric motor to spin a top at a designated spin rate in revolutions per minute (rpm) and release it onto a smooth surface. Table 1 shows the measured precession rate (in rpm) for several spin rates.

Table 1	
Spin rate (rpm)	Precession rate (rpm)
250	16
500	8
800	5
2,000	2

Experiment 2

The height (h) of a top is defined as the distance from the point of the top where it meets the surface to the top's center of gravity. Scientists varied the height of the top shown in Figure 1 by extending a lightweight stem from the tip of the top. The electric motor was used to spin the top at a rate of 800 rpm for each trial. The precession rates are shown in Table 2.

Table 2	
h (inches)	Precession rate (rpm)
1	2.5
2	5.0
3	7.5
4	10.0

Experiment 3

Scientists used a falling platform to simulate a reduction of gravitational force acting on the top from Experiment 1. The gravitation force was reduced to 0.5 times the gravity of Earth. The scientists found that for a spin rate of 2,000 rpm, the precession rate was 1 rpm.

1. Which of the following graphs best represents the change in precession rate with the change in spin rate for the top tested in Experiment 1?

A.

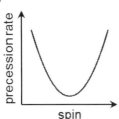

C.

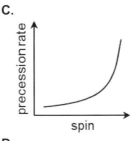

B.

D.

2. According to Experiment 2, a top with a height of 6 inches would have a precession rate of:

   F. 7.5 rpm.
   G. 10.0 rpm.
   H. 12.5 rpm.
   J. 15.0 rpm.

3. Which of the following experiments should a scientist perform to investigate the effect of a top's mass on the precession rate?

   A. Measure precession rates of tops of equal mass but different shapes, while keeping spin rate constant
   B. Measure precession rates of tops of equal mass but different shapes, while varying spin rates
   C. Measure precession rates of tops made from different metals, while keeping spin rate constant
   D. Measure precession rates of tops made from different metals, while varying spin rates

4. Based on the results of Experiment 2, what is the most likely value of *h* for the top used in Experiment 1?

   F. 5 inches
   G. 4 inches
   H. 3 inches
   J. 2 inches

Continued ←

5. Given the information provided in Experiment 3, if a scientist wanted to test the hypothesis that precession rate is related to gravity, the scientist should repeat the experiment by:

   A. varying the acceleration of the falling platform.
   B. varying the velocity of the falling platform.
   C. varying the spin rate of the top.
   D. varying the height of the top.

6. In Experiment 1, the top was likely released onto a smooth surface in order to:

   F. maintain a constant precession rate while the spin rate was measured.
   G. maintain a constant spin rate while the precession rate was measured.
   H. accurately determine the difference between spin rate and precession rate.
   J. accurately measure the height of the top.

Page intentionally left blank.

Passage III

A *battery* is a device used to supply electricity. A *resistor* is a device that controls the flow of electricity by resisting the flow of current. A *capacitor* is a device that accumulates and stores a charge of electricity. Students set up an electrical circuit consisting of a 12-volt (V) battery, a resistor, a capacitor, and a switch (see Figure 1). The students used a *voltmeter*, a device that measures voltage across a circuit, to study several characteristics of the circuit.

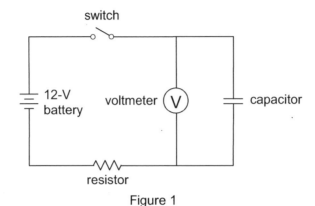

Figure 1

Experiment 1

A capacitor is measured by its *capacitance*, which is a measure of the maximum electrical charge and electrical energy that a capacitor can store. Students created a circuit as shown in Figure 1 with a 5×10^4 ohm (Ω) resistor and a 1×10^{-3} farad (F) capacitor. The switch was closed at time zero and the voltage across the capacitor was recorded. The results are shown in a best-fit curve (see Figure 2).

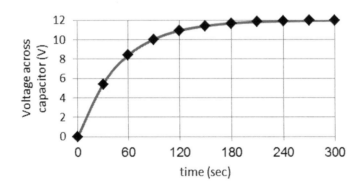

Figure 2

Experiment 2

Students set up the circuit shown in Figure 1 with a 5×10^4 Ω resistor and a 2.0×10^{-3} F capacitor. The students closed the switch and recorded the length of time until the voltage across the capacitor reached 12 V. They performed the experiment with several other capacitors. The results are shown in Table 1.

Table 1	
Capacitance ($\times 10^{-3}$ F)	Time to reach 12 V across capacitor (sec)
2.0	549
2.5	686
3.0	823
3.5	960

Experiment 3

Students set up the circuit shown in Figure 1 with a 4×10^4 Ω resistor and a 1.0×10^{-3} F capacitor. The students closed the switch and recorded the length of time until the voltage across the capacitor reached 12 V. They performed the experiment with several other resistors. The results are shown in Table 2.

Table 2	
Resistance ($\times 10^{14}$ Ω)	Time to reach 12 V across capacitor (sec)
4.0	220
3.0	165
2.0	110
1.0	55

1. The *time constant* of a circuit is a measure of time equal to the product of the circuit resistance (in ohms) and the circuit capacitance (in farads). If the voltage across the capacitor at this time was 7.6 V, which of the following is closest to the time constant for the circuit used in Experiment 1?

   A. 30 sec
   B. 50 sec
   C. 70 sec
   D. 90 sec

2. According to Experiments 1 and 2, if a 1.5×10^{-3} F capacitor had been used, the time required for the voltage across the capacitor to reach 12 V would have been closest to:

   F. less than 300 sec.
   G. between 300 sec and 549 sec.
   H. between 549 sec and 960 sec.
   J. greater than 960 sec.

3. Based on Experiments 1 and 2, and assuming a circuit as shown in Figure 1 with a 5×10^4 Ω resistor, which of the following capacitances and times would yield the highest voltage across the capacitor?

   A. 1.0×10^{-3} F at 300 sec
   B. 2.0×10^{-3} F at 400 sec
   C. 3.0×10^{-3} F at 500 sec
   D. 4.0×10^{-3} F at 600 sec

4. The main purpose of Experiment 3 was to determine how varying the:

   F. capacitance affected the time required to reach a certain voltage across the capacitor.
   G. voltage across the capacitor affected the resistance at a given time.
   H. time to reach a certain voltage across the capacitor affected the resistance.
   J. resistance affected the time required to reach a certain voltage across the capacitor.

Continued ←

5. The placement of the voltmeter in Figure 1 allowed the students to measure the voltage across the capacitor. Which of the following circuits would have most likely given the same results as those obtained in Experiments 1-3?

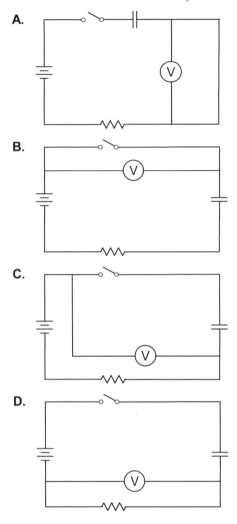

A.

B.

C.

D.

6. The students claimed that they did not need to measure the voltage across the capacitor of Experiment 1 for longer than 300 seconds. Do the data in Experiment 1 support their claim?

F. Yes; the time was sufficient to reach the minimum voltage across the capacitor.

G. Yes; the time was sufficient to reach the maximum voltage across the capacitor.

H. No; the time was not sufficient to reach the minimum voltage across the capacitor.

J. No; the time was not sufficient to reach the maximum voltage across the capacitor.

IV
CONFLICTING VIEWPOINTS

Conflicting Viewpoints passages present usually two viewpoints (occasionally more) on a given topic. The questions test your understanding of the topic and each viewpoint. Some questions will ask you to compare the viewpoints.

1. CONFLICTION VIEWPOINTS INTRODUCTION

Conflicting Viewpoints passages are visually different from Data Representation and Research Summaries passages because they typically don't rely on figures—no graphs or tables. The passages are mostly *text*, with few, if any, figures. This can make them more difficult, especially if the preceding chapters have you feeling comfortable interpreting the data found in figures. Conflicting Viewpoints passages don't display results. Rather, they introduce usually two theories or hypotheses based on some specific observable phenomenon.

The following clues should help you identify Conflicting Viewpoints passages:
- Conflicting Viewpoints passages typically include the viewpoints of different *people*, that is "scientists," "students," "researchers," etc., or you might see different "hypotheses." Generally, each viewpoint will be indicated with an italicized heading within the passage.
- While there are exceptions, these passages usually have few, if any, figures. Thus, most of a Conflicting Viewpoints passage is usually *text*.
- Each passage typically has **6-8** questions (usually 7).

To get a feel for what these passages look like, go ahead and check out some of the Conflicting Viewpoints passages in the ACT book. You should notice the following:

1. An introduction, which will usually clearly explain what the scientists are debating.
2. Two or more *viewpoints*.

IDENTIFY THE SUBJECT OF THE DEBATE

For most Conflicting Viewpoints passages, the specific *subject* of the "debate" is clearly written in the introduction, often near its end. Underline it. Understanding the subject of the debate will give you a head start toward understanding the viewpoints.

READ THE PASSAGE

Here's another big difference between Conflicting Viewpoints passages and the other passages on the Science Test. Up until now, we've done a lot of *skimming* but not much actual *reading*. On Conflicting Viewpoints passages, however, you should probably *read* the passage. This doesn't mean you'll have time to slowly read every word and understand every detail. Rather, just quickly read through the passage. While you read, circle identifiers and underline any defined terms.

AN EXCEPTION (SKIMMING)

If time is a major issue, you can try reading just the first sentence or two of each paragraph and *skimming* the rest. While skimming, look for and circle identifiers. This approach will give you more time for the questions and help you get through the test in time.

READ IN PARTS

Just as with the Research Summaries passages, we do *not* recommend reading the whole passage right away. **Most of the questions on Conflicting Viewpoints passages relate to only *one* of the viewpoints.** Use the method below:

ONE VIEWPOINT AT A TIME

1. As with Research Summaries passages, quickly look through the questions and for each one write down the the number or numbers of the viewpoints being tested.
2. **Read the intro.** Don't forget to underline the subject. If the intro is long, don't be surprised if it is directly tested by one or more of the questions (at this point, answer any of these questions).
3. Read the viewpoints one by one and answer appropriate questions after each one.

This approach should help you focus your attention on the relevant viewpoint in the passage.

EXCEPTIONS

If you ever find that you've mislabeled a question when you get to it, just skip it and come back to it after you've read the pertinent part of the passage. Also, if you ever come across a Conflicting Viewpoints passage that is not clearly arranged as a series of viewpoints, just read the passage straight through and tackle the questions in order.

A WORD OF WARNING

Because you will be going out of order, don't forget to be very careful when you fill in the bubbles on your answer sheet. **Always match the question number in your test booklet with the question number on the answer sheet.**

THE FIRST VIEWPOINT

FIND THE MAIN ARGUMENT

When you read the first viewpoint (Scientist 1), the most important thing to look for is the *main argument*. What is the scientist's position on the subject? **Usually, the scientist's main point is found in the first sentence. Underline it.**

OTHER MARKUPS

You should also circle identifiers and underline statements that you think are particularly important. By now, after going through the Reading section of the tutorial, you should be comfortable identifying and marking up important information while you read.

THE SECOND VIEWPOINT (AND SO ON)

Don't forget, you won't read the second viewpoint until you've answered all questions that refer only to the introduction or the first viewpoint. As you read, as described above, look for and underline the main argument of the viewpoint and mark up identifiers and other important parts of the passage. In addition, now you can start to *compare* the two viewpoints.

SIMILARITIES AND DIFFERENCES

When you get to the second viewpoint, you can start thinking about *similarities* and, more importantly, *differences* between the two viewpoints. How are the main arguments different? What are the differences in evidence used by the two scientists? Are the viewpoints the same in any way? Is some of the evidence the same but the *interpretation* of the evidence different? You can bet that some of the questions will require you to compare the viewpoints.

Remember, you'll read these passages in *parts*. For convenience, the questions and examples following the passage will go in the order of the passage (Introduction → Scientist 1 → Scientist 2 → Both). Keep in mind that the questions on the ACT will *not* be in any particular order, which is why you'll have to skip around. For now, just read the introduction below and move on. You might want to tear this page out so you can refer to the passage for future questions in this chapter.

The Doppler effect describes the perceived shift in frequency of acoustic or electromagnetic radiation emitted by a source moving relative to an observer. The shift is to higher frequencies when the source approaches and to lower frequencies when it recedes. Two scientists discuss how the Doppler effect helps reveal the nature of the Universe.

Scientist 1

The Universe is expanding. Observations show that there is a Doppler shift in the light spectra from distant stars and galaxies. Just as the frequency of sound decreases as two objects depart, decreasing the sound's pitch, the frequency of light decreases, creating what is known as a red shift of the light. No matter what direction we aim our telescopes, the light from distant stars is "seen" at a lower frequency than what would be seen from a static star. So the Universe must have started as a point in space. And at this beginning, a "big bang" sent all matter expanding in all directions.

Scientist 2

The Universe is contracting. The idea of our three-dimensional Universe expanding indefinitely in all directions creates the uncomfortable mathematical notion of infinity. Also problematic is the idea that the Universe stops (what would be on the "other side"?). The most likely scenario is that our three-dimensional Universe is bent into a fourth dimension that we are unable to observe. To help imagine this scenario, consider a two-dimensional Universe in the shape of a globe, a Universe with a finite size and no ends. The tiny two-dimensional beings on this globe have no sense of the third-dimension (just as we have no sense of the fourth-dimension). Now imagine that a "big bang" occurred in the North Pole of this globe. All matter would begin heading to the South Pole. One might think that as an object approaches the South Pole, the objects around it would appear to draw closer together, but this in not the case. Because of the gravitational pull of the slowly accumulating objects in the South Pole, objects closer to the pole will accelerate faster than objects farther away. So in a contracting, post-"big bang" Universe, the Doppler effect would still show stars and galaxies moving away from us in all directions.

2. DIRECT QUESTIONS

As we said, most of the questions test just *one* part of the passage (usually one of the two viewpoints, and sometimes the intro). These passages are similar to Reading Test passages in that you must answer questions using *context*, that is, the information given in the passage. Like most of the ACT Science Test, the subject will often sound very complicated. But, again, don't worry about your knowledge of science. Just worry about the information given on the test. The information you need to answer direct questions is found in the passage. Let's look at an example. Make sure you've read the introduction from the previous passage.

(EX) Which of the following figures best represents the relationship of movement and perceived frequency described by the Doppler effect?

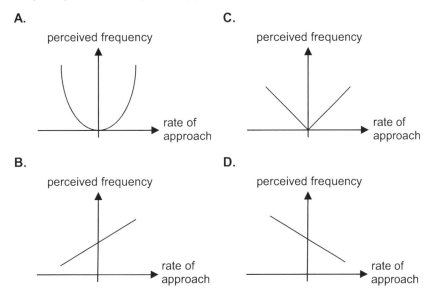

A.

perceived frequency

rate of approach

B.

perceived frequency

rate of approach

C.

perceived frequency

rate of approach

D.

perceived frequency

rate of approach

Notice that this question doesn't mention either scientist. There's a good chance that the answer is found in the introduction, so it would make sense to answer it before you read either of the two viewpoints. The intro describes the Doppler effect: "The shift is to higher frequencies when the source approaches and to lower frequencies when it recedes." Now let's understand the graphs. To the right of the *y*-axis, the rate of approach is positive, and to the left of the *y*-axis, the rate of approach is negative (the objects are departing). The actual frequency (when there is no movement) would be found at the point where the line crosses the *y*-axis. Notice that in **B**, the frequency is greater during approach and less during departure, as described in the introduction.

Now read the first viewpoint and try Question 1. Answers start on page 776:

1. Which of the following does Scientist 1 suggest is evidence of an expanding Universe?

    A. The light from nearby stars is perceived at a lower frequency than the light from more distant stars.

    B. The light from distant stars is perceived at a higher frequency than the light from closer stars.

    C. The light from distant stars is perceived at a lower frequency than the light from a theoretical star not moving away from the Earth.

    D. The light from distant stars is perceived at a higher frequency than the light from a theoretical star not moving away from the Earth.

3. INDIRECT QUESTIONS

Some questions will require you to interpret information given in the passage. These are similar to the reasoning/inference questions found in the Reading Test. The information is still in the passage, but you might have to *interpret* that information to find the correct answer. Look at the following example. This one refers to the second viewpoint, so go ahead and read it now:

(EX) Scientist 2 likely uses a two-dimensional world to illustrate his views because:

    A. the Earth-space is actually two-dimensional.
    B. all matter in the Universe moves only in two dimensions.
    C. a three-dimensional space would have to extend infinitely in all directions.
    D. readers would not be able to imagine the added dimension in a three-dimensional world.

Scientist 2 describes the fourth dimension as one that we are "unable to observe"—one that we "have no sense of." Thus, it makes sense that he uses a two-dimensional model so that his readers can understand and hopefully visualize his points. The answer is **D**. The passage does not directly support the answer; rather, the support is *indirect*. If the answer is not clear, you might have more luck eliminating answer choices.

Eliminate:
A. False—you hopefully know that this isn't true. In any case, Scientist 2 does not mention this.
B. False—Scientist 2 uses a two-dimensional model as just that: a model. He never states that all real matter moves in two dimensions.
C. False—Scientist 2 finds the idea of infinite expansion "problematic." The author states that rather than extending infinitely, the "three-dimensional Universe is bent into a fourth dimension."

Try the following question:

2. According to Scientist 2, which of the following affects the relative speed of two objects?

    A. The initial velocity of objects after a "big bang."
    B. The relative proximity to a gravitational pull.
    C. The distance between the two objects.
    D. The number of space dimensions in which the objects are found.

4. COMPARISONS

DIFFERENCES

The ACT calls these passages *Conflicting* Viewpoints, so it's no surprise that some of the questions will ask you to identify *differences* between the viewpoints. Some questions will ask about differences in the main arguments of the scientists. Harder questions will focus on specific details, such as the specific evidence used by the scientists. Look at the following example:

(EX) One of the primary differences between the two viewpoints is that:

    A. Scientist 1 uses direct observations while Scientist 2 uses a theoretical model.
    B. Scientist 1 uses evidence of a Doppler shift to explain his viewpoint while Scientist 2 considers the evidence false.
    C. Only Scientist 1 believes that all matter originated from a "big bang."
    D. Only Scientist 2 believes that a multi-dimensional Universe exists.

Scientist 1 uses direct observations (the Doppler shift in the light frequency) while Scientist 2 uses a theoretical model ("a two-dimensional Universe in the shape of a globe"). The answer is **A**. If the correct answer doesn't jump out at you, try eliminating answer choices.

Eliminate:
~~B.~~ False—Scientist 2 says, "the Doppler effect would still show stars and galaxies moving away from us in all directions."
~~C.~~ False—Scientist 1 explicitly states that a "big bang" occurred. Scientist 2 implies that a "big bang" occurred by using it in the theoretical model. In any case, there is certainly no evidence suggesting that Scientist 2 does *not* believe in a "big bang."
~~D.~~ False—Scientist 2 may be the only one who believes in a *fourth*-dimension. Both scientists undoubtedly believe in multi dimensions (more than one).

SIMILARITIES

Some questions will ask you to identify similarities in the viewpoints. Try the following question:

3.   The views of both scientists are similar in that they both agree that:

    A. the Universe is expanding.
    B. the Universe is contracting.
    C. stars and galaxies appear to be moving away from us.
    D. because there is no observable fourth dimension, the Universe must be infinite.

5. STRENGTHS AND WEAKNESSES

STRENGTHS

You might be asked to discuss the *strengths* of a viewpoint, or to identify evidence that *supports* a viewpoint. Look at the following example:

(EX) In 1965, two radio astronomers discovered a background "hiss" of stray microwaves in whatever direction they aimed their receiver. Scientists at the time said that these background microwaves were evidence of radiation left over from the "big bang." If this discovery were true, would it support the primary viewpoint of Scientist 1?

    A. Yes, because background microwaves would show measurable Doppler shifts just as light does.
    B. Yes, because the discovery provides evidence that all matter originated at a point in space.
    C. No, because Scientist 1 uses light waves, not microwaves, to provide evidence of a "big bang."
    D. No, because the discovery weakens the idea of an expanding Universe.

> Scientist 1 argues that "the Universe must have started as a point in space. And at this beginning, a 'big bang' sent all matter expanding in all directions." The discovery in the question supports the idea of a "big bang" without weakening any of the scientist's other claims. The answer is **B**.

WEAKNESSES

Alternatively, you might be asked to identify *weaknesses* in a viewpoint. These could be a result of *assumptions*, as discussed in the introduction, or you might be asked to look at *evidence* that weakens a viewpoint. Try the following question:

4.   According to Scientist 2, a major flaw in Scientist 1's viewpoint is the notion that:

    A. the shift in light frequency between departing objects is red.
    B. the Universe must have started with a "big bang."
    C. the Universe is infinite.
    D. stars that appear static are actually moving away from us.

CONFLICTING VIEWPOINTS SUMMARY

The following outline summarizes the approaches to Conflicting Viewpoints passages:

- Identify the *subject* of the debate in the introduction.
- Plan to *read* the passage (skim if time is a major issue).
- Read in *parts*.
  - Next to each question, write the number or numbers of the scientists (if any) tested by that question before you start reading the passage.
- Scientist 1: Look for the *main argument*, *evidence*, and *assumptions* while you read.
- Scientist 2: Look for the above, and also look for *similarities* and *differences* between the viewpoints.
- Answer *direct questions* using context.
- Answer *indirect questions* by *interpreting* the context.
- Be prepared to *compare* the viewpoints. Think about *similarities* and *differences*.
- Be prepared to identify *strengths* and *weaknesses* in the viewpoints. Consider assumptions and evidence in the passages.

6. CONFLICTING VIEWPOINTS PROBLEMS

PRACTICE PROBLEMS

The Real ACT Prep Guide, 3rd Edition offers 1 Conflicting Viewpoints practice passage with 5 questions, starting on page 110, and 1 additional passages (that we'll use for practice) from Test 1. Another Conflicting Viewpoints passage (with the expected 7 questions and the more-typical 2 viewpoints) can be found on the following pages. Tackle the first passage or two *out of time* so you can review the techniques taught in this chapter. Save at least the last passage below for *timed* practice.

- ☐ Sample Passage III* (page 110 of *The Real ACT Prep Guide*, 3rd Edition)
- ☐ KlassTutoring Sample Passage (following pages)
- ☐ **Test 1**: Passage VI*

*See Step 3 under "Test Corrections" below.

PRACTICE TEST

40-hour program: Now is a good time to take **Test 4** in the ACT book. You might want to first review the Timing chapter. Make sure you have a timing strategy in place before you take the test. Don't forget to correct any missed questions after you grade the test (see below). If you have time after you have completed and corrected Test 4, take **Test 5**.

TEST CORRECTIONS

After each practice test is graded, you should correct Conflicting Viewpoints problems that you missed or left blank. There are three steps to correcting the practice tests:

1. The Conflicting Viewpoints questions for each test are listed below. Go back to your answer sheet for the corresponding test and circle the question numbers below that you missed (or guessed on, if you kept track of your guesses).

    - ☐ **Test 2**: 29, 30, 31, 32, 33, 34, 35
    - ☐ **Test 3**: 23, 24, 25, 26, 27, 28, 29
    - ☐ **Test 4**: 23, 24, 25, 26, 27, 28, 29
    - ☐ **Test 5****: 6, 7, 8, 9, 10, 11, 12

    **Note: The layout of this passage is different from the ACT's *usual* layout for Conflicting Viewpoints passages. It is very likely that the Conflicting Viewpoints passage that you'll actually see on the real test will look more like those in this tutorial and elsewhere in the ACT book. However, this particular passage should give you an idea of the different kinds of passages you *might* see on a real test.

2. Correct the problems in *The Real ACT Study Guide*. As you correct the problems, go back to the tutorial and review the techniques. The idea is to: (1) identify techniques that have given you trouble, (2) go back to the tutorial so you can review and strengthen these techniques, and (3) apply these techniques to the specific problems on which you struggled.

3. If you have trouble identifying the best technique to use on a problem, see the Techniques Reference information in Chapter VI, starting on page 757.

Page intentionally left blank.

CONFLICTING VIEWPOINTS PASSAGE

Bark beetles bore through the outer bark of trees and attract mates. The female beetles carve galleries in the inner bark to lay eggs. When the eggs hatch, the larvae burrow deeper into the inner bark and spread a fungus. Eventually, the fungus can spread to the *sapwood* of the inner tree, which is the part of the tree that conducts water from the roots to the leaves or needles. If the tree cannot fight off the beetles with enough resin to force them out or drown them, the fungus will eventually cut the veins that carry the water, and the tree dies. Two scientists discuss the impact of bark beetles on forests in the Western United States.

Scientist 1

Bark beetles increase the risk of wildfires by killing trees, leaving them dry and susceptible to wildfires. When trees die, they drop their needles to the ground. The risk may be short-lived, but as long as the needles still contain resin, the potential for surface fires is greatly increased. In addition, there is an increase in the potential for a crown fire in the early stages of a beetle epidemic, when the forest is a mixture of dead, dying, and living trees. Over the past twenty years, the beetles have spread across more than 100 million acres of forest, leaving dead and dying pine, spruce, and fir trees in their wake. These dead trees quickly lose moisture, and, combined with rising temperatures and less precipitation, leave the forests of the West in a state of great fire danger.

Scientist 2

Rather than increase the risk of wildfires, bark beetles actually reduce the risk by thinning tree crowns. As pine trees die, they drop their needles, needles that otherwise would fuel fast-moving wildfires from treetop to treetop. Without this tree-crown fuel, wildfires are slower-moving and easier to contain. Furthermore, there is no evidence to suggest that the fallen needles have any effect on wildfires. Wildfires feed on larger sources of fuel, such as fallen branches and larger limbs of the trees. To study the effects of bark beetles, scientists set up "dummy" trees to attract the beetles and then used computer models to predict fire behavior in the areas infested by the beetles. The models showed that the beetles actually reduced the threat of wildfires, even as surrounding areas, unaffected by bark beetles, showed greatly increased wildfire threats because of drought and higher temperatures.

Answers to the following questions begin on page 776:

1. One of the major points of difference between the two scientists is that:

   A. Scientist 1 is more concerned about the short-term effects of beetle infestation than is Scientist 2.
   B. Scientist 1 believes that beetles are killing trees while Scientist 2 does not.
   C. Scientist 1 discounts the role of crown fires in the spread of wildfires while Scientist 2 emphasizes the role of crown fires.
   D. Scientist 1 uses computer models as evidence while Scientist 2 references historical records.

2. According to the passage, which of the following would most likely help a tree survive during an infestation of bark beetles?

   F. Increased resin production
   G. Thicker outer layers of bark
   H. Reduced needles production
   J. Denser wood in the inner bark

3. New data suggests that the intensity and duration of wildfires in the Western United States has increased over the past twenty years even though the average temperature has remained the same and average precipitation has increased. Based on the information provided in the passage, this finding would most likely *weaken* the primary viewpoint(s) of:

   A. Scientist 1 only.
   B. Scientist 2 only.
   C. both Scientist 1 and Scientist 2.
   D. neither Scientist 1 nor Scientist 2.

4. According to Scientist 2, which of the following is NOT a factor in wildfire danger?

   F. Fallen tree limbs
   G. Drought and higher temperatures
   H. Fallen needles and leaves
   J. Thinning tree crowns

5. Scientist 2 would most likely agree that wildfire danger is *decreased* as:

   A. tree foliage is increased.
   B. bark beetle populations are decreased.
   C. tree density is decreased.
   D. dead-tree moisture is decreased.

Continued ←

6. According to the passage, both scientists would agree that the risk of wildfires, at least in part, is increased by:

    F. an increase of needles on the forest surface.

    G. the spread of fungus in trees' sapwood.

    H. environmental factors other than bark beetles.

    J. human's encroachment into previously protected forests.

7. Scientist 1 claims that living trees:

    A. help counteract the effects of dead and dying trees in high fire-danger areas.

    B. are part of a complex network of factors that may increase fire danger.

    C. are less susceptible to beetle infestation than are dead trees.

    D. are more susceptible to crown fires than are dead trees.

V
TIMING

The previous chapters discussed the types of questions you'll see on the Science Test, but perhaps just as important is how long you have to answer these questions. This chapter will help you finish the test *in time*. No matter what program you're following, it is important to practice these timing techniques as you take practice tests in the ACT book.

1. TIMES

Of all the sections on the ACT, the Science Test is probably the most difficult to finish in time. Like the Reading Test, you'll see 40 questions in **35 minutes**. That's less than 1 minute per question. The timing approach below should help you maximize your score.

GENERAL APPROACH

As on the English and Reading Tests, we will use *deadlines* to help you avoid falling behind as you take the test. Because the number of passages of each type (Data Representation, Research Summaries, Conflicting Viewpoints) and the number of questions per passage have been varying on recent ACTs, the deadlines will not be based on *passages* (as with the English and Reading tests) but on sets of *questions*, specifically: **four sets of 10 questions** (40 questions total). The Reading Test is also based on four sets of 10 questions, but while the Reading deadlines coincide with actual *passages*, the challenge of the Science Test is that your deadlines will usually *not* coincide with the ends of passages.

SCIENCE DEADLINES

Since the test is 35 minutes long, you have 8 minutes and 45 seconds for each 10-question set. To be safe, let's round this down to **8:30**. Your times will probably vary, but the 8:30 number should give you a general idea of how long to take for each 10-question set, and you'll have a minute of cushion, in case you start to fall behind. Here are the deadlines; make sure to memorize them:

Science Deadlines	
Start Test	**00:00 (min:sec)**
Finish Question 10	**8:30**
Finish Question 20	**17:00**
Finish Question 30	**25:30**
Finish Question 40	**34:00+***

*You can fall up to a minute behind.

WORK UP TO IT

As we said, the Science Test can be very difficult to finish in time. If you find that you fall behind, or if you make a number of mistakes because you're rushing through the passages too quickly, you won't be able to tackle every question, at least not right away. The trick is too skip questions if you start to fall behind. Below are the questions to consider skipping:

- **Research Summaries method questions**: These are questions that don't test graphs or tables. Luckily, most of the questions on Research Summaries passages *do* test graphs or tables (just like Data Representation questions), but each Research Summaries passage will have a few questions that ask about the experimental *method*. These questions tend to be more difficult than basic table/graph questions and might be worth skipping.

- **Long questions**: Just because a question is long does not necessarily mean it will be hard, but these questions, not surprisingly, tend to take more time to answer than other questions. Consider skipping them.

- **Questions with new information**: As described in the Data Representation section, some questions will provide information that is not found in the passage. These questions are often more difficult, not to mention longer, than other questions.

- **Conflicting Viewpoints questions**: Many students find the Conflicting Viewpoints passage the most difficult passage on the test. We don't recommend skipping it entirely, but skipping some of its harder questions might help you either get ahead (if the passage shows up early in the test) or make up time (if the passage shows up later).

Besides the questions above, any question that has you stumped or seems to be testing a part of the passage you found difficult can be skipped. Needless to say, you'll probably answer more questions on easier passages than on harder passages.

And of course, you can (and should) go back to a skipped question if you find yourself ahead of a deadline.

TIMING YOURSELF ON INDIVIDUAL PASSAGES

As you practice individual passages, you'll start to get a feel for how many questions you should probably plan to skip. But how long do you have for each passage? The table below gives you time estimates for each passage type (based on the number of questions per passage).

Times per passage (for practice only)	
5-question passage (usually Data Representation)	4:15 (min:sec)
6-question passage (usually Research Summaries)	5:15
7-question passage (usually Conflicting Viewpoints)	6:00

These time estimates are just that: *estimates*—some passages will certainly take longer than others—but they should help you practice. If you have to skip a number of questions at first as you start practicing, that's OK. Just push yourself to move as quickly as you can, and with practice, your speeds should increase.

SKIMMING TIMES

DATA REPRESENTATION

We talked about skimming Data Representation passages before you start answering the questions. Depending on the passage, this should take you anywhere from **30 seconds to at most 1 minute**. Remember, you just want to get a general idea of the information presented in these passages, so get to the questions as quickly as you can.

RESEARCH SUMMARIES

The Research Summaries section discusses skimming these passages in *parts* (depending on your program, you'll cover this soon), so you probably shouldn't worry too much about the actual skimming time (since it'd be hard to keep track anyway)—just move as quickly as you can. If you're interested, however, we've found that the *total* time to skim the passage ranges from **1 to 1.5 minutes**. (Some students prefer *not* to skim in parts—they are more comfortable skimming the whole passage before looking at the questions. If this is you, then make sure to spend no more than 1.5 minutes skimming the passage before you start tackling the questions.)

USING A STOPWATCH

As you take practice tests, we recommend using a stopwatch to keep track of your times. Start your watch at the beginning of the test, and stick to the deadlines for whatever timing step you are on. Note: Practice timing when you take *practice* tests, *not* when you take the real ACT. The ACT folks do not allow any beeping noises during testing, so they probably won't let you use a stopwatch. The important thing is to get a feel for your timing when you *practice* so you know how quickly you need to work during the real test.

MOVING FASTER THAN THE DEADLINES

(!) **Just as on the English and Reading Tests, the times above are all *deadlines*—you don't *have* to take this long. If you move faster than these times, great! Don't slow down!** The extra time may come in useful on one of the later passages. The deadlines just ensure that you won't fall behind.

———

2. *HARD PASSAGES*

NOT ALL PASSAGES ARE CREATED EQUAL

Passages of the same type (Data Representation, Research Summaries, or Conflicting Viewpoints) will have variations in difficulty. The important thing is to be *aware* that you'll probably see one or more passages that seem *much harder* than the others. This awareness will hopefully encourage you to battle through on the hard ones—take comfort in knowing that easier passages are probably right around the corner. Make sure you watch your times carefully so you don't spend too much time on the hard passages.

SKIP MORE QUESTIONS ON HARDER PASSAGES

As stated earlier, you'll probably want to skip more questions on harder passages than on easier ones. Remember, you're always trying to maximize your score, so tackle the questions that you have the best chance of getting correct. These questions usually show up on passages that you find easier.

ONE HARD ONE

We've found that on many tests, there is *exactly one* "really hard" passage. We can't guarantee this will be the case on your test—and some passages that seem hard for some students will be easier for others—but if you ever feel as though your head's about to explode on one of the passages, you may be on this super-hard one. You have two options:

- **Skip it**: Regardless of what part of the test you're on, you might just move on to another passage, especially if you have difficulty meeting your timing deadlines without skipping many questions.
- **Battle through**: You might try to battle through on the hard one. Just watch the clock. You can take a little longer on harder passages, but you have to make up for it on the easier passages. The point of the deadlines is to make sure you don't take too long on harder passages and thus hurt your performance on later easier ones.

3. TIMING SUMMARY

- Stick to *deadlines* while you take practice tests:

Science Deadlines	
Start Test	**00:00 (min:sec)**
Finish Question 10	**8:30**
Finish Question 20	**17:00**
Finish Question 30	**25:30**
Finish Question 40	**34:00+**

- Skip questions, if necessary, to stay on track:
    - method questions (Research Summaries passages)
    - long questions
    - questions with new information
    - Conflicting Viewpoints questions

- Time estimates for individual passages (for practice):

Times per passage (for practice only)	
5-question passage (usually Data Representation)	**4:15 (min:sec)**
6-question passage (usually Research Summaries)	**5:15**
7-question passage (usually Conflicting Viewpoints)	**6:00**

- Passages of the same type will probably have various levels of difficulty.

- Skip more questions on harder passages than on easier ones.

- Watch out for *exactly one* really hard passage per test.

All programs: If you're following one of our standard programs, turn back to Data Representation Odds and Ends in Chapter II.

VI

ACT PRACTICE TESTS: TECHNIQUES REFERENCE

The following pages show the KlassTutoring science techniques for the practice passages and test questions in *The Real ACT Prep Guide*, 3rd Edition*. We recommend that you attempt the problems on your own *before* looking at these techniques; the techniques should be helpful when you *correct* any missed questions.

The techniques listed here offer general approaches, as taught in the preceding pages, to the problems (although we often add helpful information specific to a problem). If you still have trouble with a question even after you have reviewed the technique in this tutorial, check the solutions in the ACT book. These solutions, of course, focus on the specifics of the problems.

*ACT is a registered trademark of ACT, Inc., which was not involved in the production of and does not endorse this book.

1. ACT PRACTICE TEST 1

Passage I:

1. Direct Question

2. Trends

3. Extrapolation: Note the relationship between "Length of time" and "Lava volume" in Table 1.

4. Trends

5. Graphs from Tables

6. Make Connections/Learn: Notice that the years mentioned in Study 3 (58, 66, 133 Myr) fall just before the years in Table 1 (60, 67, 135 Myr). Logically, another extinction would fall before the formation of Plateau D (192 Myr).

Passage II:

7. Direct Question

8. Trends

9. Direct Question: You might review Tables and Graphs in the Math section.

10. Direct Question

11. Direct Question/Descriptions and Headings: Note the mention of "1 pair per 10 acres" at the bottom of Table 1. Scary-looking numbers that show up in questions are often just repeats of harmless numbers found somewhere in the passage.

Passage III:

12. Direct Question

13. Trends

14. Direct Question (Restate the Question): Which wire stretches the *least*?

15. New Material/Trends/Learn: Figure 3 suggests that gas volume increases as temperature increases.

16. New Material/Direct Question

17. Changes to Equipment/Science Sense: Would a heavier weight stretch the wire more or less?

Passage IV: This passage displays a great example of "combining graphs." The graph displays *six* different variables or labels. Can you see them all?

18. Direct Question

19. Direct Question

20. Direct Question (Restate the Question): What wavelength does not reach the troposphere?

21. Trends

22. New Information/Trends: According to the question: solar radiation↑ boundary altitude↑, or, alternatively: solar radiation↓ boundary altitude↓.

Passage V:

23. Direct Question

24. Make Connections (Multiple Figures): Don't forget to look for shared units (in this case, *depth*, in meters) between multiple figures.

25. Direct Question (Restate the Question): What is the temperature at 200 m?

26. New Information/Math (ratios)

27. Make Connections (Multiple Figures): Try process of elimination.

Passage VI:

28. Direct Question

29. Direct Question/Similarities

30. Direct Question/Differences

31. Direct Question

32. New Information/Learn: The passage states that "the upward *buoyant force* acting on the gases is stronger than the downward *force of gravity* acting on them," so the smoke rises. For the smoke (or the balloon) to fall, the opposite would likely be true.

33. Trends: The passage suggests the following trend: heat↑ density↓. So it would be likely that: heat↓ density↑.

34. New Information/Indirect Question: Read Sentence 3 of Student 2.

Passage VII:

35. Direct Question/Calculations

36. New Material/Trends: The values in Table 2 are not in order, but you should note the trend: corrected absorbance↑ NO_2^-↑.

37. Interpolation

38. Changes to Equipment/Science Sense: Don't let the confusing-sounding answer choices steer you wrong. The correct answer should be apparent. You might review how a colorimeter works (in the passage).

39. Make Connections (Multiple Figures): The important information is found in Table 1.

40. Science Sense: This one can be tricky. Again, note that corrected absorbance↑ NO_2^-↑. But if something in the meats other than NO_2^- also absorbed light, the NO_2^- measurements would be higher than the actual NO_2^- concentration.

2. ACT PRACTICE TEST 2

Passage I:

1. Direct Question

2. No technique, but if you're comfortable with rounding, this question is straightforward. Make sure to focus on Table 2.

3. Graphs from Tables

4. Trends

5. New Information: Does the passage say anything about the intensity of light *absorbed*?

Passage II:

6. Direct Question

7. Methods (Procedure): Consider what *variables* should be tested to investigate the problem (in this case, the variables are amounts of CO and CO_2).

8. Make Connections (Multiple Figures)/Learn/Headings: Note the difference in temperature between Tables 1 and 2 (see the table headings). What can you learn from the results?

9. Methods (Terms)

10. Direct Question (Restate the Question): When are the CO readings the highest?

11. Methods (Mistakes)/Science Sense

Passage III:

12. New Information/Calculations: Use the given equation for M. Note that "object size" is given in the text. (You could also interpolate.)

13. Calculations: Use the same equation we used for Question 12.

14. Direct Question

15. Calculations: Use the given equation for R.

16. Interpolation

17. Methods (Equipment)

Passage IV:

18. New Information/Direct Question

19. Extrapolation

20. New Information: The question essentially states that *star radiation* behaves similarly to *blackbody radiation*, so compare the answer choices to the figure in the passage.

21. Interpolation: Interpolation usually applies to tables, but here we see an example with a graph. Note that the brightness peaks at 500 K and 400 K fall above and below, respectively, the brightness measurement given in the question (75×10^6 watts per m^3).

22. New Information/Trends: frequency↑ wavelength↓ brightness ↑↓ (move right to left on the graph)

Passage V:

23. Graphs from Tables

24. Methods (Equipment): Read the description on Figure 1 ("height of Hg after addition of hexane").

25. New Information/Make Connections (Multiple Figures)/Trends: Try ranking the data in each table (Table 2 and the table in the question) from least to greatest to see if there's a correlation.

26. Trends

27. Methods (Equipment)

28. Methods/Science Sense: Try using process of elimination.

Passage VI: Most students find this Conflicting Viewpoints passage difficult.

29. Direct Question: "Lower-energy shapes are more stable…"

30. Indirect Question: Use process of elimination. G-J have to do with "folds," so the protein would not be "denatured."

31. Direct Question/Differences

32. New Information/Indirect Question: Review the description of the first structure level.

33. Direct Question

34. Differences: Use a process of elimination. (1) According to the intro, "randomly coiled shape" has high energy and "most stable shape" has low energy. Eliminate F and G. (2) H agrees with Scientist 1 ("active shape… is… lowest-energy shape), so eliminate it.

35. Weaknesses

Passage VII:

36. New Information/Direct Question or Trends: If you use Figure 2, 4.9 km has mostly red clay. If you use Figure 3, note the following trend: depth↓ calc. ooze↓ red clay↑.

37. Direct Question

38. Direct Question (Restate the Question): What is the relationship between "water depth" and "$CaCO_3$"? (Use the left side of Figure 1, and eliminate answers.)

39. Direct Question

40. Direct Question: Review Tables and Graphs in the Math section.

3. ACT PRACTICE TEST 3

Passage I:

1. Calculations: 22 × ? = 88…

2. Calculations: Use process of elimination, if necessary.

3. Direct Question: Make sure to focus on Figure 1.

4. Direct Question: Don't be fooled by the "2 sec." The question is simply asking for *D* if the initial speed is 60 mi/hr, using Method 2.

5. Extrapolation: We recommend using Figure 1.

Passage II:

6. Descriptions/Science Sense: Would a high-water content make urine lighter or darker? Make sure to carefully read the description at the bottom of the table.

7. Trends

8. Trends

9. Direct Question (Restate the Question): Which student had the lowest volume of urine? ("net fluid loss" = low volume)

10. Science Knowledge or Science Sense: You must either know (or sense) that as specific gravity increases, weight increases. Not surprisingly, the correct answer also has the most "suspended solids."

Passage III:

11. Extrapolation/Descriptions: Note "100 g of H_2O" in the Table 2 description. Once again, the question merely repeats a value given in the passage.

12. Methods (Terms)

13. Trends

14. Direct Question/Make Connections: In case you didn't know, H_2O boils at 100°C, as mentioned in the intro.

15. Trends/Descriptions: See Question 11.

16. New Information/Interpolation/Ratios: This one's tricky. First, note, according to the question, that 0.1 mole of $CaCl_2$ produces **0.3 mole** of particles (review Ratios in the Data Representation section). In Table 1 (and its description), we know that 0.1 mole of NaCl produces **0.2 mole** of particles (−3.4°C), and 0.2 mole of NaCl produces **0.4 mole** of particles (−6.9°C). Since temperature change is dependent on solute particles (in bold above), the answer will be between these temperatures.

Passage IV:

17. Direct Question

18. Trends

19. Methods (Procedures): See the purpose. Choose the answer that has something to do with *glaciers*.

20. Direct Question: Note the label at the top of Figure 3.

21. Science Sense

22. Calculations: Don't let the appearance of the equation scare you. You could think of $^{18}O/^{16}O$ as a simple variable, such as *x*. Hint: If $\delta^{18}O = 0$, the numerator of the given ratio must equal 0.

Passage V:

23. Indirect Question: Keep in mind, the passage is about *extinctions*.

24. Weaknesses: See Scientist 1 ("climatic warming")

25. Direct Question

26. Direct Question/Similarities

27. Direct Question: See the intro.

28. Science Knowledge: You must know that as acidity ("acid rain")↑ pH↓.

29. New Information/Indirect Question/Similarities: Focus on CO_2.

Passage VI:

30. Science Knowledge: A straightforward question, if you're comfortable with chemical equations.

31. Science Sense: If the volume of the gas decreased (in Trial 1, it decreased to 0), what would logically happen to the pressure?

32. Ratios/Learn: Do you see the pattern in Table 1? H_2 and O_2 react in a volume ratio of 2:1. If the initial volumes are not of this ratio, there will be something left over.

33. Methods (Procedures): Use process of elimination, or use your "science sense."

34. New Information/Learn/Ratios: This is similar to Question 32. Study the left side of the two chemical equations ($2H_2 + O_2$ and $N_2 + 3H_2$). If $H_2:O_2 = 2:1$ (from Question 32), then, logically, $N_2:H_2 = 1:3$.

35. Methods (Mistakes)/Science Sense: If impurities are "nonreactive," then it's unlikely they will cause an error.

Passage VII:

36. Extrapolation

37. Interpolation

38. Calculations

39. Direct Question: This question sounds harder than it is. Just find Y_0 for both the earth and the moon at 0.7 sec, and subtract.

40. New Information/Make Connections: Use Table 1 and Figure 3 to make a connection between acceleration due to gravity and fall time (acceleration due to gravity↑ fall time↓).

4. ACT PRACTICE TEST 4

Passage I:

1. New Information/Direct Question

2. Direct Question

3. Just look at the second parts of the answer choices: only one is true!

   Alternate solution: New Information/Trends/Make Connections: Don't forget to use arrows to keep track of trends: quality↑ larvae↑ (from the question), and BI↑ quality↑ (from Table 1), thus BI↑ larvae↑. Then use Table 2.

4. Descriptions: Read the description for Figure 1.

5. Science Sense: Would fertilizer increase or decrease water quality? (Then use Table 1.)

Passage II:

6. Graphs from Tables

7. Extrapolation

8. Direct Question/Calculations: The calculation is simple subtraction.

9. Science Knowledge or Science Sense: If you know (or "sense") that the molecules on the *left* side of the given chemical equation are converted to those on the *right* side of the equation (note the arrow direction), this question is straightforward.

10. Make Connections (Multiple Figures)

Passage III:

11. Direct Question (Restate the Question): In which trial did the scales show the same reading?

12. Make Connections: Trial 1 tells us how much Scale A weighed. Note in the intro: "identical scales."

13. Trends/Science Knowledge: Do you know the relationship between spring compression and potential energy?

14. No technique, but if you understand how the scales work (read the introduction carefully), this question is not too difficult. Trial 1 should help you eliminate two answer choices.

15. Trends

16. Equipment/Science Sense

Passage IV:

17. Trends

18. Interpolation

19. Calculations: Use process of elimination, if necessary.

20. Ratios/Make Connections/Learn: First, what happened to the octane number of isooctane when 3 mL of TEL was added? (It went from 100 to 125). Now, note that the ratio 100:900 is equivalent to 10:90. What's the octane number of this heptane:isooctane ratio? (90). We've learned that adding TEL increases octane, but it wouldn't logically increase it as much as pure isooctane. So we would expect something more than 90 but less than 125.

21. Direct Question: Read carefully about EOR.

22. Ratios/Interpolation: The ratio 2:8 is equivalent to 20:80.

Passage V:

23. Indirect Question/Make Connections: Note in the introduction that long-period comets have orbital periods of more than 200 years. Then read Scientist B's second sentence.

24. Direct Question/Make Connections: Note the *inclination* angles mentioned in the introduction.

25. Direct Question: See Question 24.

26. Science Knowledge: You must be able to pick out the "giant" planet among the answer choices.

27. Direct Question: Try process of elimination. Keep in mind that Scientist B says: "The KB does not exist."

28. Direct Question

29. Strengths and Weaknesses: Neither Scientist mentions the "Oort Cloud."

Passage VI: Pay attention to the table headings in this passage.

30. Direct Question/Headings: Use process of elimination.

31. Science Knowledge: You must be comfortable with cellular biology to get this one.

32. Trends/Make Connections (Multiple Figures): Note that NaCl, the substance varied among the tables, is also called "salt."

33. Methods (Terms)

34. Graphs from Tables

35. Methods (Terms): See the result for Question 33.

Passage VII:

36. Trends

37. Direct Question: You might try some simple numbers. For example, as B goes from 4 to 2 cm^2, R goes from 100 to 50 W.

38. Science Knowledge: This question tests thermodynamics.

39. Trends: Note that the cross-sectional area of the answer choices is constant.

40. Trends

5. ACT PRACTICE TEST 5

Passage I:

1. Direct Question/Science Sense: Hopefully you "sense" that as temperature went up, heat was *added* to the solution.

2. Trends

3. Extrapolation

4. Direct Question

5. Extrapolation

Passage II: If you think this a strange-looking Conflicting Viewpoints passage, we do not disagree!

6. Similarities/Make Connections (Multiple Figures): See Table 1 and Figure 3.

7. Direct Question: On a hard passage such as this one, you need to take advantage of these easier questions.

8. Make Connections (Multiple Figures): Use Table 1 and Figure 3. For this question, and Questions 9 and 11, you might want to review One-Dimensional Line Problems in the Math section.

9. Similarities/Make Connections (Multiple Figures): Use Figures 2 and 3.

10. Science Knowledge: You might want to review the subject of cell division.

11. Make Connections (Multiple Figures): Use Table 1 and Figure 3. Again, review One-Dimensional Line Problems.

12. Indirect/Learn/Science Knowledge: This is a difficult question. First look at Figure 1. The chromatids "involved in the crossover" are the two inner lines, which go from *ab* and *AB* ← *Ab* and *aB*. Just replace the letters in Figure 1 (*a, A, b, B*) with the letters in the question (*r, R, t, T*).

Passage III:

13. Direct Question

14. Extrapolation

15. Science Sense: Would rainfall be higher or lower during a drought? Use process of elimination.

16. Make Connections (Multiple Figures)

17. Direct Questions

Passage IV: Note that Figure 1 has more than two axis labels (review Combining Graphs).

18. Make Connections: You need to review the introduction carefully.

19. Calculations/Make Connections: Again, review the introduction, which describes the relationship between protons (*Z*) and neutrons.

20. Learn: According to Figure 1, what happens during beta decay?

21. Learn: Hint: According to Figure 1, what happens to *A* and *Z* during alpha decay?

22. Science Knowledge: You probably need some knowledge of kinetic energy and the relationship between mass and velocity (kinetic energy = $\frac{1}{2}mv^2$).

Passage V:

23. Make Connections (Multiple Figures): Compare the "peaks" of M3 with those in Figure 2.

24. Trends/Make Connections: Review "…time in the column…" in the text, and use Table 1.

25. Make Connections (Multiple Figures)/Learn: Get ready! You need to refer to three figures (in order: Figure 3, Figure 2, and Table 1). Also, from Figure 2 and Table 1, can you *learn* about the relationship between RT and AMM from Figure 2 and Table 1?

26. Make Connections: Review the part of the text that discusses *diffusion* (first sentence following Figure 1), and then use Table 1.

27. Make Connections (Multiple Figures)/Learn: See Question 25.

28. Science Sense: How would the *size* of molecules effect the *number* of molecules in a given volume?

Passage VI:

29. Trends

30. Direct Question

31. Extrapolation/New Materials: Remember that F = "failed burn."

32. Interpolation

33. Science Sense: You need to make a connection between "*crown fire*" and "needles" and between "*surface fire*" and "dowels," or "wood pieces" (see introduction).

34. Direct Question: Read the question carefully ("lost").

Passage VII: Notice that Figures 4 and 5 display five trials each (review Combining Graphs).

35. Direct Question/Descriptions: Note that a launch height of 3.5 ft and angle of 35° are just the measurements given in the description for Study 1. Don't let these numbers throw you off.

36. Direct Question: See "every 0.5 sec" in the text.

37. Direct Question (Restate the Question): For which speeds is $H > 37$ ft at $R = 310$ ft? Also, see note for Question 35.

38. Trends

39. Direct Question: See note for Question 35.

40. Math (review the *RTD* technique)

6. ACT PRACTICE PROBLEMS

Sample Passage I (Data Representation):

1. Trends/Make Connections (Multiple Figures)

2. Trends/Graphs from Tables

3. Calculations

4. Direct Question/Make Connections (Multiple Figures): Where is "sucrose"? You must *connect* to the text, which states that information about sucrose is given in Table 2 (read the intro paragraph). Hint: Make sure you compare the same *masses* of foods.

5. Learn/Make Connections (Multiple Figures)/Calculations: We don't have enough information in Table 1 to know what happens to 5.0 grams of potato, but can you *learn* something from the behavior of different masses of *sucrose* in Table 2?

Sample Passage II (Research Summaries):

6. Methods (Procedure Mistakes)

7. Trends: Find a relationship between number of bulbs and *L*.

8. Methods (Procedures): Consider what is being *varied* in each trial.

9. Descriptions/Science Sense: You should always take note of numbers given in descriptions (and headings), as described in the Data Representation Odds and Ends Section. The number 0.200 m is given in the description of the experiments, and in Figure 1. Hint: Can you find 0.446 m in the results?

10. Science Sense: Remember that *L* is found when the brightness of the Fixture-1 bulbs (see Figure 1) match the brightness of the Fixture-2 bulb ("the blocks looked equally bright"). So, if the Fixture 2 bulb is brighter, would the Fixture-1 bulbs have to move closer to the blocks or farther to show the same brightness?

Sample Passage III (Conflicting Viewpoints):

11. Calculations: The time for each gene transfer is clearly given in the text.

12. Direct Question

13. Direct Question

14. Indirect Question: Consider the replication moving in either direction for 30 minutes.

15. Calculations

VII

SCIENCE ANSWERS

The following answers are to all lesson, practice, and homework problems.

DATA REPRESENTATION LESSON PROBLEMS

1. At 5.4 Hz, potassium emits 0 J of kinetic energy. The answer is **A**.
2. If you extrapolate, as in the previous example, you will see that potassium emits a little over 5×10^{-19} J at a frequency of 12×10^{14} Hz. The only possible answer is **A**.
3. At 11×10^{14} Hz, beryllium emits about 2.2×10^{-19} J and titanium emits about 1.0×10^{-19} J. Read the hypothesis carefully. The student assumes that the emitted kinetic energy of the alloy will be greater than the *greater* of the emissions of the two separate metals (the greater of these is 2.2×10^{-19} J for beryllium). The answer is "no." Eliminate A and B. Since the tested value, 1.2×10^{-19}, is less than the emission rate for beryllium, 2.2×10^{-19}, the answer is **C**. The answer is not D because the student's hypothesis is not based on the "sum" of the kinetic energies, just the greater of the two.
4. This is a trends question. First, note that the graph does not have any information about wavelengths, but it does have information about frequency. So let's first see if there are any trends between wavelength and frequency. According to Table 1, as wavelength increases, frequency decreases. To keep track of these trends, write some simple notes: $W\uparrow F\downarrow$. Now, what happens to kinetic energy as frequency decreases? According to the graph, it also decreases. You could write: $F\downarrow K\downarrow$. So as wavelength increases, kinetic energy decreases. The answer is **B**.
5. According to Table 2, vultures can climb to 22,000 meters. Interpolate using Table 1, and you will find a corresponding pressure of about 35 kPa. The answer is **B**.
6. The atmospheric pressure at sea level (altitude = 0 m) is 101 kPa, and the atmospheric pressure at 50×10^3 m is 10 kPa. So the ratio of pressures (in this order), is 101:10 ≈ 10:1. **B**.
7. According to the graph, the only altitude where the temperature is about $-62°$ *and* the wind speed is about 8 knots is about 20,000 meters above sea level. The answer is **C**.

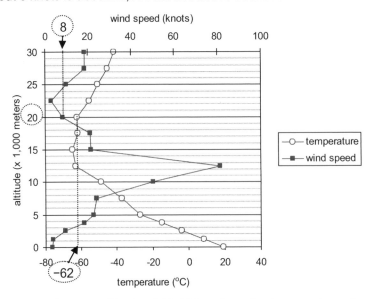

8. According to the graph, at an altitude of 20,000 meters, the temperature above all three cities is the same (a little less than $-60°C$). The answer is **D**.

9. You must use the equation for K_{eq} given in the passage: $K_{eq} = \dfrac{[NH_3]^2}{[N_2][H_2]^3}$. We know that for Trial B, the final $[N_2]$ increased, and the final $[H_2]$ and K_{eq} stayed the same (relative to Trial A). The key here is that K_{eq} did not change. Thus, since the denominator of the right side of the equation increased, the numerator $[NH_3]^2$ must also increase. The answer is **D**.

10. Since the concentrations in the question (2.0 mol/L of N_2 and 6.0 mol/L of H_2) are not listed in Table 4, we must *learn* something from the table. Consider *ratios*. According to Trial 10, we might say that when the initial concentration of N_2 and H_2 is in a 1:3 ratio, they react completely (no final concentrations). This is not surprising: we see these same numbers in the chemical equation. (The final concentrations for the trials that deviate from this 1:3 ratio are predictable. For example, in Trial 11, it is not surprising that if 1.50 mol/L of N_2 reacts with 3.00 mol/L of H_2, we end up with 0.50 mol/L of extra N_2.) Now back to the question. Since the ratio of 2.0 mol/L of N_2 to 6.0 mol/L of H_2 is the same 1:3 as in Trial 10, we would expect no final concentrations for N_2 and H_2. The answer is **A**.

11. This is a trends question. First, look at Figure 1. You can see that as the samples progress from 1 to 4, the elevation decreases. Now look at Figure 2. Which of the hydrocarbons increased in concentration as the samples progress from 1 to 4 (left to right)? The hydrocarbons o-Xylene and Toluene both increase as elevation decreases. The answer is **C**.

12. You can see from Figure 2 that Benzene and Propyl-benzene both decrease as the elevation decreases toward (and within) the water. So the answer is G or H. What about m-Xylene? This hydrocarbon does not seem to vary by elevation. Note that its concentrations in samples 1-4 are consistently less than 10 ppm. Without further evidence, we would expect the concentration at sample 5 to also be less than 10 ppm. Thus, it should be included with Benzene and Propyl-benzene. The answer is **H**.

DATA REPRESENTATION HOMEWORK PASSAGES
Passage I
1. Direct: Streptococcus lactis (or S. lactis) shows up twice in Table 1, and both times the temperature is 37°C. The generation times for the two occurrences are 26 min (for milk) and 48 min (for lactose broth), so the best answer is **C**.
2. Direct: Make sure you focus on Figure 1. The *y*-axis of the graph is scaled *logarithmically*. This can be tricky, but luckily we don't' really have to worry about it. The important thing to note is that the starting population (at time = 0) is between 10^1 (10) and 10^2 (100), so the answer must be **H**.
3. Direct: Careful. Answer choice C is tempting because the generation time (which the passage defines as the time for the population to double) for S. Aureus is 29 minutes, but the temperature is 30°C, not 37°C (read the question carefully). S. lactis in milk, which has a generation time of 26 minutes, is the correct answer answer: **D**.
4. Direct: Your first thought might be that the passage does not provide enough information to answer the question (data is simply not given for increased temperatures). So scrutinize the text. In the description for Table 1, the passage states that the temperatures are "optimal" for growth. Thus, logically, if the temperatures are increased (or, for that matter, decreased), the generation times would increase (increased generation times means slower growth). The answer is **F**.
5. Direct: The lag phase shows us that the bacteria population does not begin increasing immediately after transfer to a new growth medium (no bacterial fission). A and B are false, and C is not supported by the passage. The best answer is **D**.

Passage II
1. Trends: For all four liquids, as the object density increased, the fraction extending above the surface decreased ($D\uparrow F\downarrow$). **A**. Note: this result should not surprise you, as density is directly proportional to weight.
2. Make Connections: The connection between Table 1 and Figure 1 is *density*. According to Table 1, the density of polystyrene is 0.97 g/cm^3. According to Figure 1, a fraction of about 0.2 of this object would extend above the surface of benzine. The answer is **G**.

3. Trends/New Information/Make Connections: There are two trends to consider in this question. The first is given in the question: as temperature (T) increased, the fraction of birch wood extending above the surface (F) decreased ($T{\uparrow}F{\downarrow}$). Next, look at Figure 1 and Table 2. You can see that F decreases as the density (D) of a liquid decreases ($F{\downarrow}D{\downarrow}$). So put the two trends together: $T{\uparrow}F{\downarrow}D{\downarrow}$. The answer is **C**.

4. Make Connections/Extrapolation: Look at Figure 1. If you extrapolate, you can see that both polyethylene (0.92 g/cm^3) and polystyrene (0.97 g/cm^3) would have *negative* fractions extending above the surface of ethanol. In other words, these objects would sink. **J**.

5. New Information/Make Connections: Cedar wood has a density of 0.33 g/cm^3. The fraction of the wood extending above the surface is given as 0.8. Find this point on Figure 1. You should see that it lies between benzene and mercury. Thus, we can expect the density of the unknown liquid to be between the densities of benzene and mercury (see Table 2). The answer is **C**.

Passage III
1. Interpolation: This is a straightforward interpolation problem. Don't forget to draw a horizontal line between the relevant values (3.0/6.0 g and 142.8/285.6 kJ). Only one answer choice is between 142.8 and 285.6 kJ: **B**.

2. Graphs from Tables/Trends: As change in water temperature increased, the heat released also increased ($\Delta T{\uparrow}H{\uparrow}$). The answer is **G**.

3. Calculations: First of all, hopefully you circled "heat capacity" in the passage when you skimmed. The abbreviation is "C_{cal}." Next, look at the given equation in the passage (remember, when an equation is given, you'll probably use it at some point). The symbols q_r and ΔT are also defined in the passage. Simple algebra will lead you to **D**.

4. Make Connections: Notice that Table 1 does not give you information about how heat released varies with mass. So look at Table 2. As the mass of octane doubles, the heat released doubles. You could also show that the heat released from 3.0 g of octane (see Table 2) is exactly 3 times the heat released from 1.0 g of octane (see Table 1). The pattern is clear. So 3.0 g of methanol will release 3 times the heat of 1.0 g of methanol: $3 \times 22.8 \approx$ 68 kJ. **G**. Note: this question required you to "learn" something from the passage. We'll cover this technique more formally in the next section.

5. At first glance, this may look like an extrapolation question. Perhaps the change in temperature will be greater than that of octane, since the molar mass given in the question is greater than 114.23 g/mol. But if you look at the molar masses of, for example, sucrose and hydrazine, you will see that there is in fact no clear relationship between molar mass and temperature change. The answer is **D**.

Passage IV
1. Make Connections: All of the Outlet 2 (O2) levels for iron in Table 1 are greater than iron's allowed maximum of 3.5 mg/L (Table 2). The answer must be **D**.

2. Direct: Unsurprisingly, the flow rates for both outlets (O1 and O2), increased during the heavy rain (Day 2) and then gradually decreased during the subsequent days. The answer is **G**.

3. Trends: Notice that each marsh significantly reduced the iron content in the water. We can assume that adding a third marsh will continue this decrease. The answer is **C**.

4. Make Connections: Read the description for Table 2. The given pH value is the "minimum allowed." In other words, higher numbers are acceptable. You might also already know that as pH increases, acidity decreases. Now look at Table 1. The pH levels at Outlet 2 (O2) are safely above the minimum allowed level in Table 1 (which means the acidity was lower than the allowed level) for all 5 days. The answer is **H**.

5. New Information/Learn: The passage provides no specific information about copper mines, so we must "learn" something from the passage. In Table 1, look at the values for manganese content on days with no precipitation (Days 1, 4, and 5). The values either stay the same or *slowly* decrease as the water moves through the marshes. Only **A** shows these same characteristics.

DATA REPRESENTATION PRACTICE PASSAGES

Passage I

1. Direct: Make sure you focus on Enzyme A (the solid line). You will have to interpolate because the maximum relative activity rate (the "peak" of the graph) occurs between 40° and 60°. Look at the answer choices. Only **B**—50°C—is a possible answer.

2. Extrapolate: The x-axis stops at pH ≈ 11, so you will have to extrapolate. Go ahead and sketch the rest of Enzyme B's graph. At pH = 12, the best estimate for activity rate is 10. The answer is **F**.

3. Trends: Focus on Figure 3. At substrate concentrations below 0.3 mg/mL, relative activity rates (R) increase as substrate concentrations (S) increase. You might write the following note: "When $R < 0.3$, $R\uparrow S\uparrow$." Since the rates change as concentrations change, the rates ARE dependent on substrate concentrations. So the answer is "yes." Eliminate C and D. Notice that **B** restates the trend we discovered above.

4. New Information: Write down the most effective pH readings for each enzyme (using Figure 2 and the given table). These are the "peaks" of the graphs: Enzyme A: pH = 6, Enzyme B: pH = 10, Aspergillus: pH = 8. Notice that Aspergillus falls between Enzymes A and B. Eliminate F and G. Now, review pH (last paragraph of intro): the lower the pH, the more acidic. The answer is **J**.

5. Make Connections: Look at Figure 4. The greatest activity rate occurs at concentrations greater than about 0.3 mg/mL. (You can safely eliminate D.) Now, look at Figure 1. The peak of Enzyme B occurs at about 35°C. The answer is **C**.

Passage II

1. Make Connections: Since the mass of the chain doubles, look at Tables 1 and 3. Only Trials 1 and 10 have the same chain length (L) and momentary length (x). (The force of Trial 10 is twice that of Trial 1.) The answer is **A**.

2. Extrapolation: For a 1.0-meter chain, with $x = 0.2$, the momentary weight (MW) = 1.96 N for a 1.00 kg chain (Trial 10), MW = 1.47 N for a 0.75 kg chain (Trial 5), and MW = 0.98 N for a 0.50 (Trial 1). Do you see the pattern? Each 0.25-kg decrease in weight corresponds to approximately a 0.50-N decrease in momentary weight. So, extrapolating from Trial 1, the momentary weight for a 0.25-kg chain would be 0.98 − 0.50 ≈ 0.50 N. The best answer is **F**.

3. Trends/Calculations: First, note that as momentary length (x) increased, momentary weight did not increase or decrease consistently. Eliminate A and B. So let's look at the ratio of momentary weight (x) to the length of the chain (L). Trial 9: $x/L = 0.2$; Trial 10: $x/L = 0.2$; Trial 11: $x/L ≈ 0.33$; Trial 12: $x/L = 0.25$. The order of these ratios matches the order of the momentary weights. The answer is **C**.

4. Calculations: You might figure this one out just by looking at Figure 1. If the answer is not clear, then we'll do some simple algebra. Let's call the length of the chain not touching the scale pan y. Since we know that x is the length of the chain touching the scale pan (the momentary length), we can write: $L = x + y$. So $y = L − x$. The answer is **G**.

5. Graphs from Tables/Trends/Calculations: This is a challenging "Graphs from Tables" question. We know that as momentary weight increased, force on pan increased ($M\uparrow F\uparrow$). But this trend is true for A, C, and D. So we have to make some rough calculations to determine the relationship. Looking at Table 1, you can see that $0.98 × 3 ≈ 2.94$, $1.96 × 3 ≈ 5.89$, $2.94 × 3 ≈ 8.83$, and so on. The relationship is *linear*. The answer is **D**. (Note: you could also try scaling the graph—perhaps from 0 to 10—and plotting points from Table 1.)

Passage III

1. Trends: For a given element (Li^{+2} is the easiest to see), as n increases (left to right), I increases and E decreases: $n\downarrow I\uparrow E\downarrow$ The answer is **B**.

2. Extrapolation: The value of E for He^+ and n = 4 appears to be about 50. Since E increases as n increases, we expect E at n = 5 to be greater than 50 eV: **J**.

3. Direct: This question is actually easier than it sounds, but it does require you to dig into the text a little. The passage explains that protons have positive charges and electrons have negative charges. We also know that each of the three elements have **one** electron. Thus, if Z, the number of protons, is greater than the number of electrons, the atom will have a

positive charge, as we can see in Table 1 (the superscripts reveal the elements' charges). The answer is **C**.

4. Make connections: First, the energy of an emitted photon is defined by the symbol E. The greatest value for E is for Li^{+2}, n=4 (Figure 2). Now look at Table 1: Li^{+2}, n=4 ← r = 2.8 × 10^{-8} cm. The answer is **F**.

5. New Information/Learn/Calculations: This can be a difficult question. The equation given in the question is important (I × c = E). The first step is to find the constant c using the information in the passage (this is where we "learn" something). Using Li^{+2} (n = 2) in Figure 2, we can write (approximately): 30 × c = 90, so c ≈ 3. Thus, E for Be^{+3} (n = 2) must be close to 54.2 × 3 ≈ 163 eV. The answer is **D**.

RESEARCH SUMMARIES LESSON PROBLEMS

1. Since Table 2 does not provide data for 17.0°C, we must *extrapolate*. The data suggests that the masses of the corn plants are most likely increasing as the thermoperiod increases past 15.0°C (eliminate F and H). On the other hand, the masses of soybean plants seem to have reached a maximum (at around 10.0°C) and are beginning to decrease. (This is not surprising when you consider that, as described in the previous question, soybean plants prefer colder temperatures than corn plants.) The best answer is **J**.

2. The low temperature for all samples was controlled (20°C). Eliminate A. Since the thermoperiods were controlled, the high temperatures must have been controlled. Eliminate B. The number of seeds per pot was also controlled (10 seeds per pot). Eliminate C. The sunlight was not controlled. The passage states that the containers were given "free exposure to sunlight." The answer is **D**.

3. The 0.0°C chamber of Experiment 2 had no thermoperiod and thus had a constant temperature of 20°C. The answer is **C**.

4. Notice that the mass of corn plants increases as thermoperiod increases. If there is an ideal thermoperiod for corn plants—as one would expect, and as suggested by the existence of an ideal thermoperiod for soybean plants (around 10.0°C)—then a weakness in the study is the fact that this ideal thermoperiod for corn plants was not found. High-enough thermoperiods were not tested. The best answer is **C**.

5. In the original experiment, the plants in Experiment 3 were part of the control group because the temperature was not controlled and all other factors in the experiment (lighting, soil, seeds, etc) were not changed. The lighting must be the same for all three experiments. The answer is **C**.

RESEARCH SUMMARIES PRACTICE PASSAGES

Passage I

1. Trends: Table 2 shows that as the T_c increases from 20°C to 40°C, the velocity decreases. Don't forget to keep track of trends with arrows, if necessary: T↑V↓. The answer is **A**.

2. In both Experiment 2 and Experiment 3, the maximum temperature is unaffected by any changes to the independent variables. The numbers may vary slightly (as one would expect in an experiment), but there are no trends displayed. The answer is **J**.

3. Science Sense: As stated in the introduction, heat is released when CH_3COONa solidifies, or crystallizes. Start with Experiment 2: The slower the velocity of crystallization, the longer until the liquid away from the "seeding point" will begin crystallizing, and thus, the greater the temperature variation between the two thermometers. So what T_c shows the slowest velocity? 40°. Eliminate B and D. Experiment 3: Table 3 shows that the greater the mass, the longer it takes to reach maximum temperature. It's reasonable to assume that this is due to the time it takes for crystallization to occur away from the seeding point (because of the larger mass of the sample). The answer is **A**, the largest mass and highest supercooled temperature.

4. Neither of these weights are listed, but according to Table 3, the heavier the sample, the longer the time to reach a maximum temperature and the longer the time to return to 30°C. Note that the maximum temperature is not affected by the weight of the sample (as in H). The answer is **F**.

5. Graphs from Tables: The data in Table 1 suggests that CH_3COOH and $NaHCO_3$ react in equal mol quantities. This is most clearly displayed in Trial 6, where equal mol quantities of

both liquids (2.0 mol) react fully (leaving no liquids unreacted). For this question, all 3.0 mol of $NaHCO_3$ would react, leaving 0.0 mol unreacted. The answer is **A**. (0.5 mol of CH_3COOH would be left over. See Trial 3.)

6. This is one of those questions that might require some general scientific knowledge. When the water vapor is no longer present, the water has likely been boiled away. If the CO_2 has a lower boiling point than H_2O, it is reasonable to assume that the CO_2 had already boiled away at this point of the experiment. Thus, there would be no need to look for it. The best answer is **H**.

Passage II

1. Graphs from Tables/Trends: According to Table 1, as spin rate increased, precession rate decreased ($S\uparrow P\downarrow$). The only answer choice that displays this trend is **D**.

2. Extrapolation: In Table 2, note that whenever h increased 1 inch, the precession rate increased 2.5 rpm. Thus, if h increases 2 inches (2 ← 4), the precession rate will increase 5 rpm (10.0 ← 15.0): **J**.

3. Methods: The Experimental Method explains that to test the effect of something, vary it, while keeping everything else constant. Varying the material of a top will vary its mass. The spin rate should be held constant. The answer is **C**.

4. Make Connections: First, note that the spin rate for Experiment 2 was 800 rpm (hopefully you circled this number when you skimmed the experiment). In Table 1, a spin rate of 800 rpm resulted in a precession rate of 5 rpm. According to Table 2, a precession rate of 5 rpm corresponded with a height of 2 inches: **J**.

5. Methods/Science Knowledge: From the passage, we know that the falling platform allowed scientists to simulate changes in gravity. Only A and B have to do with the platform, so eliminate C and D. Is gravity related to acceleration or velocity? You might know (from your physics classes) that gravity is a force, and is thus related to acceleration. The answer is **A**.

6. Methods: The keyword in the question (and the passage) is "smooth." You might imagine that if the surface were not smooth, then the top's spin rate would quickly decrease because of surface friction, thereby making measurements of the precession rate (for a given spin rate) impossible. A smooth surface would ensure a (nearly) constant spin rate. The best answer is **G**.

Passage III

1. New Information/Direct: This question (like many science questions) sounds harder than it is. We simply need to find the time when the voltage equals 7.6 V. According to Figure 2, the time is about 50 sec: **B**.

2. Extrapolation/Make Connections: The trend for capacitance vs. time in Table 1 is clear: $C\downarrow T\downarrow$. The answer must be F or G. But which one? Since the capacitance in question (1.5×10^{-3} F) is greater than the capacitance in Experiment 1, we expect the time to reach 12 V to be greater than that of Experiment 1 (about 300 sec). The answer is **G**.

3. Learn: This question requires you to learn something from the passage: Figure 2 shows that the voltage across the capacitor increases from 0 V to 12 V (the battery voltage). Of the four answer choices, only **A** would have reached the maximum 12 V.

4. Methods: To understand what is being tested in an experiment, take note of what is being **varied** (review The Experimental Method). In Experiment 3, resistance is varied (this is the independent variable). The only possible answer is **J**. Note that H confuses the independent variable (resistance) with the dependent variable (time).

5. Methods (Equipment): This question asks about the setup of the experiments. First, it's important to know that the voltmeter must "intercept" the wire that includes the capacitor (since the purpose of the experiments is to measure the voltage across the capacitor). In answer choices A and B, the voltmeter doesn't intercept any one device (when the switch is closed, it functions like a wire). In answer choice D, the voltmeter intercepts the resistor, not the capacitor. The answer must be **C**. As stated above, when the switch is closed, it functions like a wire, so C is functionally the same as the circuit in Figure 1.

6. Methods: The line graph (Figure 2) levels off at 300 seconds (at a voltage of 12 V). This appears to be the maximum voltage possible. (Science sense might tell us that this has

something to do with the 12 V battery.) Measuring the voltage for longer than 300 seconds would probably be unnecessary. The answer is **G**.

CONFLICTING VIEWPOINTS LESSON PROBLEMS

1. As we said, the answer to direct questions can be found by looking at the context of the passage. This question focuses on Scientist 1. He states: "the light from distant stars is 'seen' at a lower frequency than what would be seen from a static star." This supports **C**. Note that A and B are both saying the same thing (using different words). Both are incorrect.
2. Scientist 2 never explicitly states what might affect the relative speed of two objects, but he does say: "Because of the gravitational pull of the accumulated objects in the South Pole, objects closer to the pole will accelerate faster than objects farther away." If you have some idea of the physics of motion, you hopefully know that acceleration affects velocity (as you accelerate, you go faster). The best answer is **B**.
3. Scientist 1 states that all matter is "expanding in all directions." Scientist 2 states "the Doppler effect would still show stars and galaxies moving away from us in all directions." The best answer is **C**.
4. Scientist 1's Universe is infinite, with "all matter expanding in all directions." Scientist 2 considers this scenario mathematically "problematic." The answer is **C**. Scientist 2 would most likely agree with all of the other answer choices.

CONFLICTING VIEWPOINTS PRACTICE PASSAGE

1. Scientist 1 focuses on the "short-lived" risk of dead trees, and the "early stages" of a beetle epidemic. Scientist 2 makes no specific reference to short-term effects. The answer is **A**.
2. Note that this question doesn't reference either Scientist. You should answer it after reading the introduction. The introduction states: "If the tree cannot fight off the beetles with enough resin to force them out or drown them, the fungus will eventually cut the veins that carry the water, and the tree dies." The answer is **F**.
3. Both scientists agree that drought and rising temperatures play a role in fire danger. However, Scientist 2 claims that these are the primary reasons for an increase in fire danger. Scientist 1's secondary claims of "rising temperatures and less precipitation" are certainly weakened, but his *primary* claim (that bark beetles increase the risk of wildfires) would be supported because the bark beetles would become a more likely culprit for the increased fire danger. The best answer is **B**.
4. Scientist 2 states: "there is no evidence to suggest that the fallen needles have any effect on wildfires. Wildfires feed on larger sources of fuel…" The answer is **H**. Watch out for J: thinning tree crowns *are* a factor in wildfire danger—they *reduce* it.
5. This question may not have a direct answer, but you should be able to interpret the information in the passage. Scientist 2 claims that thinning tree crowns reduce the threat of the fast-moving fires that move from "treetop to treetop." A forest with trees farther apart— one that is less dense—would, according to Scientist 2, logically decrease wildfire danger. The answer is **C**.
6. Scientist 1 states: "…rising temperatures and less precipitation" increase fire danger. Scientist 2 states that wildfire threats increase "because of drought and higher temperatures." The answer is **H**.
7. Scientist 1 states that crown fire danger is increased "when the forest is a mixture of dead, dying, and living trees." This supports **B**.

Made in the USA
San Bernardino, CA
22 January 2016